Fraud

Fraud

AN AMERICAN HISTORY FROM
BARNUM TO MADOFF

Edward J. Balleisen

PRINCETON UNIVERSITY PRESS

PRINCETON AND OXFORD

Published by Princeton University Press, 41 William Street, Princeton, New Jersey 08540

In the United Kingdom: Princeton University Press, 6 Oxford Street, Woodstock, Oxfordshire OX20 1TR

press.princeton.edu

ISBN 978-0-691-16455-7

Library of Congress Control Number: 2016935601

British Library Cataloging-in-Publication Data is available

Jacket art: Background images courtesy of Shutterstock. Portraits illustrated by Anne Karetnikov

This book has been composed in Minion Pro text with Madrone Std display

Printed on acid-free paper. ∞

Printed in the United States of America

10 9 8 7 6 5 4 3 2 1

For Stanley Katz,
David Brion Davis, and
Cynthia Herrup

Contents

ഏഉൟ

PART V:
The Market Strikes Back (1970s to 2010s)

Illustrations

❧❀❧

Figures

Table

Acknowledgments

೧ᕲᕳನ

I n recent years, I have had the good fortune to take part in several interdisci-
plinary collaborations on the workings and impacts of modern regulatory
governance. By contrast, *Fraud: An American History from Barnum to Madoff*
reflects a more traditional sole-authored work of history. The creation of such
volumes still typically depends on the steadfast, creative contributions of many
other people, as well as funds for research trips and time off from teaching. This
one is no different.

Several organizations extended financial support for my research and writing. The American Council of Learned Societies provided me with a yearlong
Burkhardt Fellowship that I took to the National Humanities Center, where I
found good fellowship and a wonderfully conducive environment for reading
and analytical thinking. I spent a delightful and productive semester at the Harvard Business School as the holder of the Thomas McCraw Fellowship in United
States Business History. In addition, I enjoyed two separate leaves from the
Duke History Department (one partially supported by the Hunt Family Fund),
as well as small research and conference travel grants from Duke's Trinity College of Arts & Sciences.

Library and archival staff proved invaluable direction for navigating far-
flung collections and the ever-burgeoning resources available digitally. I would
like to single out Ellen Zazzarino and Coi Drummond-Gehrig at the Western
History Department of the Denver Public Library, Janet Linde at the New York
Stock Exchange Archives, Laura Lenard of Historical Collections at the Harvard Business School's Baker Library, Eliza Robertson of the National Humanities Center, and, at Duke, Elizabeth Dunn, Lynn Eaton, Carson Holloway, Kel-
ley Lawton, and Jacqueline Reid.

A number of current and former Duke students have furnished superb research assistance, identifying digital sources, chasing down leads, and scoping
out secondary literature and archival holdings. These include former/current
undergraduates Maura Freedman, Alex Hoy, Sarah Kerman, Sarah Patterson,
Kate Preston, Franklin Sacha, Nick Shelburne, and Alex Wade, and former/
current doctoral students Deborah Breen, Mitch Fraas, Abby Goldman, Daniel Levinson-Wilk, Christy Mobley, and Daniel Papsdorf. In the past year,
doctoral student Ashton Merck has both dealt expertly with a number of issues concerning book illustrations and helped me to conceptualize what
I hope will be a companion website for the book. Duke administrative staff
members Jamie Hardy, Cynthia Hoglen, Carla Ivey, Robin Pridgeon, and

Gloria Taylor-Neal have handled logistics deftly around RA assignments, research travel, and grants.

I have received benefit from constructive feedback during research presentations or seminars given at Oxford's Said Business School; Harvard Business School; Duke's Fuqua Business School; the New York City Market Cultures group; the University of Pennsylvania Economic History Workshop; the Bairoch Institute for Economic History at the University of Geneva; Duke's Economic Sociology Workshop; Duke's Sanford School of Public Policy; the University of Chicago Law School; the University of British Columbia Law School; Duke Law School; the University of Minnesota Legal History Workshop; the Triangle Legal History Seminar; the Max Planck Institute for European Legal History in Frankfurt; the German Historical Institute in Washington, DC; Sorbonne University–Paris 3; and annual meetings of the American Society for Legal History, the Business History Conference, the European Business History Association, the Policy History Conference, and the American Council of Learned Societies. I am especially grateful to Duke's Kenan Institute for Ethics, led by Noah Pickus and Suzanne Shanahan, which funded a crucial daylong workshop on the entire manuscript early in 2015, and to Walter Sinnott-Armstrong and Amber Diaz Pearson, who organized that event.

Many individuals helped me develop a workable approach to a sprawling topic, suggested useful scholarship, and/or commented on chapter drafts. Close to home, I have counted on my Duke History colleagues Sally Deutsch, Laura Edwards, Margaret Humphreys, Reeve Huston, Gunther Peck, Alex Roland, and Phil Stern; a slew of other Duke faculty, such as Dan Ariely, Lawrence Baxter, Sara Sun Beale, Rachel Brewster, Sam Buell, Tim Buthe, Guy Charles, Ronnie Chatterjie, Wes Cohen, Deborah DeMott, Gary Gereffi, Kieran Healy, Lisa Keister, Kim Krawiec, Fritz Mayer, Ralf Michaels, Wayne Norman, Dirk Philipsen, Jed Purdy, Arti Rai, Barak Richman, Martin Ruef, Steve Schwarcz, Sim Sitkin, and Pate Skene; and current or former graduate students Fahad Bishara, Elizabeth Brake, Deborah Breen, Tom Cinq-Mars, Mercy DeMenno, Jon Free, Abby Goldman, Will Goldsmith, Anna Johns, Dan Levinson-Wilk, Ashton Merck, Andrew Ruoss, and Shana Starobin.

Within the broader Research Triangle, my interlocutors/readers/critics included Kevin Anderson, Tom Birkland, Al Brophy, Mary Beth Chopas, Tony Freyer, Geoffrey Harpham, Melissa Jacoby, Julia Rudolph, Benjamin Waterhouse, and David Zonderman. Among those further afield, I am indebted to Peter Baum, Hartmut Berghoff, Susanna Blumenthal, Holly Brewer, Fabrizio Cafaggi, Dan Carpenter, Cary Coglianese, Jonathan Coopersmith, Marc Eisner, Neil Fligstein, Patrick Fridenson, Christy Ford, Robert Gordon, Joanna Grisinger, Per Hansen, Will Hausman, Roger Horowitz, Robert Horwitz, Richard John, Geoffrey Jones, Pam Laird, Naomi Lamoreaux, Marc Levinson, Jonathan

Levy, Stephen Mihm, Brad Miller, Sharon Murphy, Bill Novak, Saule Omarova, Julia Ott, Lynne Paine, Dan Raff, Mark Rose, Malcolm Salter, Laura Phillips Sawyer, Phil Scranton, Dick Sylla, James Taylor, Steve Usselman, Sean Vanatta, Dick Vietor, Dan Wadhwani, Elizabeth Warren, Barbara Welke, Mark Wilson, JoAnne Yates, and Christine Zumello.

David Gilmartin and the late Jonathon Ocko helped me set issues about the rule of law in a comparative context. Wendy Woloson graciously shared excellent primary sources on dodgy nineteenth-century businesses, as well as her keen understanding of historical discourse over marketing deceptions. During my stint at the National Humanities Center, Karen Carroll furnished constructive suggestions on early draft chapters. Daniel Ernst, Walter Friedman, Leif Haase, and Mary O'Sullivan supplied especially detailed commentary on the full manuscript.

After I spent a couple of years' research on a different book project, Lawrence Friedman convinced me to drop it and pursue this one instead. I am grateful for his persuasiveness about the imperative of researching and writing a lively kind of legal/policy history that speaks to nonacademics as well as a broad audience of scholars. Roughly a decade ago, I embarked on two longer-term conversations that had profound implications for this book. One was with Christopher McKenna, then launching his own inquiry into the history of business fraud. Through many discussions, Chris and I clarified how each of us would tackle dimensions of an enormous subject, shared methodological challenges, and pushed each other to sharpen arguments and narrative approaches. A second series of exchanges took place with David Moss, which led to inter-disciplinary projects on regulatory policy and engagement with policymakers. The resulting collaborations, first with the Tobin Project and then at Kenan Institute for Ethics with the Rethinking Regulation group, have allowed me to see more clearly how historical analysis can engage with other social science disciplines and inform contemporary policy deliberations.

Since 2010, I have worked closely with Jonathan Wiener, a legal scholar, and Lori Bennear, an environmental economist, in creating the Rethinking Regulation group at Duke. I have learned an enormous amount from them about the nature of risk, the frequency with which regulatory interventions generate unintended consequences, the dilemmas of balancing conflicting policy goals, and the challenges of designing adaptive regulatory institutions.

The *Business History Review* has published one article, "Private Cops on the Fraud Beat: The Limits of American Business Self-Regulation, 1895–1932" (2009), and one short contribution to a "Corporate Reputation Roundtable" (2013), which appear below in revised form, with permission. My Princeton University Press editor, Eric Crahan, offered crucial advice about how to restructure parts of the manuscript, approach the difficult task of significantly pruning an initially longer draft, and think about a title. Katherine Harper did a fantastic job of tightening the prose through copyediting and then prepared a sterling index. Ellen Foos and Ben Pokross kept me on task with the production process. I wrote most of this book in public spaces, especially several Durham coffee shops, and von der Heyden Pavilion, otherwise known as "The Perk," a truly delightful glass structure adjoining Duke's Perkins Library. Some writers need solitude. I now seem to require hubbub, and I am obliged to the baristas and fellow frequenters of those establishments who have provided it.

Many years into this project, after I had begun to read some behavioral economics, I persuaded my two sons, Zachary and Aaron, to dip into that field. As soon as they encountered the psychology of precommitment mechanisms, I was in trouble. In the fall of 2013, as I embarked on a year's leave, they issued an ultimatum—finish a full manuscript draft by the start of the following school year or see them donate, in my name, to the reelection campaign of a politician whose views differ rather significantly from mine. They kept up the pressure over the subsequent twelve months, indulged me by listening to the occasional story about a given fraud episode, and even allowed one short extension. I am glad to say I met that adjusted deadline. (Zachary further brought news coverage of Operation Choke Point to my attention.) My sisters, Ellen Balleisen and Wendy Finger, my brother-in-law, Michael Finger, and my mother, Carolyn Balleisen, took gentler tacks in encouraging me; in the case of Wendy, that encouragement remained unfailing even as she lost a battle with cancer.

Karin Shapiro has lived with this book from its inception. For stretches, piles of related books and files invaded our dining room table. She has listened to even more stories about fraud episodes, helped me figure out how to manage competing projects, and always pressed me to keep a sense of perspective about the dangers of perfectionism. Her wise counsel further helped me distinguish the suggestions and critiques that commanded attention from those that seemed less important or even wrongheaded. Whatever its remaining faults, the book reflects my efforts to meet her standard of readable prose and her insistence on relating historical analysis of ideas, values, and practices to historical analysis of socioeconomic interests.

I have had the great fortune to chance upon some remarkable mentors. From my first weeks at college, I have relied on Stan Katz for advice about my intellectual and career trajectory. During and after graduate school, David Davis showed me how to adapt ethnography and the history of ideas to the analysis of institutions and political conflicts. Since my first year at Duke, Cynthia Herrup has been an expert guide to the challenges of doing legal history without a JD, and to the mysteries of navigating the research university. I hope they will each see traces of their influence in this book, which is dedicated to them.

PART I

Duplicity and the Evolution of American Capitalism

They look upon fraud as a greater crime than theft, and therefore seldom fail to punish it with death; for they allege, that care and vigilance, with a very common understanding, may preserve a man's goods from thieves, but honesty has no defence against superior cunning; and, since it is necessary that there should be a perpetual intercourse of buying and selling, and dealing upon credit, where fraud is permitted and connived at, or has no law to punish it, the honest dealer is always undone, and the knave gets the advantage. I remember, when I was once interceding with the emperor for a criminal who had wronged his master of a great sum of money, which he had received by order and ran away with; and happening to tell his majesty, by way of extenuation, that it was only a breach of trust, the emperor thought it monstrous in me to offer as a defence the greatest aggravation of the crime; and truly I had little to say in return, farther than the common answer, that different nations had different customs; for, I confess, I was heartily ashamed.

Jonathan Swift on the laws and customs of Lilliput,
Gulliver's Travels (1726)

Corruption, embezzlement, fraud, these are all characteristics which exist everywhere. It is regrettably the way human nature functions, whether we like it or not. What successful economies do is keep it to a minimum. No one has ever eliminated any of that stuff.

Alan Greenspan, interview on Amy Goodman's *Democracy Now!*,
Sept. 24, 2007

CHAPTER ONE

ᕼᘒᕼ

The Enduring Dilemmas of Antifraud Regulation

In the late fall of 1894, an up-and-coming Midwesterner gained a sharp lesson about the growing reach of the United States government. For eight years, this former railroad station manager had nurtured a succession of mail-order businesses in Chicago and then Minneapolis. Through experiments with national print advertising and wholesale catalogue distribution, he discovered an instinctive knack for mail-order marketing. Cultivating a folksy style, he combined alluring descriptions of goods, aggressive expansion, sharp discounts, and all manner of promotional hullabaloo. Within a few years, he gained endorsements from leading banks and public officials across the Midwest. Farm families responded so vigorously to his engaging sales pitches that his firm struggled to fill the orders that cascaded in with every day's post. By December 1894, this ambitious thirty-one-year-old employed over one hundred persons and had moved his main operations back to Chicago, to be closer to the manufacturers whose goods he required to meet his obligations. Then, just two weeks before Christmas, the United States Post Office threatened this mercantile impresario with the equivalent of a commercial death sentence. On December 11, the postmaster general issued a fraud order against his firm. The recipient of this administrative notice was Richard W. Sears, the creator of the "Dream Books" that came to rest on hundreds of thousands of kitchen tables across rural America, and the driving force behind Sears, Roebuck & Co. in its first two decades.

After the issuance of this order, anyone sending the firm correspondence would receive it back with a mark of public shame affixed, like the one in Figure 1.1. The same fate befell any mail sent out by an individual or firm under a fraud order. This administrative sanction represented a far greater commercial peril than civil lawsuits alleging deceptive business practices, or even criminal fraud proceedings, for it threatened to destroy consumer confidence. A fraud order proclaimed that the American state had adjudged a firm's business practices to be illegitimate. For most mail-order concerns, such a declaration augured crippling losses even if customers' trust somehow survived the rebuke, because it halted commercial correspondence. As we shall see (and as Sears, Roebuck's extraordinary growth in the decades after December 1894 would

Figure 1.1: "FRAUDULENT" stamp on a 1906 letter returned to sender because of a postal fraud order. Reproduced with the permission of the Smithsonian National Postal Museum, Washington, DC.

suggest), Richard Sears found a way to make the fraud order go away. But his encounter with postal regulators reflected several interrelated problems that US businesses, policymakers, and citizens have confronted since the advent of modern capitalism—how should Americans define fraud, how much should they worry about it, and how should they structure institutional responses to it?

This book retraces how Americans wrestled with these questions for the better part of a century before Richard Sears's confrontation with the Post Office and for more than a hundred years after it. Throughout those two centuries, Americans of all socioeconomic groups had to navigate the challenges posed by lying promoters and cheating retailers. From generation to generation, the upward swings of the modern business cycle have encouraged investment scams and creative corporate accounting that press at legal and ethical bounds. After the bursting of economic bubbles, journalists, academics, and governmental officials dissect the preconditions for widespread malfeasance in the nation's commercial and financial firms. In periods of both boom and bust, some enterprises have tried to attract business through misleading or false claims.

Our own generation has confronted several acute episodes of commercial deceit. Millions of individuals have experienced identity theft. The internet has facilitated thousands of marketing scams. Few investors avoided losses from the accounting misrepresentations associated with a string of colossal corporate bankruptcies, such as those of Enron and WorldCom. During and after the global financial meltdown of 2007–08, the business pages chronicled tales of prevarication and corruption at the heart of the American financial system. Deception became endemic within the chain of financing for the residential mortgage market. Manipulation became standard operating procedure in several markets, from the setting of benchmark interest and currency rates to commodities trading to the techniques of high-frequency stock trading.

Some economic deception is, of course, endemic to all modern capitalist societies. Throughout the world, business transactions depend on trust in far-flung counterparties across lengthening divides of space, beyond the social constraints of family, neighborhood, and religious community. The complexity of economic relations has created openings for those firms willing to take advantage of the enduring psychological vulnerabilities that behavioral economists have shown to be common to most investors and consumers. (Chapter Two of this book links the consistent psychological structure of economic deceit to these cognitive and emotional susceptibilities.) As a result, industrialized and industrializing societies on every continent have confronted the problem of how to handle financial and commercial misrepresentation.

Nonetheless, business fraud has occupied a large public footprint in the United States. Many of the world's most ambitious and expensive frauds have occurred in America; so too have some of the most far-reaching and innovative responses to financial and commercial deceit. From the American Revolution onward, the country's lionization of entrepreneurial freedom has given aid and comfort to the perpetrators of duplicitous business schemes. Enterprising risk-takers have enjoyed leeway from the arbiters of social norms, the makers of socioeconomic policy, and the practical operation of law, even when enthusiasm encouraged shading the truth or cutting legal corners.

The result has been latitude for processes of economic innovation in the United States, whether based on technological invention, new forms of organization, or the reimagination of the sorts of goods and services that might be offered for sale. But openness to innovation has always meant openness to creative deception. With every technological wonder, with every newfangled financial instrument or mode of organizing business ventures, with every beckoning new market, came bounteous prospects for dissemblers, operators, and downright swindlers. American popular culture, moreover, has retained a soft spot for charismatic grafters and oily-tongued salesmen, evincing admiration for their audacity, ingenuity, and capacity to land on their feet. Social commentators have often paired this appreciation with disapproval of the suckers who proved incapable of resisting pitches that were too good to be true.

And yet, the prevalence of economic deception has also always prompted anxieties about the dangers it posed to the health of American markets, about the possibility that unchecked duplicity might unleash "self-destructive tendencies" in economic life.[1] These concerns have generated recurring antifraud campaigns within the American business community, the American state, and the quasi-public domains between the two. American elites, it turns out, have abhorred regulatory vacuums about business fraud, especially at moments in which its social and economic costs have prompted wider public anxieties about the legitimacy of capitalist institutions. Since the early twentieth century, such efforts have been amplified, and sometimes challenged, by antifraud initiatives with more popular roots.

The chapters that follow explore American ambivalence about economic deceit from the early nineteenth century to the present. Since the first years of the American Republic, fraud has posed enduring commercial, political, and legal conundrums. American business owners, investors, consumers, elected officials, jurists, public servants, lawyers, accountants, journalists, and social activists have all tried to resolve dilemmas about how to cope with the problems of commercial and financial diddling, and thus how to constitute key features of capitalist marketplaces. How much freedom should firms have in trying to lure investors to part with their savings, or entice consumers to purchase their goods or services? What sorts of redress should be available if businesses overstep prevailing boundaries, venturing too far away from expectations of candor in their assertions and promises? The perennial issue, whether through common-law adjudication, informal standard-setting, statutory reform, or administrative rule-making, has been how to differentiate illicit chicanery from enthusiastic puffery. Making this distinction has never been easy, either to set overarching policy or guide day-to-day administration and enforcement, as it raises contentious disputes about economic justice and the appropriate boundaries of commercial liberty.

Since the consolidation of independence during the War of 1812, the regulation of American business fraud has gone through four phases. After the two introductory chapters, the four remaining sections of this book grapple with each of these distinctive eras of policymaking and law. For each period, I explore prevailing views about the nature of fraud and the threats that it posed to the commonweal, the emergence of new modes of regulatory governance to cope with those threats, the impacts of those policies, and the critiques that they provoked, which shaped the historical transitions from one era of policymaking to the next.

Part II, "A Nineteenth-Century World of *Caveat Emptor*," explores the relationship between antifraud law and business culture from the early nineteenth century into the 1880s. Well after the Civil War, the practical law of business fraud made it difficult to sustain many civil and criminal allegations of deceit. Reflecting a broader ethos of individualism and commercial permissiveness, this legal environment gave economic actors strong incentives to cast skeptical eyes on the firms and individuals with whom they conducted business. It also encouraged robust public discourse about prevalent misrepresentations and swindles, as journalists and editors found strong demand for coverage of business fraud and advice about how to avoid becoming a fraud victim.

Part III, "Professionalization, Moralism, and the Elite Assault on Deception," explores a series of legal and institutional challenges to *caveat emptor* that began in the mid-nineteenth century and accelerated in the Progressive era. Calls for greater regulatory paternalism came from many quarters—businessmen seeking to entrench their economic positions; professionals looking to solidify their social standing; social reformers and their political allies in both major parties, who argued that government had a duty to protect many social groups (the aged, the ill-educated and poor, recent immigrants, women, children) who were vulnerable to gross imposition; and individuals from all of these groups who, at some moments, viewed business fraud as a menace to economic and even social order. The resulting coalitions produced a cluster of antifraud initiatives targeting specific markets, such as commodities grading, the marketing of securities, mail-order retailing, and advertising, as well as growing organization of these efforts on a national basis.

Part IV, "The Call for Investor and Consumer Protection," examines the more ambitious and cohesive assaults on business fraud that policymakers fashioned during the New Deal and in the three decades following World War II. Triggered at first by the enormity of the Great Depression and the ensuing recalibration of government authority, these endeavors moved formal policy toward a stance of *caveat venditor*—let the seller beware—and relied more heavily on the national government. After 1960, a waxing consumer movement pushed elected officials to impose a yet wider array of disclosure requirements on businesses, and to expand the means by which disgruntled consumers and investors could seek redress through the legal system. Although this expanding web of antifraud regulation fell short of its architects' aspirations, these policies did circumscribe the scale and societal impact of business fraud.

Part V, "The Market Strikes Back," traces the partial resurgence of *caveat emptor* since the mid-1970s, as policymakers became convinced that economic growth required a much lighter regulatory touch. The resulting legal and bureaucratic shifts opened the door for a dramatic expansion in large-scale frauds, committed not just by marginal firms, but by some of the most important corporations in the global economy. It is possible that since the Global

Financial Crisis of 2008, antifraud regulation in the United States has entered a fifth phase, marked by revived skepticism about the reputational concerns of large corporations and renewed faith in the exercise of governmental power.

Throughout the book, I use fraud as a way to investigate the evolution of business-state relations and regulatory policy. Contemporary discussions of economic regulation often frame it in binary terms—there is "the market," on the one hand, and the state's "regulatory bureaucracy," on the other, with the latter constraining the former in the hopes of redressing some unfortunate by-product of market activity. But this framing mischaracterizes institutional realities. The efforts of nineteenth- and twentieth-century Americans to deal with the issue of economic misrepresentation show how markets and regulation have always been interconnected. Capitalist production, finance, and exchange depend on complex webs of regulatory policy. From the earliest phases of modern capitalism, regulation has defined property rights and guided contractual relationships by furnishing legal defaults. It has created modes of governance and stipulated social hierarchies for economic units—from the family farm and plantation to the sole proprietorship, partnership, corporation, and holding company, to the cooperative and the labor union. It has set standards for available products and services and demarcated the range of permissible business practices. Law and administrative regulation, in other words, have never stood apart from markets. Instead, they have always constituted them.[2]

In order to make sense of how prevailing antifraud policies have shaped American business, and how those policies have changed, in part because of pressures from business and other groups, it helps to think in terms of "regulatory ecology." At any point in time, that ecology includes many antifraud institutions. Many of these entities—legislatures, courts, regulatory agencies—operate inside government, whether at the local, state, or national level. But in the United States, a panoply of intermediary institutions have also helped to formulate and implement regulatory policy, including nongovernmental organizations (NGOs), industry trade associations, and the press. Self-regulatory organizations (SROs, in the parlance of management scholars and political scientists) have often served on the front lines of American efforts to promote truthful commercial speech and to identify and sanction those firms who stray from prevailing standards. The Better Business Bureaus stand out in this regard from their creation in the early twentieth century, and so receive extensive attention in this narrative.

In any given era, one must consider the missions, interests, capacities, and tensions that characterized all of these institutions, whether they resided inside, outside, or alongside the edges of "the state." One has to remain alert to the emergence of new institutions and the possibility that older ones may shift focus, both because of novel pressures and eroding imperatives. And one has to trace the *interactions* among this evolving set of regulatory players. This last task calls for close attention to moments in which officials jockeyed for jurisdictional control and competed to shape policy goals, strategies, and tactics. But it also requires analysis of the periodic attempts to coordinate legal reforms, build enforcement networks, and move or respond to wider public sentiment.[3]

Attempts to police business fraud tell us much about the wider history of American business regulation. From colonial settlement onward, efforts to ensure candor in commercial speech have occupied a key element of the nation's regulatory architecture, at first through the medium of patronage-based inspection regimes for exported commodities. Since the mid-nineteenth century, antifraud initiatives have often emerged at the leading edge of regulatory innovation. During the postbellum decades, antideception campaigns prompted the states and the federal government to develop techniques of modern administrative governance, in contexts that ranged from fertilizer certification to mail fraud law enforcement. Each of the resulting antifraud bureaucracies received broad delegations of power from legislatures and depended on forms of technocratic expertise. The Progressive era, the New Deal, and the Great Society spawned numerous regulatory experiments aimed at curbing economic deceit. Almost every one of these initiatives produced not only powerful new administrative agencies within the state, but also new private and quasi-public institutions devoted to fighting business fraud. The long-term performance of these institutions speaks to the enduring role of economic interests in shaping regulatory policymaking and administration. But it also demonstrates the power of ideas to influence regulatory strategy, as well as the capacity of professionalism and public-spiritedness to guide decision-making.

In part because attempts to combat fraud spawned new forms of regulatory authority and novel enforcement tactics, the arena of fraud fighting also exposed a crucial tension in American legal culture concerning the requirements of due process. The most effective modes of enforcement involved techniques of moral suasion and swift mechanisms of regulatory redress—the "fraud order" that denied Richard Sears and his company access to the US mails, or a "cease and desist" order from the Federal Trade Commission, or a declaration by a local Better Business Bureau that a company's advertising was "Not in the Public Interest." The firms whose connections, networks, and behavior did not measure up to such scrutiny often took issue with the lack of procedural protections associated with antifraud regulation. Their complaints drew sympathetic responses from many legal elites committed to Constitutional traditions of divided and accountable authority, and often culminated in the formalization of procedure. By slowing down antifraud enforcers, however, the turn to proceduralism muddied efforts to combat the prevaricators and outright cheats of the business world.

Business fraud has cut a wide enough swath through the American past that no volume with a two-century-long narrative arc could hope to be comprehensive, much less exhaustive. One key issue concerns the types of fraud under consideration, a second the evolving social and legal meanings of "fraud," a third the challenges of braiding dozens of particular stories of fraud and specific attempts to regulate it into an overarching analytical narrative. A few words are in order about each of these analytical choices.

My focus is on regulatory responses to fraud committed *by* business firms against external counterparties—suppliers, creditors, customers, and investors. Readers will find little discussion of fraud committed by consumers against businesses, as when forgers passed bad checks or policyholders cheated insurance companies, or about fraud committed by individuals against the government, whether through hiding income from the tax man or lying to gain access to public programs. I also sidestep the rich history of embezzlement committed by employees against their employers, whether public or private, as well as deceptions and gross impositions perpetrated by firms against their workers, such as the short-weighting of coal cars by nineteenth-century mining companies or the attempts of twenty-first-century retailing giants to avoid overtime payments to employees. Furthermore, I steer clear of most of the classic swindles directed at individuals by con artists, such as bunco steering (directing marks to a rigged game of chance) or the many types of advanced fee scams (promises of inheritances from long-lost relatives or other implausible tales that use the prospect of some unexpected windfall into making up-front payments).[4]

In terms of sociological theory, the book offers historical analysis of "organizational fraud"—fraud committed on behalf of firms against others—rather than "occupational fraud"—white-collar crime directed at businesses themselves by their employees. This distinction is far from airtight. The looting of firm assets by business managers, for example, has major collateral impacts on firm counterparties. Known among legal scholars as "control fraud," this form of managerial duplicity has been at the heart of significant episodes that do receive attention here.[5] I concentrate on organizational fraud because it exposes instructive historical conflicts within the business community. On the issue of fraud against businesses by consumers, or that of employees finding some new way to stick their hands into corporate tills, the business establishment has coalesced around the need for stern regulatory constraints and substantial investment in enforcement mechanisms. In the case of alleged deception perpetrated against workers, the business establishment has fought against legal reforms. By contrast, with organizational fraud, representatives of business have split into factions with clashing views about appropriate regulatory policies.

Several linguistic complications swirl about the phenomenon of business fraud. One can think of words such as "fraud" and "swindle" in either a colloquial or a technical sense. In the language of ordinary conversation and popular culture, to call a person or a business a "fraud" is, and has been for centuries, to make an accusation of ill-treatment or injustice, founded on deceit. A swindler pretends to be one thing, or to sell one thing, but is someone very different, or vends something of lesser or even no quality. In Noah Webster's 1817 *A Dictionary of the English Language*, "fraud" meant "deception or breach of trust with a view to impair the rights of another, a dishonest transaction"; to be "fraudulent" was to be "deceitful, trickish"; to "swindle" was to "cheat or defraud grossly or with deliberate artifice"; and a "swindler" was "one who lives by defrauding."[6] These meanings have retained their salience over the subsequent two centuries, joined by a slew of related Americanisms. Everyday language about business chicanery has often served as a rhetorical club. Disaffected consumers fulminated about encountering "a racket" as a way to bristle at an unsatisfactory purchase. Embattled business owners invoked the language of duplicity as a means of launching broadsides at nettlesome competitors. Alongside such elastic linguistic usages, however, one finds the much more circumscribed idioms and usages of law.

Fraud has an ancient pedigree in Anglo-American jurisprudence. Through centuries of cases at common law and equity, as well as countless legislative statutes, fraud acquired precise technical meanings. An allegation of "fraud" occurred in specific legal contests. It might be the basis for a civil suit that asked for damages: "so and so has defrauded me in commerce, and must therefore redress this wrong through monetary damages." It could constitute the defense of a litigant who sought to stymie enforcement of apparent contractual obligations: "I did sign that promissory note, but only because of illegal misrepresentations about the land that I purchased, and so I should not have to pay." It might be the substance of a criminal indictment: "Peter Funk is charged with one felony count of obtaining dry goods through false pretenses."

Each of these allegations required exacting standards of proof. To substantiate a claim of fraud, a litigant or prosecutor had to demonstrate several distinct propositions about economic behavior. At common law, and according to the requirements of many fraud ordinances and statutes, a showing of misrepresentation constituted a necessary element to such a case, but not a sufficient one. The legal demonstration of fraud also required evidence that the falsehood concerned existing facts, rather than predictions about the future; that the party guilty of misrepresentation knew the claim was false and intended to mislead; that the other party in the transaction believed the false claim and then relied on it; and that the other party, further, had exercised appropriate diligence in assessing the false claim's plausibility. At each link of this logical chain lay pitfalls for those who sought to prove an allegation of economic deceit. Perhaps the teller of an economic tall tale believed his own pitch. Or maybe a seller's false statement was such a whopper that a judge and jury could not believe anyone with half a brain could be taken in by it. Or perchance the buyer did not avail himself of easy steps to check the seller's reputation or the veracity of his statements. As in so many other legal matters, standards concerning fraud created uncertainties that skilled lawyers could exploit.

From the early nineteenth century up to the present, popular ways of talking about economic duplicity have often diverged from technical concepts governing legal consideration of allegedly fraudulent behavior. At times, however, legal concepts have shaped the beliefs and norms of ordinary citizens. I try to remain alert to the crosscutting influences of popular and legal talk about fraud, as well as the moments when reformers attempted to mobilize more popular notions to reform legal standards and regulatory architecture.

Readers of this history are going to encounter many individual stories of business fraud, a wide array of measures to combat it through retrospective mechanisms of justice or prospective modes of regulation, and varied strategic responses to those attempts. Along the way, they will meet scores of dodgy businesses—both the worst fly-by-nighters and some pillars of the establishment—and a like number of officials in prosecutors' offices, government agencies, SROs, and consumer organizations. This approach runs the risk of eliciting frustration. Brief examinations of fraud incidents may prompt a desire for more extensive exploration of personal motivations and societal impacts. Almost every previous history of business fraud takes the opposite tack, burrowing into the details of a specific episode in one market, one community, one business, or the life of one ill-fated entrepreneur, teasing out the complex personalities of central figures in a confined narrative. That approach lends itself to compelling storytelling and clean plotlines.[7] But it obscures longer-term trends and institutional development. My hope is that readers will see how all the capsule stories build on each other, suggesting enduring patterns, pointing to pivotal inflection points, and evoking broader implications for contemporary policymaking.

For more than two hundred years, Americans have struggled with how to balance the impulse to foster entrepreneurial innovation against the felt need to attack the most damaging commercial and financial dissembling. No matter how state and nongovernmental institutions have set about corralling the perpetrators of business frauds, those figures have proved to be elusive quarries, both as objects of regulatory policymaking and subjects of regulatory discipline. No matter how insistent skeptics of heightened regulatory authority have been in arguing that antifraud regulations placed excessive burdens on legitimate firms, new coalitions have appeared to demand regulatory action. The resulting patterns of rule-making, public education, and regulatory enforcement offer decision-makers instructive guides about how to foster the social confidence on which complex modern economies depend.

We will soon dig into American battles against economic misrepresentation and the worst forms of swindling, from the age of P. T. Barnum, the peerless promoter of nineteenth-century humbug, to that of Bernard Madoff, the post-1990 hedge-fund wizard. Along the way, we will have the chance to explore fundamental transformations in the institutional bases of American capitalism. First, however, the mental frames of deceit in modern marketplaces bear some consideration. Economic actors, it turns out, at least some of the time have an "error-prone, suggestible, and fallible nature."[8] An appreciation for these cognitive vulnerabilities, and how some businesses have taken advantage of them through commercial truth-stretching and more blatant frauds, provides crucial context for the modern struggles to prevent such behaviors or blunt their corrosive impacts.

CHAPTER TWO

The Shape-Shifting, Never-Changing World of Fraud

Since the earliest years of American independence, the most prevalent business frauds have occurred over and over again, even if dressed up in different garb or framed in newfangled terms. The "new smooth sell," an observer of the American business scene noted in the early 1960s, "often consists of ancient gimmicks in shiny new packages, tailored to the modern age."[1] A *Harper's Weekly* cartoon captured this key insight nicely the better part of a century earlier, in the spring of 1884 (Figure 2.1). It depicted two "financiers" conversing about the recent failure of "Smash Bang & Co.," a reference to the celebrated collapse of Grant & Ward, a New York City brokerage firm that included former President Ulysses Grant as a passive senior partner. Promising high returns from investment schemes and intimating that it had the inside track on lucrative government contracts, Grant & Ward attracted millions in capital from prominent investors. Two of the partners—Ferdinand Ward and James Fish—along with several confederates, appropriated the firm's assets to maintain lavish lifestyles, finance their own stock and real-estate speculations, and cajole big loans from banks and financiers, even as their financial positions became more and more desperate. To the cartoonist, the bankruptcy of "Smash Bang" was nothing but "An Old (s)Wine(dle) in a New Jar(gon)," a repetition of a long-established style of financial perfidy by business insiders.[2]

The *Harper's Weekly* caricaturist, Charles Green Bush, had good reason to expect his readers to get the joke. For the previous two decades, Americans had encountered a steady dose of scandals involving corporate officers or partners of investment firms who deceived the public about their businesses' financial condition while lining their own pockets. Transcontinental railroads, investment banks, and insurance companies all followed the basic script, even if not every incident culminated in the worst examples of "Smash Bang."[3]

This chapter peers into the "Old Wine" forever occupying these and other American marketplaces, offering a compendium of the major varietals of business fraud. The staying power of the dominant forms of deception reflects enduring dilemmas about whom and what to trust in a complex, integrated economy shot through with inequalities of access to information. It also speaks to

Figure 2.1: Smash, Bang & Co., *Harper's Weekly*, May 24, 1884, courtesy of David M. Rubenstein Rare Book & Manuscript Library, Duke University.

the cognitive and emotional dimensions of economic decision-making in modern capitalist societies, themes that in recent years have attracted a rich experimental and analytical literature in behavioral economics. Once we have grappled with the persistent psychological dynamics of modern business fraud, we will be much better positioned to explore the shifting currents of American antifraud policies.

Persistence in Flim-Flammery

Old Swindles in New Jargon recur throughout American history. But they have been especially evident in sectors dominated by complex products or services and characterized by transactions among strangers. Four domains convey the key patterns: the selling of investment opportunities; goods retailing; the marketing of personal economic opportunities, whether for education/training, employment, or credit; and the managerial looting of companies.

From the rise of stock-jobbing in late seventeenth-century England, the quintessential capitalist investment scam has been the "pump and dump."[4] This type of fraud preyed on public fascination with some novel outlet for investment—in nineteenth-century America, stock in a land company that intended to sell off pieces of the Ohio Country or the Yazoo region of the Mississippi Valley, or maybe shares in a Gilded Age industrial corporation operating in some promising field. Its perpetrators stoked public expectations about the new terrain for money-making, while directing attention to a specific enterprise that served as the vehicle of deception. Once all the vociferous pumping had elicited sufficient investment to drive up land prices or the value of a target company's stock, insiders dumped their assets onto the market.[5]

This basic strategy has had innumerable variants. Sometimes the goal was less to sell at the top then to create favorable conditions for selling a stock short, using futures contracts to bet on a fall in value. At other moments, the plan was reversed, as market manipulators spread rumors that, if true, would presage big declines in the worth of some company or sector. Once the "hypocritical growling of the bears" had prompted "simulation of things dark instead of bright," operators bought up shares on the cheap (or used futures contracts to bet on rising values).[6] Furthermore, the specific means of "pumping" has evolved over the centuries. In the nineteenth century, fraudulent stock promotions relied heavily on duplicitous pamphlet literature and planted puffs in metropolitan newspapers.[7] During most of the twentieth century, the chief conduits of manipulating market sentiment were mass-marketed tip sheets and telephone boiler rooms—offices crammed with desks, phones, and a battalion of stock salesmen who spent long days imploring prospects to take a plunge.[8] In recent decades, the internet chat room has become a leading instrument for the marketing of dodgy securities.[9] Yet the mode of operation remains little changed. First, use strategies of deception to influence public opinion about a financial asset, thereby shifting demand for it. Second, take the contrarian, and profitable, side of the ensuing trades, ahead of inevitable price corrections.

A second type of investment fraud, the pyramid scheme, also has retained its fundamental structure. Americans have named this type of swindle after the Italian immigrant Charles Ponzi, whose short-lived Boston finance firm, the Securities Exchange Company, dominated national headlines in the summer of 1920. A charismatic charmer, Ponzi offered Bostonians 50 percent interest for the use of their money for between forty-five and ninety days, a return supposedly made possible by arbitrage in an obscure financial instrument, international postal reply coupons. For several months, Ponzi fulfilled his promises, stimulating a torrent of deposits attracted by word of mouth from ecstatic early investors. He soon became a celebrated Boston entrepreneur, acclaimed by the public and able to purchase a major stake in a venerable local bank. Ponzi, however, paid off older investors with funds provided by new ones, a practice that could only work as long as the influx of deposits exceeded maturing obligations. This form of financial engineering invariably collapses under its own weight. In Ponzi's case, a series of newspaper stories in the *Boston Post* exposed his scheme's rickety underpinnings, triggering criminal investigations and a panicky rush by depositors to reclaim their capital. Only briefly able to stem the now-outgoing financial tide, Ponzi's company soon failed.[10]

Ponzi has had numerous emulators since 1920, with a spate of pyramid schemes emerging in the first decade of the new millennium, none bigger or more notorious than that engineered by Bernard Madoff, the New York City capitalist whose promise of steady returns through mysterious hedging strategies attracted thousands of investors, and billions of dollars of investments, from the early 1990s through 2008.[11] But Ponzi also had sundry predecessors. Scores of nineteenth- and early twentieth-century stock promoters adopted this path, promising lofty dividend payments and then delivering them through capital furnished by later investors. So too did a series of financiers operating outside the formal banking system.

Indeed, if historical priority determined idiomatic expression, Americans might well have reacted to the Madoff scandal by describing it as yet another "Franklin Syndicate," "Fund W," or "Ladies Deposit," rather than the latest Ponzi scheme. The Franklin Syndicate was the moniker of an 1899 pyramid scheme based in Brooklyn, for which a twenty-one-year-old clerk, William Miller, served as front man. Fund W operated out of Chicago earlier that decade, attracting over $1 million in deposits from investors all over the United States and Canada. Based in Boston from 1877 through 1880, the Ladies Deposit Savings Bank was run by Sarah Howe, a respectable-looking New Englander in her fifties. The Ladies Deposit only permitted investments from unmarried women of modest means, the total of which exceeded $500,000 by

1880. Each of these enterprises, with the exception of Sarah Howe's Savings Bank, advertised as mutual funds that would pool the savings of small investors, and then rely on access to inside information to earn enormous profits through speculation on the nation's exchanges. (Howe claimed that bequests by wealthy Quakers had created a surplus fund from which to pay interest to thrifty single females.) Each concern guaranteed ample payoffs (interest of 8 percent per month by the Ladies Bank, the ability to double or triple one's money within a year by Fund W, dividends of 10 percent a week by "520% Miller"), honored at first through the kind intercession of investing latecomers.[12] For at least 135 years, purveyors of pyramid schemes have followed a common script. Promise attractive, and often spectacular, returns. Rely on injections of capital to make good on those promises. Then sit back and watch as early investors become pied pipers, attracting exponential growth in investments, which those in charge skim off the top.

Such constancy in the scripts for business frauds applies as well to duplicitous retail marketing, which has involved mainly variations on the "bait and switch." Whether through reliance on window displays, newspaper advertisements, marketing circulars, catalogue copy, radio spots, television commercials, websites, or spam, this routine has begun with the same opening gambit—bombast. Amid the bustle and clutter of daily life in a capitalist society, find a way to grab consumers' attention, to persuade them to invite a salesperson into their homes, or to drive traffic into a store—sometimes located in a customer's own neighborhood, sometimes in a call center, and by the late twentieth century, in cyberspace. The bait involves some fabulous deal, a discounted price or a claim of fantastic quality that may seem too good to be true. In the most straightforward of these deceptions, consumers purchase the advertised good or service, only to discover a yawning gulf between promised attributes and actual value.

All too often, however, the initial come-on has served as prelude. Once consumers crossed the threshold of a retail establishment or invited some hawker into their living room, salespersons moved on to the "switch." The advertised sewing machine, or refrigerator, or set of dancing lessons, or MP3 player, inexpensive to be sure, was out of stock, no longer available, or really not a good deal after all because of its inferior quality or functional limitations. At this juncture, the goal became convincing customers to prefer a costlier alternative, which represented, when considered from every relevant angle, a much better value. In making this case, salespersons used all the wiles of the hard sell.[13] Known as "trading up" in the discourse of mid-twentieth-century consumer marketing, and "upselling" since the 1980s, this tactic often raised complicated questions about how to differentiate aggressive selling practices from intentional deceit. Was the advertised special completely unavailable, or only available to a lucky few? Did salespersons sing the praises of more expensive models, or deprecate the advertised item as a shoddy, even worthless imitation? As observers of the commercial scene periodically noted, "there is a fine line between a bait and switch and a trade up."[14]

No such ambiguity surrounded a related sales tactic—the making of oral promises at odds with the fine print of written sales contracts or the quality of provided goods and services. Such divergence has proved common in the vending of high-ticket goods and services on credit terms, in part because of a longstanding precept in American law, known as the "holder in due course" doctrine. From the 1842 case of *Swift v. Tyson* through the mid-1970s, this doctrine shielded innocent third-party holders of debts created by the sale of consumer goods. If the original creditor committed fraud in enticing a consumer to sign a contingent sales contract or a promissory note, and then sold that financial instrument to another person or firm who remained unaware of the original deceit, then the consumer could not avoid payment to the new creditor on the grounds that the original transaction was tainted by fraud. Sale or transfer wiped clean any legal stain left by sales misrepresentations.[15]

The holder in due course doctrine encouraged aggressive misrepresentation by sellers of consumer goods on credit. Salespersons and agents could shade the truth or lie outright in order to wheedle contractual signatures out of consumers, knowing that the contract imposed different terms and conditions. Perhaps the fine print incorporated fees or expensive insurance coverage, or specified a different base price, order quantity, or interest rate. Alternatively, customers who might think that they had taken merchandise on a trial basis left stores, according to the documents they had signed, as contingent owners who had just agreed to sales on installment plans. Once customers signed their name to a sales contact, firms could then transfer the resulting financial obligations to a loan broker or finance company at a heavy discount, leaving consumers to fend off uncompromising debt collection from these financial intermediaries.

Such schemes bedeviled the twentieth-century consumer marketplace. They became commonplace amid the explosion of debt-financed durable goods during the 1920s, sending streams of disgruntled urban consumers to seek the help of the country's new legal aid societies.[16] After World War II, American suburbia and the older terrain of small-town rural districts each spawned scores of home improvement companies and auto dealerships that worked versions of this racket; so did inner cities, with furniture stores, home security companies, electronics retailers, and sellers of frozen-food plans all garnering notoriety in this regard.[17]

The template for such duplicitous extension of consumer credit, however, reached well back into the nineteenth century. As early as the 1860s, scores of businesses in the emerging home improvement sector had embraced the mix of false oral promises, tricky fine print, and reliance on the holder in due course doctrine, carrying off schemes of misrepresentation every bit as sophisticated as those undertaken by their latter-day counterparts. The key players were lightning-rod companies, whose traveling representatives bombarded town and countryside with dire warnings about the risk of fire from every summer storm, while touting the new metal devices that could protect dwellings and outbuildings from heaven's angry bolts.

For these firms, bait and switch became standard operating procedure. Their agents lowballed estimates of installation costs and misrepresented any insurance coverage accompanying the sale of a rod system, while tucking expensive terms into sales contracts. In rural counties, salesmen explained to farm families that because their firms had just entered the area, they required a fine set of well-located buildings to demonstrate the quality of their rods, and so were willing to erect them for a big discount. (This enticement would be emulated a century later by purveyors of aluminum siding, swimming pools, and other home improvements.) Once a lightning-rod man cajoled or frightened some farmer into signing a purchase agreement, he would be followed some days later by an installation crew, and then by the firm's collecting agent. The collector would demand a much greater sum than the one to which the owner thought he had agreed, point out clauses in the fine print of the contract, and threaten legal action if the owner did not pay, or at least sign a note for the amount due. If the farmer agreed to the latter option, the company would sell the note to a local broker, leaving the farmer to grapple with the finer points of the holder in due course doctrine.[18] The rod "game" was emulated by sellers of "plows, horse rakes, or almost any kind of a rake that will rake in its victims."[19]

As with investment swindles and consumer rackets, the fraudulent marketing of educational courses, access to credit, and commercial openings has demonstrated great continuity. Such scams dangled some big opportunity before the public. It might be the chance to learn, in mere weeks, the essentials of bookkeeping or telegraph operation. It could be an opening for agents to represent some late nineteenth-century consumer goods manufacturer, with the chance not only to earn commissions from sales, but also royalties by recruiting other agents. Perhaps it involved an offer of a low-interest home loan in the years after World War I, the prospect of listing homes for sale with a real-estate agency that "guaranteed" results in the 1950s, or an exclusive franchise for an expanding national chain in the 1970s. In the midst of the exploding growth in household debt since the 1980s, it might involve the means to consolidate and refinance mounting credit card debt, or to furnish some form of "foreclosure rescue" to homeowners crushed by the housing collapse of 2008–09.

In all of these contexts, whenever a seeker of self-improvement, credit, business opportunity, house sale, or employment evinced interest by responding to an advertisement, details speedily followed. Without fail, the more extensive descriptions of the wonderful training course, generous loan terms, or well-remunerated employment would be accompanied by a notice of the need for some kind of payment up front—money for books and other materials, purchase of the exclusive right to sell a patented manufactured good in some rural county, a bill for a case of samples, charges for loan referrals or running a credit check. Such outlays, the "high pressure . . . big promise boys" would explain, constituted minimal, but unavoidable, investments in opportunity. Upon remittance of these "advance fees," as antifraud professionals have termed them since the early twentieth century, duped Americans soon experienced the bitterness of dashed expectations. Sometimes the "opportunity" turned out to be inferior to advertised promises. The exclusive license to sell a patent right would only confer the privilege of vending a useless invention. Guarantees of home sales, in the end, translated only into guaranteed listings in a real-estate brochure with no circulation. At least as frequently, fly-by-night enterprises took the money and ran.[20]

The reoccurrences of managerial fraud have followed comparable storylines. Amid the late-antebellum frenzy to build railroads and develop Appalachian coal mines, the officers of several companies staved off their own looming financial difficulties by selling thousands of shares of unauthorized stock. In the 1870s, the failure of several New York City life insurance companies brought revelations that they had placed fake policies on their books in order to paper over worsening finances, and so legitimate handsome salaries and ongoing dividend payments. During the great Florida real-estate boom of the 1920s, developers gained control of key banks in both Florida and Georgia, and proceeded to shower loans upon themselves and their associates, all the while insisting, often with the help of bribed state bank examiners, that their institutions remained paragons of financial prudence. Toward the end of the Great Depression, the American business establishment was rocked by an accounting scandal at the drug company McKesson & Robbins, in which corporate insiders faked inventories and purchase orders from a Canadian subsidiary as a way to appropriate the parent firm's profits.

The citadels of American capitalism continued to confront high-profile managerial control frauds in the decades following World War II. In the immediate postwar period, financial wheeler-dealers such as Lowell Birrell and Alexander Guterma made a fine art of looting the midsized industrial corporations that they controlled through complex stock and loan machinations associated with mergers. One crucial tactic for both was to use corporate stock as collateral for loans from high-interest moneylenders and then to default, allowing the creditors to dump shares on the market without public disclosure. During the Savings and Loan crisis of the 1980s, dozens of financial institutions relied on inflated appraisals of real estate to maintain a façade of strong earnings, which provided cover for huge salaries and bonuses. And around the turn of the millennium, a slew of large telecommunications, energy, and consumer products companies, among them WorldCom, Enron, and Sunbeam, manipulated their reports of financial performance to meet stock analysts' predictions and buoy stock prices. The most common tactics involved immediately booking expected streams of future revenue, shaving cost tallies, and even pretending that some ongoing liabilities actually constituted capital assets. In most cases, this fiddling was abetted by external auditors whose firms had come to depend on consulting contracts with the same companies.[21]

As these truncated descriptions indicate, the precise nature of deception varied from scandal to scandal, reflecting the evolution of corporate institutions, governance structures, and regulatory oversight. Whatever the details, the crux of deceit remained the same. Managers cooked the books to convey false impressions about corporate finances and prospects. Public misrepresentations provided rationales for munificent remuneration, as well as cover for self-dealing, the granting of sweetheart loans or contracts to cronies, and/or the unloading of shares controlled by executives. In the most egregious instances, such insider pilfering resulted in bankruptcy. Over and over, it was the tale of Smash Bang.

One might multiply these examples of recurrent motifs in deception within the history of American business, considering, for example, fictitious-pricing scams (the setting of falsely high "original" prices so as to create the appearance of bargains), the counterfeiting of branded goods, the running of mock auctions, or the tendency of some failing enterprises to defraud creditors, thereby transforming insolvency into a profitable enterprise. But the preceding overview suffices to establish the broad point. Most swindles have fallen into a discrete number of recognizable types, with little alteration of fundamental method.

THE MODERN PROBLEM OF TRUST IN THE MARKETPLACE

In light of such continuity, one might wonder about the inability of Americans to wise up over the past two-hundred-plus years. A Texas newspaper editor framed the issue in 1859 as he mused over the "perennial crop of fools" that fell for "plausible cheats": how could it be that "the man of to-day, with all the lights of the past to guide him, is just as much of a credulous idiot as at any time since the fall of Adam?"[22] This question should only be sharpened by Parts II through V of this book, which explore the substantial efforts to combat the problem of business fraud over two centuries, not least through strategies of public education. William H. Crosby, a lifelong swindler, encapsulated this historical puzzle in the 1923 book *Confessions of a Confidence Man*. "Every few months," Crosby pointed out to journalist Edward H. Smith, who actually penned the *Confessions*, "the newspapers and periodicals expose some sort of bunko game. The courts are continually sending our fellows to jail. The people are much better educated than they used to be. . . . But the confidence game is greater than ever."[23]

One crucial explanation involves the imperfect transmission of economic memory from generation to generation. In the short term, prevailing scams become so widespread as to gain notoriety, limiting their effectiveness. Such was the case with lightning-rod companies. By the 1870s the "lightning-rod man" had become an iconic character of commercial shiftiness and the hard sell, lampooned by writers such as Mark Twain, used by journalists and social commentators as a figurative emblem of economic trickery.[24] But Americans coming of age do not necessarily imbibe the lessons that their parents have learned. Business frauds, moreover, have never needed to fool all of the people all of the time. They result in acceptable returns so long as even a small percentage of individuals take the bait. Duplicitous lightning-rod agents found customers to fleece through the end of the nineteenth century and beyond.[25]

At a deeper level, business frauds exhibited such striking strategic continuities in the United States because the individuals who carried them out recognized the implications of a key feature of economic life in industrialized societies—asymmetries of information. Such imbalances intensified an omnipresent sociological dilemma. When transacting business, whom should one trust?

The dilemmas posed by differentials in relevant knowledge between counterparties, of course, have existed as long as there have been markets. Every premodern civilization had to grapple with the fact that sellers, and sometimes buyers, possessed informational advantages, and throughout most of recorded history, the mercantile classes have confronted popular resentments about a perceived penchant for misrepresenting wares. But the process of industrialization exacerbated inequalities in access to pertinent economic information. Technological complexity in the manufacturing of goods and the performance of services left consumers confronting daunting challenges of quality assessment. Revolutions in transportation and communication expanded the geographic scope of commercial activity, and so multiplied the quandaries associated with trading/investing at a distance and dealing with strangers. Innovations in financial instruments generated complex contracts whose legal implications often confounded the individuals and firms using them, while an explosive expansion in the use of credit generated tough questions about how to evaluate the trustworthiness of counterparties. And with the advent of the modern corporation, a growing proportion of transactions took place between large-scale organizations, whose bureaucracies possessed much knowledge about goods, business practices, and legal precepts, and often far less about small businesses and individual consumers. Without the pervasiveness of uneven access to information, none of the most common strategies of business deception would have found a sustainable niche.[26]

Practitioners of business fraud have often targeted demographic groups likely to suffer from informational gaps or to lack the savvy that accompanied long-term participation in modern transactional environments. In antebellum Eastern cities, operators of mock auction houses, gift enterprises (stores selling bundled discount goods that included prizes), and "bargain" stores licked their chops whenever newcomers from the country crossed their thresholds, a recurring scene captured in an 1858 *Harper's Weekly* cartoon of a "verdant countryman" (Figure 2.2).[27] As European immigrants poured into the United States during the nineteenth century, most encountered sharpers seeking to separate them from the savings with which they hoped to make a new start.[28] The more recent upsurge in immigration since the 1960s engendered innumerable scams that singled out Hispanics, Asians, or other newcomers.[29] From the Gilded Age onward, "work-at-home" schemes targeted poor women who lacked understanding of commercial law.[30] In the post–World War II inner city, bait-and-switch retailers preyed on the urban poor, who possessed low levels of formal education and confronted local retail monopolies.[31] Late twentieth-century financial and telemarketing fraudsters pursued America's growing elderly population; lonely and isolated, and sometimes facing cognitive impairments, a significant minority of the aged proved to be credulous about deceptively characterized goods, services, and investments.[32] Even educated native-born Americans might be the preferred targets of financial scams, as degrees and

VERDANT COUNTRYMAN. "Great Jerusalem! a Gold Ring and Livingstone's Travels for a Dollar! Ain't I lucky to have come just in time for sich a Bargain?" (*Goes in and Subscribes.*)

Figure 2.2: The antebellum "Verdant Countryman" enticed by the bargain. *Harper's Weekly*, April 17, 1858, courtesy of David M. Rubenstein Rare Book & Manuscript Library, Duke University.

professional careers did not ensure familiarity with the securities markets. Teachers, ministers, doctors, and middle-class widows have long had a reputation among fraudulent promoters as prone to bite at a good investment pitch.[33] In part, the history of American business fraud has constituted an unending search for economic novices.

Encounters with all the misrepresentations and swindles in the American marketplace, of course, spawned wariness, a dynamic well understood by the more adept practitioners of commercial and financial deceit. Many economic actors, including one-time greenhorns, came to recognize their disadvantages in access to relevant commercial information, as well as the pervasive threat of marketing falsehoods and exaggerations. Having witnessed or suffered through the indignities that came with a retail fleecing or a financial scam, they put up their guards.

This reality gave novel twists to the age-old imperative of earning trust. As the economy became ever more integrated on a continental and international basis, long-term profitability depended on reputations for reliability, quality, service, and value. From the mid-nineteenth century onward, Americans developed a slew of institutional strategies to assess the reputation for goods, services, assets, and business entities. These innovations ranged from trade journals, credit reporting firms, investment analysts, and bond rating agencies to product testing organizations, consumer groups, and corporate efforts to shape public associations with products and services, known as "brand management."[34] Yet the very success of these adaptations spawned new opportunities for misrepresentation and fraud. Within any modern process of fashioning trust lay a blueprint for how to simulate it, how to appear to possess some trusted mark of integrity so as to carry out fraud against economic neophytes and sophisticates alike.[35]

Again, the key patterns among swindlers and more legitimate firms that developed deceptive business practices recurred over time. Three stand out— social mimicry, personalization amid bureaucratization, and deflection. These strategies could overlap, as American firms that embraced deceit as a fundamental business strategy often relied on the first two, and sometimes on all three. Nonetheless, it is helpful to separate these economic charades.

To point out that American business frauds have depended on elaborate acts of impersonation risks belaboring the obvious. But Herman Melville's 1857 novel *The Confidence-Man* furnishes an important clue about the deeper historical significance of this dimension of economic deception. Its setting, the steamboat *Fidele*, symbolizes the emerging commercial world of distant linkages and anonymous counterparties. As the *Fidele*—an invocation of the Latin root *fides*, meaning trust or belief—makes its way down the Mississippi River, crossing the regions of America's midcontinent, it takes on hundreds of passengers from every racial and ethnic group and every social status, all milling together in one floating microcosm of a larger society. Aware of how difficult it has become to assess the trustworthiness of all the strangers and deal-making around them, passenger after passenger manifests an abiding skepticism about everything and everyone. The prevalence of deceit had left Americans of Melville's time already inclined to look askance at wares and projects offered in the public marts, and the hawkers who pushed them. Thus as Melville's Satanic (or, as some interpreters have argued, Christlike) Confidence Man saunters about the steamboat, he continually confronts the challenge of overcoming ingrained distrust. To prepare the way for the impositions that he visits on various passengers, he must perform one "masquerade" after another. From scene to scene, the Confidence Man seems to change shape, assuming the persona of a wizened and disabled African American man, a Mason fallen on hard times, a well-dressed traveling agent for a new charity for the Seminoles, the president of a coal mining company, and several others. In describing the serial misrepresentations that take place on the *Fidele*, Melville summons the world of theatre. As one distrustful character in the novel insists, "To do is to act; so all doers are actors."[36] Swindlers, Melville realized in the early years of America's encounter with economic relationships rife with information asymmetries, must look the part, possess the right props, know the right cues. This basic truth has structured business frauds from Melville's time to our own.

The simplest forms of dramatic imitation appropriated name and place. As soon as nineteenth-century manufacturers began to develop brand awareness among consumers, opportunists passed off counterfeit goods as the original. Many businesses tried to siphon off trade by adopting a commercial moniker that resembled that of a well-regarded enterprise, or that communicated an image of solidity and respectability. For the same reason, architects of business frauds appreciated the marketing power of location. If the public associated an industry with a single city, or neighborhood, or street, then it made good sense to set up shop there—or at least appear to do so. Up until the 1920s, for instance, New York's financial district was home not only to the nation's leading investment banks and brokerages, but also a motley assortment of short-lived bucket shops and dodgy mutual funds that touted their geographic respectability. A Wall Street address, like the one that the bogus New York City brokerage house Baxter & Co. trumpeted on the front of its 1870s marketing circulars (Figure 2.3), usually paid dividends.[37]

More subtle techniques of emulation concentrated on the general trappings of commercial success, rather than the specific markers of well-regarded firms. Promoters of financial swindles were especially inclined toward such tactics. Like the leading characters in the 1973 movie *The Sting*, most maintained offices "fitted up with great elegance" and lived the high life in order to convey an aura of wealth and social standing.[38] Before the adoption of the New Deal, dodgy financiers frequently enticed local dignitaries to serve as company directors, with "deacons of churches, bank presidents, provost marshals, and eminent lawyers" serving the purpose, should ex-governors or former Civil War generals not be available. These "decoy ducks" would receive a few thousand dollars' worth of shares in exchange for the use of their names. The hope, often realized, was that potential investors would view these celebrities' participation as endorsements of legitimacy and credibility, and so "bring others near

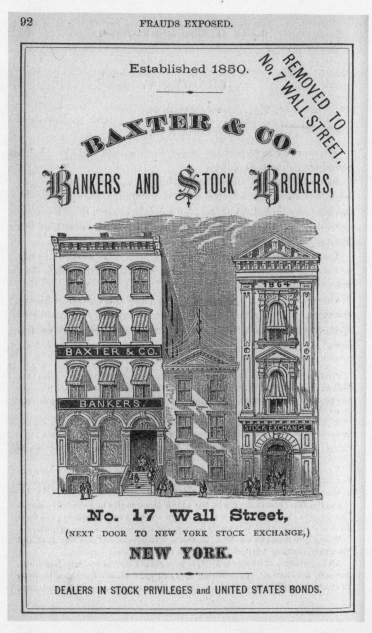

Figure 2.3: Front page of Baxter & Co. circular, circa 1878, in Anthony Comstock, *Frauds Exposed: How the People Are Deceived and Robbed, and Youth Corrupted* (New York, 1880), 92. Note that the image at once emphasizes the firm's proximity to the New York Stock Exchange and depicts the NYSE as housed in a smaller and less substantial structure.

enough to be made game of."[39] In some cases, even a bogus prominent person could do the trick. One fraudulent Texas oil trust estate in the 1920s used as its public face "General" Robert A. Lee, an elderly former janitor whom the enterprise claimed to be related to Robert E. Lee. By sending out a torrent of courtly letters from "General Lee" and placing his stately image on every trust certificate, this outfit lured thousands of white Southerners to throw away their savings by investing in the venture.[40]

The most powerful means of getting people to view a fraudulent investment as legitimate, however, remained the payment of initial dividends and the manufacture of upward price movements. Since the advent of modern securities markets, nothing has persuaded investors to take a flyer on a corporation, place their funds at the disposal of a brokerage house, or jump into a pyramid scheme more than beguiling evidence of its capacity to generate returns. Whether in the form of capital appreciation or payments dressed up as income distributions, tangible markers of market sentiment and earnings struck many Americans as economic omens that commanded respect, even when accompanied by warnings that past results offered no guarantees of future prospects.[41]

The deceptive firms that turned to social mimicry exploited modern badges of upright economic conduct. They forged a trademark, appropriated the high standing that a firm had built up with credit bureaus, traded on the esteem enjoyed by renowned directors, basked in the protection of "independent" audits, or simulated the behavior of successful businesses. By contrast, the method of personalization harkened back to much older means of demonstrating trustworthiness. This technique still required satisfying dramatic performances. But alongside attention to convincing backdrops and costumes, many practitioners of fraud recognized the value of having key actors carry off roles with emotional plausibility.

For a host of American businesses that relied on deceitful practices, oral communication and person-to-person encounters remained crucial tactics of misrepresentation. Almost every version of the bait and switch incorporated this approach. Whatever the nature of the bait, the switch depended on personal interactions between salespersons and customers. The pivotal assertions and assurances came through rehearsed lines and gestures. Artful pitches had the aim of eliciting confidence, not just in the goods or services for sale, but first and foremost in the flesh and blood sellers. When nineteenth-century lightning-rod agents worked their magic, 1950s used-car salesmen touted different and more expensive sedans from those featured in television spots, or early twenty-first-century mortgage brokers dangled exotic subprime mortgages before prospective homeowners, the first rule of selling was always in effect: before deceptive economic actors could sell the product or service, they had to "sell themselves," to "gain the friendship" of the customer or client and convey the air of someone whose word deserved credit.[42] The effective pitchman of phony investment vehicles, a Midwestern newspaper noted in 1910, was not only "always well groomed, always redolent of the fragrance of daily tubbing, massaging, and the barber shop route," but also possessed of a "dazzling smile and ingratiating manners." As the German sociologist Niklas Luhmann has put it with regard to the more general problem of gaining social confidence, "whoever wants trust must take part in social life and be in a position to build the expectations of others into his own self-presentation."[43]

Adding a personal touch to schemes predicated on deception was a straightforward matter for firms that conducted business face to face. But this approach also beckoned to entrepreneurs who hoped to pull off misrepresentations from a distance. During the first several decades of mail-order selling, the voluminous marketing literature unleashed by fraudulent firms struck a familiar tone, emulating the down-to-earth communications of the era's most successful firms.[44] Several promoters of fraudulent stocks in the early twentieth century cultivated close relationships with their investors. In pamphlets, market letters, and editorials, they portrayed any trials and tribulations that afflicted their companies as shared troubles, and solicited investments on the basis of emotional bonds forged through years of mutual risk-taking.[45] Most pyramid schemes pursued a more indirect approach to cultivating trust through personal links, relying on either the marketing skills of commission agents, who tapped their own social circles, or the cadre of satisfied early depositors. After receiving the first round or two of promised dividends, the latter made themselves into informal investment barkers who bragged about their good fortune and encouraged friends and family to follow their lead.[46]

Ties born of shared social circumstance or worldview facilitated such strategies. Members of an ethnic or racial group, religious organization, profession, or political persuasion have proven vulnerable to scams perpetrated by individuals with the same demographic characteristics or cultural markers. In the late 1980s, regulators and financial journalists termed this pattern "affinity fraud." As one California state official explained in 1992, "normally suspicious people substitute their faith in their group for their own independent judgment on the merits of a deal." Pyramid schemes in the late twentieth and early twenty-first centuries exploited this tendency to rely on the supposed wisdom of one's social networks. In its early years, Bernard Madoff's fake hedge fund, Ascot Partners, cultivated Jewish investors, both individuals and institutions; similar, if less gargantuan, frauds ensnared Seventh-Day Adventists, African American Baptists, Utah doctors, Masons, conservative Republican activists,

Hispanic and Indian immigrants, even alumni from and parents of students attending elite universities.[47]

There is some evidence that the incidence and scope of affinity fraud increased during and after the 1980s, a phenomenon perhaps related to the growing fragmentation of American society and the related sharpening of social identities. Extensive immigration and expansion in the number of tightly bound religious communities each fostered the development of close-knit social worlds that defined boundaries between trusted insiders and the rest of society. Such circumstances heightened opportunities for individuals within a given communal circle to lure their fellows into some commercial or financial trap.[48]

This kind of chicanery, however, had numerous precursors. The depredations of Sarah Howe's Ladies Deposit Savings Bank fit this pattern, as female depositors manifested enormous faith in their benefactress.[49] So too did a decades-long string of religiously based investment frauds.[50] Every burst of immigration also generated scams perpetrated against particular nationalities by their countrymen.[51] The early twentieth-century racket in bogus remittance banks represented a ruthless example of this type of fraud. Focused on one ethnic group, these businesses advertised their capacity to transfer funds across the Atlantic in the foreign-language press and used immigrant agents from the region in question. Each year, as one Western newspaper reported in 1905, these fake firms "filch millions of dollars out of the pockets of the most ignorant and helpless immigrants."[52] Even if the term "affinity fraud" emerged only toward the end of the twentieth century, the practice had a venerable American lineage.

The third and least common method of garnering reputation for integrity pursued the most indirect tactics, cloaking deception behind a public posture of fraud-fighting. In a sector that had gained notoriety for legerdemain, such as the installation of lightning rods, sales agents might, as some did, begin their pitch by deprecating "the trickery of some agents" and proclaiming that, unlike their competitors, their firm did "business on the square."[53] Similarly, ads by nineteenth-century purveyors of quack medicine might caution consumers to beware of unscrupulous competitors who injured patients with spurious elixirs, even while explaining that their in-house physicians made "a specialty of all chronic diseases of men and women," and had great skill in diagnosing and treating individuals by mail (Figure 2.4).[54]

Far more elaborate efforts to demonstrate probity emerged in the nation's securities markets. Several early twentieth-century promoters of fraudulent stocks and commodity-investment vehicles circulated market letters and fi-

CAUTION.

Beware of Fraudulent Advertising Doctors and Medical Companies who Advertise to Give Free Samples of Medicines, Free Prescriptions and Cheap Medical Treatment

The Best is the Cheapest—Skill, Honesty, Experience and Reliability in Your Physicians is What You Need—Dr. Hathaway & Co Are Permanently Located in This City Have Been for Years, and Have the Confidence of the Public,

Figure 2.4: Segment of Dr. Hathaway & Co. advertisement, *San Antonio Express*, Feb. 12, 1899, 12, courtesy of America's Historical Newspapers, Digital Edition published by Readex, a division of NewsBank, Inc.

nancial publications that warned investors about bogus companies, in addition to pushing worthless companies they themselves owned. Thus the Bankers' and Merchants' Guarantee Credit Exchange (BMGCE), a fraudulent New York City brokerage firm that operated around the turn of the twentieth century, boasted in its pamphlets that its mission was to "crush out all unprincipled concerns and direct the public to reliable firms." To identify the duplicitous, BMGCE explained, "we employ men of sterling integrity who are virtually detectives." The brokerage further directed its subscribers to a fake mercantile agency, the Investors Protection Bureau, which for two dollars would send out "a report on brokers, merchants, and manufacturers," enabling investors "to protect [themselves] against loss by fraud, failure and otherwise."[55] This technique of "concealing [one's] own sins by a loud denunciation of the sins of others" became commonplace among the financial tip sheets of the 1910s and 1920s.[56] The idea with such diversions was to fend off potential charges of knavery against one's own business by casting aspersions elsewhere. Consumers and investors, the thinking went, would let down their guard when dealing with a firm that furnished such clear evidence of public-spirited concern for fair dealing.

These three strategies for solving the problem of trust recurred because they tended to work in the short term. Successful practitioners of deceit recognized that Americans, facing so many information asymmetries, developed rules of thumb to distinguish businesses in which one might place some degree of confidence from those best left alone. By embracing the poses of commercial mimicry, personalized salesmanship, and/or deflection, these operators took advantage of such informal guideposts. Success in commercial deception, then, required an appreciation for the psychology of coping strategies amid the dizzying hurly-burly of modern economic life. Indeed, in every era since the United States gained its independence from Great Britain, business fraud has required a keen grasp of human sentiment and behavior. As the secretary of the Colorado State Horticultural Society noted in an 1887 paper about duplicitous tree peddlers, swindlers who thrived at their craft were not only unscrupulous, shrewd, and "endowed by nature with the 'gift of the gab'"; they were also "well versed in all the foibles of human nature."[57] Those foibles deserve some exploration in their own right.

DECEPTIVE PRACTICES AND THE PSYCHOLOGY
OF ECONOMIC DECISION-MAKING

Over the past decade, a growing number of historians have made emotional life a central subject of inquiry. The emotions, these scholars have shown, have a history—they are contingent upon social and cultural context and are learned as well as experienced, perhaps in equal measure. Transformations in society and culture, such as the French Revolution and its aftermath, can so powerfully remake public touchstones of value that they refashion the very sensation and awareness of sentiment.[58] But the fact of some, or even much, emotional change does not imply processes of wholesale emotional transformation. A further explanation for the tendency of the same basic frauds to bedevil American marketplaces across the centuries lies in the ability of their perpetrators to rely on a fixed set of psychological nudges. From the age of P. T. Barnum to that of Bernard Madoff, social commentators have identified an enduring set of affective tendencies that made Americans susceptible to humbug and imposition.

Some of the psychological impulses that show up again and again in the history of business fraud reflect widespread aspirations or anxieties. None received more attention, either from swindlers or observers of market behavior, than the passion for easily attained wealth. Investment frauds catered to this dream and the gambling instinct that it fostered, celebrating "the desire for gain," which, as a circular by one fraudulent Gilded Age brokerage put it, was "the strongest impulse of the human heart." In a society that produced overnight fortunes and disseminated rags-to-riches narratives, promoters could count on interest in plausible schemes to "sweep [individuals] to riches" and render investors "independent for life."[59] Many investment cons intensified such appeals by offering a way to become "insiders" within the byzantine world of finance. The fake blind pool around the beginning of the twentieth century, like the sham hedge fund around its conclusion, claimed to take advantage of special market intelligence or investment opportunities that were not readily available. "We employ SPECIAL CROP EXPERTS," screamed one New York City brokerage firm's 1897 advertisements for participation in a "SPRING WHEAT POOL" that was privy to "EXCLUSIVE INFORMATION" and operated "for the sole benefit of our active customers." Such swindles promised exclusivity as well as routes to wealth.[60] Healthcare swindles, by contrast, played on fundamental fears. Bogus nineteenth-century patent medicines, like quack mid-twentieth-century cancer cures, dangled hope in front of those laid low by disease, correctly anticipating that the afflicted desired talismans of optimism.[61] Whether conjuring up visions of Easy Street or medical miracles, swindlers exploited proclivities toward fantasizing and wishful thinking.

Findings within psychology, and especially within the burgeoning literature of behavioral economics, point the way toward a more refined understanding of why so many venerable frauds have maintained niches within American business culture. Since the 1970s, behavioral economists have conducted psychological experiments all over the world to assess how subjects choose between economic alternatives. This research has documented patterns of behavior that diverge from the expectations of "rational" economic decision-making. Such conduct, the researchers argue, suggests an array of cognitive tendencies and emotional dispositions that do not fit longstanding assumptions about motivations for economic action. The relevance of this research for the history of business fraud lies in the striking correspondence between these modes of thinking/feeling and recurring features of economic deceit.

Behavioral economists explain nonrational modes of economic assessment in terms of biases (filters that shade how individuals make sense of experience) and heuristics (mental shortcuts that people use when confronted with a massive amount of information to process).[62] None of the habits of mind identified by behaviorists represents a full picture of economic decision-making. They encompass a set of common intuitions and initial impressions, which interact with other cognitive perceptions, emotional responses, and perceived norms, and which individuals often revise or reject in light of analysis and sober second thought. A number of scholars argue that these biases and intuitive shortcuts emerged over the long history of human evolution because they allowed people to cope with complex social situations.[63] Regardless of whether such cognitive tendencies originated in the deep past or emerged with more complex civilizations, and whether or not they reflect the hard-wiring of brain chemistry or cultural processes of learning, they have made modern humans vulnerable to deception.

The pervasive faith in "social proof," for example, helps to account for the nature of investment frauds. A key element of most pump and dump swindles and all pyramid schemes is that once a critical mass of suckers takes the bait, their example prompts others to follow in their wake, often after hearing about the opportunity from acquaintances who exult in their good fortune. Most latecomers place their faith in the investigation done by those who preceded them (going along with the herd), especially, as in the case of affinity fraud, when the people they emulate come from the same trusted social group.[64]

Strategies of commercial imitation dovetail with a thought process that behaviorists refer to as the "representativeness" heuristic. This mental habit leads individuals to emphasize anecdotal social cues and markers when making judgments of economic value, particularly when access to alternative kinds of evidence is limited, or that evidence requires extensive and complicated analysis. Whenever these signals have a salience—whenever, that is, initial impressions are strong because of effective presentation—many people assume that they convey all the information they need to know. They presume, in other words, that the signals stand for or represent underlying reality.[65] In any social environment characterized by extensive reliance on this cognitive benchmark, some percentage of economic actors will remain susceptible to fraudulent schemes that pull off convincing shows of social mimicry.[66]

A third mental shortcut, the "availability" heuristic, encourages individuals assessing the merits of economic alternatives to place great weight on easily recalled events and memorable personal experiences. Several abiding characteristics of investment frauds track this method of cognitive evaluation. Promotions of spurious companies invoke examples of firms whose rapid growth brought tremendous fortunes to investors who had the good sense to get in early. The choice of exemplars shifted from era to era, from mining and oil ventures, to the daring speculative exploits of the late nineteenth-century financier Jay Gould, to Bell Telephone and Ford Motor, to Microsoft and Intel. But the goal remained that of associating the fraudulent firm with others that had burst into prominence and extraordinary profitability by laying out precise, often exaggerated calculations of the returns earned by those who purchased shares in such companies at the earliest opportunity.[67] Early dividend payments by fraudulent investment schemes have similarly taken advantage of the availability heuristic, which gives investors or depositors a strong nudge toward seeing the enterprise as legitimate.

The prevalence of this cognitive tendency further helps to account for investment swindles' cyclical character. Every speculative boom since the American Revolution has invited financial frauds, from phony early nineteenth-century land companies to the creation of supposedly AAA-rated collateralized debt obligations amid the housing bubble of the early 2000s. This same correlation has emerged elsewhere since the seventeenth century. Whenever asset values shoot up, fantastic claims find more receptive audiences, because investors see evidence of rapid accumulations of wealth all around them.[68]

Many retailing frauds have taken advantage of a fourth cognitive rule of thumb, the "anchoring" heuristic, through which individuals fix a value to some asset, opportunity, or situation, and then use that value as a reference point for later assessments. Pervasive reliance on evaluative anchors helps to account for the psychological pull of sales and discounts, including offers of "free" bonuses; the special deal appears to require much less of consumers than does the anchored price.[69] Anchoring similarly helps to explain the long-standing capacity of dodgy retailers to pull off fictitious pricing or "bait and switch" techniques. With the former practice, retailers construct an artificially high "normal" price, whether through claims about manufacturers' list prices, misleading comparisons to prices at other retailers, or inflated presale "original prices." So long as consumers lack awareness of prevailing prices, the fictitious values set a mental reference point, encouraging sales that would not have otherwise occurred.[70]

In the case of "bait and switch" tactics, the "bait" invokes economic reference points that already exist, such as customary prices, attracting attention because of the dramatic difference between those anchors and advertised specials. The "switch" seeks, in part, to exploit the psychological expectations created by the bait. Firms carrying out this bit of chicanery hope that consumers who have already invested time and effort, and who have convinced themselves that they have located special deals, will be loath to walk away empty-handed. This emotional investment makes them susceptible to the switch. There is always, of course, the opposite possibility: that consumers will be so angered by manipulative tactics that they leave in a huff. But bait and switch operators have calculated that any harm to their reputations would not stem the influx of more malleable shoppers.

Behavioral economists refer to this last example of mental anchoring as "loss aversion." In experiments that ask subjects to make choices that involve assessments of risk, most people view economic losses as more painful and memorable than equivalent gains. As a result, consumers and investors often prove susceptible to how marketers frame opportunities and risks, demonstrating greater motivation to act if they see themselves as avoiding or preventing monetary harm rather than pursuing reward.[71] In some contexts, such as real-estate development or securities investments, loss aversion would seem to complicate rather than assist fraudulent promoters' efforts. Leeriness about losing what one has would hardly appear to encourage chasing after the latest road to riches. Yet even in the realm of speculative investment, savvy marketers have exhibited an intuitive grasp of psychology. They priced the stock of bogus companies or misrepresented home-sites cheaply, and allowed investors to purchase on the basis of margin or installments. Sometimes they drew suckers in with offers of "bonus shares" of some security as a means of inculcating a sense of ownership.[72] All of these maneuvers lowered perceptions of cost. They also framed sales pitches around the avoidance of regret alongside the attainment of gain. A postbellum ad for town lots in some new Western settlement, or a prospectus for an early twentieth-century airline company, might plead with readers not to miss out on that rare chance to get in early, when the really huge gains were possible. As the early twentieth-century journalist Arthur H. Gleason recognized, this kind of pitch could sound like a revivalist sermon. The fraudulent promoter, Gleason argued, was

> a professional trafficker in spasms. He must create an emotional crisis in a multitude of persons, and must repeat the same intensity of effect many hundreds of times. He deals in breathless excitement, the peremptory demand for an immediate decision from sinner or sucker, the Last Chance for Salvation or Big Profits, To-Night and Now the Time.[73]

To hold back, to keep the checkbook in one's breast pocket, was to court regret, or as one promoter framed the issue in 1917, to miss out on the "Foresight [that] makes Millionaires," to identify oneself as a "groveling *WISHER*, always *wishing* for something BIG to turn up," who, "when the *chance* does come never [has] the COURAGE to grasp that chance."[74]

Even after a fraudulent investment failed, promoters dangled analogous rationales for throwing good money after bad. Such techniques, known as "reloading," emerged during the post–World War I Texas oil boom. Promoters would explain to loyal followers that even though the oil company in which they held shares had entered bankruptcy, there was a fantastic opportunity to recoup losses by launching a new company that would buy the old one's assets on the cheap, as well as those of other insolvent oil firms. So long as investors provided additional capital, surefire profits remained only a gusher or two away. Thousands of defrauded investors responded to such appeals, which allowed them to put off psychological acceptance of losses, and to retain faith that their initial decisions would be vindicated.[75]

Throughout the nineteenth century and most of the twentieth, the Americans who adopted deceptive business practices obviously did not craft their misrepresentations with the research findings of behavioral economists in

mind. Even toward the end of the twentieth century, few if any architects of
deceptive marketing practices or unambiguous business fraud were conversant
with the technical language of "mental accounting" and "cognitive heuristics."
But over the decades, outright swindlers and firms that practiced forms of deceit carried out their own investigations into consumer and investor psychology, testing which tactics and messages worked with a sufficient number of
targets to make chicanery pay. As Bates Harrington put it in his 1878 book
How 'Tis Done (which portrayed itself as an exposé of the various con games
visited upon the American countryside, but reads in many respects as a how-to
guide for aspiring swindlers), the most adroit practitioners of economic deceit
had reduced their endeavors to "a science. Every possible weakness of human
nature, every loophole of ignorance, every assailable point where advantage
may be gained, is studied with utmost care."[76] These informal marketing trials
generated techniques that dovetailed with the economic psychology revealed
by the more rigorous studies of the past two generations.

An episode from the history of Gilded Age financial speculation suggests
that at least some Americans grasped the significance of cognitive guideposts
such as the availability heuristic. After one fraudulent New York City brokerage had invested large sums to entice people from across the continent to speculate in its investment pools, it received numerous letters from individuals offering to serve as local agents. Many of these enterprising souls, like one
Presbyterian minister from rural Pennsylvania, proposed that they would send
in an increasing series of investments, with the brokerage sending out a series
of even-larger checks in turn, demonstrating its capacity to live up to all the
wondrous promises of its circulars. As the minister recapped his plan:

> If I send you immediately $20, will you in 30 days send me your check for $40?
> Then if I send you as another operation $50, will you send me in 30 days $100?
> Next, if I send you as a third operation $100, will you send me in the end of
> thirty days, $200? If you will do this, I can have sufficient grounds to go upon, in
> my efforts to arouse some of my rich farmers who would not listen unless the
> evidence perfectly satisfactory and sure while they were yet ignorant of the meth-
> od and details.[77]

This correspondence leaves unclear whether the minister intended to shear his
parishioners, or rather hoped only to fleece the fleecers with a bit of their own
technique. Either way, the proposition speaks to a keen appreciation of how
bait dividends could inspire trust.

****

The affective dimensions of economic life changed enormously as Americans moved from farm to city to suburb, uprooted the institution of slavery, helped to fashion and learned to cope with large-scale corporations and unions, and encountered the technologies that spilled out of industrial research facilities, the increasingly sophisticated campaigns cooked up by advertising agencies, and the ever-greater abstractions of financial markets. As the United States evolved from a nineteenth-century society predicated on production to a twentieth-century society structured around consumption, to take just one far-reaching process, the emotional texture of Americans' daily economic endeavors underwent huge transformations.[78]

The most captivating purveyors of business fraud have always remained attuned to these shifts, recognizing that deceptive marketing rests on plausible storytelling. Credible mimicry, charismatic personalization, and persuasive deflection all presume a deft grasp of social context, a capacity to tap into personal aspirations and set people at ease. One cannot pull off such masquerades without careful updating so that sales pitches evoke the lived experiences and emotional realities of targeted consumers and investors. The character of Robert A. Lee, for example, would have brought little demand for oil shares in the 1850s or the 1970s; amid the early twentieth-century flowering of Lost Cause ideology and entrenchment of segregationist white supremacy, this figure struck thousands of white Southerners as the sort of regional capitalist to whom they should deliver modest investments.[79] The inventiveness and social adeptness among the perpetrators of business fraud has left its mark on American language. As they applied longstanding modes of deception to new economic and social situations, they fashioned slang to describe their practices. Each generation has produced an argot of fraud, a wealth of evocative terms that convey prevailing practices of imposition and intentional misrepresentation.

For all of the narrative specificity that marked business frauds as characteristic of specific times, and often specific demographic and geographic communities, the psychological structures of misdirection did not shift much. These consistent strategies point to cognitive vulnerabilities that endured underneath shifting sensibilities, reconstructed economic lives, and the always-fresh storytelling that underwrote the most effective fraudulent schemes. The extent to which American policymakers recognized these cognitive vulnerabilities, however, did not remain constant. Nor did prevailing judgments about how much policymakers should be concerned about business fraud, or ideas about how the government and other institutions should try to constrain it. In the early nineteenth century, which the rest of this book takes as its point of departure, American law contained numerous formal restrictions on deceitful economic behavior, which were rooted in centuries-old Anglo-American legal precepts. It also contained some specialized regulatory institutions charged with the responsibility of safeguarding reputations for commercial truthfulness. But on the whole, and for the individuals who possessed the full rights of democratic citizenship, the antebellum legal system expected people to look sharp.

PART II

A Nineteenth-Century World of
Caveat Emptor (1810s to 1880s)

CHAPTER THREE

The Porousness of the Law

In 1854, having achieved celebrity as the exhibitor of the dwarf General Tom Thumb, the promoter of Swedish opera singer Jenny Lind, and the proprietor of New York City's American Museum, P. T. Barnum penned the first of his three autobiographies. In *The Life of P. T. Barnum*, this already larger-than-life figure characterized his childhood as an apprenticeship in the wiles of the American marketplace. Growing up in rural Connecticut, a nursery of Yankee commercial culture, Barnum was given repeated lessons in the dangers of relying on the claims of counterparties, including his own relatives. At the age of nine, he witnessed his grandfather pull off a successful lottery for a local church through deceptive marketing (promising that every ticket would receive a prize worth no less than one-half its price, and then providing almost no other prizes), which cemented his reputation as "a regular old cheat." Three years later, the young Phineas Taylor learned that he had been the butt of a family joke for years, as his "patrimony," a patch of "valuable" land called Ivy Island, was not only isolated and tiny, but also swamp-ridden. Throughout his childhood, he encountered jousting between crafty rural residents and the itinerant peddlers who sought to fleece them.

Barnum received additional lessons in deviousness after his father's death, when, at the age of fifteen, he became a store clerk. Here he became privy not only to the hard bargaining that went on between his employer and local farmers and farm wives, but also to all manner of "dishonest tricks and unprincipled deceptions," from debased bundles of rags to short-weighted loads of agricultural produce. While local hatters passed off their "inferior furs with a little of their best," young Barnum learned to adulterate "sugars, teas, and liquors." In the "dog eat dog" world of the rural marketplace,

> [o]ur cottons were sold for wool, our wool and cotton for silk and linen; in fact nearly everything was different from what was represented. The customers cheated us in their fabrics; we cheated the customers with our goods. Each party expected to be cheated, if it was possible. Our eyes, and not our ears, had to be our masters. We must believe little that we saw, and less that we heard. Our calicoes were all "fast colors," according to our representations, and the colors would gen-

erally run "fast" enough and show them a tub of soap-suds. Our ground coffee was as good as burned peas, beans, and corn could make, and our ginger was tolerable, considering the price of corn meal. . . . If we took our pay in clocks, warranted to keep good time, the chances were that they were no better than a chest of drawers for that purpose—that they were like Pindar's razors, "made to sell," and if half the number of wheels necessary to form a clock could be found within the case, it was as lucky as extraordinary.[1]

In this memoir, the commercial milieu of Barnum's youth was one of counterpoised imposition and vigilance, a world in which every economic actor—merchants, consumers, laborers, manufacturers, employees, investors, promoters—shaded and shaved, and presumed to be treated in kind. Again and again, individuals managed to put one over—sometimes on a visiting peddler, sometimes on the supplier of raw materials or finished goods, sometimes on a partner or clerk or employer, in turn on a neighbor or relative or stranger. Whoever the parties might be, the deceivers reveled in triumph that overcame sustained suspicions, while the deceived gave the deceivers their due. Barnum depicted these episodes as jokes, and presumed that readers would recognize and share the humor. At no point in his narrative, moreover, did the duped discuss legal threats, much less initiate legal process. Rather, they drove a harder bargain if they discovered a false pretense, mumbled face-saving excuses if their own falsehoods came to light, and, whenever sharp practice became evident after a transaction, complimented the perpetrator on his acumen.

Barnum's remembered society was a domicile of *caveat emptor*—a Hobbesian economic world in which buyers had to beware, lest they lose their shirts, or purchase ones that would lose their sheen and fall apart after a good washing. The residents of Bethel, Connecticut, who appear in *The Life of P. T. Barnum*, like those of New York City, where Barnum came to base his operations, and throughout the nation, where he toured with his entertainment acts, accepted this principle. That is, they assumed that adults should be able to look out for themselves; that if individuals suffered losses through clever misrepresentations, they had no one to blame but themselves; and that such experiences prepared Americans for the rough-and-tumble of market exchange. Barnum's reflections, moreover, did not constitute an unusual portrayal of American business relations. The era's novels and nonfiction accounts of urban life, such as John Chumasero's *Life in Rochester* and George Foster's 1849 volume *New York in Slices*, were filled with analogous anecdotes and commentaries.[2]

Ever the showman, Barnum surely embellished some of these recollections for dramatic or comedic effect. Indeed, any treatment of *The Life of P. T. Bar-*

num as a window on antebellum economic culture must remain cognizant of its author's aims. By the early 1850s, Barnum had fashioned a nationwide reputation as a master of humbug through well-told hoaxes and deft acts of public misdirection, which nonetheless furnished value as commodified entertainment. He had every reason to highlight the penchant of his fellow Americans to cast suspicious eyes on what was before them, as well as their propensity to be taken in regardless. His core business model, both in early traveling exhibitions and his American Museum, rested on giving his customers shared experiences in the perplexities of looking sharp. The people who experienced Barnum's spectacles knew that they were going to encounter many contrived illusions; much of the attraction lay in distinguishing genuine oddities from artful impostures. Barnum, then, had strong incentives to emphasize Americans' good-natured, tough-minded embrace of *caveat emptor*. Thus one might plausibly discount his depiction of antebellum trade as an unending battle of wits between cheats, and antebellum economic culture as sanctioning such contests as markers of the good society. Similar considerations might lead one to treat the era's other depictions of commercial and financial dealings as exaggerations.[3]

This chapter cross-examines Barnum's account of American commercial culture, considering the law of business fraud during an era bracketed by the War of 1812's conclusion and the country's retreat from Reconstruction (though at points the discussion glances before or after this sixty-year stretch of Barnum's own life). In the years after 1815, American commerce reconnected to Europe and state legislatures began to finance the internal improvements and create the banking institutions that drove regional economic integration, which sped up the long march of Americans from countryside to city and farm to factory. By its end, the nation's expanding railroad network had accelerated processes of industrialization and the vertiginous growth of large-scale corporate enterprise, as well as the emergence of a truly nationwide market for ever more goods and services. Throughout this period, the premises of a face-to-face economic world came under assault, battered by the growth of cities filled with strangers, expanded circulation of goods with cloudy origins or characteristics that were difficult to assess, and the need to deal with counterparties who possessed uncertain pedigrees. The pressures of an integrated continental economy, along with currents of professionalization, would eventually transform the legal institutions that dealt with the problem of commercial deceit. But one can usefully probe American fraud law across much of the nineteenth century—across the span of P. T. Barnum's own life—as a story of continuity.

One part of that narrative involves the tendency of formal law to frown on many of the petty deceptions that recur throughout Barnum's recollections, as well as the more serious swindles that bedeviled the world of commerce. The common law contained numerous criminal prohibitions against economic duplicity and provided several avenues for disgruntled counterparties to pursue claims of misrepresentation through civil litigation. American statute books and municipal ordinances amplified these customary principles of antagonism to commercial or financial deceit. Thus the formal rules of the nineteenth-century American marketplace sought to vindicate economic candor and buttress confidence in contracting and the transaction of business.

Barnum's autobiography nonetheless points to the practical weaknesses of antifraud laws before 1880. Daunting legal standards, challenging evidentiary barriers, and ambivalent cultural attitudes combined to weaken legal restraints on fraudulent behavior. America's legal elites tried to balance longstanding norms that upheld truthful commercial speech against their age's commitment to entrepreneurial activity and rapid economic growth. The latter priorities, encapsulated in the concept of "Go-Aheadism," counseled leeway for salesmanship and showmanship, respect for the free flow of commercial speech, and reliance on the ability of consumers and investors to look out for their own interests.[4] Such concerns left a big imprint on legal institutions and legal culture, opening up room for dissemblers and swindlers to maneuver. Even in the face of the strictest formal rules, nineteenth-century Americans often encountered a de facto realm of *caveat emptor*.

LAW ON THE BOOKS

Nineteenth-century America has long had a reputation of being a bastion of *laissez-faire*. In the decades that preceded Progressivism and the New Deal, this way of thinking goes, governments left businesses to their own devices, other than keeping public order and offering means of enforcing contracts, the classic roles of the "night watchman" polity. This notion of a "weak American state" elides the enormous impacts that governmental policy had on the shape and direction of US capitalism. In addition to defining basic property rights, including the entrenchment and then abolition of property in slaves, American legislatures, executives, and courts sought to promote economic growth and also respond to at least some of the social harms that accompanied it. The former aspiration manifested itself in public funds for transportation infrastructure, chiefly canals and railroads, as well as protective tariffs, incorporated banks, general incorporation statutes, and interpretations of tort law and the law of eminent domain that protected the interests of transportation companies and manufacturing firms. The latter impulse animated many regulatory constraints on economic behavior, especially with regard to the broad areas of public health, public safety, public morality, and public markets. Each of these centuries-old regulatory concerns made their impact on nineteenth-century American understandings of unwritten common law, as well as much municipal, state, and federal legislation. Within the broad ambit of legal rules concerning moral economy resided numerous provisions antagonistic to misrepresentations in commercial speech.[5]

The Americanized version of the common law permitted both civil and criminal actions against mercantile and financial deceit. Throughout the nineteenth century, local, state, and federal legislatures enacted numerous anti-fraud provisions, often in response to particular swindles that shocked the political establishment into action. To appreciate the thicket of legal rules pertaining to deceptive actions in this era, one need only thumb through treatises such as Melville Bigelow's 1877 *The Law of Fraud*, whose hundreds of pages testify to the enduring commonwealth tradition of maintaining a well-ordered marketplace.[6] As in almost all areas of American law, legal definitions and process varied from jurisdiction to jurisdiction. Nonetheless, the broad contours of fraud law were largely the same across the nation.

Depending on the circumstances, disgruntled buyers of merchandise, land, or intangible financial assets could pursue many legal avenues if they believed that counterparties had cajoled them into a purchase through false representations. If such a transaction involved credit terms, the purchaser might simply refuse to pay, and then, once sued, seek to avoid a judgment on the grounds of fraud. In legal parlance, defendants could plead a defense of fraud as a bar to the suit. Creditors who extended loans on the basis of false assurances from third parties as to a debtor's solvency could sue those individuals for the resulting losses. If debtors sought to avoid payment by fraudulently conveying assets to confederates, creditors could bring suit in an equity court to void such transfers. After real-estate deals, purchasers who alleged fraud could tender the land back to the seller, and, if the latter refused to refund the purchase price, bring an action in a chancery court for rescission of the contract. In the case of other completed bargains, such as those for commodities, supplies, consumer goods, or financial instruments, aggrieved parties could sue the seller for deceit, seeking monetary damages in a common-law court for the economic harm wrought by deception.[7]

These legal actions all involved civil disputes—controversies that, in the eyes of state officials, did not constitute fundamental threats to the broader social and economic order. Nineteenth-century Americans also had the option of bringing criminal fraud complaints. Under the common law, a wide range of "cheats," such as adulteration of goods or deceiving others through the use of "false tokens" (counterfeited correspondence, false trademarks, etc.), constituted misdemeanors, so long as they involved deception against the marketplace writ large. Other fraud-related criminal accusations looked to statutorily defined offenses such as obtaining goods or money through false pretenses, conspiracy to defraud, and engaging in fraudulent bankruptcy, either by hiding assets from creditors or secretly transferring assets to other parties on the eve of failure. Thus the 1833 Georgia criminal code declared that an individual who made use of "deceitful means, or artful practice" to defraud a counterparty "shall be deemed a common cheat and swindler," subject to "fine or imprisonment in the common jail, or both."[8]

The nineteenth-century American legal landscape further included myriad regulations targeting deceptive business practices in specific economic sectors. In metropolises such as Philadelphia and towns such as Fredericksburg, Virginia, auction houses had to obtain licenses.[9] Throughout the country, peddlers, traveling salesmen, and insurance agents confronted county-level requirements that they post good-behavior bonds before attempting to find local customers.[10] A host of goods markets were also shaped by regulatory schemes that sought to ensure product quality, many of which had longstanding origins in colonial economic policies. America's urban food and energy markets employed weighers, measurers, and inspectors who had the statutory authority to police the daily business of selling produce, meat, wood, and coal to retailers and consumers.[11] Because export industries such as tobacco, salted pork, and pickled fish depended on good reputations with foreign purchasers, leading figures in those industries lobbied for the creation of formal quality standards and the appointment of state officers to uphold them. Most of the resulting statutes required that sellers prepare their wares in standard dimensions and that the goods receive a mark from an official inspector who certified their purity and/or grade.

Michigan established a typical set of regulatory requirements for its leading export commodities. As of 1857, its legislature had specified detailed standards for the preparation of beef, pork, butter, hog's lard, fish, flour, leather, pot and pearl ashes, beer, ale, cider, and barrel staves. Before sending wares out of state, producers of these goods had to have them examined by county inspectors, who assessed quality grades and adherence to packing requirements. If manufacturers or merchants evaded inspections, counterfeited inspection marks, or altered the contents of already-inspected containers, they risked fines and forfeitures.[12]

Such institutional arrangements offered the prospect of more substantial impacts on business practices than did general legal provisions concerning economic duplicity. Unlike civil litigation or criminal complaints, licensing and inspection regimes did not depend on alleged victims of fraud to initiate proceedings. Instead, they vested authority in public officials to survey the metes and bounds of marketplaces, and to levy sanctions on economic actors who violated statutory mandates. Licensing and inspection systems established bureaucratic capacity.

Nineteenth-century American law, then, teemed with legal rules and institutions that attempted to prevent fraudulent practices or give modes of redress to fraud victims. But identifying formal legal requirements constitutes only the first step in any assessment of the impact that law has had on social and economic arrangements. Once one considers the judicial application of laws relating to business fraud, it becomes clear that the general nineteenth-century legal restraints against commercial or financial deceit were hemmed in by procedural and evidentiary rules. In many contexts—as, for example, the cotton trade—purchasers who wished to lodge formal accusations of duplicitous conduct by sellers had to do so soon after becoming apprised of imposition. To wait even a few months proved fatal to lawsuits, for delay compromised the ability of middlemen to make similar claims against their suppliers.[13]

Judicial standards for determining when particular acts of duplicity crossed the boundary of legally permitted behavior also tended to be exacting. Complainants had to show that misrepresentations were material facts related to the transactions in question. Discussions of contingent circumstances or assessments of future events (such as predicted price movements) were, by definition, opinions, not facts. Pledges of future payment, no matter how insincere, constituted mere promises, actionable through civil, but not criminal, process. To be "material," falsehoods had to be clearly related to the decision to go ahead with the deal. Individuals who levied allegations of fraud further had to demonstrate that they had been taken in by the false assertions, that they had actually relied on them in choosing to agree to the sale or purchase or extension of credit, that they had no ability to check the veracity of the untrue assertions or had taken reasonable steps to verify them, that reliance on a falsehood had occasioned economic loss, and, most dauntingly, that the falsehoods represented intentional efforts to defraud. Taken together, these rules created a legal gauntlet.[14]

The adoption of tough evidentiary filters for fraud claims reflected elite commitment to economic growth and individual self-reliance as fundamental social values. Providing easy means for Americans to revisit transactions on the grounds of duplicity, lawyers and judges argued, would throw too much sand into the gears of commerce. As Chief Justice John Bannister Gibson of the Pennsylvania Supreme Court argued in an influential 1839 opinion, capacious definitions of fraud "would put a stop to commerce itself in driving every one out of it by terror of endless litigation." Solicitousness toward fraud allegations would gum up civil and criminal dockets, overwhelming the courts with disputes.[15] The bar and judicial fraternity similarly tended to shy away from legal doctrines that might destroy the incentive for individuals to look out for themselves—to learn from ill-advised purchases of seeming bargains, investments that appeared to be too good to be true, or unwarranted extensions of trust. John Appleton, a Maine Supreme Court judge, encapsulated this view in an 1878 opinion concerning a debtor's effort to avoid payment to an innocent third party holding his promissory note, because the debtor had drawn the note under false pretenses. In such instances, Appleton insisted, "the foolish and the deceived must bear the consequences of their folly and imbecility and not impose on those who relied on their assertions, the penalty which nature always attaches to negligence or want of caution."[16] Judges such as Appleton grafted the ethos of *caveat emptor* onto the more restrictive general law of business fraud.

This judicial skepticism signified a departure from the dominant tendencies of early modern Anglo-American jurisprudence. In England and America, from the sixteenth century into the early years of the nineteenth, purchasers who alleged deceit tended to receive more sympathetic judicial hearings. When buyers bought from artisans or merchants in a regulated public market and paid a price customarily associated with a standard of fine workmanship or quality, judges imputed an implicit warranty of merchantability, and even soundness, to the transaction. There were scattered exceptions to this pattern, which eventually furnished key precedents for nineteenth-century jurisprudence. On the whole, though, early modern courts in the British Isles and the American colonies protected purchasers of shoddy merchandise even when sellers plausibly contended that they were unaware of defects.[17]

The point here is not that nineteenth-century American legal restrictions on duplicitous business practices disappeared entirely through the hocus pocus of judicial hermeneutics. But American judges and treatise writers of the time, like their English counterparts, narrowed those curbs. For the common-law or statutory rules to bite by the mid-nineteenth century, the deception had to be especially "skillful," designed to overcome the diligent, even vigilant, investigations of economic actors. In the case of a sale of adulterated or shoddy goods, the defects had to be "latent," hidden in such a way that buyers could not readily detect them. If promoters of some new company made fanciful claims and predictions about its future potential and manifested enormous enthusiasm about the quality of its assets and management, investors were supposed to know that such claims would not sustain fraud lawsuits. The nineteenth-century American law of business fraud typically reached only devious chicanery, not, as a Boston newspaper editorialized in 1834, "the *white lies*, exaggerations of the truth, and concealment of some particulars" that "by universal consent and common usage" helped to facilitate investment and mercantile trade.[18]

An 1847 New York appeals court case, *People v. Crissie*, typified the judicial inclination to hem in the legal constraints on fraud. The case concerned a criminal prosecution under the New York false pretenses statute, occasioned by the sale of a flock of sheep. The purchaser in question, a farmer named Brock, had asked the previous owners about the poor condition of several sheeps' hooves, which the drovers had explained as the temporary consequence of a recent journey over difficult ground, even though they knew that the flock was diseased. A lower court had set aside a conviction, arguing that Brock should not have placed any faith in the explanation. In his majority opinion, Democratic Judge Freeborn G. Jewett disagreed, but in doing so, stressed the limited reach of New York's false pretenses statute. Jewett conceded that the goal of the legislation was to "protect the weak and credulous against the wiles and stratagems of the artful and cunning." But he simultaneously proclaimed that for a falsehood to trigger criminal liability, it needed "to be an artfully contrived story, which would naturally have an effect upon the mind of the person addressed—one which would be equal to a false token or false writing—an ingenious contrivance or unusual artifice, against which common sagacity and the exercise of ordinary caution would not be a sufficient guard." The fraud statutes, Jewett insisted, did not absolve individuals from the obligation to scrutinize products and counterparties.[19] Similar concerns guided the decision-making of British courts in fraud cases, especially those related to misrepresentations by the era's burgeoning corporations. From the 1820s through the 1870s, British judges applied exacting evidentiary standards to allegations of corporate deception, out of worries that they might provide excessive legal protections to speculators. In both civil and criminal fraud proceedings, Great Britain's judiciary refused to weaken the incentives of investors to look askance at extravagant promises.[20]

As in so many areas of Anglo-American jurisprudence, the law of fraud contained numerous exceptions. Legal evolution with regard to commercial deceit was not neat and tidy, uncomplicated by contrary rulings and opinions. If nineteenth-century judges tended to look askance at most allegations of fraud, they could reverse their interpretive predispositions when alleged victims lacked what they perceived as the physical, social, and/or economic markers of republican citizenship. Widows, recent immigrants who did not speak English, the illiterate, the "weak-minded," youths, "ignorant Negroes," sailors (whom the law treated as "standing upon the same footing with young heirs and expectants"), in some cases, the aged and the intoxicated—all these groups received more charitable treatment from the courts in fraud controversies. According to the era's jurists and legal writers, these social types lacked the experience, savvy, or mental faculties to fend for themselves and so merited paternalistic protection. As a result, the judiciary articulated a different set of evidentiary rules for them, lowering the requirements to mount successful fraud-based defenses, bring fraud-based civil actions, or initiate criminal fraud prosecutions. These people, judges argued, deserved greater legal safeguards.[21]

Underlying these judicial distinctions was a set of understandings about the relationship between social identities and the capacity to gain access to relevant economic information and evaluate its implications. An "elderly, uneducated woman in humble life" who sold a choice piece of real estate to "a person far above her in station" was not, in the eyes of most nineteenth-century American legal elites, someone who could read the land market and judge the reasonableness of the latter's assertions and offer. According to this same line of thinking, courts should furnish means of redress to a newly arrived immigrant taken in by a real-estate operator selling land to which he lacked good title, or a poorly educated African American who paid a doctor to remove the poison that the physician insisted was all about his home. For these persons, the law need not insist upon the same degree of prudence before economic action. As Tennessee Supreme Court judge Peter Turney explained in an 1876 opinion laced with racism, when judges and juries considered the decision-making of dupes in fraud-related cases, they should expect only the "caution as we may naturally and reasonably expect to exist under the circumstances and conditions of life of the person practiced upon. The question is, what caution is he capable of exercising?"[22] Posing the question this way allowed legal elites such as Turney to reinforce prevailing social prejudices as they considered allegations of fraud, underscoring the supposed inability of women, working-class immigrants, and African Americans to look out for their own best interests. Even so, this formulation did expand the effective range of legal regulation of commercial speech.

Analogous considerations prevailed across the Atlantic. When duplicitous business managers targeted the British working class, the legal establishment proved far more likely to bring fraud prosecutions, judges proved far less solicitous of defense arguments and motions, and juries proved far more likely to convict. Indeed, most of the significant English fraud convictions before 1880 involved misrepresentations by savings banks and insurance companies, whose failures brought grievous losses to working-class depositors and policyholders.[23]

Judicial concern about structural asymmetries of information could even extend to some legal controversies that entangled literate adult white men in full possession of their faculties. When one party to a transaction possessed far better access to relevant intelligence about market conditions, the intrinsic qualities of property, or even the moral character and financial standing of economic actors, courts lent a more sympathetic ear to fraud allegations. Thus, if only one side to a bargain possessed particular expertise—such as a miller who was selling a flour mill—American judges tended to grant the other side more legal slack. The same inclination led legal elites to evince concern for individuals who alleged that they had been defrauded after reasonably relying on the guarantees of undisputed experts, or on third-party assurances about the solid financial standing of credit applicants who turned out to be insolvent.[24]

The nineteenth-century judiciary, then, embraced a rebuttable presumption that courts should not undo private bargains because one side raised the hue and cry of fraud. In most contexts, judges looked askance at such charges. But if the level of deception impressed, if courts viewed complainants as members of a social group meriting heightened legal protection, or if the deceiver possessed informational advantages, litigants might overcome judicial reluctance to interfere with the consequences of mercantile or financial transactions. An antebellum humorist, James Kirke Paulding, conveyed this pattern nicely in an 1839 tale, "The Perfection of Reason." In this satire, the narrator, a well-born young man with formal legal education, receives a rude introduction to the perplexities of the common law, courtesy of lawsuits involving deception claims. As a plaintiff asking for damages resulting from two deceitful horse trades, the purchase of shoddy boots from a notorious cobbler, and the acquisition of a poorly constructed ship, the narrator learns that he has the responsibility of "governing himself by the maxim *Caveat emptor*." Having neglected to undertake sensible investigations before making his purchases or to demand written warranties, the narrator loses each suit. Bitter about his losses, he resolves to adjust his transactional outlook, which leads him to take advantage of an elderly neighbor in a horse trade. This unscrupulous act, however, only lands him in a deeper legal thicket. In the resulting civil action, he discovers that courts will indeed protect the interests of an old woman with poor sight when she is shamefully imposed upon.[25]

In fashioning this interpretive scaffolding for antifraud law, nineteenth-century American judges had concerns beyond encouragement of entrepreneurial efforts and avoidance of cluttered court dockets. The judiciary also tried to accommodate the law of business fraud to the dominant understandings of republican citizenship. There was a dimension of political ideology to the waxing judicial embrace of *caveat emptor*. The era's judges and legal writers came of age in a society that prized manly self-reliance and celebrated abstract ideals of political and social equality among the ranks of its prototypical white male citizens. These legal elites inhabited a cultural milieu that lionized the aggressiveness of politicians such as Andrew Jackson, merchants such as John Jacob Astor, and showmen such as P. T. Barnum.[26]

Law in Action—The Civil and Criminal Courts

Law on the books may prove to be a dead letter, a vibrant shaper of beliefs and behavior, or something in between. Determining where a given body of law fits along that spectrum is no easy task. Ideally, it requires intensive study of mundane legal records across time and space, as well as the range of social experiences that intersect with legal rules, mechanisms of enforcement, and modes of dispute resolution.[27] Although historians have only completed scattered case studies along these lines, one can also draw on voluminous press coverage of fraud-related criminal proceedings, which offers extensive evidence about prevailing social norms and the typical workings of legal institutions. These sources suggest that before the last quarter of the nineteenth century, American law only fitfully circumscribed duplicitous marketing practices.

For one thing, individuals who viewed themselves as victims of illegal deception often did not make formal complaints against businesses and/or business owners, through either civil or criminal process. One obstacle was the possibility that the defrauded individuals had manifested intent to break the law in the course of the scam, as in the case of the counterfeiting-related swindles known as "green goods games." Such victims might eschew public complaints because of their own legal jeopardy. If they did seek out legal redress, courts ruled that fraud complainants had to enter the halls of justice with clean hands. As the New York Court of Appeals explained in a pivotal 1871 case, American courts would not engage "in the protection of rogues in their dealings with each other."[28]

In many other contexts, financial losses incurred by victims of duplicity were minimal. An instance of the sort of petty cheating described in P. T. Barnum's autobiographies would have sent few Americans to the insolvency court or the poorhouse, while most financial frauds extracted small stakes from large numbers of disappointed investors. Such circumstances raised significant economic barriers to legal action, which required expenditure of both time and money. Carrying out a civil suit or a criminal prosecution to its final conclusion, even in relatively simple matters, meant incurring $50–100 in attorney's fees and court costs, which could balloon to much greater amounts if the parsing of legal issues or the amassing of relevant evidence became complicated. (Measured in terms of an unskilled worker's wage, these sums would be the equivalent of approximately $8,000–16,000 in 2016.) As a New York City newspaper observed in 1882, the typical victim of a minor swindle became "disheartened and worn out. Having no money to go to law with he abandons all thoughts of redress and disappears."[29] In the phraseology of modern economics, legal responses to business frauds confronted collective action problems.

Of course, Americans have never engaged solely in dispassionate cost-benefit analysis when deciding whether to initiate civil suits or criminal complaints. Emotional considerations—anger at perceived mistreatment, desire for revenge, anxiousness for the commonweal—could prompt the filing of lawsuits or the making of indignant statements to law-enforcement officers, even when accusers had little chance of financial gain. In an 1833 New York City prosecution for real-estate fraud, for example, one witness described the complainant as "vindictive" and "in a violent passion," intent on having the defendant "sent to the state prison."[30] The tug of emotion, however, might also lead a victim of economic deceptions to remain quiet even when possessing a solid legal case. Dupes might keep mum, either because they did not wish to come to terms with their gullibility or because they hoped to avoid the Barnumesque public ridicule that it might elicit. Thus, in 1862, the *New York Tribune* surmised that a full 90 percent of fraud cases remained hidden from public view, because defrauded individuals were "ashamed to have it known that they have been so easily victimized." Throughout the nineteenth century, accounts of far-reaching frauds presumed that most defrauded individuals would stay silent.[31]

Even if most victims of duplicitous business practices did choose to "lump it," thousands of Barnum's contemporaries did not stay silent in the face of commercial chicanery or unabashed swindling. Formal allegations of fraud, however, neither received a uniformly welcome reception from legal institutions, nor readily translated into damage awards, convictions, and jail sentences. The legal treatment of nineteenth-century civil suits seeking compensation for fraudulent misrepresentations remains murky at the trial level, because we lack the fine-grained historical studies of particular jurisdictions that can yield quantitative measures of outcomes. Appellate decisions, along with scattered newspaper coverage of civil disputes, make clear that plaintiffs could recover at least some damages through deceit actions or use the defense of fraud to fend off debt collection suits—especially when they possessed a respectable social status, could afford expert legal counsel, and could substantiate that the misrepresentations met legal requirements.[32] But evidentiary standards stymied many civil actions for deceit when allegations pertained to complex transactions like those that occurred in the transatlantic cotton supply chain. Antebellum Southern juries and arbitration boards tended to discount claims by middlemen that they had suffered losses as a result of "falsely packed" cotton, which hid inferior-quality staple inside a bale with an outer veneer, or "plate," of the highest grade. In such cases, plaintiffs had to establish the precise character of the deceptions, as well as who was responsible for them.[33]

Victories at the bar, moreover, often did not generate significant compensation for fraud victims. As one New England lawyer and disgruntled purchaser of a horse discovered to his chagrin in 1861, a verdict against the seller on the grounds of deceit meant little if the defendant lacked the resources to pay, or was willing to go to jail rather than make good on a judgment.[34] Scores of defrauded Americans learned a similar lesson as a result of a "great land swindle" by Niels Frederiksen, a Danish immigrant capitalist based in Chicago. Frederiksen's company purchased thousands of acres at state tax auctions, as well as options on large tracts of railroad lands. It then resold the lands to Scandinavian immigrants on the installment plan, withholding titles until the company had received full payment; created bogus mortgages on the same plots; and sold those fake obligations to investors in Eastern and Midwestern cities. After the firm's 1889 collapse, it faced an avalanche of civil suits seeking damages, and lost all of them. But by this point, Frederiksen and his son had already transferred their American assets to favored creditors as collateral and decamped for Europe, taking along a hefty sum of cash. As a result, the filers of all the lawsuits merely threw good money after bad.[35]

Evidence about criminal fraud prosecutions is easier to amass; the press at this time covered criminal proceedings more closely than civil suits and some state governments compiled relevant statistics. Attempts at swindling, along with the appropriation of goods or money via false pretenses, comprised regular entries on the nineteenth-century urban criminal docket, though these crimes never constituted a leading preoccupation for policemen and prosecutors. The monthly arrest reports of the Baltimore police in the late 1860s illustrate this: fewer than 1 percent involved charges for commercial or financial deception.[36] A significant fraction of successful fraud prosecutions, moreover, involved charges brought by corporations or retail businesses against custom-

ers, or by individuals against other individuals, rather than by consumers, investors, or other counterparties against firms. Insurance companies, for example, regularly went after policyholders whom they suspected of filing
fraudulent claims, while storekeepers periodically filed false pretense charges
against consumers, and other criminal cases resulted from spats over personal
loans.[37] Still, nineteenth-century prosecutors and judges handled criminal
fraud cases against business owners year in and year out, especially in larger
cities. During 1868, the Baltimore police charged about twelve persons a
month with fraud-related offenses, of which fewer than half resulted from allegations of illegal deception against business enterprises.

Initiation of a criminal fraud case against a business owner did not, of
course, ensure conviction or punishment. The era's criminal justice system
gave most felony defendants ample opportunity to dance out of trouble,
whether the charge involved some kind of fraud, other crimes against property, or physical acts of violence. Many arrests did not lead to indictments; indictments did not always culminate in prosecutions; prosecutions sometimes
ended with acquittals rather than guilty verdicts; appellate courts had little
compunction about overturning convictions if judges could identify procedural shortcomings; and governors displayed a penchant for commuting sentences and issuing pardons, often at the behest of the juries and local prosecutors who sent individuals to prison. One telling measure of the porousness of
America's nineteenth-century criminal justice system lies with the treatment of
African Americans accused of criminal actions in the slave South. Unable to
present testimony from African American witnesses, often bereft of competent
legal counsel, and forced to confront all-white juries, black defendants in antebellum Southern states had the legal deck stacked against them. Yet between
1819 and 1860, African Americans in South Carolina were found guilty only
two-thirds of the time. For white defendants throughout the nation, rates of
conviction tended to be far lower, with some jurisdictions producing guilty
verdicts in as few as one in five trials.[38] Fraud-related prosecutions produced
outcomes on the lower side of this scale, if the postbellum prosecutorial statistics compiled by Michigan's attorney general mirrored outcomes elsewhere. In
the year ending June 30, 1866, three in ten Michigan false-pretense indictments led to convictions, less than half the conviction rate for larceny. Six years
later, the state's conviction rate in false pretenses cases was only 17 percent,
well below the 61 percent rate of conviction for larceny prosecutions.[39]

Even when victims came forward with specific allegations that fit relevant
legal categories and definitions, criminal convictions for business fraud did not
come easily. Amassing compelling evidence was often difficult, especially if deceptions had been communicated orally. When swindles operated within the

growing networks of national trade and finance, jurisdictional complications bedeviled prosecutors, who had to grapple with distant witnesses and thorny questions about who had the authority to try individuals suspected of criminal deceit. If the businessmen charged with fraud had the wherewithal to retain leading attorneys, as many did, they benefited from the ample procedural and substantive loopholes of nineteenth-century American criminal law. Defendants who confronted strong cases could also just skip town, especially before initial arraignments. And in the unlikely event that a businessman with money and social connections received a guilty verdict and had little hope of a successful appeal, he could always petition for a pardon. One can best appreciate these obstacles to punishment by retracing the careers of a few businessmen who underwent high-profile business fraud prosecutions. Three such vignettes follow, concerning a notorious mock auctioneer, a large-scale mercantile credit fraud, and a serial promoter of phony businesses.

From the late antebellum period into the late 1870s, Zeno Burnham developed a reputation throughout New York City as a consummate perpetrator of retailing fraud. After a stint operating an oyster saloon in the early 1850s, during which he faced a charge for stealing illuminating gas by illegally tapping a local utility's main line, Burnham found his calling in the auction business.[40] From the emergence of auctioneering in New York City after the War of 1812, some firms had specialized in deceptive business practices, including the switching of displayed merchandise, misrepresentation of goods, and use of shills, often called stool pigeons, cappers, or "Peter Funks," to force up bids. Prevalent in sales of dry goods, jewelry, and watches, these tactics soon spread to the vending of horses and furniture. Rigged furniture sales were advertised as resulting from some wealthy person's death or imminent move from the city, which ostensibly required a quick liquidation of "fancy" appurtenances, and occurred in "stuffed flats" filled with shoddy "gingerbread" furnishings.[41] Burnham turned the mock furniture auction into an art form, taking in hundreds of bargain-seekers during the 1860s and sidestepping several criminal allegations, often through reliance on expert legal counsel.[42]

In the fall of 1865, a white, married female customer of Burnham's filed yet another criminal complaint, alleging that he had altered the invoice for her furniture purchase to increase the amount due, and then refused to return her deposit of government bonds, worth far more than the $300 purchase price. An assistant district attorney prosecuted Burnham under a new criminal statute that specifically targeted frauds in auctions. Burnham's "profession," the prosecutor insisted, was "one of iniquity—it lives, thrives, and prospers on deception." If the jury acquitted this "king of the mock auctioneers," he announced, they would "say in the same breath to the rest of the fraternity, 'Go and do likewise.'" If they rather "dethrone[d]" him, "his people [would] fall." Burnham lost this round, with the jury rendering a guilty verdict and the presiding judge sentencing him to thirty months in the state penitentiary, an outcome that led the local press to marvel that a "wealthy ruffian" had ended up in jail.[43] But Burnham remained in prison only a matter of weeks. Drawing on his social networks and allegedly showering the right people with several thousand dollars, he soon conjured up a pardon, based on attestations from prominent attorneys that his conviction resulted from unfair prejudice, and a prison doctor's assessment that his health was poor. For the next fifteen years, Burnham continued to ply his trade as a mock furniture auctioneer, though now acting behind the scenes, with a confederate as legal proprietor. He confronted further criminal investigations, but managed to dodge them, partly because of haziness about who actually ran his enterprises.[44]

The theme of ambiguous legal responsibility similarly complicated a prosecution arising out of the business's failure by Folger & Tibbs, a New York City dry-goods firm that carried out a classic scheme of credit fraud. In the fall of 1866, the firm convinced wholesalers to sell them $100,000 worth of goods on credit. (As a share of the overall economy, this sum would equal well over $100 million in 2016.) Once the partners received shipments of merchandise, they sent them on to auctioneers in Baltimore and Cincinnati with orders to sell for cash at fire-sale prices. Within a few months, some creditors became aware of the scheme and initiated criminal proceedings that alleged a conspiracy to defraud. By this time, however, Messrs. Folger and Tibbs had departed for Europe. As a result, prosecutors could only charge clerks and agents who had arranged the original purchases and later shipments, as well as the Cincinnati and Baltimore auctioneers who disposed of the goods. A two-month investigation and trial revealed the suspicious nature of these transactions, which included nonexistent recordkeeping and an emphasis on immediate sale at any price. But the formal indictment only mentioned the specific goods sold by the single mercantile complainant, a lot of handkerchiefs. In light of the nonappearance of several key witnesses and a lack of evidence that linked all of the defendants to a specific conspiracy concerning those particular kerchiefs, the judge dismissed the case.[45]

In addition to exemplifying the capacity of swindlers to flee from legal process, this episode highlights the evidentiary barriers to fraud-related convictions, even in a case that involved brazen duplicity. Demonstrating the knowledge and criminal intent of employees and agents who facilitated a duplicitous business scheme was no easy matter. Who could say where an underling's obligation to obey his employer or an agent's duty to follow his principal's instructions shaded over into criminal enterprise? The "Alleged Great Dry Goods

Swindle," as one newspaper termed it, further illustrates the potential liability that lurked behind any attempt to pursue criminal fraud charges. In the aftermath of the directed acquittal, one of the vindicated Cincinnati auctioneers brought a civil malicious prosecution suit against the New York merchant who had charged him with conspiracy. Eighteen months later, he obtained a jury award of $5,000 for the indignity of spending six days in jail, and the resulting "injury to his character."[46]

The swindling career of James H. "Doc" Langley, like that of Zeno Burnham, extended over several decades, in his case from the early 1870s through the first years of the twentieth century. Although Langley at one point dabbled in patent medicines, he came to specialize in the promotion of spurious investments and business opportunities. One line of his business focused on peddling shares in bogus companies, including such ephemeral enterprises as the Mexican Guano and Fertilizer Company, the Medical Instrument Company, the Anti-Friction Car Box Company, and the United States Construction and Investment Company, which promised to assist railway inventors in obtaining and marketing patents. Langley deployed all of the leading tactics of late nineteenth-century stock swindlers, including elaborate prospectuses, carefully prepared samples, stock certificates that "were elegant in appearance," decoy directors, and offices "furnished in a sumptuous manner." A second income stream came from the distribution of agencies associated with such concerns, which required some form of advance fee—either investment in the company, the provision of a loan, or some form of deposit for "good behavior."

One of Langley's key strategies was constant movement. At one time or another, he based his operations in Worcester, Boston, Rochester, New York City, Chicago, Richmond, and Galveston, as well as several other cities. This willingness to relocate helped him evade the clutches of the law, despite repeated arrests and indictments. Whenever he faced criminal charges, he would post bail and flee. Langley assumed, correctly, that the infrequent sharing of information among police and prosecutors from different jurisdictions would allow him to begin anew without interference. In 1897, however, a Boston jury found him guilty of fraud in connection with the promotion of an industrial life-insurance scheme, a conviction that did lead to a multiyear jail term.[47]

As Burnham's and Langley's convictions suggest, the masterminds of large-scale swindles in the nineteenth-century United States were not immune from criminal prosecution. In some circumstances, fraud indictments and convictions of prominent business figures were especially likely. If deceitful business practices antagonized a respectable constituency, the victims might not only raise funds to prosecute those responsible, but also lobby state legislatures to tighten legal prohibitions. The emergence in the 1850s of scams targeting recent immigrant populations, for instance, prompted concerted efforts along these lines by the Emigrant and Benevolent Societies of New York City. These organizations persuaded Albany legislators to enact a statute prohibiting the sale of steamship passenger tickets by unauthorized agents, and then helped to prosecute violators.[48]

The failure of a financial institution with substantial numbers of depositors or policyholders also tended to trigger sufficient popular anger to concentrate the minds and investigative energies of local prosecutors. When such insolvencies resulted from the looting of corporate assets and prosecutors could amass evidence that managers had issued false financial reports while seeking to cash out before the inevitable crash, criminal proceedings became the norm rather than the exception, with convictions often following. Thus Thomas W. Dyott, a wealthy Philadelphia drug manufacturer and private banker, faced prosecution for fraudulent insolvency after his Manual Labor Savings Bank failed during the Panic of 1837. The authorities showed that Dyott had concealed tens of thousands of dollars in assets from the state insolvency court and conveyed valuable property to relatives on the eve of the bank's failure. The eventual result was a conviction and a three-year prison term.[49] Such outcomes became more common after 1850, as executives of Northeastern banks and insurance companies periodically received jail sentences for criminal fraud associated with corporate failures.[50]

But for every conviction of corporate executives, there were instances in which legal technicalities or ambiguities about fraudulent intent led to quashed indictments or jury acquittals. Prosecutions against corporate managers might founder because it was hard to demonstrate all the legal elements that added up conspiracy to defraud, so that juries could distinguish fraudulent misrepresentations from misfortune tinged with wishful thinking. Although T. W. Dyott encountered the cold confines of Philadelphia's Eastern Penitentiary, the well-connected Baltimore lawyers and political operatives whose financiering led to the Bank of Maryland's 1834 failure had little difficulty deflecting fraud prosecutions, even though their use of deposits to fund their own speculations had led to widespread harm.[51] Sometimes individuals at the center of a large-scale banking fraud were even able to negotiate legal immunity in exchange for helping to untangle all the accounting knots that they had created, in order to maximize payments to depositors and shareholders.[52]

In other cases, despite clear evidence of deception about a corporation's financial position, executives could point to steadfast efforts to buoy stock prices. Rather than securing their own financial positions prior to the collapse, or even profiting from failure, these officials suffered heavy losses along with depositors, policyholders, and/or investors. Such individuals, like the officers of the National Cordage Trust, an enterprise whose attempt to create a monopoly in rope manufacturing ended in bankruptcy during the early 1890s, typically avoided guilty verdicts.[53] Furthermore, in order to build a fraud case against the managers of corporations, prosecutors usually had to undertake "months of preparation, the engagement of costly experts, and a vast amount of legal and clerical labor." Because such cases involved statutes filled with "vague and general" language, savvy defendants could avail themselves of "loop-holes for escape," either at trial or on appeal. In light of the herculean efforts required to gain convictions, nineteenth-century prosecutors tended to press only the most convincing cases.[54] As the *New York Times* summed up the situation, the cheating of an American company's stockholders "entails little or no inconvenience, save upon its victims."[55]

Even in cases that resulted in tens of thousands of dollars in losses to hundreds of depositors, investors, or policyholders, fraud convictions rarely led to more than a year or two of jail time. Nineteenth-century legislatures and judges did not see crimes of economic deception as deserving the same kind of punishment as violent crime or physical theft. Tellingly, the disgraced banker T. W. Dyott managed to slice more than a year off his unusually long three-year prison sentence, garnering a pardon from Pennsylvania's governor in 1841 on the grounds of his advanced age, and, at least according to the newspapers, because so many other swindling executives of failed banks had recently avoided criminal convictions.[56] Appropriators of fence rails or chickens might end up with far longer jail terms than would the bank cashier or insurance-company president who brought losses to thousands of investors and policyholders.

In light of the low conviction rates and minimal formal penalties, one might be tempted to characterize the criminal treatment of nineteenth-century American business fraud as all but toothless, especially for larger-scale operators. There is much to be said on behalf of such a conclusion. But a focus solely on the decisions rendered by juries and judges can obscure the full social and economic impacts of criminal proceedings. Arrests, indictments, and the resulting press coverage damaged reputations even in the absence of prosecutions, convictions, and jail terms. Corporate fraud scandals in Victorian Britain often destroyed the social standing of once high-flying entrepreneurs, even when they avoided jail sentences and civil judgments.[57] In cases of more prosaic duplicity, a false pretenses charge might still find its way into a credit report, serving as a caution to prospective counterparties.[58]

The point of criminal complaints, moreover, was often not to put deceitful businessmen in jail, but rather to increase the likelihood that they would agree to terms as the price of making complaints go away. Sometimes prosecutors withdrew criminal fraud cases because the accused and accuser had reached a settlement. Such negotiation usually occurred in private communications between counterparties or their legal counsels, and so left little public trace. Nonetheless, press coverage of fraud arrests and trials sometimes ended with a bland declaration that authorities had discontinued proceedings in light of a settlement between the parties, or because prosecuting witnesses had disappeared, possibly—perhaps probably—after a compromise. More frequently, newspapers noted an arrest or indictment without any subsequent mention of trial. We can presume that at least occasionally, defendants agreed to cough up partial payment.[59] When alleged perpetrators possessed high social standing, they might be compromised by mere threats of arrest or indictment. Thus, according to one Alabama newspaper, cotton exporters who detected fraudulently packed bales of cotton usually shied away from lodging formal charges. Given "the trouble and expense of prosecuting the guilty party," middlemen tended to "prefer a compromise," which resulted in the controversy being "hushed up."[60]

Nineteenth-century urban police forces also played roles as mediators between business owners and citizens who alleged that they had been the victims of duplicitous treatment, especially in cases that involved small sums. Keepers of employment agencies and proprietors of retail auction houses, for instance, developed the habit of responding to police investigations with at least partial refunds to disgruntled customers. Such activities were common enough that the police sometimes reported statistical overviews. During the first four months of 1862, the New York mayor's office informed newspapers that it had received 101 complaints about mock auctions, which prompted investigations that in turn led to refunds totaling almost $3,000.[61]

There is no way to quantify the incidence of such accommodations with precision. According to an 1847 contributor to the *New York Legal Observer*, hardly a week went by in New York City without someone putting "the machinery of the criminal law . . . in operation for the purpose of enabling the prosecutor to drive the defendant to a settlement of some civil litigation." Some twenty years later, a correspondent of the *National Police Gazette* asserted that similar efforts were commonplace in Pittsburgh.[62] It seems safe to conclude that compromises occurred with sufficient frequency to impose a measure of accountability for deceptive firms.

And yet, this use of criminal process to redress losses from deceit also reinforced official skepticism about some allegations of fraud—especially those emanating from creditors who claimed that debtors had lied to obtain loans. Misrepresentations by borrowers about their financial standing had bedeviled

America's credit system since at least the late eighteenth century. The least controversial circumstances involved outright credit swindles, such as the one perpetrated by Folger & Tibbs. When an individual or a partnership pretended to be launching a mercantile business, received supplies of goods on credit, secretly sold those goods, concealed the resulting funds, and then refused to pay creditors, arrests and convictions would follow, so long as the perpetrators hung around long enough to face trial.[63] But matters became murkier if an established business suffered losses and had either shaded the truth when arranging initial orders or obscured worsening finances to maintain a flow of credit, perhaps more out of self-delusion than as a scheme to harm creditors. So long as a creditor could mount a plausible case that a failed debtor had engaged in illegal deception, a criminal complaint might persuade the latter to scare up the funds to pay the debt. Throughout the nineteenth century, this logic, along with a more general antagonism toward the willingness of so many Americans to skirt financial obligations, convinced some merchants and bankers to file formal allegations of credit fraud.

Using criminal charges as levers to pry out debt repayments, however, elicited grousing from hinterland debtors and their political allies. To Americans who depended on credit from wholesalers in New York City, Boston, or Chicago, debt collection via a criminal fraud prosecution represented abuse of legal process, especially when it involved extradition to unsympathetic faraway courts. Boston creditors who took such steps, a New Hampshire Democratic newspaper argued soon after the Panic of 1837, were just as responsible for rural mercantile failures as were bankrupts, because they had "urged [them] to buy goods" that turned out to be unprofitable. Rather than accepting their share of a general misfortune, the paper complained, Boston merchants cynically exploited a Massachusetts "trap" law that made false oral representations by debtors a felony. Their goal was to "persecute" the insolvent storekeeper "for the purpose of coercing his friends to pay his debts, when the man had done nothing wrong, and gave as fair and honest an account of his situation as he could." Such arguments dovetailed with the opposition to imprisonment for debt that reshaped state debtor-creditor laws in the 1840s and 1850s.[64]

A second criticism focused on the public character of criminal process. Anglo-American legal theory had long understood criminal actions as targeting behavior that had an impact on society as a whole, rather than just the interests of private parties. As William Blackstone explained in his canonical treatise *Commentaries on the Laws of England*, "private wrongs, or civil injuries" only affected individuals. Crimes, by contrast, were "a breach and violation of the public rights and duties, due to the whole community, considered as a community, in its social aggregate capacity." They struck at "the very being of society, which cannot possibly subsist, where actions of this sort are suffered to escape with impunity."[65] This understanding did not foreclose attempts by complainants to use criminal process to mediate personal conflicts, in rural and urban jurisdictions alike. But as professionalization began to reshape American legal institutions in the mid-nineteenth century, the separation of civil and criminal actions became more distinct in fact as well as theory. Urban district attorneys and judges came to frown on private parties who tried to direct the machinery of criminal justice toward personal ends.[66]

These complementary arguments encouraged distrust of debt-related criminal fraud complaints, especially if transactions took place in interstate mercantile trade. Although such cases generated extradition requests, governors did not always comply with them. When they did go along, hinterland debtors often challenged extradition orders in state courts, filing applications for *habeas corpus* as they faced imminent transportation across state lines. These legal motions argued that the accused had not fled from criminal proceedings in another state, a key requirement for extradition. Judges sometimes proved sympathetic to this argument, releasing debtors from custody.[67]

In a pivotal 1847 case, *Fay and Collins v. Oatley and Blodgett*, the Wisconsin Supreme Court went further. This controversy arose out of Fay's 1845 mercantile failure in Milwaukee and the unwillingness of Oatley, a Buffalo creditor, to agree to a compromise offer. Instead, Oatley gained a false pretenses indictment against Fay in Buffalo, persuaded his state's governor to request extradition, brought the papers to Wisconsin, and used them to compel Fay's arrest. Once in manacles, "menaced with being run out of the State without the opportunity of consulting with counsel," Fay agreed to execute a series of promissory notes to Oatley, cosigned by his solvent brother-in-law, in exchange for his freedom. When Oatley attempted to collect on these debts, the Wisconsin courts refused to give them legal effect. In an opinion upholding a lower court's ruling on this point, the state Supreme Court maintained that for years, extradition proceedings had been "scandalously perverted" by Eastern creditors, and held that Oatley's behavior was "such a gross abuse of criminal process as to preclude its sanction by any court of law or equity."[68] By 1887, widespread dissatisfaction with such cases led appointees from nineteen state governments and the District of Columbia to raise bureaucratic barriers for those who wished to pursue fraud-related extraditions. The new recommended "rules of practice" required that extradition applications include a formal affidavit that the prosecution was "made in good faith, for the sole purpose of punishing the accused," and that the creditor did "not desire or expect to use the prosecution for the purpose of collecting a debt."[69]

Nineteenth-century opinion-makers and legal elites further advocated exacting evidentiary standards for debt-related business fraud cases. Throughout
1847 and 1848, for example, the *Philadelphia Public Ledger* decried the "unprincipled creditors" who resorted to such tactics "as a means of extorting payment" from insolvents. "The object of the criminal law," the *Ledger* reminded
its readers, was "to punish public wrong, not to adjust private disputes between
man and man." Almost a decade later, the *Chicago Tribune* similarly dispar-
aged the motives of creditors who brought criminal false pretenses charges.
Too many creditors did so either "to gratify private pique or revenge, or for the
purpose of 'squeezing out' property which civil process cannot reach." The authorities, the *Tribune* implied, needed to reread their Blackstone on the distinction between civil and criminal actions, and so redouble efforts to filter out
such "vexatious and frivolous controversies." Leading lights of the Northeastern judiciary picked up on this theme as well.[70]

Such sensibilities influenced the handling of debt-related fraud prosecutions. A legal writer for *Hunt's Merchant's Magazine* observed in 1857 that
"there is no [other] offense, which prosecuted, is so difficult to obtain conviction upon." District attorneys, "magistrates and grand jurors," and trial jurors
all knew that these allegations were frequently "frivolous or avaricious." As a
result, they all tended to manifest prejudice toward debt-related charges of
conspiracy to defraud or obtaining goods through false pretenses. In these
cases, the protagonists within the criminal justice system focused on the complainant's "pecuniary interest" and therefore "regard[ed] the evidence with
mistrust."[71] Prosecutors could and did overcome such wariness when the accused came from a disreputable social background, adopted a false identity as
part of a scheme to borrow or buy on credit, or engaged in such extensive
misrepresentations that multiple creditors came forward demanding prosecution.[72] But if defendants had purchased goods "in a regular way" and could
mobilize social networks to testify to their social standing and good reputation, convictions were unlikely.[73] And on the rare occasion when creditors engineered criminal fraud convictions against failed debtors who could lay claim
to respectability, appeals courts might find grounds to overturn guilty verdicts.[74] Even as settlements occasioned by criminal complaints extended the
legal reach of Americans who saw themselves as victims of deceit, they simultaneously curtailed options for redress.[75]

Conciliation also enabled deceitful proprietors to go about their business.
Indeed, the willingness of disgruntled counterparties to reach settlements gave
repeated lifelines to career swindlers such as the mock auctioneer Zeno Burnham. His knack for eluding pressure from police and district attorneys reflected not only careful exploitation of legal ambiguities, but also discreet pay-

ments to persistent complainants. Before and after his 1866 conviction, he defused the anger of customers who had lodged formal complaints by getting out his checkbook. Even Burnham's early release from prison was contingent on a full refund to the woman who had initiated prosecution.[76] Compromise extended a measure of justice to insistent victims, but at the cost of leaving some of the most duplicitous operators free to cheat another day.

LAW IN ACTION—ADMINISTRATIVE REGULATION

Civil and criminal proceedings did not constitute the only forms of authority that the perpetrators of business fraud might encounter in nineteenth-century America. As we have seen, localities and states created administrative mechanisms to foster honesty in commercial dealings. Evaluation of how these licensing and inspection regimes functioned is again hampered by the fact that historians have undertaken few detailed case studies. But press coverage, along with scattered government reports and occasional political debates, allows for some conclusions.

The regulatory institutions that maintained the strongest record in combating deceptive business practices were inspection regimes in states that had commodity export sectors. In tobacco states such as Virginia and Maryland, planters and merchants shared an interest in trustworthy evaluations of cured leaf, which created enduring political support for meaningful regulation. Building on inspection regimes that had begun in the early eighteenth century, these states mandated that prior to export, state inspectors had to examine the contents of shipping barrels to ensure merchantability and furnish judgments about quality. This process called for a tobacco inspector and his assistants to open a random barrel at a central warehouse, remove samples from several places in it, and then assess the samples' quality. Northeastern states such as Massachusetts maintained similar inspections of pickled fish, while Pennsylvania retained compulsory inspection of exported flour.

Up through the Civil War, many public inspection regimes maintained reputations for effectiveness, especially among larger-scale producers. In the colonies around the Chesapeake Bay, inspection laws improved European demand and prices for tobacco. Buyers in Britain, France, and Germany continued to rely on the judgments made by Virginia and Maryland tobacco inspectors for decades after the Revolution.[77] By the 1840s, the work of these appointed officials had become interwoven into the region's commercial practices, occasioning newspaper commentary only via matter-of-fact reports about monthly or annual inspection statistics. As the Missouri tobacco industry began to expand in the early 1840s, local elites, many of whom had grown up in Virginia or Kentucky (another tobacco inspection state), took it for granted that the emergence of St. Louis as a tobacco center depended on trustworthy public inspection. Without it, they assumed, far-flung buyers would look elsewhere.[78]

The Massachusetts system of fish inspections similarly sustained industry reputation at home and abroad. "There is no doubt," one writer maintained in 1843, "but the fisheries of Massachusetts have derived great advantage from our Inspection Laws." Public fish inspections ensured that "the public are protected . . . from imposition in purchasing an article with which they are not familiarly acquainted, and which they would not purchase at all, were it not for the character stamped on them by the State."[79] From the 1810s through the 1850s, flour exported from Baltimore and Philadelphia—cities in states with strict inspection requirements for that commodity—traded at a premium compared to flour exported from states without such stringent monitoring. Mercantile observers consistently attributed this market advantage to the "integrity" of Maryland and Pennsylvania inspectors.[80]

State inspection regimes, however, faced a growing chorus of objections from the early 1840s onward, voiced both by Jacksonians and some Whigs and then Republicans. Critics depicted inspection as costly, oppressive, and rife with the cronyism associated with the rise of machine-style democratic politics. Instead of choosing competent inspectors, opponents argued, governors selected party activists who had expended great effort on behalf of a winning electoral ticket. Such individuals, the critics alleged, cared far more about milking offices for fees than upholding quality standards. As a result, they indulged marginal lumbermen, millers, fishermen, or tobacco planters, passing suspect goods or inflating their quality. Instead of protecting the public against fraud or sustaining the reputation of American commodities in foreign markets, inspection requirements gave unsophisticated buyers a false sense of security, while imposing de facto taxes on commerce. An inspector's stamp of approval, moreover, often absolved manufacturers and dealers from legal responsibility for goods that they sold, leaving disgruntled purchasers few options but to sue inspectors for dereliction of duty. The *National Police Gazette* summed up this viewpoint in 1846, depicting inspection laws as "a farce, by which the community are swindled under cover of law."[81]

Adversaries of compulsory public inspection did not have to scrape the bottom of regulatory barrels to find instances of inaccurate appraisals or political maneuvering in appointments. In 1847, for instance, the combination of a poor catch and intense pressure from local fishermen led Massachusetts fish inspectors to expand their definition of No. 1 pickled mackerel, much to the consternation of Philadelphia fish dealers. When pressed by state legislators responding to public outcry, the Massachusetts inspectors conceded that their work during the season had been characterized by "negligence and carelessness," and quickly promised reforms. During the early 1850s, San Francisco flour inspectors caused an uproar among inland communities by approving the merchantability of any barrel that purported to contain a substance called flour, no matter how sour or musty.[82] Every so often, commercial victims of poor inspections found their legal position compromised, as critics warned they might, by the fact that tainted goods had passed official muster. Because the sellers could plead an affirmative state inspection as a defense, they often skirted liability for the sale of adulterated or spoiled commodities.[83] And sometimes, as with Chicago's decision to create the new office of "city flour inspector" during the Civil War, the driving force behind a new regulatory authority was furnishing a valuable office to an influential politico.[84]

Opponents of public inspection linked such evidence to the wider critique of government that emerged in the wake of the financial panics of the late 1830s and the resulting debt crises that paralyzed so many state and local authorities. They further stressed the increasing importance of large-scale American manufacturers, whose attention to quality exceeded government standards and whose reputation sustained premium prices without official stamps of approval. All of these arguments had left their imprint on public policy from the mid-1840s through the postbellum era, nowhere more than in New York. There, the 1846 state constitutional convention prohibited the legislature from creating public offices for weighing, measuring, and otherwise inspecting articles of trade, a policy confirmed by the subsequent constitutional convention of 1867–68. Buyers or sellers who wished to avail themselves of inspection services in the state had to rely on private parties who operated without color of state authority. Other states exempted out-of-state goods that came to their ports for transshipment elsewhere. Still others made at least some commodity inspections voluntary rather than compulsory. These provisions allowed buyers and sellers either to bypass inspection altogether or to rely on private certification firms rather than public facilities.[85]

Advocates for these reforms linked them to an ethos of *caveat emptor*. Americans, according to delegates at New York's 1846 convention who spoke against state inspections, "were sharp-sighted to see their own interest" and "perfectly capable of taking care of themselves in all the transactions of life." Just over two decades later, the most vociferous proponent of maintaining New York's constitutional ban, Thomas G. Alvord, placed his faith in the workings of what twenty-first-century economists would call reputational capital. When businessmen tried to cheat, this prominent attorney and recent lieutenant governor proclaimed, "it is bruited about in the community," causing the cheaters eventually to lose far more than any short-term gains. Alvord concluded that New York would be well advised to rely on "the old doctrine of *caveat emptor*. Let a man's eyes be his guide." The *Baltimore Sun* agreed with this logic as it campaigned for an end to Maryland's system of tobacco inspection in 1876. To argue for inspection of any article of trade, the *Sun* maintained, was to commit oneself to "inspectors for everything" and "offices for everybody." It made much more sense to "depend less and less upon government . . . guardianship of men's private dealings," trusting instead to "personal character and men's sense of their own interests."[86] Here was a vision in tune with P. T. Barnum's approach to political economy.

That vision did not fully vanquish nineteenth-century inspection regimes. Although Kentucky and Virginia both ended compulsory tobacco inspection during Reconstruction, the Maryland legislature continued to ignore the shrill pleas from the *Baltimore Sun* for similar action into the 1880s, listening instead to the numerous tobacco growers who preferred mandated public assessments of leaf.[87] Many commercial states, such as Massachusetts, Ohio, and Louisiana, retained a robust and wide-ranging inspection system for at least some goods, while taking steps to limit conflicts of interest among inspectors.[88] As we will see, the growing economic importance of many products that defied easy certification of quality led to new inspection laws after the Civil War. Nonetheless, the pullback from compulsory commodity inspection reduced the states' role as arbiters of fair commercial dealings.

In addition to inspection laws, nineteenth-century American states, cities, and counties also maintained myriad licensing schemes as ways to curb duplicitous business practices. Local governments could deny licenses to traveling salesmen, auctioneers, or keepers of intelligence offices whose background raised serious questions about their probity; they could also threaten to revoke or actually rescind the licenses of miscreants. Public officials could use these powers to sanction individuals whose customers had accused them of fraud. Even after receiving his pardon, for instance, Zeno Burnham was unable to regain a New York City auctioneer's license.[89] Furthermore, city governments combined these official means of enforcement with more informal strategies. In the 1840s, the police in New York City emulated a tactic that local authorities in London had deployed as early as 1812: they paid young boys to stand in front of notorious mock auction shops wearing large placards that warned, "STRANGERS, BEWARE OF MOCK AUCTIONS." City authorities in New Orleans soon pursued a similar strategy, employing "negros," perhaps free, perhaps enslaved, to "parade the streets with boards. On one side is 'Beware of Mock Auctions,' and on the other is 'Beware of Peter Funks.'"[90] Early in the Civil War, New York City stationed police in front of known mock auction houses to warn off potential customers, threaten arrests, and pressure proprietors to provide refunds.[91]

When pursued with sufficient vigor, these approaches reshaped urban geography. The 1862 operation against New York's dodgy auction trade in watches and jewelry cleared the Broadway, Chatham Street, and Maiden Lane shopping districts of these establishments.[92] But such campaigns by no means rid the city or nation of the individuals who ran those firms. Many mock auctioneers who cleared out of the downtown retail districts joined Zeno Burnham in the uptown auction furniture trade or turned to rigged auctions of cigars or horses. Others moved to new cities, with their own supplies of strangers and greenhorns ripe for picking. Even the refusal to grant licenses did little to stop determined perpetrators of business fraud. One might simply open for business without a license like many, if not most, nineteenth-century intelligence offices, or, like Zeno Burnham after his conviction and pardon, operate through a front man.[93] Indeed, just a year or so after the extensive 1862 police campaign against New York City mock auctioneers, the police commissioner observed that concerted efforts to compel settlements with complaining customers turned out to be "futile." "The rogue," he pointed out, "will continue to rob as long as he loses only the amount of the robberies in the few cases where he is detected, and gains the amount of the robberies in the many cases where he is not." To land a real blow against mock auctioneers, the commissioner called for systematic, ongoing license revocation.[94] Sustained administrative focus on antifraud campaigns, however, proved to be the exception among postbellum urban police forces.

One further antifraud policy adopted at this time deserves at least a brief mention: legal requirements to improve the disclosure of pivotal economic information in a particular market. An important antebellum policy of this sort emerged as a response to the problem of falsely packed cotton. Complaints from Northeastern and European merchants about bales filled with trash, stalks, seeds, sand, dirt, and/or stones, or made heavier through judicious use of water-soaked cotton, rained down upon US exporters in the twenty years that followed the War of 1812, especially during periods of strong demand and high prices. One key problem was that middlemen in the global supply chain struggled to identify who was responsible for such tricks. The connection between a particular bale and the original planter or gin-owner whose workers had pressed it was often lost amid the flurry of activity on river landings and in seaports on both sides of the Atlantic. Difficulties in fixing responsibility for deceptive packing encouraged the practice.[95]

Southern elites might have addressed this problem by instituting a system of cotton inspection. But close examination of the inside of a several-hundred-pound bale was no easy matter. An alternative idea, pushed by US seaport exporters and British importers alike, called for statutory requirements that every cotton bale include an external mark specifying the planter or ginner who sold it. Because this would greatly assist middlemen in enforcing claims of false packing, the thinking went, it would help to deter the practice. Alabama enacted such legislation in 1832, and other states may have followed suit.[96] But grumbling from American and European textile manufacturers continued. Indeed, renewed high prices during the 1850s led many Southern planters to ignore the duty to brand their bales amid expanded volume and a more hectic trade. Complaints about fraudulent packing once again reached a crescendo, with renewed pleas for tougher regulatory action from mercantile organizations on both sides of the Atlantic.[97]

In Barnum's America, then, administrative mechanisms to combat business fraud made duplicitous business practices more difficult and less remunerative in some sectors. Yet large chunks of economic activity remained outside the jurisdiction of administrative officers, while the dynamics of political patronage and the shifting of executive priorities blunted the effectiveness of regulatory schemes. Like the checks of the civil and criminal law, bureaucratic restraints on fraudulent enterprises, whether involving goods inspection, licensing, or standards of information disclosure, bound deception-minded American proprietors only so tightly.

✳✳✳✳

The living, breathing law of American marketplaces did not quite map onto P. T. Barnum's published recollections. Individuals and firms who suffered economic losses and attributed their misfortune to duplicity did not find themselves bereft of all legal protections and levers. But given the monetary and social costs of taking fraud allegations to the courts, the degree of institutional and popular skepticism about such allegations, jurisdictional limits, and capacity constraints on public bureaucracies, the showman's autobiographical reflections did not fall wildly short of the mark. The legal environment of his world tilted toward the premises of *caveat emptor*.

The nineteenth-century United States, of course, encompassed several regions—remote rural sections and bustling urban districts, Yankee New England and the cotton states. It was further riven by social fractures based on race, ethnicity, gender, and class. The legal handling of business fraud reflected these geographic and social divisions. Antebellum appellate judges in Southern states that imported slaves proved more sympathetic to civil fraud suits by slave purchasers than did their counterparts in Virginia or Kentucky, where slave-owners were far more likely to be sellers than buyers.[98] It mattered that Zeno Burnham's accuser in 1865 was a respectable, middle-class white woman, just as it mattered that the corporate officers who faced criminal fraud charges could pay for the very best legal representation and enjoyed the benefit of the doubt accorded to high social position. Despite the salience of these differences in social identity, the legal treatment of American business fraud generated some broader commercial and financial risks that confronted Barnum's contemporaries from all social backgrounds and in every part of the country. Their economic world was filled with deceit.

The antebellum countryside indeed teemed with sharpers—peddlers seeking to unload shoddy wares, rural farmers and storekeepers who engaged in running battles over adulterated goods and manipulated weights and measures, slave-owners who attempted to disguise the ailments of the seriously ill men and women whom they wished to sell, land claimants who played fast and loose with legal requirements to secure a slice of the public domain, and land dealers who misrepresented the market value of their real estate or the strength of their claims to ownership. Commercial practices in the antebellum city were, if anything, even less predicated on candor. In addition to the routine deceptions of retail trade, the typical metropolis contained plenty of mock auctioneers like Zeno Burnham and quite a number of mercantile firms that did not hesitate to stretch the truth in their circulars and advertisements.[99] Would-be borrowers lied about their finances, persuaded third parties to lie on their behalf, and lodged already-pledged or fraudulent collateral, all to make credit flow. Everywhere, the nineteenth-century economy was awash in counterfeits—bogus imitations of branded goods, forged securities, impostors who posed as legitimate business agents, and above all else, fake currency.[100]

Rapid growth in the scale and reach of corporate enterprise from the 1840s onward magnified the possibilities for economic legerdemain. Promoters of new corporate securities issued prospectuses that promised fabulous returns and indulged in the grossest of financial evasions, especially in industries whose stocks were greatly in demand, such as mining and oil drilling. The secondary markets remained rife with insider manipulation, and as financial corporations became fixtures of the American economy, so too did sham banks and insurance companies that siphoned off a fraction of deposits and premiums. With far greater regularity, incorporated businesses suffered losses from embezzlements and endemic self-dealing among corporate managers.[101]

During the early 1850s, the German journalist, translator, and travel writer Moritz Busch came to the United States for a year's sojourn. Like many European visitors, Busch took on the task of explaining the new republic to his countrymen and -women. After months spent in cities, on steamboats, and in rural hamlets, Busch concluded that "ganz Amerika ist eine einzige ungeheure Mock-Auction!"—"all America is one gigantic Mock Auction."[102] This generalization, like Barnum's autobiography, was exaggerated. And yet, there was little doubt that the land between the Hudson and the Mississippi, and beyond them as well, remained locations of much gulling and grafting, in which people were well advised to seek whatever channels of information might help them distinguish the trustworthy from the Peter Funks.

CHAPTER FOUR

Channels of Exposure

Opportunities for fraud exist in any economy. But they were particularly salient in the nineteenth-century United States, where technological breakthroughs, transformations in finance and business organization, and the rapid creation of an integrated national economy sparked a series of economic booms, and where migration and the shifting boundaries of social class loosened traditional forms of communal authority. These conditions encouraged the flowering of a booster ethos suffused with thoroughgoing optimism and celebration of the rapid accumulation of wealth; they also fostered the emergence of pervasive information asymmetries. Optimism bred credulousness and willingness to take on risk. Profound differences in access to market intelligence limited the ability of investors and consumers to assess the claims of the parties with whom they contemplated doing business. This combination increased the payoffs and lowered the costs associated with fraud.[1]

Such conditions, along with the de facto legal environment of *caveat emptor*, led many business owners who felt victimized by some commercial imposition or financial fraud to engage in modes of self-help, a strategy long enshrined in Anglo-American law and social practice. Instead of turning to lawsuits, British and other European importers of falsely packed cotton might demand monetary compensation from their American mercantile correspondents, who often complied, realizing that a delay in payment would gravely damage important long-term economic relationships.[2] Rather than rushing to the police after being taken by a mock auctioneer, visitors to the big city occasionally sought, and sometimes received, redress through a personal show of force.[3] Sometimes fraud victims banded together in larger social actions to voice their displeasure. Thus, in 1835, hundreds of working-class Baltimore depositors, outraged by the Bank of Maryland's failure after brazen managerial speculations, initiated a full-scale riot. Animated by a centuries-old tradition of crowd action as a means of vindicating popular moral economy, these disgruntled casualties of bank fraud destroyed the homes of several bank directors.[4]

The problem of business fraud led greater numbers of nineteenth-century Americans to explore preventative strategies. One common impulse was to cultivate networks of commercial intelligence that gave businessmen access to more than their own eyes and ears as they assessed the trustworthiness of people, goods, and intangible assets. Within communities, webs of local knowledge fixed reputations, as with one shifty Cincinnati storekeeper, whose establishment was described by a judge in a midcentury legal controversy as "fairly hedged in by information. Eshelby, looking from his shoe store over the way, sees rascality; Rooney, a very quiet man, knows all about it; the sheriff is on his guard, and creditors are besieging the premises." The image here is striking—a proprietor with proclivities for trickery, fenced in by the shared observations and suspicions of neighbors.[5] The Eshelbys and Rooneys had their counterparts in every village, hamlet, and urban commercial district across the North American continent.

Local surveillance, however, proved far less effective as the scale and scope of impersonal economic relationships in the United States expanded, prompting entrepreneurs to develop several institutional strategies to cope with the threats posed by fraud. These usually had the goal of reducing information differentials between counterparties or between principals and their agents, or of providing some form of insurance against fraud-related losses. Some of these approaches encompassed the development of entirely new business niches, including confidential credit reporting, the provision of credit insurance, and the emergence of investment banks as mechanisms to discipline corporate managements. Others entailed the fashioning of new methods of monitoring within large-scale corporations, such as stiffer internal accounting controls to limit opportunities for forgery or embezzlement, and innovations in marketing, such as the cultivation of brands or the provision of money-back guarantees.[6]

There was also a complementary if more diffuse nineteenth-century response to fraud as an economic dilemma—a growing realm of public commentary about commercial and financial deceit. The constant reminders to Americans to beware of all the goods, services and opportunities floating around them encouraged demand for public information about prevailing deceptions. A group of self-appointed commercial policemen among the nation's journalists, writers, and publishers took it upon themselves to meet this demand. These guardians surveyed the American marketplace for swindles and swindlers and then tried to warn "the public"—in some cases targeting the broader marketplace and society, in others seeking out participants in a single industry or sector. As a result, the era's newspapers, magazines, and bookshops teemed with commentary about frauds and fraudsters. In the resulting public discourse about imposition and humbug, Barnum's contemporaries, and Barnum himself, devised their most substantial, if still quite imperfect, regulation on behalf of truthful commercial speech. Ironically, the resulting public discourse about fraud soon reverberated through American business culture, prompting the evolution of ever more sophisticated modes of economic deceit, and buttressing, for a good many decades, middle-class and elite commitments to the premises of *caveat emptor*.

MAKING MARKETS FOR FRAUD INTELLIGENCE

Public discourse about economic deception had roots in the colonial period, when newspapers and pamphleteers tracked the exploits of tricksters and confidence men.[7] With the growth in complex economic relationships based on impersonal trust, nineteenth-century writers explored a widening set of issues about business fraud. The most extensive investigations, particularly in urban newspapers and national periodicals, concerned large-scale financial scandals. When a leading American entrepreneur such as Benjamin Rathbun became embroiled in charges of financial malfeasance—in Rathbun's case because of allegations that he had propped up his real-estate developments in mid-1830s Buffalo by forging endorsements—local and national press closely followed the events. Later scandals, such as Robert Schuyler's fraudulent overissue of New Haven & New York Railroad Company stock in the early 1850s, the Credit Mobilier contracting scandals of the 1860s, and the financial collapses of a series of fraudulent New York City life-insurance companies during the 1870s, attracted even more intensive reporting and analysis.[8] This close attention reflected competition among a multiplying number of news outlets, as well as the increased economic fallout of large-scale fraud. American journalists also emulated the example of their British peers. Instances of corporate malfeasance, such as those associated with the railway promotions of the 1840s, the bank and insurance failures of the 1850s, or the stupendous collapse of the Overend and Gurney bank in 1866, generated massive coverage from Fleet Street.[9]

Public surveillance of allegedly duplicitous commercial activities, whether in Britain or America, reached far beyond retrospectives on the most consequential frauds and defalcations. The urban press provided a fraud blotter. Day after day, month after month, readers learned about embezzling bookkeepers and bank tellers, the discovery of forgery rings, efforts to launch bogus banks and insurance companies, and arrests or trials related to criminally prohibited misrepresentations. When private complaints or police investigations identified swindlers who had escaped the porous constraints of the legal system, publications such as the *National Police Gazette* further made a habit of publishing their physical descriptions or photographs, a nineteenth-century precursor of the all-points bulletin.[10]

Coverage of specific frauds also prompted more general reflections about how employers, customers, suppliers, creditors, policyholders, or investors could detect it. Articles on one incident recalled analogous dodges and articulated rules of thumb for spotting duplicitous marketing, fraudulent investments and credit applications, or employee behavior that signaled looming defalcation. As early as the 1830s, demand for such commentary supported the emergence of pamphlets and books that detailed the tactics of unscrupulous merchants, stockbrokers, and company promoters. In subsequent decades, publishers produced a steady supply of book-length fraud exposés. Some were memoirs of personal encounters with suspect practices in one segment of the American economy. Others offered up general catalogues of trickery that advised readers how to avoid the fate of the fleeced.[11]

Antifraud discourse, then, had a broad footprint in America from 1830 onward, taking up space in just about every newspaper, the commercial press, and more specialized trade journals, as well as on the shelves of book dealers. Of course, it shared that space with an enormous amount of puffery that all too often abetted fraudulent practices or schemes. Local newspapers in areas greatly desirous of outside investment capital became notorious for boosterism that buoyed the extravagant claims of associated land speculators and corporate promoters. Trade journals manifested a promotional outlook and a willingness to tout the virtues of leading businesses within the relevant industry. Organizers of midcentury gift enterprises—firms that disposed of hard-to-sell goods through promotional premiums—paid rural editors to place favorable "news items" about their businesses. Some even created separate newspapers or magazines as thinly veiled marketing vehicles. Up into the 1890s, many papers and journals remained heavily dependent on advertising from the makers of patent medicines, and so displayed scant concern over the fantastic nature of those concerns' assertions and promises.[12]

Commodity and securities speculators also concocted all manner of schemes to use news channels as an element of their strategies for manipulating price movements in the nation's markets. Early efforts along these lines involved planting stories in the press that, in combination with coordinated campaigns to circulate rumors, would likely move stock prices in a desired direction. Nearly every Western mining boom of the 1860s and 1870s was accompanied by heavily managed promotional campaigns in local newspapers. In his 1872 account of the previous decade's gold and silver booms, *Roughing It*, Mark Twain explained the basics of journalistic corruption. Reporters received shares in new mining ventures as a matter of course, and returned the favor with optimistic accounts that "frothed at the mouth as if a very marvel in silver discoveries had transpired," all to feed the speculative temper of outside investors.[13] By the latter decades of the century, some speculators published their own tip sheets and financial newspapers to gain a stronger hold on the financial rumor mill. The large-scale speculator Jay Gould went so far as to purchase a respectable publication, the *New York World*, to facilitate his maneuvers in the stock market. Through the *World*, Gould could engineer support for his takeover attempts by having the paper run stories that encouraged investors to dump the stocks of the companies in which he was interested.[14]

Behavior of this sort horrified the nation's Protestant establishment. In 1854, a Philadelphia clergyman, Henry Boardman, published a collection of sermons/lectures that gave voice to religious concerns about prevailing commercial ethics. *The Bible in the Counting-House* meticulously flayed the duplicitous behavior of American merchants, expressing contempt for efforts to justify cheating through appeal to commercial customs. Boardman's goal was to contrast prevailing deceptions and the mores that tolerated them with the demands of Christianity, thereby convincing the nation's businessmen to subordinate their Machiavellian instincts to the higher norms of Jesus' teachings. In a country in which "young men will flock, as they have done, to the marts of business," and in which those marts set the key patterns for society and culture, the only way to secure religious truth and national honor was to "go directly into the abodes of commerce, and publish to the great army of traffickers, the high requisitions of Christianity." In other words, in Barnum's America, as went the spiritual lives of the merchants, so would go the spiritual life of the country.[15]

The great majority of cautions about fraud in this period were rooted in far more prosaic considerations. Most obviously, the sentinels of commercial flimflam and financial skullduggery perceived a vibrant demand for their reporting, evaluations, and advice, and hoped to profit from that demand. In a commercial world filled with tricks and masquerades, discussion of the latest forgery or confidence game furnished compelling copy, particularly for the penny dailies and popular weekly sheets such as the *New York Herald* and the *National Police Gazette*, which catered to mass readerships. Fraud helped to sell papers. For decades, the *Police Gazette* titillated its readers with the daring exploits of notorious quacks, sharpers, and confidence men, giving their most prominent place to the counterfeiters or swindlers who demonstrated a knack for eluding police or escaping from jail, and exhibiting particular fascination for female con artists or male swindlers who managed to gain the trust of social elites. As in so many other cultures, incidents in which a trickster fooled the high and mighty resonated with less-prosperous readers, who in this case had the disposable income to consume tales of comeuppance through commodified newsprint.[16]

The pecuniary impulse to gain from public announcements of swindles and humbugs, however, took on an array of manifestations, and these patterns suggest intriguing conflicts over cultural authority within the American marketplace. One important impetus for public warnings about fraud came from well-entrenched businesses whose managers worried about deceptions that siphoned off demand for their offerings. Manufacturers of branded goods were the most important targets of imitations, and by the late nineteenth century, they increasingly fought them through trademark infringement suits.[17] But legal action required the expenditure of significant resources and often entailed risks. As a result, aggrieved businesses often responded to counterfeit goods by engaging in a form of self-help. They placed advertisements that put the members of the public on their guard.

Thousands of such advertisements appeared in nineteenth-century newspapers and periodicals. The pleas were to "Beware of Fraud!" when purchasing Hyde Winship & Co. Soap, because a Baltimore distributor was passing off "common White Soap, cut into very thin flakes, and a small quantity of perfume applied to the outside" as the genuine product; or to "LOOK OUT FOR FRAUD" when searching for Blake's Patent Fire Proof Paint, because its popularity had enticed "scores of unprincipled individuals" to "throw . . . into the market all kinds of worthless, counterfeit stuff, much of it no better than dirt from the street"; or to purchase the Ostermoor Elastic Felt Mattress only from the manufacturer via mail-order, because in retail establishments, "only frauds are offered—not the Ostermoor."[18] Little changed in this advertising genre over three-quarters of a century, aside from the occasional introduction of basic graphics and the eventual references to unauthorized dealers selling knockoffs.

More communal impulses toward economic self-defense also prompted public commentary about swindling and systematic deceit. A nineteenth-century newspaper sometimes gave intense coverage to fraud allegations out of concern that endemic misrepresentations were damaging its city's standing in regional, national, or international trade. This concern drove an effort by the *New York Times* during the mid-1850s to prod the city's Corn Exchange to implement new rules to govern the inspection of flour. After the prohibition of state offices for goods inspection by the 1846 state constitution, a system of private inspection emerged in Manhattan, in which those shippers who desired some kind of quality determination paid for inspection firms to rate their flour. But the system was so riddled with conflicts of interest that the quality of flour shipped from New York deteriorated, leading the *Times* to spearhead efforts to improve standards of private grain grading.[19]

On other occasions, public analyses of fraud represented still-subtler forms of commercial self-protection. Businessmen who faced questions about the legitimacy of their business practices, or even of their core business model, sometimes responded to this kind of criticism by trying to redirect the public spotlight onto even more disreputable enterprises, a version of the strategy of deflection. P. T. Barnum serves as a case in point. Throughout the first few decades of his career, Barnum had to contend with recurring complaints about the more outrageous of his stunts and exhibitions. Many leading social and religious figures denounced Barnum's offerings as swindles, characterizing them as barefaced misrepresentations that gave the visitors to Barnum's American Museum nothing of value in return for the price of admission.

This criticism reached a crescendo in the aftermath of Barnum's 1854 autobiography, and of his personal insolvency just over a year later. To the *Southern Quarterly Review*, Barnum's reflections on his life were those of a "thimblerigger who has cheated the public" and who had the effrontery to seek more profits from "an exposition of his own roguery." The *New York Times* complained that the only difference between Barnum's systematic dependence on false pretenses and those of common counterfeiters was that the former had not learned "the advantage of doing things on a grand scale and with the flourish of trumpets." Religious commentators were equally scathing. The reviewer for the *Christian Examiner* condemned the proprietor of the American Museum as having made "quackery" a fine art, and as possessing an extraordinary "vulgarity of aims" and "a low and unscrupulous cunning." One contemptuous English commentator encapsulated all of these attacks in 1859. Barnum, a writer in the *British Advertiser* thundered, had raised himself up as a false prophet, a dangerous cultural icon who

> tells us that to cheat is no longer a wickedness, that to lie is no longer a condemned expedient; that to gull the public is the beginning and the end of all wisdom; . . . that mammon worship is the true devotion, and that hypocrisy, deceit, lying, perjury, and fraud are the legitimate arts of worship.

By the eve of the Civil War, Barnum had become a lightning rod for transatlantic anxieties about the impact of modern capitalism on social mores.[20]

The impresario's spectacular insolvency in January 1856 only heightened this dynamic. Barnum failed because he agreed to serve as an endorser for a Connecticut clock manufacturer that, unbeknownst to him, was on the verge of bankruptcy. After he found himself unable to pay hundreds of thousands of dollars of the manufacturer's notes, many of which Barnum alleged were forged, editors across the country happily crowed about a deceitful scoundrel getting his comeuppance. "The deposed King of Humbug," one Albany paper wrote, had been able to "evade the law" and "delude the clergy," but his relentless attempts to gain "notoriety without paying for it" had finally and appropriately "exploded" in his face.[21]

Barnum anticipated most of these attacks in his first autobiography, insisting that he provided his customers with excellent value. In addition to the genuine curiosities and quality theatrical shows in his Museum, his skeptical visitors had the entertaining experience of evaluating the authenticity of his spurious exhibits, and of trying to figure out how Barnum managed to put things over on his audiences. Some commentators on his place in American culture picked up on this theme. Thus in defending the showman in the immediate aftermath of his failure, the New York Tribune insisted that "in law and morals, there is a great distinction, and justly so, between white and black lies." Only costing his customers "extremely moderate" sums, Barnum's exhibitions succeeded eminently in "gratifying the sentiment of wonder." The Tribune concluded that "every person who visited" the American Museum "got his money's worth."[22]

Barnum's 1865 book Humbugs of the World extended this line of argument. In this treatise on scams in American commerce, religion, and medicine, the showman contrasted his techniques of promotion and jovial misdirection, which he depicted as legitimate, with contemptible varieties of swindling and imposture. The wholesalers and grocers who adulterated foods, the mail-order lottery dealers who touted rigged drawings, the promoters who peddled worthless shares of bogus oil companies, the mediums and spiritualists who faked access to the world of the dead, and the quacks who conjured up contrived testimonials from Civil War generals for their "Hasheesh Candy" or "Preparation of Turkish Roses"—all these deserved the appellation of swindler, and many a few years in the penitentiary. By comparison, a purveyor of entertainment who "attract[ed] crowds of customers by his unique displays," and who sent these customers home satisfied with the experience of puzzling over their authenticity, had done nothing but divert his audience with an afternoon's enjoyable respite.[23]

During the postbellum decades, several respectable New York City stockbrokers and speculators, including William Henry Fowler and Henry Clews, undertook a similar approach with regard to the often-mysterious business of Wall Street. These financial insiders decried the techniques of unscrupulous stockbrokers and bucket shops. Such operators often only pretended to execute the trades ordered by their customers, shaved off profitable returns through false reports on actual trades, and reported initial phantom profits on investments in order to attract more substantial deposits. Fowler and Clews similarly explained and excoriated the strategies that speculating rings used to disseminate false rumors among investors eager for some inside dope. The most direct message of these publications was that individuals tempted to enter the fray of the securities markets should ignore the wild promises of unsolicited stock circulars. But another dominant theme harped on the enormous difference between the multitude of swindling brokers and the high-toned firms with close links to the New York Stock Exchange, an institution described by one pamphleteer as "unquestionably honorable, legitimate, and thoroughly reliable" and providing "the most complete protection against irresponsibility."[24] Once again, the strategy here was to deploy scathing critiques of purveyors of deceit as a way to legitimate related businesses that faced significant public complaint.

Not all nineteenth-century American publicists of fraud were businessmen who perceived themselves to be targeted by counterfeiting miscreants, local elites anxious over threats to regional economic reputation, or entrepreneurs who faced sufficient criticisms of their own practices to prompt attempts to redirect public criticism elsewhere. In many segments of the American economy, strategically placed individuals took advantage of their knowledge and access to commercial intelligence to set themselves up as cultural authorities and de facto arbiters of when economic behavior overstepped acceptable boundaries. The publishers of counterfeit detector manuals, which proliferated from the 1830s up to the Civil War, took on this role. Their imposing lists of all the spurious and doubtful bank notes in circulation were sent to subscribers by a shifting band of metropolitan note brokers, such as New Yorker John Thompson. These financial middlemen recognized that their expertise about a heterogeneous antebellum money supply allowed them to furnish the broader public with detailed descriptions that distinguished trustworthy from bogus currency.[25]

Few other spheres of American commerce generated as extensive efforts to institutionalize fraud coverage as the circulation of paper money, although some came close. From its inception, *Scientific American* paid close attention to methods for masking imitations of manufacturing materials, strategies for manipulating the weights and measures of commodities, and patent swindles, including the marketing of bogus inventions such as the Keely motor, said to run on mysterious "etheric" energy.[26] The emergence and rapid technological evolution of photography was accompanied by all manner of photographic snake oil—slight tweaks to established approaches that did nothing to improve performance, magical new methods that failed outright, fake licenses to actual or even nonexistent patents. Such tactics prompted the creation of journals such as the *Philadelphia Photographer*, which informed subscribers about the latest chemical impostures.[27] Trade journals aimed at druggists, physicians, and chemists similarly took aim at worthless patent medicines and practices of food adulteration.[28] From the Civil War onward, the *Engineering and Mining Journal* policed fake mining processes, the promotion of fraudulent mining stocks, and efforts by insiders to manipulate price movements on mining exchanges.

Nineteenth-century trade journals performed many functions. In addition to providing fraud-related intelligence, they covered technological and organizational innovations, discussed public policies that impinged on their economic sector, compiled and disseminated statistics about sales and markets, and furnished a vehicle for advertisers to reach a sectoral niche. But fraud-fighting at least occasionally topped this list with regard to marketing strategy. Thus in the mid-1890s, a new weekly called *Electricity* marketed itself primarily as a means to keep abreast of fakes in a technical marketplace undergoing a dizzying pace of technological innovation. Aware that subscribers to trade journals had come to expect intelligence about business frauds, the promoters of *Electricity* directed their advertising dollars toward such periodicals, placing ads that highlighted the value of its fraud coverage. Although its advertisements also promised to convey news about developments in electrical research in a "non-technical and popular manner," the journal's greatest selling feature was its promise to redress information asymmetries for "those whose knowledge of electrical matters is limited," thereby protecting them from "all forms of humbuggery, quackery and fraud" (Figure 4.1).

For several postbellum publications, the fraud beat became an entrenched feature, an editorial department on which readers could depend. American honey producers who subscribed to *The American Bee Journal* or *Gleanings in Bee Culture* received not only ongoing coverage of recent developments in the "Patents" column, the proceedings of state beekeeper "Conventions," and novel ideas for "Marketing Honey," but also the latest news of "Adulteration in Honey" and "Swindles and Humbugs."[29] The latter ranged from tracking the movements and enterprises of noteworthy operators, in some cases for years, to detailing the most recent commercial hoaxes targeting beekeepers. In Orange Judd's *American Agriculturist*, the most influential weekly for the nation's vast farming population, subscribers from the 1850s on encountered regular exposés of "Sundry Frauds and Humbugs." Occupying almost a full newspaper page, this feature achieved a national reputation as a foe of fakery. As the *American Journal of Dental Science* put the consensus view in 1879, the *Agriculturalist's* "persistent caustic exposures of Humbugs and Swindles are of great value to all its readers."[30]

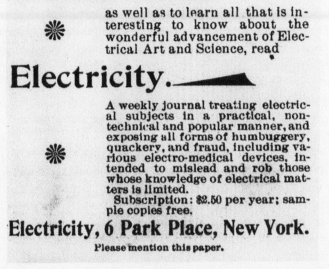

To Keep Yourself Posted on all
Electrical Frauds and Humbugs,

as well as to learn all that is interesting to know about the
wonderful advancement of Electrical Art and Science, read

Electricity.

A weekly journal treating electrical subjects in a practical, non-
technical and popular manner, and
exposing all forms of humbuggery,
quackery, and fraud, including various electro-medical devices, intended to mislead and rob those
whose knowledge of electrical matters is limited.
Subscription: $2.50 per year; sam-
ple copies free.

Electricity, 6 Park Place, New York.

Please mention this paper.

Figure 4.1: Advertisement in *Gleanings in Bee Culture* 23 (May 15, 1895): 419.

The regular sections about economic deceit in rural America had a strongly democratic flavor, as they depended on the active participation of readers. Subscribers sent in hundreds of letters describing encounters with fraud, expecting them to be printed as warnings to the broader farm population. J. E. Moore sent along a typical missive to the *American Bee Journal* in March 1878, cautioning readers about "The Crystal Honey Fraud" and its promoter, a Mr. Chidester of New York City, who was offering sales agencies a fake method to make candy out of honey.[31] Farmers also bombarded these publications with queries about unsolicited business propositions, unfamiliar marketing tactics, and novel products, seeking authoritative assessments of whether a company or advertised machine was aboveboard. Editors sometimes pursued their own research to furnish readers with answers, especially if the inquiry involved a firm that had advertised in their journals. On other occasions, they convened informational clearinghouses, publishing letters of inquiry in the expectation that far-flung readers would chime in with helpful responses. These journal-based communities were nineteenth-century versions of tightly moderated internet bulletin boards, in which editors selected both initial postings to the community and then the contributors to subsequent threads of sometimes contentious discussion resulting from crowd-sourced investigation.

Persistent efforts to warn Americans about the swindles in their midst re-flected an editorial assumption that fraud monitoring paid dividends by help-ing to convince readers that they received value for subscription dollars. As the *Genesee Farmer* noted during its 1855 coverage of prevailing frauds in the dis-tribution of guano fertilizers (made from seabird droppings harvested from Chilean and Peruvian island rookeries), "the agricultural press is never more usefully employed than in watching the interests of farmers and guarding them against the frauds of dishonest speculators. Let the farmers see that their *trusted friends* are sustained." When circumstances allowed, as they often did, editors crowed about their triumphs in clearing the marketplace of swindlers and shams.[32]

As the *Genesee Farmer* plea also suggests, however, the ethos of fraud pre-vention embraced a more communitarian sensibility. Among agricultural journals that made fraud coverage a specialty, the Departments of Humbug manifested a language of "friendship." A. I. Root, the longtime editor of *Glean-ings in Bee Culture*, tagged his section on "HUMBUGS AND SWINDLES Per-taining to Bee Culture" with a reminder that "we respectfully solicit the aid of our friends in conducting this department, and would consider it a favor to have them send us all circulars that have a deceptive appearance. The greatest care will be at all times maintained to prevent injustice being done to any one." Beekeepers who desired information about a company, salesman, product, or business opportunity accordingly addressed their queries not to "Editor," or even A. I. Root, but rather to "Friend Root." Root responded in kind, address-ing his published replies to "Friend P." or "Friend B." This practice personalized the answers that he furnished to F. A. Parsons of Oconoe, Washington, or to D. D. Brewer of Springfield, Arkansas, both of whom wrote Root in 1886 to in-quire about the supposedly patented "Golden Bee-Hive." (Root was happy to oblige, explaining that "the patent right man is trying to come the old trick over you.") Such a familiar mode of address simultaneously connected Parsons and Brewer to the hundreds of other farmers who read his *Gleanings*. Together, this band of beekeepers kept one another abreast of a continental market, lean-ing on the intercession of a trusted editorial intermediary to facilitate a collec-tive means of protection against the wiles of patent right agents and other dodgy operators.[33]

In the case of many trade journals, such as *Iron Age* and *The Railroad Ga-zette*, the inclination of editors to set themselves up as inveterate enemies of imposition and fraud went hand in hand with professionalization. Eager to secure the social and economic status of experts, the era's spokesmen for chem-ists, pharmacists, and engineers portrayed their lines of work as having an ethic of truthfulness resulting from rigorous technical education and the social obligation to expose falsehood and quackery. This responsibility included not only vetting the legitimacy of new ventures and spreading the word about dicey business practices such as deceptive accounting tricks, but also informing readers about migratory charlatans who posed as experts, or novel scams cooked up by employees to bilk their employers. Assiduous reporting on such matters put readers "on their guard against further swindling."[34]

Throughout the postbellum decades, the *Engineering and Mining Journal* furnished especially detailed articulations of the premises that undergirded expert surveillance of the marketplace. The journal's editors, Richard Rothwell and Rossiter Raymond, proclaimed independence from all conflicts of interest, all "entangling alliances" with mining speculations or stockbrokers. In issue after issue, they professed commitment to the values of professional expertise in the assessment of existing and proposed mines and mining corporations, and the obligations that all geologists and mining engineers had to the broader public, even when employed by mining promoters. They further pledged that their publication was the inveterate "enemy of all fraudulent mining ventures," and that it would "give such disinterested information as may put investors on their guard against the bogus or overvalued enterprises that are already seeking to beguile the confiding of their money." To those ends, Rothwell and Raymond emulated the community-building techniques of the agricultural papers, cultivating a far-flung network among subscribers, who were primarily mining professionals and investors. The editors solicited cautions about suspicious mining promotions and queries about the legitimacy of new and often isolated mining ventures, while also requesting readers to respond on the basis of their professional competence and local knowledge.[35]

All this surveillance, the editors insisted, had the ultimate goals of stabilizing the flow of capital into the American mining industry and so sustaining entrepreneurial opportunities in that sector. By exposing swindlers who sought to unload stocks in phony mines and companies that hawked bogus mining processes, the journal promised not simply "to render them harmless," and so to save investors from embarrassing losses; Rothwell and Raymond further hoped to buttress public confidence in the mining sector, since "every dishonest enterprise is a standing warning against the investment of capital" by Americans and Europeans alike. Systematic exposure of swindling mining promotions, then, promised to counteract the all-too-common equation of mining investments with "wildcats" and "a form of gambling in which the 'outsider' stood but little chance of winning."[36] Such regulatory impulses mirrored earlier justifications for the methods adopted in American credit reporting, where networks of watchful reporters sent in assessments about local firms and business owners. By identifying the scoundrels who sought credit, the Mercantile Agency's Lewis Tappan had hoped in the 1840s, his network of informants would "check knavery, and purify the mercantile air," making it easier for honest enterprises to attract the oxygen of credit.[37] For Tappan, like the trade journal editors, modern markets rested on public trust, which in turn rested on a base of social norms and regulatory structures (in this case, outside the bounds of the state).

For the trade journals, antifraud stances represented a targeted expression of commercial oversight that reached only a single economic sector. Several agricultural weeklies claimed a broader jurisdiction, recognizing that farm families confronted scams directed at them as producers, consumers, and investors; but these papers tended not to cover the kind of retailing and investing swindles that predominated in America's burgeoning cities. Metropolitan newspapers took on those frauds. Like Orange Judd's *American Agriculturist*, urban dailies such as the *Boston Herald*, *Philadelphia Public Ledger*, and *New York Times*, and national weeklies such as the *National Police Gazette*, covered all kinds of commercial deception. Small-scale depredations by local auctioneers and grocers received attention alongside swindles perpetrated through mail-order marketing and the fraudulent machinations of corporate insiders. In reflecting the larger purposes of such reporting, newspaper editors claimed the mantle of commercial guardians and popular educators, on behalf of not just one particular slice of the American population—farmers, or pharmacists, or mining investors—but of the nation's most important marketplaces, of their cities' populaces as a whole. The *Times* evinced great pride in its "warnings" and "cautions," characterizing itself in the mid-1870s as a champion of "the commercial honor of the community," with the "right to bring a great fraud to light in whatever way we can." The *National Police Gazette*'s editor similarly thumped his chest as a guardian of truthful commercial communication, proudly recalling in 1880 that since its inception several decades earlier, the publication had had a policy of attacking "all classes and kinds of frauds... , strip[ping them] of their veneering and expos[ing them] to the contempt which they merited."[38]

These endeavors shaped popular understandings of the role of the press as monitors of economic candor. By the 1870s, letters from alleged victims of fraud poured into urban newspaper offices. One such missive from "Policy Holder" arrived on the desk of the editor of the *New York Times* in May 1873, noting that a competing paper had just begun to report on "high-handed corporate mismanagement in life-insurance corporations." Observing that "the

Times has already rendered lasting benefit in fraud exposures," "Policy Holder" implored the paper to direct its investigative powers toward this question, especially as most "insurance journals" published only "purchased puffs and flattering notices." Governmental officials became so accustomed to the press alerting the public to prevailing scams that they sometimes sent their own "cards" to newspapers to issue a fraud warning. By this point, urban residents and officials had developed settled expectations that newspapers served as sentinels of trade and finance, sounding the alarm about all manner of fraud and imposition.[39]

Taking on the role of guardianship against commercial duplicity earned nineteenth-century writers and publications more than a little enmity. In the antebellum decades, reports of circulating counterfeits or fraudulent financial reports triggered vigorous complaints from bank officers, who denied the existence of the former and the veracity of the latter.[40] When a newspaper exposed sharp practices or outright swindles involving the management of publicly traded corporations, the incident might elicit whispering campaigns that its editor had been bought off by a syndicate looking to execute a bear raid on the company's stock.[41] In some instances, aggrieved corporations either threatened or instigated libel suits against trade journals that had raised serious questions about the truthfulness of financial reporting.[42]

The lurking possibility of libel actions led most editors to take care before publishing correspondence that alleged some kind of fraud. Orange Judd's *American Agriculturist* stressed in 1872 that it ignored all anonymous accusations, refused to publicize charges against "names and business enterprises" without "sufficient evidence," and, in the case of any "error" caused by the "deception" of a malicious correspondent who wished to "vent his spleen," would "make [a] prompt correction or retraction."[43] But the occasional controversy and lawsuit did not forestall the emergence of a vigorous public conversation about the swindles and beguilement swirling about American marts of trade. Indeed, Judd boasted that despite frequent attempts at intimidation through libel suits, his weekly had exposed over fifteen hundred swindles in its first thirty-one years, or nearly one every week. In one sense, attacks on fraud exposés deepened nineteenth-century antifraud discourse, because they encouraged some editors around the turn of the next century to open their journals to critics who wished to challenge a given accusation. By giving "both sides of a question a fair hearing," the press would furnish Americans with the most compelling arguments about how to distinguish legitimate businesses and business practices from unwarranted puffery or contemptible chicanery.[44]

The Paradoxes of Gatekeeping

Orange Judd and his fellow nineteenth-century editors and economic writers took on roles as guardians of American commercial speech. Through specific warnings and more general instruction, these self-appointed gatekeepers extended the number of metaphorical placards paraded before the domiciles and advertisements of dodgy enterprises, imploring strangers to BEWARE of some particular PETER FUNK, or simply of general PETER FUNKISM. Their collective efforts had tangible impacts. When publications built up a strong community of readers committed to a shared project of market surveillance, they hemmed in duplicitous marketers. By calling out operators and shining a light on emerging schemes and scams, they deprived swindlers of the oxygen of trust and plausibility, and so speeded up the process by which a given swindle burned out. Through the media of newspapers, magazines, and coordinated correspondence, these informal communities greatly expanded the geographic reach of watchfulness. They multiplied the pairs of eyes—the Eshelbys and Rooneys—that might not only spot commercial or financial knavery, but also bring it to the attention of a larger, and in some cases continental, neighborhood. Such actions enabled Americans to recalibrate their judgments about the individuals and firms with whom they might do business, improving reputational checks on duplicity.

And yet, the dissemination of so much commentary also furnished new opportunities for fraud. The capacity to use publicity and mechanisms of informal public education to contain the threats posed by economic deception depended on the good faith of journalistic gatekeepers. But could one truly trust the Orange Judds and Rossiter Raymonds of the age's commercial public sphere? As soon as figures developed reputations as trustworthy brokers, the American marketplace faced new dangers of corruption and novel possibilities for corrosive mimicry. The same set of threats emerged with other institutional strategies to combat economic misrepresentation, such as the development of internal accounting and efforts to screen employees for fidelity. Every new form of institutional monitoring to combat business fraud could itself become a vehicle for imposture.[45] Indeed, the informal culture of surveillance and public exposure served as a feedback loop to those contemplating economic deception, a low-cost channel of intelligence about prevailing schemes and public awareness of them. All the writing about swindles and measures to prevent fraud thus furnished not only a basic curriculum in deceptive tactics, but also signals to swindlers about when to change modes of operation, as well as blueprints for how to exploit the trust created by new methods of inhibiting duplicity.

Direct evidence for this kind of dialectic is sparse. But descriptions of scams in the press, like more comprehensive book-length overviews of deceit on Wall Street or in the retailing trades, were just as available to the rogue and the hard-pressed entrepreneur as they were to the excessively credulous investor, farmer, or store owner. As a result, coverage of swindles and more comprehensive inventories of deceptive strategies might furnish anyone contemplating the adoption of these practices with a quick course of instruction as to how they might proceed. A midcentury explanation in *Hunt's Merchants' Magazine* about the most common techniques by which grocers doctored their commodities could turn consumers into more savvy judges of vinegar and sugar, or tutor retailers in the finer points of padding profit margins. When agricultural papers published the detailed recipe used by a shady fertilizer company to adulterate guano in 1855, one can certainly wonder whether its impact was limited to placing farmers more effectively on their guard, or whether it also helped to launch new schemes to "palm off on the credulous farmers of our broad domain a comparatively worthless article, at a high price, and under a *false name*."[46]

Cognizant of the often-contradictory impulses toward credulity and suspicion bred by an economy prone to boom psychology and characterized by widespread deception, some nineteenth-century scam artists embraced the trust-manufacturing strategy of deflection. These dodgy proprietors directed public attention to competing frauds as the route to push their own. In the late 1880s, the Pulvermacher Company of New York pursued an elaborate version of this strategy, distributing free copies of *Health and Strength Regained*, a "complete Encyclopedia of information for suffering humanity." This compendium promised to "expose . . . the frauds practiced by quacks and medical imposters," including "sham curative articles," and to furnish simple tests for detecting increasingly fashionable but "spurious . . . electric belts," all the while pointing readers to how they might achieve "permanent health." That key to such an outcome for the afflicted lay in their finding out "how to treat their own cases at home by electricity," using "the *Pioneer* and *only reliable Electric Belt*," which Pulvermacher would be pleased to send along at half-price. Here was just the sort of elaborate scheme that the purveyors of *Electricity* would soon promise to uncover.[47]

The use of exposés as a means of pitching a swindle was especially common within the burgeoning field of patent medicines and health nostrums. But in many other sectors of the economy, a still more complicated dance ensued between people who sought to make economic deception more difficult, and so restore the foundations of impersonal commercial trust, and those who kept a keen eye on novel opportunities for transforming such trust into dangerous credulity. In sectors such as antebellum currency distribution, postbellum mining promotion, and late nineteenth-century financial services, complex systems for detecting and preventing fraud produced ever more elaborate masquerades.

The codependent evolution of counterfeiting techniques and anticounterfeiting schemes began as soon as Americans embraced chartered banks and paper currency in the early nineteenth century. A proliferation of banks generated a blizzard of befuddling banknotes of various denominations, sizes, colors, and degrees of reliability. When the presence of so much "rag" paper led to near-obsessive coverage of known fraudulent bills in newspapers, banking journals, and, by the 1830s, counterfeit detectors, counterfeiting rings rapidly adapted to the new environment, finding ways to manipulate the confidence bred by authoritative catalogues of bad notes. The manufacturers and distributors of bogus currency learned to time their distribution of notes so that they came just after the publication of a local or regional catalogue. Some put out a small batch of a counterfeit with an obvious defect in order to stimulate warnings about a given issue, and then, once those cautions had become widespread, flooded the market with an altered version of the fakes. Bribing the editors of counterfeit detectors to look the other way seems to have occurred with some frequency, at least in light of allegations made by competing publications. Most brazenly, some counterfeiters published their own bogus counterfeit detectors, which both masked particular counterfeits and, in combination with all of the controversies over the honesty of more established organs, sowed public skepticism about the utility of all available detectors.[48]

Dodgy financing of postbellum mining corporations, particularly in the Rocky Mountains and the Far West, gave rise to a similar process of heightened fraud surveillance followed by adjusted modes of swindling. As Western mining took off in the aftermath of the Civil War, the sector gained notoriety for misrepresentations and outright swindles. The most duplicitous practices included the promotion of phony mining stocks and insider schemes to manipulate the stock prices of genuine mining companies, which often involved the spreading of false information about their output. But the truly sophisticated approaches emerged only over several decades.

During the 1860s, promoters of fraudulent Western mining companies followed a relatively simple recipe. They issued prospectuses that envisioned fabulously rich veins of ore, enticed prominent figures to become company directors through the granting of stock allocations, and exhibited fake sample ores at mining bureaus in San Francisco or large Eastern cities.[49] These tactics soon attracted criticism from both technical and nontechnical publications. (*The American Mining Index* produced a telling spoof of fraudulent promotions in a satire on the "Hunkidora Silver Mining Company," which was headed by Treasurer Gideon Graball and President Jeremiah Blowhard, whose directors included Major General D. Bility and Adjutant General P. Q. Lation, and which obtained legal advice from the firm of Sneak, Quibble, and Steele.) A stream of news stories about the machinations of mining companies, in combination with widespread losses by outside investors, bred deep-seated skepticism. Americans began to joke that a mine was "a hole in the ground owned by a liar" or "a hole in the ground sold by a lying promoter to a stupid investor." Such perceptions, in part the result of journalistic exposés, slashed the supply of capital for all mining ventures.[50]

Over the course of the 1870s and 1880s, genuine mining promoters adopted several strategies to buttress public confidence. In addition to touting the assessments of independent geologists and mining engineers, they delayed public offerings until ventures began significant mining operations, placed a premium on early payment of dividends to demonstrate earning capacity, and circulated financial reports. In turn, shadier mine promoters crafted novel forms of deceit. Alerted by the mining press to these attempts to display trustworthiness, the swindling community crafted more sophisticated schemes of theatrical emulation. They distributed glowing analyses from sham experts, or "salted" mines with ore samples in order to fool legitimate mining engineers about a location's prospects. They initiated at least some actual mining operations in an unexplored spot, or revived production at an abandoned mine on the basis of a supposedly newfangled mining process, and then paid early dividends out of capital. They further made it worth the while of local newspapers, and in some cases, national mining journals, to print positive commentaries on their speculations, marking their undertakings as aboveboard and stoking expectations of gain. Finally, in the aftermath of endemic bankruptcies among Western mining companies, promoters bought up the resulting wreckage on the cheap.[51]

The *Engineering and Mining Journal* tracked all of these developments, which led the publication to refine its rules of thumb for mining investors. In the late 1870s, amid a renewed interest in mining stocks that sustained the refloating of Eastern mining stock exchanges, the journal consistently reminded its subscribers that "rock or specimen assays . . . are worthless," and fancy promises in prospectuses, glowing newspaper columns, and the endorsements of prominent directors little better; that no mine should receive serious attention unless a reputable legal authority vouched for its holding uncontested legal title to its claims; that investors should consider only producing mines with incontrovertible profits; and, most importantly, that no investment should proceed in the absence of "consultation with professional mining engineers." This latter recommendation required further elaboration, as the turn to such precautions had encouraged the proliferation of "quacks and impostors" posing as reputable engineers. As a result, capitalists had to screen their mining advisors carefully—and of course, the best way to do so was to scrutinize the *Engineering and Mining Journal*.[52]

Within the wider financial services industry, the emergence of more complex schemes of misrepresentation also took place over several decades. Initial gambits involved paying newspaper and magazine editors to run stories that placed promotions in a favorable light. Every so often, a big-city newspaper would delight in demonstrating the compromised ethics of a rival, touting the latter's corruption in its coverage of an investment scheme. Thus in 1857, the *New York Times* sought to prick the *New York Herald*'s pretensions as an authority on public virtue, running several stories on its rival's longstanding attempts to goose investment in the fraudulent Parker Vein Coal Company of Maryland, which had failed spectacularly three years before.[53] As early as the 1860s, some editors had advocated that publications forswear the corrupt placement of promoters' financial news stories or related editorial squibs, a stance that attracted growing support among national publications desirous of social respectability. In the case of the *New York Sunday Mercury*, the uncovering of journalistic corruption and corporate deceit underpinned the paper's efforts to build a loyal readership. Unlike its "moribund" competitors, who hawked access for "one dollar a line" and sold "editorials, at five dollars a column," the editor of the *Mercury* proclaimed that his paper maintained an unswerving independence. Rather than emulating the many "servile tools" of corporate interests, the *Mercury* pledged a "war upon wickedness and fraud in high places," alongside a "repudiation of bribery in any form, whether as an advertisement or a purchased puff."[54]

By the late 1880s and 1890s, the depth of misrepresentation in the financial markets had helped to spawn several business models predicated on closing the informational gulf that separated insiders from the investing public. These new firms ranged from financial newspapers such as the *Wall Street Daily News* (founded 1879) and the *Wall Street Journal* (founded 1889) to investment analysts and bond raters such as Standard & Poor's and Moody's. The financial press cast beady eyes on the legitimacy of new stock issues and the propriety of managerial decision-making at leading corporations. These publications sought, as one reader of the *Wall Street Daily News* noted in its first year of operation, to give investors "some idea of the movements in the market, and other information that will guard the public against imposition."[55] The emergence of such intermediaries inspired deceptive embellishments, turning the perpetrators of stock frauds toward schemes of deflection. During the early twentieth century, promoters of bogus stocks distributed newsletters, tip sheets, and weeklies that purported to warn readers about scams afoot in the securities markets, all to cover their own misrepresentations.[56]

In casting aspersions on the press's role in hyping products and investments, the era's critics did not allege that editors and journalists were rotten to the core. The occasional acceptance of compensation in exchange for the publication of planted news stories or editorial endorsements did not mean a complete absence of journalistic integrity. Nor did many newspaper editors possess the capacity to check the veracity of the accounts and stories that crossed their desks. As the *Engineering and Mining Journal* observed in May 1877 with respect to the evaluation of mining corporations, few publications had sufficient "facilities for separating the wheat from the tares," for "pass[ing] correct judgment on the thousands of opinions expressed on the subject of mining."[57] Yet whether public misrepresentations emanated from corrupt self-interest or a mixture of credulousness, optimism, and ignorance, they greatly complicated economic decision-making. The profusion of published puffery and countervailing exposés could be dizzying, leaving Americans unsure of what to believe or whom to trust.

Nineteenth-century frauds gave rise to private monitoring of business communications, which in turn begat new forms of deception, new corruptions of trust, and, eventually, new surveillance mechanisms and certifications of trustworthiness. With the emergence of every new community guardian came yet another set of possible theatrical roles and backdrops, yet more concerns about potential impostures. This cycle, so indicative of the "ingenuity" that went into the "preparation and execution of frauds," did not emerge so early nor with such sophistication in every economic sector.[58] To some extent, this cycle had a self-limiting quality. Ever more elaborate swindles depended on ever greater investments; one could not produce compelling counterfeit banknotes, fake mining ventures, or several months' worth of a financial newspaper without access to meaningful startup capital. Once the requirements of effective misrepresentation became more daunting, swindlers faced barriers to entry. Nonetheless, the pattern occurred with enough frequency to sustain healthy demand for intelligence about economic deceit throughout the century, and beyond.

Fraud Sentinels and the Case for *Caveat Emptor*

Nineteenth-century editors and writers who sought to combat economic chicanery faced an additional dilemma: the continued credulity of consumers, business owners, and investors. Despite the upsurge in public scrutiny of commercial deception, the American marketplace remained full of swindling. Many leading antifraud beacons marveled at the resilience of duplicity around them. "Notwithstanding the hundreds of warnings of the Press," one writer pointed out in 1872, swindlers seemed to have little trouble maintaining a steady business. Even if broadly disseminated alarms broke "up a few firms for the time being," accomplished con artists moved on to territory that had not yet encountered sustained press coverage of their brand of artifice. Alternatively, they cooked up some new scheme, often a variation on some venerable scam, launched it under new names, and continued on their merry way. Despite all the cautions, another commentator fretted a few years later, Americans demonstrated an "amazing gullibility . . . to enter into mechanical and financial schemes of enormous promise and certain failure."[59]

Contemporaneous explanations for the American public's enduring susceptibility to fraudulent pitchmen turned in part to psychological themes. Postbellum commentators homed in on the depth of ambition for wealth in the United States. Some writers argued that, aware of the enormous fortunes created by periodic booms, and attracted to schemes that offered democratic access to riches, Americans' "greed for sudden gain blinded them to the possibility of disappointment, and prompt[ed] them to the most reckless waste of their hard won savings."[60] Here lay a large obstacle before the self-appointed commercial mandarins who sought to watch over the marketplace and alert their readers whenever some roguish plot was afoot. The vision implicit in most antifraud discourse was of dispassionate assessment of risk and reward, of careful evaluation of available information and competing arguments, of sensible reliance on disinterested experts, of individuals who would learn from mistakes and cultivate healthy suspicion of promises that seemed too good to be true. This approach presumed a reflective public sphere, driven by rational assessment and sober calculation.[61]

But even before the advent of psychology-driven sales campaigns in the early twentieth century, American marketing was suffused with emotional appeals—most-obviously to fantasies of easily attained luxury and promises of regained health, but also, in some cases, to the desire to recoup past losses through a new roll of the dice. As early as the 1860s, promoters of fraudulent insurance had learned the effectiveness of the roll-up: that they could lure many holders of stocks or policies in insolvent corporations to buy into new enterprises that had purchased the assets of the failed concerns.[62] Through trial and error, veterans of marketing swindles and more legitimate business enterprises learned how to appeal to the cognitive vulnerabilities catalogued in recent decades by behavioral economists. The pervasiveness of what often seemed like transparently foolish economic behavior raised a central problem for postbellum fraud sentinels—what to do if their warnings were not enough to stem the tide of deceit, especially beyond the ranks of those vigilant correspondents who made up some editors' far-flung, informal antifraud police force.

For the most part, America's social elites and middle-class opinion-makers responded to the stubborn reality of endemic duplicity by rededicating themselves to the values of economic self-reliance. Many incidents of deception recalled by memoirists or covered in the press had entertainment value because of the admiration that so many Americans had for a well-executed scam, or because of the humor and *schadenfreude* elicited by a sucker's misfortune. If the promoters of a fake California diamond mine managed to fool several legitimate geologists and mining professionals by salting the area with diamonds, who then convinced prominent capitalists to jump in with both feet, many journalists felt bound to give the swindlers their due—their duplicity being "a well-laid, skillfully executed, ingeniously arranged and managed affair." In discussing the problem of falsely packed cotton, a postbellum Georgia newspaper might, rather than scold its readers or sermonize about the threat to Southern commercial reputation, advise that "farmers who wish to cheat buyers" rely on rocks and iron rather than "wet cotton," because the former was less easily detected, and the latter had less pernicious impact on the remainder of the bale. When insiders revealed the nature of financial-market manipulation, they might describe themselves as a "vigilance committee of bubble prickers." But their accounts exuded appreciation for the audacity and artfulness exhibited by veteran speculators and pool operators, who often came from modest circumstances, resolutely maintained the secrecy of their maneuvers, and found clever ways to bend public sentiment to their purposes.[63] Within limits, the minders of economic probity could pay their respects to a good dodge and a successful dodger. The dodgers demonstrated not just coolness, calculation, and self-control, but also a passion for self-advancement, a canny ability to negotiate the social demands of an industrializing culture, and an adaptability to momentary reversals of fortune.[64]

With even greater regularity, nineteenth-century writers evinced little or no sympathy for the victims of fraud. The staple jokes about the dismal prospects of outsiders who dabbled in mining investments carried such connotations; so too did the expressions of near-disbelief about the naïveté that Americans displayed in so many other contexts. *Scientific American* marveled at credulous inventors who ought to be "shingled for stupidity" for making no effort to assess the reputations of swindling patent agents who had solicited their business. Orange Judd, who so assiduously compiled reports of fraudulent doings in the *American Agriculturist*, expressed occasional astonishment at the folly of rural consumers, whose chasing after impossibly cheap deals merited contempt rather than pity. Postbellum observers of the financial markets wondered at the ability of "the outside public [to] forget how they have been bamboozled by these bogus companies," suggested that "the public loves to be humbugged," and argued that "it is not advisable to keep a fool and his money together." Meanwhile, reports on health-related swindles chronicled how "our susceptible young men" so were easily "duped by the specious advertisements in country newspapers into the belief that for some fancied secret ailment they will find a remedy."[65]

As far as most Gilded Age commentators were concerned, if creditors or investors or consumers plunged into some transaction without the most basic effort to investigate its legitimacy, they had little justification for pointing fingers anywhere but at their own breasts. The prevalence of fly-by-night storekeepers in the Northeast, who persuaded wholesalers to deliver large orders on credit and then skipped town, prompted one editorial reflection that captured the sentiment nicely: in this sort of situation, "all we can say is that [the credulous merchants] deserve to suffer for it." Similar premises guided the most common prescriptions for how American society should cope with "rampant quackery"—more suspicion, greater prudence, more investigation, and closer attention to the burgeoning sources of economic surveillance such as credit reporters, reputable stockbrokers, and the fraud-fighting press.[66] Here, the sensibilities of American commentators echoed the inclinations of the nineteenth-century British establishment. However much London opinion-makers railed against duplicitous managers in the aftermath of some colossal corporate bankruptcy, they heaped equal scorn on the middle-class and elite stockholders whose inattention and fanciful projections had "brought their losses upon themselves."[67]

Edward Youmans, the editor of *Popular Science Monthly*, encapsulated this Anglo-American view in an 1874 commentary on the "celebrated Tichburne case" in England. This legal controversy involved a fraudulent claim to an inheritance, which, despite abundant evidence of imposture, led to seven years' worth of court cases and popular controversy. Youmans used this instance of widespread public folly to reflect on the reach of "deception and fraud" in his own nation. He produced a litany of "false pretenses" much like the one proffered by Barnum twenty years earlier, taking note of every type of retailer and artisan—"the falsified foods of the grocer" and "the swindling textures of the dry-goods man," the flimflam of "unscrupulous shoemakers" and "dishonest hatters," the "builders of fraudulent houses" and "sham furniture," the gas man who "sell[s] us one thing and furnishes another." Even more directly than Barnum, Youmans observed that "overreaching, and circumventing, and the attainment of ends by false pretenses" had taken on the character of accepted, even admirable conduct, "organized in our blood." Such " 'smartness' and 'sharpness' have acquired new meanings and are openly commended, and nothing is more common than the remark that a little humbug is indispensable in all successful management."[68]

Appreciation for clever imposition and impatience with those who should have known better fed into debates about the nature of economic deception, and about who should have authority to distinguish sharp practices from unacceptable and illegal deceit. Nowhere can one see this influence more clearly than with regard to the question of how Americans should apply social norms about duplicity to novel forms of business enterprise, such as the urban spectacles championed by P. T. Barnum or the modes of stock, bond, and commodities investments emerging on New York's and Chicago's financial exchanges. As we have seen, Barnum and the emerging financial elite both took the trouble to highlight prevailing swindles and impositions as a means of differentiating such reprehensible practices from their own endeavors, which, because of their supposed benefits to society, deserved respectable status. But to unabashed critics of Barnumesque entertainment or Wall Street financiering, such attempts at legitimation differed little from the techniques of deflection embraced by the era's especially savvy swindlers.

For Christian moralists who classed Barnum as the false prophet of Mammon and stock operations as inveterate gambling, *Humbugs of the World* had the same character as the "CAUTION!" that the sophisticated marketer of bogus patent medicines issued about his equally spurious competition. Each reflected commercial sleight of hand, a conjurer's trick of distraction that built trust on a false foundation of apparent concern for the commercial commonweal. Some reviewers of Barnum's 1865 volume made such arguments explicit. According to the *Boston Advertiser*, the showman was a "Mephistopheles" who "glories in the tricks and deceits by which he has grown wealthy," one of the "wolves" who "must don sheep's clothing before they can enter the fold at all." A reviewer for one literary journal used more urban metaphors, likening Barnum to a "thief" who, "when pursued by a crowd will sometimes shout 'Stop Thief!' and, thus deceiving his pursuers, escape."[69]

Such disputes demonstrated the historically contingent nature of what constituted fraud and who qualified as an authoritative interpreter of commercial culture, especially in domains of economic life characterized by a great deal of entrepreneurial innovation. Was the self-promoting puffer for novel goods, services, and/or business practices a public benefactor or a devilish shape-changer? When did a permissible "white lie" or mere humbug shade over into a confidence-sapping imposition? Nineteenth-century Americans frequently disagreed about where to draw the cultural, linguistic, and legal answers to such questions, and even which public voices possessed the integrity to consider them. As a result, the burgeoning market for public commentary about economic deceit reflected more than just attempts to supply intelligence about the details of acts that essentially everyone agreed to be swindles, and the business operations of individuals universally viewed as swindlers. This part of the American public sphere was additionally characterized by ongoing arguments about how to define swindling itself, and who had the standing to join in that discussion.

In Barnum's case, adroit management of public relations—which extended to writing his autobiographies and *Humbugs of the World*—allowed him to neutralize the most vehement charges of deceit. Who better to expose the deceivers, he stressed, than one so well versed in good-natured deception, and whose bankruptcy resulted from his own inability to spot a swindle? Who better to school the public in the talents of keeping eyes peeled and ears pricked? A key element of the era's public discourse on fraud, moreover, was humor, often directed at the folly of those Americans who found themselves bested by misrepresentation. Barnum knew how to deflate his cultural, and legal, antagonists through a good joke.

During the immediate fallout of his insolvency, after facing day after day of public questioning from the lawyer of an especially piqued creditor who suspected Barnum of deceitfully secreting assets from his creditors, the showman received a query about his current business. "My occupation at present," he replied, was "tending bar." This surprising bit of information, after a shocked pause, prompted the further inquiry, "How long have you been occupied in this business?" to which Barnum deadpanned, "Ever since the lawyers have been pulling me up to the bars of the different courts." This exchange received coverage in newspapers from New England to Missouri, indicating the extent to which newspaper editors, and presumably many of their readers, appreciated the one-liner. Barnum's clever moment of comedy helped to shift public scrutiny away from his successful efforts to transfer a chunk of his assets into his wife's name.[70] Such deftness allowed him to solidify his standing within American society. Along with the increasing receptiveness of his fellow citizens to an urban culture predicated on consumption of goods, services, and the "experience" of commodified entertainment, it allowed Barnum to squeeze his ventures into the social mainstream and sustain his position as a cultural arbiter of swindling. That triumph, in turn, narrowed the grounds on which consumers of entertainment might allege a cheat.

In some contexts, though, exposés of fraud suggested a greater degree of empathy for individuals who found themselves duped. Here, one sees a clear parallel to the bifurcated dispositions of judges and juries in fraud cases. Rural Americans who fell for midcentury scams sometimes received expressions of "sympathy rather than censure" because of their "uncultured intellect," and because "farmers as a class are more easily deceived than others, because being less crafty themselves, they are not suspicious or on the look out for fraud"; so too did women who were taken in by one "Dr. Skinem" or another, because, as one writer argued, the sex was "proverbially credulous." Analysts of the financial markets also voiced enduring concerns about corporate secrecy, which facilitated market manipulations by insiders privy to information about an enterprise's performance and prospects. This tendency was especially pronounced if the losers, by some questionable financial failure, turned out to be members of the urban working class, as in the case of savings banks. In all these areas, at least some members of the nation's informal economic vigilance committee counseled the wisdom of heightened governmental regulation, either out of paternalistic concern for supposedly less-savvy groups or because entrenched asymmetries of financial information presented more sophisticated investors with loaded dice.[71] Indeed, by the 1870s, heightened concern about insufficient access to financial information led British newspapers and politicians to advocate sterner criminal penalties for corporate fraud, as well as greater investment in public enforcement of criminal fraud statutes.[72]

When such calls for stiffer governmental oversight of truthfulness in commerce or finance had the strong backing of some cohesive and influential economic interest, or of newly organized professional societies eager to flex their social and political clout, they could result in extensions of governmental responsibility. As we will see shortly, concerns over structural barriers to the detection of fraud drove the successful postbellum movements for state regulation of grain storage in Illinois, the accounting practices of mining corporations in California, and the quality of agricultural fertilizers in states throughout the country, as well the federal prohibition of fraudulent schemes dependent on the United States mails. But arguments for reliance on the state to combat commercial and financial deception commonly faced significant opposition from the country's self-appointed band of informal fraud police, out of concern that governmental efforts to certify economic activities as legitimate would only create powerful new openings for swindling. The fear, especially with regard to areas such as banking and insurance, which already faced regulatory regimes by the 1870s, was that monitoring by the state resulted in decreased public vigilance, and that swindlers would point to regulatory oversight as a guarantee of corporate solvency.[73] Distrust of reliance on the state to combat fraud was further amplified by recognition that swindlers so frequently avoided prevailing legal sanctions.

Antagonism to regulatory mechanisms of fraud reflected both worldview and self-interest. Connected to elite economic and social networks and to the politics of Liberal Republicanism, many editors and writers put even more effort into exposing governmental corruption than they did into tracing the duplicitous schemes of shady businesses.[74] These reporters of the economic scene tended to harbor skepticism about the ability of government officials to stick to appointed tasks or carry them out well, a tendency that spilled over into the postbellum assault on compulsory government inspection of commodities. Lack of confidence in the institutions of government was often accompanied by awareness that the press benefited from its status as a central source of guidance for Americans who wanted to arm themselves against the artifices of grocers, quacks, and stock peddlers. For many informal guardians of the economy's public sphere, any decision to champion the creation of government regulatory institutions carried a risk—that those private guardians might no longer play such a central role in protecting Americans from the unpleasant experience of becoming some sharper's mark.

These concerns appear to have governed how editor Edward Youmans answered the question of how Americans should cope with "all this multifarious imposture" around them. A devotee of the British conservative Herbert Spencer, Youmans had no faith in governmental efforts to handle the problem of ever-present "calculating knaves." To this social Darwinist, democratic modes of governance were also characterized by the "rankest fraud," in the guise of "demagogism" and electoral machinations. Any reliance on the regulatory power of the state was accordingly doomed to failure. Instead, the only solution to the problem of commercial deceit lay in the realm of public education. "There is but one thing," he asserted, "that can protect people against the thousand-fold insidious and plausible impostures to which they are continually and everywhere exposed, and that is a resolute mood of skepticism, and an intelligent habit of sifting evidence that shall become a daily and constant practice." For this popularizer of scientific method and discovery, the only way to inoculate ordinary people from the rampant fraud around them was to educate them properly in the careful routines of "observation, inference, [and] judgment"—a task to which his humble journal had, of course, devoted itself.

✳✳✳✳

Any analysis of responses to economic deceit in the nineteenth-century United States runs the risk of overstating the incidence and salience of business fraud. The willingness of millions of Americans to trust one another through a burgeoning web of impersonal networks and far-flung business organizations did not always, or even usually, result in some barefaced swindle. Innumerable economic decisions were guided by deserved reputations or repeat transactions that built up reserves of confidence. The success of almost all frauds in America's industrializing economy depended not only on the optimism floated by long-term economic growth, but also on perpetrators' ability to emulate legitimate, successful, and trustworthy enterprises, to strike persuasive commercial poses. As a London mining magazine observed in 1872, fraudulent corporations were "cuckoos of the share market," interlopers whose success depended on the existence of "sound compan[ies]" to imitate.[75] The same basic dynamic occurred with most frauds. If at any juncture deceit became too commonplace, its effectiveness would almost necessarily diminish amid ever more wary economic decision-makers.[76]

One must similarly remain alert to the capacity of many savvy consumers to navigate a marketing environment suffused with misdirection and surface falsehoods. Many of the Americans who responded to wildly inaccurate patent medicine marketing no doubt had some idea of what they were getting—chiefly alcohol or some mix of alcohol and opiates. By the same token, a significant proportion of the consumers who purchased knockoff jewelry or fabrics probably understood that they were receiving a discount for imitations, often produced from cheaper materials on the basis of less-skilled workmanship.[77] In some corners of the American economy, such as the trading and sale of horses, the premises of *caveat emptor* had particularly deep cultural roots. Generations of men accepted, even reveled in the gamesmanship associated with horse-trading, so long as its participants were all adult men in possession of their faculties. They viewed the half-truths, evasions, and trickery that characterized the equine marketplace as a venue for displaying manly cleverness and acumen; occasionally getting taken in was part of the game.[78]

By the same token, the question of whether business transactions represented acts of fraud could prove to be highly ambiguous and contentious. Consider a rural consumer in the late 1860s who responded to a mail-order firm's fanciful circular by placing an order for some trinkets, perhaps linked to a gift lottery, which presented the alluring possibility of winning a gold watch. Such a customer would have paid vastly more than he might have in a city shop. But if he nonetheless was satisfied with the baubles that he purchased for his wife and enjoyed the chance to dream of a fashionable, expensive timepiece, was he a victim of fraud? Many of his contemporaries would have answered no.[79]

In the decades after the American Civil War, however, public observers of chicanery noted with ever more emphasis that the population of commercial cuckoos seemed to be on the upswing. So, too, did the numbers of credulous Americans tricked into feeding them. The multiplication of schemes and scams led a growing number of elites to view the culture of fakery and false pretense as threatening public faith in a host of newly integrated, complicated national markets. Throughout the nineteenth century and into the twentieth, swindles continued to bedevil employers, investors, and lenders, insurers and policy-holders, readers of consumer advertisements, and purchasers of drugs and foodstuffs. But the formal courts and informal modes of settlement only imperfectly tethered those Americans who were tempted to pursue businesses predicated on deceit. Responding to this state of affairs, a self-anointed "vigilance committee of bubble prickers" had provided a substantial, if flawed, means of regulating the truthfulness of economic communication. Those bubble prickers had also showered as much contempt on the duped as on those who did the duping.

Amid waxing faith in the regulatory powers of government during the Progressive era, the techniques of public exposure would strike growing numbers of Americans, including many muckraking journalists and social commentators, as inadequate to the task at hand. Many of those thinkers embraced an aspect of Edward Youmans's thinking—that effective antifraud initiatives would have to rely on scientific expertise—sometimes seeking to embed that expertise in the state, sometimes preferring to depend on nongovernmental organizations. But even as late nineteenth- and early twentieth-century reformers fashioned new institutional answers for the dilemmas posed by misrepresentation in the marketplace, older premises about individualist self-reliance would continue to influence debates over how best to define and cope with fraud.

PART III

Professionalization, Moralism, and the Elite Assault on Deception (1860s to 1930s)

CHAPTER FIVE

The Beginnings of a Modern Administrative State

In Barnum's America, the sanctions associated with antifraud statutes and common-law proscriptions constrained dishonest business practices only lightly. But from the Civil War through the 1920s, waxing concerns about deceptions and frauds prompted bureaucratic innovation. Much of this experimentation occurred inside the divided American state, on both the state and national levels, but a good deal of it also took place within several new quasi-public or nongovernmental organizations that possessed close affiliations to the business establishment. The next four chapters trace the emergence of new antifraud regulations that further confined the impulses of *caveat emptor*, as well as the construction of new institutions dedicated to combating economic duplicity.

Chapter Five begins this exploration with a survey of government antifraud efforts. In some contexts, including the oversight of Civil War military contracting or postbellum grain marketing, battles against fraud drew on long-standing strategies of public inspection. But in other domains, such as fertilizer regulation, supervision of corporate accounting and securities marketing, the Post Office's efforts to stem the tide of mail fraud, and the broad arena of advertising regulation, policymakers fashioned transformations in administrative governance. Before the early twentieth century, these endeavors remained patchy, leaving large swaths of commercial speech regulated chiefly by informal public discourse. A few regulatory initiatives also ran into the judicial buzz saw of Gilded Age constitutionalism. Nonetheless, these antifraud policies helped to lay the groundwork for the modern American regulatory state, predicated on technocratic expertise rather than artisanal rules of thumb.

Ambitious would-be regulators tended to loom large as architects of the new antifraud institutions. They not only conceptualized potential institutional strategies, but also cobbled together political constituencies to bring their plans to fruition. In at least some cases, such as the creation of mail fraud as a new legal category, regulatory entrepreneurs were motivated as much by a desire to vindicate the reputation of their organizations or emerging professions as they were by any broader economic or moral objectives. In others, such as fertilizer regulation, reforms depended on scientific advances that made regulatory schemes feasible.

Antifraud initiatives in the late nineteenth and early twentieth centuries sought to address problems created by wrenching processes of industrialization. An integrated national economy generated a higher percentage of commercial and financial transactions taking place at a distance, often between strangers. With an ever more dense web of railroad tracks, telegraph lines, and eventually radio stations; with the related expansion of manufacturers and mercantile firms operating on a regional or continental basis; with the deepening of a national capital market and the emergence of mass advertising; with all of these forces remaking American livelihoods, parties to economic transactions more frequently confronted wide differences in access to economic information. Eastern investors who invested in a Western mining company after reading a prospectus, like rural consumers persuaded by a catalogue to place an order from a far-off distributor, had limited capacity to investigate the claims that convinced them to part with their money. Recognition of pervasive informational asymmetries encouraged adjustments in how the American state tried to resolve the tension between honoring entrepreneurial freedom and discouraging marketing practices that played fast and loose with the truth.

Such adjustments, however, did not resolve the dilemma of how to distinguish unacceptable deception from the pardonable exaggerations and enthusiastic dissembling that so often characterized efforts by new firms to establish a commercial foothold. This enduring quandary has been especially prevalent in sectors at the forefront of economic change, where technological uncertainties abound, and norms about legitimate modes of competition have yet to be settled. Chapter Six examines this phenomenon and its implications for the enforcement of prohibitions against mail fraud, a process that sometimes depended at least as much on assessments of social respectability as it did on evaluation of candor in marketing techniques.

Structural economic transformations, institutional inventiveness, and, in some contexts, advancements in scientific inquiry all were necessary preconditions for the emergence of new antifraud bureaucracies. The entrenchment of these institutions depended as well on the sponsorship of some influential group that viewed fraud as an ongoing threat to its interests or the moral health of the wider society. Chapter Seven homes in on this dynamic, focusing on a decades-long campaign by key figures in urban commercial communities to build a nationwide movement against deceptive business practices, centered on pleas for "Truth in Advertising." In part, the leaders of this campaign sought statutory reforms, such as new state laws against false advertising and deceit in applications for commercial credit. They focused, however, on creating robust organizations of business self-regulation, none more important than a mush-rooming network of Better Business Bureaus (BBBs). The BBBs built capacities for public education, monitoring, and enforcement that rivaled those of local, state, and even national authorities.

Whether inside, outside, or on the always-fuzzy boundary that separated the domains of American government from those of American society, late nineteenth- and early twentieth-century antifraud institutions fashioned tactics predicated on aggressive application of discretionary power. The practitioners of business fraud did not stop being an elusive bunch. They could set up shop quickly and move on to new territory whenever regulatory authorities gained a fix on them; they could adjust marketing campaigns to skirt specific enforcement actions; when confronting legal challenges, the more successful among them could and still did retain high-powered legal representation. To make headway against commercial and financial deception, the new antifraud regulators turned to summary modes of enforcement, such as bans from the use of the mails. This flexing of administrative power in turn prompted angry complaints about how antifraud efforts violated longstanding principles of due process. Chapter Eight examines both the nature of these critiques and a series of reforms that tried to infuse antifraud regulation with greater procedural protections.

To retrace these varied streams of American regulatory innovation and re-action is to confirm the strengths of several prevailing approaches to the study of political economy in the modern industrial world. The economic theory of politics and administrative regulation points to the pivotal role of interest groups in driving many antifraud initiatives.[1] Ideas from within political science about bureaucratic entrepreneurship have great relevance for under-standing the origins and evolution of much agricultural regulation, as well as the Post Office's decades-long campaign against mail fraud.[2] Sociological analyses of business self-regulation suggest how the seriousness of private anti-fraud efforts depended on credible threats of governmental action.[3] Historical analysis of social movements furnishes instructive tools for interpreting the early twentieth-century business community's wide-ranging embrace of "Truth in Advertising" as a rallying cry.[4] But each of these conceptual approaches cap-tures only some elements of modern America's multifaceted struggles with commercial and financial deceit.

Like the establishment of regulatory policies with regard to environmental issues, labor conditions, public health, and public morality, the construction of modern American regulatory institutions to fight business fraud was a messy, protracted affair.[5] Occurring across many fronts over many decades, this pro-cess spawned diverse regulatory strategies, sometimes in fits and starts. There are overarching patterns in this narrative, but readers will find no single grand theory of regulatory politics. Instead, they will encounter the historian's penchant for methodological and conceptual scavenging—the borrowing of interpretive approaches that help to make sense of strands in a tangled past. Some patterns did tend to reappear across many of the tangles, though. As American business owners, consumers, investors, journalists, elected officials, and regulators grappled with the problem of commercial misrepresentation during the seven decades that followed the outbreak of the Civil War, they drew interrelated lessons about the centrality of confidence to modern capitalism. Healthy capitalist markets rested on widespread faith in the trustworthiness of commercial communication. That foundation of confidence, in turn, required broadly accepted communal norms about fair dealing, which had to adapt to the rapidly changing circumstances of capitalist innovation. And finally, this process of adaptation depended on a web of regulatory institutions, often public but, in the American case, often quasi-public or even private, that cultivated norms and gave them tangible meaning. Modern capitalism depended on a complex ecology of norms, standards, rules, laws, and the institutions that gave them life and force.

Extending the Realm of Inspection and Licensing Regimes

During the frantic efforts to raise and equip armies following Fort Sumter, the Union war effort was hampered by wide-ranging contracting frauds. The biggest scandals involved the purchase from Northeastern manufacturers, at high prices, of poorly made uniforms, shoes, blankets, and tents that proved unequal to the demands of military conflict. These incidents led the *New York Herald* to popularize the term "shoddy" as a way to describe inferior goods. Other exposés revealed overpriced contracts for ships to transport goods from New York City to the Virginia front lines, for construction of fortifications in Missouri, for horses in Kentucky that turned out to be emaciated and diseased, and for adulterated foodstuffs. Contracting problems resulted in part from state-based mobilization, which led to intense competition among purchasing agents. But in many instances military contracts were sweetheart deals arranged by longtime political operatives, without competitive bidding or the most cursory monitoring to ensure quality or fair value, and abetted by inspectors with close ties to suppliers.[6]

As details of the cheats and swindles came to light through journalistic and legislative investigations, pressure for action intensified. Democratic politicians highlighted every instance of apparent Republican malfeasance, demanding an end to corruption.[7] Well-established Northern manufacturers insisted that the rush to initiate military purchasing had disadvantaged them, allowing unprincipled contractors to bilk the government.[8] Republican publications hurled editorial thunderbolts at the shameless "plunderers" who profited from deceptive practices as brave soldiers risked life and limb.[9] Wartime antifraud discourse echoed longstanding complaints about the disreputable trickery of middlemen. One early (1862) poem that appeared in *Harper's Weekly* cast contractors as "Leeches," chronicling the perfidy of the sort who "loves his dear old country's flag, and Yankee Doodle Dandy / And so he shows his love for them / By selling poisoned brandy."[10]

Amid the crisis of civil war, such critiques paved the way for stringent antifraud policies. The most draconian proposal called for trials of alleged fraudulent suppliers in military courts and imposition of the death penalty on those convicted. Despite popular support for this Napoleonic approach to military justice, it did not become law, partly out of concern that the prospect of such extreme penalties would complicate enforcement efforts.[11] But the Lincoln administration did institute a series of auditing committees, which reexamined early supply contracts and imposed reductions on scores of contractors. During the winter of 1861–62, the US Army also consolidated and regularized military purchasing. It placed supply logistics in the hands of a professional Quartermaster Corps, whose purchasing agents and inspectors proved far less susceptible than politically appointed state agents to corruption and insider dealing. In addition to developing rigorous specifications for military supplies, the Corps required sealed bids and imposed payment discounts on deliveries of substandard goods.[12]

Aware of mounting public anger, Congress further enacted legislation in March 1863 "to prevent and punish Frauds upon the Government." This statute gave informants the right to institute proceedings in federal court against military contractors they could show had made false claims, and to receive one-half of any funds or fines recovered through their evidence. It further defined all military suppliers as subject to the jurisdiction and terms of military justice, while exempting court-martialed contractors from capital punishment.[13] Motivated by the desire to create a credible deterrent, military judge advocates initiated at least twenty prosecutions under this law in the final two years of the war, and used the threat of prosecution to force several contractors out of business. Northern publications hailed these attempts: after the first conviction under the 1863 law, the *New York Times* editorialized that "our prison doors gape for just such knaves."[14] They tended to gape only, however, for suppliers who lacked political connections and high social standing. When contractors with pull faced fraud allegations, they either avoided court-martial through some form of settlement or had guilty verdicts overturned through appeals.[15]

Civil War policies to thwart contracting swindles thus had some key features in common with antifraud law that had been prevalent in the United States since Independence. Like earlier state inspection regimes, wartime regulation of military contracting revolved around assessments of goods quality by public inspectors. Enforcement of the 1863 Frauds Act also continued the easy treatment of defendants with elite social status. But there was a significant departure as well. By placing authority in the hands of the Quartermaster Corps and a new group of military judicial advocates, Congress and the Department of War empowered a bureaucracy with an esprit de corps based on tough-minded opposition to fraud. In several arenas, the stresses associated with industrialization and the inventiveness of antifraud reformers encouraged even greater divergence from longstanding regulatory practices.

One crucial site of regulatory change involved the postbellum introduction of compulsory grain inspection in Illinois. Reform of the Chicago grain markets was driven by merchants, farmers, and city boosters. Members of this coalition worried about the private grading practices of the Chicago Board of Trade, which were both greatly influenced and easily evaded by grain warehouses. The operators of warehouses occupied a choke point in the grain trade, which they used to control the grading process. Critics alleged that numerous abuses resulted from this state of affairs, ranging from untrustworthy grading and weighing, to the use of inside information as a basis for commodity speculation, to the issuance of warehouse receipts far in excess of actual grain in storage. They also argued that the funny business occurring in Chicago grain elevators had undermined the confidence of Eastern and European buyers, leading to lost business and reduced prices. To restore the reputation of Chicago wheat and corn, the Illinois legislature enacted a comprehensive inspection law in 1871, acting under the instructions of the new 1870 state constitution. Although this statute furnished an initial definition of grades for all major grains in the Chicago market, it vested authority for implementing an inspection system in a new Railroad and Warehouse Commission. One of the first in a new breed of independent regulatory agencies, the Commission had responsibility to adjust grade definitions as needed, as well as power to appoint and oversee a corps of grain inspectors.[16]

Public grain inspection in Illinois became a basic element of the Midwest's economic infrastructure. By the mid-1870s, a department of more than thirty inspectors examined tens of millions of bushels of grain each year, assigning grades in accordance with the Railroad and Warehouse Commission's standards. One group performed "in-inspections," as grain arrived at Chicago railroad depots, a second group "out-inspections," as it left warehouses for points east. In 1877, merchants questioned grading decisions just 0.2 percent of the time, with only one-third of the appeals leading to revised grades. This approach to monitoring and quality certification restored Chicago's primacy as a transshipment center. The grading system stimulated trust among American and European purchasers, a development ratified by the adoption of Illinois grading standards by traders throughout the North Atlantic economy. As annual reports from the Railroad and Warehouse Commission documented, each year brought greater harvests to the city's grain elevators and warehouses. These results led Midwestern states to follow Illinois's lead, instituting independent agencies to regulate grain inspection.[17]

Despite the congratulatory tone of officialdom, day-to-day operations of state grain inspectors generated periodic grousing within the trade. According to many grain receivers, ambiguities in grade definitions still gave inspectors too much latitude. As the *Chicago Tribune*, a longtime advocate of public inspection, conceded in 1879,

> the requirement that grain must be "reasonably clean" in order to obtain admission to a designated grade is open to a wide range of interpretation by different individuals and even the same individual at different times. The eating of an overdone steak at breakfast, or a wakeful hour during the night caused by a crying baby, may be sufficient to cause even an honest man to veer in his judgment of what is "reasonable" to the extent of two or three cents a bushel.

This observation conveyed a growing dissatisfaction with indefinite rules of thumb. Even if a grain inspector was not corrupt or a partisan hack—even if he was "an honest man"—his methods remained haphazard. The *Tribune* suggested that inspectors relied more on samples that indicated the minimum quality for a particular grade as a means of ensuring consistent judgments. One member of the state legislature took this impulse even further, calling for specification of the amount of moisture allowed for various grades, and scientific testing whenever shippers chose to appeal grading determinations.[18]

By the early 1880s, complaints intensified amid perceptions that upward adjustments in fees constituted an unjust tax on grain traders and that inspectors shifted their standards depending on market conditions. Extensive investigations by the Chicago Grain Receivers' Association and by a special 1881 state legislative committee led to charges similar to those that had bedeviled earlier American inspection bureaucracies. Many inspectors, critics alleged, lacked expertise in the grain markets; a former chief inspector had improperly pocketed over $23,000 in fees; the current chief inspector did not "possess any special knowledge of the grain business" and had treated the position mostly as a sinecure, furnishing weak oversight of the inspectorate. Although attempts by a rump faction of grain receivers to return inspection to the Board of Trade failed, the partisan 1885 appointment of an unqualified chief grain inspector led to renewed complaints about unjustified variations in grading, which threatened Chicago's "standing and . . . name before the world."[19]

Late nineteenth-century debates in this area concerned not the question of whether to have state-mandated grain inspection, but rather how to ensure that inspection retained integrity and technical competence. Among grain dealers, support for the return of inspection authority to the Board of Trade remained strong throughout the 1880s, though the legislative clout of rural representatives precluded such a move. Two other common proposals were to give the Board of Trade a role in nominating a slate of potential candidates for chief inspector, and to impose "'civil-service' rules" on the inspector corps—a move that Minnesota had taken in 1889.[20] Illinois did not introduce civil service examinations as a basis for selecting grain inspectors until 1910, but as early as 1904, it created a "school of instruction for the inspectors," which "by the use of type samples of the different . . . grades," attempted "to instill in the [inspectors'] minds a greater degree of uniformity and accuracy." The inspectorate further implemented a system in which track inspectors took samples from railroad cars, and warehouse inspectors from shipments leaving grain elevators, and then brought them to a central office. This innovation facilitated rigorous comparison of samples by the most experienced inspectors, ensuring greater consistency in grading.[21]

The themes of professionalism, expertise, and bureaucratic system as checks on deceptive marketing emerged with even greater force in the movement to subject fertilizers to state inspection. Bogus commercial fertilizers plagued American farmers from the 1840s, when manufacturers began to produce phosphate-based products and merchants introduced Latin American guano. Assessment of the quality of a given batch of fertilizer depended on complex chemical analysis of its phosphate and nitrogen content, as well an appreciation for the applicability of chemical compositions to soil types. Without technical expertise, agricultural purchasers had little capacity to evaluate compounds for sale. These circumstances created openings for vendors of adulterated or spurious products. "The farmer," Yale chemistry professor Samuel W. Johnson concluded in an 1855 lecture to the Connecticut State Agricultural Society, "is entirely at the mercy of the manufacturer, or dealer."[22]

Outcry from farmers who had purchased worthless fertilizers led seaboard states to enact inspection laws for imported guano in the late 1840s and early 1850s. These statutes mandated that appointed seaport inspectors analyze samples from shipboard cargoes to ascertain their "per centage of ammonical and phosphatic compounds," and then publicize results. But inspection quality often proved to be poor, for most appointed inspectors "knew nothing of chemistry." Early enforcement practices also proved easy for merchants to circumvent, either by adulterating guano after inspection or recycling used bags with an inspector's mark. The rapid growth of domestic fertilizer manufacturing presented yet more regulatory challenges. Because early producers of artificial manures relied on different inputs and made divergent claims about their products' purported chemical makeup and agricultural performance, assessments required more sophisticated testing than with guanos. Some manufacturers also produced high-quality fertilizer to gain endorsements from private chemists and build reputations, but then adulterated products in subsequent seasons to pad profit margins.[23]

Conceptualizing institutional remedies for these problems required genuine scientific expertise. As a result, the key figures in shaping regulatory responses to deceptive fertilizer marketing were nascent professional chemists, such as Yale's Samuel Johnson, James Bennett Chynoweth, a Philadelphia scientist who had worked for numerous fertilizer companies and who coauthored a touted compendium on manures in 1871, and Dr. H. C. White, a Georgia professor and national leader of academic chemists. These individuals framed misrepresentations by fertilizer companies as tantamount to the basest forms of fraud. Maryland's state agricultural chemist, Philip T. Tyson, stressed in 1860 that in such cases, "people are punished criminally" for obtaining money "under false pretenses." Was it not, he asked, "equally criminal in morals, if not in law," to advertise "certain proportions of valuable matter in a manure," and then sell goods with far less potency? Roughly a decade later, Chynoweth decried the "wholesale Peter Funks" who had flooded farms with "bogus compounds." Depicting their actions as a "national calamity," because they perpetuated "deserved prejudices . . . against the use of commercial fertilizers," he insisted that scientists had a duty to bring fraudulent firms "to justice and punishment."[24]

In addition to building a rhetorical case against fertilizer frauds, the emerging group of agricultural chemists advocated practical strategies to make fertilizer advertising more accurate. From the late 1850s through the 1870s, chemists focused on how the state might improve information disclosure. One recurring suggestion called for the states to appropriate funds for widespread testing of "the articles *actually received* by the farmer." By sampling products at retail stores or in use on farms, governments could uncover those firms that had evaded inspection at ports of entry or domestic manufactories, or adulterated products after inspection. Testing, moreover, had to be undertaken by "*competent* and *honest* chemists," who had the knowledge and scientific technique to evaluate the composition of guanos and artificial manures. Those in-dependent scientists would inform the public of findings through regular no-tices in the press. Some chemists advocated legislation that would require fertilizer companies to furnish a "guaranteed analysis" of their products, and that firms should "be liable to prosecution if their manures fall short of the guaranteed standard."[25]

The key ideas for regulating fertilizers came from Europe, as had the tech-niques for making artificial guanos. Many leading chemists who took a public stand against adulterated composts had been trained at German universities, which exposed them to both the latest ideas about chemical analysis and the close relationship between scientists and the regulatory apparatus of govern-ments. Chynoweth made the German source of his proposals explicit, celebrat-ing the stringent inspection rules in force within the principality of Baden, which compelled manufacturers to provide detailed information about the chemical composition of their products, imposed regular testing of samples, offered free testing of any samples furnished by farmers, and mandated monthly publication of all testing results. "As a result of the rigid German in-spection laws," Chynoweth instructed his rural readership, "purchasers are protected."[26]

By forging close relationships with agricultural societies, state boards, and legislatures, chemists put regulatory ideas into practice. The first step involved scientific analyses of leading commercial fertilizers, as with the studies that Samuel Johnson undertook for the Connecticut Agricultural Society and Board of Agriculture from 1857 through 1869. After receiving local fertilizers "without their names or any mark except a number," Johnson evaluated their nitrogen and phosphate content. Such analyses received widespread attention from state agricultural departments.[27] Once chemists had demonstrated the ubiquity of low-grade fertilizers masquerading as high-quality products, they pressed for legislative enactment of state-mandated inspection requirements based on German practices, along with appointment of respected scientists as fertilizer inspectors.[28]

Agricultural chemists faced headwinds in persuading postbellum state gov-ernments to follow their suggestions. Waxing skepticism about the capacities of state inspection regimes led some commentators to depict proposals for sci-entific "police surveillance" of fertilizers as efforts by ambitious chemists to gain "a place for individual advancement," a dig that contained some truth. Rather than rely on scientific guardians, these observers retained faith in the principle of *caveat emptor*, which placed the onus on manufacturers to estab-lish brands known for "a standard of quality." This argument found favor with the occasional official, including the secretary of Maine's Board of Agriculture, who instructed farmers to search out "honest manufacturers and dealers" rather than trust to unwieldy, unreliable, and expensive inspection regimes. Through the mid-1870s, moreover, many fertilizer firms opposed new regulations as unjust impositions on their commercial liberty.[29]

Despite these critiques, postbellum farmers and the agricultural press proved receptive to the chemists' arguments, especially in regions facing problems with soil exhaustion. The debate over fertilizer inspections occurred amid the waxing agrarian indictment of transportation companies, banking institutions, and manufacturing interests, all of which farming organizations viewed as hiding behind expansive definitions of property rights and the supposed virtues of illusory market competition. In a rural America that looked to Populist organizations such as the Grange for political and economic guidance, appeals to commercial reputation as a sufficient check on chicanery fell flat. As one farmer insisted in response to an 1878 plea that fertilizer purchasers place their faith in a seller's reputation, the opportunity "for deception in the sale of a piece of calico is not comparable to a compound like a commercial fertilizer."[30]

In state after state, fertilizer regulation premised on scientific testing gained ground, though details varied. Georgia adopted a typical inspection bureaucracy through a pair of mid-1870s laws. These statutes mandated inspection of fertilizer samples before sale by six regional offices, required sellers to provide full disclosure of chemical composition and guarantees of represented contents, prohibited sale of fertilizers whose key ingredients fell below stipulated floors, and required appointment of "an experienced and competent chemist, to analyze the fertilizers" sampled by the inspectors. In addition to creating misdemeanors for violation of these provisions, the Georgia laws enabled farmers to send fertilizer samples to the state chemist for analysis, and empowered the Commissioner of Agriculture to establish additional regulations to implement the inspection service.[31]

In almost every state that established fertilizer inspection, governments tapped well-regarded scientists to implement the new regulations, usually professors of agricultural chemistry at land grant universities. Most of these chemists had studied in Germany or with American professors trained in Germany. They eagerly compared the marketing claims of fertilizer companies with the chemical composition of their products. Season after season, thousands of samples of commercial manures poured into state laboratories, sometimes provided by manufacturers, sometimes by inspectors, and at other times by farmers. Month after month, bulletins poured out, reporting on fertilizer composition and estimating commercial value per ton, based on regional prices for component chemicals.

State chemists rarely turned to the penal features of fertilizer laws, which often lacked bite. In Indiana, officials fretted that they were hamstrung by the law's reliance on lawsuits by purchasers as a means of punishing deceptive fertilizer companies. This policy, the state's chemist reported in 1892, had proven ineffective, for "the farmers are not willing to file complaints after fraud is shown" because of the time and effort required to defend the public against imposition. Official chemists also gave manufacturers opportunities to rectify outright mistakes, such as not furnishing mandated samples or marginally misrepresenting product components, "in a quiet way." The central focus of regulation was to improve the flow of public information about product quality, most commonly by educating farmers, and in some cases manufacturers, about appropriate standards for commercial manures and the best practices for assessing their value. Nonetheless, state chemists did not shy away from publicly upbraiding unscrupulous firms, nor, where they possessed the authority, from initiating legal proceedings to chase them out of their jurisdictions.[32]

Fertilizer inspectorates, like the postbellum agencies that graded Midwestern grain, shored up commercial confidence. Across the eastern half of the United States, state officials judged that regulation had improved fertilizer quality and stimulated demand. In Ohio, the Secretary of Agriculture reported in 1883 that the state's publication of results from rigorous fertilizer testing had "greatly diminished fraud," led the producers of "ten low-grade brands" either to improve their products or abandon the state, and "greatly increased the sale of high-grade fertilizers." A few years later, Georgia's chief chemist observed with pride that out of 845 annual inspections, only one fertilizer did not measure up to its purported quality, adding that the state's rigorous monitoring made it "nearly impossible to impose a fraudulent fertilizer upon the farmers" of the state.[33] State chemists had every incentive to exaggerate their effectiveness. But the agricultural press, occasional legislative investigations, and foreign observers agreed with these assessments. "Wherever this official chemical inspection is once begun," the *Maine Farmer* observed in the mid-1880s, "it increases in usefulness as it is continued from year to year," directing farmers to high-value commercial manures. The British Vice-Consul stationed in Wilmington, North Carolina, similarly observed in 1888 that due to the "vigorous enforcement" of fertilizer regulations in that state, "the trade in fertilizers has been remarkably free of evasions of the law." Encouraged by regulatory constraints on deceitful marketing, the American fertilizer market grew by a factor of almost ten between 1869 and 1889.[34]

Manufacturers also testified to the positive impact of fertilizer regulation. Once states adopted fertilizer inspections, several producers wasted little time in boasting that their goods bore the esteemed stamp of scientific officialdom.

Thus Georgians reading the *Macon Telegraph* learned in March 1881 that "the State Chemist" had rated Pendleton's Guano "higher in commercial value than any other in the market." Often firms felt no need to communicate anything other than the reported test results. What better demonstration of respectability and comparative value than a government scientist's declaration that one's product cost $33 per ton, but was worth a full $4.67 more? By 1889, fertilizer inspection had become so essential to the infrastructure of the industry that a New England fertilizer manufacturer could instruct an annual meeting of Vermont farmers that purchasers of commercial artificial manures should "consult your State Chemist . . . and the admirable tables which he publishes, to know what the different things contain."[35]

Such indications of beneficial regulatory impact did not free late nineteenth-century fertilizer regulation from all controversy. Even though implementation remained in the hands of professional scientists, early inspection practices elicited complaints from manufacturers analogous to the ones that many dealers leveled at the system of grain grading—that there was too much inconsistency in inspection methods. Throughout the 1870s and early 1880s, fertilizer companies griped that inspectors did not use the same techniques in taking samples and that state chemists employed different analytical approaches, reaching frustratingly different results. Manufacturers further opposed the tendency of many official chemists to offer assessments of fertilizers' commercial value based on estimates of prices for active ingredients. These estimates, producers maintained, were often inaccurate and so unfairly harmed reputations.[36]

State chemists recognized the threat that "the inconsistencies of agricultural chemical analysis" posed to their as-yet fragile public standing. "There is no doubt," one leading chemist noted in 1884, that such variable results "pinch all of us." These regulatory innovators quieted complaints about their work by adopting an even more ambitious strategy for engendering uniformity in inspection than the one later adopted by the Illinois Department of Grain Inspection. In the mid-1880s, through the auspices of a new national organization, the Association of Official Agricultural Chemists (AOAC), state regulators hammered out a consensus about best practices in fertilizer analysis, based on peer-reviewed appraisals of prevalent techniques. These communal endeavors shored up the new organization's prestige, which its leaders used to foster national harmonization of state fertilizer regulation.[37]

Over the subsequent quarter-century, state chemists leveraged their expertise to bring about a dramatic expansion in regulatory authority.[38] Experience with commercial manures offered a model for how to assert novel regulatory jurisdiction. Developing chemical tests for the purity of food, drugs, herbicides, and pesticides required skills and techniques analogous to those the chemists already possessed. As scientists with access to the resources and research communities at universities and experimental agricultural stations, they put their technical capacity to new uses, assessing the relative purity of butter or identifying the contents of a given medicine. In the parlance of later economic theorists and business strategists, they took advantage of opportunities to develop economies of scope.[39] They had built a technocratic recipe for cleaning up problems of adulteration and misrepresentation. As highly regarded state officials, moreover, they enjoyed connections to leading politicians and positions from which to construct alliances with interest groups such as agricultural societies, consumer groups, and manufacturers of high-quality products. They also possessed a powerful precedent on which they and their allies could rely in political debate.

Official agricultural chemists set their sights on ambitious augmentation of their regulatory responsibilities almost from the moment they had secured their position as arbiters of legitimacy in the fertilizer industry. In 1885, the president of the Ohio Board of Agriculture, Professor I. W. Chamberlain, traveled to Pennsylvania to address that state's Dairymen's Association. In addition to offering general suggestions about animal husbandry, he launched a stinging attack on systematic "adulteration" resulting from the introduction of factory methods to dairying. The Ohio official chemist proposed legislation that would compel manufacturers of dairy products such as oleomargarine and non-cream cheeses to inform consumers of their composition, and then create a scientific inspection regime to hold them to their claims. "The law," he intoned,

> should prescribe heavy penalties for false or insufficient branding, and provide for inspection, with powers and funds for chemical analysis, and for prosecution, as is now the case in regard to commercial fertilizers. If chemistry and law are made to help the manufacturer of counterfeits, they should be made to protect the producer of honest milk, butter, and cheese.

Four years later, John A. Myers, then Mississippi's state chemist and president of AOAC, used his address to the organization to make a similar argument. Municipalities and states, Myers noted, were passing legislation to combat the adulteration of dairy products, liquors, and "other agricultural products offered for sale." So long as the AOAC retained its "proper conservative attitude and strict adherence to scientific principles," he predicted that "the time is not far distant when . . . its conclusions will virtually become the law regulating the sale of nearly every agricultural and food product offered in our cities." His belief was that organized scientific endeavor would snuff out the cheats and adulterations so prevalent in American consumer markets.[40]

The vision sketched by Chamberlain and Myers came to pass, though in the end mostly through scientific bodies within the federal government. Several states did enact inspection regimes for dairy products and foods such as sugar, with New York, New Jersey, and Massachusetts taking the lead in 1881–82.[41] But regulation in these areas expanded enormously in 1906, when Congress responded to journalistic exposés about adulteration of food and medicines by passing the Pure Food and Drug Act. This law prohibited the sale of falsely labeled or misbranded foods and pharmaceuticals in interstate commerce, and vested oversight powers in the Department of Agriculture's Bureau of Chemistry. The key figure in the law's passage and its initial enforcement was Harvey Wiley, who served as the Agriculture Department's chief agricultural chemist from 1883 until 1912. Wiley's office conducted a stream of studies to determine the extent of adulteration in food and medicine, and then coordinated lobbying efforts that culminated in the 1906 Act.[42] Some of his earliest regulatory experiences, however, occurred in his capacity as Indiana state chemist during the late 1870s and early 1880s, when he led campaigns against bogus fertilizers. The path to regulatory curbs on worthless patent medicines and adulterated foodstuffs ran through chemical laboratories that scrutinized the contents of guano bags and loads of phosphates.[43]

Even more so than with fertilizer regulation, the more vigorous oversight of food and drugs fostered expectations that public testing for adulteration should rest on reproducible, standardized methods. To rid marketplaces of swill passing for milk or spurious patent medicines, the American state required not only administrative authority, but also scientific capacity. It needed state-of-the-art laboratories. It needed leading scientists who could engage in sophisticated chemical analysis, help to forge clear national standards, and hold businesses accountable through the regular testing of samples.

One can see the power of these assumptions at work in the evolution of grain market regulation. During the 1890s and 1900s, a growing number of politicians from grain-growing states advocated the imposition of federal grain inspection. Supporters portrayed this policy as a means to overcome periodic disputes between counterparties in different regions, who sometimes differed in interpreting grading definitions. They also alleged that large-scale Chicago grain elevator companies, in cahoots with the Chicago Board of Trade, had regained control over the inspection process. As a result, the elevator combination could once again manipulate grades as they had done before the 1871 grain grading reforms. Renewed European concerns over uneven US grading practices served as an additional impetus, especially in light of the emergence of significant foreign competition from the wheatlands of Australia and Argentina.[44]

The farmers and Populist politicians who campaigned for federal grain inspection confronted opposition from many grain traders and commercial elites, who preferred local grading institutions and who worried about the creation of new avenues for political patronage.[45] But advocates of centralized inspection found allies within the Agriculture Department's Bureau of Chemistry, which carried out intensive studies of grain grading from the mid-1900s through 1914. This research enabled the Bureau's chemists to propose far more precise grades, based on a sample's percentages of moisture, damaged grain, cracked kernels, and foreign substances. It also led to the development of tests for the use of sulfur or other bleaching agents and detailed instructions for effective sampling of large shipments of grain.[46] In 1916, Congress bent to political pressure and administrative expertise, passing the Grain Standards Act. This statute not only instituted federal grading for interstate shipments, but also placed it on a scientific basis under the auspices of a new National Grain Standards Board within the Agriculture Department. This board had the power to devise and implement new standards, as well as to license and supervise local inspectors, whether they worked for local exchanges or state inspection bureaus.[47]

Under the new system, federal inspectors had to pass an examination. In light of the heightened premium on scientific understanding and technique, the Agriculture Department encouraged state universities to create courses of study that would enable individuals to qualify under the new rules.[48] To facilitate public acceptance, its officials instituted a massive education campaign through demonstrations at county and state fairs, which instructed farmers about new grading techniques. By 1920, federal oversight of grain grading had become so stringent that a number of inspectors had lost their licenses for poor performance, and sufficiently accurate that it had won the support of associations of grain dealers as well as farmers.[49] The baseline for quality certification of commodities now presumed policy formulation by government experts who had the scientific knowledge to pierce the farmer's or manufacturer's veil, and so could identify grain properties with great precision.

Toughening up Corporate Accounting

After the Civil War, many states also took steps to combat fraud in local securities markets. Several legislatures constrained how corporations could raise capital, requiring that they use proceeds of stock offerings to expand tangible assets. Some state constitutional conventions further mandated that corporations open their books to interested shareholders and only raise additional capital after explicit shareholder consent.[50] Two episodes stand out as more far-reaching administrative efforts to curb fraud: California's 1880 enactment of new rules governing financial reporting by mining companies, and New York's 1881 passage of a regulatory regime for life insurance companies. As with state-mandated regimes of grain and fertilizer inspection, both of these reforms were preceded by several years of critical news coverage and deepening complaints among market participants. Unlike those contemporaneous extensions of American regulatory authority, the forays into public accounting regulation were triggered by dramatic scandals and business failures rather than just an accumulating sense of injustice.

In California, pleas for stricter reporting rules were prompted by the endemic machinations of mining capitalists and large-scale speculators on the San Francisco Stock Exchange.[51] Without regular flows of public information about labor activity or the quantity and quality of output, mining insiders could quietly buy or sell shares on the basis of inside information, as well as engage in charades to move markets either up or down. One of the more elaborate frauds involved the staged "shutdown." Because information about deep-level Western mining strikes was at such a premium, mine-owners closed down the exit points of shafts whenever workers began to develop a new part of the mine. By restricting miners' ability to pass word of a new ore vein to the neighborhood and wider world, the owners hoped to be able to buy up company shares on the cheap. This practice soon taught speculators to watch out for shutdowns, which possibly signaled big mineral strikes. In response, one set of unscrupulous owners initiated a shutdown in 1872 despite a lack of new mining activity. After speculators inferred that this action presaged an ore strike and piled into the mine's stock, insiders dumped their own shares through confederates. In other cases, mining executives conveyed false information in annual reports, skimmed off profits by channeling ore to their own privately owned mills, or sold mine assets to business associates for pennies on the dollar.

Such manipulations bilked outside investors, sometimes precipitated full-blown company failures, and undermined public confidence in the San Francisco market for mining stocks. By comparison, the skullduggery that went on inside grain elevators or fertilizer manufactories exacted only minor tolls on the marts of trade. As early as 1870, the San Francisco Board of Brokers developed formal recommendations for state legislation that would mandate regular information disclosure by mining companies. Like their elevator warehouse counterparts in Chicago, however, Western mining magnates tenaciously opposed challenges to their freedom of action. When pressures mounted for state regulation in 1874, mine-owners deflected the most far-reaching proposals, conceding only that mining corporations would have to abide by the informational requirements of their own bylaws, whatever those might be, and that minority shareholders had the right to inspect mine property.

Only in 1880 did a more robust statute clear the legislature and statehouse, after several additional scandals and bankruptcies, a number of market busts, a relentless reform campaign by San Francisco newspapers, and the emergence of a competing New York City mining exchange. This legislation made insider looting more difficult by requiring that corporate officers receive approval from two-thirds of shareholders before selling, leasing, or mortgaging company assets. It also required regular reporting to stockholders of expenses, labor, and output, according to uniform accounting standards. Shareholders also gained the right to bring along a geological or mining expert when visiting mines. Nonetheless, California required neither regular reports to a state bureaucracy nor independent audits. The focus of regulatory action was empowering shareholders to obtain better information so that they could better protect themselves.

New York's life insurance reforms followed a spate of bankruptcies in the wake of the Panic of 1873. The sector grew quickly in the late 1860s, fuelled by new products from mutual companies that gave policyholders the prospect of speculative gains, as well as far more aggressive sales techniques. The establishment of state insurance departments in places such as New York and Massachusetts also reassured many policyholders about the industry's safety. Strong demand encouraged the entry of new insurance providers, including incorporated stock companies, incorporated mutual companies (owned by their policyholders) and, after the mid-1870s, scores of nonprofit fraternal associations. This last group eschewed strict actuarial methods, assessing members for payments to make good on promises after a death.

Many of the new insurers took a "high-pressure" route in the scramble for policyholders. They opted for cut-rate premiums and generous commissions to agents, encouraged aggressive selling tactics, and invested assets speculatively, in the search for sufficient returns to meet burgeoning obligations. Managers at several underwriters engaged in blatant self-dealing, deceptive accounting, and embezzlement. Even before the Panic of 1873, a few of the more dodgy life insurers failed. After the Panic, crashing asset values and plummeting demand exposed financial vulnerabilities, with more than thirty companies and fraternal organizations careening into insolvency and nearly twice that number winding up their affairs. Even after insolvency, predatory behavior continued, as corporate insiders gained positions as receivers and either wasted assets or arranged for mergers with other overextended firms on terms that disadvantaged policyholders.[52]

Subsequent investigations by the New York Insurance Department exposed the depth of managerial abuses, as did a string of fraud prosecutions (attempts that, as we have seen, almost always failed to put insurance executives in jail). These inquiries and court proceedings were all seized upon by the Northeastern press. Journalists and editors took particular umbrage because of the demographic groups hurt by life insurance company failures. Unlike duplicity in the market for mining stocks, which hurt speculators and gamblers, the life insurance depredations had victims more worthy of sympathy. To *The Independent*, a weekly that catered to the Northern Protestant middle class, the behavior of failed insurance companies constituted "fraud of the worst stripe, because it was the swindling of dependent families." Once again, fraud against the innocent and vulnerable elicited heightened concern from the arbiters of public opinion.

Against this backdrop of public concern, a New York State legislative committee held lengthy hearings into life insurance, drafting a bill that brought the new and heretofore unregulated fraternal insurance schemes under state regulation. Incorporated stock companies already had to submit annual reports and deposit $100,000 in assets with the insurance department as a reserve fund. The new legislation required that "charitable" organizations receive a license from the Insurance Department before opening. Like the stock-based companies, cooperative organizations would now also have to submit detailed accounts of their business to the state regulators; they would be subject to liquidation if regulators found their operations in gross violation of members' interests.[53]

The goal of this legislation, state Superintendent of Insurance Charles Fairman explained, was to safeguard both New York policyholders and legitimate insurers from "swindling frauds designed to enrich ... managers and owners under the garb of benevolence and charity." The "legitimate and honorable associations," Fairman added, had supported reform because they realized that the threat that they faced from

> unknown and irresponsible associations without assets and without capital, worse than the wildcat banks of Michigan or the bubbles of the South Sea, which promise fabulous endowments in fifty years hence out of impossible reserves calculated in total disregard of all mathematical or mortality tables.

Protection would come from the staff of Fairman's department, who would bring dispassionate actuarial science to bear on the applications and reports that came across their desks.[54]

By raising barriers to entry, the 1881 New York insurance reform law prevented the most rapacious frauds by New York life insurers. It was followed by several other reforms, sometimes emerging in legislation, sometimes resulting from judicial opinions in legal challenges to insurance company practices. The most important of these changes imposed surrender values for policyholders whose premium payments had lapsed, held companies liable for actions by sales agents, and streamlined the process to close down duplicitous insurance companies or associations.[55]

These reforms, however, did not touch many misrepresentations and financial abuses. Later investigations, such as the New York Legislature's 1905 Armstrong investigation, demonstrated that managers at the largest insurers were still lining their own pockets through high salaries and the channeling of investments into businesses in which they had an interest; they also used company funds to curry favor with legislators and other public officials. Reliance on expensive sales commissions continued as well, encouraging "twisting"—a practice in which sales agents contacted policyholders of other companies and misrepresented contractual terms to convince them to switch insurers, a move that incurred high and undisclosed transaction costs.[56]

The Armstrong revelations spurred yet more regulatory action, including limits on executive compensation, prohibitions on speculative insurance contracts and speculative company investments, constraints on excessive commissions to agents, prohibitions against twisting, and the adoption of more rigorous accounting standards. This last reform mandated not only detailed tracking of selling costs, mortality payouts, and investment returns, but also independent audits and regular reports to the Department of Insurance and policyholders.[57] As the headquarters for America's largest insurance companies, New York set a national regulatory tone. Numerous states followed its lead, imposing analogous accounting regimes over local companies and fraternal organizations.[58]

During the first two decades of the twentieth century, a further rash of corporate frauds prompted new state-level administrative mechanisms to oversee securities markets. In California, the impetus for reform came from swindles that took advantage of the state's early twentieth-century oil boom. Elsewhere, concern arose from a wider slate of fraudulent promotions, from mining and real-estate companies to banking and manufacturing enterprises, as well as recurrent exposés of transportation and utility companies' stock-watering (that is, floating additional shares to pay for new capital investments at inflated valuations). Because a growing number of Americans had begun to invest in stocks and bonds, the resulting financial losses reached more deeply into farming communities and the urban middle class. Throughout the first three decades of the twentieth century, muckraking journalists turned a spotlight on the "pirates of promotion" who roiled securities markets. Over the same decades, financial elites became more anxious about fraudulent stock operators. In agricultural states, commercial bankers fretted about losing deposits to the siren call of the stock market and the insistent pleas of get-rich-quick artists. From 1911 through 1932, almost every state responded to the resulting political pressures, adopting laws that targeted shady stock promoters and deceitful brokerages. The predominant impulse was to create a regulatory filter for the investment markets.

Kansas's legislature led the way in 1911, enacting a statute that required corporations that sold stocks or bonds in the state to submit extensive financial data to the Bank Commission. This agency would grant a license to market securities so long as the firm was a legitimate enterprise that offered investors a "fair promise" of a return and had prepared truthful prospectuses and advertising materials. Most states soon followed Kansas's lead. Some placed responsibility for licensing securities with their banking commission, others with a new Bureau of Corporations or a Division of Securities within the Secretary of State's office. Some legislatures created new licensing requirements for brokerage firms operating within their borders and gave the relevant state agency power to sue for injunctions against misleading marketing campaigns. These "blue-sky" laws—so named for their goal of checking stock pitches without any basis other than the azure vistas surrounding their unscrupulous promoters—gave state officials authority to distinguish firms with viable business plans from those that lacked decent prospects or represented pure swindles.

New York, by contrast, eschewed prospective administrative approaches. Confronting intensive opposition to blue-sky approaches from Wall Street, Albany legislators instead enacted a new criminal fraud statute, the 1921 Martin Act. This legislation, pushed by a new association of the largest nationwide securities underwriters, the Investment Bankers of America, created specific prohibitions against financial frauds and enabled the state attorney general to seek injunctions to stop ongoing fraudulent promotions. It further gave that official extraordinary investigative authority, including wide subpoena power and the capacity to compel testimony from corporate executives and stock promoters. To enforce the statute, the attorney general's office established a separate fraud division that would investigate and prosecute fraud committed by promoters who operated outside established stock exchanges.[59]

The flurry of antifraud regulation in financial services represented an important shift in thinking about the state's responsibility to protect investors and policyholders. Blue-sky laws and creation of antifraud bureaucracies reflected the presumption that government had the obligation to ensure truthful communication in these markets. In states with a strong current of Populism, this impulse extended even further, embracing the provision of more detailed guidance to Americans in their choice of investments.

INVENTING MAIL FRAUD

Late nineteenth- and early twentieth-century American inspection regimes took their lead from counterparts across the Atlantic, hewing closely to European examples of close cooperation between scientists and public regulatory institutions. The development of corporate accounting regimes and requirements of greater transparency from life insurance companies also borrowed to some extent from British examples.[60] By contrast, the legal construction of postal fraud was very much an American invention. Yet in this context, too, the key sculptors of regulatory policy were ambitious officers of the state.

The continental economy that emerged during the lifetime of P. T. Barnum depended on revolutions in both transportation and communications, including rapid improvements in the mails. Dependable, affordable postal service, whether reliant on stage, canal, or rail, encouraged business owners to expand their geographic horizons. It eased the gathering of commercial intelligence and opened a channel to faraway customers without the intercession of local middlemen. For thousands of manufacturers, merchants, and promoters, the Post Office facilitated regional or national marketing strategies. These firms sent out circulars through the post that described products or investments; they received and filled orders the same way.

But mail-order business also attracted deceptive practices, for it could not rely on checks available to participants of a neighborly economy. As soon as legitimate enterprises began to work out mail-based marketing schemes in the 1850s, unscrupulous ones developed mail-based scams. Some of the most prominent involved fake lotteries and gift enterprises. After compiling addresses from directories, these concerns mailed tens of thousands of circulars that stressed the excellent odds associated with their drawings. Many recruited postmasters as local selling agents and persuaded country editors to place advertising bombast. All too often, replies surged into post offices as far-flung Americans took the bait. Occasionally, proprietors of these businesses would distribute paltry tokens to some wagerers. Usually, they sent word that participants had not won this time, but encouraged them to try again. Thousands of other fraudulent businesses pretended to offer cheap goods or profitable business opportunities as a means of separating "the public from its superfluous cash."[61]

After customers of these fly-by-night firms received shoddy products or realized that no goods or legitimate employment opportunities would be forthcoming, most suffered their losses in silence. But some wrote to the police or the mayor where the fraudulent business claimed to be located, pleading for assistance. Once city governments got wind of fraudulent mail-order firms, they often assigned detectives to investigate, who sometimes arrested clerks responsible for receiving and responding to incoming mail orders.[62]

But successful fraud prosecutions of swindlers who relied on postal transactions turned out to be even rarer than in false pretense cases that involved local defendants and complainants. As with any fraud case, prosecutors confronted the enduring problem of defendants who skipped bail, as well as the perennial challenge of amassing evidence to satisfy the rigorous standards of American criminal law. There were even thornier prosecutorial obstacles in cases of fraudulent schemes operating via the mail. Victims had to expend time and money to institute formal criminal proceedings in distant courts. In light of the small sums at issue, few dupes were willing to follow through with the requirements of the criminal justice system. Even clear-cut cases might fail because "none of the actually swindled persons" were present in the city "to enter a formal complaint."[63] The principals of nineteenth-century mail scams, moreover, often lurked in the shadows, far away from the metropolitan addresses listed on marketing literature. If urban police managed to track down these elusive figures, they often took advantage of local networks to evade legal process. As a result of such barriers, few criminal investigations into postal swindles progressed to actual trials. On those rare occasions in which detectives forced fraudulent proprietors to close businesses, they proved adept at shifting their base of operations and starting anew.[64]

Faced with limited avenues for exacting punishment, city governments turned mail fraud incidents into opportunities for public education. After the New York police shut down one swindle in 1858, they returned outstanding letters, enclosing whatever sums they had contained. An explanatory note informed senders that the would-be recipient had "been arrested in this city" and advised them to "be on your guard against gift enterprises, lotteries, and other bogus businesses, as they are designed to defraud the unwary." A decade later, New York City mayor A. Oakley Hall mobilized the nation's newspapers for a more systematic educational campaign. Frustrated by scores of complaints about the city's mail-order businesses, Hall distributed a "Caution" to editors around the country. The message warned rural readers against mail-related swindles emanating from New York City, imploring them to steer clear of "dollar stores, or any other possible scheme whereby property . . . is promised greater than the price asked to be paid."[65] Such endeavors multiplied the earlier official signs outside mock auction houses that instructed strangers to "BEWARE OF PETER FUNKS," now warning greenhorns against the frauds that might seek them out, via the mail, in the comfort of their own homes.

Such episodic attempts to inoculate consumers from mail-order impositions struck postal officials as inadequate to the task at hand. Swindling through the mails was becoming a more common occurrence, and the Americans who fell for these scams had begun to direct their ire at the Post Office itself, which they often assumed was responsible for losing letters or shipments. Some savvy swindlers encouraged this conclusion by denying that they had received orders or insisting that they had long ago mailed the goods in question. One serial perpetrator of mail frauds informed disgruntled correspondents that because the New York Post Office was so rife with theft, he had "discontinued his box"; he then suggested that customers send all monies by express. Such tactics generated an avalanche of official complaints from defrauded Americans who attributed "their losses . . . to the defective organization of the Post Office Department." Through poses of innocence, one postal official observed, sharpers had managed to transfer "the odium of the fraud . . . to the government."[66]

Post office leaders viewed this situation as an unacceptable affront to institutional reputation. One promising option was to take an expansive view of a postal rule that prohibited letter delivery to fictitious addressees. The postmaster general, Joseph Holt, had instituted this regulation in 1857; the next year, he ordered all officeholders to interpret it broadly as a way to curb fraudulent schemes. Enforcement of the rule temporarily shut down fraudulent lotteries, gift enterprises, and other assorted scams in cities such as New York, Albany, and Philadelphia. Once police received complaints about bogus mail-order firms, they asked local postmasters to send any mail addressed to those concerns to the Dead Letter Office. This action enabled the police, in conjunction with postal workers, to return funds to at least some duped customers.[67]

Such a broad exercise of federal authority, however, did not sit well with the businessmen who lost access to the mails, some of whom challenged its legality. It also attracted scathing criticism from Democratic editors, who worried that making postmasters into censors would lead to "abuse which may seriously infringe upon the rights of innocent parties." In light of these complaints, Postmaster Holt requested a formal legal opinion about his policy from Attorney General J. S. Black. In an October 1860 letter, Black reasoned that "the right of the Post Office to make a regulation which will prevent the service from being prostituted to purposes of fraud, has never been denied." But he also noted that postal officials did not possess "any authority to carry on an extended inquiry into private affairs of persons who receive letters by mail." To justify denial of access to letters, he suggested that "the fraudulent intent ought to be clear."[68]

This opinion created ambiguity about the extent of postal authority. It also gave protection to fraudulent businessmen who did not hide behind false names. In the midst of the Civil War, such issues receded far into the political and bureaucratic background. But with the fall of the Confederacy, they re-emerged in the shape of a formal 1866 request that Congress expand the Post Office's regulatory power. The proposed legislation would allow postal officials to intercept mail sent to individuals or businesses engaging in intentional schemes "to deceive and defraud." It also criminalized use of the mails to fur-ther fraudulent lotteries or gift enterprises. These proposals were endorsed by New York's mayor and police chief, who saw no other way to curb the inter-state swindles that left them inundated with complaints.[69]

Although the impetus for anti–mail fraud reforms came from a federal bu-reaucracy intent upon protecting its own standing, it found support among Northern evangelicals. For social conservatives, postal regulations constituted an attractive vehicle to impose censorship on a rapidly changing society in danger of losing its religious moorings. Northern moralists viewed lotteries, investment swindles, and commercial frauds as part of a larger assault on pub-lic morals by illegitimate businesses, including purveyors of abortifacients, prostitution, and pornography. All of these enterprises had used the mails to forge national markets and circumvent state and local regulations. All of them supplied, in the words of the *Philadelphia Age*, "intelligence of a highly im-proper character . . . to young men," leading "them into crooked and question-able paths." With the right kind of postal regulations, and the right kind of enforcement, evangelicals believed that they could redeem the emerging na-tional marketplace, expelling corrosive lines of trade. The need, the *American Agriculturist* explained in an 1866 discussion of fraudulent lotteries, was for the "strong arm of the law to crush these pests of society." Such confidence re-flected the national government's recent triumph in eradicating the evil of slav-ery, a powerful example of how national authority could remake economic institutions and social norms.[70]

Despite warm advocacy by Northern reformers, the mail fraud bill lacked the political backing to make it through Congress, even one stacked with Re-publicans supportive of vigorous articulations of federal power. As a result, the proposal languished in the Postal Committee for more than five years. But starting in late 1870, Congress undertook an overall codification of postal law, which offered a legislative vehicle for prohibition of mail fraud. Enacted in the spring of 1872 without fanfare, the postal revision statute gave the department the authority to close the mails to "any person, firm, or corporation" that ran a "fraudulent lottery or gift enterprise," or that otherwise operated "any other scheme or device for obtaining money through the mails by means of false or fraudulent pretenses, representations, or promises." So long as the postmaster general received evidence "satisfactory to him," he could issue a fraud order that took away access to registered mail and postal money orders. The law also created a new misdemeanor for anyone using the mails as part of a "scheme or artifice to defraud."[71]

One potential limitation of the reform law concerned enforcement. Without a corps of dedicated inspectors to investigate allegations of mail fraud, the statute would have minimal impact. The department had more than fifty postal inspectors in 1872, but they had their hands full with mail-theft rings and embezzling postmasters. As soon as Congress enacted the new postal statute, however, several evangelical reformers figured out how the Post Office could flex its administrative muscles without further taxing the federal budget. This group was led by Anthony Comstock, a young New York City salesman with a strong commitment to conservative Protestant theology and social values, several years of informal leadership within the Young Men's Christian Association, and a mission to rid Victorian America of disreputable commerce. Comstock saw the new postal law as a cudgel to use against immoral businesses, which he viewed as grave threats to the souls of young urban dwellers who had lost their moorings amid the corruptions of the fast-paced metropolis. Within months of its passage, he helped to found the New York Society for the Suppression of Vice (NYSSV), receiving financial backing from a group of evangelical business elites. He then offered his services to the Post Office as a special agent, without pay, since the NYSSV would provide him with a salary. Similar arrangements soon emerged in Boston, St. Louis, Chicago, and San Francisco, with the leaders of new private antivice organizations taking on official roles as investigators of interstate mail-order businesses. These individuals beefed up the ranks of postal inspectors and infused the department with a deep commitment to do battle against mail frauds.[72]

The mandarins of late nineteenth-century fertilizer regulation and early twentieth-century food and drug regulation were professional scientists who could make uncontested claims to technical expertise, so long as they spoke with one voice. By contrast, the self-appointed guardians of the United States mail possessed no such foundation of technical knowledge. Instead, they constructed regulatory authority out of moral indignation, the willingness to experiment with enforcement practices, and, over time, an accumulated understanding of swindling schemes and swindlers' social networks. Rather than sitting back to wait for complaints to find them, Comstock and his fellow inspectors developed more aggressive investigatory tactics. They scoured the nation's publications for advertisements that bore the telltale marks of duplicity. They then replied to those ads, often sending letters of inquiry under fictitious names so as to occasion no suspicions. Thus, after learning in early 1877 of a fraudulent Hoboken, New Jersey, business that had advertised for sales agents, Comstock arranged for a decoy letter of inquiry to be sent from a nonexistent person in Pittsburgh.[73] This mode of proceeding allowed Comstock and his fellow postal inspectors to collect evidence that would sustain fraud orders or prosecutions.

During the 1870s and 1880s, postal officials directed investigations toward fraudulent lotteries, gift enterprise schemes, and "green goods" operators who offered to sell counterfeit currency. These businesses struck the mail inspectors as especially grave threats to the country's moral health. Interstate investment swindles received close attention as well, as did purveyors of quack medicines, mail-order firms that sent customers "goods of greatly inferior value to what they represented" in ads, and advance-fee scams that promised employment or educational opportunities.[74] By the mid-1890s, the postal authorities issued roughly two hundred fraud orders each year; they also pursued criminal prosecutions. Anthony Comstock and several subordinates made hundreds of fraud-related arrests from the 1870s through the close of the century and investigated many more fraudulent schemes, often convincing their proprietors to cease operations through threats of legal proceedings.[75]

At several junctures, moreover, postal inspectors went after and shut down large-scale enterprises with political clout. Campaigns against the nation's largest lotteries from the 1870s through the early 1890s stood out in this regard, as did a crackdown on bogus brokerage firms in the late 1870s and early 1880s, and a concerted effort in the mid-1890s to close patent medicine and cosmetics firms operating out of South Bend, Indiana.[76] The maneuvers against fake brokerage firms deserve more extended discussion, as they illustrate both the enduring obstacles to fraud prosecutions and how bureaucratic innovations could clear some of them away.

During the mid-1870s, several New York City investment firms blanketed the country with newspaper ads for investment pools that promised to combine funds from small investors and place them under the control of insiders who could safely navigate the arcane, risky world of Wall Street. By reporting excellent returns, they played on the tendency of investors to give great credence to recent events when making financial decisions. These tactics persuaded thousands of Americans to invest, always to their detriment. After a month of two of paper gains, the brokerages informed customers that unexpected market fluctuations had resulted in disastrous losses. Having never invested the pools of capital in the first place, the firms used the funds to pay for marketing expenses and pocketed the remainder.

Complaints about these early, if fake, versions of mutual funds soon inundated Orange Judd's *American Agriculturist*, the financial press, the New York City police, and the New York Stock Exchange (NYSE). Worried about the impact that "combination" brokerages were having on popular sentiment toward financial markets and more respectable firms, the NYSE's Law Committee hired outside legal counsel to investigate the bogus brokerages in 1878. The Committee charged attorney Ralph Oakley to amass "all the information possible concerning the firms that were using the mails and the press to defraud the public by means of fake transactions in stocks, and to use all legal means to secure the convictions of the offending parties." As this statement indicates, the NYSE hoped to overcome the collective action problems that stymied most nineteenth-century fraud prosecutions.[77]

Oakley had little difficulty collecting circumstantial evidence against the cuckoo brokerage firms. Through surveillance of offices, he showed that they did not send runners out to place sell or buy orders, as legitimate brokerage firms did, and that their clerks did nothing but receive and send mail. After placing newspaper ads asking for information from disgruntled investors, he received ample examples of marketing circulars that promised "golden harvests," as well as correspondence that reported initial paper profits and then catastrophic losses. But he struggled to obtain more direct substantiation of intentional misrepresentations that would underpin criminal prosecution in the face of determined legal defenses. Finding a stationer who was owed a debt by one of the firms, Oakley persuaded him to file a collection suit, hoping to force a judicial order for examination of its books. When asked by the court to file an indemnification bond, however, the stationer balked, withdrawing his action. Like so many other would-be prosecutors, Oakley struggled to find individuals who were willing to lodge criminal charges. Most unhappy investors, he found, "refused to . . . sacrifice themselves" by undertaking such a time-consuming endeavor. Instead, like Oscar Moltke, a resident of Yorkville, South Carolina, who lost $211 with the firm of Lawrence & Co., they remained focused on getting back the funds that were "justly due" to them. As Moltke stressed in a December 1879 letter to the *Wall Street Daily News*, his priority was to attain redress of a private grievance, to gain assistance for a "poor man" who was "in absolute need of the money" that Lawrence & Co. had tricked out of him. This white Southerner did not care a fig for the vindication of a public wrong. In the few instances in which defrauded investors initiated criminal process against proprietors of bogus brokerage firms, they accepted settlement offers. Finding himself "balked at every point," Oakley chose not to bring fraud prosecutions.[78]

The mail fraud statute, however, gave Oakley an alternative mode of proceeding. The legal standard to ban firms from the mails was far less stringent than criminal proceedings, for postal inspectors only had to furnish evidence that the postmaster general ascertained to be "satisfactory." In late 1879, the lawyer gave Anthony Comstock his evidence; the latter then initiated a separate inquiry, visiting eight brokerages that received and sent hundreds of letters a month, but that appeared to transact no stock trades. These firms refused to give Comstock access to their books, to substantiate claims that they had thousands of satisfied investors, or to demonstrate that they had generated profits for any single investor. Comstock's report convinced the postmaster general to issue fraud orders, which shut down these firms.[79] A few years later, an investigation of the multi-million-dollar Chicago-based Fund W pyramid scheme culminated in both fraud orders and criminal convictions of two fund managers.[80]

Enforcement of the postal fraud statutes did not eradicate misrepresentations by American mail-order firms. Criminal mail fraud prosecutions encountered many of the same problems that bedeviled fraud prosecutions in state courts. Coordinating the testimony of distant complainants and developing sufficient evidence against ringleaders turned out to be difficult. If indicted mail-order swindlers did not make themselves scarce, they often drew on the talents of the defense bar's most accomplished members. Local juries also sometimes viewed duplicitous mail-order firms sympathetically, as they brought much-needed business to a town or city. For years, there was no way to gain guilty verdicts against the managers of the Louisiana Lottery in New Orleans or its agents in Washington, DC.[81] Federal convictions, when they occurred, also tracked outcomes in state fraud trials. Prison sentences for the largest postal swindles rarely exceeded eighteen months, with even those terms sometimes cut short by pardons, as occurred in the Fund W case.[82] Several operators of fraudulent lotteries came to view fines for mail fraud, which could not exceed $500, "as nothing more than a mild license which an agent of the Lottery could well afford to pay once in every thirty days."[83]

Administrative fraud orders also had important limitations. Postal officials conceded that many recipients of these directives restructured their businesses around reliance on express companies or changed the names and locations of their firms to maintain access to the regular mails. As Anthony Comstock himself admitted, American "swindlers were the hardest people in the world to run down. . . . They have so many aliases and addresses."[84] Several of the largest lotteries responded to fraud orders by moving to locales in Mexico, Canada, or the Caribbean, from which they returned to the business of flooding US mailboxes with circulars.[85] Such adjustments, however, did not necessarily protect dodgy operators from subsequent fraud orders. They also increased the fixed costs associated with deceptive marketing practices, and so helped to stem their incidence.[86]

By the early twentieth century, the federal government had built up a corps of career inspectors, special agents, and attorneys who had spent years, and in several instances decades, investigating postal frauds. This experience conveyed a wealth of knowledge about the pivotal figures among the nation's duplicitous mail-order enterprises and their most effective tactics. Congress periodically furnished these officials with additional enforcement tools. In 1890, it prohibited the mailing of any promotional materials related to lotteries, gave postal inspectors the authority to arrest suspects without warrants, and permitted prosecution of mail fraud where its perpetrators sent mail, as well as where it originated. An 1895 statute gave the postmaster general power to bar firms from sending or receiving mail, whether registered or not, and also outlawed the sending of illicit materials by express.[87] Together, the cultivation of a seasoned inspectorate and extensions of regulatory authority allowed the Post Office to mount nationwide campaigns against prevalent business frauds. These crackdowns targeted fraudulent bond investment schemes in the 1890s, quack medical treatments early in the new century, and bogus Texas and California oil companies in the 1910s and 1920s. Each of these operations closed down scores of firms and resulted in high-profile convictions, despite the still-daunting obstacles that faced fraud prosecutions.[88]

The Post Office's assault against deceptive marketing extended well beyond efforts to bar swindling firms from the mails or to deter misrepresentation through criminal actions. In addition to deploying coercive power, postal officials sought to forestall frauds through public education. One key policy targeted the nation's corps of postmasters. Swindlers had long recognized the pivotal role that postmasters played in the national circulation of goods and ideas, and so often solicited their assistance in marketing schemes.[89] After the Civil War, officials in Washington sought to keep pace with duplicitous mail-order firms. They distributed circulars so that postmasters might in turn alert their customers, in the case of one 1866 handbill, to "TAKE WARNING! Beware of Jewelry and Lottery Swindlers!" To keep track of peripatetic miscreants, the Department maintained a running list of those accused of mail fraud, which it published, along with aliases and descriptions of schemes, in its monthly *Postal*

Guide. In addition, officials fired several "colluding postmasters" who abetted business frauds.[90]

Not content with internal audiences, postal officials jumped into the extensive public discourse about business fraud. No individual took on this task with more gusto than Anthony Comstock. In addition to publishing *Frauds Exposed* (1880), a book that chronicled the depredations of mail-order swindlers and valorized his ongoing struggles against them, Comstock cultivated close relationships with journalists and editors close to the Republican Party and the Protestant establishment. These connections allowed him to place dozens of magazine articles about his crusades against fraud and obscenity, and to attract hundreds of newspaper accounts of his work as a postal inspector.[91]

The close nexus between postal officials and the print media further transformed enforcement actions into means of public education, as the issuance of fraud orders or the filing of criminal charges triggered extensive news coverage of duplicitous business practices. In the first two decades of the mail fraud law, the press focused on large-scale cases, such as those against the Louisiana Lottery or the Fund W scheme. By the 1890s, an accelerating tempo of mail fraud actions was matched by more systematic appearance of journalistic accounts, which in turn stimulated popular awareness of the Post Office as a regulatory minder of commercial speech. Waxing popular consciousness in turn generated more lodged grievances against mail-order firms, from working-class urban neighborhoods and rural homesteads alike. Comstock had encouraged such communication in *Frauds Exposed*, pleading with "every reader" of the volume "to co-operate, by sending any knowledge or information in the shape of circulars, or otherwise, of any scheme to rob or defraud the people." The nation's editors echoed this call, redirecting fraud inquiries to postal officials. Thus, in 1904, *The Youth's Companion* pleaded with its hundreds of thousands of subscribers "to call the attention" of local postmasters to any "fraudulent schemes afloat," and to suggest that the postmasters notify superiors in Washington. "To do this in every suspicious case," the magazine explained, "is a duty which every honest man owes to his neighbor as well as to himself."[92] These appeals mirrored the calls for coordinated vigilance against deception made by trade journal and newspaper editors such as Friend Root, but now instructed the country's neighborly sentinels to direct their information to the public monitors of the mail service.

Thousands of Americans heeded this advice. Some wrote to the Post Office Department to inquire about the legality of a particular business's methods, much as they had sought out the advice of trusted magazine editors. Others sent in evidence of what they viewed as deceptive marketing, usually to ask for

Figure 5.1: The Post Office Department as "guardian angel" to the "easy." *Harper's Weekly*, Jun. 10, 1911, courtesy of David M. Rubenstein Rare Book & Manuscript Library, Duke University.

assistance in obtaining refunds and occasionally to demand that the Post Office pursue enforcement actions. On the eve of World War I, the federal government received over thirty thousand inquiries and allegations annually.[93] This torrent of grievances testifies to the expanding sense of rights consciousness among Americans, as well as the tendency to look to the federal government as guarantor of those rights. A 1911 illustration in *Harper's Weekly* (Figure 5.1) captured the growing inclination of American investors and consumers to look to the Post Office for redress. Pictured in the center of the illustration is an upstanding postman, in rigidly starched attire, with an angel's wings. Behind him, held back by a strong left arm, are four disgruntled citizens leaning forward with either imploring hands or clenched fists—a prim middle-class woman, perhaps a schoolteacher; a farmer, maybe the victim of a patent right scheme; an elderly gentlemen with a handkerchief falling loosely out of his pocket, as if it had been picked; and an elderly woman clutching a bankbook, emblematic of devastating losses. In front of the guardian postman, ignoring the plea of his stiffly bent right arm, are four grasping swindlers, one holding up a patent medicine bottle, another a "Get Rich Quick" circular, a rotund businessman holding firmly to a "no doubt dubious stock certificate," and a fourth pitchman of some indeterminate scheme.

American postal regulation of commercial speech had its origins not in such acts of social protection, but rather in institutional self-defense. The Post Office took on this task because its officials wished to safeguard their own reputations from the lies of deceptive mail-order businesses. This impulse remained a leading regulatory motivation for many years. In 1883, the *New York Times* could insist that because Americans were "not living under a paternal Government," the object of mail fraud enforcement "is not so much to protect the people as it is to protect the mail service." As late as 1890, postmaster general John Wanamaker pleaded for tougher legislation against lotteries on the grounds that the flouting of existing rules by the Louisiana Lottery had "humiliated" and "demoraliz[ed]" his department.[94]

With the injection of Protestant moralism into the department by Anthony Comstock and his fellow special agents, and the greater incidence of public requests for fraud investigations, the rationale behind mail fraud policy more commonly referenced harms to consumers and investors. In *Frauds Exposed*, Comstock evinced concern for those "honest and simple-minded persons" duped by "the multitudinous schemes and devices of the sharper"—the "verdant" Americans who were taken in by green goods men, unscrupulous danglers of nonexistent commercial agencies, and pitchmen for worthless patent medicines and bogus investments. Six years later, another long-time postal inspector described the department's antifraud work as a reflection of "paternal solicitude . . . to protect the ignorant, the weak, and the unwary from the wolves who stand ready to devour them."[95] By the early twentieth century, this perspective suffused official pronouncements about mail fraud. As Woodrow Wilson settled into the White House, the Post Office Department's solicitor proclaimed that "the old rule of *caveat emptor* cannot apply to mail-order sales." Given the way that "the conditions of business in this country have been revolutionized," with "sales being made at a great distance from the purchaser," the state had to embrace its role as policeman of national commercial speech. Such talk percolated down the ranks. One of the Post Office's pivotal duties, the superintendent of the mails at Trenton, New Jersey, explained in a May 1914 newspaper article, was to "protect the public from itself," to safeguard "the people from the temptation to become a victim of fraud."[96]

****

The Post Office's expansive endeavors against mail fraud, such as the state inspection regimes and the legislative moves against duplicitous corporate reporting, gained an institutional footing during an era in which American courts cast a skeptical eye on many regulatory endeavors. Drawing on aversion to legislatively bestowed economic privileges that dated back to the Jacksonian period, late nineteenth-century American judges struck down numerous exercises of regulatory authority that they characterized as "class legislation." If litigants could show that the intended purpose of a regulatory policy was to benefit narrow interests, and that it imposed burdens on firms engaging in interstate commerce, federal judges would often void the legislation as unconstitutional.[97] Sometimes regulation that proponents depicted as antideception measures ran afoul of this standard. Licensing requirements aimed at out-of-state salesmen, for example, tended to raise judicial hackles, even if they tar-geted fly-by-night commercial sharks. Thus federal courts struck down Min-nesota and Alabama laws that required the licensing of agents for out-of-state tree nurseries, despite a clear pattern of misrepresentations and outright fraud, because they did not impose the same standard for local agents.[98]

American judges, however, proved to be at least as respectful of regulatory efforts to curb business fraud as they were of most exercises of police power on behalf of public health, public safety, or communal morals. Despite many legal challenges, the federal judiciary upheld the constitutionality of administrative mail fraud proceedings and almost always rejected challenges to criminal mail fraud convictions.[99] State grain grading, fertilizer inspection, and life insurance regulation similarly passed constitutional muster. So too did statutes that pro-hibited the sale of oleomargarine colored to resemble butter, antiadulteration laws that targeted compromised medicines and swill milk, and occupational licensing laws that claimed to protect American society from quacks, pettifog-gers, and other unqualified riffraff masquerading as professionals. The courts accepted arguments that endemic duplicity threatened the confidence that floated so much commercial activity. As a result, judges held that the public interest in fostering honesty in economic transactions gave a wide berth of ac-tion to legislatures, including the delegation of rule-making and enforcement powers to administrative agencies.[100]

Postbellum courts manifested the same concerns in trademark enforce-ment. The basic structure for its regulation was set, like mail fraud's, by a Reconstruction-era congressional statute. Rather than looking to a bureau-cratic mode of enforcement, however, the Trademark Act of 1870 created a means for businesses to sue infringing competitors in the federal courts. Over the following four decades, the enterprises with national brands that sought to protect their marks found sympathetic ears on the federal bench. In fashioning a conceptual framework for trademark cases, federal judges carved out a sig-nificant exception from the norms of *caveat emptor*. When it came to deciding whether competitors had closely mimicked the names or packaging of Pills-bury Flour or Dr. C. MacLean's Celebrated Liver Pills, the courts did not pre-sume that consumers were careful or discerning. Instead, they treated them as "unwary purchasers"—often harried, distractible, inclined to rely on quick ap-praisals of how an item appeared on the store shelf, and so liable to make er-rors when they made choices on the basis of brand preferences. This approach did not guarantee victories for plaintiffs. Judges sometimes ruled that the de-gree of similarity between names or logos did not justify damage awards, be-cause they did not believe that ordinary purchasers would be led astray. But trademark law remained hospitable terrain for business complaints against imitators.[101]

As with other nineteenth-century legal exceptions to the precepts of *caveat emptor*, the intellectual assumptions guiding trademark law reflected judicial prejudices about social types. The familial arbiters of urban consumption by the 1880s and 1890s tended to be women, a group of economic actors whom judges viewed as requiring paternalistic assistance. Yet the character of litigants mattered at least as much. Many federal judges were disposed to respect the large-scale businesses that filed trademark actions. These companies, like the Chicago meatpackers whose lawsuits upended local regulatory statutes requiring local inspection of live beef, also hired top legal talent who developed compelling legal strategies and pursued them through a series of cases.[102]

Judicial deference accorded to antifraud initiatives gave state and federal bureaucrats room to construct expansive policies during the five decades following the Civil War. The result was not a single cohesive plan for responding to economic deceit, but rather a diverse set of institutional strategies, each tailored to the dilemmas of specific markets, each shaped by the ambitions and ideologies of key regulatory protagonists. With army contracting, grain grading, fertilizer inspection, and reporting requirements for insurance companies and the sale of corporate securities, the goal was improved information disclosure. Purchasers of these goods and financial instruments demanded disinterested assessments of quality, which a growing number of Americans believed could only occur through the auspices of the state. With mail fraud, officials placed an administrative turnstile in front of the country's primary channel of communications, allowing them to block access to those firms and individuals whose business practices sullied the Post Office's reputation and threatened public morals.

In all of these regulatory contexts, the architects of antifraud policies paid close attention to mechanisms of coercion, defining new crimes and administrative penalties and building up enforcement mechanisms. But their most far-reaching impacts turned as much on redirecting social norms as on fashioning credible shows of regulatory force. The regulations that sought to constrain commercial misrepresentations entailed the fashioning of new standards—for the quality of grain and fertilizers, or the obligations that mining and life insurance companies had to investors and policyholders, or the limits of acceptable puffery in mail-order marketing. This process built on informal regulatory communities already established through the nation's print culture. State and federal regulators looked to the press to spread the news of rule-making and enforcement actions, an expectation generally met by the trade journals and newspapers with fraud beats. Many regulators replicated the relationships that fraud-fighting editors had forged with subscribers, soliciting intelligence about business frauds and emphasizing public education. These endeavors solidified the legitimacy of antifraud regimes, strengthening the position of officials now charged with policing the line between forceful salesmanship and shameless imposition, and reinforcing social mores against rank duplicity.

Appeals to individual self-reliance did not disappear in the face of this co-ordinated assault on commercial tricksters. Among American sharpers, this sensibility remained commonplace. One young mail-order entrepreneur who ran afoul of the new postal law a few years after its passage typified this defiant stance. This twenty-two-year-old widely advertised the sale of a "low priced seven-shooter" made possible by economies of scale in manufacturing, but then filled orders with cheap popguns. Upon being confronted by a postal inspector, the young promoter explained that he had "read Barnum's life, and accepted the doctrine that the American people like to be humbugged." Observing that his ads had said nothing about supplying an actual firearm, he insisted that "if anybody is green enough to suppose I meant a revolver, that's his lookout."[103] The question of how to demarcate the boundaries of business fraud continued to be a vexing problem, nowhere more so than with regard to innovative firms that operated on untested commercial ground, and that shared the young popgun seller's aggressiveness in marketing.

CHAPTER SIX

Innovation, Moral Economy, and the Postmaster General's Peace

The new regime of mail fraud regulation ensnared hundreds of American businesses a year by the 1890s, including, as the opening passage of this book noted, Richard W. Sears. It is now time to return to his run-in with the Post Office, which extended from December 1894 into the summer of 1896. The episode constitutes more than a colorful addendum to Sears's already iconic entrepreneurial biography: it reveals complex connections between entrepreneurial innovation and sociolegal understandings of fraud. As such, it provides a crucial angle of vision on the dynamics of fraud enforcement as policymakers fashioned new tools to target commercial and financial cheats.

Sears played a crucial role in transforming the world of American consumption, along with several other innovative retailers—department-store moguls such as Macy, Fields, and Wanamaker; the creators of discount stores such as Woolworth and Kress; the entrepreneurs who applied the logic of the chain store to supermarkets and pharmacies, such as Michael Cullen and Charles Walgreen; consumer goods manufacturers such as H. J. Heinz and James B. Duke; and advertising executives such as J. Walter Thompson. Over several decades, these businessmen and scores of managers in their companies focused collectively on realizing efficiencies, whether through cutting out middlemen, adopting new technologies that would enhance productivity, or achieving economies of scale and scope. Even more importantly, they recognized the latent consumer demand created by America's demographic growth. Their marketing practices helped to forge the mass consumption that became a defining characteristic of American life. In the process, this interlocking directorate of marketing innovations swept away older methods of distribution, traditional lifestyles, and a great many firms stuck in old ways of doing business.[1]

This chapter juxtaposes Sears and the mail-order behemoth he founded with a different and mostly far less well-known cast of entrepreneurial characters from the late nineteenth and early twentieth centuries. These individuals include Modelle Miller, a young woman from New Carlisle, Indiana, who owned a company that manufactured cosmetics and herbal remedies and sold them through a far-flung network of female sales agents; A. S. Burrell, a Marshalltown, Iowa, publisher who created an early debt-collection and consumer credit rating agency; Edward Gardner Lewis, a publisher, sometimes-banker, and real-estate developer, based initially in St. Louis and then in Atascadero, California; George Graham Rice, a controversial stock promoter who helped to democratize America's securities markets in the first few decades of the twentieth century, primarily from a base in New York City; B. H. Lambert of Louisville, Kentucky, who joined the stampede of American capitalists into the early automobile industry; Madame C. J. Walker, the creator of numerous successful beauty products and services for African American women; J. Overton Paine, a New York City investment analyst and tipster who helped to create the nascent field of economic forecasting; and Charles H. Young, a Korean immigrant who settled in Chicago and developed a wholesale trade in secondhand clothing, particularly for the African American market in the South. Like Sears, this cast of business owners pushed the boundaries of commercial practice, envisioning new markets and developing novel ways to transact business. Like Sears—and so many other American entrepreneurs before and since—they exuded confidence and readily broadcast optimistic puffery. Like Sears, they created businesses that depended on the postal system to distribute their marketing pitches and deliver goods or services. Like Sears, and thousands of other American firms between 1890 and 1930, they ran afoul of the nation's postal inspectors and confronted administrative fraud proceedings.

Most firms that attracted such scrutiny either ran prohibited lotteries or pursued out-and-out swindles with varying degrees of sophistication. When the proprietors of such enterprises received notice of pending or actual fraud orders, they typically closed up shop, though often only to change location and business name before relaunching similar schemes. By contrast, the subjects of this chapter—all either manufacturers or distributors of consumer goods, or providers of financial services—occupied more contested legal ground. In the eyes of some Americans and key postal officials, they overstepped the boundary between permissible hyperbole and prohibited charade. And yet, they pursued innovative business strategies and offered novel goods or services that eventually percolated into the commercial mainstream, while engaging in a style of commercial communication not unlike that of many competitors.

The encounters that these various firms had with the postal fraud order suggest the profound challenge that capitalist innovation offers to prevailing conceptions of commercial morality. Entrepreneurial experimentation raised new kinds of ethical and legal dilemmas for which entrenched standards of economic behavior offered only ambiguous answers. This pattern emerged far earlier than the late nineteenth century, and has hardly been confined to the United States. Nonetheless, American fraud order cases bring the conundrums that innovation posed for the definition of business fraud into especially clear view, at a time when the principles of *caveat emptor* confronted powerful new critiques.

Those cases further indicate that the federal government's treatment of entrepreneurial firms remained highly contingent, dependent on legal savvy, the ability to mobilize networks of social and political capital to vouch for integrity, and the extent of perceived threats to entrenched and politically influential interests. In this realm of economic regulation, the American state retained a form of process that strikingly mirrored centuries-old mechanisms of keeping the peace, in which legal outcomes were structured by informal modes of investigation and personal methods of weighing reputation.

Sears, Roebuck at the Bar of the Post Office

Richard Sears's enterprise ran afoul of the Post Office because of its promotions—chiefly offers of prizes to the first group of customers who ordered merchandise from a particular state, or to the first one hundred correspondents who furnished advice about how to reach customers in their neighborhoods. The surviving records of the mail fraud investigations into Sears, Roebuck do not indicate who initially complained to the government about these overtures. But one can get a sense of the communications that provoked concern from a May 29, 1894, mass letter that went out to previous customers, seeking to elicit interest in a deal on shoes. "We believe if we can induce you to read this circular," the handwritten missive predicted,

> you will favor us with an order at once. True, you may not get the $500.00 piano or even a $50.00 gold watch, yet considering the small number of these offers we are sending out, you ought at least to be in time for a gold watch if you answer at once. But, in case you do not get the piano, or a watch, you are sure to get some nice present. *And* the shoes we send you at $2.75 are worth nearly three times the price asked. If you will fill out the enclosed order blank and send it to us at once, with $2.75, for a pair of shoes described, we will see that you get a nice present, and if first, the piano; if not first of all, but first from your state, a $50.00 gold watch.[2]

Premiums of this ilk struck turn-of-the-century Midwestern postal inspectors and their superiors in Washington as thinly disguised, inherently deceptive lotteries. Having dealt serious blows to big gambling concerns, postal officials did not wish to see popular demand for games of chance receive new outlets. This way of thinking generated the fraud order against Sears, Roebuck.[3]

Flirting with prohibited lotteries, however, was not the only complaint that postal authorities received about Sears's business. In the months that followed the original fraud order, customers forwarded several additional grievances, mostly from small rural towns such as Eskridge, Kansas, and Pegram, Mississippi. Sears, Roebuck, these individuals alleged, had engaged in classic bait and switch tactics, promising merchandise of a given quality, such as a fourteen-carat gold chain, and delivering something decidedly inferior; or it had failed to send already paid-for goods. As one Maine complainant put it, the mail-order firm was a "Nest of Swindlers," deserving of "prompt Steps to prevent them from using the U. S. Mails to Defraud People."[4]

Given Sears, Roebuck's business practices throughout the late 1880s and 1890s, one might have expected a deeper range of accusations. The mail-order house characterized its wares as "the best in the world" and frequently engaged in Barnum-like come-ons, such as an 1889 newspaper advertisement that offered, for a limited time, a sofa and pair of chairs for only ninety-five cents. Although the ad included the word "miniature" in tiny print, there was no explanation that Sears meant only doll furniture. Illustrations in the firm's ads often implied that pictured items were available at extremely low prices, when those sums rather constituted down payments or only fetched models of lesser quality. Sears slipped endorsements from the "Editor" into the text of his print advertisements. The firm sometimes shipped unsolicited goods to businessmen around the Midwest, priced at intentionally high figures, and then responded to refusals of delivery by trying to convince railroad-station managers or express agents to take over the goods, selling them at steep discounts from inflated initial prices. Beginning in 1896, Sears, Roebuck also aggressively marketed patent medicines and health devices on the basis of unsubstantiated claims about efficacy. In addition, the company filled orders with substitutions whenever heavy demand for items swamped the firm's inventory.[5]

Nonetheless, it would have been hard in the 1890s to substantiate characterization of Sears, Roebuck as nothing but "a nest of Swindlers," no different from the worst fly-by-nighters preying on the credulous. The firm boasted tens of thousands of satisfied customers, all of whom could inspect goods before accepting delivery; it furnished guarantees of customer satisfaction backed up by a generous return policy; it often took advantage of economies of scale and speed to sell at prices well below its competition; it enjoyed the support of leading Chicago banks and dozens of Midwestern manufacturers. All of these features militated against complaints by customers who felt misled by the company's more extravagant pitches. Any charge of fraud against Sears, Roebuck remained open to question.[6]

Richard Sears wasted little time in presenting such arguments to federal authorities. Within hours of learning about the fraud order, he boarded a train to Washington, DC, where he met with postal officials to inform them about his business and challenge the exclusion from the mails. Sears pledged to halt all objectionable promotions and pleaded for notice of any future complaints, so that the firm might rectify identified problems. On the basis of these promises, the Post Office Department suspended its order on December 22, just eleven days after it had gone into effect.[7] For the next year and a half, though, postal inspectors kept close tabs on the firm, assessing how it responded to customer complaints. Sears personally handled these matters to demonstrate that his business had cleaned up its act.

Like all mail-order retailers, Sears, Roebuck faced the challenge of how to take advantage of railroad expansion and the dramatic decline in manufacturing costs resulting from industrialization. Like his competitors, Sears embraced contradictory commercial strategies. Drawing the attention of as many rural Americans as possible was essential, even if doing so sometimes required a healthy dose of "huckstering," but so too was building a reputation for trustworthiness. As the country's commercial mores shifted around the turn of the century, and as the goal of fostering repeat business overtook the imperative of finding new customers, the company toned down its carnival barking. Instead, it opted for a more consistently straitlaced approach to advertising in catalogues and newspapers alike, a shift ratified by Sears's retirement from managerial duties in 1908. In light of this progression, the significance of the mail fraud case would lie primarily as a powerful nudge toward that strategic shift, much like the adoption of stronger federal regulation of food and drugs, which led the company first to offer a disclaimer that it did not warrant that its patent medicines would achieve results promised by manufacturers, and then to discontinue that line altogether in 1913.[8]

This way of framing the mail fraud investigation against Sears, Roebuck has much to be said for it. But it also misses some crucial dimensions of the incident, which involve enduring linkages between processes of business innovation and the emergence of fraud. To appreciate these connections, we need to take a bit of a detour onto the ground of entrepreneurial experimentation and its implications for both outright swindling and the inclination of businesses to bend commercial truths.

Innovation, Puffing, and Moral Ambiguity

The ideas of the Austrian political economist Joseph Schumpeter offer a useful point of departure. For Schumpeter, capitalist societies were defined by the leeway they furnished to entrepreneurs, a small subset of the business owners and corporate managers who attempted to maximize profits. Most members of the business class, Schumpeter argued, were traditionalists, conservative in outlook and drawn to tried-and-true methods, however much they might strive for pecuniary gain or pursue speculative gambles. Even in the most dynamic capitalist societies, small-scale proprietors and executives typically desired rents—predictable flows of income from stable structures of production and distribution. They shared the mindset of Adam Smith's "people of the same trade" who "seldom meet together, even for merriment and diversion, but the conversation ends in a conspiracy against the public, or in some contrivance to raise prices."[9]

By contrast, Schumpeter contended, entrepreneurs viewed prevailing markets, commercial networks, and economic institutions as stale and ripe for transformation. These venturesome souls envisioned untapped markets, novel products or services, new ways of organizing business activity. Then, often with obsessive focus, they set about trying to make that imagined reality come to pass, an endeavor that depended on access to significant investment capital. Entrepreneurs sought to rip up prevailing economic cultures and fashion new ones on the broken foundations of the old, a process that Schumpeter called "creative destruction." This analytical framework has great salience for the historical study of American business fraud.[10]

Creativity in the worlds of manufacturing, commerce, and services has repeatedly furnished swindlers with novel businesses and commercial practices to emulate. Deceit in business has a distribution across the sectors that make up a society's economy. Because misrepresentation and organizational fraud constitute illicit practices, there is no way to calculate this distribution with precision. No government has conducted a decennial census of marketing distortions and unambiguous swindling. But scrutiny from the media and officials charged with law enforcement offers clues, indicating that duplicitous business practices have disproportionately characterized economic sectors at the forefront of economic change. Modern processes of innovation attract schemes and scams.

Investment swindles stand out in this regard. When Americans have staked out some new terrain of economic activity, phony offerings have sprung up alongside legitimate enterprises. The early Republic's relentless efforts to open

Western lands to settlement spawned endemic land frauds, just as the era's fervor for banking encouraged the creation of grossly undercapitalized wildcat banks. Mining and oil booms were notorious for attracting spurious ventures, from the goldfields of California and the Petrolia of western Pennsylvania onward. The emergence of transformative technologies has invariably generated bogus startups seeking to skim off some proportion of capital made available by the investing public.[11] Business opportunity scams have tracked commercial innovations just as much as schemes predicated on worthless securities, which in the mid-nineteenth century mostly involved sham agencies to sell patented manufactured goods.[12]

Deception in goods markets similarly tracked fundamental economic transformations. As soon as New York City importers fashioned an auction system to disburse a post–War of 1812 glut of British imports, for example, buyers had to contend with the "mock auctions" run by the likes of Zeno Burnham.[13] The development of breakthrough financial services elicited parallel frauds. As life and fire insurance companies gained footholds in antebellum America, they confronted phony competitors.[14] Around the turn of the twentieth century, Americans had to cope with fake deposit insurance for banks, pretend patent agents, and firms that masqueraded as investment banks, falsely promising to assist small firms with incorporation and the raising of capital on public securities markets.[15]

Several aspects of business innovation made it a magnet for hucksterism and swindling. Novel goods or ways of doing business attracted public interest from consumers and business owners, at least once initial prototypes seemed to deliver on early promises. The ethos of "Go-Aheadism" within the broad middle class encouraged an optimistic equation of invention and entrepreneurial initiative with social improvement and individual opportunity. An accelerating pace of scientific and technological invention, moreover, intensified popular expectations that fabulous new means of consumption and investment would regularly present themselves. American investors have also long recognized that the most spectacular returns have accrued to enterprises that exploited some new geographic or technological frontier. At the same time, new markets, products, or business practices almost always created marked asymmetries in information, a crucial prerequisite for most strategies of economic deceit. Almost by definition, novel commercial terrain lacked familiarity to many economic actors.

The career of the Arctic Refrigerating Company, a firm based in Cincinnati during the late 1890s, illustrates how fascination with technological progress created tempting incentives for deception. Touting a new system for household refrigeration, Arctic recruited selling agents through nationwide ads. Boasting hundreds of testimonials from its far-flung sales force, the company "guaranteed" that its "Cooling Refrigerators," which supposedly made use of a secret chemical compound, were "indestructible," "75% cheaper than ice," and able to "keep perishable articles indefinitely."[16] Such claims did not hold up to scrutiny, such as that undertaken by the son of a man who had paid for an exclusive Arctic Refrigerating agency in northeastern Texas. After traveling to Cincinnati, the son reported to his father that the firm was an obvious fake, with a tiny headquarters, no listing with major credit reporting firms, and office staff who refused to demonstrate the product. Eventually, the US Department of Agriculture's Bureau of Chemistry confirmed this assessment, establishing that the "secret compound" was actually Glauber's Salts, which alchemists had used for centuries in the attempt to turn base metals into gold. Rather than extending the life of ice, Arctic Refrigerating's product actually accelerated melting. And yet scores of Americans eagerly responded to the firm's circulars, snapping up exclusive selling territories.[17]

Arctic's grandiose promises resonated so widely because of the tremendous allure of refrigeration. From the 1870s onward, a phalanx of tinkerers in the United States and elsewhere experimented with ways to manufacture the cold. Hardly a season went by without news stories that marveled at an inventor's new process or a company's exploits in keeping perishable products fresh.[18] By 1898, tens of thousands of Americans knew that firms were refining techniques for refrigeration through novel uses of chemical substances, such as pressurized liquid ammonia. Detailed grasp of the underlying science, however, was far less common. This gap between popular enthusiasm and technical comprehension gave Arctic Refrigerating room to play fast and loose with the truth.

Economic deceit has thrived on America's entrepreneurial margin because businesses such as Arctic Refrigerating did not hesitate to exploit limited familiarity with new products and services. Indeed, the savviest practitioners of misrepresentation have shifted from scheme to scheme in tune with the latest developments in the American marketplace, sometimes over decades. The career of Charles H. Unverzagt exemplifies this chameleonic capacity. Unverzagt, whose last name appropriately means "unabashed" in German, danced his way across the US financial scene from the early 1880s into the 1920s, organizing a bewildering series of shady insurance, loan, and investment vehicles that left behind a trail of disgruntled investors. Operating from Baltimore, Chicago, and then New York, his first schemes took advantage of interest in new insurance products such as tontines and whole life. By the 1890s he was creating complex firms that mimicked building and loan societies. Over the subsequent decade and a half, he rode the upward trajectory of mining booms, especially in British Columbia. After gaining control of companies such as the Great Cariboo Gold Mining Corporation, he churned out circulars that falsely asserted that the Canadian government had certified the promising nature of his mines. He also offered investors the chance to buy "gold futures" that would furnish fabulous returns just as soon as he had sufficient working capital to realize the potential of his mining claims.[19]

Regardless of whether the concocters of deceitful commercial strategies hewed so closely to novel industries and products, they were typically among the first Americans to appreciate the transformative implications of new communications technologies. This pattern has proven especially strong within the realm of financial fraud. In the postbellum decades, for instance, the peddlers of spurious stock offerings and the proprietors of bucket shops latched onto the telegraph and the stock ticker as essential tools for hoodwinking investors. The former offered a means of spreading rumors and imploring potential investors to act before market prices moved away from them; the latter facilitated market manipulation by rapidly transmitting engineered price movements, a key element in the creation of market momentum that allowed insiders either to dump assets or buy them on the cheap.[20] In the 1910s and 1920s, the marketers of Texas or California oil leases quickly sensed the power of moving pictures, commissioning films that showcased the oil fields as part of high-pressure sales presentations.[21]

The Unverzagts of the American business world gravitated toward the newest developments in consumption, investment, or finance because such contexts offered the most favorable conditions for imposture. Similar calculations drove less nimble merchants of deceit as they latched onto the latest mechanisms for reaching potential customers, clients, and investors. Herein lies a further explanation for the continual reappearance of so many standard forms of deception, such as the pump and dump investment scheme, or some marketing version of the bait and switch. As journalist Edward Smith pointed out in his 1923 Confessions of a Confidence Man, "every development of civilization, every social change, every notable invention brings to life a fresh manner of parting the sucker and his money. It may be and usually is only a disguised evolution of an older swindle, but it is new to the victim and therefore effective."[22]

Edward Smith's reflection about the tendency of business fraud to target commercial environments undergoing rapid change presupposed a distinct line between legitimate and duplicitous marketing practices. Indeed, the examples in his Confessions represented clear-cut, intentional efforts at fraud, the kind that could plausibly convince a nineteenth-century jury to agree on a guilty verdict. But the uncertainties associated with new fields of economic endeavor complicated the already often-tangled question of how to distinguish commercial dishonesty from enthusiastic promotion or misjudged optimism.

Young firms attempting to construct a viable business on the outer fringes of economic change confronted a host of uncertainties—about the course of technological innovation, the evolution of consumer tastes, the effectiveness of marketing strategies, and modes of managerial coordination. Because they operated in an economic sector widely perceived as having enormous potential, they almost always had significant entrepreneurial company. Thus, even though firms in immature markets did not have to worry about an entrenched set of leading companies, they nonetheless faced stiff competition and a lack of clarity about the strategies that would yield profits. Entrepreneurs developing new business models have often had to feel their way, looking for sales pitches that appeal to would-be customers and assessing which product lines or marketing tactics find favor. And because their firms started with constrained capital resources and access to credit, they had only limited time to achieve profitability.

Such circumstances encouraged entrepreneurs to push the bounds of their claims, whether about the advantageous nature of their services, the quality of their wares, or anticipated returns for investors. This tendency dovetailed with the psychological profile of American entrepreneurship. The proprietors of nineteenth- and early twentieth-century startups rarely lacked for self-belief, especially when staking out ground on new commercial terrain. Behavioral economists would be inclined to characterize these risk-takers as prone to overconfidence—a common predisposition to overrate one's capacities—and so inclined to presume that even though the great majority of business ventures failed, theirs would prosper.[23] Certainly, novel business sectors in the United States have never lacked for sanguine individuals willing to try their commercial luck with other people's capital.

One can see this dynamic in the early history of Richard Sears's domain, mail-order marketing. American firms had done at least some of their business by mail as far back as the eighteenth century. But this method of distribution only began to achieve a significant foothold with the dramatic postbellum expansion of the national rail network, and only boomed after the 1890s, when the Post Office slashed first the cost of mailing catalogues, and then the charges for delivering goods to rural households.[24] Prospective mail-order firms could now envisage truly national markets for their goods. To tap the potential mass market, however, they had to worm their way into the consciousness of far-flung consumers, even as the advertisements of thousands of other businesses clamored for attention.

This challenge prompted all sorts of hullabaloo. Like Sears, Roebuck, mail-order businesses across the country offered free or heavily discounted merchandise to readers who distributed promotional material or who sold items to their friends and neighbors. These firms similarly offered the chance to win prizes and paid for testimonials and editorial squibs that touted extraordinary discounts, without disclosing the financial relationship that accounted for the endorsements. Their catalogues included deceptive illustrations and made fantastic claims for available goods, including false assertions that the low price of loss leaders resulted from savings associated with bulk purchasing.[25] Even relatively well-capitalized newcomers to the mail-order trade, such as the Chicago furniture company Spiegel House Furnishings, exhibited a penchant for exaggeration. Spiegel's early twentieth-century catalogues falsely boasted of millions of dollars in capital, factories of its own, an ability to compel suppliers to cut prices because of gargantuan buying power, and possession of "twenty-five mammoth stores in the principal cities of the United States." As the firm branched out into new product lines, its communications to customers invented jousting matches with monopolies such as the "Watch Trust," all to convey the impression of a firm committed to the people's interests.[26] The notoriety of deceptive marketing by mail-order firms led one early twentieth-century legal guide to comment that "the various offers which have converted advertising into means of fraud are past all reckoning, and it is quite beyond the purview of this volume to give illustrations of questionable announcements in the mail-order field alone."[27] The unequivocal falsehoods were mingled with half-truths, exaggerations, and other forms of puffery. In the struggle to become early movers amid American's transition to a thoroughly integrated consumer society, almost every mail-order businesses engaged in some misrepresentations.

This reality reflects a more general relationship between highly competitive economic environments and reliance on deceptive marketing practices. The exaggerated boosting of mining areas, oil regions, and new agricultural ventures in places such as Arizona and Florida, for example, reflected efforts to stand out with international investors who had many options. Imported capital paid not only for the sinking of shafts and wells, the digging of desert canals, and the planting of groves, but also real-estate development in nearby towns and transportation infrastructure that linked them to outside markets. Many Westerners had no problem with the distortions and barefaced falsehoods broadcast by promoters, so long as they slaked voracious local thirst for capital. Views might change once the sour taste of fraudulent bankruptcies lodged in distant investment markets, whether in San Francisco, New York, or Antwerp. But amid the heady days of prospecting and town-founding, local residents saw little harm in truth-stretching or even far more cynical promotional falsehoods.[28]

In sectors characterized by numerous players and a lack of mutualism, such as the early twentieth-century apparel industry, the willingness of some firms to embrace deceptive strategies made it difficult for others to eschew such tactics. Facing intense competition, metropolitan clothing retailers regularly made false claims about the fiber content of their apparel and adopted misleading trade names for furs.[29] In such environments, there was a Gresham's Law of marketing, as misdirection and deceit displaced candor.[30]

At an even more fundamental level, processes of commercial and financial innovation could throw into question what counted as duplicity. The fashioning of new products and the development of novel marketing practices and accounting techniques often generated methods that struck many constituencies as unacceptably deceptive. In at least some cases, the resulting finger-pointing came to look like the foolish, unimaginative, or self-serving conservatism that frequently accompanies the emergence of disruptive economic innovation. One can see such an example from the early years of the US mail-order industry. In the fall of 1873, the *Chicago Tribune*, its editor perhaps egged on by concerned rural retailers, perhaps irked by a dearth of advertising placements, printed a stern caution about Montgomery, Ward & Co, which would soon become the largest retailer in the United States. This business, the *Tribune* confidently explained, was obviously a "swindling firm," for no business could sell such a broad range of goods at such low prices. Such false accusations (which the *Tribune* soon retracted, prodded by threats of a libel suit) could muddy popular thinking about commercial deceit.[31]

Sometimes, moreover, prevailing legal rules and business customs furnished few guidelines about the permissibility of novel business practices. One can get a sense of this ambiguity by considering debates set off by the accounting strategies of Gilded Age railroads. In addition to amassing unprecedented agglomerations of capital and fixed assets, railway corporations assembled complex financial structures that intermingled mortgage bonds with equity. Their managers had to devise ways of accounting for the depreciation of equipment, the differences between fixed costs and working capital, and the projections of revenues from dispersed operations. The creation of regional systems through mergers and integration of branch lines raised additional perplexities about how to relate the assets, liabilities, and income of subsidiaries to those of the main line. Finally, railroads faced the task of communicating convoluted financial positions to stock- and bond-holders, as well as potential investors across North America and northwestern Europe.[32] For several decades, railroad managers encountered few clear-cut rules about how they should go about such tasks, beyond the insistence of the commercial press and European holders of American securities that they owed investors detailed, audited financial accountings.[33]

Railroad insiders possessed huge informational advantages in this environment, which many exploited, often through strategies of deception. Highly profitable lines sometimes characterized construction costs as recurrent expenses, so as to fend off pressures for rate cuts by reducing apparent profits; at other junctures, they inflated expenses to justify lower dividends, or held back word about a special dividend so that insiders might first buy up shares cheaply. Struggling railroads assigned operating costs to the construction account, so as to disguise ongoing financial difficulties. When managers wished to buttress bond and share prices despite a lack of profitability, they might withhold data about the full extent of indebtedness or refuse to account for depreciation of engines, cars, and track.[34] Such financial humbug led farming interests and journalists to raise the cry of imposition and deceit. "The temptations to fraud on the part of railway directors are now enormous," the *Merchants' Magazine* concluded in 1870, "and checks upon them are trifling."[35] Some contested practices within railroad accounting, however, represented novel approaches to problems that lacked obvious precursors. The treatment of depreciation and the handling of non-construction fixed costs were initially subject to such wide discretion because no one had previously confronted such issues.

The questions posed by accounting for the maintenance of gargantuan railroad networks took economic actors onto *terra incognita*. There were more- and less-familiar features on those economic landscapes, with enough of the former that many counterparties and observers raised the hue and cry of misrepresentation. But the strangeness of new economic worlds made it easier for entrepreneurial actors to contend that they lacked authoritative cultural or legal maps. To shift from a terrestrial metaphor to the seafaring language of behavioral economics, these novel situations lacked clearly established, unambiguous moral anchors. Such contexts intensified incentives to profit from information asymmetries, while offering individuals ample ground to argue, to themselves and others, that they had not transgressed any established norms.

THE INDETERMINACY OF MAIL FRAUD

Recognizing the perplexities of fraud at Schumpeter's entrepreneurial margin helps to clarify the challenges confronted by turn-of-the-twentieth-century postal inspectors. Many of the businesses accused of violating the mail fraud statute, such as Sears, Roebuck, operated in relatively immature markets whose promise had attracted numerous entrants, but that had yet to develop leading firms, or clarity about the business strategies that would yield dependable profits. That is, they faced strong incentives for exaggeration, whether about discounts, quality of wares, or commissions earned by sales agents. For an enterprise such as Modelle Miller's Indiana beauty company, extravagant assertions about the wonderful properties of its Oriental Curling Fluid, Famous Lily Bouquet, or Meadow Leaf (a remedy for "Female Weakness") were indispensable means to standing out among competing concerns. The same impulse lay behind the Walker Manufacturing Company's ebullient characterizations of its leading product, a "Hair Grower." To break into the quickly evolving automobile market on the eve of World War I, a relatively undercapitalized entrepreneur such as B. H. Lambert, the president of two short-lived Louisville car companies, had little choice but to promise potential dealers and investors that his factory would soon be churning out reliable vehicles, even if his design had encountered significant engineering problems.[36]

The struggle to become an early mover amid America's transition to an integrated consumer society often pushed businesses to flirt with misrepresentation. The fashioning of new products and the development of novel marketing practices, in other words, frequently generated claims that struck observers as unacceptably misleading, even if those assertions were not necessarily proscribed by prevailing legal rules or business customs. As postal inspectors waded into mail fraud investigations, they found themselves trying to get their bearings amid the resulting legal ambiguities.

Consider the case of Charles Young, the Korean immigrant who built up a business wholesaling used clothing in post–World War I Chicago. After receiving a secondary education in Hawaii and spending a few years in San Francisco as a servant, Young traveled to the Midwest to pursue a college education. After receiving his degree from Indiana University, he worked for several years as a traveling salesman for a firm that manufactured a carpet-cleaning device. This employment alerted him to business opportunities within Chicago's used clothing trade, which he entered on his own account in 1924. At first, Young restricted his field of vision to the local market. He bought inventory at bankruptcy auctions, had his staff of native-born, white American women clean and repair individual items, and then resold the spruced-up goods to retailers on Chicago's South Side who catered to the city's burgeoning African American population. Within a year of getting started, however, heightened urban competition led Young to seek out business from rural storekeepers in the Midwest and the South. A crucial dimension of his business model involved grading his inventory, as he offered clothing merchants various bundles of used goods, with so many items of No. 1, No. 2, or No. 3 quality. In the eyes of several retailers who complained to the Post Office, the Chicagoan did not fulfill his promises. Instead, he foisted off shoddy garments as more valuable lightly worn attire and falsely promised that storekeepers could make as much as $75 a day from rummage sales.[37] But who was to determine what distinguished one grade from another, either in theory or with regard to the day-to-day categorizing of repaired trousers and restitched dresses? And how was one to judge the plausibility of estimations about demand for secondhand clothes?

The challenge of building up distribution networks that skirted the nation's prevailing system of small-scale retailers prompted analogous conundrums. Mail-order firms dependent on local sales agents, for instance, often fashioned incentive structures similar to what would later come to be known as multilevel marketing. These schemes encouraged agents not only to sell a firm's products, but also to pitch the commercial opportunities presented by sales agencies, and furnished long-term payments to agents who recruited others to the sales network. In some cases, as with Modelle Miller's beauty company, the manufacturer focused as much on promoting agencies as goods, offering extensive advice on how to tap social networks in order to sell the firm's products.[38] To critics, including postal inspectors, these practices represented nothing more than duplicitous lotteries: they promised outsized returns to a small number of agents, with scant regard to the poor chances of success.[39]

Yet such methods had ample precedents in American commercial culture. Life insurance companies had employed similar tactics for decades, enticing the purchasers of "tontine" policies with the possibility of especially large returns if they outlived a group of fellow policyholders, and compensating agents heavily on the basis of sales by their subagents. For all the bluster about the insidiousness of multilevel marketing, many Americans viewed it as an acceptable way to give individuals who lacked capital a chance to attain independent proprietorship. As one federal judge argued in striking down a 1925 fraud order against a New York City hosiery company's "chain" method of marketing, the firm's "scheme . . . may or may not be a wise business proposition, but the Post Office Department is not the guardian of the people of the United States in the respect of what they shall go into in the way of business." As this comment suggests, distinguishing permissible inducements from illicit hazards of chance was far from an obvious endeavor.[40]

The heightened tempo of economic activity in industrializing America prompted further legal ambiguities, even in circumstances that might seem relatively straightforward, such as when firms allegedly did not deliver goods for which customers had made payment, or allegedly delivered unauthorized substitutes. Charles Young in 1927, like Sears, Roebuck in 1895, faced such charges. Both firms responded by noting that the complaints were not necessarily legitimate and that mistakes, on the part of both consumers and supplier, were inevitable once one attained a large scale of business. Thus Young maintained that some disgruntled customers had either tried to return goods the firm had not sold, or fraudulently sent back rags, threatening to report him to postal inspectors if they did not receive full refunds. As Richard Sears argued in one letter to the postal authorities, it was "impossible to avoid complaints," given the notorious impatience of farmers "restless" for their goods, and the fact that his company now filled orders worth "about $150,000 per month."[41] The key question, Sears and Young argued more than three decades apart, turned on the system that a business had created to evaluate and respond to customer grievances. But who was to say whether a given complaint system met the standards of mercantile fair dealing closely enough to sustain access to the postal network?

Within the financial markets, efforts to sell securities or investment advice to a mass market posed similarly vexing questions about appropriate norms of candor. Such dilemmas emerged especially clearly in the mail fraud proceedings brought against Colorado's Orphan Boy Extension Mine in 1895, and the Newark, New Jersey–based Paine Statistical Corporation and its president, J. Overton Paine, in 1916. Promoters N. C. Merrill and Frank P. Arbuckle were the key figures behind Orphan Boy, which they boomed in Eastern newspapers as a potential silver and gold bonanza that had attracted prominent Coloradans to serve as company directors. In order to entice investors of modest means, Merrill and Arbuckle followed the practice of most late nineteenth-century mining corporations, pricing shares at $1. In recommending a fraud order against Orphan Boy, the Denver postal inspector, William McMechen, insisted that the government had to view such offerings with abiding skepticism. Every year, McMechen argued, more "so called Mining Companies" appeared, and it was nearly impossible to bring legal action against fraudulent promoters in Western jurisdictions because of "lax local laws in this regard" and the "loose custom" associated with selling mining securities. In light of the 25 percent commission going to Eastern agents who sold Orphan Boy's shares and the sharp criticism that several experts had voiced about its prospects, the postal inspector viewed the mine as "Utopian" and its officers as undeserving of access to the mails.[42] Exactly how, though, were federal officials supposed to distinguish the hopelessly "Utopian" mine from the legitimately speculative one? And why should the opinion of unnamed experts keep a mining company from mailing circulars to Americans who might want to furnish it with capital?

The postal investigation of J. Overton Paine reflected a similar expression of paternalistic concern for "innocent" and easily "beguiled" investors. In the late 1890s, Paine became a leading New York City speculator who specialized in identifying and then profiting from the era's endemic attempts at market manipulation. After parlaying killings in Rapid Transit and American Sugar into a large-scale brokerage firm, he absorbed big losses from investments in an automobile company and several inventions. Amid turn-of-the-century allegations that his brokerage was nothing but a high-toned bucket shop, he ceased to act as a securities broker. Instead, he began to provide financial analysis through market letters and alerts, offering subscribers evaluations of overall market conditions and specific stocks. In circulars that advertised his services, as well as the market letters and telegrams themselves, Paine characterized his expertise as resting on the accumulation of economic data, mostly purchased from new firms such as Roger Babson's Statistical Service, and the sophisticated assessment of those data. Paine pledged that his "advice" was not related to his own stock operations, warned that his commentary represented only opinion and was not guaranteed to generate positive returns, and recommended that subscribers trade only with reputable brokers. Should subscribers find themselves dissatisfied with his analysis, they had the right to ask for refunds.

And yet Paine's advertising simultaneously embraced aspects of America's "Get Rich Quick" tradition. His literature expressed confidence in the capacity of ordinary people to make a "FORTUNE IN THE STOCK AND WHEAT MARKETS," while touting a track record of incisive advice that had enabled "thousands" to "profit from my daily market letter." He also frequently dangled "a VERY SPECIAL piece of information" about a stock or commodity, implying that he possessed inside dope about the operations of some investment pool.[43] Did Paine's mode of operation represent sanguine puffery by an aggressive businessman trying to fashion a new form of financial services, which open-eyed American investors should know to take with a grain of salt, especially in light of the rampant rumor-based manipulation in US securities and commodity markets? Or did it rather constitute cleverly braided misrepresentations that would lead unsophisticated investors to incur substantial losses?

From the 1890s into the 1920s, such questions forced postal authorities to grapple with the moral economy of marketing in an industrializing economy, and so to reconsider the difficult balance between respecting entrepreneurial freedom and sustaining the state's responsibility to protect the American marketplace from sharpers. The effort of federal officials to strike this balance was complicated by the tendency of sectors at the forefront of economic change to attract a disproportionate share of outright scams. In light of the way that capitalist innovation attracted sophisticated swindlers, Post Office officials had ample reason to emphasize consumer and investor protection and the safeguarding of public confidence in commercial speech. The religious and ideological predispositions of postal inspectors who had joint appointments with metropolitan antivice societies, such as Anthony Comstock, reinforced this line of thinking. In light of their profound commitment to late nineteenth-century Protestant moralism, and the resulting intensity of their opposition to liquor, gambling, and prostitution, these officials were alarmed by marketing strategies that remotely resembled lotteries, including "chain" methods of recruiting agents.[44]

The depth of the resulting bureaucratic paternalism is nicely encapsulated by an 1894 memo from a Keokuk, Iowa, postal inspector who recommended a fraud order against the State Mutual Life Insurance Company of Illinois. This corporation was one of many bond-investment schemes that sought to fill the vacuum created by the Post Office's successful war against the Louisiana Lottery. These companies operated much like tontines and pyramid schemes. They promised immediate large payouts to investors who received low serial numbers on their bonds, and provided significant returns to other purchasers only if a large number of bondholders who bought on installments did not complete their purchases. The inspector, W.G.D. Mercer, argued that the State Mutual Life's bonds were predicated on fraudulent promises of randomly generated bonus payments. Characterizing the company's product as a newfangled lottery scheme that cheated Americans out of hard-earned savings, Mercer evinced "great pride in stepping in between these sharks and the unsuspecting victims who have been tempted to risk their little all in the vain hopes of obtaining the price of a house."[45]

In some contexts, the moralism of postal officials encouraged striking expansions of "fraud" as a legal concept, something the Iowa publisher A. S. Burrell discovered in 1896. Burrell had developed an integrated set of business services for regional storekeepers. Those merchants could keep abreast of credit conditions by subscribing to his *Interstate Tracer*, a newsletter that combined regional economic news and listings of deadbeat consumers. Retailers could also turn to Burrell's Credit Rating System, a proprietary service that offered confidential assessments of individual creditworthiness through a "Commercial Reporter," and to a companion debt-collection service, the Iowa State Businessmen's Association. When firms forwarded a notice of a delinquent debtor, the Businessmen's Association would send that debtor a letter, explaining that failure to pay would trigger circulation of a poor credit rating through the *Interstate Tracer* and Burrell's confidential credit bulletin. Several debtors complained about this arrangement to postal authorities, who issued a fraud order on the grounds that the collection letters represented blackmail. Fraud, in this and related cases, encompassed not just misrepresentation, but also economic communication that smacked of coercion.[46]

Antagonism to marketing practices with the slightest tinge of gambling or to coercive tactics in debt collection nonetheless left a considerable area of fuzziness over which transgressions truly merited loss of access to the mail. Individuals and firms confronting fraud order proceedings magnified the stakes associated with this administrative action, because it threatened their ability to pursue entrepreneurial livelihoods. Lawyers for one small Ohio cosmetics firm informed Washington officials in 1896 that the Post Office was threatening to "crush the life" out of their client. J. Overton Paine characterized the matter even more dramatically twenty years later: "Issuing a fraud order against any man of standing," he insisted, "is a thousand times worse than a sentence of death," portending "absolute ruin and disgrace forever."[47] The residents of early twentieth-century American prisons would have surely disagreed with this sentiment; but fraud orders did severely threaten commercial reputations and business prospects.

The Sears case suggests how action by the Post Office could reverberate, multiplying the contexts in which a firm had to defend itself from allegations of misrepresentation, and turning an initial determination of fraud into a self-fulfilling prophecy. Most immediately, the fraud order against Sears, Roebuck kept some customers from receiving orders, prompting a new round of complaints. Even after the order's revocation, it still influenced assessments of commercial probity, much like a later newspaper retraction not seen by many readers of the original story. Toward the end of 1895, one elected official who had previously vouched for Sears, Roebuck wrote to inform postal authorities that "the firm's methods are of such a character at the present time that I do not feel warranted in allowing anything that could be construed as an endorsement of them to remain a matter of record." More worryingly, lingering news of the initial order led a prominent rural periodical to warn its readers that Sears, Roebuck's promotions were "absurd" promises that "simply can't be carried out," and that the Post Office had branded the outfit as a fraud. Here was a powerful instance in which a legal category had profound implications for economic reputation and identity, channeled through the nation's journalistic fraud monitors.[48]

Mindful of that stark reality, the Post Office frequently accepted settlements with businesses that possessed many of the characteristics of upstanding firms, but had adopted arguably deceptive tactics. When "legitimate enterprises are so advertised as to mislead the public," but "without intention to defraud," the postal department declared that its policy was to allow "adjustment of the matters complained of," either through settlements with aggrieved customers or, more commonly, formal assurances that firms would "eliminate" objectionable marketing practices. Hundreds of adjustments occurred in the late nineteenth and early twentieth centuries, often, as in the case of Sears, Roebuck, through revocation of an existing order.[49] And yet, compromise was by no means inevitable, as the experience of two prominent American businessmen, Edward Gardner Lewis and George Graham Rice, attests.

Both of these promoters and inveterate salesmen could lay claim to significant entrepreneurialism. Lewis, like Sears, spotted the potential of the rural market. Born and educated in Hartford, Connecticut, he had several sales positions before starting his first large-scale enterprise, based in St. Louis, which involved heavily promoted and deeply discounted magazines. Relying on advertising for revenue and catering especially to rural women, these periodicals achieved circulations that rivaled those of the country's leading magazines, with Lewis's flagship *Woman's Magazine* attaining a peak circulation of well over one million. By 1905, growing awareness of rural frustrations with limited financial options led him to found the nation's first mail-order banking institution, the People's United States Bank. This institution offered savings accounts, small loans, and inexpensive money transfers. A similar recognition of rural educational aspirations prompted the creation of the People's University, which offered correspondence classes. Lewis sought to integrate these endeavors through local real-estate development in suburban St. Louis, as he directed the construction of University City, a planned community that became home to his printing establishment, bank, college, and later, the American Woman's League, an umbrella organization for woman's clubs that coordinated the marketing of magazine subscriptions.

George Graham Rice had experience as a journalist for New York City newspapers and as a horse-racing tipster in New Orleans around the turn of the century, useful apprenticeships for later attempts to bring investing to the masses. Between 1905 and 1908, Rice promoted Nevada mining companies through a news service that supplied Eastern papers with coverage of the Western mining scene. In 1908, he moved back to New York City. Over the next quarter-century, he became the dominant force in several brokerage houses that specialized in mining and oil stocks and used discounted commissions to attract far-flung investors of modest means. He simultaneously helped to popularize finance through a succession of investing dailies—the *Mining Financial News,* the *Industrial and Mining Age,* the *Wall Street Iconoclast,* and the *Financial Watchtower*—some of which reached hundreds of thousands of subscribers.

The enterprises of these two innovators attracted the Post Office's sustained enmity, in each case for over two decades. Lewis received a fraud order in 1905 that threw his bank into turmoil and eventually led to its demise. Over the subsequent seven years, he faced a series of criminal indictments and trials for mail fraud. Although he avoided conviction, the financial and reputational costs associated with these prosecutions crippled his publishing, educational, and real-estate ventures in greater St. Louis. In 1912, Lewis moved to California, where he turned again to magazine publishing and real-estate development in the town of Atascadero, mixed in with several mining, transportation, and oil ventures. His appeals to investors for these endeavors once again came under postal scrutiny, which led not only to another fraud order, but also a criminal conviction for mail fraud. Rice found himself under fraud investigations by postal authorities even more consistently. He received a fraud order in 1903, then faced criminal mail fraud indictments in 1909, 1918, and 1927. The indictments, alleging either fraudulent treatment of brokerage clients or misrepresentations in securities promotions, resulted in three successive convictions.[50]

Lewis and Rice would never have been mistaken for paragons of business ethics. Before building his St. Louis empire, Lewis had a checkered career working for companies that sold patent medicines and insecticides, experiences that alerted him to the power of advertising and led him to enter the publishing business. Thereafter, he faced recurring accusations that he had inflated circulation numbers for the *Woman's Magazine*. In order to persuade his rural subscribers to purchase stock in the People's United States Bank, which they did in the thousands, he solemnly pledged that the new financial institution would be overseen by outside directors with substantial banking experience, that he would invest one million dollars of his own funds, and that neither the bank's capital nor deposits would be loaned to Lewis's other businesses. After launching the bank, Lewis violated each of these promises. In subsequent years, he repeatedly milked a core group of loyal investors, always pleading for one last injection of capital to keep their joint dreams of riches afloat.[51] Rice specialized in touting Western mining and oil stocks in which he had acquired a controlling stake. His mode of operation included relentless puffing about his companies' prospects, as well as sophisticated market manipulation to generate upward price movements that encouraged momentum-oriented speculators to purchase his securities. In addition, his brokerage firms repeatedly faced accusations from clients about bucketing of orders, nondelivery of shares, and misappropriation of securities deposited as collateral for margin purchases. By the early 1920s, Rice had earned a reputation as a preeminent "Pirate of Promotion," the "king of the tipsters."[52]

Yet both men could point to exculpatory dimensions of their businesses similar to those highlighted by Sears, Roebuck and other enterprises that settled mail fraud allegations. Lewis's *Woman's Magazine* was one of the first publications in the country to guarantee protection to its subscribers against frauds committed by its advertisers. In court and in print, Lewis insisted that he had scrupulously avoided paying dividends on any of his companies' stock, preferring to reinvest profits, and that he resolutely intended to fulfill the pledges that he made regarding the People's Bank. His ability to make good on those promises, he maintained, had been delayed by unexpected hitches in the appointment of outside directors, and an unanticipated liquidity shortfall precipitated by news of the mail fraud investigation, which necessitated bridge loans to other holdings so as to sustain the financial integrity of interlocked enterprises. Those loans, he observed, were backed by excellent collateral and were financing extensive and valuable real-estate development. Finally, he stressed his bank's record of prudent management, confirmed in 1906 by an independent assessment. Even in liquidation, the institution met all of its obligations to depositors and 87 percent of those to stockholders, despite the extraordinary damage caused by the fraud order and a subsequent state receivership.[53]

In Rice's earliest run-ins with the Post Office, he emphasized the small number of complaints relative to his firm's overall business, as well as its efforts to redress grievances. He further portrayed many complaints as sour grapes from investors who did not follow instructions to take profits, and insisted that any printed falsehoods did not reflect fraudulent intent. As he argued in a confessional 1911 memoir, no one should assume that

> because a promoter represents the chances of profit-making in a mining enterprise to be enormous, and you later find his expectations are not realized, that the promoter is ipso facto a crook. Big financiers are apt to make mistakes and so are little ones. Undoubtedly grave misrepresentations are made every day, and insidious methods are used to beguile you into forming a higher opinion regarding the merit of various securities than is warranted by the facts. But mine promoters are only human, and honest ones not infrequently are carried away by their own enthusiasm.

In both this memoir and later financial publications, Rice consistently offered an insider's view of how the financial markets actually operated, revealing the manipulations and conflicts of interest so common in that era. From his earliest ventures, he warned investors that he held stakes in the firms that he touted; he also reminded them that they put down money at their own risk. Rice further denied that he engaged in pump and dump schemes, noting that he always used profits to support share values once boom turned to bust; and he vigorously maintained that his tactics of manipulating share prices, whether through the dissemination of news stories or market operations, did not differ a whit from the typical methods of Wall Street.[54]

The marketing practices of E. G. Lewis and George Graham Rice, then, arguably fell within a zone of legal ambiguity. They had constructed substantial, innovative enterprises, while simultaneously manifesting less-than-punctilious regard for candor in commercial speech and behavior. Their treatment by the federal government was contingent, not foreordained by business conduct. But a stress on legal contingency suggests an intriguing historical puzzle. How can we explain the willingness of postal officials to forge settlements with firms such as Sears, Roebuck, Modelle Miller's beauty concern, and Paine Statistical Corporation, given the tenacious enforcement actions against Lewis's bank and Rice's brokerage firms?

A savvy legal posture certainly helped in fending off mail fraud allegations. The ability to contextualize grievances that had prompted official inquiries represented one way to convince postal authorities to hold off issuance of a fraud order or to suspend one already in force. Sears, Roebuck and Charles Young effectively took this tack in their interactions with the Post Office, both by emphasizing that high volume made some degree of customer dissatisfaction inevitable and by explaining their systems of redress. Such arguments worked best when accompanied by expressions of contrition and deference to federal authorities. Those officials typically expected some form of apology for putting out "florid" newspaper ads, disseminating "excessively alluring circulars," relying on chain marketing, or otherwise crossing into what the Post Office adjudged to be deceptive commercial speech.[55] They similarly assumed that firms would respond assiduously to customer complaints, as Richard Sears did throughout 1895 and 1896. Tellingly, Sears took care to voice his appreciation for being "afforded this opportunity of showing your department that we are willing and anxious to carry out any suggestion emanating from that source."[56] Most importantly, prosecutors required that firms enter into stipulations that they would discontinue objectionable practices—the combination by A. S. Burrell of credit reporting and debt collection; claims by the Walker Manufacturing Company that its Hair Grower actually caused hair growth; the Crown Motor Car Company's solicitation of additional agents in advance of actual car production; J. Overton Paine's incantation that financial riches were within any man's reach.

Business owners on the mail fraud docket who wished the Post Office to cut them some slack also did well to rely on influential legal representatives, even if, as was often the case, they did not possess detailed knowledge of mail fraud proceedings. Several of the entrepreneurs who arranged settlements secured prominent lawyers to represent them: Richard Sears retained a leading Washington, DC, attorney; J. Overton Paine hired a former United States Attorney for New Jersey; the estate of C. J. Walker relied on a former governor of Indiana. These individuals brought the weight of their own social and political standing to bear on the scales of postal justice, lending credence to assurances of reformed marketing practices.

Plausible legal arguments, willingness to adapt business practices to directives from federal officials, and august legal representation, however, did not always produce settlements with the Post Office. Both E. G. Lewis and George Graham Rice were able to make strong legal cases, especially regarding the question of fraudulent intent. Both men also cooperated with authorities, at least initially, giving postal inspectors extensive access to their books and manifesting some willingness to adjust business practices. Lewis discontinued a magazine's multilevel marketing promotion, and in the wake of the 1905 fraud order, followed through on promises to attract outside financiers to his bank's board. Rice became increasingly explicit about alerting the readers of his tip sheets to his interest in the stocks that he puffed. The two promoters also depended on legal heavyweights for representation. In 1910, Rice's legal team was headed by a former New York City district attorney; in the 1920s, his counsel included a former New York governor and a one-time United States Attorney. Lewis retained several leading lawyers, including one former high-ranking postal official intimately involved with the case against him.[57]

Another likely possibility is that social identities influenced how postal investigators assessed allegations against firms. In light of the comparatively short legal shrift given to members of marginal groups during this period, one might expect that nonwhites, immigrants, and non-Protestants would face tougher scrutiny from postal inspectors. Indeed, the tenor of mail fraud proceedings suggests heightened suspicions about firms not run by native-born Protestant white males. The Chicago postal inspector who probed the affairs of Charles H. Young, for example, ignored repeated invitations to visit his secondhand clothing business, see the wholesaler's system of quality control, and interview the employee who handled dissatisfied customers. Instead, the inspector recommended a fraud order solely on the basis of complaints from white shopkeepers, along with a brief interview that he conducted with the Korean merchant at the Chicago Post Office. As an Asian businessman, Young almost certainly received less benefit of the doubt than similarly situated white wholesalers. By the same token, George Graham Rice confronted close scrutiny in part because of his social origins and a history of criminal behavior. Originally named Simon Jacob Herzig, Rice was the son of a Jewish immigrant, albeit a wealthy furrier. The promoter extraordinaire changed his name after serving jail sentences for forgery and theft in the 1890s.[58]

But Young's case also reveals that individuals who faced allegations of mail fraud could rebut the Post Office's assumptions about commercial integrity, or the lack thereof. At his hearing, Young offered extensive evidence of his respectability through testimony by the Washington, DC, Commissioner for the government of Korea, and through affidavits from his native-born white female employees. Young additionally underscored his reliance on a leading Chicago advertising firm in developing the circulars that he sent to rural storekeepers.[59]

Indeed, a common theme running through the firms that came to some sort of settlement with the Post Office was their ability to mobilize a set of economic and political patrons to vouch for their legitimacy. Richard Sears took care to document an extensive list of manufacturers, wholesalers, and bankers who placed their trust in him. Modelle Miller not only persuaded her former employer, the New Carlisle postmaster, to send a character reference to the postal officials in charge of her case, but also circulated a petition among local businessmen calling for a suspension of her fraud order and successfully orchestrated a letter on her behalf from a former congressman. A. S. Burrell went so far as to organize correspondence by Iowa businessmen to the state's members of Congress, who then wrote to the Post Office Department to explain that Burrell enjoyed the confidence of upstanding citizens in his region.[60]

The salience of social contacts in mail fraud proceedings underlines the crucial role that access to such networks played for entrepreneurs who wished to seize the opportunities and sidestep the risks posed by an industrializing and ever more integrated national economy. In addition to easing access to credit, commercial intelligence, and sources of new business, social networks also constituted a handy bit of insurance if one ran afoul of the law. Mail fraud investigations thus mirrored the handling of pardon applications in nineteenth-century America, or the efforts of that era's insolvent business owners to get back on their feet. Like prisoners seeking pardons or bankrupts trying to restart careers, the goal of entrepreneurs who faced allegations of mail fraud was a second chance, a reprieve from punishment and stigma, an opportunity to reclaim or shore up a more honorable social identity. In all these contexts, the route to a fresh start involved the marshalling of personal expressions of support from relevant elites, whether through petitions or commercial endorsements.[61]

For a company such as the State Mutual Life Insurance Company of Illinois, the high standing and connections of its officers and directors led to a revocation of an 1894 postal fraud order even though the company sold savings vehicles that closely resembled lotteries. Through its attorney, the firm fired off an indignant protest about the federal government's willingness to "blacken the character and business of honest, respectable citizens of this state," including a former governor, while simultaneously pledging to desist from any marketing practices that the government adjudged problematic. In this case, the Post Office quickly relented. By contrast, the owners of small-scale businesses who lacked sufficient pull to persuade local notables to speak up on their behalf struggled to reverse the loss of mail privileges. Such was the experience of Laura Thomas, the operator of a mail-order cosmetics firm in Elkhart, Indiana, whose business practices greatly resembled Modelle Miller's. Unlike Miller, however, Thomas had no blizzard of testimonials to point to, and her plaintive appeals during the winter of 1895 fell on deaf ears.[62]

And yet, like the turn to seasoned legal advice, the mobilization of accumulated social and political capital also had limits. George Graham Rice and E. G. Lewis both played this card. Despite his criminal record, Rice attracted well-regarded individuals to serve as company directors, and was able in 1920 to convince highly regarded journalists and a former Comptroller of the Currency to join his managerial staff. These maneuvers lent his operation a greater patina of respectability, but not immunity from prosecution.[63] After receiving the fraud order against his bank in 1905, Lewis garnered full-throated endorsements from two former Missouri governors, leading lights of the St. Louis business community, thousands of subscribers and investors, and several members of Congress, who took pains to emphasize the promoter's longstanding Republican Party credentials. Over fifteen thousand people and "twenty-one manufacturing, mercantile, and civic organizations" signed one petition on his behalf, but such efforts did not persuade the Post Office to lift its fraud order.[64] Effectively deploying one's business networks was another crucial response to charges of commercial duplicity by the Post Office Department; but again did not, by itself, always diffuse the threat of a fraud order or mail fraud prosecution.

For Lewis and Rice, the path to some sort of legal settlement turned out to be particularly arduous because of the nature of their competition. Lewis, as he and his many supporters never tired of arguing, worried numerous entrenched interests—Midwestern publishers, including, most importantly, the owners of the St. Louis Post-Dispatch and the St. Louis Mirror, who were threatened by Lewis's intention to start a competing newspaper; the country's major express companies and banks, who did a substantial money transfer business; and the Post Office itself, which sold money orders and was planning its own foray into postal banking. Rice stepped heavily on the toes of leading Western mining syndicates, respectable Eastern brokerage houses, mining journals, and investment banks. He repeatedly castigated these bastions of the country's economic establishment in print, and his recurrent efforts to manipulate stock markets, along with his exposés of similar activities by financial elites, made him many enemies.[65]

One need not presume that postal officials slavishly did the bidding of secret corporate paymasters to conclude that determined competitors tipped the scales of postal justice. Lewis's troubles began with exposés in the local papers, drawn largely on information provided by a disgruntled former partner, which led to a full-scale federal investigation. His budding commercial empire then received an enormous jolt even in advance of the issuance of the fraud order against him: another St. Louis daily printed a leaked postal inspector's report about his activities, which stoked a crisis of confidence in his concerns and drastically curtailed his access to credit, complicating his ability to make promised investments in his mail-order bank.[66] In 1909, rival promoters, the *Engineering and Mining Journal*, which faced a libel suit by Rice's brokerage firm, and a private detective working for the NYSE all funneled information about Rice to postal inspectors. During the 1920s and 1930s, evidence provided by the financial establishment again enabled federal prosecutors to move against the mining promoter.[67]

The key dynamic here was a combination of intense persistence by commercial antagonists, knowledge of the regulatory preoccupations of postal authorities, and a capacity to amass or broadcast incriminating evidence. In the right circumstances, even relatively small firms could make significant interventions into mail fraud deliberations. Indeed, recipients of fraud orders who arranged settlements with the Post Office sometimes played this role. After his experience with a fraud order, the retail credit reporter A. S. Burrell took it upon himself to become a postal sentinel, apprising officials in Washington about every other credit reporting firm in his region that threatened to publicize nonpayment as a debt collection tactic. Burrell had the satisfaction of prompting several fraud orders against competitors. A northern Indiana cosmetics maker who received a fraud order in the early 1890s similarly became the chief conduit for evidence about deceptive behavior by other firms in the industry. Ironically, running the gauntlet of mail fraud proceedings gave some business owners the capacity to become de facto postal policemen for their corners of the American marketplace.[68]

Pressure from competitors by no means ensured that the postal authorities would produce or maintain a fraud order. Businesses under investigation frequently tried to undercut accusations against them by noting that they had been instigated by commercial rivals. And even influential complainants might find the Post Office unmoved by calls for action if enterprises had sufficient commercial standing. Such was the result of a 1907 attempt by a Southern member of Congress to prod the Post Office into a fraud investigation of the New York Cotton Exchange (NYCE). Southern agricultural and commercial interests argued that the Exchange was allowing its members to settle futures contracts on high-quality cotton by substituting inferior grades, a deceptive practice that depressed prices. This charge closely paralleled the attacks against Chicago grain elevator operators that had culminated in a new state inspection regime. But the NYCE's president haughtily brushed off this broadside against his organization. "It is deplorable," he declared in a public letter, "that such assault upon . . . a chartered institution of over thirty-five years standing, founded by merchants of this city, or that such implication as to the integrity of its members, should be made under any pretext or for any purpose whatsoever." Postal officials agreed, finding no wrongdoing. For members of the business establishment, barriers to a fraud order could be quite high.[69]

When confronted with a hard case at the margins of economic change, then, postal authorities often responded vigorously to compelling evidence assembled in part by business interests, especially if those interests were well connected and the accused enterprises lacked strong links to commercial elites. This way of conceptualizing the Department's handling of mail fraud helps to account for its treatment of Sears, Roebuck. The Chicago mail-order house did encounter at least one legal objection from a retail storekeeper whose business it substantially threatened. Surviving 1895 complaints about the burgeoning company included several from a Leavenworth, Kansas, bicycle dealer, whose business had felt the impact of Sears's cut-rate offerings, and who insisted that Sears passed off shoddy merchandise as quality goods.[70]

But this isolated intervention proved little more than an annoyance, given Sears's ability to point to the quality guarantees that his company demanded from its suppliers and, even more crucially, his cultivation of personal relationships with officialdom. After arranging a revocation of the fraud order against his firm, the former railroad stationmaster took great care to satisfy any concerns that the federal government raised about his business. He paid regular visits to Chicago's chief postal inspector, inquiring about any new complaints from customers and personally handling disputes as they arose, even if they involved as little as one dollar's worth of merchandise. At the same time, he maintained close contact with officials in Washington, on at least one occasion sending them copy of a proposed promotion to make sure that it did not cross any legal lines. (Several other firms similarly responded to mail fraud investigations by asking the Post Office to vet marketing materials.) Richard Sears responded to the mail fraud investigation by extending the reach of his networks into the bureaucracy of the federal government. Rural storekeepers may have groused about Sears, Roebuck, but in its early, most vulnerable years, they lacked the kind of national trade organization that might have mounted a more substantial legal campaign against the mail-order concern's more duplicitous forms of marketing.[71]

For all the legal arguments and connections that Lewis and Rice could place on one side of the Post Office's scales of justice, they could not stop their well-established commercial antagonists from exerting pressure on the other one. The resulting suspicion among postal officials decreased the likelihood of settlements, premised as they were on the establishment of trust. Furthermore, neither man managed to pull off the attentive ingratiation of postal officials expected of defendants who asked for revocations of fraud orders. In light of the shadier aspects of Rice's and Lewis's business practices, the sustained legal pressure from commercial antagonists and a brashness of manner precluded compromise.

✳✳✳✳

In the end, should we view E. G. Lewis and George Graham Rice as prototypical scoundrels, forever adjusting their pitches to keep the suckers interested, constantly striving to stay a few steps ahead of the law, taking cynical advantage of the rights accorded to criminal defendants? Or should we rather see them as not so different from other aggressive Americans in the marketplace of their time—but as picking enemies poorly and reaping the consequences? Had the postal authorities given them a bit more slack, might they, like Richard Sears, have toned down their tactics and prospered, perhaps eventually joining the upper tiers of the business class? These are difficult questions without obvious answers; they underscore the complex moral and legal issues raised by entrepreneurial innovation.[72]

A *New York Times* reporter observed toward the end of a 1912 article on mail fraud enforcement that "It's hard to draw the lines between the knaves and the enthusiasts." Edward G. Lewis pushed this point even further in 1911, suggesting that even in a country such as the United States, which had so welcomed inventions of all sorts, truly innovative commercial ideas often encountered profound antagonism. "If something is new," Lewis suggested as part of an explanation for the government's assault on his business career, "it is pronounced impossible, a fake, a fraud, and everything in the dictionary of the human barker."[73]

The preceding tales of mail fraud on the entrepreneurial margins, in which postal officials had to draw such barely visible lines and attempt to distinguish the knavish barkers from the enthusiastic seekers of commercial grails, have implications for historical understandings of both American law and American business. Before the twentieth century, criminal process in the United States often turned out to be as much about assessing reputation as it was about sifting evidence and evaluating its legal import, and the point of criminal proceedings was frequently to adjust personal disputes informally rather than to assign guilt or innocence. Such patterns held in the rural South and the teeming neighborhoods of Northeastern cities. When the son of a North Carolina farmer faced an allegation of theft in the 1830s, or an Irish immigrant woman sought out a Philadelphia alderman in the 1850s to lay an assault charge against her husband, the key questions involved who the protagonists were, how the relevant legal authorities saw them as related to the larger social order, whether they evinced the right kind of deference to those authorities, and how those authorities thought they could best maintain a degree of social equilibrium, reintegrating legal protagonists into their communities.[74]

Up into the early twentieth century, mail fraud enforcement had a similar character, especially when investigated firms inhabited the ambiguous moral terrain that surrounded so many business innovations. In cases that did not involve unalloyed gambling or obvious scams, postal inspectors and prosecutors wanted economic peace between distributors and consumers, wholesalers and retailers, and promoters and investors. These officials relied first on informal assessments of the behavior and social standing of the firms that faced complaints. When confronted with vigorous objections to initial judgments, they considered not only the persuasiveness of legal arguments, but also the social and political pull of the accused business owners and complainants. The key questions involved who the business owners were, how they related to the larger economic and political order, whether they showed the right kind of respect toward authority, and how officials thought they could maintain commercial equilibrium. As Postmaster General George Cortelyou explained in 1907, when disputes over marketing practices involved firms with "integrity," the Post Office would serve as "peacemaker" and "adjust the difficulty."[75] Even within the heart of America's industrializing economy, the legal system sometimes accommodated the values of social reintegration and personalized justice so often associated with premodern and non-Western legal mores.[76]

Sears's dexterity in convincing postal officials that he met this standard for restoring commercial harmony suggests an additional dimension to his entrepreneurial success. Sears struggled to lead his company after it achieved gargantuan scale; indeed, only with the 1895 entry of the clothing manufacturer Julius Rosenwald into the firm did Sears, Roebuck shore up its capital base and managerial capacity, enabling it to handle the strains of extraordinary growth.[77] But it was Sears who oversaw relations with the Post Office during that pivotal period in the company's expansion. His knack for reading the aspirations and fears of customers was paralleled by an instinctive grasp of postal officials' concerns. Sears, Roebuck dodged the bullet of the fraud order because its founder convinced postal attorneys that he was a trustworthy merchant who would adjust business methods to accord with their sensibilities.

As it happens, 1896 did not mark the end of Sears, Roebuck's troubles with the federal government over marketing methods. In 1907, the company was hit with a mail fraud indictment in Des Moines, Iowa, related to allegations of misleading catalogue descriptions. Eleven years later, well after the Barnumesque showman Richard W. Sears had relinquished managerial duties, the firm faced complaints about exaggerated claims concerning the quality of its coffees and teas, as well as deceptive marketing of loss leaders, which they falsely claimed reflected volume discounts. From the mid-1900s onward, moreover, Sears, Roebuck confronted coordinated hostility from rural retailers, whose antagonism was now expressed by the Home Trade League of America, an umbrella organization for the countryside's commercial associations.[78] By this point, however, the "Great Firm" brushed off such legal attacks with ease, adapting to more stringent standards in the event that its formidable legal department lost cases before administrative agencies or in court.

One can measure this process through a telling moment in a mail fraud proceeding some years later, when the attorney for Korean immigrant Charles Young unknowingly emulated Richard Sears's performance at the bar of the Post Office. As the lawyer cross-examined the Chicago postal inspector who had investigated the used-clothing wholesaler, he stressed that leading firms such as "Montgomery Ward, Sears, Roebuck, National Cloak and Suit Co. all receive complaints" like the ones leveled at his client, and then asked, "that does not necessarily show that their business is fraudulent, does it?" The Inspector's answer was emphatic—"Oh, no, no."[79] Transmuted by sustained expansion and internal transformation into a landmark of commercial rectitude, Sears, Roebuck had become the standard by which to judge where other enterprises resided within the moral economy of modern America.

CHAPTER SEVEN

The Businessmen's War to End All Fraud

On hot mornings in the summer of 1933, the residents of Dallas, Texas, could count on a daily radio bulletin, Sundays excepted. This report did not ruminate about bleak chances for rain nor offer the latest intelligence from swooning cotton markets. It provided no details about upcoming church socials, no listings of used goods for sale, no chronicle of New Deal political maneuverings in Austin or Washington, DC. Instead, it furnished commentary and counsel about commercial tales so tall that they crossed the line of acceptable economic behavior. The shady pitches included local offers of "Free Lots" that came with a big catch, a "Business Stimulator" method that its promoter guaranteed would bring orders to struggling firms, and a sham employment scheme.[1] The inclusion of a fraud report in the Dallas radio lineup was not an idiosyncratic decision by a lone station manager desperate to fill airtime. Similar segments occurred on radio stations across the nation in the 1920s and 1930s, all courtesy of officials working for local Better Business Bureaus (BBBs), nonprofit organizations dedicated to exposing commercial flimflam and providing consumer and investor education.

In the first decades of the twentieth century, business fraud became more sophisticated and extensive, mirroring the growth of truly large-scale enterprise. By the 1920s, American marketers had become sufficiently familiar with the psychology underpinning popular consumption and investment to craft emotive sales pitches that played on modern enticements and anxieties, further complicating the question of what counted as deceptive commercial speech. The resulting advertisements included images of soap that somehow anointed its users with sex appeal, depictions of mouthwash that ostensibly functioned as a talisman against halitosis, and visions of fractional shares in oil wells that would magically transport their owners into the ranks of the wealthy.[2]

Amid this vexing economic environment, Americans increasingly identified prevailing antifraud regulations as insufficient to the tasks at hand. The most influential early twentieth-century reformers came from a key segment within the country's business elites, who crafted a far-reaching plan to combat economic duplicity. Concerned about the impact that swindles and misrepresentations were having on commercial culture and economic growth, scores of executives within advertising, marketing, and finance collectively mounted a full-scale campaign against business frauds. Cementing an alliance with the national Republican Party, antifraud reformers created several nonprofit organizations to combat the procurement of credit through provision of fabricated financial information, fraudulent bankruptcy, the sale of spurious medical treatments, false advertising and other deceptive marketing practices, and securities swindles.

This chapter probes the business establishment's diagnosis of the "fraud problem" and its chief remedies for it—campaigns of public education, such as the Dallas radio spots, legal reforms that more carefully defined the requirements of truthfulness in commercial speech, and private policing of those limits, all overseen by novel nonprofit organizations that had close ties to the corporate world, the Better Business Bureaus chief among them. Closely connected to state authorities, these organizations opened up new fronts in America's ongoing struggles with business fraud. As they did so, they further blurred the lines between public and private regulation.

The early twentieth-century crusade against fraud suggests the need for more refined understandings of how the era's business elites viewed economic governance. In the broad arena of commercial speech, most of those elites did not want government to remain on the sidelines, nor preferred that the state focus only on industry standard-setting, nor placed their faith in co-optable administrative agencies. Rather, business leaders prodded public servants at all levels to sharpen statutory prohibitions against misleading commercial communication and to beef up criminal enforcement of those measures, though with a big helping hand from the new nongovernmental institutions dedicated to the fight against deception in the marketplace. Here was a particularly vigorous effort to create "associationalism"—a mode of government-business relations in which the state facilitated substantial intra-industry, and even inter-industry, cooperation, with the goal of stabilizing market conditions and solving other socioeconomic problems.[3]

The businessmen's fight against commercial duplicity further points to the enduring strengths and weaknesses of business self-regulation as a mode of governance. Antifraud organizations quickly developed effective administrative capacity, at least some bureaucratic autonomy, and considerable goodwill among business owners and managers. These assets constituted the hard-won fruits of a social movement of sorts within America's commercial classes, and they enabled the movement's leaders to design and carry out a comprehensive strategy to attack commercial misrepresentation. As a result, the campaigns for truthful commercial speech often successfully challenged longstanding entrepreneurial practices that privileged secrecy and promoted narrow short-term economic calculation, thereby fostering more transparent communication between buyers and sellers in many markets. At the same time, key participants in those campaigns often manifested an ethnocentrism that targeted immigrants and flirted with the rhetoric of eugenics. Close relations between dominant corporations and key figures in the antifraud movement, moreover, compromised those leaders' collective vision, encouraging them to ignore some of the era's most serious instances of economic deceit. This episode thus underscores both the allure and the dangers of vesting authority in private regulators, especially when they retain attachments to business elites.

A CADRE OF PROFESSIONAL FRAUD-FIGHTERS

From William McKinley's election in 1896 to Herbert Hoover's defeat in 1932, Americans confronted recurring assessments that fraudulent behavior pervaded their society. Although such evaluations had ample precedents, the early twentieth-century discourse on commercial fraud conceptualized the problem differently. Observers now considered the impact of duplicity on a more clearly defined national economy, imagining and even calculating its systemic costs. By the 1920s, government agencies and business organizations placed impressive dollar figures on the price tag imposed by fraud. Credit scams ostensibly amounted to between $250 million and $400 million per year. Insurance swindles reportedly bilked companies out of at least a billion dollars annually, while securities fraud allegedly removed at least that amount from ordinary Americans, and possibly twice that. Estimates of total annual costs from organizational fraud, which also included consumer frauds and real-estate swindles, typically topped three to four billion dollars, a figure that, if accurate, equaled roughly 1 percent of the US gross domestic product. Although the factual basis for these estimates was murky, they passed into conventional wisdom, repeated in editorials, news reports, and cartoons, as with a 1927 depiction of the credulous suckers who bit at fraudulent stock pitches (Figure 7.1).[4]

Newspaper coverage and periodical exposés further made clear that American perpetrators of fraud methodically developed more refined schemes of social mimicry. In the nineteenth century, credit fraud occurred with some frequency but typically represented a one-off response to looming insolvency. By the late 1890s, nationwide rings of "credit trimmers" had emerged, which sought repeatedly to bamboozle manufacturers and wholesalers who sold wares on the basis of unsecured trade credit. These rings first established members of the conspiracy as independent retailers, either by providing falsified

Figure 7.1: The popularization of fraud cost estimates in the 1920s. Reprinted from *Commerce, Finance, and Industry*, May 1927, courtesy of the *Los Angeles Times*.

references, buying out existing businesses, or launching stores with names similar to those of well-regarded firms with solid credit. Once these front enterprises cajoled distant manufacturers or wholesalers to furnish them with substantial inventories, the rings would spirit the goods away for sale by confederates elsewhere. Indebted retailers then either disappeared or falsely declared bankruptcy before moving on to new towns, taking on new commercial identities, and beginning the scheme anew.[5]

Securities fraud similarly came to require significant capital and organizational capacity. As early as 1910, the most effective peddlers of dodgy stocks published financial newsletters and dailies that offered conventional assessments of the securities markets, but also relentlessly puffed selected issues controlled by the promoters who owned the tip sheets. Relying on ever more finely tuned compilations of sucker lists, which concentrated on individuals who had previously fallen for securities scams, fraudulent promoters employed crews of clerical workers to distribute their newsletters and other promotional materials to tens of thousands of potential investors. They also oversaw teams of high-pressure salesmen who either operated out of boiler rooms or through revivalist-style investment meetings and tours. The latter proved especially common in the sale of oil stocks and real-estate investments. In some cases, large-scale stock swindlers even created or gained control over regional stock exchanges, such as the Boston Curb Exchange, to facilitate the market manipulations that persuaded investors that individual stocks were in the early stages of a boom.[6]

The most expansive flotations of sham companies went to great lengths to convey their bounteous prospects. No self-respecting swindler would attempt to cash in on an oil boom without setting up shop in close proximity to known gushers and constructing impressive-looking derricks and storage tanks. A few of the more enterprising operators "salted" a creek by infusing it with petroleum from buried barrels.[7] Fraudulent promoters in the early automobile industry, such as the Pan Motor Company of Minneapolis, employed even more expensive attention to theatrical optics. Pan Motor's promoters built a mammoth factory and a handful of cars, all to impress visiting journalists and the recipients of the firm's photograph-laden prospectuses.[8]

To business leaders, legal thinkers, and prominent financial journalists, the all-too-rapid evolution of American swindling posed dangers beyond the most direct financial costs to consumers, investors, wholesalers, and insurers. The sap who invested in a fraudulent automobile company withdrew assets from a legitimate savings bank and did not invest in reputable enterprises, thereby increasing the latter's costs of capital. The dupe who purchased worthless items from a fly-by-night mail-order concern or who responded to the deceptive advertising of a local piano store reduced the profits of law-abiding retailers. Through sales of stolen goods, the credit fraud ring brought losses to legitimate retailers and higher overhead costs to defrauded suppliers. At the same time, successful deceptions set dangerous examples for the legions of American young men on the make, who "learn[ed] to think that there is a better way of getting money than by earning it" and who focused on "making plenty of money and keeping out of jail."[9]

Perhaps the greatest threat posed by fraud concerned the public faith in America's most important marketplaces, or, as one leading spokesman for the business world put it, "the capital of confidence upon which all progress depends." When department stores touted discounts on goods that turned out to be unavailable, marketing executives fretted that such bait and switch schemes fed public skepticism about advertising in general. Opinion-makers within finance worried that duplicitous marketing of stocks and bonds would spawn "sectional prejudice against 'money centres,'" perhaps even "bitter and unreasoning suspicion" of all securities, leading potential small investors to "thrust many a dollar down deeper in the sock." By the 1920s, Wall Street had become more reliant on investing by ordinary Americans, needing infusions of capital from the socks (and savings accounts) of wage- and salary-earners.[10]

Some observers of the economic scene even expressed the fear that deceptive practices ran the risk of souring ordinary Americans on capitalism altogether. In February 1919, during a severe wave of securities swindles that targeted individuals with modest financial resources, witnesses at a federal government hearing depicted such crimes as "a prime cause of social unrest." Amid the early years of the Russian Revolution and a postwar period of intense labor conflict, as well as unprecedented political success by the American Socialist Party, business elites feared that the pervasive experience of becoming a sucker created political openings for radicals. The danger was only sharpened by the tendency of fraudulent stock promoters to levy sharp public attacks on the power of industrial corporations and New York City investment banks. As the headline writers at the *New York Times* framed the possibility, "Stock Frauds Seen as Spur to Bolshevism."[11]

One might question how much the specter of unbridled swindling threatened to turn large numbers of post–World War I Americans toward the Leninist banner. But leading capitalists became sufficiently anxious about the issue of deceptive commercial speech to create a series of nonprofit business organizations between the mid-1890s and the early 1920s, all primarily dedicated to rooting out fraud in the American marketplace. In 1896, the executives responsible for credit extension by manufacturers and large wholesalers founded a new professional organization, the National Association of Credit Men (NACM), which sought to reduce credit fraud. Roughly a decade and a half later, a group of prominent advertising executives joined forces through the Associated Advertising Clubs of the World to create a "truth in advertising" movement, which emerged out of a series of local "vigilance committees" organized by urban advertising associations. Within a few years, the Investment Bankers of America had instituted an analogous committee focused on the challenges of securities fraud, followed by the New York Stock Exchange's (NYSE) creation of the Business Men's Anti–Stock Swindling League. In the early 1920s, these institutional responses to deceptive merchandising and investment-peddling merged into a nationwide network of metropolitan Better Business Bureaus (BBBs), coordinated by a National Better Business Bureau (NBBB).[12]

All of these initiatives predated the "second wave" consumer movement, which was triggered by the seminal muckraking exposés *It's Your Money* (1927),

100,000,000 Guinea Pigs (1933), and *Skin Deep* (1934), and given real momentum by the creation of independent advocacy groups such as Consumer Research (1929) and the Consumers Union (1936). Consumer activists eventually launched withering attacks on mainstream advertising practices, which intensified the inclination among business leaders to bolster confidence in advertising through mechanisms of self-regulation. But such critiques came too late to motivate the initial movement to foster greater honesty in marketing.[13]

There were abundant precedents for American business organizations to tackle the problem of economic deceit. One important touchstone involved the stock and commodities markets, an important sponsor of several new antifraud groups. Since the 1870s, the nation's leading stock and commodity exchanges had maintained internal rules against "obvious fraud," whether attempted against other exchange members or outside customers.[14] As memoirs and exposés by participants in the financial markets attest, such prohibitions did little to protect investors from gross manipulations by insiders.[15] But especially egregious duplicity, such as appropriating a client's funds or adulterating already-inspected loads of grain, did occasionally lead exchanges to expel members.[16] Urban chambers of commerce also sought to curtail misrepresentations in trade or investments, as with the creation of arbitration boards by several Southern chambers to address allegations of fraudulently packed cotton. Many of these rule-making and disciplinary bodies had short lifespans, however, and almost all of them were limited to oversight of firms that belonged to parent organizations.[17] By contrast, the NACM, BBBs, and American Medical Association (AMA), which began to target quackery and medical swindles in the early twentieth century, embraced much more ambitious goals. These organizations wished to combat duplicitous commercial practices throughout the economy, among member and nonmember firms alike.

Funded through annual subscriptions, mostly by large corporations, the new antifraud institutions soon came under the direction of individuals who built careers on the work of curbing commercial deception. J. Harry Tregoe and H. J. Kenner illustrate this pattern. Tregoe initially worked in banking and as the credit manager for a Baltimore shoe company, jobs that exposed him to the costs resulting from dishonest debtors. In the three decades after helping to found NACM in the 1890s, he served the organization as president, executive secretary, general manager, and editor of its primary publication.[18] Kenner spent his early career as a North Dakota retailer, serving as an officer for a local mercantile association. In 1914, at the age of twenty-six, he was tapped by Minneapolis ad executives to direct their new vigilance organization, making him the first person to receive a salary for such work. After a year of regional travel preaching the gospel of truthful advertising, he took a job with the National Vigilance Committee (NVC), an early coordinator of local groups. In the early 1920s, he moved to New York City to head its new BBB, which he proceeded to manage for the next quarter-century.[19]

Constructing a vision of fraud prevention as a calling, Tregoe, Kenner, and their fellow antifraud specialists arrived at similar conclusions about commercial fraud's origins, as well as the most effective means of addressing it. Their sensibilities reflected the era's pervasive embrace of professionalization. Like so many other highly educated economic and cultural brokers, ranging from industrial engineers, accountants, and personnel managers to social workers and public-health officials, antifraud careerists claimed that expertise and commitment to the common good prepared them to tackle the problems created by rapid economic and social change.[20]

Like other early twentieth-century experts, the band of nascent antifraud professionals began with systematic analysis of causes before constructing programs of action. In doing so, they echoed many arguments common within the previous century's commentary about business fraud, while more deeply probing the relationships among deceptive marketing practices, socioeconomic structures, and social norms. Swindling flourished in modern America in part, they reasoned, because the growth unleashed by industrialization had put savings and disposable income in the hands of unsophisticated consumers and investors. These neophytes struggled to navigate the informational challenges of a modern economy, and they often chased after the latest consumer goods or investment fads on the basis of cursory investigation. Whether unscrupulous retailers tried to attract customers to mail-order offerings or retail stores, their beguiling ads zeroed in on the allure of the bargain. Financial hucksters similarly took advantage of pervasive aspirations for affluence in a society that lionized Horatio Alger figures but had narrowed paths to independent proprietorship. Focusing on the latest technological wonders or booms in oil, mining, or real estate, these promoters pitched penny stocks to "the discontented janitress and the ambitious elevator boy," to the salaried clerks and struggling professionals "who are obsessed by an easy road to wealth."[21]

Antifraud professionals stressed that the financing of America's participation in World War I accelerated this process, as the mass marketing of Liberty Bonds acculturated millions of wage- and salary-earners to the securities markets. From the first days of peace, swindlers sent brigades of "chipper salesmen" to go "from door-to-door in city and farming communities, enticing Liberty Bonds from hiding and giving in return lithographed certificates bearing marvelous artists' dreams of derrick after derrick, gusher after gusher, spreading as far as the eye can see." Yet credulity and situational ignorance, antifraud organizations argued, extended far beyond those Americans who were less accustomed to the ways and wiles of twentieth-century capitalism. In bulletins and annual reports, the BBBs continually marveled at "the gullibility of the business public," who were frequently burned by the pitchmen for sham collection agencies and fake commercial directories. NACM officials constantly harped on the susceptibility of so many suppliers to fraudulent requests for credit. Even the New York Stock Exchange had to caution its employees against their propensity for playing the sucker, biting at some spurious "inside" tip or seeking to ride a wave of public fascination with a worthless stock, hoping to get out at the top.[22]

Antifraud crusaders further emphasized that prevailing legal prohibitions against duplicitous commercial speech posed only slight risks to swindlers. Institutional and cultural dynamics that had stymied nineteenth-century fraud prosecutions continued to shape the criminal justice system. The ethos of *caveat emptor* retained a strong allure among many early twentieth-century Americans, who still prized individualism, identified citizenship with the ability to look after their own affairs, and viewed governmental paternalism with abiding skepticism. As a result, con artists frequently received "admiration" for their "cleverness and dexterity," as in George Randolph Chester's best-selling novels about "Get-Rich-Quick Wallingford." Swindlers operating petty mail-order scams sometimes mocked the individuals who fell for their pitches, explicitly informing them that they had been taken for a ride and suggesting that they had received something of value for their money—a bit of experience that would wise them up for the next commercial go-round. Given these widely held social norms, a swindler's victim might be more likely to experience psychological denial (especially in the case of investments gone awry or medical treatments that proved worthless) or keep quiet to avoid the embarrassment of "advertis[ing] the fact that he had permitted a 'slicker' to best him."[23]

When individuals nonetheless did complain to the authorities about instances of alleged swindling, successful prosecutions proved to be the exception rather than the rule, for much the same reasons as during the 1840s or the 1880s. Early twentieth-century fraud cases often turned on complex factual questions about the nature of misrepresentation and the evidence showing fraudulent intent. As a result, convictions depended on investigatory and prosecutorial expertise, which was often in short supply at every level of government. Moreover, in the rare circumstances in which authorities charged individuals with fraud, prosecutors all too often found themselves outgunned by high-priced defense attorneys, while juries frequently protected local businessmen whose deceit attracted outside capital into their communities. In the even rarer instances in which fraud prosecutions culminated in convictions, the judiciary almost always handed out fairly minimal sentences—either modest fines or relatively short jail stints. If convicted swindlers possessed good political connections, as they often did, even those slight penalties could be wiped away by pardons. As one early twentieth-century legal expert observed, the perpetrator of credit fraud "may be punished with no greater severity than the man who expectorates on the floor of a public conveyance." The result, critics complained, was that fraud enforcement still only slightly increased most swindlers' requirements of working capital, essentially imposing a "license fee."[24]

Antifraud organizations identified one further contributor to widespread economic duplicity: the tendency of business owners to respond to short-term incentives, without regard to the long-term implications of their actions for broader commercial culture and public confidence. In this regard, the early twentieth-century analysis of fraud incorporated a more sophisticated appreciation for economic sociology than was present in prior discourse about commercial deceit. Especially within NACM, activists observed that the pressures of competition encouraged far too many wholesalers to extend commercial credit without sufficient investigation, making them likely candidates for credit fraud. Analogous pressures pushed far too many retailers and promoters to flirt with deceptive advertising, and far too many newspapers and magazines to accept such ads. When business owners were taken in by scams, they often proved willing to accept compromise settlements from a swindler's "squawk fund," securing their own financial interests rather than insisting upon criminal prosecutions that would improve the deterrent value of fraud laws.[25]

These diagnoses guided NACM and the BBBs as they developed strategies to protect American markets from duplicitous commercial speech. In their early years, antifraud organizations focused particularly on lobbying state and federal governments to tighten legal prohibitions against deceptive economic conduct. Thus NACM's central purpose during the 1890s was to agitate for a new federal bankruptcy law that its leaders hoped would curb fraudulent conveyances and the concealment of assets by failing debtors, an endeavor that yielded legislative success in 1898. In addition to calling for periodic amendments to the federal bankruptcy code, NACM moved on to press for uniform state laws that would criminalize two common tactics of credit fraud schemes— the signing of a false financial statement in order to obtain credit and the selling of retail inventory in bulk without furnishing notice to commercial creditors. By the same token, the Associated Advertising Clubs of the World (AACW) concentrated much of its initial energy on pushing a model state statute to punish false advertising claims. Spearheaded by the advertising journal *Printer's Ink*, this campaign led to the passage of statutes in forty-three states by 1930. Throughout the 1920s, moreover, the Investment Bankers Association, the NYSE, and the BBBs all worked for the adoption of state securities laws that would facilitate prosecutions of fraudulent stock promoters.[26]

At the national level, antifraud organizations also pressed the new Federal Trade Commission (FTC) to interpret its jurisdiction as including the authority to combat duplicitous business practices. The chief impetus behind the commission's 1914 creation lay with worries about the waxing power of monopolies and trusts, as well as more specific frustrations with a series of Supreme Court opinions, including the 1911 decision in the Standard Oil case, that narrowed the reach of the Sherman Anti-Trust Act and fostered uncertainty about which anticompetitive strategies the courts would view as illegal. Section 5 of the FTC Act, however, also empowered the new agency to investigate "unfair methods of competition," language that at least some members of Congress assumed would encompass misleading or untrue marketing claims. These members of the antitrust coalition viewed the emergence of concentrated corporate power as at least partly the result of pervasive deceptions and frauds committed by aggrandizing monopolists.[27]

Almost immediately after the passage of the FTC Act, the AACW's National Vigilance Committee (the precursor to the National BBB) lobbied the new commission to tackle cases involving false advertising, sending it a series of formal complaints. Stymied by the federal courts in many of its attempts to regulate industrial structure, but allowed in most cases to proceed against duplicitous business tactics, FTC lawyers gradually made deception cases a central element of their docket. By the mid-1920s, they brought several hundred such cases a year, involving misrepresentations of product quality, quantity, newness, or origin, or falsehoods about business status, supposed testimonials, or fictitious price cuts. By the end of the decade, nine of ten docketed cases were of this type.[28]

In addition to these efforts to expand the ambit of antideception policies, antifraud organizations embarked on massive public education campaigns. If a pivotal explanation for pervasive fraud lay with insufficient skepticism and savvy among ordinary Americans, then surely any sensible attempt to prevent fraud had to teach those people how to resist the siren song of the swindler. As one financial journalist with years of experience covering fraud argued in 1919, the most sophisticated antiswindling statutes could not "safeguard people from their own foolishness, and in the last analysis, education in these matters is the individual's best and surest protection."[29]

The BBB network pursued that goal with a vengeance. During the 1920s the antifraud publicity blitz was impossible to avoid in urban America. From Los Angeles to Atlanta to Boston, industrial workers encountered a rotating stream of posters on factory bulletin boards and educational articles in company mag-

Figure 7.2: A typical BBB billboard, St. Louis, 1926. From St. Louis Better Business Bureau, *Telling the Public,* courtesy of NACM.

azines. BBB messages bombarded commuters on buses, trains, subways, and streetcars, while its billboards repeated key slogans for the benefit of automobile drivers and passengers. Individuals who visited banks to make deposits or withdrawals found BBB advice cards tucked into their account books. Newsletters and bulletins from local Bureaus filled the nation's mailbags, mirroring the prodigious output of swindling stock tip sheets and fraudulent mail-order catalogues. As the pitchmen of worthless stocks and boom-related real-estate ventures turned to revival-style sales lectures, BBB officials countered with hundreds of annual speeches to women's clubs, business groups, labor organizations, and civic associations. Thousands of newspapers, magazines, and trade publications donated advertising space to the "truth in advertising" movement and ran articles written by BBB leaders. Once radio stations gained a commercial footing, they quickly followed suit, offering free access to the airwaves for short spots and longer segments.[30]

One can get a more concrete sense of this publicity onslaught by considering its scale in the city of St. Louis. In 1926, the local BBB claimed that each month it placed the equivalent of thirty-eight full newspaper pages of free commentary in fifty-one different papers, which included three major metropolitan dailies, the local African American paper, twelve foreign-language publications, and a host of suburban weeklies. Together, these sheets counted over 290,000 subscribers. Thousands of free ads in trade journals, labor sheets, company magazines, and religious newspapers amplified the message, as did a slew of billboards (such as the one in Figure 7.2) and neon signs, over one hundred talks by BBB officials to community groups, free movie announcements and placements in theatre programs, and regular radio chats by representatives of the Women's Advertising Club. Finally, through close relationships with newspaper editors and the managers of the St. Louis News Service,

BBB officials ensured that their work received ongoing coverage in regional news outlets.[31]

These media blitzes mirrored the strategic approaches of nineteenth-century publications that regularly exposed frauds and humbugs. Like those earlier sentinels, twentieth-century organizations broadcast specific cautions about prevailing scams and misrepresentations, warning the public to avoid specific stores, investments, business deals, and promoters. The BBBs also disseminated general advice about how to invest and consume wisely, emphasizing the crucial importance of eschewing retailers who offered supposedly first-rate goods at enormous discounts, promoters who dangled visions of easily attained wealth, or anyone who made a big show of offering something for nothing. Above all else, antifraud campaigners pleaded with the public to rely wherever possible on expert assistance, particularly when selecting investments. "Before you invest, investigate," became the BBB's best known mantra, by which its officials meant that Americans should have the good sense to follow the advice of respectable bankers or brokerage firms in deciding where to place their savings.[32]

An analogous logic underpinned more focused endeavors to reshape America's commercial culture. Here, antifraud activists again broke new conceptual and strategic ground. Because entrenched business practices aided and abetted those who perpetrated scams, antifraud organizations also tried to persuade firms to reject such practices. NACM leaders continuously advocated the adoption of credit policies that accorded with its view of the shared long-term interests of all wholesalers and manufacturers. At its annual conventions and through its monthly publication, the association's leaders called for more sustained scrutiny of credit requests and greater willingness to exchange intelligence about the creditworthiness of retailers, including the creation of cooperative credit bureaus that would provide more up-to-date information than did standard credit-reporting firms. With regard to merchandising, the BBB network pressured newspapers and periodicals to reject advertisements that did not meet strict standards for candor, and eventually helped to organize a series of trade conferences in order to adopt unambiguous standards for the categorization of materials such as furs, textiles, and woods.[33]

The Imperative of Organized Vigilance

For all the faith that early twentieth-century antifraud reformers placed in reconfigured statute books and educational campaigns, they also viewed the parlous state of law enforcement as requiring urgent attention. By the early 1900s, the NACM had set up local investigating committees composed of volunteer credit men to examine instances of questionable behavior by debtors, and passed along evidence of credit fraud to relevant authorities. Beginning in the 1910s, advertising clubs created similar mechanisms to look into allegations of false advertising, deceptive merchandising, and fraudulent securities promotions. "Putting swindlers in jail for what they have done," the president of the NYSE explained in a 1922 speech, "will give far more protection to the public than a hundred laws warning criminals of what they may not do."[34]

These moves into private law enforcement, like the efforts to create clearinghouses for news about prevailing swindles and scams, built on longstanding American traditions. In addition to the periodic turn to organized vigilantism in places as varied as northern Indiana, central Texas, Montana, San Francisco, and throughout the South, nineteenth-century Americans frequently turned to nongovernmental associations in order to supplement government policing, in many cases with explicit sanction from state legislatures. The anti–horse thief associations in late nineteenth-century America stood as examples of this impulse, as did banks' anticounterfeiting associations and, later, antivice societies such as the New York Society for the Suppression of Vice and the New England Watch and Ward Society, which played such a central role in the Post Office's campaigns against mail fraud and obscenity. Typically, such initiatives came from elite and middle-class Americans who embraced the use of law to constrain what they saw as socially or economically dangerous expressions of individual license, but who despaired of the government's capacity to enforce law on its own, either because of endemic corruption or lack of capacity. These self-appointed enforcers also wished to retain influence over the investigative and prosecutorial process.[35]

In the years surrounding World War I, corporations in several industries that confronted serious crime problems updated this strategy, as did a number of new voluntary agencies concerned about working-class family dynamics or a perceived rise in urban lawbreaking. Within the business world, railroad corporations established a detective bureau to break up freight thefts by rings of insiders. Fire insurance companies did the same to investigate arson gangs, guarantee companies to look into cases of embezzlement, and department stores to combat shoplifting. At roughly the same time, middle-class reformers were creating nationwide "desertion bureaus" to track down husbands who had abandoned their families, as well as local groups such as the Chicago Juvenile Protection Association. The latter organization sought to reshape the rules governing the treatment of adolescent criminal offenders and to provide a battalion of social workers who could take psychological profiles of defendants and monitor convicted teens on probation, thereby magnifying the disciplinary capacity of urban courts.[36]

As occurred with most of the era's enforcement campaigns by nongovernmental groups, antifraud organizations experienced a steady process of expansion and professionalization. The early volunteer committees soon found themselves overwhelmed by complaints, mostly from affected businesses, but also from disgruntled members of the general public. They responded to a crippling workload by lobbying successfully for the creation of independent organizations with salaried staffs, all funded by subscriptions, primarily from big business. After years of debate over issues of practicality and institutional control, NACM supplemented its local vigilance groups in 1916 with a national committee, for which it raised $25,000. By 1926, the newly renamed Investigation and Prosecution Department boasted a multiyear Prosecution Fund of nearly two million dollars—an equivalent share of American GDP in 2016 would be around $330 million—regional offices throughout the country, and a corps of forty experienced investigators who could draw on the services of local credit men's associations in more than forty states. This unit pursued as many 750 investigations annually and referred hundreds of cases to state and federal prosecutors, with most resulting in indictments and convictions. The local and national BBB network, though starting later than the NACM, also built hefty administrative capacity. In 1916, the AACW's National Vigilance Committee, the direct forerunner of the National BBB, ran on a shoestring budget of $15,000 and had two employees, while many local Bureaus still operated primarily on a voluntary basis. By the mid-1920s, total annual expenditures by all the BBBs approached $1 million (roughly equal to $165 million as a share of 2016 GDP), as forty-three local bureaus, spread across nineteen states, handled tens of thousands of complaints about securities fraud, catchpenny scams, and misleading or false advertising. Most also maintained "shopping systems" to monitor retail establishments in their communities, sending out paid female shoppers in order to assess the extent to which department stores and other retailers lived up to advertised promises and followed ethical sales practices.[37] These multifaceted initiatives dwarfed the endeavors of the late nineteenth-century editors who carved out a role as arbiters of legitimate mail-order enterprise.

BBB spokespersons such as Boston department store executive Louis Kirstein emphasized that scrutiny by independent shoppers served as a salutary check on retail marketing campaigns. These evaluations, Kirstein stressed, offered a means of correcting inevitable mistakes and demonstrated to smaller competitors that the BBB commercial standards applied to all sellers in the urban marketplace. The mechanics of the shopping systems, however, suggest that they additionally sought to police the behavior of a growing retail work-force, including not only in-house advertising staff, but also buyers and sales personnel. In Boston, for example, the form that Bureau shoppers had to fill out included numerous questions about the deportment and level of service provided by salespersons, as well as the queries, "Did representations of S. P. [salesperson] agree with representations in advertisement?" and "Did S. P. misrepresent merchandise?" Employees of large-scale retailers often received commissions as an element of their compensation, and so had strong incen-tives to move merchandise, even if their characterizations of goods or other sales tactics violated store policies. The shopping system thus furnished a means of keeping store workers from ignoring dictates about the treatment of customers, compensating for imperfect lines of authority. As such, it con-stituted a companion mechanism to the pervasive reliance on store de-tectives, whom managers charged with preventing both shoplifting and em-ployee theft.[38]

Especially in the case of the BBBs, the emphasis on independent monitor-ing and policing also reflected an attempt to make public education campaigns more effective. For specific cautions about prevailing scams to have real value, they had to occur before too many individuals had taken the bait. "If the infor-mation comes to the Bureau only after a number of prospects have already parted with their money," an article in a trust company magazine explained in 1927, it would be much more difficult "to retrieve for them their vanished funds," or to "save loss for others." Such timeliness depended not only on effi-cient channels of communication, but also on an extensive warning system of "listening posts" that would allow fraud monitors to pick up early signals of commercial or financial chicanery, and on the willingness of the "public . . . to report immediately anything that appears at all questionable or doubtful."[39]

Antifraud organizations further recognized that heightened enforcement was a crucial precondition to strengthening deterrence against fraud, and that such enforcement would have to overcome the daunting barriers to collective action that were rooted in administrative incapacity and an individualistic commercial culture. The tendency of fraud victims to avoid the time and ex-pense associated with criminal proceedings, especially if they were able to ex-tract some restitution from a swindler's squawk fund, presented companion difficulties for law enforcement. Silent suckers furnished authorities with no basis to launch an investigation, no oral testimony or documentary evidence on which to base a prosecution.

In their public education initiatives, antifraud institutions repeatedly chipped away at the common disinclination to bring swindlers to justice.

NACM leaders implored members to maintain good recordkeeping practices, which eased evidence-gathering should any debtors turn to fraud. It also extolled the civic-mindedness of executives who treated credit swindlers with the contempt that they deserved, and heaped scorn on those who ignored their civic responsibilities by accepting compromise offers in fraud cases. "DON'T let apathy and supinity rule when you have been victimized by a credit crook," the editors proclaimed in one 1914 issue. "Remember, he has made a raid, not on you alone, but on the great business organization of which you are but a part. Arouse yourself; do all in your power, cost it little or much, to rid the commercial commonwealth of those who would assault that relationship of faith and confidence . . . which is the basis of solid business growth." The credit man with a spine, the manly credit man, worked to send fraudulent debtors to prison, even at significant short-term cost, just as the manly retailer lived up to the promises in advertising spreads.[40]

Even when defrauded individuals or businesses wished to assist law enforcement, though, investigative complexities often strained the capacity of early twentieth-century police forces and prosecutors' offices, especially when swindles operated across state lines. By building up a corps of professional investigators, many of whom had experience in district attorneys' offices or as postal inspectors, antifraud organizations attempted to match the sophisticated tactics and geographic reach of the most successful perpetrators of fraud. By the early 1920s, both NACM and the NVC had developed national evidentiary clearinghouses. They kept track of evolving scams and the careers of prominent swindlers and maintained "Rogues' Galleries" in the form of photographic collections that helped identify individuals who had a penchant for skipping town and changing names and life stories (Figure 7.3). The national antifraud network thus facilitated the sharing of intelligence about transient fraud and fraudsters. Once antifraud investigators amassed what they viewed as clear-cut evidence of criminal activity, they passed along the findings to governmental officials in the appropriate jurisdiction.[41]

The cultivation of investigative capacity dovetailed with the NACM's and Better Business Bureaus' goals of public education. A network of seasoned detectives facilitated arrests, indictments, and prosecutions, all of which received extensive coverage from a sympathetic press corps. The resulting stream of enforcement-related stories offered additional opportunities to inform the public about the telltale signs of fraud, while signaling to both outright swindlers and legitimate enterprises that deceptive marketing brought consequences. Such attention, BBB officials maintained, generated "public indignation," which in turn "spurred prosecuting authorities and juries to a less lenient frame of mind where swindlers are concerned." Fundraising campaigns, such

Figure 7.3: An NACM investigator compares a photograph of a credit-fraud suspect with the pictures in the organization's Rogue's Gallery, which it kept in New York City. From *Credit Monthly*, March 1928.

as the NACM's effort to raise nearly $2 million to support investigative efforts in 1925, furnished similar opportunities to heighten awareness of antifraud messages.[42]

By keeping initial fraud monitoring and investigations within their own institutions, antifraud organizations maintained flexibility in law enforcement—and likely far more than would have been feasible through a strategy of lobbying to place more public detectives and prosecutors on the fraud beat. In cases where an established firm embarked on a marketing campaign that flirted with misrepresentation, the BBBs initially approached it quietly, "endeavor[ing] to impress the advertiser with the desirability and the advisability of raising the standard of his own copy." Most of the time, managers accepted proposed adjustments, even agreeing to retract advertising. BBB publications teem with overviews of these settlements achieved through "friendly persuasion." The 1928 Annual Report of the Kansas City Bureau, for instance, reported that it had "secured changes in 670 inaccurate advertisements," ranging from instances of "Underwear Over-valued" and "Furniture Cut Deceptive" to "Deceptive Comparative Prices" and "Real Estate Exaggerations." If advertisers rebuffed efforts at moral suasion, Bureau officials often progressed to public disclosure, using their publications, connections, and public relations to shine a spotlight on a given business's problematic tactics. Cases went to state or federal prosecutors only when BBB administrators confronted what they viewed as recalcitrance, which occurred only once or twice for every hundred legitimate complaints.[43]

One needs to keep the scale of the business establishment's war on fraud in perspective. After two decades of rapid expansion, the persons collectively employed by the BBB network likely totaled fewer than a thousand, a workforce roughly similar in size to that employed by a single large-scale advertising firm such as N. W. Ayer & Co., and less than 3 percent of the employees at a leading national retailer such as Sears, Roebuck & Co.[44] At no point did the bureaucratic resources of NACM and the BBBs approach those of the largest corporate enterprises. Indeed, the corps of store detectives working for the nation's large urban department stores probably exceeded the full complement of BBB employees and NACM's Prosecution and Investigation Department combined, while the force of private railroad police, totaling ten thousand in 1930, certainly did so.[45] Nonetheless, the number of fraud monitors and educators compared favorably with the administrative infrastructure at the Federal Trade Commission. In 1930, the FTC employed only 450 persons and possessed an annual budget of approximately $1.5 million, with which it had to carry out its legal mandates to enforce not only federal prohibitions against deceptive advertising, but also violations of the antitrust laws. If one adds the considerable in-kind contributions of advertising space by publications and radio stations to the BBBs, the educational and disciplinary footprint of the antifraud organizations greatly outstripped that of the pre–New Deal Federal Trade Commission.[46]

THE SCOPE OF CAPITALIST COLLECTIVISM

Suffusing all of these various activities—lobbying to extend statutory prohibitions of deceptive commercial communications; campaigns to inoculate the public against scams and schemes and convince businessmen to resist the inclination to adopt or accommodate such deceptions; articulation and dissemination of commercial standards and best practices; construction of private, professional antifraud bureaucracies—was an extraordinary degree of confidence. Leaders of the maturing antifraud establishment were not bashful about asserting their expertise in matters concerning fraud, which they expressed most commonly in the idiom of public health. NACM officials characterized their endeavors as "sanitary work" or "organized credit hygiene," and insisted that "communities should be vaccinated against commercial crime just as they are against smallpox." *Credit Monthly* represented the association's spokespersons as credit physicians who safeguarded the country's businesses from the

Figure 7.4: Dr. NACM takes on the credit crook. *Credit Monthly* cover, February 1926.

poisonous depredations of the "credit crook." BBB managers received an analogous message from NYSE President E.H.H. Simmons in September 1927. The Bureaus, Simmons declared, had obligations in the "economic and business field closely resembling [those] which medical men [have] in the field of public health and sanitation." Just as physicians had "educated the public in matters of health . . . rendering it immune to the scourges of disease which formerly worked such havoc with human life," so antifraud leaders had the fundamental tasks of "educat[ing] the American investor into a similar condition of immunity from . . . the swindling profession, and . . . clear[ing] up the conditions where these parasites on our national business establishments lurk and breed." Like public health officials who combated the environmental conditions that bred tuberculosis, yellow fever, and malaria, antifraud professionals portrayed their labors as rooted in scientific understanding and aimed at protecting the public from dangerous scourges.[47] Depictions such as a 1926 rendition of "Dr. NACM" (Figure 7.4) expanded upon the rhetoric that had animated regulation of adulterated fertilizers and foodstuffs. Now all antifraud work took on the sheen of science.

Accompanying such self-presentations were insistent claims that antifraud organizations represented the United States writ large and looked out for the "public welfare" without fear or favor. NACM publications characterized its members as crusaders for the economic commonweal, on occasion depicting them in the garb of medieval Crusaders, upholding the ancient virtues of *Vigilantia* and *Fidelitas*. BBB officials proclaimed that they had "no axe to grind" and no interest to protect, that their "methods have been scientific," that, perhaps most strikingly, they were "literally of, by, and for the public." The Oklahoma City Bureau declared in 1930 that the organization was "[u]nprejudiced, unbiased, and adher[ing] strictly to its own work and purposes" and that it "never allowed its facilities or influence to be used to further selfish or personal rights." One president of the National BBB similarly pronounced that antifraud work sounded "the undoubted note of patriotism . . . which adds to the general prosperity of our country."[48] Indeed, antifraud professionals often asserted de facto jurisdiction over fraudulent behavior, a move that the media tended to ratify, as through a 1926 *New Orleans Times Picayune* cartoon depicting NACM as a motorcycle cop hot on the heels of a band of commercial swindlers (Figure 7.5). The cartoonist added a "U.S.A." nameplate and titled his drawing "The National Policeman," clothing this private association of business executives with the legitimacy of the state.[49]

Throughout the 1920s, America's dominant Republican Party blessed the quasi-public character of antifraud institutions, with the country's highest officials giving them full-throated endorsements. President Calvin Coolidge observed that "wherever deception, falsehood, and fraud creep in, they undermine the whole structure," a calamity to "our commercial life" that could only be prevented "by the businessmen themselves." His successor, Herbert Hoover, praised the BBB network for greatly "contributing to the economic stability and progress of the country." Treasury Secretary Andrew Mellon, Attorney General John Sargent, Secretary of the Post Office Harry New, and many lower-level political appointees expressed similar sentiments.[50]

The standing of antifraud professionals with Republican leaders translated into influence over key legal appointments. The New York City and National BBBs, the Investment Bankers of America, and the NYSE all had significant say over prosecutorial positions in their bailiwicks, such as the United States attorney for New York's Southern Federal District or the New York State assistant attorney general responsible for enforcement of securities fraud law. Government detectives and prosecutors who had experience with fraud cases also frequently accepted employment at private antifraud agencies. With such strong connections, it should come as no surprise that the era's law enforcement officials leaned heavily on these organizations, especially when embarking on high-profile fraud crackdowns such as the Post Office's campaigns

Figure 7.5: NACM as the national vindicator of the law. *New Orleans Times Picayune*, reprinted in *Credit Monthly*, May 1926.

against fraudulent Texas oil companies and Florida real-estate scams during the 1920s.[51]

The antifraud crusade wished to remake commercial culture across the United States. As such, it constituted something of a social movement within the confines of American business, though one emanating from the ranks of the elite, rather the social or cultural margins. The campaign's leaders and troops embraced the challenge of convincing corporate bigwigs, small-scale entrepreneurs, middle managers, securities promoters, and advertising professionals that they should eschew the quick buck, and rather act with regard to long-term reputation, the stability of their industries, and the health of the

Figure 7.6: Attendees at a 1929 Better Business Bureau Conference in San Diego.
Courtesy of Western History and Genealogy Division, Denver Public Library.

broader economy. As the members of the antifraud vanguard fine-tuned this pitch, they put forward numerous sober arguments. But they also conjured evangelical visions of manly commercial fellowship and self-consciously infused their creed into the business establishment's evolving social rituals.

Toward these ends, NACM and the BBBs annually convened national conventions, like the 1929 BBB meeting in San Diego depicted in Figure 7.6, where members of the antifraud fraternity deliberated over new tactics, expanded networks of information-sharing, and mutually testified to the righteousness of their "Crusader Spirit" and "nation-wide effort." They made periodic fundraising campaigns into collective expressions of esprit de corps, through which participants could offer tangible evidence of commitment. Even more frequently, local chapters held lunches and dinners or dispatched speakers to the monthly meetings of Rotary Clubs. At such gatherings, business leaders shared a good meal at a local hotel, and then, "after cigars had been lighted," listened to a talk that harangued the fraudster and those who abetted his machinations, while extolling the business community's exertions to rid itself of confidence-killing deception. Tellingly, antifraud activists did not shy away from the language of communitarian action, characterizing their initiatives as a "movement" for truth-in-advertising. The commercial establishment's fight against fraud depended as much on personal contexts of fellowship as it did on sophisticated lobbying campaigns, impressive public relations machinery, and ever more extensive bureaucratic techniques of commercial surveillance.[52]

Movement-building events could attain an impressive scale, reflecting the seriousness and financial commitment that undergirded the early twentieth-century antifraud war. A gala annual dinner thrown by the St. Louis BBB in the spring of 1941 exemplified pivotal dimensions of communal occasions. On the main floor, BBB leaders and invited guests sat at head tables on the side, while representatives from BBB member firms and local dignitaries shared tables in the center. On the mezzanine level, scores of students from more than fifty high schools had the chance to listen to the speechifying, and to begin the process of identifying with the battle against cheats and swindlers. Large American flags festooned the mezzanine railing, reminding participants that the antifraud fight was America's fight. Over one thousand St. Louisans purchased tickets to this gathering, a testament to the "sincerity and determination on the part of legitimate business to rid the community of improper practices."[53]

The early twentieth-century drive against commercial fraud tracks patterns evident in most social movements. Whether arising out of evangelical rejection of prevailing institutions and practices, working people's demands for greater economic security and political power, disfavored social groups' insistence upon equal citizenship rights, or the concerns of economic elites about pervasive commercial humbuggery, such collective undertakings have faced similar challenges. The historical enemy might be slavery, alcohol consumption, unequal bargaining power, discrimination on the basis of race/gender/sexual orientation, or business fraud. In all these contexts, movement leaders had to fashion a new sense of identity around issues of shared concern and build deep commitment to the cause, often by creating new kinds of emotional experience. Invariably, modern social movements have sought to subordinate individual concerns and interests to broader communitarian norms. Such endeavors have always required the construction of engrossing narratives that pull individuals into the movement, connect personal identities to the cause, and convince participants that their actions will make a difference.[54]

To purge American marketplaces of chicanery, officials such as J. Harry Tregoe and H. J. Kenner tried to reframe the emotional stakes of day-to-day marketing practices. Through their organizations' publications, public narratives, and social events, these standard-bearers sought, in the language of behavioral economics, to leaven "market norms" with "social norms," to inject communal values into business culture.[55] In doing so, antifraud leaders contributed to a broader effort by interwar business interests to impose order on the dizzying transformations within America's industrial economy, chiefly by confining the channels of permissible competition.[56]

In many respects, the work of the NACM and the BBBs reflected the antipathy of corporate America to administrative agencies that could bog down enterprises with endless rules and bureaucratic processes.[57] The new business-funded antifraud organizations, like so many of their corporate patrons, rejected most proposals to create large and intrusive government bureaucracies as a strategy of addressing the social ills, economic instability, or other externalities generated by modern industrial economies. In the securities arena, for example, BBB leaders vigorously criticized any suggestion that the state ought to protect investors by licensing stockbrokers or, even worse, by vetting public securities offerings to ensure their legitimacy. Indeed, the founding of the New York City BBB formed a central element of Wall Street's efforts to deflect state legislative proposals for "blue-sky" legislation that would create such administrative authority. As the AACW argued forthrightly in 1919, "if an industry does not clean house for itself, the law will do it, and the law often operates in such a manner as to injure the legitimate while seeking to stop the faker."[58]

Visceral antagonism to the heavy-handed administrative state was accompanied by a hearty embrace of the post–World War I Republican call for associationalism. NACM's efforts constituted a leading example of the Republican preference for trade groups that responded to economic challenges through mutualistic standard-setting (in this case, with regard to evaluating credit requests and exchanging credit intelligence). Although the BBBs had a much wider purview than most trade groups, they facilitated associationalism in a host of contexts. Most importantly, the Bureau network defined and continually refined principles for truth in advertising, which they disseminated among newspapers, magazines, radio stations, advertising agencies, and frequent advertisers, such as urban department stores. In the latter half of the decade, the National BBB also joined with the Federal Trade Commission to convene conferences among leading retailers of furs, furniture, and numerous other lines of goods, to hammer out transparent standards for the use of trade names that would avoid confusion among manufacturers, dealers, and the buying public.

Again and again, the antifraud establishment characterized their initiatives as forms of "home rule" by American business, paralleling the sentiments that drove associationalism in so many other corners of the post–World War I American economy. As H. J. Kenner emphasized in a 1926 speech, the organized business community had pledged to keep "its own house in order." Through the BBB's educational efforts, impartial monitoring of the marketplace, and disinterested cooperation with the authorities in law enforcement, Kenner argued, "[b]usiness will impress Government and the public alike with its determination to police its own domain. Respect for Business and for Law will then grow apace." This preference for commercial and financial self-government greatly influenced the BBB's approach to fraud policing, which stressed, wherever possible, flexible adjustments or reliance on the pressure of public disclosure, rather than a turn to the all-too-cumbersome disciplinary power of the state.[59] In fashioning a discourse of "home rule," the antiswindling brigade mirrored the contemporaneous language of Southern segregationists. Like their political counterparts in the Southern Democratic Party, who demanded unchallenged jurisdiction over race relations in their states, business elites asserted their right to deal with issues related to fraud on their terms, through their own administrative and investigative authority.[60]

The dilemmas posed by duplicitous commercial speech, however, convinced a broad cross-section of American business leaders of the need for an additional layer of governmental oversight. The specter of diminished public confidence led corporate leaders, especially within the sectors of large-scale retailing, finance, and the media, to turn to the state for retrospective economic regulation through the criminal code. Through vigorous enforcement of a tighter set of criminal fraud laws, the business establishment expected to clamp down on dodgy small-scale enterprises and outright fly-by-night firms. Such enforcement centrally involved the state—indeed, it entailed increased resources for investigative and prosecutorial manpower and led to the creation of several new divisions focused specifically on fraud, such as within the offices of New York's attorney general and the US attorney in Southern New York. Such public fraud-fighters, however, worked in conjunction with the new nonprofit organizations created by business elites. Those entities often had greater financial resources and administrative capacity and increasingly served as an investigative filter, handling initial complaints and deciding which cases merited governmental attention.

The cozy relations between antifraud organizations and law-enforcement officials faced no sanction from the American judiciary, in sharp distinction to the cold shoulder that the era's judges gave to price-fixing agreements and efforts to share information about prices and costs. American cartels and open-price associations had to struggle against age-old legal suspicion of restraints of trade.[61] NACM and the BBBs, by contrast, could and did portray their endeavors as attempts to vindicate American law, to breathe life into longstanding common-law precepts against economic deceit that had remained mainly dormant because of practical barriers to fraud prosecutions.

In both state and federal courts, judges typically endorsed such activities. As one member of the federal bench argued in a 1941 case concerning the obligation of the Oklahoma City BBB to pay Social Security taxes,

> The Bureau carries on a continuous campaign of fraud prevention work. It warns the public against fraudulent plans and schemes. It endeavors to induce the local advertising agencies not to accept advertisements from the promoters of such

plans and schemes. Through newspaper advertisements, radio talks, bulletins, and posters, it acquaints the public with fraudulent practices. It exposes specific fraudulent practices being carried on in Oklahoma City. It also endeavors to induce merchants to refrain from misleading advertising, extravagant claims, and price comparisons, and to conform to a high standard of business ethics. It endeavors to educate the consumer to buy wisely.[62]

This supportive depiction might as well have been authored by a BBB official. In 1929, New York City magistrate George W. Simpson penned a perhaps even more revealing note to H. J. Kenner in advance of the latter's appearance at a Rotary Club luncheon, imploring Kenner to "enlist Rotary in our cause," by which he meant the effort not only to "stop outright fraud," but also to "head off . . . border-line fraud." Simpson signed the note, "Fraternally yours," an epistolary gesture that helps to explain judicial deference to the strategies of public-spirited businessmen and antifraud professionals, who, after all, possessed similar socioeconomic and educational backgrounds as the prototypical mid-twentieth-century American jurist.[63]

Unsurprisingly in light of such sentiments, American judges shied away from placing roadblocks in the path of the antifraud campaign. When businessmen shamed by Bureaus for fraudulent practices brought libel suits, courts rejected them.[64] As a result of this legal acceptance, early twentieth-century business-government associationalism reached its apex in the arena of regulating commercial speech. Here, the cooperative impulse among business elites skirted the typical judicial preference for economic competition. Here, the relationship between business and the American state more closely approximated the situation across the Atlantic, where European governments tended to ratify price-fixing agreements in order to stabilize a tumultuous economic environment.

Because the early twentieth-century antifraud campaign received such strong support from American government, it represented an ambitious experiment in business self-regulation. Its champions did not hesitate to trumpet its successes, which they depicted as a vindication for business "home rule" and "self-government." Antifraud leaders missed few opportunities to broadcast achievements, especially in bringing the individuals, businesses, and rings who engaged in fraud to face the criminal justice system. Both NACM and the BBBs kept careful track of investigations through monthly updates and annual reports, partly to justify their effectiveness to business subscribers. The two institutions also highlighted evidence of significant contributions to law enforcement, and even some indications of deterrence. Between 1925 and 1929, the labors of NACM's Investigation and Prosecution Department resulted in nearly 1,600 indictments from either state or federal grand juries; of the cases that had gone to trial by June 1929, prosecutors had secured more than 734 convictions, achieving a success rate of over 80 percent. Government prosecutors reported that this showing reflected considerably better conviction rates than before NACM began assisting in evidence-gathering, both for fraud cases and for criminal complaints generally.[65] It certainly reflected a vast improvement over the paltry nineteenth-century conviction rates for fraud-related prosecutions.

Over the course of the 1920s, BBB managers could point to an even wider array of accomplishments. In addition to the standardization of trade names through industry conferences, local and national Bureaus had assisted the print media and radio stations in assessing suspicious requests for advertising space, culminating in the rejection of thousands of proposed ads, including nearly all pitches for "get-rich-quick" schemes in respectable publications. They had collectively handled several million complaints about either securities promotions or the marketing practices of advertisers, and had negotiated tens of thousands of adjustments in marketing policies by urban retailers in every region of the country. Such adjustments occurred more readily because of the credibility that the Bureaus possessed in local business communities, and because of their capacity to operate flexibly and, when they so chose, outside the glare of publicity. Like NACM, the BBBs also made a significant mark on the enforcement of fraud laws. Investigations undertaken by Bureaus across the country led to hundreds of indictments and convictions, especially under the federal mail fraud statutes and state securities fraud laws such as New York's Martin Act, which criminalized deception in securities promotions.[66]

The nation's chief fraud opponents further claimed that their undertakings had cut down the numbers of suckers taken for a ride and dramatically improved business ethics. NACM oversaw the founding of dozens of credit exchange and adjustment bureaus across the country, which its officials portrayed as reducing the susceptibility of suppliers to credit fraud. Repeated BBB warnings helped to limit public losses in a host of post–World War I investment and employment scams. Within the realm of merchandising, executives at several large department stores became convinced that the Bureau's outside monitoring of advertising served as a useful check on store practices, leading to "the improvement of retail stores as public institutions." As a result of the outside prodding, these executives encouraged their buyers and division managers not only to exercise greater care in formulating advertisements and to cooperate with any BBB investigations, but also to engage in their own surveillance of competitors.[67]

Antifraud professionals could even point to indications that their labors had created a more substantial deterrent to commercial skullduggery. According to NACM, tighter credit standards and heightened prosecution of credit fraud resulted in a 32 percent decline in the number of cases referred to its Investigation and Prosecution Department between 1925 and 1928. As early as 1926, the group's general manager, J. H. Tregoe, assured its members that "'Watch your step' has become the motto of the commercial crook." The BBBs pointed to assessments of retail advertising in St. Louis that reported only 2 percent error rates by the mid-1930s, and a study of two fraudulent stock promotions that found a disproportionate number of suckers lived outside the areas served by a Bureau. According to BBB officials, such findings suggested that swindlers had learned to avoid their territory.[68] Whether or not all of these assertions had a solid factual basis, they gained currency in the nation's print media, as suggested by a 1929 cartoon in the *New Orleans Times Picayune* (Figure 7.7). Depicting the apprehension of a "credit crook" by a robust "Credit Men's Association," figured again as a policeman, the cartoon includes as onlookers both a very pleased representative of "New Orleans Business" and a fearful "potential credit crook."

By the mid-1920s, the growing influence of the American antifraud movement encouraged some of its key leaders to think in transnational terms. Within NACM, officials envisioned an international credit bureau that would monitor relations between commercial creditors and debtors across national boundaries, while fostering "international co-ordination of credit methods and ideals." Leaders in the "truth in advertising" movement similarly wished to expand abroad, targeting Europe, and especially England, as propitious ground for antifraud bureaus. Such confident proposals for extensions of "soft" American power dovetailed closely with the dramatic expansion of Rotary International and the effort to bring US retailing strategies to Europe during the 1930s. The latter initiatives broadly shared the ideological predispositions of the campaign for economic truthfulness, as well as the participation of many of the same business elites. To commercial leaders such as Louis Kirstein, American "self-government of industry" deserved emulation by other industrialized nations.[69]

For all the successes of the Credit Men's Associations and the BBBs, the handling of deceptive commercial practices through self-regulation and retrospective law enforcement had some serious limitations. NACM's entreaties that credit managers no longer prefer short-term profits to the longer-term health of the overall commercial credit system clearly did not persuade a great many executives. Otherwise, the *Credit Monthly* would not have had to continue issuing insistent pleas throughout the 1920s for credit managers to per-

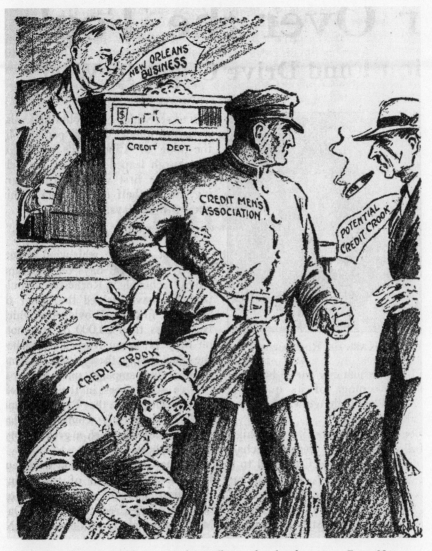

Figure 7.7: A portrayal of deterrence from effective fraud enforcement. From *New Orleans Times Picayune*, June 1929, courtesy of NACM.

form due diligence in vetting potential mercantile customers, to share their knowledge about problematic debtors, and to refuse to accept compromise payments from dishonest debtors. All of the BBB's public warnings, all the rejected advertisements and negotiated adjustments of marketing policies, all of the arrests and convictions, did not put that much of a dent in BBB estimates of overall fraud incidence. Cut off from easy access to established media organs, swindlers merely turned in greater numbers to the production of their own tip sheets and financial papers, which they distributed widely throughout the country. No longer able to unload a given worthless stock or real-estate development because of public exposure, promoters moved on to another town, another scheme, often pursuing some twist on well-known scams that kept the sucker bait fresh. At no point in the 1920s did either law enforcement officials or representatives of antifraud organizations estimate actual declines in the annual losses resulting from fraud. Furthermore, the onset of economic depression sharpened the incentives for deceptive advertising, as retailers chased ever more elusive consumer dollars and created new avenues for stock swindling, chiefly through attempts to reorganize bankrupt companies.[70]

Throughout the interwar period, antifraud campaigners sought to solidify their newly gained authority, often through a kind of rhetorical alchemy. These individuals had to show a business constituency increasingly drawn to quantitative assessments of success that contributions to antifraud organizations led to appropriate and predicted results. But they also had a predisposition to find new threats to commercial confidence and to magnify the nature of such dangers. Like "police" in a variety of contexts, and like modern organizational consultants, antifraud professionals had a powerful incentive at once to crow about their impact and warn about the fearful consequences of not receiving ongoing funding and support.

In addition, antiswindling campaigns consistently cast suspicions on Americans from the commercial and social margins. These undertakings were funded by large-scale enterprises whose managers believed that small firms constituted the gravest threat to standards of fair-dealing. Leaders at NACM and the BBBs came from America's native-born, Protestant establishment, and their worldviews were shaped by the values and expectations of that establishment. J. Harry Tregoe, the most important leader at NACM during its first thirty years, offers an instructive example. A fixture of Baltimore's Presbyterian community and a stalwart Republican, he devoted considerable attention to his city's (Baltimore) Young Men's Christian Association, expressed deep-seated hostility toward alcohol consumption, and imbibed the waxing nativism of the post–World War I era. His political and cultural sensibilities had a great deal in common with that of a nineteenth-century antifraud crusader such as Anthony Comstock. To Tregoe, the basis of American civilization was under siege from both the "low-thinking foreigner" and the labor radical. As he explained when denouncing the labor leader Samuel Gompers for criticizing a Supreme Court decision in 1922, "the safety of America is threatened by barbarians like those who caused the downfall of Rome."[71]

Such ethnocentrism lent antifraud campaigns an anti-immigrant animus, just like the public health initiatives that its publicists so frequently held up as models. To be sure, antifraud organizations targeted immigrant communities for educational messages about the best practices for consumers and investors. But in working to fashion a nationwide "vacuum cleaning system," a network powerful enough to remove what one NACM mandarin saw as the "Unclean . . . lepers" that imperiled domestic economic health, these institutions often focused investigative resources on immigrant communities.[72] The Syrian mercantile community received especially close scrutiny, reflecting its reputation for incorporating recently arrived compatriots into fraud rings. Eastern European Jews also featured prominently in the rundowns of arrests and convictions published by *Credit Monthly*, as well as its accounts of the detective work that brought commercial crooks to justice. As NACM's chief investigator, C. D. West, made clear in one such profile of a Russian Jew who was a serial credit swindler, the organization sought to "free business of the parasite, . . . the dishonest immigrant who believes that a change of name and a little American veneer will bring him a fortune overnight."[73]

In an analogous vein, BBB staff expended most of their energies on combating commercial untruths by con artists and smaller businesses that pushed the limits of acceptable puffery, hyperbole, and bombast. With the exception of some large-scale retailers that relied heavily on newspaper advertising, the Bureaus left alone the big corporations whose executives sat on their boards of directors. As a result, at no point during the 1920s stock boom did the BBB network identify the era's egregious conflicts of interest or misrepresentations within the reputable finance industry, all of which came to light amid the congressional investigations of the early 1930s. Bureau investigators steered clear of securities listed on the major exchanges and pressed ordinary investors to place their trust and savings in the hands of "expert" counselors from the banking industry. BBB managers issued no warnings about the deceitful tactics used by most leading investment banks to push hundreds of millions of dollars worth of exceedingly risky Latin American bond issues on their customers. They published no cautions about the stock manipulations and insider dealing undertaken by several leading New York City banks. They offered no admonitions about the duplicitous marketing of Kreuger & Toll bonds to thousands of small investors, nor the beguiling promises associated with the bond flotations of the Insull public utilities empire.[74]

In response to a 1927 inquiry from a New York financial reporter, one BBB employee did voice some concerns about the high overhead costs and questionable management practices of the new investment trusts (later known as mutual funds). By the early 1930s, it would become clear that this early warning was prescient. A number of investment trusts engaged in rank manipulations of stocks controlled by their executives. Others operated on the "Fund W" plan, issuing false statements of results and paying dividends to early investors out of the capital of those who came later. But the day after the BBB employee's comments appeared in the press, H. J. Kenner issued a clarifying public letter, insisting that these remarks were "merely . . . his personal views on the subject," and that the Bureau had no institutional position on the advisability of placing funds in investment trusts. The BBB, Kenner reminded the public, confined itself to "facts" about "companies which may appear to be under suspicion."[75]

Despite hundreds of bulletins about shady investments, the nation's most prominent antifraud organization remained blind to the seamier practices of the investment banks and brokerage firms that bankrolled it. Tellingly, in 1930 the New York City BBB placed Richard Whitney, then NYSE president, on its advisory board. Like the rest of the country, the Bureau remained oblivious to the financial improprieties surrounding his brokerage firm—chiefly the appropriation of trust funds to his own use—that would eventually land him in prison.[76] Implicitly convinced of their patrons' respectability and honor, BBB officials simply could not entertain the possibility that their chief backers might be major contributors to the problem of duplicity in the American marketplace. They did not so much willfully ignore evidence of financial deceit in high places as never go looking for it. For Kenner and other leaders of the antifraud movement, fraud crept in on the feet of outsiders.

✴✴✴✴

Where post–World War I antifraud organizations such as NACM and the BBBs chose to tread—in clarifying commercial rules for advertising, merchandising, and granting credit, or in putting unambiguously fraudulent promoters and brokerage firms under close surveillance—their close links to prominent businesses and prosecutors, along with their ability to handle disputes flexibly, allowed them to make significant headway. A 1925 speech to employees by Sheldon Coons, the advertising manager of Gimbels Department Store, encapsulates many of these advantages. The Better Business Bureau, Coons assured his audience, "is not a police organization. It is not an organization run by somebody trying to interfere with our business. It is an organization designed and financed by New York stores and investment houses. Our membership is costing us several thousand dollars a year. We are members of this Bureau because we want an outside check upon our activities."[77] For Coons, the BBB was a friend, rather than a bureaucratic enemy, and deserved cooperation and respect. But the circumscribed territory in which antifraud organizations chose to exercise their jurisdiction also ensured some rather glaring failures; and with those failures would eventually come a turn to far more vigorous forms of governmental regulation during the Roosevelt administration.

The resulting embrace of an ever more ambitious set of antifraud regulatory objectives will receive extended attention in Part IV. But first, the legal environment ushered in by Progressive-era policy innovations merits a closer look. Day-to-day efforts to strike at economic duplicity not only threatened to stifle entrepreneurial ingenuity; at times, they also endangered longstanding procedural commitments to the rule of law.

CHAPTER EIGHT

Quandaries of Procedural Justice

The modes of American fraud policing that emerged from the early 1870s through the 1920s augmented regulatory power. Both within and outside of the state, antifraud organizations developed an unprecedented capacity to monitor economic misrepresentations and sanction the individuals and firms responsible for them. Ranging from chemical laboratories to nationwide information clearinghouses, the new regulatory infrastructures boasted pools of trained, experienced manpower, including scientists, inspectors, and detectives. These fraud-fighters did not sit back and wait for allegations of fraud to come to them. They randomly tested the composition of agricultural inputs, impersonated customers to amass evidence against sham mail-order firms, and sent shoppers to see if marketing practices lived up to the promises of advertising copy. In order to overcome the collective action problems that so often stymied fraud prosecutions, they built investigative networks that matched the geographic range of sophisticated swindling rings and deceptive promoters. Finally, antifraud organizations developed far-reaching remedies for economic deception, imposing new quality standards, cutting off access to the mails, and limiting access to advertising channels.

These new forms of bureaucratic power did not sit well with some Americans. Previous chapters have offered glimmers of this discontent. Through 1910 or so, the most vocal protests came from businesses who perceived themselves as unjustly treated by antifraud institutions, although Democratic newspapers and champions of civil liberties from both major parties sometimes chimed in. By the advent of the Wilson administration, anxieties over antifraud tactics were increasingly expressed by a conservative faction within the legal profession, who viewed discretionary administrative power with abiding suspicion. One recurrent complaint emphasized a lack of consistency in regulatory determinations, as had occurred in response to variable fertilizer analyses or grain grading. A second and even more powerful objection targeted invasive investigative techniques and unaccountable methods of adjudication, which opponents of antifraud efforts portrayed as harmful to competition, undemocratic, and even un-American. These latter grievances arose particularly in the contexts of administrative mail fraud enforcement between the

1880s and early 1900s, and the later enforcement activities of the Better Business Bureaus during the 1920s and early 1930s. Postal officials and BBB leaders vociferously defended themselves against their detractors, but eventually modified internal procedures to assuage critics, chiefly through more formal protections for due process.

The resulting adjustments anticipated a broader mid-twentieth-century effort to accommodate evolving administrative institutions to the longstanding formalities and values of American legal culture. In the federal government, this process culminated in the passage of the Administrative Procedure Act of 1946, which compelled federal regulatory institutions to adhere to exacting procedural standards in both rule-making and enforcement actions. But it was evident as well in the early history of the Federal Trade Commission (created in 1914), which from its first decades embraced modes of proceeding that hewed much more closely to common-law protections than had the Post Office Department before 1913. Procedural reform in antifraud efforts thus served as a prologue to more general administrative law reform.

Insofar as late nineteenth- and early twentieth-century antifraud initiatives achieved their aims, success often depended on the power to act quickly and with discretion. One key virtue of postal fraud orders and informal agreements to exclude advertisers from leading publications was that officials could implement them rapidly, before fraudulent firms reached many victims. In addition, threats to rely on these remedies persuaded numerous firms that had used marginally deceptive tactics to discontinue them. These advantages were hallmarks of effective regulatory governance. But when both the Post Office and the BBBs eventually agreed to reshape their methods of handling disputes, they reduced their disciplinary impact. Such adjustments testify to the enduring force of America's common-law legal culture, even as the United States came to terms with the pressures of modern capitalism.

Anti-Comstockery

The first broadsides directed at the Post Office arrived almost as soon as it began to enforce the 1872 Postal Reform Act's provisions targeting objectionable materials in the mails. Opponents of Anthony Comstock's moral crusade complained that his techniques violated American norms of fair play. By adopting fictitious personas to gain evidence against the senders of illicit mail, critics charged, Comstock embraced means that were as immoral as his antagonists' businesses. One Democratic editor insisted at various points in the mid-1870s that the New York City postal inspector stooped to "lies and forgeries" by sending his decoy letters in search of illegal goods; he made "his living by lying, swindling, and deceiving the people in the name of the God and morality party"; against "all true law and manly decency," he systematically relied on the same sort of "false pretences" as his far-flung suspects.[1]

Comstock's campaigns against distributors of pornography provoked the loudest condemnations of his enforcement practices, though few voices defended the rights of publishers to disseminate literature with sexual content. But many New Englanders, including a number of nonevangelical ministers and avowed free-thinkers, objected to the vice reformer's aggressive investigations in much the same fashion as the Chicago newspaperman. A New York City minister objected to "the whole system of spies and the lying thereby enacted" by the use of decoy letters, while a Boston intellectual argued that "a lie or fraud perpetrated in behalf of morality or religion is just as truly a lie or a fraud as is one prompted by the Father of lies." One New York City publisher whom Comstock arrested for selling pamphlets that contradicted Christian revelation and discussed sexual reproduction, D. M. Bennett, compared his mode of operation to that of the Spanish Inquisition. To Bennett, the postal inspectors had embarked on a "nefarious business" founded on "falsehood, deception, traps, and pitfalls for the unwary." This approach might furnish evidence against many ne'er-do-wells, but at the cost of ensnaring innocent individuals as well. Such critiques persuaded over seventy thousand Americans to petition Congress in the late 1870s to repeal the obscenity portions of the Postal Reform Law.[2]

Qualms about Comstock's practices paralleled concerns about the surveillance instituted by private credit reporting agencies in the mid-nineteenth century. Credit reporters did not engage in such subterfuges. Instead, the agents for R. G. Dun, Bradstreet's, and other such businesses compiled financial details about individuals, as well as prevailing opinions about their creditworthiness and character. Yet the creation of a nationwide system of surveillance over commercial debtors struck many Americans as a disreputable "spy system" that intruded into private lives. Other commentators objected to the "secret service manner" in which commercial agencies did their business, because the identity of credit reporters remained a mystery, as did the process by which they formulated their judgments.[3]

Nineteenth-century credit reporters and postal inspectors attracted reproach for similar reasons. Both worked for national organizations that wielded potentially crippling power over individuals and firms. Both pursued investigations in secret and made decisions without fear of legal accountability. Underlying the uneasiness with credit reporting and mail fraud enforcement lay ambivalence about the way that the creation of an integrated national economy tended to bring about concentrations of power, minimally constrained by legal or democratic oversight. As Philadelphia economics writer Edward Freedley articulated the concern in 1853, mercantile agencies were "in the hands of a few men, self-constituted umpires, . . . subject to the errors of ignorance and mistakes of carelessness, with no guaranteed exemption from the influence of malice, favouritism, bribery, or corruption."[4] Cautions such as Freedley's embodied suspicions of unchecked authority that had animated American politics since the Revolution.[5]

Credit reporting firms and the postal inspectorate mostly parried the thrusts of their adversaries. The former emphasized their role in preventing reckless speculators and unsavory characters from gaining access to established channels of credit, as well as their facilitation of such access to reputable firms. Mercantile agencies further insisted that the pressures of an intertwined national credit system necessarily limited the privacy rights of would-be debtors.[6] Postal officials stressed the difficulty of building evidentiary cases against proprietors of illicit businesses operating across state lines, which justified some tactical deceptions. "Officers who deal with corrupt men," the Reverend Henry Ward Beecher argued at the 1885 annual meeting of the New York Society for the Suppression of Vice, "must adapt themselves to the finesse, the courage, and the trickery of their game." As Anthony Comstock stressed, those who complained about the postal laws primarily had run afoul of those prohibitions; they were not "the merchant, banker, or business man engaged in open, legal traffic." Comstock further emphasized that there were strict limits to the inspectorate's "finesse" and "trickery." At no point did they violate the "sacred seal" of mail in transit. They simply ordered and purchased goods from firms identified by suspicious advertisements, extraordinary postal volume, or specific complaints from members of the public. In doing so, they used "test" letters, not "decoys." Official duplicity extended only to the fabrication of identities for the purpose of initiating orders.[7]

Many Republicans and evangelicals, including key figures within the nation's commercial elite, joined the defense of virtuous creditor reporters and heroic soldiers against vice. Organs of the business establishment, such as *Hunt's Merchants' Magazine* and *Bankers' Magazine*, offered early and full-throated support to nascent credit-reporting firms. Once they became established in the 1840s and 1850s, metropolitan business leaders and social commentators portrayed them as a pillar of the country's economic infrastructure. The mercantile agency system, *Bankers' Magazine* concluded in 1858, safeguarded honest businessmen from "the ruinous competition of the inexperienced, the incompetent and the fraudulent," while redressing "many evils incident to the credit system." According to the *Philadelphia Inquirer*, credit reporters labored "not only for the benefit of the general commerce of the country, but for the benefit of their neighbors and friends." By the 1880s, the role of credit reporting in "protecting merchants and manufacturers against fraud and imposition" had become commonplace among leading businessmen.[8]

This elite consensus helped commercial agencies fend off libel lawsuits from the 1850s through the 1880s, as well as regulatory proposals in several states. Legal actions were initiated by businessmen who alleged that false credit reports had occasioned commercial losses. In the federal courts and Northeastern state courts, judges consistently held that when credit reporters provided information to customers on a confidential basis, they were not liable for damages resulting from inaccuracies made in good faith. Elsewhere, Dun lawyers sought to frustrate libel litigants through procedural objections and delaying motions, pressure on mercantile witnesses not to testify, and enticements to plaintiffs' lawyers to drop suits. If strongarm tactics proved insufficient, the agency settled cases to avoid adverse judicial opinions. During the 1870s and 1880s, especially after financial crises that led to widespread bankruptcies, state legislators throughout the nation proposed tough regulations on credit reporting. The most common bills either made intentional dissemination of a false credit report a crime, or required commercial agencies to post heavy bonds as checks against losses resulting from false reports. Outside of South Dakota, which in 1890 passed a bond requirement, credit reporting firms found sufficient legislative allies to keep such ideas from becoming law.[9]

The Northeastern establishment similarly endorsed the Post Office's attempts to regulate fraudulent marketing and the trade in obscene literature. Comstock's *Fraud Exposed*, explicitly written to counter attacks on mail fraud and obscenity enforcement, received laudatory reviews in the religious, commercial, and Republican press. The *Boston Advertiser* typically characterized Comstock's "ruses" as the "only way yet discovered to track and convict the scoundrels" who defrauded Americans through the mails. [10] Publication of annual reports from the country's urban antivice societies, which tallied arrests and other enforcement actions, prompted similar commentary. The objectives of the flagship New York organization, the *Christian Advocate* explained, were "of the highest value to every Christian community and every family home," while its "indefatigable . . . Secretary, Mr. Anthony Comstock," was "doing a work of real Christian heroism" by battling "the mercenary fiends who are preying upon the morals of the body politic."[11] Persuaded by Comstock and his backers, the nation's business and political leaders brushed off periodic calls for Congress to prune back the regulatory powers of postal authorities, or for the postmaster general to muzzle his eager special agents. Comstock also side-stepped an attempt on his life in 1874, as well as legal actions for libel and false arrest.[12]

Although attacks on Anthony Comstock and his fellow inspectors did little to change investigative practices in mail fraud cases, a quarter-century's worth of complaints about administrative adjudication of mail fraud allegations encouraged procedural adjustments. The assault on the Post Office's internal legal process was spearheaded by relatively deep-pocketed businessmen who faced fraud order proceedings. The first effort along these lines, undertaken in 1879 by the extremely well-resourced Louisiana Lottery, challenged the fraud order's constitutionality. After a federal court rejected this gambit, attention turned to the specifics of how officials evaluated evidence collected by postal inspectors and then made determinations to bar individuals or firms from receiving mail.

The 1872 Postal Reform Law furnished few guides about such matters. Until the mid-1890s, the department's practice was to have a postal inspector or special agent write up a report on a case, which he would then send to the assistant attorney general for the Post Office. After reading the report and any supporting documents, that official would make a recommendation to the postmaster general, who almost always followed his advice. This approach meant that very few subjects under investigation received the benefit of a hearing prior to the issuance of a fraud order. Indeed, from 1872 through 1896, very few individuals even received notice that the Post Office was considering action against them. Like Richard Sears, fraud order recipients usually learned about the Post Office's concerns only once they were barred from the mails. Although most subjects of fraud orders responded with flight, those on the entrepreneurial margin often, again like Richard Sears, appealed for revocations. The Post Office generally granted hearings in these circumstances, and, as we have seen, demonstrated a willingness to revoke fraud orders if lawyers could show that their clients had the backing of significant local elites and would discontinue any problematic marketing practices. After the issuance of fraud orders, however, the legal burden rested on recipients to show why the Post Office should rescind them. During the 1890s, the government agreed to as many as sixty-four revocations a year.[13]

That same decade, attorneys for the bond investment companies hit with fraud orders excoriated the Post Office's disregard for basic principles of due process. Thus J. T. Hanna, an attorney representing Illinois' State Mutual Life Insurance Company, wrote to the acting postmaster general in July 1894 to express shock at the Post Office's treatment of his clients. The Department, Hanna maintained, "has seen fit to 'brand' the business of this company as 'fraudulent,' upon information secretly transmitted to you, without giving it any notice thereof, or an opportunity to meet the charges." Adding insult to injury, it then refused to explain the basis for its action. The lowest criminal, the attorney observed, received more substantial procedural respect. Such treatment occasioned stinging rebukes from the trade press of the advertising industry. To the editor of the *Advertisers' Guide*, the "underlings of the Post Office" had set themselves up as "petty tyrants" who were every bit "as autocratic" as "the Czar of Russia or the Sultan of Turkey." Rendering the US Constitution "a dead letter," they had instituted "a star chamber tribunal," in which the system "hangs men first and tries them after."[14]

Late in 1896, members of the federal judiciary joined the chorus condemning the slipshod legal process within the Post Office Department, prompted by legal actions that bond investment firms and brokerages brought to challenge fraud orders. That September, several Chicago brokerages received fraud orders on the grounds that they were bucket shops. One firm challenged the action in federal court, arguing that it had received no prior notice and had no chance to defend itself. At the resulting hearing, District Judge Peter Grosscup took pains to emphasize that the postmaster general's authority to issue fraud orders was settled law. But he voiced disapproval of the one-sided nature of the department's investigative sifting of facts. "I do not think," Grosscup explained from the bench, "that an *ex parte* statement of some postal inspector should be the basis of an order that might destroy a man's business." A week later, the judge refused to grant an injunction against the Chicago postmaster, though not without remarking that the "great" authority vested in the postmaster general "ought to be restricted."[15]

Officials in Washington could pay little heed to the yelps of dodgy mail-order businesses or the screeds of advertising journals that profited from deceptive ads. After all, the late nineteenth-century American legal system tolerated many summary processes in which defendants possessed few of the procedural rights enshrined in the state and federal constitutions. The handling of vagrancy charges by urban and Southern rural courts stood out in this regard, as did federal hearings to consider the exclusion of would-be immigrants.[16] But a sharp lecture from an esteemed federal judge who had a track record of ratifying the Post Office's regulatory efforts was not so easy to ignore. After the Republicans had regained the White House and control over federal appointments in the 1896 election, the new assistant attorney general for the Post Office, James Tyner, revised fraud order policy. Henceforth, postal officials would conduct hearings in Washington before issuing fraud orders. Legal process would remain far more informal than civil suits or criminal trials, and defendants would not necessarily receive access to evidence against them. But postal officials would no longer act against businesses on the basis of allegations made by "one aggrieved person," and they would furnish a "memorandum of the charges" to assist the mounting of a legal defense.[17]

These procedural concessions ushered in a six-year period in which the Post Office issued fraud orders far less frequently, in some years barring fewer than fifty individuals or firms from the mails. Officials publicly explained the reduction as a reflection of more careful vetting of cases, along with a disinclination to issue fraud orders in doubtful cases. The new standard led the Department to revoke a number of fraud orders, including several that targeted bond investment companies, on the grounds that federal courts had not adjudged their operations to be so deceptive as to constitute fraud.[18]

By expanding the zone of legal ambiguity surrounding the fraud order, the McKinley administration heightened opportunities for corruption with the office of the assistant attorney general for the Post Office. As a subsequent two-year internal investigation documented, James Tyner's deputy and nephew, Harrison Barrett, along with another departmental lawyer, Daniel Miller, used the new procedures to operate a de facto protection racket. After notifying firms that they were under investigation, Barrett and Miller intimated that the owners could deflect legal action by amending their business practices. The key step, they then explained in letters to corporate attorneys, was to retain outside legal counsel who possessed the expertise to guide them. Through the close of 1900, Barrett directed mail-order firms to a Baltimore lawyer with whom he had close relations; he then resigned his position and entered into a partnership with that attorney. Thereafter, Miller suggested that businesses that needed to revise marketing literature to meet postal standards hire Barrett. Tyner subsequently lost his job, and both he and Barrett faced a 1904 criminal trial for conspiracy to defraud the government, which resulted in an acquittal attributed chiefly to Tyner's advanced age and poor health.[19]

Such influence-peddling extended beyond the confines of the Post Office Department, reaching as far as Congress. A few months before the Tyner-Barrett trial, Senator Joseph Burton of Kansas was convicted on a bribery charge stemming from his efforts to forestall a fraud order against a St. Louis investment firm. In exchange for a $500 monthly retainer, Burton agreed to act as the investment firm's attorney, using his influence to intercede with postal authorities. The senator made no attempt to deny this arrangement. Instead, he argued that his legal services constituted a more formal version of the good word that members of Congress regularly communicated to the Post Office Department on behalf of constituents under suspicion. Burton's trial, in conjunction with the Tyner-Barrett revelations, suggested that irregularities had become commonplace within mail-order proceedings.[20]

These scandals gave adversaries of the fraud order additional ammunition, and they wasted little time in using it. As in the 1890s, the leading dissenters were high-profile businessmen who faced postal scrutiny. Led by oilman H. H. Tucker and publisher and banker E. G. Lewis, these critics sharpened the arguments against the Post Office's allegedly autocratic practices and disseminated them to a national audience. They simultaneously cultivated influential new allies among civil libertarians and members of Congress.

Tucker, one of the colorful early twentieth-century stock promoters who invoked a language of democratic capitalism, sought to cash in on a succession of oil booms in Kansas, Oklahoma, and Texas through the Uncle Sam Oil Company. Attracting thousands of investors through puffing newspaper advertisements and prospectuses, Tucker promised not only to develop wells in emerging fields, but also to build refineries and a transport network. The oilman initially cultivated investor loyalty by depicting his enterprise as an inveterate opponent of the Standard Oil monopoly. He then cemented attachment to Uncle Sam by explaining any legal setbacks, including a 1907 mail fraud prosecution and 1908 fraud order, as the result of dirty work by Standard Oil's political and legal errand boys. Insisting that the Post Office was persecuting him at the behest of the oil giant, Tucker avoided a guilty verdict in 1907 and then took his attacks to Congress, President Theodore Roosevelt, and the press. At every point, he lambasted postal officials, and especially R. P. Godwin, Tyner's successor as assistant attorney general. Godwin, Tucker's company argued in a 1908 petition to Congress, had maliciously disregarded evidence presented by Uncle Sam at its fraud order hearing, and then authored a report on the case that was "untrue and incorrect and wholly unsupported." In addition to asking for relief from the fraud order, Tucker called for a congressional investigation into postal regulation that would expose "the outrages and injustices as have been perpetrated upon this company," create a basis for the punishment of "misconduct in office," and formulate legislative reforms that would "prevent such injustices in the future."[21]

Lewis, the St. Louis-based mail-order entrepreneur who mixed an eye for innovative business opportunities with an elastic conception of truthful marketing, responded even more vigorously to the Post Office's regulatory tactics. He excoriated the department in his magazines' editorial pages, then, through his publishing company, distributed two books that fleshed out his critiques. He cooperated in the production of a third volume about his travails, authored by a former high-ranking postal official who dissented from the department's treatment of Lewis. Through his political connections, he also pushed legislation to establish a legal mechanism to appeal fraud orders in the federal courts.

Like Tucker, Lewis alleged malfeasance, claiming that the postal protection racket had continued after Tyner's firing and was now run by Leonard Goodwin, a Chicago attorney specializing in mail fraud cases and the brother of the new assistant attorney general. Lewis alleged that Goodwin had promised to make his troubles with the federal government disappear. For the right retainer, he would show the publisher how to word his marketing materials so as to meet any objections from the Post Office.[22] Such machinations were possible, Lewis argued, because every step of the fraud order process remained shrouded in secrecy. Even when accorded a hearing, defendants had no access to the evidence, inspectors' reports, or legal justifications that underpinned fraud orders. "If a man uses the mails," Lewis defiantly pronounced in 1905, "he has no right of any sort that a Post Office Inspector has to respect." The publisher and banker portrayed himself as a victim of "secret Russian methods," a man who had been "crucified from coast to coast as a fraud and swindler."[23]

On their own, the transparently self-interested views from shifty entrepreneurs on the margins of American capitalism were unlikely to influence the direction of postal regulation. But the arguments put forward by H. H. Tucker, E. G. Lewis, and other mail-order businessmen received amplification from the occasional trade journal affiliated with the sector. They also resonated with a collection of writers, lawyers, and politicians who either worried about individual civil liberties or opposed waxing centralization of federal authority, as well as some conservative Republicans who winced at their party's flirtation with paternalistic regulation. The periodical *Health*, which catered to a sector that attracted numerous fraud orders in the 1900s, encapsulated the key arguments against Post Office legal culture in a 1909 editorial. Fraud order proceedings, *Health*'s editor fulminated, were "arbitrary," a "gross travesty of justice," even "un-American." The assistant attorney general for the Post Office had become "a veritable Pooh Bah" who took on the roles of "prosecutor, judge, and sheriff." This official decided whether the initial evidence collected by postal inspectors warranted a hearing, oversaw that proceeding, and then determined whether to recommend a fraud order. This mixing of legal functions, the editor proclaimed, violated basic Anglo-American norms about justice and the rule of law.[24]

An eclectic group of public intellectuals picked up on similar themes. The anti-imperialist editor Louis Post saw fraud orders as a type of "persecution," given that they occurred "without trial or accusation, upon the mere *ipse dixit* of a postal clerk at Washington." Such power harnessed "autocratic" impulses on a par with the extension of American political control over territories recently wrested from Spain. Franklin Pierce, a prominent New York City attorney and Democratic legal reformer, identified the lack of due process in mail fraud deliberations as a prime example of "federal usurpation" also evident in growing reliance on appointed commissions and the summary conduct of immigration cases. Even with the procedural reforms initiated in 1897, the Post Office retained authority to institute temporary bans on mail service pending hearings. Such action, Pierce maintained, shared much in common with lynching, as the postmaster general first went about "destroying a man's business" and then gave him the courtesy of "a hearing [to] ascertain whether he is guilty," in front of the same official who judged the case as meriting action. For Edward Frederick Browne, a conservative Republican author, the Post Office's antifraud "system of paternalism" had put "even the Empires . . . of Europe into a second class," portending an ominous illustration of "the present socialistic tendency to build up the executive power."[25]

With such varied opponents of a vigorous national government training their sights on the fraud order, Lewis, Tucker, and other similarly situated businessmen had little difficulty finding congressional advocates for curbs on the Post Office's antifraud powers. The leading champions of reform included Edward Crumpacker, a former Indiana judge and House Republican, and William A. Ashbrook, an Ohio Democrat. An ardent opponent of racial disenfranchisement, lynching, and the treatment of African Americans by the Southern legal system, Crumpacker viewed the fraud order through the prism of procedural fairness. The Postal Department, he explained to the House of Representatives in 1906, ran "a system of . . . espionage" in which hundreds of "secret emissaries" used "dark lantern methods" to produce "secret reports," which then became the basis for "blasting forever" the "business reputation" of firms. Such proceedings, he argued, were "absolutely inconsistent with the spirit of free institutions." From 1905 through the early 1910s, he pushed legislation that would have allowed the recipients of provisional fraud orders to appeal in federal district court. The Post Office would then have fifteen days to make its case before a federal judge and jury, whose assent would be required for any appealed fraud order to go into effect. In federal court, common-law procedural protections would be in effect, allowing accused business owners to see investigative reports and to present and cross-examine witnesses.[26] After the Democrats' 1910 electoral victory placed Ashbrook in the chairmanship of the House Committee on Post Office Expenditures, he convened hearings on the department's treatment of E. G. Lewis and the Uncle Sam Oil Company. Taking place over several months, the Lewis hearings furnished the publisher with ample opportunity to air his version of events to a national audience, placing an official spotlight on the implementation of antifraud policies.[27]

As in the late nineteenth century, leading figures within the Post Office mounted a robust public relations campaign to counter attacks on their handling of fraud orders. The department's annual reports insisted that postal officials exercised "great care" in assessing firms alleged to be violating the mail fraud law. No firm or individual lost access to the mails without a "thorough review" of the relevant evidence by both the assistant attorney general and the postmaster general. Whenever "legitimate enterprises" disseminated "misleading advertisements" without a clear intent to deceive, the department afforded them the chance to discontinue misrepresentations, clean up ad copy, and "adjust" any outstanding complaints from customers. In pamphlets and magazine articles, officials such as Postmaster General George Cortelyou further pointed out that only one in eighty recipients of fraud orders challenged them. They also insisted that the loudest calls for constraining Post Office discretion emanated from "those who have been hampered in nefarious undertakings through the issuance of fraud orders," men who naturally saw the mail fraud law as "autocratic and tyrannical." Above all else, postal officials stressed the indispensability of "promptness" in fraud order proceedings. Delay "for any appreciable time" meant that a "scheme could run its fraudulent course or transfer its affairs to other names and destinations before it could be obstructed by official interference." By contrast, the existence of a "summary" process protected the public from "hordes of rascals" whose transgressions, because of the evidentiary challenges that had bedeviled prosecutors for decades, defied criminal prosecution.[28] The establishment press, including trade periodicals, professional journals, mass-market magazines, and leading metropolitan newspapers, echoed the Post Office's stance on these issues.[29]

Whether or not federal judges paid attention to the controversies over the fraud order, they mostly continued to defer to bureaucratic judgments about which marketing practices were sufficiently deceptive to justify this remedy. In 1902, the Supreme Court did chip away at postal regulation of medical treatments. In *American Magnetic School of Healing v. McAnnulty*, the tribunal directed a lower federal court to grant a temporary injunction against a fraud order, and to entertain legal arguments about whether the school's claims about its capacity to heal patients through the use of magnetism actually constituted mail fraud. Writing for the majority, Justice Rufus Peckham ruled that assertions about the efficacy of healing methods involved matters of opinion rather than fact, and so did not easily fit within the legal framework of fraud. But in another case two years later, the Supreme Court reiterated that the fraud order was a Constitutional exercise of power, and that the judiciary would not second-guess the postmaster general's findings absent clear indications of legal improprieties.[30] The lower federal courts, moreover, continued to reject almost all requests for injunctions against fraud orders, finding that the identification of "fraudulent schemes" was a factual matter, and that Congress had authorized postal officials to assess such facts. Even when a federal judge indicated that he would have ruled differently in a fraud order proceeding, as Circuit Court judge Learned Hand did in one 1909 case, this disagreement was not enough to overturn postal authority. So long as "there be any evidence at all" sustaining the postmaster general's position, Hand concluded, that officer's decision was "final" and unreviewable. For the courts to void a fraud order, it would have to be "a clear case of error" in which "no one can reasonably conclude anything else."[31] Such a high legal standard meant that reform would have to occur through the political branches.

The legislative high-water mark of efforts to subject fraud orders to judicial review came in January 1907, when the House of Representatives passed the Crumpacker Bill on a voice vote. But intensive lobbying from George Cortelyou, along with a veto threat from President Roosevelt, doomed the proposal in the Senate.[32] Despite this legislative outcome, the tirades against postal autocracy eventually nudged the Post Office to adjust its policies. In 1910, a new postmaster general, Frank Hitchcock, decided to deemphasize the fraud order in favor of criminal prosecutions. The stated rationale for this shift was that fraud orders did little to hamstring the savviest swindlers, as "a man who was put out of business by such a fraud order might very easily move across the street into another office building and begin his work over again under the name of another bogus company." To take down such adaptive promoters, Hitchcock explained, the Post Office had to invest the time and resources to build cases that could withstand the rigors of criminal trials. The continual comparisons of postal officials to secret police, czars, and sultans surely helped to convince him to take this step.[33]

The Post Office Department's new tack dramatically increased the number of individuals whom it arrested, prosecuted, convicted, and sent to prison for mail fraud. Before 1910, the department did not keep comprehensive statistics on its criminal fraud cases; it likely did not prosecute more than fifty a year. But from that year through the end of the Taft administration, the tempo of prosecutorial activity quickened, as Table 8.1 suggests. Over these three years, postal authorities sent well over a thousand mail fraud cases into the federal courts, including several high-profile prosecutions of New York City brokerage firms that floated fraudulent stocks, such as Continental Wireless, a corporation that falsely promised to create a nationwide network of wireless telegraphy stations (a vision of what would eventually become radio).[34]

To facilitate more intensive enforcement, Hitchcock reorganized the postal inspectorate. In addition to placing the inspector corps under the "immediate

Table 8.1: Criminal Mail Fraud Cases Handled by the Post Office Department, July 1910 to June 1913

	Indictments	Convictions	Cases Nolle Prosequied	Acquittals
1910–11	529	184	36	12
1911–12	537	263	85	51
1912–13	554	304	100	36

(From Post Office Annual Reports, 1911–13)

supervision" of his office, he created an elite unit of investigators to handle complicated cases, demanded more coordination among regional offices, and instituted a policy of geographic rotation. This last innovation attacked the parochialism of many senior inspectors, who had developed inappropriately "cozy" relationships with businessmen in their cities, including some individuals who had displayed a penchant for deceptive marketing. Hitchcock further deepened cooperation with other federal agencies with an antifraud mission, such as the Agricultural Department's Bureau of Chemistry, which enforced the Pure Food and Drug Act.[35] These initiatives enabled the Post Office to bring off a high percentage of mail fraud convictions. From July 1910 through June 1913, the ratio of convictions to acquittals was better than seven to one, a much greater prosecutorial success rate than had been the norm in nineteenth-century state fraud cases.

And yet, "Mr. Hitchcock's War on Swindlers," as *The Independent* dubbed it, soon bogged down amid investigative fatigue and the obstinate realities of the criminal justice system. By the fall of 1912, the Post Office Department was groaning under the strain of over four thousand fraud investigations, leading to a formal request that Congress move responsibility for such inquiries to the Justice Department.[36] Even though only about one out of every eight investigations led to indictments, and roughly one-fourth of indictments resulted in trials, mail fraud cases also began to clog the federal courts. The reorganized and reinvigorated postal inspectorate could now more readily grapple with the sophisticated strategies of deception and misrepresentation employed by large-scale mail-order businesses. But as the relevant evidence became more voluminous and intricate, and as a wealthier class of defendants hired specialized legal counsel, mail fraud trials became ever more complicated. Turning on complex matters of fact and law, they often took months to complete. As Chief Postal Inspector Robert Sharp observed in 1912, mail fraud actions had "practically filled the dockets of the courts and exemplified the inadequacy of the present judicial machinery to promptly dispose of the various cases." Once Postmaster

General Hitchcock directed his inspectors to aim for criminal convictions rather than administrative fraud orders, federal prosecutors complained that their offices could only handle the new fraud workload "to the exclusion of other matters of public importance." Faced with lengthening backlogs, US attorneys called for state officials to take charge of these cases.[37]

Postal officials, moreover, soon expressed concern about judicial approaches to mail fraud trials, which tempered the impact of high conviction rates. "The discouraging feature to the department in its fraud crusade," Chief Inspector Sharp lamented in 1912, was "the character of sentences imposed by the courts." Individuals who defrauded thousands of Americans frequently avoided prison terms, getting off with "small fines, ranging from a few dollars to $3,000"; men who "robbed the people of millions of dollars" left courthouses with "sentences of only a few months." According to Sharp, most judges did not appreciate the national implications of mail fraud, and so viewed the offense as meriting only "light court sentences."[38] The expense of these trials raised additional concerns, as journalists contrasted their tens of thousands of dollars in costs with the minimal jail terms and fines that they produced.[39]

Disquiet over the shortcomings of criminal prosecution prompted yet another redirection of enforcement policy. The Democratic postmaster general appointed by President Woodrow Wilson, Albert Burleson, articulated the need for fresh strategic thinking. His Republican predecessor's single-minded focus on criminal prosecution, Burleson proclaimed, left too many Americans vulnerable to mail fraud. Characterized by continuances, lengthy trials, and appeals, fraud prosecutions were "necessarily slow" and their "execution of sentences had been deferred for long periods." During this interval, which the flood of mail fraud cases had only exacerbated, many fraudulent companies "had continued to reap a harvest" from investors or customers. Even worse, light sentences created minimal deterrence; short jail terms and low-level fines barely disrupted the operations of many swindling enterprises. Predicating antifraud strategy solely on criminal prosecution, the Wilson administration's new team contended, left the American public "at the mercy of swindlers."[40]

Burleson maintained that the sensible response was to pursue both fraud orders and criminal prosecutions, because the former had immediate preventive impact. Even when firms went through the hassle of restarting their operations under newly created front companies, fraud orders reduced their profits and slowed the process of finding new customers or investors. Mindful, however, of the longstanding aspersions cast at fraud order proceedings, the new administration instituted yet another procedural overhaul. Henceforth, the assistant attorney general for the Post Office would no longer personally review the reports and recommendations made by postal inspectors, nor decide whether to pursue fraud orders, nor draw up formal "citation[s] of charges," nor present cases at hearings. Instead, lawyers in his office would undertake that work on their own. The assistant attorney general would take on a judicial role, presiding over fraud order hearings, assessing all relevant evidence and argument, and preparing memoranda for the postmaster general's consideration. This new arrangement, postal leaders argued, addressed longstanding concerns about the unfairness of having the same person serve as prosecuting attorney and authoritative assessor of facts.[41]

Reconfiguring fraud order proceedings to look more like common-law trials did not eliminate public attacks, as the occasional author or lawyer still raised the hue and cry of governance by fiat.[42] But the Post Office Department's moves defused politically salient critiques. Complaints about postal secret police and American Star Chambers no longer echoed from the House of Representatives nor reverberated across the telegraphic reports of the Associated Press. Indeed, the ramping up of nongovernmental antifraud organizations such as the NACM, the BBBs, and the AMA gave the Post Office influential and vocal supporters. These organizations lauded the department's endeavors and expanded its disciplinary scope, their private investigators cooperating closely with federal authorities.[43] From 1913 into the 1920s and 1930s, postal inspectors and attorneys went about their business, while the solicitor of the Post Office Department (formerly the assistant attorney general) took on his new role of administrative judge.

Greater attention to legal formalities, however, brought costs. Fraud order hearings evolved into elaborate affairs, with motions, presentation of voluminous evidence, and punctilious production of official records. Departmental lawyers took increasing care to prepare for hearings, as did the Washington attorneys who specialized in mail fraud cases. By the late 1910s, fraud order hearings could take several weeks. This slower pace made it impossible for the department to handle the same number of formal hearings as it had under Postmaster General Cortelyou. The annual number of fraud orders accordingly declined, ranging between twenty-seven and seventy-six between July 1913 and June 1919, even as mail-order business boomed. These figures understated the reach of enforcement actions, as postal officials simultaneously negotiated a much larger number of stipulations that committed otherwise legitimate businesses to stop deceptive practices. The department also continued to prioritize criminal prosecutions, with annual cases approaching one thousand a year by America's entry into World War I. Nonetheless, by lengthening the administrative gauntlet for fraud orders, the new procedures encouraged a much finer internal filter for identifying commercial deceptions that merited action. In the 1919 fiscal year, tens of thousands of complaints and hundreds of investigations produced only sixty-one formal administrative hearings, with fewer than half leading to fraud orders.[44] After its reforms, the Post Office no longer confronted noisy controversies about the legitimacy of its antifraud work. But the department became less nimble in its efforts to disrupt swindling through the mails, beset into the 1930s by a caseload that threatened to overwhelm an understaffed cohort of investigators and prosecutors.[45]

THE "CLUE CLIQUES CLAN" OF COMMERCE

The nation's network of Better Business Bureaus also encountered sharp public questioning of methods and motives. During the 1920s, and even more after the onset of the Great Depression, the Bureaus faced claims that they cared only about extending their influence and furthering their corporate funders' interests. According to their antagonists, the BBBs sometimes functioned like the protection racket allegedly run by Post Office lawyer James Tyner. The accusations were that the BBBs extorted subscriptions from businessmen, in some cases relying on solicitation agents who employed the same boiler room tactics that BBB leaders decried in the securities markets. If local concerns refused solicitations, critics argued, those firms found themselves subject to BBB investigations and then public shaming, which often caused irreparable commercial harm. Fearful of such treatment, many businessmen decided to "pay for immunity."[46]

At other times, the BBBs' detractors maintained that they kept new firms from gaining footholds through sharp competition or inventive puffery, pointing to examples in the Denver dry-cleaning industry and the St. Louis personal-loan market. Another complaint was that the BBBs ignored the unethical or even illegal commercial practices of the large corporations on which the organizations depended for much of their funding. Anti-BBB literature of the early 1930s noted repeatedly that the NYSE and the Investment Bankers of America had furnished tens of thousands of dollars in assistance to the Bureaus. A common allegation compared the Bureau network to the more sophisticated tip sheets of stock swindlers, which railed against all the fraudulent promotions clogging the nation's mailbags even as they flogged their own valueless schemes. To its critics, the antifraud network "served the purposes of the Stock Exchange by throwing suspicion outward, which served also . . . to prevent scrutiny inward."[47] An illustration in a 1931 exposé of the antifraud organizations (Figure 8.1) encapsulated this latter contention, portraying BBBs as the exceedingly good "pal" of business elites. With these lines of attack, the antagonists of private antifraud organizations extended a libertarian critique of gov-

Figure 8.1: The Better Business Bureau as good friend of the Establishment. A cartoon from Edward Riegel's 1931 anti-BBB pamphlet, "The Indictment of the Better Business Bureau Conspiracy."

ernmental administrative regulation to the economic establishment's preferred mechanisms of "home rule." In either case, regulatory institutions turned out to be the pawns of entrenched businesses, and so created indefensible barriers to entry for would-be competitors.

Skeptics about the BBB network further condemned its pretensions to "quasi-public" status, calling it an "invisible government" without accountability or oversight. This strand of anti-BBB discourse echoed nineteenth-century attacks on credit reporting and the decades-long complaints about fraud orders. Like the foes of nineteenth-century commercial spy systems and secret postal investigations, the adversaries of interwar antifraud organizations rejected their vaunted surveillance networks and influence over prosecutors and the press. Such methods once again attracted the charge of being "un-American," because they required a "system of espionage that is more vicious than the fraud it professes to suppress" and ignored principles of due process. As a longtime BBB adversary put this argument in 1933, the Bureaus had supplanted "the legitimate agencies of investigation, prosecution, and protection." They had placed such powers in the hands of "unelected, irresponsible men, as well as unlicensed snoopers," mostly "despicable" female "quasi-purchasers," who "inject themselves into retail stores, to find, if possible, something derogatory to the merchant." The BBB's financial dependence on many of the businesses that they monitored elicited similar complaints.[48]

Even the name of the organization came under assault. The word "Bureau" was "a delusion and a snare," falsely suggesting to ordinary Americans that it had official, public status, that it was even "a quasi-judicial body of our government." "Vigilance Committee," the institution's original moniker, implicitly struck one antagonist, the iconoclastic social commentator Edwin C. Riegel, as more appropriate, because its extralegal mode of operation was reminiscent of the Ku Klux Klan. He dubbed the BBBs the "Clue Cliques Clan of Commerce." Leaders of the Truth-in-Advertising movement had repeatedly invoked the language of "home rule," portraying BBBs as institutions by which the business establishment could take the lead in policing candor in the marketplace. For Riegel, parallels between the antifraud campaign and the cause of white supremacy extended far beyond strategies of rhetoric.[49]

The National Businessmen's Protective Council, a short-lived competitor to the BBBs, brought most of these charges together in a striking cartoon (Figure 8.2) that illustrated a promotional pamphlet. The cartoon's central figure, a heavily muscled man symbolizing "Oppressed Business," is bound by a clownish "Professional Snooper" and throttled by a venomous, two-armed snake, representing "Better Business Bureaus and Other Rackets." Over the "Snooper's" shoulders, a "Racketeer" whispers instructions. All the while, in the dis-

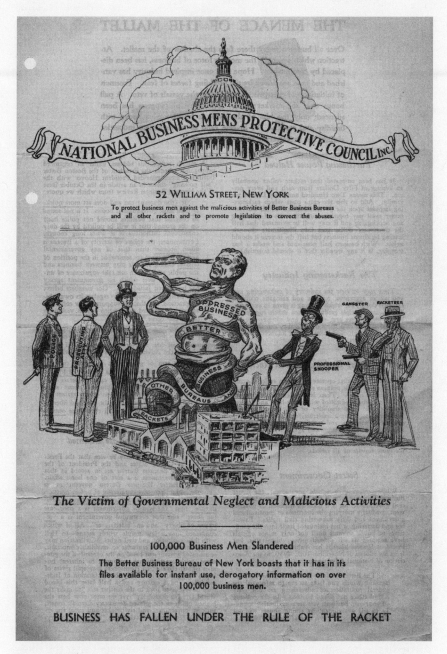

Figure 8.2: The Better Business Bureau as a two-armed poisonous snake. National Businessmen's Protective Bureau pamphlet, 1931. Consumers' Research Papers, Special Collections Library, Rutgers University.

tance, governmental officials either look away or glance bemusedly at the go-
ings-on. Here was a vision of trade and industry "under the rule of the racket,"
and of the BBBs as antithetical to American traditions of liberty, law, and free
enterprise.

BBB officials responded to these various jibes in much the same way that
credit reporting agencies and the Post Office had. In public commentary, they
defended their methods as judicious institutional innovations that prevented
economic duplicity. Both they and their political allies also attacked the credibility of their critics, whom Bureau defenders described as falling into one of
three groups. The first comprised businessmen who pursued questionable
marketing tactics and hoped to deflect attention from "their own malprac-
tices." This group included the stock promoter George Graham Rice, whose
encounters with postal fraud allegations had led him to hone a populist rhetoric. In the wake of his first fraud order in 1904 and then his later mail fraud
convictions, the inveterate promoter levied withering assaults on postal regulation, arguing that the country's financial elite, and especially the Guggenheim
mining syndicate, used it as a means to crush their antagonists. In later years,
his stock tip sheets denounced the Post Office, the New York Stock Exchange,
and the nation's BBBs, all of which he characterized as doing the bidding of
Wall Street.[50]

A second source of criticism, BBB leaders suggested, came from professional agitators and cranks such as Frank O'Sullivan and Edwin Riegel, who
owed their livelihoods to windmill-tilting against the central institutions of
modern American society, or from seemingly upstanding civic leaders who
were hiding shady pasts, such as Logan Billingsley. A small-scale Chicago publisher and author, O'Sullivan specialized in florid detective literature and exposés of the criminal underworld. A self-taught libertarian economist, Riegel
operated through an outfit known as the Consumers Guild of America, which
was little more than a shell organization to dress up its president's periodic
rants against both big business and big government. After a career in Seattle as
a bootlegger, during which he faced allegations of involvement in two mur-
ders, Billingsley moved to New York City, where he dived into real-estate development. In the early years of the Great Depression, he gained control of the
moribund Bronx Chamber of Commerce and Manhattan Board of Commerce,
building up their public profiles by falsely claiming to have attracted prominent businesses as members. Like George Graham Rice, Billingsley sought to
discredit the institutions of the "truth in advertising" movement after the BBBs
exposed his own deceptions and evasions.[51]

Finally, antifraud organizations pointed out that they were occasionally targeted by populist politicians such as Iowa's Republican senator Smith W.

Brookhart. These politicos repeated the usual anti-BBB charges, seeing the issue as a chance to burnish their credentials as opponents of concentrated economic power. Given the sources of the complaints about BBB methods, its representatives advised that the public treat them as untrustworthy grumbling. Such gripes about the techniques of antifraud organizations were, the Columbus BBB explained in the early 1930s, nothing more than "the squealing of a stuck pig."[52]

The squealing, however, sometimes contained an element of truth. Throughout the 1910s and the boom years of the 1920s, the BBBs had focused far more on identifying and publicizing the deceptions of fly-by-night firms than on the misrepresentations of large-scale retailers or leading investment banks. One exception to this generalization concerned price-related advertising by some metropolitan department stores, which BBB leaders highlighted as a further refutation of the claims made by its chief antagonists. The most prominent incident involved a public spat over the price claims of R. H. Macy & Co., which played out over the course of 1925 and 1926. This controversy would eventually push the BBBs, like the Post Office, to introduce procedural reforms.

For decades, Macy's had cultivated a reputation for low prices, boasting, as in one typical 1880 advertisement, that "OUR PRICES ARE BELOW COMPETITION." By the 1920s, this claim had become far more precise. "Macy prices," the store proclaimed in a 1925 ad, "are at least 6 percent *less*, every day of the year, on every article of merchandise," including both regular and sale items. The department store could meet this promise, executives claimed, because Macy's purchased goods in large quantities for cash or extremely short credit terms, and sold only for cash, thus avoiding the bad debts and high return rates associated with credit sales. Prompted by a chorus of complaints from competitors, the New York City BBB's merchandising division sent its professional shoppers into Macy's over several months in 1925, in line with its policy of checking the advertising claims of all retailers, including member firms. The shoppers then compared the prices of identical items at other retailers, discovering dozens of items elsewhere that were the same price or even cheaper. Several meetings between BBB officials and Macy's executives ensued, as the Bureau pressed the company to redress the alleged inaccuracy in its core advertising message. But Macy's management rejected any suggestion that its ads were fundamentally "inaccurate," characterizing the Bureau's demands as intrusive attempts to dictate marketing policies.[53]

The dispute between Macy's and the New York City BBB closely paralleled a key point of contention between the Post Office and Sears, Roebuck in the mid-1890s—how to interpret the significance of unfilled or wrongly filled orders. Sears had emphasized that his firm's enormous volume of business and large number of employees rendered some mistakes inevitable, and that the company had created an internal mechanism for identifying and correcting errors. Percy Straus, Macy's vice president, took a similar tack in responding to the BBB's allegations about his firm's ad copy. His department store, Straus pointed out, sold thousands of items, with prices for many changing regularly. In order to adhere to Macy's policy of selling below its competitors, the establishment maintained an internal "Comparison Bureau," which sent out employees to other retailers to survey prices. Macy's also encouraged customers to bring lower prices to its attention, and charged its hundreds of sales clerks with "report[ing] prices conflicting with our Policy." Whenever Macy's management became aware of a price differential, Straus insisted, they adjusted the store's prices downward. But in light of the enormous range of its offerings and the size of its workforce, some mistakes and oversights were inevitable. In many cases, moreover, thorny questions arose over whether particular goods were "really directly comparable or equivalent," which required time-consuming "technical analysis" and internal debate. Straus further explained that in all instances of ambiguity, Macy's erred toward "giving to our customers the benefit of the doubt."[54]

Macy's and the New York BBB possessed very different understandings about what counted as an advertising "inaccuracy," and who should have the authority to apply that standard and fashion remedies for violations. The department store's executives did not object to the BBB's shopping checks; indeed, they welcomed them and promised to adjust prices whenever the Bureau pointed out discrepancies. They also readily adjusted the wording of their advertising copy, including an explicit concession, adopted in early 1926, that "We are not infallible. Others may on occasion cut our price—may on occasion sell merchandise for one reason or another at prices lower than we, until we find it out." But they refused to give ground on their central marketing claim—that they systematically offered the lowest prices in New York, and so were "the store of the thrifty—of those who pay as they go." To concede this point, Percy Straus insisted, would amount to tacit approval of the BBB's extending its jurisdiction far beyond the mission of combating fraud. The result of such a concession would be all manner of "dangerous meddling" in the delicate and difficult process of "competition in business." Rather than accept this *diktat*, Macy's resigned its membership in the New York City Bureau.[55]

The controversy over Macy's pricing policy simmered for several more years. BBB officials wished to demonstrate their willingness to stand up to a large corporation; they were fortified in that impulse by the encouragement of several Macy's competitors, such as Gimbels and Wanamaker's, which viewed their rival's claims of perennial underselling as misleading. For several years after Macy's resignation, BBB leaders looked upon the department store with suspicion. In the late fall of 1930, for example, the head of the Detroit BBB confidentially reported rumors that Macy's was bankrolling the activities of Logan Billingsley's Manhattan Board of Commerce, which had included attempts to place anti-BBB billboard ads in Detroit. At the national level, the BBB network forged standards for advertising copy that frowned on the use of universal claims of underselling such as those pushed by R. H. Macy & Co. In its 1932 *Guide for Retail Store Advertising*, the Affiliated BBBs described such assertions as "impossible of fulfillment," because no advertiser could "have complete and accurate knowledge of all prices in all other stores by all merchants at all times."[56]

Nonetheless, Bureau officials felt compelled to handle its scrap with Macy's in a much less confrontational fashion than its response to the organizations and individuals who criticized its operations most vehemently. Percy Straus was no George Graham Rice. The Macy's vice president was a well-respected member of the nation's business elite who managed an iconic retail establishment, not a shifty promoter with a criminal record and a history of running businesses that, at best, pressed the bounds of propriety and honest marketing. In January 1926, at the height of the dispute over the "6 percent" claims, the New York City BBB offered to send the Macy's advertising case to an ad hoc review panel, appointed by the president of one of three organizations—the Merchants Association of New York, the New York State Chamber of Commerce, or the Bar Association of the City of New York. This approach, the BBB head Bayard Dominick suggested, would permit "the fullest possible determination of all the facts as to whether [Macy's] advertising slogans . . . are accurate as applied to your business, or whether they are misleading to the public and unfair to your competitors."[57] Dominick's proposal conceded that the Bureau's mode of enforcement was open to the same kind of objection so often lobbed at fraud order proceedings before the 1913 postal reforms—that the BBB vested the role of investigator, prosecutor, and judge in the same institution, and sometimes the same person.

Macy's declined to participate in arbitration relating to its advertising strategy, but the idea of instituting some type of appeal process to an impartial body remained alive within BBB circles. As the public attacks on its methods intensified amid the early years of the Great Depression, procedural reform of this sort became more attractive. An additional prod in this direction came from the increasing integration of the BBB network into the formal policy-making and enforcement activities of the federal government. During the late 1920s, the Federal Trade Commission had called upon the National BBB and the Affiliated BBBs to coordinate trade practice conferences to set standards in several industries, including one on national periodical advertising. This initiative culminated in the 1933 adoption of "Code of Advertising Practices," which largely tracked the 1932 *Guide to Retail Advertising*.[58]

To fortify its case for the adoption of such codes, and perhaps to make them more palatable to its large corporate funders, the National BBB proposed the creation of "a Review Committee on Fair Business Practices" in 1931. Comprising representatives of advertisers, the advertising industry, and media, this board would furnish an appeal tribunal to advertisers who disagreed with NBBB findings. Although its jurisdiction would be informal, akin to voluntary arbitration, its procedures would mimic many legal conventions. After advertisers requested a hearing, the NBBB would furnish it with "a brief designating the alleged practices and setting forth the reasons why the practices are considered by the Bureau to be unfair to competition or detrimental to [the] public interest in advertising." The appellant would next file a "written answer" within fifteen days, and the NBBB would set a date for a hearing. Although that proceeding would "be conducted in an informal manner," the board would have the power to confine discussion to the precise dispute at issue, both sides would have the opportunity to introduce "expert testimony," and each party could ask legal counsel to present arguments. Edward Greene, the NBBB's general manager, depicted this setup as "a sound application of quasi-judicial opinion applied to business conduct." In combination with the surveillance and moral suasion furnished by the National BBB, Greene contended, the new tribunal would "provide a broad and equitable system of self-regulation by business."[59]

With the incoming Roosevelt administration in view, Greene found sufficient support from the publishing, broadcast, and advertising industries to begin preparations for a review board in late 1932. Over the next several months, the NBBB persuaded trade associations representing these industries to appoint members to the board, and announced in late spring of 1933 that it would soon begin operations.[60] This initiative quickly faded from public view, however, displaced by the chaotic activity of the National Recovery Administration (NRA). As part of the New Deal economic recovery strategy, the NRA asked industries, including advertising, to adopt and then enforce fair business practices. The codes that emerged for retail advertising followed the script laid down by the NBBB's work from the late 1920s and early 1930s. Throughout the country, moreover, the new federal agency turned to the BBB network for assistance in enforcement, borrowing several BBB officials to help run metropolitan compliance divisions, and drawing on a number of local BBBs to undertake the work of code monitoring and enforcement. Now, instead of the planned Advertising Review Committee, firms who chafed at a

BBB interpretation or decision could gain a formal hearing before an NRA Code Administrator.[61]

Unlike the Post Office Department, then, the early twentieth-century BBB network did not actually implement extensive procedural protections for its mode of handling instances of marketing deceptions. As we will see, the truncated history of the Advertising Review Committee foreshadowed institutional evolution after World War II by both the National BBB and many of its local bureaus. On its own terms, the episode from the early 1930s still suggests the influence that common-law procedural norms had on antifraud initiatives. From the inception of the "truth in advertising" movement, bureaus had stressed the advantages of informal investigations and negotiations taking place outside of the public spotlight, so long as firms demonstrated a willingness to defer to their assessments of fair dealing. But in the face of sustained criticism about secret methods and unaccountable arrogation of power, and wishing to bring along heavy corporate advertisers whose executives and legal counsel wished to maintain freedom of commercial action, BBB leaders looked to defuse criticism through procedural adjustments. Their proposals reflected longstanding ideals about the rule of law—notice, specification of charges, the chance to present and rebut evidence, the opportunity to rely on legal counsel, and judgment by individuals who did not participate directly in the initial investigations. Edward Greene stressed that any hearings by the Advertising Review Committee would "be conducted in an informal manner," and that the rules governing its operation were indeed much more informal than a court proceeding. Even within the realm of business self-regulation, however, American legal culture left its stamp on institutions. The *New York Times* did not miss the legal implications of the advertising review panel. Its headline for the story reporting on its adoption informed readers that the "Advertising Field" was about to get a "High Court"—though this august body would function entirely outside the ambit of the state.

Early Fraud-Fighting at the FTC

As Federal Trade Commission officials began to combat deception in interstate trade during the mid-1910s, they skirted the political assaults that the Post Office Department had endured, and that critics would later direct toward the BBBs. They did so in part by paying attention to issues of procedural fairness from the start, adopting rules that insulated the commission from charges that it operated like Russian secret police. Unlike the Post Office, which could bar access to the mails and initiate criminal fraud prosecutions, the FTC's arsenal consisted mainly of "cease and desist" orders, which directed firms or individuals to stop specified practices. Officials at the commission, moreover, could only issue such orders after a lengthy administrative process that incorporated several features of common-law adjudication. After receiving an initial complaint about a business, usually from a competitor, or encountering evidence of wrongdoing through direct monitoring of the marketplace, the FTC would assign one of its staff attorneys to conduct a preliminary investigation. Typically involving at least some field interviews, this inquiry resulted in a written report that recommended either closing the case or initiating a formal hearing. A review board of two senior FTC attorneys and one FTC economist would then consider the recommendation, evaluating whether the firm in question participated in interstate or foreign commerce, whether its activities were sufficiently deceptive to violate the FTC Act, and whether formal administrative proceedings were in the public interest. This last requirement hinged on the applicability of other means of legal redress. If the board viewed the investigation as sufficiently thorough and believed that further FTC action was called for, it would ask the commissioners for authorization to launch a more formal consideration of the allegations. With that authorization, the FTC would send the target of the investigation official notice of an impending hearing to consider charges that it had engaged in unfair methods of competition, including a summary of the allegations against it. Before the hearing, the enterprise would have the opportunity to file a written answer to the charges, laying out the contours of any defense. The hearing would usually be conducted by a trial examiner not involved in any aspect of the investigation to this point, and would give respondents the opportunity to present evidence, cross-examine witnesses, and rebut arguments. After the hearing, the trial examiner prepared findings and a recommendation either for a dismissal or for the issuance of a cease and desist order, to which lawyers for the respondent and the FTC could reply through formal briefs. Finally, the full complement of five FTC commissioners would receive the complete record of the case, hold a further hearing for oral argument from the parties, debate its merits, and vote on its disposition.[62]

The FTC, then, gave ample notice of its actions and furnished access to the evidence amassed by investigators. It also took pains to separate the officials who investigated and prosecuted cases from those who ruled on them. FTC proceedings did not offer the full panoply of common-law protections available in the regular courts; they allowed a wider range of admissible evidence and limited respondents' opportunity to enter procedural motions available in traditional legal disputes.[63] Inquiries into allegations of unfair competition remained exercises in administrative law. Some legal observers would have preferred an even greater institutional separation between FTC prosecutors and trial examiners, especially in light of the occasional practice of asking prosecuting counsel to prepare formal findings for consideration by the full Commission.[64] Nonetheless, early FTC deception cases reflected the Wilson administration's general concern for procedural niceties, evident in its reform of the fraud order process.

Indeed, adherence to the formal requirements of exacting procedural rules frequently compromised the FTC's ability to strike quickly at firms engaging in methods of unfair competition. During its first decade, numerous commentators reproached the FTC for its protracted process. The Commission itself noted that many preliminary inquiries entailed "long, extensive, and painstaking investigation of the facts." Although subsequent hearings were supposed to take place within forty days of legal notice, a crowded docket made months-long delays all too common. As a result, the issuance of a cease and desist order often took a full two years. And if a firm defied such an order, the FTC had to go to federal court to compel its enforcement, a process that required still more time.[65]

Some respondent corporations grumbled that the slow pace of FTC decision-making forced them unfairly to contend with bad publicity before they were exonerated. Delays also meant that some fraudulent enterprises continued operations for months or even years while cases against them wound their way through the FTC bureaucracy. Perhaps the most problematic category of deception cases involved securities frauds. Because of the factual complexities and wide geographic reach of such swindles, the taking of testimony proved especially time-consuming. In the case of Samuel E. J. Cox, a notorious peddler of worthless Texas oil stocks who eventually faced federal prosecution for mail fraud, the FTC took almost four years to move from an initial 1919 complaint to the filing of a cease and desist order. As the legal scholar Gerard Henderson observed, "if the facts found by the Commission are true, one is tempted to ask how many gullible citizens were separated from their savings while the case was in progress!"[66] The FTC's legal process, then, often led to the shutting of commercial or financial schemes long after swindling schemers had moved on to new locales.

When control of the FTC passed over to Republican appointees in 1925, Chairman William Humphrey instituted several policies that sought to redress the FTC's version of the "slows." One pair of administrative changes sought to facilitate negotiated agreements between the commission and investigated businesses, akin to the turn-of-the-century stipulations arranged by the Post Office with firms that possessed good reputations but had flirted with misrepresentation. Under Humphrey's direction, the FTC no longer docketed formal complaints nor publicized cases immediately after initial investigations. Instead, it allowed firms facing allegations to make provisional responses to them in closed, informal hearings. If, after this step, FTC attorneys still felt disciplinary action was appropriate, they tried to dispose of most false advertising cases through negotiated settlements. The most common arrangement required a business's acceptance of a formal stipulation to cease those practices that FTC lawyers saw as problematic. In such instances, the FTC publicized only the relevant facts, keeping the names of stipulating companies from public view.[67]

According to Humphrey, these reforms allowed the FTC to dispense much fairer administrative justice, while enabling it to "quit playing tag with fraud." Businesses that faced an unjust complaint from some competitor no longer had to deal with negative publicity in the months and years that it took for an action to make its way through administrative process. With stipulations, disposition of deceptive practices cases occurred within months rather than years. The much greater emphasis on negotiated compromises, Humphrey also stressed, moved FTC proceedings closer to the workings of the traditional court system, where most controversies ended with settlements. Such arrangements had the further advantage of freeing up investigators and lawyers to focus on truly fraudulent companies and unscrupulous media firms, against which the FTC chairman vowed not simply firm enforcement, but a "war of extermination."[68]

In a similar vein, Humphrey greatly expanded the investment of FTC resources in trade practice conferences, which had begun soon after the conclusion of World War I. These meetings of firms in a particular industry identified unfair commercial tactics that had become commonplace and then adopted rules against such practices. Although these statements of industry custom lacked the force of law, their articulation helped to create commercial standards and norms that influenced managerial behavior. Even before the new FTC regime, Gerard Henderson had concluded that "the educational influence of a single trade practice submittal is as valuable as the coercion of a host of formal complaints and orders." The agreements that resulted from trade conferences also helped FTC officials with enforcement actions. Industry rules of the road facilitated assessments of whether particular complaints about unfair methods of competition deserved attention. And because those rules reflected "the expressed sentiment of the trade," they extended the capacity of FTC lawyers to use moral suasion against firms that had allegedly violated them. The FTC convened dozens of such conferences in the 1920s and 1930s, often in conjunction with the National BBB.[69]

A further initiative concentrated on direct monitoring of national print advertising. In 1929, the FTC created a Special Board of Investigation, headed by three attorneys, which reviewed thousands of sampled ads every week. This new unit operated in much the same fashion as the nation's BBBs. Like the Bureau network, the FTC developed a close working relationship with publishers of national magazines. When an official identified an advertisement that appeared to be deceptive, the FTC would contact the relevant publisher or station manager and request substantiation of marketing claims. If unsatisfied by the reply, officials suggested that the publication or station make adjustments or refuse the ad. If neither action was forthcoming, the FTC could authorize formal investigations of the advertiser as well as the relevant advertising agency and media outlet. This informal mechanism of regulation, the FTC claimed in its 1931 annual report, led advertisers, agencies, and print publications to agree to stipulations 95 percent of the time. The commission calculated that "over 10,000 false and misleading advertisements have been discontinued" as a result of its work.[70]

The FTC's regulatory ethos under Chairman Humphrey, then, reflected a strong commitment to both common-law proceduralism and the Republican philosophy of business self-rule. Each of these impulses called for a more restrained approach to false-advertising and other deception cases, though one still presupposed an active administrative state. This version of associationalism retained the tension between adherence to formal legal process and informal administrative problem-solving. For William Humphrey, the key to resolving this tension lay in a more sympathetic regulatory stance toward legitimate enterprises. The Republican FTC chairman remained confident that his legal staff and fellow commissioners could identify outright swindlers when they saw them, treating them differently from honest businessmen who occasionally engaged in misrepresentation. Humphrey believed, like Postmaster General Cortelyou, that his agency could serve as a trustworthy keeper of the commercial peace. At the same time, he shared the growing concern of many early twentieth-century observers about vulnerable consumers within industrial economies. The FTC, he proclaimed in 1926, was charged with making "it impossible for the frauds and fakers, swindlers and scoundrels, with the help of dishonest, unprincipled, and mercenary publishers, who share in the fruits of their crime, to rob the sick and unfortunate, the credulous and the ignorant, of hundreds of millions of dollars annually."[71]

Humphrey's procedural innovations found favor within the business community, which appreciated curbs on investigative publicity. But some influential legal thinkers viewed the FTC's turn to informal dispute resolution as an affront to procedural justice. To Henry Ward Beer, a professor at Brooklyn Law School and one of the nation's foremost trade lawyers, Humphrey's FTC had fashioned "short cuts" that violated "the first principles of legal procedure," as

well as the explicit terms of the FTC Act. That statute, Beer insisted, only authorized formal complaints, public hearings, and public rulings. Informal inquiries, "secret" stipulations, and trade practice conferences had no firm legal
basis; they replaced fair-minded judgment with the worst kind of arm-twisting
by officialdom, which few firms would resist, regardless of the merits of a given
case. "As a people," Beer protested, "we are not content to have our rights tried
by administrative fiat." As a result, he argued, it would be far preferable to have
"much fake advertising . . . go unpoliced . . . than to have one honest business
man put out of existence" through informal mechanisms that masqueraded as
"as a substitute for its legal authority to proceed by complaint and finding of
facts."[72] Despite such carping, the FTC adhered far more closely to Anglo-
American conceptions of the rule of law than most agencies of the early
twentieth-century federal government, including the pre-1913 Post Office. As
with the Post Office Department, however, deference to procedural norms
meant a slower pace of formal justice, and so more time for opportunistic marketing strategies that employed deception.

✳✳✳✳

The direction of institutional evolution within late nineteenth- and early
twentieth-century antifraud organizations underscores the attraction that
many American elites had to the philosophy of administrative law articulated
by the influential Victorian-era British legal scholar Albert Venn Dicey. For
Dicey, the emergence of modern administrative agencies posed a grave threat
to Anglo-American conceptions of liberty, because they so often took away the
right to gain a review of state action by a member of the regular judiciary,
under the rules and interpretive practices of the common law. As Dicey put the
argument in his widely read lectures on the British legal system, the rule of law
required that when a regulatory agency took some action that harmed private
interests, it acted on the basis of "a distinct breach of law established in the
ordinary legal manner," with recourse in all cases to "the ordinary Courts of
the land."[73]

In the first half of the twentieth century, Dicey's views found favor among a
segment of America's legal establishment that saw the emerging administrative
state as a threat to the rule of law. Many American legal thinkers, among them
University of Chicago law professor Ernst Freund, embraced a conservative,
substantive version of Diceyism. Freund insisted that US constitutional values
required far-reaching checks on administrative discretion, including the ability
to appeal all administrative decisions in federal court. He wished to establish
"an American *Rechtsstaat*," in which administrators applied clearly articulated,

legislatively enacted rules and remained subordinate to the judiciary. This vision appealed to middle-class urbanites who associated public policy with the corruptions of boss-run political machines, as well as to prominent members of the bench and bar, who equated liberty with legal rituals and process.[74]

An alternative position was staked out by a group of eminent legal figures, most of whom were based in either America's financial capital, New York, or its seat of politics, Washington, DC. This group included corporation lawyer, Republican governor of New York, and Supreme Court justice Charles Evans Hughes; Henry Stimson, the Republican who served as Presidents Taft and Roosevelt's Secretary of War and Hoover's Secretary of State; John Foster Dulles, a leading business lawyer and eventual Republican Secretary of State, and, perhaps most importantly, Felix Frankfurter, Harvard law professor, policy counselor, and Roosevelt appointee to the Supreme Court. These attorneys recognized the implausibility of asking courts to review the nitty-gritty of administrative fact-finding, and so viewed flexible administrative decision-making as indispensable to the resolution of economic controversies within an industrialized society. But they sought to infuse regulatory agencies with respect for due process, and called for members of the legal profession to become watchdogs of the administrative state, ready to cry foul when discretion transmuted into unprincipled, unfair "arbitrariness."[75]

These ideas would become fundamental premises of American regulatory design, enshrined in the 1946 Administrative Procedure Act, and the analogous legislation later passed by most state legislatures. Earlier experimentation with antifraud measures, however, demonstrates the longstanding gravitational pull of procedural reforms. To ignore them in the construction of regulatory organizations was to court antagonism from affected entrepreneurs and public censure from conservative lawyers and politicians. By contrast, grafting elements of regular court procedures into regulatory operations enabled agencies to fend off critics. Provision of notice and specific charges, formal hearings, separation of investigation, prosecution, and judgment, opportunity to appeal—these policies cemented the legitimacy of administrative antifraud adjudication within state agencies and quasi-public institutions such as the BBBs. In fits and starts, from the 1870s into the 1930s, antifraud regulators blunted political critiques by embracing procedural protections.[76]

This pattern did not emerge at the behest of a judiciary jealously guarding its prerogatives, for the courts deferred to administrative muscle-flexing against deceptive business practices. Instead, the demands came from a motley crew of journalists, iconoclastic social commentators, and the targets of fraud investigations—all of whom usually drew on a popular legal culture that distrusted governmental power. Specters of "Star Chambers" and secret police connected the critique of antifraud regulation to the nation's revolutionary past, updated to distinguish American liberty from the dictatorial dispositions of Eastern Europe and Asia. Eventually, opponents of administrative antifraud techniques fashioned a more professionalized discourse that reflected the norms of elite legal education and the emergence of specialized legal practices. Those opponents received support from many large-scale businesses, which embarked on a concerted effort to slow down the ever more wide-ranging American regulatory juggernaut, and to compel less ambiguous directions from regulatory agencies.

The disputes over basic procedural questions in American fraud law has important implications for historical understandings of "the rule of law"—that complex, evolving, and ambiguous cluster of ideas and attitudes about justice that has helped to shape legal institutions in numerous societies over the past several hundred years, from Great Britain and its far-flung colonial possessions, to the continental powers of Western Europe, to late imperial and Republican China, to the United States.[77] Modern conceptions of governance enshrined such values as clarity and effective dissemination of rules, impartiality in official judgments, provision of appeal, and universal application of law, regardless of social position.[78] As the evolution of American antifraud institutions suggests, these norms were hardly shibboleths. They connected elite debates over bureaucratic design to more popular conceptions of law and justice; and appeals to these values often carried weight in the construction and refining of institutions, public and private. But their precise implications remained the subject of intense political jockeying amid the efforts to adjust institutions to the challenges of industrialization and the emergence of integrated, national economies.

To think about "rule of law" historically, then, one must do more than define its key elements and how they changed over time. One must also locate the sources of ideas and sensibilities, whether within the circles of legal elites, or among social groups, or in the ambit of a more diffuse, popular legal culture. One must further identify when established "rule of law" tenets receded in the face of competing political and legal priorities, or once again came to the fore, often with new twists or points of emphasis. And one must assess the social and economic consequences resulting from fidelity to these norms.[79]

Greater procedural protections within antifraud organizations slowed up their legal machinery. This shift hardly took away the ability of the Post Office, the FTC, or the BBBs to arrange stipulations with firms under investigation. Indeed, each of these organizations became a savvier practitioner of informal regulation, more appreciative of how industry-wide deliberations over fair practices and judicious settlements could attain regulatory goals with targeted use of scarce institutional resources. But the emergence of slower and more expensive formal procedures furnished businesses that relied on deception with more room to maneuver. Unscrupulous enterprises enjoyed more time before they felt enough pressure to close up shop and move, or before authorities were able to shut them down. In evaluating behavior on the margin between puffery and misrepresentation, public institutions such as the FTC may have shied away from confrontation with deep-pocketed corporations, or settled for easier terms, because the alternative would likely involve protracted legal proceedings with uncertain outcomes.

Concerned about the social costs of business fraud, late nineteenth- and early twentieth-century American policymakers experimented with the techniques of modern administrative regulation. They did so in some cases with the hope of burnishing professional credentials, but in all instances with the expectation of bypassing the frustrations associated with attacking deceit through the regular courts. Although several decades of legal counterattacks did not fully remold antifraud regulation according to common-law precepts, the critiques did encourage regulatory officials to take procedural fairness far more seriously. With the resulting institutional adjustments came heightened protections for the civil liberties of entrepreneurs and companies, greater authority for business lawyers, and more courtlike rituals within administrative adjudication; but also a sometimes less aggressive enforcement posture, and more regulatory disappointments akin to those that characterized Barnum's America.

PART IV

The Call for Investor and Consumer Protection (1930s to 1970s)

CHAPTER NINE

Moving toward *Caveat Venditor*

Shortly after Franklin Delano Roosevelt's inauguration in March 1933, he sent a special message to Congress that called for federal regulation of the securities markets. Taking note of the "severe losses" that investors had incurred "through practices neither ethical nor honest on the part of many persons and corporations selling securities," the new president asked for legislation that would require comprehensive disclosures by marketers of stocks and bonds. The enormity of the Great Depression, he argued, demanded new standards for communication by public corporations, investment bankers, and other players in financial markets. In order to restore "public confidence" in mechanisms of capital allocation, Congress had to place "the burden of telling the whole truth on the seller." Without oversight that ensured candor by the vendors of investments, Roosevelt proclaimed, stock exchanges and the bond markets would remain moribund, as shell-shocked investors shunned public securities.[1]

Roosevelt's plea represented a turning point in the policing of business fraud in the United States. After some wrangling over details, Congress acceded to his request, creating a powerful agency to supervise America's capital markets, the Securities and Exchange Commission (SEC). Along with the 1938 Wheeler-Lea Act, which extended the FTC's jurisdiction over duplicitous marketing, the creation of the SEC vastly expanded federal responsibility for regulating the truthfulness of economic speech. During the New Deal, the nation's elected officials pledged to redress informational asymmetries within America's industrialized, continental economy. They chose to act through robust bureaucracies that would monitor national marketplaces and combat deceptive business practices. These developments ushered in a half-century of intensive public action to constrain economic duplicity. Congress, statehouses, and city councils passed legislation that attacked such deceit, both in general and with respect to specific markets such as retail trade, franchising, and consumer credit. From the late 1950s through the 1970s, states and municipalities also launched new agencies charged with combating business fraud.

One must be careful not to overstate the degree of change associated with post–New Deal antideception regulation. Legislators and other policymakers had many earlier experiments upon which to build, and the fraud-fighting endeavors of the mid-twentieth century retained key features of those precursors. The waxing insistence that sellers face stricter standards at no point meant forsaking the assumption that economic actors had to be able to fend for themselves. Roosevelt explained that his call for tighter securities regulation did not absolve buyers from the duty to keep a sharp lookout. Rather, the proposal "adds to the ancient rule of *caveat emptor* ['Let the buyer beware'] the further doctrine: 'Let the seller also beware' [*caveat venditor*]." The crafting and implementation of New Deal securities legislation adhered to this formulation. Indeed, almost all of the antifraud policies enacted by American legislatures and regulatory agencies between 1933 and the 1970s were premised on due diligence by economic actors. Those policies also reflected abiding anxieties about extending too much power to administrative bureaucracies, whether through overgenerous budgetary allocations or the granting of undue discretionary authority. As a result, even at the height of the more expansive mid-twentieth-century American state, nongovernmental and self-regulatory organizations continued to play key roles in the antifraud regulatory environment.

The Roosevelt administration's embrace of *caveat venditor* nonetheless signaled a shift in political discourse and policy. For the following four decades, American legislators and regulators from both political parties gave less credence to assertions of economic freedom, and worried more about preserving popular confidence in markets or treating economic actors fairly. They also framed antifraud policies in terms of consumer and investor protection. Indeed, only with the New Deal did those phrases come into common currency.[2]

The next three chapters survey American fraud policing from the New Deal through the 1970s. This chapter considers antifraud efforts into the early 1960s, focusing on federal regulation of the financial markets and retail marketing, as well as related undertakings by Better Business Bureaus. Chapters Ten and Eleven grapple with the impact of consumerism on antifraud regulation from the late 1950s through the late 1970s. Together, these three chapters document wide-ranging attacks on commercial deception through legislative statutes, administrative rule-making, and, in some contexts, judicial interpretation. They also chart the bipartisan construction of a much denser and more integrated network of antifraud institutions, both public and outside the state. Despite enduring constraints on the reach and effectiveness of antifraud regulation, all of this activity circumscribed the scale, scope, and impact of marketplace deceptions.

Institutional Designs and Intellectual Foundations

New Deal antifraud regulation was born out of anxieties about the securities markets, which focused on decades-long patterns of self-dealing, manipulation, and misrepresentation, given new intensity by the post–World War I boom and subsequent stock market crash. During the dramatic run-up in stock prices from 1920 to 1929, Wall Street depended on a wider base of shareholders. Having become accustomed to investment through the World War I Liberty Bond campaign, and bombarded by the hard-sell techniques of fast-growing brokerages such as Merrill Lynch, several million middle-class Americans joined the investing class.[3] These newcomers purchased not just the securities of established sectors such as banking, insurance, transportation, and mining, but also shares in manufacturing, retail firms, and investment trusts, as well as foreign bonds. The mix of strong demand, unsophisticated purchasers, and weak regulatory constraints generated powerful incentives for deceit.

As Chapter Five demonstrated, mail fraud enforcement had targeted stock and bond swindlers since the late 1870s, and interstate investment fraud became a more substantial priority for the Post Office Department in the 1910s and 1920s, resulting in scores of prosecutions and convictions. During World War I, the Treasury Department's Capital Issues Committee received the authority to scrutinize proposed initial public offerings and to disallow the marketing of any issues deemed to be inconsistent with the war effort. Far more substantial regulatory legislation occurred at the state level, with the outpouring of blue-sky laws.

Rather than truly discriminating filters, however, state regulatory schemes proved to be at once porous and overly restrictive. The former problem resulted from legislative exemptions, either for sectors such as utilities and banking, or for companies with listed securities. The Investment Bankers of America (IBA), founded in 1913 to fend off the threat posed by blue-sky laws, worked hard to establish safe harbors for stocks and bonds sold on exchanges. Woeful bureaucratic limitations further hampered state regulation. Legislative appropriations often allowed only cursory enforcement, and even the best-funded agencies did not constrain the tip sheets and telephone boiler rooms that drove interstate sales. At the same time, promoters inveighed against blue-sky licensing requirements. To these apostles of enterprise, the new rules created legal "shackles" that only reinforced the power of established stock exchanges and investment banks, while placing a "strait jacket [on] industrial development."[4]

Even New York's far-reaching attempts to curb securities fraud through the 1921 Martin Act and the creation of a dedicated Bureau for the Prevention of Fraudulent Securities (BPFS) faced important limits. From 1925 onward, it distributed compulsory questionnaires to promoters and stock brokerages, so that it might learn about questionable practices even without specific complaints from investors.[5] BPFS attorneys initiated thousands of fraud investigations during the 1920s and 1930s, pursued hundreds of injunctive proceedings to force firms out of business, and brought scores of criminal prosecutions. Its success rate in the courts, moreover, represented a distinctive break from the hapless record of nineteenth-century state antifraud enforcement actions. As with requests for mail fraud orders, most BPFS motions for injunctions and the appointment of receiverships went uncontested; the Bureau usually prevailed when promoters or brokerages opposed it in court, and its criminal fraud prosecutions, while far less common than injunctive proceedings, typically resulted in convictions.[6] BPFS could and did point to successful enforcement actions against large-scale investment frauds. Attorneys general and their deputies took every opportunity to crow about their fearless takedowns of the New York's Consolidated Stock Exchange during the mid-1920s, George Graham Rice's promotion of the Idaho Copper Mine, Charles Bob's looting of a mining investment trust, and many other financial frauds. Officials also stressed that the Bureau's impact extended beyond putting investment swindlers out of business or in jail, because initial inquiries from staff attorneys often convinced securities firms to reform their marketing practices.[7]

Despite official breast-beating, contemporaries questioned how much enforcement of the Martin Act curbed the hawking of fraudulent investments. There were too many dodgy promoters for a few dozen investigators, attorneys, and clerks to track down, leading to laments from attorneys general about stingy appropriations and an impossible workload. Too often, critics such as the Progressive lawyer Samuel Untermeyer argued that enforcement under the Martin Act would merely "lock the stable door on these promotion frauds after the stock had been distributed and the thieves had bolted with their swag." Furthermore, court orders to dissolve fraudulent securities firms, again like mail fraud orders, did not prevent seasoned operators from relaunching scams through new firms. And Martin Act investigations targeted fringe operators—outsiders who dealt in unlisted stocks. Like the investigators of the Better Business Bureaus, the BPFS rarely scrutinized national financial elites.[8]

Amid the prosperity unleashed by World War I, as well as a heightened pace of technological diffusion and a rapid expansion of consumer credit, shady practices became endemic in Wall Street. Large public corporations such as the

Insull utilities' holding companies took advantage of permissive accounting standards to inflate income statements, thereby facilitating the marketing of new securities.[9] Corporate insiders and the managers of stock pools relied on a corrupt press corps to disseminate news favorable to their trades and manipulated prices directly through wash or matched sales—transactions in which they arranged to have confederates purchase shares to create the appearance of intensifying demand and increasing prices. Floor traders and specialists at the NYSE took advantage of knowledge about pending orders to engage in "front-running." As these insiders received large orders that would affect prices, they first placed trades on their own account that would appropriate some of the economic value from those price movements.[10] The investment trusts that sprang up during the 1920s created a culture of secrecy that abetted misrepresentation. Although fund managers claimed to have adopted sophisticated portfolio strategies that minimized risks, they often used investor funds to prop up struggling companies that they controlled, skimmed profits through undisclosed management and underwriting fees, and amplified risks by purchasing securities on margin.[11]

Investment banks and stock brokerages indulged in both conflicts of interest and deceptive practices. When underwriting initial public offerings of stock, investment bankers underpriced shares and reserved placements for corporate insiders and other favored clients, including members of the nation's political and legal elite.[12] In marketing the sovereign debt of struggling Latin American countries such as Peru, banking syndicates characterized the securities as low-risk, despite internal reports that warned of parlous fiscal situations.[13] Banks and brokerage firms that sold securities to the broad middle class, such as National City, adopted several practices of the boiler room brigade. In addition to training salesmen in high-pressure tactics and implementing commission-based remuneration policies that encouraged stretching of the truth, they trimmed the firms' losses on poorly performing stocks in their portfolios by instructing sales personnel to push those securities on retail customers.[14]

On the eve of the Great Depression, New York Attorney General Hamilton Ward conceded that prevailing regulations, including his own state's Martin Act, did little to prevent the most barefaced securities frauds. "The Martin Act," Ward observed, "is no protection against the common thief who claims to be a broker or salesman and deals in worthless securities. From the petty grafter to the gang of high-pressure salesmen with plenty of money who open a big office, there is a large field in which the remedies provided by the Martin Act help but little." Amid the wreckage strewn about the post-1929 financial landscape, the most ambitious forms of state antifraud legislation appeared even more insufficient.[15]

Malfeasance in the financial sector attracted public critiques before the New Deal, whether through the tell-all memoirs of stock operators Thomas Lawson, George Graham Rice, and Jesse Livermore, the analyses of academics such as economist William Z. Ripley, or the coverage of muckraking journalists such as John T. Flynn.[16] But only with the Senate Banking Committee's hearings on the securities markets did many Americans learn about the seamier side of the 1920s stock boom. These hearings, which began in the spring of 1932 and picked up momentum after Roosevelt's election and the selection of Ferdinand Pecora as lead counsel, received saturation press coverage. The evidence presented by Pecora demonstrated the questionable ethics and behavior of vaunted firms, including National City Bank and J. P. Morgan. The hearings undercut Wall Street's image, set off a political furor, and laid the groundwork for the Securities Act of 1933 and the Securities and Exchange Act of 1934.[17]

This pair of statutes remolded the marketing of securities. Although some Roosevelt administration officials and congressmen wished to create a federal "blue-sky" law, the chief drafters of the legislation, including Harvard law professors Felix Frankfurter and James Landis, viewed state regulatory approaches as failures. Instead of vesting the federal government with the obligation to certify new stock issues as reasonable propositions, Frankfurter and Landis joined two separate strategies of regulatory governance. The first involved bans on insider trading, market manipulations, and deceptions in initial public offerings and the secondary shares market. Here the architects of reform emulated the approach of the Martin Act, as well as state false pretenses laws and the federal mail fraud statute: they presumed that vigorous criminal prosecutions would deter outlawed behavior. The second strategy followed the longstanding logic of British financial regulation, which emphasized transparency in accounting and truthful marketing claims. The New Deal securities laws imposed rigorous disclosure requirements on public corporations, investment banks, and stock brokerages. But American legislators also extended the British approach. Across the Atlantic, the government depended on investors to identify wayward companies and promoters. Congress instead created an administrative regime to oversee provision of financial information, lodged in a new oversight body, the SEC.

Before investment banks could sell new securities to investors, they had to register proposed offerings (first with the FTC and, starting in 1934, with the SEC) and then wait twenty days before making sales. Registration documents had to furnish information about past performance, future strategy and prospects, assets and capital structure, and underwriting fees and sales commissions. If questions arose about veracity or completeness, firms could amend statements during the waiting period. If the SEC judged the information to be incomplete or untruthful, it could issue an administrative stop order that blocked offerings. Public companies further had to submit quarterly and annual statements about earnings and financial conditions, audited by independent accountants and consistent with accounting standards approved by the SEC in conjunction with the American Accounting Institute. The legislation furnished exemptions for small-scale stock offerings, closely-held companies with fewer than one thousand shareholders, and corporations with only in-state investors; but it reached most stocks and bonds owned by American investors.[18]

Three later pieces of legislation completed the New Deal architecture of securities regulation, each designed in light of SEC investigations and hearings. The 1938 Maloney Act mandated the creation of quasi-public regulatory organizations to oversee America's hundreds of brokerages as well as the "over-the-counter" (OTC) market, which took place through telephone trades based on privately circulated price sheets, and which handled secondary bond transactions, stock purchases by large institutional investors, and trading in shares of unlisted companies. The new quasi-public associations would have authority to license brokers. They would further set training standards and rules of practice, monitor compliance with these rules, hear complaints from customers, and penalize brokers and firms that misled or mistreated investors. The SEC retained supervisory authority over self-regulatory institutions, as well as its own direct powers of rule-making, monitoring, and enforcement. After the passage of the Maloney Act, the industry settled on a single self-regulatory organization (SRO) to fulfill these roles, with the IBA reconstituting itself to become the National Association of Securities Dealers (NASD).[19]

Two years later, Congress enacted the Investment Companies Act and the Investment Advisers Act, which established regulatory oversight of investment trusts and the new fields of investment counselors and portfolio managers that had emerged after World War I. The first of these two statutes prohibited self-dealing in the selling and investment practices of mutual funds. It also barred individuals who had been sanctioned for securities fraud from serving as investment company directors or officers, required investment companies to register with the SEC, and mandated that those corporations provide investors with detailed updates about holdings, financial structure, and strategy. The second statute required advisers to register with the SEC and disqualified individuals who had participated in securities fraud; it further forbade material misrepresentations and mandated disclosure of potential conflicts of interest.[20]

On occasion, the SEC extended rules against deceptive practices, as in 1942, when it adopted Rule 10b-5. This regulation clarified the 1933 Securities Act's

prohibition of fraud in securities transactions, declaring that it covered purchases as well as sales, omissions of material facts that made claims misleading,
and any other kind of deceitful "device, scheme, or artifice." For almost two
decades, Rule 10b-5 remained a minor element of securities regulation, ignored by SEC enforcement staff and securities lawyers. But in 1961, more aggressive officials adopted an interpretative opinion that this rule prohibited
stock trading by corporate officers who were taking advantage of nonpublic
information, as well as the provision of such information to others who then
traded on it.[21]

All of this legislative and administrative action was premised on the use of
regulatory power to reshape the business environment. The central goal of disclosure requirements on corporations and investment banks, like the licensing
mechanisms for stock brokerages, stock dealers, and investment advisers, was
to remake the structure and culture of the financial markets. Toward this end,
legislative framers, along with SEC staff, enlisted the help of financial professionals. Policymakers concentrated on private gatekeepers such as corporate
attorneys, who had the responsibility to oversee compliance with the new requirements, and public accountants, whom the legislation anointed as monitors of corporate financial statements. This strategy of administrative prevention retained punitive features. Failure to abide by disclosure requirements
made corporations subject to civil and criminal penalties, as did adoption of
deceptive or fraudulent marketing practices. The Securities Acts also gave investors standing to sue for damages if corporations had made false claims or
withheld material information, and if investors had suffered losses due to reliance on false or incomplete representations. But their central aim was to construct a new set of norms and practices about communicating truthful financial information.[22] The apex of regulatory power in this system lay with the
SEC and its hundreds of government lawyers, economists, and bureaucrats.
Nonetheless, its designers remained leery of gumming up the securities markets with excessive red tape. As a result, they delegated extensive responsibility
for regulatory compliance to the long-established stock exchanges, the newly
created NASD, and the legal and accounting professions.[23]

As with securities law, post-1933 regulation of duplicitous retailing built on
institutional forerunners and involved more robust activity by the national
government. The most important federal agency in this policy arena remained
the FTC. During the 1910s and 1920s, FTC lawyers had investigated thousands
of businesses to determine whether they had violated Section 5 of the FTC Act,
which outlawed "unfair methods of competition." Its inquiries generated hundreds of "cease and desist" enforcement actions, as well as many more stipulations—written pledges to discontinue objectionable business practices. At no

point, however, did the FTC enunciate the marketing transgressions that would trigger investigations. FTC administrative law judges and commissioners rather laid out principles piecemeal in case opinions.

Through this common law–like accretion, the pre–New Deal FTC identified clusters of disfavored marketing deceptions. Misleading claims about the quantity, quality, or newness of goods raised the eyebrows of FTC officials, as did false assertions about place of origin, the nature of ingredients/components, and the seller's status within the business community. Other enforcement triggers included unjustified disparagement of competing firms; deceptive claims about prices, such as fake "going out of business" sales and the touting of big discounts from fictitious high list prices; and phony testimonials. The trade practice conferences of the 1920s and early 1930s, which hammered out voluntary codes of fair competition, applied these broad principles to the specific contexts of individual industries.[24]

From the onset of the New Deal through the 1960s, the FTC took a very dim view of these marketing tactics. As its investigators, hearings' officers, and commissioners evaluated allegations of commercial misrepresentations, they used a much lower evidentiary standard than that required for criminal fraud allegations. The issue of fraudulent intent did not factor into FTC assessments, at least as they substantiated cease and desist proceedings in court; nor did the question of whether purchases had been influenced by deceptive claims. Instead, as the Supreme Court ruled in the 1919 case of *Sears Roebuck v. FTC*, the Commission only had to find that advertising or other aspects of marketing "had a capacity or tendency to injure competitors directly or through deception of purchasers."[25]

Later action by the courts and Congress expanded the reach of FTC regulation. Just a few months after President Roosevelt decisively shifted the Supreme Court's political balance through the appointment of Justice Hugo Black, that tribunal further lowered evidentiary requirements in FTC deception proceedings. The pivotal case was *FTC v. Standard Education Society* (1937), an appeal from an FTC cease and desist order against an encyclopedia distributor. According to the FTC, the firm's army of door-to-door salesmen falsely claimed that prominent figures had either contributed to or endorsed the encyclopedias; they told prospective purchasers that they wished to give them a set of volumes as a gift in order to gain access to their homes, before explaining that they would also have to pay for a ten-year subscription to monthly supplements; and they mischaracterized the regular purchase price as a steep discount. To argue its case in the federal courts, the Standard Education Society retained Henry Ward Beer, the fervent and long-time critic of expansive FTC administrative action. A federal appeals court vacated several elements of the

FTC's order, resting its judgment on the logic of *caveat emptor* laid out by Beer. "We cannot," the lower court argued, "take too seriously the suggestion that a man who is buying a set of books and a ten years' 'extension service' will be fatuous enough to be misled by the mere statement that the first are given away, and that he is paying only for the second." This opinion echoed the nineteenth-century jurists and editors who marveled at the stupidity of some Americans. On this view, if hopeless rubes insisted on ignoring telltale signs of imposition, courts had no business protecting them. After the FTC took the case to the Supreme Court, Justice Black rejected this contempt for the credulous sucker. "The fact that a false statement may be obviously false to those who are trained and experienced," Black reasoned,

> does not change its character, nor take away its power to deceive others less experienced. There is no duty resting upon a citizen to suspect the honesty of those with whom he transacts business. Laws are made to protect the trusting as well as the suspicious. The best element of business has long since decided that honesty should govern competitive enterprises, and that the rule of caveat emptor should not be relied upon to reward fraud and deception.

Black's opinion for the Court accordingly upheld the FTC order in its entirety.[26]

Like the post-1937 federal judiciary, Congress enlarged the FTC's fraud beat. During the 1920s, the Supreme Court had ruled that the FTC only possessed jurisdiction over duplicitous sales practices if it could show that they constituted "unfair methods of competition" that brought harm to other businesses. The 1938 Wheeler-Lea Act removed this limitation, prohibiting "deceptive practices" in interstate commerce regardless of losses incurred by other firms, and enhancing the FTC's powers to act against deceptively marketed food, drugs, and cosmetics.[27]

Buoyed by these moves by the Supreme Court and Congress, FTC hearing officers and commissioners pushed out the boundaries of illegal deception. From the 1940s through the mid-1960s, they continued to convene trade practice conferences, encouraging firms and trade associations to hammer out sectoral codes of fair competition. In the late 1950s, the Commission conducted economywide campaigns against fictitious pricing, bait and switch advertising, and deceptive guarantees. After distilling the broad principles that had underpinned cease and desist orders in these areas, it disseminated official guides and made them investigative priorities.[28]

These endeavors received deferential treatment from the federal courts. Midcentury appellate judges shied away from overturning FTC assessments in deceptive practices cases, even without evidence that customers had been deceived or that anyone had suffered quantifiable monetary harm. Members of the federal bench presumed that FTC experts could be trusted to look out for the "careless" and "least sophisticated" readers of advertising, identifying the tricky or ambiguous claims that would trip up easy marks. If those public servants found that descriptions of hair dye as "permanent" went beyond the legal pale, because the dye would not impact new growth, the courts would not upend their judgment. Nor would they overrule FTC findings that a company's "buy one, get one free" promotional campaign was deceptive, on the grounds that the firm had never sold the item at the stipulated price; or its rejection of a television shaving-cream advertisement that claimed the product could soften sandpaper, because the ad relied on "camera tricks" and a "simulated prop" made of Plexiglas covered in sand.[29] As the eminent federal judge Learned Hand summed up the FTC's discretion in deception cases, it had the authority to require "a form of advertising clear enough so that, in the words of the prophet Isaiah, 'wayfaring men, though fools, shall not err therein.'" FTC staff well understood the leeway that they enjoyed. The Commission's 1966 *Manual for Attorneys* described its mission as protecting the "most ignorant and unsuspecting purchaser." This objective required that investigators assess the "general impression" of ads and promotional materials, but did not hinge on showings of intent and gave investigators flexibility in building cases, because establishing deceptiveness was not amenable to "any general or all-purpose rule of investigative procedure."[30] This paternalistic vision represented a stark reversal from the presumptions that defined transactions a century, or even a half-century, earlier.

With America's entry into World War II, the national government refocused antifraud policy on military contracting and the regime of consumer price controls. As manufacturers retooled factories to meet the insatiable demand for weapons, munitions, tanks, and planes, reports surfaced of overbilling and other abusive practices. Federal officials responded by scrutinizing the work and billing practices of contractors and subcontractors. The armed services adopted stringent rules about quality control and cost structures, and backed them up with thousands of civilian inspectors and auditors who spent most of their time within factories. Congressional committees held a series of hearings to keep administration officials attentive to the task of keeping contractors honest. This oversight encouraged jawboning over charges and contract renegotiations. Where such informal pressure did not generate satisfactory outcomes, the Defense Department initiated dozens of high-profile prosecutions, which in most cases led to convictions.[31]

The crucial arbiter of the wartime retail economy was the Office of Price Administration (OPA), which had the task of enforcing rationing systems and price controls on consumer goods. In Washington, OPA economists and scientists set price ceilings and quality standards for a bewildering variety of consumer goods, and then constructed rationing regulations for crucial items such as gasoline and meat. Across the nation, local OPA officials, many of them former BBB leaders, enlisted hundreds of volunteer advisory groups and tens of thousands of local board members to assist with the formulation and implementation of regulations. A companion army of volunteer "price assistants," mostly housewives, monitored compliance with price and quantity controls in retail outlets.[32] Fraud enforcement represented only a minor aim for this gargantuan bureaucracy, which remained focused on tamping down inflation and ensuring the fair distribution of essential goods. But the organization nonetheless spearheaded hundreds of investigations across the country into ration-coupon counterfeiting, as well as the fraudulent sale of highly in-demand rebuilt radio sets and used cars, leading to scores of arrests and trials.[33]

In the decade and a half after World War II, Congress passed a series of other statutes that targeted specific forms of commercial deceit, including the 1951 Wool Act and Fur Products Labeling Act, the 1958 Textile Fiber Products Identification Act, and the 1958 Automobile Information Disclosure Act. These statutes embraced the central regulatory strategy that animated New Deal securities law: information provision. Each specified several types of truthful information that businesses had to provide to their customers and defined standards for presenting that information. Together, they solidified the federal government's commitment to acting against misleading and fraudulent forms of commercial speech, while also signaling an ongoing preference for enhancing the capacity of individuals to look after themselves.[34]

Post–World War II national policymakers exerted analogous efforts to rein in fraudulent educational institutions. Such concern reached back into the 1910s, when Better Business Bureaus, state prosecutors, and federal postal inspectors all began to wage battles against diploma mills. The creation of national higher-education grants and guaranteed loans through the GI Bill, however, gave the problem of educational fraud new salience. Now the issue was not just protecting the credulous or safeguarding the value of legitimate degrees and the standing of reputable educational institutions, but also preventing raids on the Treasury. After the 1944 passage of the GI Bill, there were periodic scandals involving fly-by-night vocational schools and more respectable institutions that misled prospective students about instructional quality or graduates' career trajectories. The federal government's primary regulatory response, heralded first in the 1952 Veterans' Readjustment Assistance Act, depended on state and regional accrediting agencies. These nongovernmental organizations took on the role of certifying that universities, colleges, and proprietary vocational schools furnished bona fide educational programs, and so deserved eligibility for federal loans and grants. As with oversight stock brokerages, which relied on NASD scrutiny, attempts to combat fraud in higher education delegated key regulatory functions to quasi-public entities.[35]

Companion antifraud efforts occurred outside Washington, DC, as state and local governments added their own statutes and ordinances targeting consumer fraud. During the 1940s and 1950s, much of this legislative barrage singled out problems in specific economic sectors, such as marketing practices in the insurance industry (which was not subject to federal regulation, with the contested exception of advertising in national publications), or licensing and bonding regimes for occupations. The number of states that made instances of false advertising subject to prosecution as a misdemeanor also grew. By 1956, forty-three states had enacted such laws, with thirty-one mandating that prosecutors did not need to establish either knowledge or intent to obtain convictions.[36]

In one longstanding arena of antideception regulation—mail fraud enforcement—the judiciary did prune federal power. In a pair of cases, the Supreme Court ruled that the Post Office had to demonstrate fraudulent intent to justify the issuance of fraud orders, and that postal officials had to take greater care in framing the scope of such orders, so that they reached only activities shown to be fraudulent.[37] These rulings, however, were premised on concurrent expansion of FTC authority, which gave the federal government an alternative administrative sanction for deceptive marketing practices—the FTC cease and desist order. The Post Office also retained authority to investigate allegations of mail fraud, initiating criminal prosecutions where appropriate.[38] Thus, from the onset of the New Deal into the 1960s, tighter antifraud regulation represented a consistent feature of the American political economy.

There was no epochal event such as the 1929 stock market crash to serve as a generational touchstone for regulatory moves against duplicitous retail marketing. At no point did the specter of consumer fraud seem daunting enough to crash the entire economy. On occasion, smaller-scale incidents galvanized national concern over the willingness of businesses to shade the truth. In 1958, revelations that the major television networks had scripted popular game shows such as *Twenty One* and *The $64,000 Question* shocked elite commentators and ordinary viewers alike. A few years later, public disclosures that music companies showered DJs with inducements ("payola") to play their records on radio programs produced similar reactions. These episodes generated high-profile congressional hearings, sparked some policy shifts, such as a federal law criminalizing payola, and encouraged the FTC to embrace a more aggressive posture toward deceptive business practices.[39]

In the absence of scandals, Americans continued to learn about the ongoing problem of consumer and financial fraud from commercial watchdogs. At no point did metropolitan newspapers cease to cover fraud prosecutions. As early as the 1930s, columnists such as the *New York Post*'s Sylvia Porter guided investors through the maze of modern capitalism, including advice on how to avoid financial swindles. The midcentury embrace of long-term investigative reporting produced numerous series on prevailing cheats, such as Jim Foree's five-part June 1957 exposé for the *Chicago Defender* on sleazy automobile sales practices. Mid-twentieth-century national magazines also emulated their predecessors. Publications as various as *Better Homes and Gardens*, *Reader's Digest*, *Nation's Business*, the *Saturday Evening Post*, and *Changing Times* ran compendiums of business scams and recycled general cautions about the telltale signs of fraudulent marketing.[40] A number of these journalists, such as Ralph Lee Smith, Frank Gibney, and Sidney Margolius, reached national audiences through books on frauds and rackets that drew on their careers covering consumer issues.[41]

Antifraud sentinels in the press continued to have allies in the nation's network of Better Business Bureaus, which became even more entrenched during the postwar decades. The BBBs retained a focus on public education, as indicated by a massive campaign at the end of World War II to warn Americans about a flurry of investment frauds (Figure 9.1). By the 1950s, though, the BBBs put more effort into combating consumer fraud, a reflection of the deepening institutional framework of securities regulation. As Americans moved to the suburbs, BBBs followed right along, opening up offices in fast-growing new communities. By 1962, there were bureaus in 122 American cities and towns. They distributed a torrent of consumer guides to suburbanites, explaining how to look after their interests when dealing with a landscaping company, ordering television repairs, or purchasing an appliance on credit. In several cities, they produced radio and television segments that highlighted enduring problems of consumer fraud—three thousand radio and television episodes and forty thousand shorter public-service advertisements a year.[42] In Chicago, for example, the long-running radio programs *Hello Sucker* and *It's Your Money* ran weekly in the 1950s, warning listeners about frauds in automobile showrooms, among door-to-door salesmen, and through the marketing of franchising opportunities and residential developments.[43] These campaigns rivaled the scale of BBB efforts in the 1920s.

National consumer organizations founded during the Great Depression, such as Consumer Research and Consumers Union, also monitored deceptive business practices as part of efforts to educate the parents of baby boomers and other postwar adults about how best to spend. As these organizations evalu-

Figure 9.1: A BBB poster beseeching investors to remain vigilant in the face of post–World War II investment and charity frauds. W. Dan Bell Papers, Denver Public Library, Western History Collection. Reproduced with permission.

ated product quality, they remained alert to marketing that pressed at the boundaries of acceptable puffery. Their newsletters and magazines then informed subscribers about products, services, and companies that flattered to deceive.[44]

Some of the most insistent post–World War II pleas for combating business fraud came from middle-class women, who took advantage of the growing tendency of economic discourse to feminize "the consumer" by picturing this abstract individual as a middle-class housewife. Cultural linkage of American household consumption to female decision-making had longstanding origins. The nineteenth-century birth of consumer education was bound up with the invention of home economics, a highly gendered undertaking. Mail-order houses, early department stores, and advertising agencies all directed marketing to potential female purchasers.[45] But the equation of women with consumption decisions became even more common after World War II, as the figure of "Mrs. Consumer" became a common stand-in for the spending public, addressed in ads, referenced in the business pages, and depicted in anti-fraud literature, such as an early 1950s BBB poster that showed a skeptical housewife deflating the confidence of a door-to-door salesman by invoking the need to check out his firm with the local Bureau (Figure 9.2). "Mrs. Consumer" took on the gloss of the capitalist economy's true sovereign, the maker or breaker of corporate profitability. Through mounting consumer complaints to businesses, BBBs, and government officials, middle-class women deployed this rhetoric with regard to numerous consumer issues, including deceptive marketing. They organized as well, joining myriad neighborhood organizations that lent popular heft to consumerism.[46]

Figure 9.2: A skeptical Mrs. Consumer in a 1950s Better Business Bureau cartoon. Illustrated by Wilson Cutler as part of a series of educational slides commissioned by the Better Business Bureau.

Heightened expectations by consumers and investors encouraged diffuse support for antifraud regulation. Ongoing media coverage raised awareness of commercial deception and at least sometimes fostered public outrage over economic injustices. A steady increase in the number, kind, and reach of NGOs dedicated to fighting business fraud broadened the chorus of voices calling for antifraud measures, as well as the research base about marketing practices and consumer behavior. These developments swelled popular pressures for government action against commercial deceit and enlarged the stock of ideas about how to execute such regulatory campaigns. But the adoption of antifraud regulations between 1945 and the early 1960s rarely reflected vigorous grassroots mobilization.

During these years, regulatory action against misrepresentation was pushed by business interests, much as had been the case in nineteenth-century debates over fertilizer adulteration or the early twentieth-century campaign against false advertising. Adoption of more stringent labeling regimes for furs and textiles in the 1950s, for example, came at the behest of fur raisers, wool and cotton growers, and upscale manufacturers and retailers. Other than officials from regulatory agencies, representatives from these sectors were the only witnesses who testified before congressional committees considering labeling reforms. These groups alleged that discount sellers were engaging in rampant mislabeling that undercut public confidence in higher-quality goods; they also contended that many consumers were duped by such tactics, and needed protection that only strong public regulation could provide.[47] Similarly, major record labels instigated the late 1950s payola investigations in the hopes of beating back inroads by independent producers. The latter had turned to payola as one way to introduce R&B, rock music, and African American artists to a wider public, focusing on new local radio stations that coveted young listeners. Even though the established music distributors also furnished DJs with gifts and favors, they calculated correctly that investigations into the industry's endemic bribery and kickbacks would hamstring independents such as BMI and Ace Records.[48]

Advocacy for postwar antifraud regulation, however, did not always equate to regulatory capture, in which corporate puppeteers lay behind more stringent regulatory action, pulling the strings of public officials in order to fend off competitive threats.[49] With some initiatives, such as moves against bait advertising and misleading pricing practices, antifraud professionals within the business establishment—BBB careerists, aided by counterparts at national advertising trade associations—stood out as the key figures driving regulatory agendas. From the 1930s onward, local BBBs and the National BBB identified such marketing practices as deserving of priority attention. During hundreds of trade practice conferences, BBB leaders hammered out detailed specifications about what constituted bait and switch tactics, false comparisons with competing retailers, and fake assertions about sale discounts. By the early 1950s, the Bureaus had developed comprehensive standards in these areas, whether for consumer goods such as vacuum cleaners and automobiles, or for services provided by home improvement companies and insurance companies. These codes served as templates for the FTC's regulatory rule-making and enforcement priorities, which targeted bait advertising in late 1958, deceptive pricing in 1959, and deceptive advertising of guarantees in 1960.[50]

Postwar BBB officials, moreover, articulated an expansive antifraud philosophy that reflected an institutional mission distinct from that of their corporate funders. C. W. Dessart, a trade practice consultant specializing in the regulation of car marketing, articulated this stance in a sharply worded 1957 letter to a Texas auto dealer who had opposed more stringent antifraud rules for the industry. "As a dedicated automobile man, and as a Better Business Bureau Trade Practice Consultant," Dessart explained to the dealer,

> we admit to a kind of bias. For we are biased against the petty thief who filches pennies from a blind man's cup; we are biased against the "shopper" who lies

about what the "other dealer allowed him" for his old "heap" and the merchant whose business ethics and "law" is that of the shady business jungle, and whose theme song is "CAVEAT EMPTOR"—"let the buyer beware;" we are most decidedly biased against the merchant in any line—including automobiles—whose technique is to trade upon and exploit human ignorance and credulity, and who as an automobile "Medicine Man" pitches his "snake oil" by mass advertising to today's Mortimer Snerds, instead of to the yokels from the tail-gate of a horse drawn wagon as in the earlier days.[51]

For Dessart, sharp practices in retailing had no place in modern America. This mindset percolated throughout the national network of long-serving BBB professionals.

The voices raised up against American business fraud during the Great Depression, World War II, and the immediate postwar period, then, reflected important continuity. As was the case during the Progressive era, some business interests continued to see deceptive sales cultures either as a short-term competitive threat or a longer-term menace to consumer confidence. And a cadre of antifraud professionals often took the lead in formulating legal reforms and setting enforcement priorities. Indeed, Presidents Truman and Eisenhower refrained from the full-throated critique of *caveat emptor* that had framed New Deal securities regulation.

To be sure, Harry Truman treated consumer welfare and the equitable distribution of America's economic bounty as policy lodestars for his "Fair Deal." These broad goals shaped his thinking about using fiscal policy to tame the business cycle and extending prosperity to a wider circle of Americans through national health insurance, expansion of Social Security, stronger protections for labor unions, federal aid for education and housing, stricter antitrust enforcement, and civil rights legislation. But at no point did Truman make consumer protection a centerpiece of his domestic agenda.[52] While in office, Dwight Eisenhower signaled concern that American businesses faced too much heavy-handed governmental oversight. "The great economic strength of our democracy," he proclaimed in his first message to Congress, "has developed in an atmosphere of freedom. The character of our people resists artificial and arbitrary controls of any kind." This philosophy guided Eisenhower's legislative priorities and appointments to regulatory agencies such as the SEC and FTC.[53] Thus, it should come as little surprise that the pace of major federal antifraud initiatives slowed in the decade and a half after World War II, or that antifraud legislation adopted by Congress in this time period, such as the Textile Fiber Identification Act, came at the behest of business interests.

Toward the end of Eisenhower's time in office, however, the television quiz show and payola scandals elicited a few presidential echoes of FDR's rhetorical shots against unscrupulous stock promoters. Ike denounced the quiz show frauds "as a terrible thing to do to the American public" and described payola as an affront to "public morality." In both cases he called for investigations and prevention of reoccurrences, which nudged Congress to pass legislation criminalizing fakery over the airwaves.[54] These responses presaged more sustained presidential engagement with deceitful marketing and business fraud as national problems.

Challenges of Enforcement

New Deal and post–World War II antifraud statutes, of course, did not immediately transform legal culture and day-to-day economic relations any more than the formal legal reforms of the previous century. Policy innovations do not magically elicit adequate enforcement. Once again, we need to consider law in action—the meanings of all the new statutory requirements and administrative rules to aggrieved consumers, embattled firms, and consumer watchdogs; the legal system's mediation of fraud-related disputes; and the impact of new legal norms on the beliefs and values that influence economic behavior. With the pivot toward the legal principle of *caveat venditor*, American policymakers filled in the latticework of a modern antifraud state. By 1960, thousands of individuals worked for antifraud institutions, deepening organizational capacity, constructing enforcement networks across jurisdictions and agencies, and encouraging professionalization of antifraud regulators. In some arenas, such as securities regulation, these endeavors achieved significant improvements in the trustworthiness of commercial speech. Wrestling with the flim-flam man, however, continued to require constant monitoring, patient investigation, shrewd deployment of resources, and unwavering vigilance, and the wrestlers did not always live up to these exacting requirements.

Mid-twentieth century antifraud enforcement efforts confronted numerous obstacles that had deep historical roots. Echoes of longstanding popular attitudes toward hucksterism represented one complication. Despite the shifts away from the premises of *caveat emptor* in American law, many corners of society retained contempt for the sucker and grudging admiration for those who took advantage of them. Post–World War II overviews of prevalent consumer and investor scams often marveled at the wondrous gullibility of those "suckers" who bit on the truly "preposterous," "incredible," "astonishing," "fantastic swindles" lurking about the American marketplace. Accounts of specific fraud scandals, such as the 1948 implosion of Arthur Knetzer's Ponzi-like car deposit scheme in southern Illinois, or the 1961 collapse of David Farrell's guaranteed trust deed investments in southern California, elicited analogous amazement at just how "eager" and "naïve" investors and consumers could be.[55] American linguistic practices also still communicated a disfavored status for those taken in by bait and switch advertising or investment scams. Even when seeking to warn consumers and investors about the need for skeptical appraisal of puffery, mid-twentieth-century commentators tagged those who lacked such habits with unflattering monikers. One list included "come-on, flyflat, John, juggins, or pigeon"; another "apple, bates, boob, chump, clown, easy mark, addle-cove, addict, egg, fink, lily, mooch, mug, pushover, top, [and] sweet pea."[56] Such turns of phrase did not imply abiding concern or respect.

The picaresque confidence man also continued to receive frequent billing in popular culture. W. C. Fields's 1939 film *You Can't Cheat an Honest Man* became a mainstay of postwar television, repeating the message that those preyed on by financial bilkers had only their own greed to blame. It was joined by such hits as *A Day at the Races* (1937), *The Rainmaker* (1955), and *The Music Man* (1962). These productions offered sympathetic characterizations of grifters who relied on their wits to navigate unforgiving worlds. As one writer observed about the ongoing cultural status of the confidence man, he remained "an eccentric, a source of anecdote, a joke quickly told." Even within the consumer movement, more conservative spokespersons such as Frederick Schlink of Consumers Research opposed stringent antifraud regulation, repeating the argument that it was impossible to hornswoggle "an honest man," and worrying that regulatory paternalism would render consumers unthinking "wards of the state."[57]

These undercurrents of mockery toward fraud victims and approbation for tricksters were not as powerful as in the nineteenth or early twentieth century. Most post–World War II discussions of swindles and commercial impositions stressed the psychological vulnerability of consumers and investors to well-constructed deceptions. A 1960 article in *Changing Times*, a personal finance magazine aligned with moderate Republicanism, conveys this common interpretive stance. The author of this catalogue of prevalent swindles and marketing trickery declared that "No one is safe" from commercial and financial fakery; that "[a]nybody can be a victim"; that "fraud operators can strike anywhere and anyone." [58] By the same token, perpetrators of business frauds received scorn as "heartless" criminals.[59]

Still, wonderment at the credulity of American consumers and investors remained a feature of public discourse and private attitudes, as did some ambivalence about the "golden fleecers" who so artfully separated them from their savings. Such sentiments could hinder antifraud prosecutions. Amid lingering norms that harkened back to the age of *caveat emptor*, the psychology of embarrassment or denial still led many shorn Americans to keep quiet. According to Nathaniel Goldstein, New York attorney general in the mid-1950s, the vast majority of defrauded investors fell into this category, letting "pride keep them from filing complaints against the sharpers."[60] Even when victims were not dissuaded from making public complaints, there might be considerable delay between the moment of deception and its recognition by the consumer or investor, complicating any investigation. As in previous eras, the tiny stakes of many scams constituted a further barrier to action. Because many consumer frauds filched only small sums from individual purchasers, most victims did not chase after satisfaction.[61]

In both financial and consumer fraud cases, moreover, key actors in the American justice system viewed allegations of marketplace deceptions with jaundiced eyes. Outside the ranks of specialized antifraud agencies and divisions, the legal fraternity often retained personal standards that hewed closely to those of W. C. Fields, or even P. T. Barnum. In the decades before the emergence of public-interest law firms and a plaintiff's bar that specialized in class-action suits, American attorneys were more accustomed to the perspective of business interests than that of consumers or investors, and so tended to sympathize with that viewpoint. Thus, if disgruntled consumers or investors sought out legal advice about how to handle some allegedly deceptive transaction, they were likely to be counseled against pursuing criminal complaints. For similar reasons, many mid-twentieth-century prosecutors were disinclined to bring fraud-related charges against businessmen. Moving in the same social and political circles as retailers and real-estate developers, and often contemplating returns to private practice, they had incentives to avoid antagonizing future clients.[62]

Prosecutors also knew that criminal fraud cases were often hard to win, for the same reasons as in earlier periods. The artful dodging of duplicitous businessmen, so vexing to late nineteenth-century postal inspectors and early twentieth-century BBB managers, continued to trouble antifraud enforcers. Pitchmen of mid-twentieth-century get-rich-quick schemes proved no less capable than their predecessors of moving boiler rooms from location to location, or of seeking out friendly jurisdictions from which to operate. Improvements in communications even expanded their geographic options. After the creation of the SEC, Canadian cities became popular bases for peddling penny stocks to American investors over the phone.[63]

The wide expanses of the United States also still offered escape routes for the purveyors of consumer frauds, as was made clear by the decades-long predation by a clan of several hundred petty swindlers known as "The Travelers" or "The Terrible Williamsons." This set of related Scottish families maintained a nomadic lifestyle, moving from town to town pitching "bogus goods and services," such as the cheapest textiles passed off as fine imports, shoddy driveway resurfacing, or ineffective roof sealing. The Williamsons took care to "stop in one location just long enough to bilk the local citizenry out of as many hard earned dollars as possible" before a chorus of complaints raised the alarm with local police. In those unusual circumstances in which members of the clan stuck around long enough to face arrests and criminal charges, they had little compunction about skipping bail. As a result, postwar BBBs officials and journalists issued repeated public warnings about their exploits.[64]

When victims were willing to file complaints and testify in court, and law enforcement officials were able to corral alleged perpetrators, prosecutors still had to weigh the drain on resources that fraud cases often entailed. Although the post-1945 judiciary accommodated antifraud reforms that lowered evidentiary burdens in administrative enforcement actions, the legal requirements for criminal fraud convictions remained steep. Just as in the previous century, much investigative legwork was necessary to substantiate fraud prosecutions. Establishing the false claims that underpinned marketing deceptions, as well as reliance on those falsehoods by victims and the fraudulent intent of defendants, often required interviews with far-flung witnesses and, in financial cases, expert accounting analysis. Prosecutors might have needed weeks to present such evidence before grand juries or in court, which meant that fraud cases clogged criminal dockets. The nature of the evidence at issue further gave well-prepared defense counsel opportunities to slow matters down with procedural challenges. These considerations shaped case selection even among prosecutors who made fraud cases a priority.[65]

Mid-twentieth-century criminal fraud prosecutions also ran into difficulties with juries and trial judges. The former could struggle to keep track of complex evidence about obscure financial transactions, manifest skepticism about the extent to which defendants had meant to deceive their counterparties, or demonstrate reluctance "to stigmatize a man as a criminal" because sales pitches had taken a few liberties with the truth. The latter often refused to see fraud charges as meriting the degree of concern shown to instances of violent crime, or went out of their way in jury instructions to emphasize that fraud convictions required a showing of fraudulent intent beyond a reasonable doubt.[66] These stubborn dimensions of the legal system meant that some criminal sanctions against hucksterism went unused. Despite the steady passage of statutes criminalizing false advertising, prosecutions almost never occurred, because prosecutors viewed indictments as disproportionate responses to deceptive marketing.[67]

In addition, charismatic businessmen accused of fraud retained their penchant for avoiding criminal penalties, even after business failures that resulted in losses to investors, employees, and creditors. The 1949–50 trials of automobile impresario Preston Tucker suggests how the best defense attorneys had a knack for leading judges and juries to see their clients as sympathetic if flawed entrepreneurs. After World War II, the Tucker Corporation developed a new motor car, the Torpedo, in the hopes of cashing in on voracious demand created by rising household incomes and a wartime production ban. This vehicle possessed several technological innovations, but was beset by cost overruns and the gargantuan capital requirements of launching a new automobile firm. To raise cash, Tucker sold hundreds of dealerships to local businessmen and thousands of purchase options to consumers, while regaling potential investors with his company's prospects. After national magazine stories raised questions about corporate financial practices and a series of engineering difficulties, the firm spiraled into bankruptcy.

At this juncture, officials at the SEC, Post Office, and FBI became convinced that Tucker was emulating several fraudulent interwar carmakers, such as the Pan Motor Company of St. Cloud, Minnesota, which built factories and prototypes as part of elaborate schemes to bilk investors. As a result, they charged Tucker and seven other corporate officers with mail and securities fraud. Two high-profile trials led first to a mistrial and then acquittals. In the second trial, the judge instructed jurors about the high legal bar for fraud cases, informing them that they could convict only if they found that the defendants had made false statements and promises out of "a purpose and design to cheat." Jurors rejected the prosecutor's argument that a mix of unrealistic projections, aggressive salesmanship, and generous executive compensation met such an exacting standard.[68] Versions of this script recurred through the Cold War decades, as judges and juries declined to follow the lead of prosecutors in fraud cases brought against flamboyant leaders of failed corporations.[69]

Even when prosecutors won fraud cases, they often despaired over continuing judicial leniency. Whether fraud convictions came under state false pretense laws, the federal mail fraud statute, or prohibitions against securities fraud, defendants received minimal sentences. More often than not, unsavory characters who had filched large sums received only "wrist slaps": probation, suspended sentences, or jail terms of a few months.[70] The disinclination of judges to "rap their knuckles a little harder" when staring down at individuals convicted of business fraud had ramifications for plea bargaining. Because defense lawyers knew the score, plea deals rarely imposed jail time and often mandated only consent decrees that accepted findings of legal violations without admission of guilt.[71]

In earlier decades, frustrations with criminal fraud prosecutions had encouraged innovations such as the postal-fraud order and informal pressure on publications to reject advertising from offending firms. These tactics had elicited howls about creeping despotism, prompting adoption of procedural protections, which, in turn, had limited the effectiveness of administrative remedies. Proceduralism became even more deeply ingrained after World War II. Within the criminal courts, the dominant trend, driven by a Supreme Court concerned about civil liberties, was to give defendants greater access to legal representation and to ensure observance of procedural safeguards. Tougher appellate scrutiny of criminal convictions sometimes meant the overturning of fraud convictions on procedural grounds.[72] That possibility expanded the tactics employed by defense attorneys in business fraud cases, because trial judges operated in the shadow of the appellate bench.

Heightened concern for procedure also cramped administrative enforcement. Here, the legal terrain was reshaped by the 1946 Administrative Procedure Act, which mandated extensive opportunities for public comment as part of the rule-making process and required that administrative actions mimic criminal process. Parties facing enforcement actions had to receive ample notice of specific allegations; they enjoyed rights to legal representation, access to incriminating evidence, and reasonable accommodation in preparing defenses; they could expect that hearing officers, investigators, and prosecutors would all be separate individuals, and that hearing officers would explain the legal basis of findings to them. Such protections, embraced as well by state Administrative Procedure Acts, extended the time and resources needed to pursue administrative orders against firms accused of deceitful marketing.[73]

Given sufficient bureaucratic capacity, the extensions of American commitment to the rule of law need not have presented insuperable enforcement problems. Some antifraud agencies, moreover, were able to build sizable organizations. The SEC began the post–World War II era with a budget of $4.6 million, which enabled it to maintain a staff of nearly 1,200, including more than three hundred employees in regional offices. But even at the most well-funded agencies, antifraud officials often still felt hard-pressed to meet their responsibilities in light of the growing population and economic activity. The SEC's budget did not keep pace with the explosive growth in securities origination and trading in the fifteen years after World War II, and budget cuts under

Eisenhower forced the Commission to slash its staff by a quarter. Appropriations for the FTC's regulation of antideceptive practices did increase at a rate comparable to that of economic growth between 1945 and 1965. But its deceptive-practices unit struggled to handle thousands of annual complaints about false advertising and misleading sales techniques.[74]

Even more so than in the 1920s, administration action at the postwar FTC became notorious for its languid pace. Investigations often took months or years and then had to go through secondary reviews by staff attorneys.[75] Consideration of formal cases by hearing officers and then the full commission took even longer, as high-level staff evaluated the analyses and conclusions of investigators and prevailing rules encouraged continuances. Every few years, an FTC chairman would declare war on internal delays and preside over speed-ups that would reduce bottlenecks. But a "dilatory and over-legalistic" institutional culture would then reassert itself. Although the courts mostly upheld FTC findings, appeals tacked on more time. In one convoluted case brought against Carter's Little Liver Pills for dubious health claims, the interval between the first investigation and the last court challenge was sixteen years. More often, three to five years elapsed before the conclusion of all appeals, far longer than the typical length of advertising campaigns. In addition, once FTC cease and desist orders became final, the agency allocated minimal resources to check on compliance. The agency developed a reputation for "snail-like procedures" and a "comatose spirit," becoming known to the capital's chauvinistic wags as the "old lady of Pennsylvania Avenue."[76]

The regulatory odyssey of Michigan's Holland Furnace Company suggests the capacity of some larger corporations to exploit these bureaucratic shortcomings. Holland Furnace had franchises in most states. Working door-to-door, its sales agents would create the impression that they were either government safety inspectors or private heating engineers, and ask to see the furnace. If homeowners agreed, agents would disassemble it and then spin grave tales of impending disaster via cataclysmic explosion, asphyxiating fumes, or engulfing conflagration. Next would come high-pressure pitches for replacement models, along with refusals to reassemble the old unit on the grounds that salesmen would not be "accessories to murder." Holland managers gave salesmen extensive training in these tactics; the company also structured compensation incentives to encourage the hard sell.[77]

Holland executives pushed this selling scheme beginning in the mid-1930s. Scores of consumer complaints led the FTC to issue a cease and desist order against the firm in 1936. But the sales force ignored it. Years of additional complaints prompted another FTC investigation in 1954, which after four grinding years of procedural challenges culminated in a second cease and desist order.

Holland personnel gave this order and a subsequent court decree the same short shrift. The firm continued to advertise for branch sales agents, whom it promised to "teach our business," enabling them to make "above average wages while you learn and higher wages once you are experienced." Holland management also scoffed at fraud investigations by state and local agencies, raising every conceivable legal objection. Only in 1965, when a federal judge found the corporation in criminal contempt of the court decree, sentenced the former company president to a short prison term, and levied a fine of $100,000, did the firm take meaningful steps to root out abusive practices.[78]

Daunting practical realities confronted mid-twentieth-century enforcers of laws against business fraud: reticence among the fleeced; migratory swindlers; echoes of the world of *caveat emptor* that ricocheted around some corners of the criminal justice system; hyper-legalism; budgetary allocations that failed to match legislative aspirations. But regulatory officials were not without their own resources in coping with such challenges. Just as the history of American business fraud foreshadowed these problems, it also suggested regulatory rejoinders. Every facet of early twentieth-century American campaigns against business fraud reappeared in post–World War II initiatives, at a greater scale and intensity.

FORTIFYING THE ANTIFRAUD STATE

Aware of their limitations, postwar antifraud organizations looked to maximize monitoring capacity and efficiently deploy resources for enforcement. One priority was to improve coordination and information-sharing among the agencies with jurisdiction over business frauds—an echo of the *American Agriculturist*'s network of correspondents, the NACM's "rogue's gallery," and the compendiums of quackery and quacks put together by the AMA's Bureau of Investigation. As soon as the SEC opened its doors, officials forged close relationships with federal postal inspectors, state securities regulators, and criminal investigators and prosecutors. Within months, the SEC collected sufficient data to construct a comprehensive set of "securities violation records." This "central index and clearing house" maintained details on about fifteen thousand Americans and Canadians who had faced allegations of securities fraud. In addition to keeping the index up to date, the SEC sent out a "monthly confidential bulletin" to its bureaucratic partners and contacted them about thousands of individual cases. By 1950, the fraud register comprised details on over fifty-three thousand stock promoters, brokers, and salesmen. SEC staff also analyzed the records to spot "overall pattern[s]," and always made the files

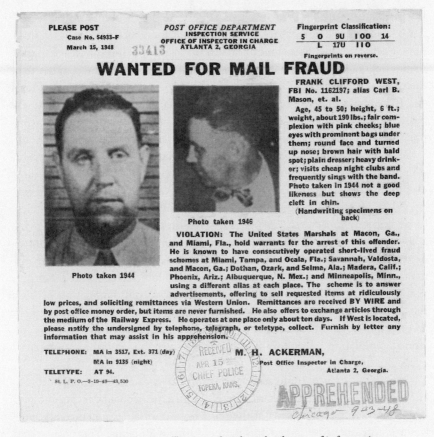

PLEASE POST
Case No. 54933-F
March 15, 1948
33413

POST OFFICE DEPARTMENT
INSPECTION SERVICE
OFFICE OF INSPECTOR IN CHARGE
ATLANTA 2, GEORGIA

Fingerprint Classification:
5   O   9U   I OO   14
L   17U   I IO
Fingerprints on reverse.

WANTED FOR MAIL FRAUD

FRANK CLIFFORD WEST, FBI No. 1162197; alias Carl B. Mason, et. al.

Age, 45 to 50; height, 6 ft.; weight, about 190 lbs.; fair complexion with pink cheeks; blue eyes with prominent bags under them; round face and turned up nose; brown hair with bald spot; plain dresser; heavy drinker; visits cheap night clubs and frequently sings with the band. Photo taken in 1944 not a good likeness but shows the deep cleft in chin.

(Handwriting specimens on back)

Photo taken 1946

Photo taken 1944

VIOLATION: The United States Marshals at Macon, Ga., and Miami, Fla., hold warrants for the arrest of this offender. He is known to have consecutively operated short-lived fraud schemes at Miami, Tampa, and Ocala, Fla.; Savannah, Valdosta, and Macon, Ga.; Dothan, Ozark, and Selma, Ala.; Madera, Calif.; Phoenix, Ariz.; Albuquerque, N. Mex.; and Minneapolis, Minn., using a different alias at each place. The scheme is to answer advertisements, offering to sell requested items at ridiculously low prices, and soliciting remittances via Western Union. Remittances are received BY WIRE and by post office money order, but items are never furnished. He also offers to exchange articles through the medium of the Railway Express. He operates at one place only about ten days. If West is located, please notify the undersigned by telephone, telegraph, or teletype, collect. Furnish by letter any information that may assist in his apprehension.

TELEPHONE: MA in 3517, Ext. 371 (day)
MA in 9135 (night)
TELETYPE: AT 94.
St. L. P. O.—3-19-48—43,530

M. H. ACKERMAN,
Post Office Inspector in Charge,
Atlanta 2, Georgia.

RECEIVED APR 15 CHIEF POLICE TOPEKA, KANS.

APPREHENDED
Chicago 9-23-48

Figure 9.3: A Post Office "Wanted" poster, detailing the degree of information collected, and hinting at its national distribution (with receipt by the Topeka, Kansas, police, and a notation of the suspect being apprehended in Chicago). Author's collection.

available to state and local officials to assist with "current enforcement problems."[79] The postal inspectorate developed analogous information systems, as well as national distribution of "wanted" posters. The latter, such as a 1948 bulletin for Frank Clifford West, "alias Carl B. Mason" (Figure 9.3), included not only photographs, but also capsule biographies (in West's case, consumer fraud schemes in seven separate states), fingerprints, and even handwriting samples. These national information systems facilitated the tracking down of even the most migratory swindlers.

Postwar antifraud agencies extended their reach through heavy reliance on self-regulatory organizations. New Deal securities regulation incorporated private regulatory gatekeepers from the start. The SEC leaned not only on securities exchanges and the NASD, but also on corporate accountants and attorneys. Exchange staff closely monitored transactions for indications of market manipulation. The NASD's inspectors visited brokerages far more often than their SEC counterparts, and its officials could levy punishments on individuals and firms that unfairly treated investors, including fines, suspension, and expulsion. Accountants and attorneys had professional obligations to keep corporations attuned to the new set of regulatory rules.[80]

As investor confidence returned during and after World War II, cooperation from self-regulatory institutions and professional gatekeepers became ever more crucial. By the late 1950s, the annual value of shares traded on registered exchanges eclipsed that of the 1930s by more than 300 percent. Investors could buy more than 7,500 stock issues on those exchanges or over the counter, while the number of brokerages approached five thousand, accompanied by nearly 1,500 firms that offered investment advice.[81] Faced with the enormity of the American financial markets, SEC officials presumed that prevention of securities fraud would have to rest on a solid foundation of "self-regulation," "self-discipline in the brokerage community," and a commitment among lawyers and accountants to foster "compliance with the law." The relentless circulation of capital threatened to overwhelm centralized regulatory oversight.[82]

Outside of finance, trade associations for broadcasters, news publications, and advertising agencies took on responsibilities for keeping deception out of major marketing channels.[83] But the most important NGOs involved in anti-fraud enforcement remained the Better Business Bureaus. The post–World War II BBBs continued to encourage consumers with grievances against businesses to contact them. Millions of Americans internalized these pleas, bombarding BBB offices with letters and phone calls that raised questions or concerns. Although most complaints did not allege fraud, a significant fraction did so. A steady stream of BBB members complained about advertising and marketing tactics by competitors. These two streams of accusations prompted over thirty thousand annual investigations nationwide. In addition, BBB officials scanned newspaper and magazine advertisements and then sent out a corps of several hundred professional shoppers to discover whether enterprises lived up to their marketing promises. This ongoing policy of "shopping the ads" triggered additional inquiries. BBB activities amplified the monitoring activities of state agencies such as the FTC, which could only invest limited resources in surveillance of broadcast and print advertising.[84]

In hundreds of civil and criminal cases at every jurisdictional level, BBB officials coordinated with government investigators and prosecutors. BBB offices further responded to regular requests from governmental officials for assistance with enforcement efforts. During the early years of the New Deal, for instance, the Missouri commissioner of securities, resident in Jefferson City with no budget for investigative staff, pleaded with the St. Louis, Kansas City, and Springfield BBBs to forward intelligence about firms dealing in securities without licenses, or about "duly licensed dealers and brokers who may be adopting shady or questionable methods in the distribution of securities." After World War II, the Federal Housing Authority asked for BBB assistance in policing the submission of "completion certificates" by construction and home improvement companies, which were required for homeowners to receive FHA mortgages. The FHA's deputy commissioner went so far as to ask every office to "establish a working relationship with the local" BBB, because such "close cooperation . . . will serve as one means of maintaining a close watch over . . . operations in your area."[85]

The post–World War II BBB network never enjoyed statutorily sanctioned authority like that of the NASD in securities regulation, though BBB leaders sometimes hoped for such formal delegation. As the head of Denver's BBB mused in an early 1960 memo, "Maybe we could dare to propose that BBBs be set up like Eric Johnston's operation in the movie industry; or NASD's operation in the securities business, the Commissioner of Baseball, etc."[86] Such tentativeness suggests minimal confidence in achieving official grants of power. Nonetheless, the BBBs' post-1945 activities meant that the line between public and private business regulation continued to blur, as efforts by public and private agencies shaded into one another, even without explicit legislative delegation.

By the 1950s, the more established antifraud organizations, whether inside or outside the state, boasted numerous long-serving career professionals. These individuals had familiarity with marketplace deceptions, kept abreast of new variations, and knew how to conduct fraud investigations. The best of these careerists appreciated the challenges of navigating criminal and administrative enforcement actions and grasped the importance of sensible prosecutorial discretion, given limited institutional resources. They also enjoyed strong personal relations with their peers in other agencies.

Long tenure as a fraud fighter by itself did not guarantee legal savvy or implementation of effective enforcement techniques. The FTC developed a reputation for having bureaucratic "deadwood," with timid staff attorneys cowed by the tendency of the pre–New Deal judiciary to overrule more expansive FTC actions. From the 1930s onward, many of its most powerful career attorneys owed appointment and promotion to connections with members of Congress serving on oversight committees. Dubbed "cronies" by critics, these civil servants perfected the art of the drawn-out investigation, demanded procedural meticulousness, and often set agendas more on the basis of how much competitors groused about a business's advertising than on sustained analysis of harm to consumers. Tellingly, the 1966 FTC *Manual for Attorneys* furnished detailed instructions about how to handle complaints from competing enterprises, because staff "not infrequently" learned about "alleged violations" from those quarters. By this point, the FTC had developed a reputation for fecklessness, inertia, and leniency toward powerful corporations.[87]

By contrast, at the SEC, within the postal inspectorate, and among the ranks of federal prosecutors, appointments and promotions more often reflected talent and performance. A few biographical sketches suggest the ability of veteran antifraud enforcers in these agencies to cultivate high standing among policy elites and the wider public. Irving Pollack typified the SEC's dedicated corps of lawyers who hewed to meritocratic norms. Arriving at the SEC in 1946 a few years after graduation from Brooklyn Law School, Pollack was one of the few staff lawyers who had not attended an Ivy League university. Over more than three decades, he participated in almost every aspect of fraud regulation, from monitoring new issue registration statements to fraud prosecutions. As he moved into managerial positions, he created an indexing system of SEC cases to streamline the process of linking evidentiary findings to prosecutorial arguments. Because of his breadth of experience, Pollack took on a key role in conceptualizing the early 1960s Special Study of Securities Markets, a mammoth assessment of regulatory policy amid rapid changes on Wall Street. Throughout the Cold War era, the reputation established by high-ranking SEC officials such as Pollack helped the organization attract the nation's sharpest law school graduates.[88]

At the Post Office and Justice Departments, the careers of Nathaniel Kossack and Henry Montague illustrate the accrual of expertise in fraud cases. Kossack joined the fraud division in 1952 as a prosecutor after serving as an FBI agent known for excelling in the "painstaking research" and "patient detective work which fraud cases require." He became divisional chief in 1953 and then deputy assistant attorney general in 1965. These positions afforded opportunities to plan and carry out nationwide antifraud campaigns, which required coordination of personnel from multiple jurisdictions and agencies.[89] Originally a postal clerk in Poughkeepsie, New York, Montague lacked the professional education of fraud prosecutors. But after becoming a postal inspector during World War II, he received an extended tutorial on how to locate perpetrators of business frauds. After a decade of fieldwork, he became head New York inspector in 1951 and then chief postal inspector a decade later, a position that he occupied until his retirement in 1969. Montague's office was an early adopter of computer processing to improve investigators' access to mail fraud complaints and invested in forensic laboratories to speed analysis of handwriting and typewritten evidence. Throughout his tenure, he forged deep networks with other federal agencies and US attorneys.[90] By the time he left his post, exacting hiring standards and rigorous professional training had allowed the postal inspectorate to cultivate a reputation as "among the most effective of all federal investigators."[91]

Self-regulatory organizations depended on an analogous accumulation of professional experience. Most of the key figures in the postwar BBBs were careerists. Men such as W. Dan Bell came of age in the 1920s or the Great Depression, found a niche in the early bureaus, and stayed on for the bulk of their working lives. Beginning his BBB work by monitoring Chicago auto ads for compliance with NRA regulations, Bell worked as an automobile marketing specialist for the Cleveland BBB in the late 1930s, managed first the Peoria and then the Buffalo BBB during World War II, and took over the revived Denver Bureau in 1951, presiding over it until he retired in the mid-1970s. At the national level, bureau leaders such Kenneth Willson and Victor Nyborg spent most of their adult lives with the organization. Scores of BBB officials who served during the mid-twentieth century had similar résumés.[92]

The professional identities of BBB leaders were based not only on the status hierarchies of a continental network of local organizations and national umbrella institutions, but also on fidelity to its mission of fostering honesty in communication with consumers and other firms. High-level BBB staff viewed themselves as deputized by the business establishment to serve as arbiters of fair competition. Kenneth Barnard summed up this self-perception in a March 1960 letter to Clyde Kemery, then the manager of the Oklahoma City BBB. Granting that "Better Business Bureaus are the creation of the business community," Barnard refused to "concede they are its vassals. Indeed, the record shows that businesses created them as the umpires of business advertising."[93] The story was much the same at other self-regulatory bodies, such as the AMA's Department of Investigations, with the partial exception of the NASD, which into the early 1960s relied on volunteers from member firms to fulfill enforcement functions.[94]

This generation of antifraud specialists was influenced strongly by the Great Depression and World War II. The majority came of age during this fifteen-year stretch; some served in the military. Manifesting allegiance to public service, they valued antifraud work as a lifelong calling. Despite close links to the business establishment, they viewed themselves as resolute defenders of the trust that underpinned capitalist marketplaces, and so "the integrity and strength" of the American economy.[95] If they hungered after distinction, it was for the esteem of peers in the growing fraternity of antifraud investigators, prosecutors, and regulators.

Like their predecessors in the "truth in advertising" movement, postwar antifraud regulators placed a high priority on refashioning and reinforcing social mores about manipulative and deceptive marketing. This impulse drove the many trade-practice conferences convened into the 1960s by BBBs and the FTC. Republican regulators favored this mode of antifraud regulation, because it involved minimal public expense and placed the onus for regulatory action on business. As with so many other features of the antifraud state, the goal of trade codes was to improve the quality of information that structured purchasing decisions. With manufacturers incorporating so many new materials, novel production processes, and other technological innovations, opportunities for misrepresentations in selling emerged all the time. The fashioning of complex service products and complicated credit terms created further avenues to mislead purchasers. Trade practice conferences gave communities of businessmen the chance to hammer out principles of fair competition that would make miscommunication, misdirection, and deception less common.

The often tedious business of code-making laid out exhaustive standards for information provision. Rules articulated by the Chicago BBB in 1965 for the local advertising of plastic slipcovers convey the impulse. The slipcover code not only prohibited bait tactics, price quotes excluding labor, porous guarantees, misleading claims of low overhead, and use of asterisks or excessively small print; it also set out complex definitions for quality (at least 8 grade clear plastic, with no Poly or Poly-plastic), and specified norms for the allowable size of furniture to be covered ("tight back, loose cushioned sofas up to 90 inches, sections to 65 inches and chairs approximately 34 inches in width"), unless firms described variations in their ads.[96]

The thousands of marketing codes drafted from the 1940s through the mid-1960s had important implications for regulatory enforcement actions. Codes often clarified the specific nature of alleged misrepresentations. They also offered touchstones as enforcers engaged in moral suasion, because firms had participated in code formulation and had consented to the rules. The tone of BBB bulletins, for example, mixed communal boosterism with ministerial preaching that called wayward congregants back to the straight and narrow path. A 1957 bulletin from the Pittsburgh BBB to its members typified this rhetorical style. As part of a national campaign against deceptive car marketing, it had convinced over one hundred area car dealerships to sign a new code of conduct. The report on this "Campaign for Integrity in Auto Advertising" applauded firms that had shown a "VAST IMPROVEMENT" in the candor of their advertising copy and reminded dealers that they had agreed that it was "*more desirable* to compete in a *clean competitive environment.*" It also contrasted the admirable dealer who "didn't hem and haw" when a BBB official pointed out questionable advertising claims, who was "a *man*" and so quickly agreed to run a correction, from the backsliding dealer who continued to push exaggerated price claims—"the other kind of bird" who "tries to talk *around* you instead of *to* you, and is most interested of all in comparing himself to advantage with the dregs of *other* advertisers."[97] With such messages, Bureaus staked out ground as independent arbiters of best commercial practice, called on businessmen to live up to professed ideals of commercial morality, and infused those ideals with an ethos of manliness.

Implicit in this framework of self-regulation was a faith in voluntary fulfillment of regulatory directives. The facilitators of trade practice conferences hoped that deliberation about the boundaries of legitimate marketing would lead participating firms to embrace the resulting standards and embed those rules in commercial routines. Insofar as the detailed rules of codes became general practice, one did not need to worry so much about compliance. Earl Kintner, a Republican FTC commissioner appointed by President Eisenhower in the late 1950s, elaborated on this approach in speeches to Chambers of Commerce, trade groups, advertising conventions, and BBB meetings. "By every means at its disposal," Kintner explained, "the Commission is attempting to fan the coals of conscience into a fire hot enough to burn the impurities out of ads." Advertising agencies had to find the "courage" and "pride" to prefer "professionalism" to "short-termism" and "the rat race," demonstrating that they had "the guts to put these principles over billings." Media outlets should not "be blinded by short-sighted visions of shady profits." Such pronouncements tinged self-regulatory endeavors with Protestant evangelism, harkening back to the nineteenth-century pleas of H. H. Boardman and the moralism of Progressive-era "truth in advertising" acolytes. Kintner presumed that the Bible belonged not only in the modern counting house, but also the marketing department and advertising agency.[98]

This approach to antifraud regulation could reconfigure competitive environments, as the FTC's moves against deceptive claims by mail-order health insurance firms illustrate. The private health insurance industry mushroomed after World War II, stimulated by wartime tax policies that made employee benefits tax-deductible, the failure of Truman's plan for public insurance, advances in medicine, and rising household incomes. Amid this surge, dozens of insurance companies looked to sell policies through the mail. By the mid-1950s, these firms provided coverage for three million Americans, bringing in nearly $70 million a year in premiums. Competition was fierce, encouraging expansive promises in promotional materials about benefits, which skirted exclusions, coverage limits, and policy termination triggers (though the actual policies mentioned these contractual features in fine print). As early as 1949, several larger companies had asked the FTC to sponsor a trade practice conference to root out misleading advertising tactics. The resulting meeting produced a sectoral code of conduct, but many firms refused to abide by it. Then, after a mammoth ten-month nationwide investigation in 1954 that belied its reputation for timidity, the FTC charged forty-one companies with false and deceptive advertising, including several leading insurers.[99]

Through the 1945 McCarran-Ferguson Act, Congress had vested insurance regulation with the states unless they had abdicated oversight. The charged corporations used this statutory provision to challenge FTC jurisdiction in the courts. Aware that the companies had a strong case, the FTC convened a second conference to forge a revised set of industry standards, inviting not only insurers and the Health Insurance Association of America (HIAA), but also state regulators and the National Association of Insurance Commissioners, which had developed its own statement of best practices for mail-order ads. The United States Senate also began to consider legislation to tighten federal regulation of mail-order insurance marketing, as did individual states. Faced with these pressures, more established companies subscribed to a code of ethics and pledged that they would help to "eliminate the 'bad apples' in their industry." To sustain HIAA membership, companies now had to eschew misleading ad copy. Over the next several years, cut-rate mail-order insurance firms continued to pop up. But they had a harder time placing advertisements, as regulators circulated lists of licensed insurers to publishers, convincing many to accept ads only from these companies.[100]

Coordinated action by BBBs could result in similar reforms. Early in the Eisenhower administration, Bureaus in Los Angeles and Chicago spearheaded an initiative to clean up marketing by large discount-car dealerships, which had adopted abusive sales practices such as "bushing" (increasing prices after an initial oral agreement) and "packing" (including overpriced "extras" in packaged car deals).[101] In the late 1950s, nationwide cooperation among BBBs exposed systematic misrepresentation and overcharging by auto collision insurers, which in turn prompted multi-million-dollar refunds.[102]

Despite these demonstrations of the potential to reshape commercial norms through self-regulation, most postwar antifraud officials recognized that there would always be a population of dissemblers and swindlers who would prey on gullible Americans. As a result, every antifraud bureaucracy responded to budgetary constraints and procedural gauntlets by constructing internal filters to guide prosecutorial discretion. Veteran enforcement officials at the SEC and the Post Office acquired a fine-grained sense of the circumstances that facilitated successful prosecutions. Unless prosecutors saw evidence of callous deceit that would raise the hackles of judges and juries, they declined to seek indictments. The vast majority of complaints or referrals did not generate docketed investigations, while investigations leading to criminal prosecutions tended to hover at around 1 percent. Civil enforcement actions were more common, but still represented a small fraction of official inquiries.[103] Prosecutorial selectivity, in combination with accumulated savvy in presenting fraud cases, resulted in impressive conviction rates. From World War II through the 1960s, US attorneys won criminal cases referred by the SEC more than 80 percent of the time. Mail fraud cases were even more likely to result in guilty verdicts: the postal inspectorate's meticulousness helped federal prosecutors to convict nineteen out of twenty defendants.[104] Such outcomes represented even greater prosecutorial successes than during the early twentieth-century campaigns against business fraud.

Furthermore, when circumstances brought wider public attention to nodes of commercial chicanery, antifraud agencies had the capacity to mount coordinated campaigns with bite. In the mid-1950s, officials at the SEC and Justice Department became alarmed by boiler rooms that floated sham mining and high-tech stocks amid a booming market, as well as mutual-fund managers who unloaded worthless securities on their investors. Federal regulators ramped up securities fraud investigations, with annual indictments and convictions between 1959 and 1965 increasing 400 percent as compared to the previous fifteen years.[105] Many of these cases targeted peddlers of dodgy Canadian uranium mines or corporate shells masquerading as producers of the latest electronics wizardry. But federal prosecutors also went after more sophisticated promoters, including Walter Tellier, Lowell Birrell, and Alexander Guterma. These individuals organized complex multi-million-dollar frauds involving mergers, acquisitions, and the burgeoning corporate strategy of conglomeration.[106]

One can point to numerous enforcement drives against other arenas of business fraud. Toward the end of the 1950s, several members of Congress were alerted by constituents to an upsurge in interstate advance-fee schemes, which dangled alluring franchising opportunities, promises to find buyers for those wishing to sell small businesses or residential properties, or offers to arrange loans for small-business owners in need of capital. The resulting congressional hearings triggered multiyear investigations mounted by the Department of Justice's Fraud Division and the postal inspectorate, generating dozens of successful prosecutions.[107] During the early 1960s, officials at the Federal Communications Commission cooperated with their counterparts at the DOJ and the Post Office to clamp down on US mail-order scams that ran ads on high-powered Mexican radio stations.[108] Throughout the 1960s, Federal agencies also launched extended campaigns against credit fraud rings, interstate real-estate scams, and a spate of managerial frauds at Savings and Loans.[109]

Even the most gung-ho enforcers, however, had to be mindful of resource constraints. Ever-present budgetary and staffing limitations allowed only so many expensive, time-consuming investigations and interagency campaigns. As a result, post–World War II antifraud cops, just like their interwar predecessors, relied heavily on negotiated settlements. When evidence seemed serious enough to warrant official attention, the first option was always to enter into informal discussions with a firm whose business practices were skirting the lines that separated puffery or aggressive reliance on informational advantages from fraud.

Enforcement strategies at postwar BBBs typified reliance on a graduated system of sanctions. Bureau officials encouraged disgruntled purchasers to seek out resolutions such as partial refunds that would allow both sides to avoid implications of impropriety. If BBB staffers judged ads or sales techniques to violate standards of fair dealing, they would request revisions, turning to sterner measures only when businesses rebuffed these interventions. For firms that did not follow through on promises to clean up their marketing, the next stage involved drawing up formal stipulations. In April 1952, the Logan Appliance and Furniture Mart signed off on a typical "voluntary" agreement with the Chicago BBB, pledging to foreswear advertising "which has the tendency . . . to mislead" and all "bait practices." They also agreed to furnish fuller information than they had about credit terms.[110] Such declarations, like the act of signing on to an industry code, committed firms to the moral force of BBB standards and the legitimacy of ongoing BBB oversight. BBBs further asked some firms to run corrective advertisements that apologized for past deceptions.

If firms rejected overtures for quiet adjustments or signed stipulations only to violate their terms, BBBs again turned to the weapon of publicity. Every local branch published newsletters calling out firms that had strayed too far from BBB principles. A still more pointed step was to give local media outlets details about a firm's repeated violations and intransigence in the face of requests for reform, and to proclaim that "further advertising by this source is not in the public interest." Although not every publisher or broadcaster abided by such "NIPI" declarations, many, including leading publications such as the *Chicago Tribune* and the *Los Angeles Times*, did. Radio and television stations, which had to worry about FCC license renewals, also abided by Bureau directives. "NIPI" declarations functioned like postal fraud orders, cutting lines of communication between businesses and customers. The most common outcome of such proclamations was a toning down of marketing, which led the BBB to lift its objections. According to the Chicago BBB's automotive trade consultant, Carl Dalke, NIPIs were much "more effective than to haul someone into the local state attorney's office for a hearing. What we do is not only a lot tougher, but it's faster, and it works."[111] As a result of Bureau jawboning, firms ran corrections to thousands of ads (150 in Chicago alone during 1957), and adjusted thousands more. In 1962, businesses complied with requests from the National BBB for such adjustments 93 percent of the time.[112] In addition, BBB investigations could, and did, help authorities send fraudulent businessmen to jail.[113]

At the same time, BBBs emulated public antifraud agencies through greater concern for procedural rights. Although pushed by the consumers and competitors who complained to them, Bureau officials remained representatives of the business community, eager "to protect the business man." They further had to worry about retaining membership. As a result, BBB officials extended the benefit of the doubt to established firms. The always present threat of civil suits for conspiracy and libel fortified this inclination. From the 1930s through the mid-1960s, local BBBs faced more than a hundred such lawsuits, which reinforced a preference for "quiet investigation and patient persuasion."[114] Concerns about due process eventually led BBBs to revisit the idea of an appeals process, with several local Bureaus forming advertising review boards. Before a NIPI directive went into effect in these markets, an affected enterprise could ask for a hearing before a tribunal of prominent BBB members. After sustained debate within national BBB structures, the organization endorsed such forums in late 1952. By the end of 1960, twenty-six BBBs had one, with a further sixteen in the works.[115]

The extension of proceduralism into self-regulation created openings for business cheats in much the same fashion as had the punctiliousness of FTC cease and desist hearings. Consider the saga of Fritzel Television Repair. For almost two decades, owners of televisions and radios complained to the Chicago local BBB about Fritzel, alleging unauthorized, unnecessary, and faked repairs, shoddy work, overcharges, and rank coercion, as employees refused to return radio or television sets until bills were paid in full, regardless of pending complaints. Fritzel customers pleaded with the BBB to make the firm accountable for its abuses and to warn others about it. "I keep wondering," a (Mrs.) Andre Chervence wrote in June 1954, "how many other people are being 'done in' as I was. . . . I don't like to feel that such dishonesty can go unchecked." Into the 1960s, Bureau staff regularly contacted the company to mediate on behalf of consumers like this North Side housewife. Fritzel accommodated BBB overtures, reaching numerous settlements with disgruntled customers, but not changing its business practices.[116] Only after the Illinois Bureau of Consumer Fraud began a 1964 investigation did the BBB go after the firm, assisting with a sting operation that demonstrated a pattern of fake repairs, in which Fritzel technicians replaced working components with second-rate or even faulty ones.[117] Here was another Holland Furnace Company, operating on a local scale.

Cases like Fritzel recur throughout the Chicago BBB files. Although complaint mediation frequently happened within days, BBBs often took years to adopt tougher measures, especially when businesses did not make the mistake of brushing off BBB staff. Even a steady stream of mediated compromises, ad corrections, and stipulations might not lead to less deceptive marketing. As with FTC disciplinary action, a far-sighted marketing department could easily cope with BBB finger-wagging. By the time that a BBB staffer objected to an ad, firms could cheerfully comply, because they were about to roll out a different, though analogous pitch. BBB methods did not necessarily work better than those of the administrative state.[118]

Beginning in the late 1950s, some BBBs tried a more preventive tack by offering advance assessments of advertising campaigns. The vetting of proposed ads allowed businesses to receive clearer signals about the interpretive boundaries of BBB and media codes of conduct. This "opportunity to iron out wrinkles before the fact," Bureau officials insisted, did not constitute "precensorship"; it was merely a sensible mechanism to ward off deceptive pitches before they "reach[ed] the public's ears and eyes."[119]

On occasion, persistent preaching led to conversion. The postwar Chicago BBB could point to numerous examples in which years of jawboning persuaded an aggressive discount house to clean up its advertising. Bargaintown, U.S.A., for instance, tussled with the head of the Bureau's Home Furnishings Division for nearly five years in the late 1950s and early 1960s. On several occasions, BBB officials demanded ad corrections by this local toy store chain; three times, they issued three NIPI directives because of disputed comparative price claims. Bargaintown treated BBB officials with deference and complied with these requests. Eventually, its owner-managers also agreed to cease making claims about markdowns from manufacturers' suggested list prices, on the grounds that the ongoing revolution in American distribution had so intensified price competition as to render them "meaningless and confusing," producing "a lack of confidence by the consumer in ourselves as merchants and in the toy industry in general." BBB officials could not hope for a clearer recitation of the "truth in advertising" catechism.[120]

From the 1920s up to the late 1960s, the FTC, SEC, and Post Office disposed of its fraud-related caseload in similar fashion. If inquiries convinced FTC lawyers that a firm's marketing promotions had the capacity to mislead, they looked to negotiate pledges to stop the offending practices.[121] In order to encourage compromises, the FTC in 1951 stopped requiring that businesses agree to findings of illegal marketing as a condition of stipulations. Beginning in 1962, it followed the BBB's lead and set up an advisory service to dispense guidance about the legitimacy of new marketing strategies.[122] SEC and postal regulators likewise looked to give firms the chance to correct problems before initiating the creaky wheels of formal legal process. If registration documents for an initial public offering lacked important details or included misleading text, SEC officials would send a "deficiency letter" that laid out the problematic features and asked for revisions. After "a process of give and take by conferences, telegraph messages, telephone conversations, or correspondence," the commission would draft a voluntary agreement setting out necessary amendments. SEC staffers also issued advisory opinions to corporate lawyers who asked for guidance about the legality of promotional materials. Within the Post Office, most fraud investigations led not to fraud orders or indictments, but rather stipulations in which firms promised to discontinue objectionable marketing.[123]

This posture reflected realities that confront all regulatory bureaucracies. But for BBBs and many officials at federal antifraud agencies, they also represented deeper philosophical commitments amid the era's epochal conflicts with Soviet communism. BBB leaders remained dedicated to an ideology of business self-regulation, in which regulators, ideally, handled marketing deceptions outside the glare of publicity. This style also suited the leadership of the postwar FTC and SEC. Convinced that most businessmen were trustworthy and well-meaning, these officials gave reputable firms considerable leeway. There would be, Earl Kintner and later Democratic FTC chair Paul Rand Dixon agreed, no "commercial Gestapo" as the United States engaged in the "battle" between "individual freedom and state slavery."[124]

****

The sentiments expressed by these two FTC commissioners spoke to broader impulses that underpinned antifraud policies from the early New Deal through the first years of the Kennedy administration. During these three decades, most new antifraud regulations and enforcement campaigns were pushed either by business interests or policy entrepreneurs within antifraud agencies. Corporate interests, such as textile manufacturers, worked to root out what they saw as unfair competition. Policymakers sometimes worried about systemic threats that fraud posed to capitalist markets, nowhere more so than in securities regulation, as the Great Depression left an enduring imprint. In other contexts, such as the post–World War II moves against diploma mills, legislators and regulators looked to protect the government itself, much as the Reconstruction-era Post Office had moved against mail fraud to safeguard its own reputation. These efforts were often inflected by deeper faith in the value of candor in commercial speech; they always depended on dense networks that linked national and state governments with self-regulatory organizations. In all of these contexts, antifraud regulators stressed the importance of looking out for consumers and investors who lacked the information or sophistication to sidestep misleading and fraudulent pitches.

But before the 1960s, consumer perspectives rarely drove either antifraud politics or policy. In the 1940s and 1950s, organizations such as Consumers Research and Consumers Union did help educate Americans about marketing deceptions, but they lacked the bureaucratic capacity, strategic vision, and standing to set regulatory agendas. Amid the heightened socioeconomic expectations that accompanied the postwar boom, however, a resurgent consumer movement would increasingly bring its own analyses of business fraud to Washington, DC, state capitol buildings, and city council chambers. Buoyed by the more general political activism of the 1960s and greater awareness that specific demographic groups continued to be the victims of abusive marketing practices, advocates of consumerism would soon inject a new sense of urgency into public efforts to beat back the scourge of business fraud.

CHAPTER TEN

Consumerism and the Reorientation
of Antifraud Policy

The postwar tightening of laws against business fraud occurred during a period of remarkable prosperity. Rapid economic growth between 1940 and 1970 moved tens of millions of Americans into the middle class, raising social expectations. Although America's consumer society had deep historical roots, the embrace of consumption took on new dimensions after World War II. Politicians and other arbiters of public values came to define social aspirations in terms of home ownership, possessions such as cars and televisions, and the capacity to pursue chosen lifestyles. Such messages were amplified by advertising barrages from corporations and ubiquitous depictions of material plenty in radio dramas, movies, and television shows. This perspective privileged technologically driven improvements in living standards and a concomitant widening of consumer choice. Over the same decades, the nation's leading financial institutions, led by the NYSE, developed comprehensive public relations programs to bring the masses into the financial markets. This renewed drive to democratize investment, along with the expanding scope of institutional investors such as pension funds, insurance companies, and mutual funds, meant that by 1970, a majority of American families had a personal financial stake in the securities markets.[1]

For some business elites and their political allies, the valorization of consumer culture and democratic participation in modern financial capitalism had deeper political purposes. One goal was geopolitical—to sharply differentiate the US economy, with its capacity to distribute the fruits of capitalism to a broad middle class, from its Soviet antagonist. A 1952 DuPont Chemicals advertisement that posed the question, "Which Marx Gets the Biggest Laugh?—Karl or Groucho"—encapsulated this line of argument. It lampooned the Marxist "joke" about "the impoverishment of the people" under capitalism, which "[y]ou don't get . . . until you try to find a place to park, down-town amid all the impoverished people shopping like mad in the department stores," or until "you see newsreels of the new Russian automobile," which would "be sneered off any used-car lot in America." Related messages focused more on domestic political economy. Through public relations and advertising that extolled free enterprise, the corporate establishment hoped to deflect calls by more militant labor unions for a greater say in the management of enterprise. Business elites further wished to constrain the broader New Deal focus on providing economic security and to forestall more substantial roles for the public sector, such as nationalized healthcare or expansive public housing projects. Such efforts did limit the place of government in American capitalism.[2] But in nudging popular mores toward the imperatives of consumption and the views of Groucho Marx, the tribunes of free enterprise sharpened popular dissatisfaction with perceived duplicity by manufacturers, retailers, and financial firms.

The mid-twentieth-century consumer economy, moreover, provided unscrupulous American firms with ample opportunities to generate dissatisfaction. American inner cities remained home to businesses that riffed off the venerable strategies of bait and switch advertising, high-pressure selling tactics, and reliance on deceptive credit terms. In the process of unleashing new frontiers for consumption, post–World War II suburbanization created further avenues for consumer fraud, with home improvement, automobile sales, electronics repair, and real-estate scams topping the list. By the 1960s, dramatic growth in the elderly population encouraged scams targeting seniors. After World War II, the panoply of available investments continued to include Ponzi schemes and scores of get-rich-quick stock promotions.

With so many targets remaining for would-be reformers, and with heightened popular sensitivities to duplicitous marketing, the embrace of antifraud initiatives allowed one to claim the mantle of consumerism. Savvy politicians across the country recognized this opportunity, as did a slew of community-based consumer organizations. The result was a renewed and reconfigured antifraud coalition, pushed by consumer activists and informed by sociological and legal research, with significant participation from leaders of both major political parties, including three successive US presidents. New antideception laws and agencies proliferated at all levels of government, reflecting the imperatives of consumer and investor protection. Nonetheless, macroeconomic challenges during the 1970s meant that public investments never quite matched rhetorical flourishes. Those same economic pressures set the stage for a conservative backlash against the most ambitious advances of the antifraud state.

Expansion of the Antifraud Coalition

The impetus to redirect antifraud regulation toward consumer interests sprang from the discontent that ordinary Americans expressed as they navigated the postwar economy. All the paeans to technological improvement and the good life heightened expectations about consumer experience, even as the concerted efforts of social movements deepened American commitments to individual rights. As racial minorities, women, and other social groups pressed their claims through popular discourse and constitutional litigation, a larger fraction of the populace felt emboldened to demand their due, and so disinclined to remain silent suckers. The BBBs and law enforcement agencies reaped the resulting whirlwind, embodied in tens of thousands of annual consumer complaints that accused businesses of misleading or untruthful marketing pitches.

As in earlier eras, journalists played a central role in identifying the contours of business fraud and making them visible to the public. National magazines, such as *Ebony* and *Better Homes and Gardens*, along with leading newspapers, such as the *Chicago Tribune* and the *New York Times*, continued to cover business fraud. Every year, their journalists churned out hundreds of stories that alerted readers to the latest deceptions, covered enforcement actions, and dispensed advice about how to avoid scams or seek redress. Prominent writers also updated the messages of *Confessions of a Confidence Man* and *The Bargain Hucksters*, publishing books that focused on the latest marketing depredations in urban neighborhoods and suburbia.[3]

By the 1960s and 1970s, a growing number of urban newspapers and television stations gave individual reporters and columnists the opportunity to become local consumer sentinels. At the *Philadelphia Tribune*, a paper that focused on the local African American community, journalist Len Lear put together in-depth series on scams by home-improvement firms, used-car dealers, unscrupulous or phony doctors, and predatory life insurance companies. The paper also created "Mr. Help," a service desk that readers could contact to ask for assistance in dealing with consumer complaints.[4] Christine Winters, who wrote for the *Chicago Tribune*, pumped out dozens of articles on the consumer frauds prevalent in the Windy City. In Atlanta, station WAGA gave its consumer relations editor, Paul Reynolds, wide latitude to put together regular segments on automobile repair rip-offs and mail-order frauds. Television viewers in Washington, DC, received regular news coverage of consumer scams on three different local channels: the ABC and NBC affiliates and independent station WTTG.[5] These reporters, joined on the fraud beat by counterparts throughout the nation, offered troubleshooting services for disgruntled consumers, much like those provided by BBBs.

Investigative journalism was accompanied by a growing corpus of social science research into the prevalence, dynamics, and policy responses to business fraud. In terms of sheer output, legal scholars dominated this academic discourse. The nation's leading law reviews published a steady flow of articles that documented trends in antifraud policies, evaluated their impacts, and proposed new approaches. Many of the most probing analyses came from student editors, who produced comprehensive "Notes" that detailed fraud law in action. This conversation within legal academia increased in frequency and intensity from the mid-1960s through the late 1970s.[6]

The most influential academic study, however, came from a sociologist, David Caplovitz, whose research into consumer culture in disadvantaged New York City neighborhoods came out in 1963 under the title *The Poor Pay More: Consumer Practices of Low-Income Families*. Caplovitz showed the limited choices confronting these residents and the extent to which merchants and door-to-door salesmen took advantage of them through "shady practices." His catalogue of predatory retail tactics received extensive notice from national opinion-makers. It also helped to shape the agenda of the Kerner Commission on the race riots of the 1960s, whose 1968 report stressed commercial misrepresentations and abuses as contributing to urban unrest.[7]

By the early 1970s, a host of newer consumer groups had joined the antifraud fray. In almost every state, activists founded councils that focused on consumer education and policy work. From 1968 onward, these state-level groups were linked through national umbrella organizations such as the National Consumer Law Center and the Consumer Federation of America. In this same period, numerous community-based organizations were founded in the nation's largest cities. Usually possessing shoestring budgets and sometimes keeping their doors open for only a few years, these advocates were based in poor urban neighborhoods and manifested the creative activism that characterized the era's wider social movements. To the leaders of San Francisco's Consumer Action, Chicago's Community Thrift Club, or Philadelphia's Consumer Education and Protective Association (CEPA), governments needed to do far more to combat the cruelest scams, which targeted individuals with limited formal education and low incomes, often in inner-city African American and Latino communities.[8]

Nonprofit consumer groups, however, did not initially take the lead in translating popular anger into concrete proposals for new antifraud policies. Instead, elected officials staked out this ground, with a few state attorneys general playing prominent roles. These officials had the responsibility of enforcing criminal fraud laws and recognized the political payoffs that might accrue to consumer champions. One way to cultivate such a reputation was to create antifraud bureaucracies. The first effort along these lines was instigated by New York Attorney General Louis Lefkowitz, a lifelong Republican stalwart.

Hailing from an immigrant neighborhood on Manhattan's Lower East Side, Lefkowitz found himself inundated by consumer complaints about shady businesses and outright frauds after gaining office in 1956. The next year, he established a Consumer Frauds and Protection Bureau, which he made an internal funding priority. This new office developed ambitious strategies of public outreach, and increased its capacity to investigate complaints from disaffected New York consumers. It put out newsletters, pamphlets, and educational films, and issued a blizzard of press releases. Hardly a legislative session went by without Lefkowitz calling for the passage of some new law to deal with a dimension of consumer fraud that citizen complaints had brought to the attention of his staff attorneys. All of this activity received assiduous coverage from the state's news outlets and cemented the attorney general's popularity with New York voters, who returned him to office by large margins for over two decades.[9]

Lefkowitz pressed other states to address consumer fraud issues, and his long tenure in office advertised the electoral advantages of doing so. Elected officials elsewhere took note, with scores of prominent political figures seeking to position themselves as intrepid foes of consumer and investor fraud. Governors from both parties, including Connecticut's Abraham Ribicoff, New York's Nelson Rockefeller, Maryland's Spiro Agnew, and Georgia's Jimmy Carter, constructed anti–business fraud agendas. Even Ronald Reagan set out several proposals to constrain consumer fraud while serving as California governor.[10]

Attorneys general proved even more eager to build reputations as vocal defenders of the put-upon consumer. Often viewing their positions as stepping-stones to governorships or US Senate seats, they grasped that aligning themselves with a burgeoning consumer movement represented excellent politics. These ambitious politicos ranged from liberal Democrats, such as Illinois's William Clark, to more conservative members of the party, such as North Carolina's Robert Morgan, and also included moderate Republicans such as Slade Gorton and Evelle Younger, from Washington and California, respectively. Each spearheaded antifraud agendas, lobbied state legislatures for more vigorous consumer protections and greater funding for consumer fraud divisions, and chased after media coverage.[11]

National political leaders soon joined the competition to burnish credentials as consumer advocates. Of all the voices asking for sterner antifraud policies, none had a bigger megaphone than occupants of the Oval Office. President Eisenhower had used that megaphone briefly after the television quiz show scandals. Subsequent presidential administrations did so more frequently, identifying antifraud reforms as national priorities. Presidents Kennedy, Johnson, and Nixon each used their bully pulpit to amplify public awareness of consumerism as a policy framework and commercial deception as an issue demanding legislative and administrative responses.

The Kennedy administration signaled its intentions in the fall of 1961, when Attorney General Robert F. Kennedy convened a national conference for law-enforcement officials on antitrust issues, consumer protection, and investment fraud. The following year, his brother, President John F. Kennedy, articulated an expansive commitment to consumerism in a Special Address to Congress. Modern consumers, Kennedy argued, faced unprecedented informational challenges. Firms throughout the country had embraced the impersonal mar-keting techniques of mass advertising, a bewildering array of credit terms, and confusing, nonstandard packaging techniques. In addition, the president stressed, the "voice" of consumers was "not always as loudly heard in Washing-ton as the voices of smaller and better-organized groups" such as manufactur-ers, retailers, and trade associations. As a result, the federal government needed to develop a more cohesive program of consumer protection, tackling con-sumer safety, the problem of concentrated economic power, and the most prevalent versions of commercial deception. Kennedy concluded by calling for a consumer's bill of rights featuring "the right to be informed—to be protected against fraudulent, deceitful, or grossly misleading information, advertising, and labeling."[12]

Lyndon Johnson reprised all of these themes four years later in his own presidential message to Congress. For Johnson, America faced "new problems of prosperity" brought on by "new complexities and hazards" associated with "the march of technology" and marketing practices that made consumer "choices more difficult." While lauding corporate innovation and cautioning against excessive meddling in "the free enterprise system," the Texan nonethe-less demarcated an indispensable role for government in safeguarding "the consumer . . . against unsafe products, against misleading information, and against the deceitful practices of a few businessmen that can undermine confi-dence in the vast majority of diligent and reputable firms." In addition, he made federal action against business deceptions a central feature of his "Great Society" agenda, calling for legislation that would establish "new legal reme-dies" for misleading packaging, deceptive consumer lending terms, "sharp and unscrupulous" selling of interstate real estate, and conflicts of interest in the management of pension plans.[13]

Reversion of the White House to Republican control in 1969 did not prompt a wholesale rhetorical shift on these issues. Emulating his two predecessors, President Richard M. Nixon issued yet another special message to Congress, assuring the nation that "Consumerism . . . is here to stay" and that federal government remained committed to a "Buyer's Bill of Rights" that included "the right to accurate information" that enabled the consumer "to make his free choice." Nixon advocated several legal reforms designed to strengthen protections against marketplace deceptions and "dishonest . . . competitors," including easing the rules for bringing federal consumer class-action lawsuits (though also requiring that such suits could only proceed after successful criminal prosecution of a business by the Justice Department), expanding the FTC's authority to ask for injunctions against deceptive corporations, and improving disclosure of warranty terms for durable goods.[14]

Such presidential pronouncements were augmented by new consumer offices. In 1963, President Kennedy established a White House Council on Consumer Affairs; the following year, President Johnson appointed Esther Peterson, a long-time activist in the consumer and labor movements, as head of the new council and Special Assistant to the President on Consumer Affairs. Although possessing a modest budget and still having other responsibilities in the Labor Department, Peterson gave consumer advocates a point person within the White House and kept in close contact with federal agencies and elected officials who focused on consumer issues. She also traveled the country to give speeches to consumer groups and business organizations, wrote extensively on consumerism, and stood ready to testify before Congress.[15] After Peterson resigned her position in 1967, Johnson replaced her with Betty Furness, a career actress with close ties to Democratic Party leaders but far less experience involving consumer matters. Furness nonetheless developed a reputation as an effective opponent of the "rackets" that victimized "the elderly, the uninformed, the sick, and the poor."[16]

President Nixon transformed the Advisory Council into an Office of Consumer Affairs within the White House, which he characterized as obliged to "take a leading role in the crusade for economic justice." Nixon further asked Congress to create a Consumer Protection Division within the Department of Justice, which would have the authority to investigate consumer abuses, represent consumer interests before Congress and federal agencies, and coordinate enforcement efforts related to consumer protection statutes. He also urged every state that had not already done so to enact its own consumer protection law and establish a dedicated enforcement body. Nixon's appointee to head the White House office was Virginia Knauer, the former head of the Pennsylvania Bureau of Consumer Protection. Like Peterson and Furness, Knauer maintained a grueling travel and speaking schedule in order to keep consumer issues in national headlines. Through speeches and congressional testimony, Knauer depicted consumer fraud in even graver terms than had her predecessors, referring to it "as an insidious economic cancer which eats at the vitals of our society." Deception by the "white collar fraud-robber," she warned, threatened popular faith in the rule of law. It also "withers our moral fiber . . . [,] misdirects our economic resources . . . [, and] saps the strength of our free enterprise system."[17]

By identifying consumer protection as a national priority and characterizing business fraud with such stark images, the Kennedy, Johnson, and Nixon White Houses greatly enhanced the place of consumer fraud on the nation's policy agenda. Their administrations took place toward the end of a period of growing presidential influence, in which the challenges of depression, world war, and the struggle against communism had consolidated power in Washington, the executive branch, and the White House. It was also the "golden age" of broadcast television, which allowed the head of the Executive branch unmediated access to the citizenry at large. In an era in which presidents often framed public debate, their imprimaturs mattered, even if specific legislative proposals did not always meet the approval of more militant consumer organizations. Presidential insistence about the salience of any specific issue deepened public awareness of it. Such presidential blessings also stimulated more news coverage and journalistic investigations, galvanized the academics, interest groups, politicians, and career bureaucrats who most cared about an issue, and encouraged new policy ideas and more intense coalition-building.[18]

Within Congress, a cluster of long-serving members carved out complementary niches as champions of tougher consumer fraud policies. These public servants had imbibed the critique of unregulated capitalism and the positive view of governmental power ushered in by the New Deal. Democratic Senator Warren Magnuson of Washington, one of the most committed consumer advocates on Capitol Hill, encapsulated this perspective in *The Dark Side of the Marketplace*, a well-received 1968 book that assessed numerous threats to economic welfare, health, and safety. As Magnuson confidently remarked in the book's introduction, he was "certain that we all share the common conviction that . . . it is no longer a question of *whether* the consumer will be protected, but rather a question of *how*."[19] Magnuson, along with hundreds of elected officials who shared that conviction, believed that the state could redress socioeconomic problems. These national politicians, like their counterparts on the state level, also calculated that seeking out concrete strategies for combating business fraud would cement their stature and popularity. Like Magnuson, most of these congressmen and senators were Democrats who hailed from more industrialized parts of the country, such as the Midwest, Northeast, or Pacific Coast. Among senators, they included Paul Hart of Michigan, who became a key advocate for fair packaging and labeling legislation; Paul Douglas of Illinois, the chief proponent of truth in lending reform; and Harrison Williams of New Jersey, who provided leadership on the issue of fraudulent interstate real-estate developments. In the House, Democrats such as John Moss of California and Howard Rosenthal of New York City emerged as prominent sponsors of antifraud legislation. These elected officials convened the legislative hearings and sometimes asked for the agency studies that built an evidentiary case for reform. They oversaw the drafting process by staff and managed bills as they moved through committee, floor consideration, and final negotiations among congressional leaders and the White House.[20]

Despite the central role of elected officials in turning domestic policy agendas toward the problem of business fraud in the early 1960s and maintaining public focus thereafter, the strategic preferences of consumer activists increasingly shaped legislative and administrative action. Once the newer consumer organizations and lawyer-activists had gained a footing in cities, state capitals, and Washington, DC, they had perches from which to influence policy discussions. This growing clout manifested itself at every stage of the policymaking process, as illustrated by the hearings on consumer law held by a Senate subcommittee in 1969 and 1970. Convened to consider responses to legislative proposals that would strengthen the FTC's ability to fight consumer frauds, the subcommittee's witness list included trade association representatives and corporate CEOs. Unlike the discussions that produced fur- and wool-labeling legislation in the 1950s, however, Congress now invited consumer organizations to the policymaking table. Indeed, the hearings were set up by testimony from representatives of these groups—George Gordin, Jr., of the National Consumer Law Center; Walker Sandbach, executive director of Consumers Union; and Edward Berlin, general counsel of the Consumer Federation of America. As consumerism took hold in the United States, its leaders began to shape the legislative agendas and the formulation of specific policy proposals, and antifraud reforms took on a more populist hue.[21]

The individual who had perhaps the greatest role in setting the broader consumerist agenda, activist lawyer Ralph Nader, did not take the lead in channeling calls for action against consumer fraud, though he did give the issue some attention. In 1969, Nader charged a group of law students to prepare a detailed study of the FTC itself, focusing on its regulation of deceptive marketing practices. The result was a critical report that helped to lay the intellectual foundation for later FTC reforms. He also drove the longstanding and eventually unsuccessful effort to create a national Consumer Protection Agency, which would have had the power to investigate issues related to consumer fraud, monitor fraud-related enforcement efforts, and shape new regulatory initiatives. But Nader focused far more on other consumer issues, such as product safety, environmental protection, the reinvigoration of antitrust enforcement, and the selective dismantling of industry-specific regulatory structures. As a result, the consumerist challenge to deceptive marketing had more of a pluralist flavor, with studies and proposals emanating from across the new organizations that emerged in the 1960s and 1970s.[22]

A Wave of Regulatory Action

At all levels of government, elected, appointed, and career officials at once recognized and emboldened advocates of enhanced consumer protection measures. Public servants sometimes transformed the more diffuse popular sentiment for enhanced consumer protection into concrete reform proposals, and more frequently appropriated the ideas put forward by academic experts and consumer organizations. They built coalitions within legislatures and executive agencies for new antifraud policies and engineered compromises to overcome entrenched opponents of change. Argument by argument, hearing by hearing, and debate by debate, they deepened the legitimacy of using public power to beat back the unscrupulous bait and switch artist and peddler of misrepresented goods, services, and investments. The result was a groundswell of antifraud reforms adopted between the Kennedy and Ford administrations, in Washington, state capitals, and cities alike.

At both the national and state levels, regulators and legislators took aim at the decades-old problem of spurious cures and medical treatments. Officials at the Food and Drug Administration (FDA) spearheaded the most comprehensive initiatives, as when they convened three massive National Congresses on Medical Quackery with the AMA in 1961, 1963, and 1966. These meetings of medical experts and policymakers highlighted the extent to which false "medical messiahs" still preyed on the sick and terminally ill, and helped to galvanize support for tightening up marketing regulations. The most important congressional response came in the 1962 amendments to the Food and Drug Act. This legislation shifted regulatory authority over the advertising of medical products and services from the Federal Trade Commission to the FDA, mandated scientific proof of medical efficacy before firms could market drugs or other treatments, and required meticulous attention to scientific studies in the making of any therapeutic claims.[23] Within the states, more vigorous regulation of fraudulent healthcare providers occurred partly through occupational licensing boards. Several states also adopted "pure drug statutes" and regulatory oversight bodies patterned on national policy frameworks, in the hopes of rooting out adulterated, misbranded, and sham medical products.[24]

Leaning on the Democratic congressional supermajorities of the mid-1960s, consumer advocates enacted a trio of antifraud measures: the 1966 Fair

Packaging and Labeling Act, the 1967 Interstate Land Sales Full Disclosure Act, and the 1968 Truth in Lending Act. Each of these statutes again sought to redress imbalances in information by requiring businesses to furnish purchasers with truthful, standardized statements as to the quantity, quality, and cost of goods, assets, or credit; each further authorized the FTC to enforce these disclosure obligations.[25] State and local governments embraced a slew of additional antifraud proposals. One popular reform imposed mandatory cooling-off periods—two or three days in which customers could cancel purchases or contracts—in commercial sectors notorious for high-pressure tactics, such as home improvement repairs. Several jurisdictions also tightened the regulation of consumer credit arrangements.[26]

Within the realm of investor protection, more expansive governmental reforms occurred through legislation and administrative action, often driven by appointed officials and career civil servants at the SEC. The mid-1960s revamping of New Deal securities regulation, which was set up by the SEC's nineteen-month Special Study of Securities Markets, stands out for this type of policy entrepreneurship.[27] Taking place at the start of the Kennedy administration, the Special Study was a response to a fraud scandal on the American Stock Exchange (AMEX). In 1960, regulators and the press discovered that for nearly a decade, the Re brokerage firm, a leading voice in internal AMEX governance, had engaged in market manipulations and insider trading.[28] This incident might have generated a fairly narrow assessment of the shortcomings in AMEX self-regulation. Instead, SEC commissioners William Cary, Jack Winter, and Emanuel Cohen opted for a much broader inquiry. Recognizing that the financial markets had undergone profound transformations since the start of the New Deal, they convinced Congress to furnish $750,000 (as a share of the economy, roughly equivalent to $22 million in 2016 dollars), for an examination of shifting investing practices and the evolution of regulatory institutions. The commissioners asked Milton Cohen, a leading securities lawyer with SEC experience, to oversee the investigation. Its charge was to examine regulatory relationships among investment banks, corporations, and brokerage firms, on the one hand, and stock exchanges, professional gatekeepers, the NASD, and the SEC, on the other. Cohen agreed, but only after securing guarantees that the commission would not be able to demand revisions of study findings.[29]

Through confidential questionnaires to brokerage firms and detailed interviews of regulators and individuals who worked within the financial markets, Cohen's team of sixty-five veteran staffers amassed a mountain of evidence. They traced the emergence and rapid growth of institutional investors, documented the regulatory challenges posed by a quadrupling in the frequency and value of securities transactions since the 1930s, and completed several case studies of malfeasance and conflicts of interest on the part of securities promoters and stock brokerages. The team of lawyers and analysts then crafted detailed recommendations for legislative reforms.[30] Upon the completion of the Special Study, the SEC convened a liaison committee with finance leaders to draft formal legislative proposals. Although Congress did not accept every one of the Special Study's recommendations, its monumental final report established an evidentiary and conceptual basis for the next fifteen years of national legislation regarding securities regulation. The chief antifraud measures of the 1964 Amendments to the Securities Acts, including a significant expansion in the number of firms subject to disclosure rules and NASD membership, and imposition of tighter regulatory oversight of sales practices by brokerages, emerged from the Special Study.[31]

Richard Nixon's victory in 1968 did not temper the SEC's commitment to full disclosure and candor in the securities markets. Acting at the request of SEC staff attorneys who wished to expand the agency's enforcement tools, federal judges acceded to requests for disgorgement and restitution orders that furnished at least partial compensation to defrauded investors. The judiciary further accommodated the filing of private class-action suits by lawyers representing large numbers of similarly situated disgruntled investors.[32]

During the 1960s and 1970s, the clear trend remained placing higher regulatory barriers in the way of promoters, stock dealers, or corporate officers who wished to pull fast ones on the investing public. Born out of profound economic crisis, the New Deal administrative structures that sought to constrain securities fraud became entrenched features of the financial marketplace. These frameworks came to enjoy bipartisan support among political elites (though Democratic administrations in the 1940s and 1960s proved more willing to extend antifraud rules than did the Eisenhower administration). Despite initial antagonism from some parts of the financial sector, the cratering of business during the 1930s led a generation of stockbrokers, investment bankers, accounting firms, and securities lawyers to accept both the new regime of information disclosure and the more extensive prohibitions against market manipulation and insider trading. As SEC career attorney David Silver later recalled, in the post–World War II decades, "there were a lot of memories of the trials and tribulations of Wall Street, how the shenanigans of Wall Street really fit into the Great Depression. . . . [T]here was a general perception that the misbehavior of financial institutions had an awful lot to do with what happened in the country." This view was widely embraced within the halls of the SEC, whose staff shared a conviction that honest communication was not only crucial to the proper working of capital markets, but also for their broader democratic legitimacy.[33]

Deceptive claims in the booming domain of business franchising attracted similar regulatory attention. This mode of business organization had been a feature of the American economy since the mid-nineteenth century. But it burst onto the suburban landscape after World War II, as franchisors offered American consumers reliability in goods and services (branded clothing, fast food, motels) while achieving the economies of scale that came with a national or regional footprint. Purveyors of retailing concepts liked franchising because it slashed the capital costs and risks associated with expansion, while securing the entrepreneurial energies and sweat equity of franchisees. Franchise owners appreciated the business training that they received, the extensive advertising campaigns mounted by the home office, and buy-in requirements that were less than the capital needed to launch standalone small businesses.[34] The meteoric growth of postwar franchising, however, elicited duplicitous sales practices. Plenty of advance-fee scams tempted Americans to chase after the dream of proprietorship by throwing their savings at nonexistent franchisors. Many prospectuses for legitimate franchising opportunities also downplayed the number of competing franchises in an area and the implications of ongoing financial obligations, while exaggerating likely income streams.[35]

Beginning in the late 1960s, policymakers took regulatory aim at these problems. Once more, the dominant instinct was to protect would-be small-business owners with strategies of information disclosure. Through an array of civil actions brought by aggrieved franchisees, state and federal judges signaled a willingness to treat franchise contracts as investments subject to the New Deal regime of securities regulation. State legislatures also enacted laws that compelled franchisors to furnish prospects with detailed, truthful information about their training programs, ongoing financial obligations, and calculation of franchisee earnings projections. Drawing on the provisions of these state statutes, the FTC followed suit with a Franchise Disclosure Rule. This administrative action, which took a full six years to move through the rule-making process, imposed extensive informational obligations on franchisors operating in interstate commerce.[36]

The congressional pinnacle of twentieth-century efforts to curb deceptive retail marketing occurred in 1975, with the passage of the FTC Improvement Act. This legislation gave the FTC authority to combat commercial deceit through its own administrative rule-making, which could create legally binding standards for industries or even the entire economy. It also augmented FTC enforcement powers. The commission could now seek substantial fines from businesses that did not comply with cease and desist orders or that violated an FTC administrative rule, as well as financial restitution for consumers harmed by such actions. FTC officials soon flexed their new muscles, notifying scores of corporations about their potential liability for deception-related fines and considering several far-reaching substantive rules. The most consequential, adopted in 1976, did away with the holder in due course doctrine concerning debt collection. This legal standard, once exploited by nineteenth-century lightning-rod salesmen and then a mainstay of urban retailers of durable goods, had long protected third-party holders of consumer debt, such as finance companies, from legal defenses that the underlying commercial transaction had resulted from fraud.[37] Even before the passage of the 1975 legislation, FTC officials experimented with ways to exert more pressure on national advertisers, introducing a policy in 1971 that required corporations to substantiate the factual assertions in their ads and, in the case of a demonstrated lack of substantiation, to run "corrective advertising" that alerted consumers to prior "questionable claims."[38]

In addition to targeting specific marketing deceptions or extending the enforcement powers of existing agencies, states and local governments established many new bureaucratic beachheads against consumer fraud. Some states followed the path blazed by Louis Lefkowitz in New York, carving out consumer protection offices within the office of the attorney general; others created standalone consumer protection departments or agencies. By 1974, all but six states had also codified their legal regulation of consumer fraud through general consumer protection statutes, following one of three basic approaches. In thirteen states, legislatures enacted "Little FTC Acts" that borrowed the broad statutory language that had created the federal agency's antideception jurisdiction. These states all gave some department investigative authority and bestowed enforcement powers such as cease and desist orders, injunctive remedies, and restitution mechanisms. A few went so far as to proscribe "misleading" claims.[39]

Other states embraced the basic framework of two model consumer protection laws developed in the 1960s by legal scholars, legal elites, and good governance bodies such as the National Conference of Commissioners on Uniform State Laws. The first of these, the Uniform Deceptive Trade Practices Act (UDTPA), laid out several categories of prohibited marketing tactics, including "misrepresentation of the geographic origin of goods, disparagement of goods, services, and businesses, bait advertising, [and] price misrepresentation." Rather than relying solely on criminal enforcement or administrative action by a state agency, the UDTPA created private actions that could be brought by affected consumers. The second effort, the Uniform Consumer Sales Practices

Act (UCSPA), was the least common legislative template. It targeted an even wider set of commercial transactions, proscribing "unconscionable" as well as "deceptive" behavior by merchants. It further gave the state agency charged with overseeing consumer protection issues the power to bring class-action civil suits on behalf of consumers.[40]

Amid the institutional ferment and confidence in robust government that characterized the late 1960s and early 1970s, urban officials joined the anti–consumer fraud bandwagon. Major cities such as Boston, New York, Jacksonville, Louisville, Chicago, and Seattle passed local ordinances that codified prohibitions against deceptive marketing and established their own Offices of Consumer Affairs or Consumer Protection Agencies. This flurry of institution-building was matched by metropolitan county governments such as Long Island's Nassau County, Maryland's Montgomery County, and southern Florida's Dade County.[41]

The rise of consumerism also had far-reaching impacts on the realm of business self-regulation. BBB officials recognized that as unions created consumer offices to assist their members, as dozens of independent consumer groups emerged, and as more and more states and cities established consumer protection agencies, advertising and marketing self-regulation faced powerful new institutional competitors. These developments expanded both the number of voices seeking to shape antifraud policy and the potential venues for registering consumer complaints. BBB leaders such as Denver's W. Dan Bell pointed to the tide of consumer regulation as they sought to persuade local and national businesses to increase their financial support of advertising self-regulation. As early as 1961, Bell berated other BBB managers and his own membership about the grave dangers facing "the Better Business Bureau movement." The AFL-CIO's Consumer Counselling Program and the reemergence of "professional consumer groups"; the looming creation of a Colorado State Consumer Fraud Bureau, or even a federal "Department of the Consumer"; the emergence of "exposure" books such as Vance Packard's *The Waste Makers* and Frank Gibney's *The Operators*, which stoked mounting "expressions of suspicion and distrust" from consumers about American business; all of these developments threatened to "siphon away an inestimable amount of 'self-regulation' and BBB strength." Unless the business community replaced its "'token' financial backing" and "lip service" with resources to sustain meaningful self-regulation, Bell and other BBB executives warned, there was reason to worry about "the survival of the kind of economy under which America had grown to greatness—the free enterprise system."[42]

A consensus also emerged by the end of the 1960s that the BBBs required not only more funding, but also a fundamental reorganization. Centralization of authority in a new Council of Better Business Bureaus, the thinking went, would improve the consistency of operations and allow individual BBBs to receive some income from the national organization, lessening dependence on local businesses. This approach would also enable the BBB network to make substantial investments in information technology to improve management of the overwhelming bits of information that crowded into BBB offices. A 1969 management consulting study by Knight, Gladieux, & Smith called for all of these changes, ratifying proposals that had long circulated among the Bureau's leaders. The BBB network immediately set about implementing them, without significant objections.[43]

For the BBB old guard who worked either at the national level or in metropolitan areas that were part of the Northeast, the Midwest, or the West Coast, the Bureau network needed to accommodate a historical transformation that was too strong to simply oppose. These leaders, including Kenneth Barnard, Victor Nyborg, John O'Brien (who had a long career running BBBs in Akron and St. Louis), and Edward Gallagher (who had run the Boston Bureau for decades) had spent their working lives learning how to cooperate with the steadily expanding antifraud state. Their strategic sensibilities meshed with the moderate conservatism of an Eisenhower or Lefkowitz. They accepted the basic structure of the welfare state and more vigorous antifraud policing, but looked to soften public antagonism toward business. These figures had built close relationships with antifraud regulators from both parties, though they leaned toward Republican regulators such as Earl Kintner who were strong supporters of business self-regulation.[44]

To veterans of "truth in advertising" campaigns, the social and political transformations that had put Kennedy and Johnson in the White House were irreversible. With consumer protection occupying a central position on the nation's policy agenda, they argued that the BBBs had to maintain a critical distance from business and deepen working relationships with consumer groups and governmental consumer protection agencies, so that its officials might continue their roles as regulatory brokers. Unless the organization adapted to consumerism, "recogniz[ing] the permanence of this 'consumer voice' movement, and mov[ing] to join it in a more positive way," the BBBs ran the risk of becoming irrelevant. If the network did adapt, it could take advantage of its favorable reputation, indicated by both opinion polls and the frequency of public contacts with local BBBs, to shore up its position as a "respected, *independent*" guardian of commercial morality, an "even-handed . . . informal court of appeals" for "the customer." The goal, as one insurance executive with close ties to the BBB movement argued in the fall of 1971, was one of "triangulation: Find the point in the center of, but equidistant from, business, the Federal Trade Commission, and Ralph Nader."[45]

In Chicago, longtime BBB head Kenneth Barnard followed this logic in responding to proposals for the creation of an Illinois Bureau of Consumer Fraud. Barnard supported the idea, though only if the new agency would concentrate on prosecuting the worst offenders, thereby increasing the leverage that BBB officials could exert on firms. For officials such as Victor Nyborg, this kind of political flexibility would not only make antifraud work more effective, but also inoculate Bureaus against charges of "always needing to be against everything."[46]

The BBB strategy of triangulation further extended procedural protections for businesses that ran afoul of its standards for truth in advertising. In 1971, the Advertising Federation of America, the American Association of Advertising Agencies, and the Association of National Advertisers agreed to the creation of a National Advertising Review Board (NARB), which would be run under the auspices of the newly formed Council of Better Business Bureaus (CBBB). Drawing on proposals that had circulated among BBB officials since 1960, as well as a British system of advertising self-regulation that had begun in 1962, the NARB comprised five-person panels selected from fifty board members—thirty executives from national advertisers, ten representatives of the advertising industry, and ten independent experts on marketing, who were to represent the public. It heard cases of alleged marketing deception whenever advertisers disputed the findings of the CBBB's newly formed National Advertising Division (NAD), which had the responsibility of monitoring television, radio, and national publications and assessing allegations of misrepresentation. The NARB could also take jurisdiction whenever a public complainant objected to an NAD ruling that an ad was not so deceptive as to merit action.[47]

The procedural mimicry of the administrative state by the BBBs did have limits. Local BBBs did not institute formal hearings in advance of decisions to issue a NIPI directive against an advertiser, nor ensure that the official who authorized the NIPI did so without any prior knowledge or involvement in the case; most bureaus did not create review boards of any kind; and those that existed did not, like the NARB, create a public record of their proceedings and determinations. Indeed, when the Little Rock BBB's Advertising Review Board experimented in the mid-1960s with the creation of written rulings and a requirement that media outlets abide by NIPI declarations as a condition of BBB membership, the FTC ruled that such formal processes overstepped the bounds of legitimate self-regulation, shading over into the realm of illegal restraints on trade.[48] In order to skirt similar legal concerns, the ad industry limited the NARB's sanctions to publicity and formal referral to the appropriate federal agency, usually the FTC. Still, the day-to-day regulatory efforts of BBBs testify to the salience of due process as a postwar institutional ideal.

The antifraud institutions created during the late 1960s or 1970s relied heavily on young turks fresh out of college or law school, sometimes with an internship or a year or two of work for community organizations under their belts. In the state and local consumer protection agencies, many leaders were true believers with experience in the consumer movement rather than politicos who spied a popular wave. Several of these appointees came from the growing ranks of activist lawyers. Philip Schrag, consumer advocate in the New York City Department of Consumer Affairs (DCA), had served as a community lawyer working for the National Association for the Advancement of Colored People (NAACP) Legal and Educational Defense Fund. Others hailed from the journalist's consumer beat or came up the ranks of government agencies with consumer-related missions. In Minnesota, the head of the State Consumer Service during the early 1970s, Sherry Chenoweth, had covered consumer issues as a local television reporter. The inaugural head of the Los Angeles Consumer Affairs Bureau, Fern Jellison, had several decades of experience in the city office charged with regulating charities. In Chicago, Jane Byrne became the head of that city's Department of Consumer Sales, Weights, and Measures after years of Democratic Party activism and positions in city antipoverty programs.[49] One of the most prominent local consumer agency leaders, New York City Commissioner of Consumer Affairs Bess Myerson, turned to consumer protection from a career as a model and television actress that had been kick-started by her winning the Miss America pageant in 1945. Although Myerson faced derision upon assuming office, she used her celebrity status to expand public awareness of consumer programs and build political support for them.[50] Regardless of the career avenues that led to leadership in local consumer protection bureaucracies, these positions attracted energetic figures who embraced consumerism and policy experimentation.

In numerous policy domains, the New Deal and Cold War eras generated state-building predicated on linkages to a dense network of quasi-public and nongovernmental institutions. The national defense establishment drew on the analysis furnished by social scientists based in universities, think tanks, and nonprofit organizations. The New Deal farm state incorporated not only new programs within the federal Agriculture Department and companion state-level agencies, but also a complex set of organizations that spoke for farmers and farmworkers, as well as elected committees of local farmers, who had responsibilities for implementing federal agricultural programs. Regulatory gov-

ernance over the content of American film, radio, and television relied on industry self-regulatory bodies. Post–World War II federal grant programs
in healthcare and higher education depended on quasi-public mechanisms
of accreditation.[51] The elaboration of the American antifraud state mirrored
these other complex regulatory ecologies. By the mid-1970s, the antifraud terrain encompassed not only a thicket of public laws and administrative rules
adopted by every level of government, but also myriad public and quasi-public
agencies, as well as a burgeoning army of private watchdogs and gatekeepers.

Within all of these institutions, regulatory protagonists shared, for the most
part, the premises that Warren Magnuson had articulated in his preface to *The
Dark Side of the Marketplace*. Consumer and investor protection, including
protection against mendacious businesses, was a fundamental element of government. American marketplaces should not operate according to the unforgiving logic of *caveat emptor*. As FDR had argued in his message to Congress
on securities regulation, sellers had obligations to customers, competitors, and
the wider society. They, too, needed to look sharp, lest they run afoul of the
many legal prohibitions against dishonest marketing and the mushrooming
public and quasi-public institutions charged with enforcing them. Consumer
activists such as Colston Warne, the Amherst economics professor and long-
time president of Consumers Union, and business regulators, including Republicans such as Louis Lefkovitz and FTC Commissioner Paul Rand Dixon,
pressed this argument repeatedly. They insisted that "caveat emptor has now
become outmoded and *caveat venditor* must be the foundation of the marketplace"; that "protection from some business frauds cannot be afforded except
by government protection"; that "the obsolescent and socially destructive idea
of *caveat emptor* should be appropriately buried as a relic of the days of simple
markets and well-understood commodities."[52]

A diverse chorus of voices from the business community ratified this turn
away from *caveat emptor*. As early as 1960, the Advertising Federation of
America characterized the legal principle of *caveat venditor* as a "fact" that advertisers ignored at their peril. By the late 1960s and early 1970s, this premise
suffused business discourse. A Rhode Island paint dealer who wished to boast
of his quality products could title a newspaper advertisement "Caveat Venditor," while a manufacturer of construction materials could trumpet in its 1972
annual report that it had long ago replaced "caveat emptor" with the principle,
"Let the buyer have faith." Even the conservative United States Chamber of
Commerce conceded that commercial fraud was "Everybody's Problem, Everybody's Loss."[53]

The inclination to bow before the dictates of consumerism did not quash
disagreements over the best means to hold mendacity in check, nor disputes

over how tightly constraints on sellers should pinch. In his 1969 message on consumerism, for example, Richard Nixon drew distinctions between his views and those of many consumer activists and Democrats. His steadfast commitment to a Buyer's Bill of Rights, Nixon explained, "did not mean that *caveat emptor* . . . had been replaced by an equally harsh *caveat venditor*," nor that "government should guide or dominate individual purchasing decisions," a view that pleased the conservative *Chicago Tribune*.[54] The Chamber of Commerce accepted that consumer fraud was a national problem, but still worried about excessively "rigid and cumbersome" antifraud legislation and preferred solutions that depended on mechanisms of business self-regulation.[55] For all the efforts of BBB leaders to cast their organization as a "militant instrument of impartial enforcement" and a steward of "the public trust," they embraced negative conceptions of economic liberty associated with American conservatism. The BBB's core mission was to safeguard the "free enterprise system," whether from confidence-sapping swindlers and chiselers, heavy-handed government bureaucracies, or impatient and unfair consumers.[56] The politicians and interest groups with such viewpoints did not shy away from voicing their concerns in debates over fraud policies. Because of their influence, even the most aggressive antifraud legislation emphasized regimes of information disclosure that would empower consumers and investors to make better choices. And in states controlled by Republicans or conservative Southern Democrats, consumer fraud measures stressed cooperation with the business establishment.[57]

Nonetheless, it is striking how often participants in the 1960s and 1970s debates over antifraud policies framed the formal shift away from *caveat emptor* in epochal terms. In reviewing *The Dark Side of the Marketplace*, Morton Mintz, a *Washington Post* political reporter, commented that the older injunction that buyers beware "should have died centuries ago and been buried alongside those primitive deities in whose names millions of goats, sheep, and virgins were sacrificed." Before a 1971 audience of business executives, Elizabeth Hanford, Nixon's deputy assistant for consumer affairs, remarked that "the days of *caveat emptor* are past and the days of *caveat vendor* are at hand." Even a professor of marketing at a Louisiana university, writing in 1974 for a publication read chiefly by sales managers, judged that the United States had "entered a new and extended era in which the possibility of class-action suits coupled with the adequate enforcement of federal and state consumer legislation means the seller also must beware. The day of *caveat vendor* is here!" The exclamation point suggests the degree of confidence in the durability of this new regulatory world.[58]

We shall have occasion to revisit this confident prediction of a new age of legal antagonism to the business cheat in light of contrary developments over the subsequent four decades. For the moment, we should take note of its central assumptions about the educational force of new antifraud rules and the impact of fraud enforcement. New language in the statute books, the daily compilations of rules in the *Federal Register*, and the pronouncements of state and local consumer protection agencies did not necessarily transform legal and commercial culture. Policy innovations did not automatically remake norms nor elicit "adequate enforcement" in the 1970s any more than in the 1870s, 1920s, or 1950s.

Retracing Paths of Education and Enforcement

The early twentieth-century movement for "truth in advertising" had invested first and foremost in public outreach, on the theory that the best way to constrain fraud was to inoculate potential victims against the enticements of get-rich-quick promoters, slick salesmen, and deceptive ads. The BBBs had retained this focus after World War II. As consumerism gained momentum in the 1960s and early 1970s, every antifraud organization, whether established by statutory authority or private initiative, did likewise. Investments in public education were cheap and embraced by politicians across the political spectrum. Who could object to attempts to steel investors and consumers against the wiles of the shape-shifting sharper?

The flurry of informational posters, booklets, and pamphlets emanating from antifraud organizations intensified after 1960. Public education efforts turned to short films such as *The Fine Art of Fraud*, a twenty-minute overview of fraud techniques produced by the New York attorney general's office in 1966, radio and television spots, and consumer-related high school and college curricula.[59] Whatever the medium of communication, the content mirrored the basic messages conveyed by antifraud journalism. Most materials explained prevalent swindles and recommended that investors or consumers rely on professional experts to guide their economic decision-making. In case these messages did not hold the rip-off artists at bay, public education campaigns implored victims not to suffer in silence, but rather to "be public spirited and make a big squawk." Like their counterparts earlier in the century, post–World War II antifraud organizations argued that "by making known your dissatisfaction, you may save others from being victimized." The consistent plea, like the messaging of the NACM during their Progressive era battles against credit

Figure 10.1: Poster from the New York Bureau of Consumer Frauds and Protection, 1966. Reprinted from the *Albany Times-Union*, Aug. 11, 1966, with permission.

fraud, was one of social obligation—to "Help Protect others" by "making it more difficult for the . . . disreputable retailer to do business." To facilitate such communitarian goals, antifraud communications, such as a 1966 poster from the New York State attorney general's office (Figure 10.1), made a point of explaining where consumers or investors could seek assistance from nongovernmental consumer groups and state agencies. They also detailed how to put together an effective complaint.[60]

For all the heightened attention in the 1960s to commercial predation faced by the urban poor, the educational materials produced by the antifraud state targeted a middle-class audience. In beseeching readers to run investment ideas by a banker or financial adviser, the authors had professionals and small business more in mind than day laborers or the rural poor. *The Fine Art of Fraud* included dramatizations of bait and switch marketing by a travel agent hawking European vacations to a pair of white schoolteachers, as well as a high-pressure pitch for a referral-selling scheme, made by a cultured salesman to a prim white couple in their comfortable suburban home. These were not the scams operating in the Puerto Rican neighborhoods of the Bronx, on the South Side of Chicago, across the Watts neighborhood of Los Angeles, or in the hollows of Appalachia. Graphics in consumer protection pamphlets reflected comparable expectations about readership. For the Washington attorney general's office, the image of the consumer who had to watch out for bait and switch advertising was a well-coiffed middle-aged white woman. When Pennsylvania's Bureau of Consumer Protection (BCP) crafted a "buyer's bible," its choice of a prototypical purchaser was "Conrad Consumer," an "average family man" depicted in cartoon form as a young middle-class white father in a cardigan sweater.[61]

In the wake of the 1960s summer riots that devastated poor neighborhoods in many large cities, the new consumer protection agencies and older self-regulatory agencies brought educational messages more directly to those inner city communities. In addition to setting up branch offices, state and local anti-fraud organizations put out Spanish-language versions of publications, equipped mobile outreach buses that could bring pamphlets and seasoned antifraud professionals to city neighborhoods, and participated in local consumer fairs. New York City's BBB hired African American consumer specialists to staff its new Harlem branch and commissioned the film *Just Sign Here*, which focused on frauds endemic to poorer communities rather than schemes that targeted those higher up the income ladder. At the national level, the FTC established a companion Consumer Protection Office for the District of Columbia, held a series of hearings on inner-city consumer fraud, and prioritized the hiring of African Americans for the consumer protection division.[62]

Community-based consumer and civil rights organizations, which possessed far more legitimacy within poor urban neighborhoods than most state or business-linked agencies, launched their own educational efforts. In Philadelphia, CEPA's monthly newspaper, *Consumer Voice*, mixed in-depth reporting on the marketing abuses afflicting poorer consumers with a hard-edged editorial posture. In San Francisco, the antipoverty organization Bay Area Neighborhood Development (BAND) set up a network of offices to assist consumers. BAND produced booklets that warned low-income residents about all manner of consumer deceptions, imploring readers, "FIGHT BACK! DON'T LET THE GYP ARTISTS GET AWAY WITH IT!"[63] Regardless of the social milieu generating the outpouring of antifraud instruction, one might be tempted to see it solely in terms of the unending struggle to wise up individuals, whatever their ethnicity, race, gender, or social class. But a key goal of outreach, in this period as much as the Progressive era, was to buttress social norms against manipulative modes of selling.

State and local antifraud agencies also followed their predecessors in building informational networks and clearinghouses. Attorneys general built mechanisms to collect timely intelligence on fraudulent business activity in their states, and to share that intelligence with state agencies, local police departments, and prosecutors. Louis Lefkowitz's office again laid the foundation for such initiatives during the late 1950s and soon attracted imitators. In 1962, Maryland Attorney General Thomas Finan asked the State Police to establish a "special six-man intelligence unit" to aggregate information from local authorities about prevalent rackets and identify emerging statewide trends. By the mid-1960s, the Consumer Fraud Unit of the California attorney general's office had developed a far more ambitious framework, using reports that came in from local police and prosecutors as a basis for "multi-county fraud investigations" and "statewide criminal crackdowns." Other states developed variations on this approach, including policy councils that brought local prosecutors together with state officials responsible for consumer fraud, and statewide computer databases on fraud investigations and prosecutions.[64]

These more sophisticated enforcement networks facilitated a growing number of city-specific and statewide prosecutorial sweeps, which targeted the chicanery that went on in many automobile dealerships, home improvement companies, television repair shops, and purveyors of miracle health cures. On occasion, local law enforcement moved in response to specific newspaper exposés and indignant editorial demands for action. With the rising tide of consumerism, more prosecutors saw great value in gaining notice as inveterate foes of rackets.[65]

Press releases, newsletters, and annual reports from these agencies trumpeted statistics and capsule summaries of successful enforcement actions, such as criminal convictions, fines, injunctions, consent decrees, and orders of business dissolutions. So, too, did a steady stream of articles on consumer fraud enforcement produced by attorneys general, heads of Consumer Protection Offices, and district attorneys for law reviews.[66] Sometimes state-driven undertakings even zeroed in on larger business frauds with national reach. In the early 1970s, authorities in more than thirty states drew on their new antifraud powers to shut down Glenn Turner's pyramid sales schemes, which he had organized through the Koscot Interplanetary and Dare to Be Great corporations. Turner's business model involved selling cosmetics and then motivational books and tapes through multilevel distributorships, in which franchisees earned income through commissions earned by recruiting new franchisees. He pitched these distributorships through revivalist weekend-long meetings, held in convention centers. From Oregon to Michigan to Mississippi to Maryland, state prosecutors brought dozens of successful injunctive proceedings and criminal cases against Turner enterprises and midlevel franchisees.[67]

The Turner cases attest to the networks that state and local antifraud officials built to share policy ideas and enforcement techniques. Fraud fighters met at conferences convened by the National Association of Attorneys General (NAAG) and the Department of Justice. The NAAG published annual surveys of consumer fraud regulation, compiling statistics on consumer protection budgets and staffing and tracking legislative and administrative trends. Such efforts were accompanied by an uptick in academic scholarship on investor and consumer protection, as well as in news coverage. Ideas about how to combat business fraud circulated through all of these channels, encouraging national convergence of antifraud strategies.

In part because of this deepening antifraud network, the champions of consumerism remained aware of the enduring obstacles that confronted criminal fraud prosecutions and administrative antideception proceedings. By the early 1970s, the legal system's soft treatment of fraudulent business owners (and white-collar criminals more generally) was considered commonplace by prosecutors and legal sociologists.[68] Recognition of this pattern also seeped into popular sentiment, sometimes prompting indignant protest after guilty verdicts for prominent businessmen led only to trifling sentences. In 1975, after a prominent San Diego banker received a suspended two-year sentence for a multi-million-dollar bank fraud, readers of the *Los Angeles Times* seethed in anger. To the twenty-five letter writers moved to comment about legal proceedings a two-hour drive away, the case showed that "America operates two systems of justice—one for the rich and powerful and another for the poor and powerless," that " 'lectric chairs ain't for millionaires," that "you can't send Mr. San Diego to jail."[69]

The men and women charged with running consumer protection agencies knew all about cases such as Holland Furnace and were determined to avoid such outcomes by taking tougher stances toward deceptive sellers. They had fought hard to gain access to more potent enforcement tools, such as the power to ask for injunctions, dissolutions of incorporation, and mechanisms of compulsory restitution. In the most egregious cases, state and local consumer protection agencies deployed such authority to good effect, every year shutting down hundreds of abusive retailers and service providers. As with late nineteenth-century postal officials and early twentieth-century regulators at the FTC, antifraud reformers of the late 1960s and early 1970s hoped to sidestep the inefficiencies of the criminal justice system through more nimble modes of regulatory governance. Had consumer protection champions possessed a deeper grasp of history, they might have tempered their expectations. Forceful antifraud tactics tended to generate complaints about autocratic governance that ran roughshod over individual rights and American values, which then prompted adoption of procedural protections, which in turn limited the effectiveness of administrative remedies. Post–World War II proceduralism deepened the democratic legitimacy of antifraud regulation, but at the cost of extending the rights of accused businesses, whether in criminal or administrative contexts.

Such safeguards, in combination with judicial skepticism about business fraud cases, often stymied expeditious redress for consumers. Although New York City armed its DCA with the power to ask for injunctions against deceptive firms, the city's judiciary and the clerks on whom they relied for advice frowned on the rapid-fire action contemplated by Mayor John Lindsay's administration and its consumer protection officials. Even in cases with extensive documentation of predatory behavior by businesses, some members of the New York City bench harbored concerns about issuing injunctions, believing they should "only be granted sparingly" before a final court finding that firms had committed fraud. The resulting delays could sour victims on consumer protection agencies, convincing them that there was little justice to be found through recourse to the new champions of consumer rights.[70]

Once again, the effectiveness of antifraud agencies depended on the extent of funding. During the 1960s and 1970s, state legislatures in heavily industrialized states such as Illinois appropriated sums for consumer protection bureaus that allowed them to establish several satellite offices. In some of the largest cities, urban consumer protection bureaus had budgets and staffs of even greater size. A few suburban agencies, like the one in Long Island's Nassau County, received significant resources: by the early 1970s, it enjoyed a $376,000 budget, enabling it to employ a staff of almost fifty.[71]

But American proceduralism often went hand in hand with budgetary stringency for regulatory agencies. Congress, state legislatures, and city councils proved far more willing to adopt new regulatory schemes that targeted hucksterism than to appropriate generous sums for implementation. Most public agencies charged with enforcing antideception law operated on a shoestring. Consumer protection divisions within the attorney general's office or standalone consumer protection agencies usually had only a few staff members. Funding for city and county consumer bureaus proved even less munificent. The Los Angeles Bureau of Consumer Affairs launched in 1972 with only twenty-one salaried personnel to police marketing practices in a city of almost three million—"only one 'fraud catcher' for every 166,000 people." It enjoyed that many staff only because the city was able to obtain a federal grant to defray the costs. During the early 1970s, the entire city of Philadelphia relied on the efforts of a consumer affairs staff of just three people. When the Prince George's County, Maryland, Consumer Protection Commission opened its doors in 1970, it had only a single commissioner and two assistants. Most consumer agencies, moreover, had responsibility for a much wider set of consumer issues than just combating commercial duplicity.[72] At the New York City DCA, a staff of 350, around fifty of whom worked for the enforcement division, still groaned under the weight of tens of thousands of annual consumer complaints. Matters worsened considerably in the mid-1970s, when the city's fiscal woes led to budget reductions.[73]

Like public antifraud regulators, self-regulatory organizations confronted the problem of insufficient bureaucratic capacity. After years of rapid growth in the number of BBBs, member businesses, and collective financial resources, the 1960s brought relatively flat budgets, even as demands from consumers, businesses, and governmental agencies intensified. The BBB network expanded by an additional twenty-two locals between 1962 and 1972, but the total funds for operating budgets did not keep pace, approaching only $9 million in pledged memberships by 1972, just $2 million more than in 1962.[74]

Pinched budgets led to staffing shortfalls and associated declines in the quality of service. A 1971 report on the BBBs, undertaken by several law school students at the direction of New York congressman Benjamin Rosenthal, chronicled the impacts on organizational performance. Pressed to respond to all the letters, phone calls, and consumer visits, many bureaus sharply curtailed their public hours. Even though this move rationed access and created consumer frustrations, the BBBs still battled to keep track of all the information that they received. As the reliability of their files diminished, many consumers who managed to get through to BBB employees received false impressions when they inquired about businesses. The Rosenthal Report, modeled on the Nader-funded assessment of the FTC, further found that budgetary pressures had led most local bureaus to compromise some of their most basic moral commitments. Many had outsourced recruitment of new members to sales companies that engaged in high-pressure sales tactics and no longer screened new members to check on reputations, nor expelled members that repeatedly violated BBB standards. Most of these conclusions echoed the pronouncements of the confidential analysis of the Bureaus conducted by the management consulting firm, Knight, Gladieux, & Smith in 1969.[75]

Together, punctilious proceduralism and tight budgets raised the likelihood that grievances about deceptive selling practices would take a long time to wind their way through the system (widening the practical openings for "quick kill[s]") or fall through bureaucratic cracks altogether.[76] The publicity surrounding the inauguration of state local consumer protection offices, in conjunction with a more general societal embrace of consumerism, only heightened such pressures. That publicity elicited a torrent of complaints, which immediately taxed investigative and adjudicative capacities. One common strategy was to turn to volunteers who could assist with monitoring and complaint-taking, much like the nineteenth-century journal subscribers who answered the calls to become informal antifraud sentinels.

Thus, in the late 1950s, New York Attorney General Louis Lefkowitz convened a statewide committee of "100 housewives" to serve as unpaid adjuncts. These middle-class women likely had experience working with community organizations; some may have participated in the citizen networks that monitored World War II consumer price regulations.[77] Lefkowitz asked the volunteers to "observe conditions which affect the purse strings," channel consumer complaints to his consumer protection office, and serve as community spokespersons who would "alert and educate the buying public in the techniques of slick salesmen." The attorney general also drew on unpaid law student interns, who processed less complex consumer complaints. Over the subsequent two decades, most state and local consumer agencies developed similar strategies. In some cases, as in the California attorney general's office during the early 1970s, agencies recruited volunteers to serve as mystery shoppers, who visited stores to assess "the validity of advertisements [and] sales practices." Reliance on volunteers and interns extended regulatory footprints. The Office of Consumer Protection in New Jersey's Burlington County, created in 1969, had only two salaried staff members. But after the creation of a "volunteer army of 50 persons" in 1971, as well as a weekly local radio show that solicited complaints, it was able to handle a much larger caseload.[78]

Despite such measures, many of the new consumer protection agencies struggled to satisfy complainants, in much the same fashion as local BBBs. All too often, consumers encountered recurrent busy signals, delays before investigators could look into their allegations, or "referral runaround," as overwhelmed complaint-takers directed them to other consumer protection bureaucracies. Confusion over which local, state, or federal agency to approach became commonplace; so did dissatisfaction with the pace of regulatory action. In many cases, formal proceedings within local or state consumer affairs offices bogged down in a procedural morass, leading angry citizens to throw up their "hands in frustration after struggling through phone calls, letters, or visits" to multiple agencies. The most jaded consumer protection officials tried to deflect unhappy consumers as much as solve their problems; the most well intentioned often felt as if they were "sitting at the bottom of the ocean bailing with a tin cup."[79]

In spite of intention and occasional practice, the antifraud monitors came to function as a mediation service. In 1962, the Illinois attorney general had described the new Consumer Fraud Bureau (CFB) as dedicated to prosecuting "merchants who habitually employ fraud." A decade later, the CFB instead proclaimed that it was "the face-to-face legal representative" of the "citizen who feels that he has been duped or wronged in a consumer transaction," and that its chief goal was "recovering the individual's money whenever possible."[80]

The strategic preferences of consumers and businesses encouraged this bureaucratic reorientation. Although some consumers took on the roles of communitarian guardians and asked for "public-oriented remedies" such as prosecution, most prioritized the righting of their own personal injustices. In one comprehensive study of an Illinois consumer protection office, seven in eight complainants referenced only their desire to hold a business to what they perceived to be a contractual promise, or to receive their money back. Thus, only one in eight complaints voiced a desire for punishment or concern that a business not harm others. The most unscrupulous business cheats, like their counterparts in earlier periods, frequently took advantage of such inclinations to "cool the mark out"—in the language of the grafter, to "pacify a mark after he has been fleeced," often by extending partial refunds to indignant customers. When the business managers of more-reputable firms confronted allegations of deceptive behavior, they similarly looked to find some accommodation that would assuage consumer anger while minimizing financial repercussions. Limited institutional resources pressed consumer protection agencies in the same direction. Staff members at these agencies received an avalanche of complaints, most of which did not involve clear-cut evidence of misrepresentation or fraud. They had little option other than to focus on cases that seemed amenable to quick resolutions, that would offer complainants at least partial satisfaction, and that would allow businesses to sidestep admissions of bad faith.[81] Many agencies reported that nine-tenths of their staff time went into efforts to use "dialogue" to bring about "reconciliation of the disadvantaged consumer and the businessman." In the rare cases where consumer protection agencies opted for sterner legal process, such as motions for an injunction or criminal prosecution, the most common outcome was still either some form of monetary settlement for complaining consumers or a promise of more complete contractual performance.[82]

This emphasis on retrospective compromises meant that every year, tens of thousands of American consumers who asked for assistance from consumer protection bureaus received some form of redress. Over time, the data that accumulated from the stacks of individual grievance forms also allowed antifraud professionals to identify patterns of behavior by businesses that justified the expenditure of resources on sterner enforcement measures. Staff members at consumer protection bureaucracies toted up the resulting restitutions, and then pointed to those figures as concrete measures of their work on behalf of consumers. Every year during the mid-1970s, for example, Kansas consumers received several hundred thousand dollars in refunds as a result of interventions by the attorney general's Consumer Protection Division and had hundreds of contractual promises fulfilled.[83] Such figures, however, represented only a small fraction of the most common estimates of annual losses imposed on the US economy due to business fraud, which ran into the billions (though, as in the early twentieth century, the people who offered such estimates never explained their method of calculation).[84] The institutional preference for negotiated settlements further allowed a great many unscrupulous businesses to retain the longstanding strategy of the squawk fund. Rather than forsake misleading or even predatory styles of selling, they furnished refunds to insistent customers and paid the occasional fine, treating such payments as merely part of the "cost of doing business."[85]

✳✳✳✳

For the sternest advocates of consumerism, the dominance of mediation at consumer protection agencies elicited frustration and disillusionment. Philip Schrag set the tone for movement toward self-evaluation in his widely read 1972 memoir, *Counsel for the Deceived: Case Studies in Consumer Fraud.* Schrag might have subtitled the book *The Education of an Activist Regulator.* Drawing on his experience at the New York DCA, he chronicled just how hard it was to bring hucksters to heel, even with dedicated staff and the capacity to draw on significant investigative powers and coercive sanctions. Within just a few years after the launch of this expansive regulatory experiment, the initial heady expectations looked hopelessly naïve. As Schrag framed his "disappointment" with his time at the DCA,

> I had actually imagined that a good law, properly administered, could wipe out misleading sales practices altogether. Our experiences . . . suggest that given our toleration of the way in which adversary and judicial systems now operate, the amount of resources constituting "enough" would be more than any government should devote to the problem.[86]

For this young attorney turned fraud enforcer, the enduring structures of legal decision-making profoundly compromised any reformist aspirations to use regulatory power to cast the worst dissemblers and cheats out of the temples of American consumer capitalism.

This assessment, accepted across political divides, prompted a range of strategic replies by consumer activists. One response, forged on inner-city streets and borrowed from militant unions and the civil rights movement, harkened back to centuries-old strategies of legal self-help. Others, popular among intellectuals and policymakers, called for better arming consumers to look out from themselves, either before they entered into transactions or by seeking their own legal remedies if some business took advantage of them. Observers outside the ranks of the consumer movement, however, drew very different conclusions, pleading for renewed faith in the power of the market and at least a partial return to the legal premises that shaped Barnum's America. Before we take stock of Philip Schrag's pessimism about the twentieth-century antifraud state, these cross-currents deserve careful consideration.

CHAPTER ELEVEN

The Promise and Limits of the Antifraud State

Philip Schrag's account of battling consumer fraud was not all doom and gloom: the Department of Consumer Affairs achieved some early victories that he took care to document. Schrag was proudest of its takedown of Vigilant Protective Systems (given the moniker "Foolproof Protection, Inc." in *Counsel for the Deceived*). Created in 1968, this firm operated throughout New York City and its environs, selling residential burglar alarms to low-income African American and Puerto Rican families. Vigilant's African American sales force monitored police radio to learn about residential robberies. While the sense of personal violation was still fresh, they paid calls on victims. After commiserating about "soaring crime rates," the salesmen offered to install state-of-the-art alarm systems connected to the closest police precinct for a free thirty-day trial. If customers chose to keep the alarm, they would pay a monthly leasing fee of $14 ($20 if a fire alarm was included in the package), but would retain the right to cancel at will, and could expect regular maintenance as necessary. Sales agents further promised that the company would never use court process to collect in the case of nonpayment.

Every one of these claims was false. The company installed low-grade alarms made of cheap components that rang only in the apartment, and that burglars could easily disable. Contractual fine print, which many Spanish-speaking customers could not read, committed lessees to three-year contracts with no right of cancellation, did not reference a trial period, and specified that lessees would owe legal fees if Vigilant had to go to court to compel payment. Vigilant's lawyers always pursued court judgments in cases of nonpayment, often on the basis of "sewer service"—not supplying legal notices to nonpaying customers, but rather metaphorically chucking those notices into the sewer so that its debtors did not learn about hearings. The company soon became New York City's fifth most-active plaintiff. Its salesmen also ignored a New York installment sale law that required distribution of a card that alerted customers, in both English and Spanish, of a three-day cooling-off period for consumer contracts. Here was an updated version of the nineteenth-century lightning-rod sales routine and the abusive tactics honed by Holland Furnace Company.

Vigilant's president, Sol Rosen ("Sam Stone" in Schrag's memoir), had extensive experience with this kind of marketing scheme. After spending a chunk of the 1950s selling deceptive food-freezer plans, he started up a finance company that bought debt contracts from predatory urban merchants. Vigilant took his techniques of deception to a new level of sophistication. It was a subsidiary of a publicly traded holding company that skirted disclosure requirements in its financial reports; the holding company had managed to attract $1.5 million in working capital from four major New York banks, secured by its customer accounts, as well as an exclusive deal with a major department store to showcase its alarms.

All of Rosen's ventures encountered pressure from antifraud regulators. In each case, Rosen adopted the common strategies of accommodation and retreat. He accepted a plea deal against the freezer plan corporation that included dismissal of pending criminal charges, and later allowed the finance company to go out of business. Within months of its launch, Vigilant faced an investigation by the New York Bureau of Consumer Fraud and Protection. That case ended with a consent decree, in which Rosen pledged to discontinue objectionable marketing practices. He and his salesmen ignored its terms.

Schrag and his colleagues succeeded in putting Vigilant out of business by 1971, but only by eschewing time-consuming enforcement tools, such as seeking an injunction against the company. There were several twists and turns in the story, including coordination of lease cancellations by almost four hundred customers on the grounds that they had not received notice of their "cooling off" rights, a threatened business license revocation, and complex negotiations that resulted in a very tough settlement agreement. The key point is that after the DCA received evidence of the firm's ongoing violations of the settlement, it threatened a parallel investigation of the department store that marketed Vigilant alarms and facilitated extensive press coverage about the case, which hurt the reputations of the department store and banks that kept Vigilant afloat. These tactics led to a bankruptcy filing in July 1971 and stimulated enough public uproar that the district attorney brought criminal charges against Sol Rosen.[1]

Success in this case depended on creative maneuvers akin to the policy innovations that antifraud activists and organizations had concocted since the mid-nineteenth century, from the sandwich-board warnings about Peter Funks in antebellum auction districts, to postal fraud orders and "sundry frauds and humbugs" features in nineteenth-century magazines, to the NACM's prosecution fund, to the SEC's stop orders and the Better Business Bureau's NIPI declarations. As the implementation of consumer protection reforms in the 1960s and 1970s reinforced appreciation for the shortcomings of reliance on traditional legal mechanisms, opponents of business fraud continued to experiment with alternative enforcement strategies.

The takedown of Vigilant Protective Systems incorporated several approaches that mirrored the long history of American antifraud efforts. One move was to rely on the disinfecting power of public exposure. A second was to find new ways to exert pressure on the business infrastructure that allowed deceptive firms to function, described by Philip Schrag as "commercial synapses." These support-service providers included advertising agencies, media outlets, law firms, banks, accounting firms, and insurance companies. Finally, antifraud bureaucracies looked for ways to reinforce the capacity of disgruntled consumers and investors to vindicate rights on their own, such as by informing Vigilant customers that they had a right to cancel their contracts and encouraging them to do so. These strategies all had limitations; but each, in at least some contexts, was a meaningful weapon against commercial deceit.

Officials who turned to such tactics retained a conviction that the state had an obligation to protect investors and consumers from duplicitous marketing. Among American conservatives, there was a contrasting impulse to challenge antifraud measures as regulatory overreach, as just one more example of failed statism. This viewpoint found adherents within the realm of business self-regulation, and especially among a newly invigorated vanguard of conservative intellectuals. Elements of this perspective gained ground among some progressive policy elites as well, setting the stage for profound reconfigurations of antifraud policies in the final quarter of the twentieth century.

Exposing Deceit in the Civil Rights Era

Philip Schrag used the term "direct action" to describe the creative maneuvers against Vigilant Protective Systems, evoking the civil rights demonstrations that had been roiling American society since the 1950s. This idiom surely came readily to mind because of Schrag's earlier experience as an NAACP attorney. Perhaps reflecting his socialization into the legal fraternity, the New York City consumer advocate did not think to reference an even more vigorous style of collective protest deployed to pressure notorious business cheats just one hundred miles to the southwest.

In Philadelphia, the Consumer Education Protective Association (CEPA) had refined the art of securing justice for consumers, including fraud victims, through an assertive style of community self-help informed by militant unionism. This cooperative organization was founded by Max Weiner, a former real-estate broker and finance company manager who had seen the predatory side of urban marketing practices. In addition to provision of consumer education tailored for the inner city, the group urged low-income Philadelphians to inform its unpaid staff members about retailers who engaged in bait advertising, phony oral promises, abusive credit terms, and other prevalent consumer frauds. When staffers viewed complaints as meritorious, they advised the consumers in question about how to pursue informal redress. If satisfactory adjustments were not forthcoming, CEPA sent delegations of its members to accompany individual complainants in further efforts to seek accommodation. The next step involved picketing operations, which members committed to join as a condition of receiving assistance themselves. Uncooperative business owners could look forward to the arrival of CEPA members "equipped with placards, leaflets, and sometimes loudspeakers," who would "march in front of the place of business, protesting the injustice and explaining it to passersby" (Figure 11.1). From 1966 through the mid-1970s, CEPA coordinated scores of public protests against finance companies, car dealerships, furniture stores, and other retailers and service providers, both in Philadelphia and outlying communities.[2]

CEPA had the wherewithal to pursue targeted businesses for weeks and even months, garnering extensive media attention. The local African American daily, the *Philadelphia Tribune*, furnished close coverage, and other local publications ran features on the cooperative and stories on specific boycotts, with state and national outlets also taking note. This publicity drove additional consumer complaints to CEPA. It also magnified the pressure that CEPA could bring to bear on local firms, which enabled it to negotiate hundreds of settlements a year and sometimes persuade the city district attorney to file criminal fraud charges. The amounts refunded through CEPA interventions rivalled those of the consumer protection agencies created by state and local governments.[3] By the early 1970s, CEPA had set up branches in Des Moines, Cleveland, Baltimore, and Washington, DC, with community activists in other cities explicitly patterning separate organizations on Max Weiner's template.[4]

Recognizing the antipathy of most business owners to unflattering publicity, some law enforcement personnel adopted analogous hard-edged tactics. The most flamboyant was Marvin Zindler, a deputy in the Harris County, Texas, sheriff's office tasked in 1971 with heading up a new consumer fraud division. Treating "consumerism" as "up there with God, country, and motherhood," and having "an uncanny flair for publicity," Zindler wielded his own sledgehammer at Houston businesses accused of deceptive practices. In cases of even small-scale misrepresentations, he coerced businesses into compromises by threatening publicized arrests. Former work as a newspaper photographer and public relations officer in the sheriff's office had given the "nattily

Figure 11.1: CEPA activists prepare a picket sign, August 1976. George D. McDowell *Philadelphia Evening Bulletin* Collection, Temple University Libraries, Urban Archives.

attired" deputy a wide network among local journalists, as well as insights about how to command public notice. The son of a wealthy Jewish retailer, Zindler had a chip on his shoulder as a result of perceived anti-Semitic slights, as well as an insatiable desire for public recognition. "I want the public to know I'm here to help them," he explained to one journalist, "and the crooks and cheats to know I'll get them." He made his threats realistic by initiating 1,300 criminal fraud cases in the first year of the consumer fraud unit and informing television stations whenever he was on his way to make an arrest, so that cameras could record it for the evening newscast. Even though Houston prosecutors viewed his cases as unwinnable and local judges threw out most charges that went forward, fear of bad press led most businesses to agree to consumer settlements, which was always Zindler's goal. This approach attracted thousands of complaints and fawning profiles from local and national journalists.[5]

Business owners did not take kindly to such treatment, whether applied by community consumer groups or a maverick law-enforcement official. San Francisco's Consumer Action faced a libel suit from one car dealer outraged by a demonstration. CEPA faced several lawsuits seeking to enjoin them from continuing their pickets; during one moment of widespread inner-city riots, it confronted a mayoral emergency proclamation banning public pickets of more than twelve persons. Marvin Zindler attracted deep enmity from the Houston business establishment. After a new Harris County sheriff took office in early 1973, business groups exerted their own pressure, successfully campaigning for Zindler's firing (Figure 11.2). American law and journalism nonetheless proved hospitable to this form of antifraud discipline. The courts tended to give direct action by consumer organizations a wide berth, so long as they framed their motives narrowly around the redress of specific, defensible consumer grievances. Judges accepted assertions of free-speech rights by protestors of commercial injustice, in part because ordinary legal process did such a poor job of handling fraud allegations.[6] And although Marvin Zindler lost his handcuffs and badge, within weeks of his dismissal he started a new career as a reporter for the local ABC television station. Using a consumer affairs segment to retain access to a complaint phone line, he continued to excoriate "usurious merchants, unscrupulous auto mechanics, four-flushing house-siding salesmen and other con artists" in the same florid style.[7]

During this era, media action lines proliferated at urban newspapers and broadcast stations, because they tended to attract readers, listeners, and viewers. Numbering over four hundred by the late 1970s, they were headed by a consumer-affairs journalist, but relied on corps of college-student volunteers and middle-class housewives. Although they handled citizen complaints of all kinds, a portion of their work involved allegations of false advertising or de-

Figure 11.2: Houston Sheriff Marvin Zindler in his office. Reprinted from *Texas Monthly*, Feb. 1973, with permission.

ceptive marketing. As with consumer protection agencies, these media departments focused on solving problems through mediation, though always with the threat of a negative newspaper column, radio spot, or television news segment hovering in the background.[8] Very few American cities boasted a crusading figure such as Zindler, even if they possessed a media action line. Nor did every metropolitan area have a savvy neighborhood-based defender of consumer rights such as CEPA. Small towns and rural areas were even less likely to possess such guardians. Where they put down roots, however, they offered meaningful assistance to victims of consumer fraud and some measure of populist deterrence.

Pinching off Commercial and Financial Synapses

The idea of placing regulatory pressure on business counterparties of duplicitous firms hardly originated with the New York City DCA. One of the foundational premises of the "truth in advertising" movement had been to close off access of fraudulent advertisers to reputable publications. From the inception of the New Deal, federal securities regulation looked to law and accounting firms to police the truthfulness and completeness of registration statements and financial reports. In the wake of the quiz show scandals of the late 1950s, the FTC also brought some deceptive practices cases against advertising agencies as well as their clients.[9]

Before 1965, however, antifraud agencies rarely sought to target ancillary firms as a systematic strategy to constrain deceptive behavior by business principals. Thus the SEC steered clear of efforts to pursue sanctions against the lawyers who furnished services to fraudulent stock promoters unless they helped to plan and execute scams. The FTC's experience in going after advertising agencies nonetheless hinted at how a tough-minded regulatory posture could percolate through corporate practice. At the Westinghouse Corporation, for instance, closer FTC scrutiny prompted new internal rules for the development of ad campaigns. All comparative performance claims would henceforth have to "be certified by an accredited independent laboratory" and the firm's ad agency would have to keep affidavits of certification on file.[10] A growing number of regulatory agencies soon embraced the tactic of attacking business fraud through the professional gatekeepers who either facilitated it or looked the other way.

The SEC led the way in developing aggressive enforcement actions against fraud-abetting professionals, prompted by a series of cases in the 1960s that came to light as a result of corporate bankruptcies. The typical story involved corporate management who relied on legal opinions or auditor certifications to shield themselves from liability for violating securities laws—perhaps for misleading financial reports, or for delays in release of corrected financial data until after the closing of a corporate merger. Troubled by these instances in which gatekeepers skirted professional obligations, SEC lawyers explored ways to initiate charges against the lawyers and accountants who had blessed deceptive practices.

The pivotal case that encapsulated this more aggressive enforcement posture was *SEC v. National Student Marketing*, brought in 1971. The SEC had already pursued criminal charges against two auditors some years earlier for their actions in the run-up to the bankruptcy of a franchise vending machine company. But only in *National Student Marketing* did SEC lawyers charge partners in a "major law firm . . . that had an international reputation," and only in this case did the SEC articulate an expansive interpretation of the legal obligations owed by attorneys and accountants when they learned of material misrepresentations by corporate clients. In 1967 and 1968, executives at the National Student Marketing Corporation approached several large-scale corporations about their business model, which was to use part-time college students to create buzz about consumer products on campuses. The company's management used oral agreements as the basis for booking revenues on their financial statements; when most of the oral agreements fell through, they did not disclose the news, but instead rushed to complete several corporate mergers, made possible by the company's inflated stock price. Executives carried out this deception over the objections of the corporation's accountants, but with the assistance of its attorneys. For SEC staff lawyers, this case suggested the importance of laying down two basic principles of professional responsibility: attorneys and accountants had to correct financial estimates and projections as soon as they realized they were false or mistaken; they also had the "obligation to bring [such information] to the attention of the authorities" if their clients refused to act on their advice.[11]

The federal courts ruled for the SEC in *National Student Marketing*. With consumerism in the ascendancy, and with an embattled Nixon administration seeking to deflect political pressures by appointing antifraud hawks as SEC commissioners, staff lawyers felt that they could press forward with the opinion in this case as a guide. Their determination was only reinforced by several large-scale business failures in the early 1970s, including the Penn Central Railroad, Equity Funding, and Home-Stake Oil. These debacles all involved evidence of widespread securities fraud and each cost investors hundreds of millions of dollars. As a result, the SEC initiated a series of fraud and nondisclosure proceedings in the 1970s against leading New York law firms and the nation's most influential accounting companies.[12]

The avowed point of these proceedings was to buck up the legal and accounting professions, so that their members would be "more stand-upish with their clients and say no when they needed to say no." Leading architects of enforcement at the SEC, such as Irving Pollack and Stanley Sporkin, took close note of the rapid growth in the securities markets during the 1960s and were horrified by the extent of professional abdication in some of the era's bigger business failures. These developments led them to conclude that the SEC would never have sufficient resources to monitor and police the markets on their own. The only sensible approach, as one long-time staff lawyer recalled the emerging bureaucratic consensus, was to "create incentives for the people who were at the access points to the market . . . the brokers/dealers of the world, the investment bankers of the world, the lawyers and the accountants— and encourage them to police themselves." Accountants had to act in accordance with their duties to the investing public; corporate lawyers had to remind themselves that their client was in fact the corporation, not senior executives, and that the SEC, "with its small staff, limited resources, and onerous tasks is peculiarly dependent on the probity and the diligence of the professionals who practice before it."[13] Such diligence might cut off access to the financial services required for any large-scale investment deception.

The rapid expansion of mutual funds and other institutional investors during the 1960s and early 1970s, moreover, meant that a greater proportion of disgruntled bond- or shareholders had the resources to pursue legal avenues of redress. Plaintiffs' lawyers soon explored potential causes of action against defendants with sufficient assets to make civil lawsuits worth filing. After corporate bankruptcies, professional gatekeepers had the great advantage of still possessing assets that one might attack, as did creditors, investment banks, brokerage firms, and corporate directors in their personal capacity. These participants in the securities markets faced an increasing number of fraud-related civil suits, especially after the sharp stock market correction of the late 1960s. SEC regulators and plaintiffs' attorneys kept a close eye on test cases, piggybacking on each other's arguments and scrutinizing judicial opinions for indications of how to proceed with fraud allegations.[14]

In addition to pushing for expanded liability for legal counsel and accounting firms, the SEC's enforcement staff also concocted novel disciplinary mechanisms. One option was to suspend or bar individual lawyers or accountants from practicing before the commission, which in most cases would preclude individuals from working on any securities-related filings. But the SEC tended to focus on remedies that would change how firms conducted core activities. Always conscious of tight budgets, SEC lawyers preferred negotiated consent decrees to litigated cases. During the late 1960s and early 1970s, the dramatic growth in demand for corporate auditing had fostered rapid consolidation in the accounting industry, which in turn generated, as the SEC's head accountant later described it, "managerial and control problems of unprecedented magnitude." This diagnosis of auditing shortcomings shaped settlement priorities. SEC officials demanded that accounting firms commit to more searching internal supervision of auditing procedures, as well as regimes of continuing education and training for its accountants and "peer review" of its work by expert third parties. Such requirements obviated the common defense that in signing off on misleading financial statements, a firm's employees had acted on their own, without the knowledge or consent of superiors. Regulators also sought to infuse organizational culture with a stronger commitment to professional obligations and legal compliance—to gatekeeping in the public interest.[15]

Within America's legal, accounting, and corporate establishments, the new enforcement landscape occasioned loud complaint, which paralleled earlier critiques of innovative antifraud techniques. Objections focused on the alacrity with which the SEC was willing to "sully the reputations of leading figures of business, finance, accounting, and the bar," as well as the use of coercive negotiating tactics that compromised due process rights. Legal scholars, securities lawyers, and accounting specialists further raised the specter of unintended consequences. Attorneys might refuse to work for companies with financial difficulties, lest honest mistakes take on a different gloss if the businesses failed; or they might dissuade management from attempting "novel, although perfectly proper, transactions that could be the daring, imaginative business moves necessary to realize substantial profits." Executives would have to devote far more time to scrutiny of reporting statements, thereby diverting focus from managerial challenges. Fearful about the new limits to attorney-client confidentiality, they might also shy away from asking counsel about thorny disclosure questions, foreclosing the possibility that corporate lawyers would be able to head off proposed actions that might constitute illegal misrepresentation.[16] Within the accounting world, some observers raised concerns that extension of liability to auditors would lead them to reject "more challenging audit assignments," and that demands for more detailed reporting of complicated financial data might lead to "disclosure pollution"—the provision of so much information that investors would become lost in a sea of numbers and clarifying footnotes.[17]

Elite discontent prompted institutional pushback, which fed a more general antiregulatory fervor in American politics. By the late 1970s, the federal courts began to restrict the SEC's most expansive efforts to saddle gatekeepers with liability for corporate misrepresentations. SEC commissioners appointed by Presidents Carter and Reagan, such as Harrison Williams and John Shad, also toned down enforcement tactics and redirected priorities toward the investigation and prosecution of insider trading.[18]

In the short term, however, the campaign against professional facilitators of deception in the securities markets had significant institutional ramifications. Nudged by the Securities Law division of the American Bar Association (ABA) and the Bar Association of New York City, law firms moved to tighten internal oversight of securities work. They adopted "more cautious procedures for dealing with the complex issues that frequently arise under the federal securities laws," sought "to inculcate a degree of independence in responding to client pressures," and required "a review of legal opinions and registration statements by at least one additional partner."[19]

Stung by years of intense criticism, the accounting profession agreed in 1972 to the creation of a new Financial Accounting Standards Board (FASB). Unlike its predecessor, FASB would have full-time members and professional staff. Chastened later in the 1970s by yet more corporate reporting scandals and congressional inquiries that raised fears of direct federal control over accounting standards, the industry further strengthened mechanisms of self-regulation. In 1977, the American Institute of Certified Public Accountants made professional certification more stringent. It also imposed three-year peer reviews of internal quality controls at member firms and compelled periodic rotation of the main partner in charge of a corporation's external auditing.[20] Such internal governance mechanisms served as counterweights against insistent client requests that law and accounting firms approve misleading financial communications.

THE REACH OF THE CLASS-ACTION LAWSUIT

Several of the civil securities fraud cases brought against ancillary parties in the 1960s and early 1970s were class actions, in which lawyers filing the suits purported to act on behalf of all similarly situated investors. Those attorneys took advantage of a 1966 restatement of the rules of federal civil procedure, which made such cases much easier to pursue. Under the revised Rule 23, lawyers could bring a civil suit on behalf of multiple individuals so long as they had sufficiently comparable claims, their allegations raised comparable issues of law, and a consolidated hearing would enhance "judicial efficiency." The outcomes of post-1966 class actions pertained to all members of the relevant class, including parties not named in the suit, unless they asked to be excluded in a timely fashion.[21] For consumer activists disappointed by the record of regulatory agencies, the class action beckoned as a way for consumers and investors to defend themselves. It seemed to offer a way around one of the biggest impediments to curbing many business frauds—the small losses typically inflicted on any individual victim, which often did not justify the expenditure of resources necessary to seek redress. Like the securities plaintiff's bar, several public-interest lawyers began experimenting with consumer fraud–related class actions in the 1960s, drawing on experiences with civil rights suits premised on the tactic.

A 1964 case brought by a young Los Angeles attorney on behalf of the city's taxi riders suggested the potential for this form of collective lawsuit. The case involved rigged meters on the city's Yellow Cabs. In 1963, former maintenance employees alleged that for several years, the company had "deliberately set meters to run fast," resulting in systematic overcharges of between 3 and 5 percent. These charges were aired by a Miami cab company hoping to break into the Los Angeles market, which at that point remained a regulated monopoly. An eventual grand jury investigation cleared Yellow Cab owners of intentional deceit, as they had bought the company well after the meter rigging had occurred. But public testimony to the Los Angeles Board of Public Utilities created an extensive evidentiary trail about the episode.[22]

Able to draw on this record, the young lawyer, David Daar, filed a civil suit, taking advantage of a little-used provision for class actions that had been part of California civil procedure since the 1870s. Yellow Cab persuaded a state Superior Court judge to deny certification of the class, on the grounds that cheated taxi riders had suffered varying losses, and that there would be no way to identify wronged individuals or precise amounts lost, and so no way to apportion refunds. The state Supreme Court, however, reversed this ruling, accepting Daar's argument that the class action existed for such situations, that "separate actions would be economically infeasible," and that the basic issues of law and fact were the same, even if the precise amounts at issue were not. Daar eventually wrung a negotiated settlement out of the company that incorporated innovative remedies. Because direct compensation to millions of people was impossible, Yellow Cab instead agreed to reduce its fares by a total of $1.2 million over the following seven and a half years, and to allow Daar to serve, along with the city's taxi regulator, as co-monitor of the company's compliance with the agreement.[23]

News of Daar's victory circulated among consumer groups, prompting keen interest in class-action lawsuits as a means to furnish restitution to the victims of business fraud. The basic idea of enabling victims of relatively small-scale frauds to band together to pursue relief attracted support from both militant and more moderate consumer groups. If "business firms can bilk in bulk," the New York City consumer activist Mark Green argued, then consumers "should be able to . . . sue [them] in bulk so that the penalty fits the offense."[24]

It quickly became clear, however, that consumer fraud class actions would confront high legal hurdles in most jurisdictions. Concerned about a deluge of lawsuits, the US Supreme Court placed several barriers in the way of litigants trying to bring fraud-related class actions in the federal courts. For plaintiffs relying on interstate transactions to establish federal jurisdiction, each member of the class had to have a claim in excess of $10,000. The court also held in a 1974 case that plaintiffs' attorneys would have to exercise diligence in locating and notifying potential class members, which hiked pretrial costs.[25] These rulings did not foreclose securities fraud class actions. The New Deal securities statutes established federal jurisdiction regardless of amounts at issue, and the Supreme Court eased the path for many suits in 1979, when it ruled that private litigants could rely on the factual determinations of SEC enforcement proceedings as bases for their own suits, which reduced discovery costs. The legal environment was sufficiently hospitable to securities class actions that law firms began to specialize in them, encouraging a steady increase in filings.[26] By the late 1970s, initial filings and multi-million-dollar settlements in such cases had become commonplace.[27]

Attempts to bring consumer fraud class actions, however, ran into bigger legal obstacles. The $10,000 threshold for the establishment of federal jurisdiction created a key hurdle, for few individual claims reached this amount. Unlike California, most states did not possess ready mechanisms for class actions, and those that did often had cumbersome procedural rules that hindered would-be consumer fraud litigants. The judiciary in both federal and state courts also tended to be skeptical of claims that the victims of consumer frauds met the essential characteristics to justify class actions—that they had parallel legal complaints, that they constituted an ascertainable class who could learn about court proceedings, and that claims were specific enough that courts could oversee compensation. Aware of these issues, consumer advocates looked to statutory solutions, for which a bevy of legal scholars soon offered ideas. Beginning in the late 1960s, their proposals for consumer protection legislation included calls for Congress and state legislatures to relax the definitional standards for consumer fraud–related class-action suits and to widen the range of remedies, including the fluid prospective restitution that California courts accepted in *Daar v. Yellow Cab*.[28]

Some federal consumer protection laws, such as the 1968 Truth in Lending Act and the 1975 Magnuson-Moss Warranty Act, widened the door for class actions. The Truth in Lending Act did not require a minimum amount at issue, and also called for a low standard of proof—just a showing that merchants had not provided mandated information to customers. Demonstration that merchants had misled customers, or that purchase decisions had only occurred because of the lack of disclosure, was not necessary. The burden on plaintiffs thus resembled the situation in many securities fraud cases. This statute also mandated minimum awards of $100 to winning plaintiffs and allowed for generous attorney fees. As a result, legal counsel for consumer debtors filed thousands of class-action suits, many brought because they offered the best means of redressing the small-scale individual harms caused by deceptive marketing. Although some federal judges balked at certifying the largest proposed classes on the grounds that the resulting multi-million-dollar awards would impose too much harm on defendants, hundreds of suits were successful. According to many close observers of consumer issues, these cases helped to foster general compliance with the legislation by the late 1970s.[29]

The Magnuson-Moss Act established minimum standards for warranties of consumer products worth more than $10, including use of clear language and a ban on deceptive disclaimers and exceptions. In order to limit pressure on the federal courts, the legislation encouraged corporations to create informal dispute resolution mechanisms to handle warranty-related complaints. But it also established an avenue for federal class-action suits, so long as each individual claim exceeded $25, the class numbered one hundred or more persons, and the amounts at issue totaled $50,000. Federal judges, however, ruled that Magnuson-Moss class actions had to name one hundred specific plaintiffs and that plaintiffs had to pay for notice to the affected class. These impediments stymied all but a handful of warranty-related class-action filings.[30]

Consumer groups and several members of Congress hoped to lower the jurisdictional hurdles to consumer fraud–related federal class actions, but proposals to create a more plaintiff-friendly federal mechanism never became law. During the early 1970s, the Nixon administration deflected political momentum by calling for a limited class action that would only become available once the FTC had declared a business practice to be deceptive.[31] Later that decade, class-action reform become bound up with the drive by Ralph Nader and a coalition of public interest organizations to create a Consumer Protection Agency (CPA), which would have had the authority to represent consumer interests before federal agencies. As Nader envisaged it, the CPA would counterbalance business interests in regulatory rule-making and enforcement processes, prodding bureaucracies to act in the public interest. Both the proposed CPA and calls for streamlining federal consumer class-action lawsuits became lightning rods for corporate executives, who mounted furious campaigns to thwart them. To opponents such as US Chamber of Commerce president Richard Lesher, consumer class actions gave "ambulance-chasing" lawyers the capacity to shake down legitimate firms that might have done nothing but innocently violate some "obscure government rule." Such arguments resonated with enough moderate Senate Democrats to keep the liberalization of class actions from becoming law.[32]

Supporters of consumer class actions fared better in the states, even though only a few created procedural mechanisms to facilitate these suits.[33] California remained a leader in this regard. The state legislature revised its class-action framework in 1970, allowing notification of class members by public advertisement. Shortly thereafter, the state Supreme Court reaffirmed its approbation of class actions in a case that involved two hundred consumers who each alleged fraud by the same seller of freezer food schemes. Although the customers had purchased a variety of plans, the court certified the existence of a class because of a consistent pattern of falsehoods by company agents. (Establishing commonality among plaintiffs was eased by the fact that company training included memorization of the required sales pitch.) Several other states moved in California's direction, including Ohio, Illinois, and even New York, which before a legislative reform in 1980 had been unreceptive to consumer fraud class actions. Within these states, private class actions became a more viable means of redress.[34]

Regardless of how open a state's legal system was to consumer class actions, they proved less common than suits on behalf of investors. In part, this difference reflected a greater difficulty in identifying defendants with the capacity to make restitution. But it also resulted from evidentiary challenges. Plaintiffs' attorneys confronted the same problems in consumer fraud cases that so often bedeviled prosecutors. One could not always expect a would-be competitor to assist in bringing forward public testimony of a cab company's meter-rigging, nor an offending company to have its sales staff repeat, word for word, the exact same lies to every customer. When large-scale consumer fraud class actions were successful, they often relied on the investigative capacities of the antifraud state, a pattern exemplified by the 1977 engine-switching affair at General Motors.

Beset by deteriorating labor relations and facing sharp competition from European and Japanese imports, General Motors also struggled with quality control during the mid-1970s. Nonetheless, it retained a dominant position in the US market, which encouraged managerial complacency.[35] In 1976 GM executives decided to equip 1977 Oldsmobiles with Chevrolet engines, without informing consumers that the higher-priced make had a lower-priced engine under the hood. (Dealers received a cryptic notice of an engine change that did

not announce the substitution of a Chevy power train.) The company may
have been responding to production problems caused by an underestimation
of consumer demand for powerful engines, as it claimed; or it may have been
seeking to cut costs.

Either way, GM traded on customer expectations cultivated through a half-
century's worth of product differentiation and brand management. For almost
thirty years, Oldsmobile had advertised that its higher sticker price paid for a
higher-quality car, including the distinctive V-8 "Rocket" power train.
Oldsmobile headquarters even had a large sign on its roof proclaiming that
the building was the "Home of the Rocket Engine."[36] Within months of GM's
production shift, some owners learned of the switch, either because they were
mechanics who fiddled with their new engines, or because they had to take in
cars for needed repairs, only to discover that Oldsmobile dealerships lacked
parts for Chevy engines. State and local consumer protection agencies soon
received a "thunder of protests," prompting widespread investigations. One of
the first was undertaken by the Consumer Fraud Division of the Illinois attorney general's office, which soon ascertained the nationwide scope of the
engine swaps.[37]

Recognizing the depth of anger among his constituents, Illinois Attorney
General William Scott filed a $40 million class-action suit in federal court on
behalf of all affected American car owners. The value to individual consumers
overcame the usual roadblocks to federal consumer class actions, and Scott
could marshal the resources of his office to sustain evidence gathering and
meet notice requirements. This move triggered seventy additional suits, including more than twenty filed by other consumer fraud agencies and a further
twenty-five private class actions. Forty-one attorneys general also joined the
Illinois filing. In response, GM lawyers insisted that its engine swap reflected a
longstanding industry practice to exchange components as business conditions warranted. Confronted with withering publicity and formidable legal opposition, however, GM took steps in April 1977 to inform all of its customers
about the engine switch, giving them the option of exchanging their "Chevymobiles" for new cars, "less 8 cents a mile for wear and tear." Then, in late 1977,
the car manufacturer agreed to a further $40 million settlement with Attorney
General Scott, lead negotiator for the public class actions. The corporation denied any culpability for deception, but committed to furnishing a $200 pay-
ment to all affected car-owners, as well as a three-year supplemental engine
warranty.[38]

This settlement, however, represented just the end of the first phase of legal
jockeying over the Chevymobile. Only half of eligible owners accepted the
settlement, with some plaintiffs standing "on the principle of the thing." As Joe

Siewek, the retired Chicago mechanic who first brought the issue to the attention of the Illinois attorney general's office, put it, "people should be told what they are paying for. . . . I bought something and I didn't get my money's worth." One private class action challenged the settlement, convincing an appeals court that the agreement did not gain the assent of all parties to the dispute. This ruling opened the way for a 1981 jury trial on the remaining class action, which culminated in a partial victory for the plaintiffs. Car owners who had purchased Chevymobiles before GM disclosed its engine switch would be entitled to $550 payments. After GM appealed this decision, it accepted a 1984 settlement that reduced its monetary obligations to $400 per holdout.[39]

Such victories led consumer activists and like-minded legal scholars to retain some faith in postsale legal remedies as ways to discipline misleading or fraudulent selling. In the right circumstances, action by consumer protection agencies, criminal fraud prosecutions, civil suits, or some combination thereof furnished a measure of justice to victims of economic deceit, and some degree of deterrence. But in the fifteen years after Kennedy's Message to Congress on consumer issues, there were enough cautionary tales to convince many leading scholars of consumerism that preventive strategies offered the best return on scarce antifraud resources.

Two large-scale studies commissioned by the Department of Justice's National Institute of Law Enforcement and Criminal Justice put the stamp of officialdom on this viewpoint. The first of these, a *Survey of Consumer Fraud Law* produced in 1978 by lawyers Jonathan Sheldon and George Zweibel, catalogued the shortcomings that had cramped retrospective fraud enforcement. Although the authors singled out class actions pressed by state attorneys general as one promising regulatory arena, they advocated greater focus on the requirement of effective "presale disclosures" and the granting of more expansive cancellation rights.[40]

The second study, *Consumer Fraud: An Empirical Perspective*, written the following year by Jane Schubert and Robert Krug, analyzed a large sample of complaint files to government consumer protection agencies. Schubert and Krug assessed the nature of complaints, patterns of how they moved through bureaucracies, and their outcomes. Most "transactions gone bad" involved low stakes and required great effort to achieve any resolution. The social scientists thus recommended efforts to restructure the framework of consumer transactions. The goal, they argued, should be to empower consumers, whether through cooling-off periods, improved standards for warranties, or requirements of more effective information disclosure. Insofar as governments focused on postsale mechanisms of redress, the most sensible option was to improve mediation services at consumer protection agencies.[41] These studies signaled a tempering of aspirations for tackling consumer fraud, a judgment that only so much was possible in the context of American justice. They offered a coda to an era of regulatory governance born amid great anticipation and concluding with pleas for trimmed sails and curtailed aspirations.

Reinvoking the Regulatory Filters of Markets

For skeptics of concentrated state power, disenchantment with antifraud policies was to be expected. In some quarters, the expansion of the antifraud state during the New Deal and post–World War II decades had always occasioned suspicion or outright antagonism, as had expanded governmental authority over other economic realms. As the impacts of statutory reforms and enforcement campaigns accumulated, antifraud regulations attracted the critical attention of political scientists, legal scholars, and economists. This social science research was part of a more general inclination to appraise the shortcomings of modern regulatory governance, and shared a common intellectual touchstone—the implications of economic self-interest for political behavior. Many scholars who took a close look at the evolution of American regulatory institutions worried that regulated businesses invested far more effort in shaping policy than the rest of society. No other constituency cared more about regulatory outcomes, nor possessed comparable resources to shape the details of regulatory statutes and engage with administrative decision-making. The technocrats charged with carrying out regulatory missions also came in for close scrutiny, because they had incentives to care more about building administrative empires or currying favor with regulated businesses than upholding broader interests. According to the academics who studied regulatory institutions, policymakers had to worry about the dual threats of regulatory capture from without and administrative inefficiency from within.

This analytical indictment emerged from every direction of the American political compass. If there was one academic text that framed the trope of regulatory capture and set the parameters of specific agency studies, it was Marver Bernstein's 1955 monograph *Regulating Business by Independent Commission*. A centrist and Princeton University political scientist, Bernstein stressed that even if powerful business interests were neither the architects of regulatory frameworks nor the puppet masters of regulatory officials, their structural advantages allowed them, over time, to bend regulatory decision-making to their liking. Drawing on extensive archival research for his 1963 monograph, *The Triumph of Conservativism*, radical historian Gabriel Kolko came to similar conclusions. Arguing that large corporations had dictated the Progressive-era creation of national regulatory agencies, Kolko charted a line of interpretation adopted by activists Ralph Nader and Mark Green from the left, and economist George Stigler and legal thinker Richard Posner from the right. The range of perspectives that raised tough questions about the regulatory performance of federal agencies gave the resulting scholarship greater force than if censure had come from just one end of the political spectrum.[42]

The voluminous Cold War–era scholarship on American economic regulation primarily examined oversight of prices, rates, and entry in specific industries, including railroads, trucking, airlines, broadcast communications, and energy. There were, however, numerous investigations of deceptive practices regulation by academics and policy analysts within regulatory institutions. These studies put forward three overlapping critiques. The first raised questions about the benefits of antifraud policies. Several scholars argued that the impulse to strike at misrepresentation generated regulatory broadsides at "trivial" aspects of modern capitalism. Efforts by the FTC to define deceptive practices and then police those boundaries came in for the harshest scrutiny. The FTC prioritized such deceptions as inaccurate characterizations of synthetic fiber content in clothing, claims of sales discounts from misleading price anchors, and promotions that included "free" items. Between 1964 and 1968, more than half of FTC cease and desist cases addressed allegations of mischaracterized textile contents or misleading claims about a product's country of origin. But few FTC enforcement actions showed that a significant proportion of consumers were influenced by such claims or viewed themselves as harmed by them. By the mid-1960s, the lack of thoughtful priority-setting had become a common concern among scholars who examined the FTC's antideception work. In 1969, both the Nader Report and the ABA Committee that reviewed the FTC excoriated the Commission on this score.[43]

Several scholars raised questions about the supposedly beneficial impact that antifraud regulation had on commercial practices and consumer behavior. These academics took note of often-toothless FTC cease and desist orders, pervasive difficulties in making criminal fraud cases stick, and overwhelmed consumer protection staffs. In addition, some studies found that the most basic tool of the antifraud state—improved disclosure to redress buyers' informational disadvantages—had grave limitations. Information provision about credit terms under the Truth in Lending Act serves as an important case in point. As state and federal officials implemented these requirements, a number of social scientists assessed business compliance and the impact of the new rules on consumer choice. Compliance improved over the course of the 1970s, partly because of low barriers to legal challenges by consumers if sellers had not supplied mandated disclosures. But mere disclosure often did not influence buying decisions. Many consumers found disclosed credit information to be confusing. Even clear understanding of credit terms did not matter much at the time of sale compared to availability of credit and perceived capacity to make payments. As one Los Angeles banker noted at the time of the Truth in Lending Act's passage, "What concerns most people is the amount they have to pay each month," regardless of the interest rate.[44]

Evaluation of information disclosure regimes in other consumer arenas raised similar cautions. In a host of contexts, social psychologists found that consumers paid minimal attention to disclosed information if they were unaccustomed to comparison shopping, or if disclosures used complex language, presented a mass of details, or did not have obvious relevance for a purchasing decision. If prospective buyers did comprehend the basic meaning of disclosures, their retention of that information proved ephemeral and rarely shaped purchasing selections.[45] Studies by legal sociologists also suggested that disclosure did little to protect the urban poor from abuses, absent robust consumer markets that furnished meaningful competition.[46]

Skepticism about the value of mandatory disclosure regimes extended to analyses of investment markets, though here the most vociferous criticisms came from conservative scholars. The typical individual investor, critics aimed to show, lavished about as much attention on detailed historical accounting data as consumers paid to complicated disclosures of credit terms. Instead, investors relied on the advice of brokers and market letters, the opinions of friends, and recent price movements. During speculative booms like that of the late 1960s, investors paid scant attention to the prospectuses and registration statements of new firms. In periods of both boom and bust, the decision to reelect corporate directors did not represent careful appraisal of performance or fidelity to corporate interests, but was rather a "meaningless ritual" in which "the chief executive officer usually dominate[d] the process" and "apathetic" investors ratified the CEO's hand-picked slate. As compared to individuals, institutional investors took far more note of mandated disclosures. But they preferred analysis of industry trends, macroeconomic forecasts, and overall market movements rather than detailed inquiry into the corporations' SEC filings.[47] Investors in interstate real-estate properties proved even less inclined to scrutinize information required by the 1968 Interstate Land Sales Full Disclosure Act, which often came in convoluted reports "that confuse[d] many potential purchasers by their complexity." High-pressure sales tactics continued to generate ample demand for sham Sun Belt developments throughout the 1970s.[48]

The second major critique of antifraud regimes highlighted their substantial direct and indirect costs. The former were the easiest to see. Someone within corporate management and the staffs of smaller businesses had to gather the information required by consumer disclosure regulations and then prepare notices, forms, and reports. Employees had to receive training on the new regulatory environment and their responsibilities to give customers correct forms and appropriate information. In sales involving the extension of credit, mandatory disclosure meant "additional time" to complete transactions, because "loan officers or credit department employees" had to sit down with customers and "explain how rates are computed and how other provisions of the [truth-in-lending] regulation affect him." This sort of "bureaucratic red tape" increased overhead expenses, which translated into higher prices for goods and services.[49] Compliance with the disclosure regime for public securities was far more costly, involving charges for external auditors, legal reviews, printing, and distribution of reports to far-flung investors. Once the SEC initiated fraud-related enforcement actions against independent auditors and law firms, moreover, liability insurance for these professionals became far more expensive, necessitating higher fees for corporate clients.[50]

The collateral consequences of consumer and investor protection efforts raised deeper reservations. Disclosure mandates erected barriers to entry for would-be newcomers. Constraints on marketing practices or capital raising strategies curbed competition. This trade-off raised sharp dilemmas for a regulatory agency such as the FTC, which encompassed two missions in profound tension. It had the responsibility to uproot the deceptive practices that constituted "unfair methods of competition." But it also had the obligation to promote robust competition, which generated cheaper prices for consumers. The SEC faced a similar conflict between combating misrepresentation and facilitating the transformation of savings into capital formation. State and local consumer protection agencies faced analogous quandaries.

For detractors of antifraud regulation, Cold War–era regulatory agencies had sacrificed vigorous competition on the altar of sanctimonious policing of commercial candor. The legal scholars Gregory Alexander and Richard Posner developed this line of argument in separate indictments of the FTC. Writing in the mid-1960s, Alexander painstakingly documented the commission's disproportionate antagonism to aggressive marketing by discounters. The firms that most eagerly embraced advertising hullabaloo hoped to drive price-conscious consumers through their doors. These same businesses were the ones that most frequently elided descriptions of a goods' place of origin, or fought to gain the notice of consumers through offers of *FREE!* gifts or bonuses, or described sales promotions in ways that exaggerated discounts. Alexander did not reject the value of FTC policing of retailing "honesty." But he stressed that in hard cases, the FTC investigators and hearing examiners who handled deceptive practices cases too often ignored the impact of their actions on competitive conditions, thereby harming consumers in the very attempt to lend them a regulatory helping hand.[51]

Posner's analysis of the FTC, which he completed while a member of the ABA's 1969 investigatory committee, was even more scathing. Then a quickly rising star in the legal academy, Posner had spent several years as a staff attorney for FTC Commissioner Philip Elman, who had developed his own critical appraisal of the agency. Like Alexander, Posner depicted most FTC cease and desist proceedings as "nitpicking" and characterized its fictitious pricing cases as "harassing discounters." His greatest complaint, however, was the systematic burden that the FTC placed on young firms seeking to develop new products or services that would furnish cheaper substitutes for established offerings, often through importation, technological invention, or organizational innovation. Hundreds of postwar businesses had to cope with FTC investigations that scrutinized their advertising claims for novel wares, often at the behest of incumbent firms looking to beat back threats to their market share and profitability. These investigations, Posner maintained, cost upstarts millions in legal fees and had a chilling effect on competition.[52]

The financial economists and legal scholars who portrayed securities regulation as misguided and ineffective emphasized a different set of ancillary harms. To be sure, the expenses associated with public offerings could shut out some businesses from the public capital markets. By the 1960s, onerous disclosure requirements for bond issues had driven half of corporate debt placements off public exchanges. And the decision after the 1961 Special Study of Securities Markets to narrow registration and disclosure exemptions made it harder for some smaller companies to attract financing. But a bigger problem was the danger that formal disclosures might themselves become misleading. As of the early 1970s, filings to the SEC still had to eschew discussions of earnings projections and market forecasting, because these estimates represented opinions rather than historical measures of performance. But sophisticated investors demanded forward-looking assessments as a basis for decision-making, and SEC filings did not furnish that analysis.[53]

The third element in the intellectual challenge to antifraud regulation involved a reconsideration of the possibility of checking commercial and financial chicanery through the workings of markets. Did consumers and investors really need a paternalistic state that compelled information disclosure and disciplined wayward firms that strayed off the path of candor, especially through administrative sanctions such as cease and desist orders? Richard Posner, for one, had more confidence in the balancing pressures of competitive marketplaces. Consumers, he insisted, were not hapless dupes. They made reasonable assessments of economic options and relied, in a world of newfangled technologies and financial arrangements, on the "advice" of "information brokers" who had expertise about specific products and services. If on occasion consumers did get taken in, they "would learn from unhappy experiences." Sellers had plentiful reasons to worry about their reputations, which prevarication and imposture would soil. Even in impersonal markets, competitors could and would police one another, responding to false advertising with publicity campaigns to "correct any misrepresentation" and call out the miscreants. For the ever more complex world of securities, the economist George Benston and the securities law professor Homer Kripke placed their faith in the reputational considerations of intermediaries such as auditors, investment bankers, and financial analysts. Mindful of long-term interests, these experts "would afford investors protection from fraudulent or misleading financial statements in the absence of government disclosure regulations."[54]

The critics of antifraud regulation recognized that the most vigilant marketplaces were still prone to misrepresentation and outright swindles. But the appropriate policy response for the dodgy seller who posed as a reputable dealer, or the intermediary who traded on his reputation, was criminal prosecution, not administrative rules and investigations. One sees in such arguments a return to the premises of nineteenth-century approaches to business fraud—reliance on the hardening impact of tough experience or the instructive guidance of *Consumer Reports* (rather than the Argus-eyed trade journal editor); meeting misleading claims with "disparaging" comparative advertising (rather than combating the product counterfeiter with advertising pleas to look for the genuine article's trademark); trusting to the good auspices of the financial analyst and auditor (rather than the august investment banker whose most important asset was his good name).

Amid the heady days of consumerism, Elizabeth Hanford and many other political elites had proclaimed that in the United States, "*caveat emptor*" was dead. At essentially the very same moment, Richard Posner had offered as a full-throated rejoinder, "long live *caveat emptor*." Posner capped off his 1969 flaying of the FTC by calling for its abolition, because the costs that it imposed exceeded whatever social benefits it conferred. He suggested that the loosening of common-law evidentiary standards to establish liability for commercial deceit had been a fundamental policy error, as had the construction of administrative processes to police those more easily demonstrated violations of truthfulness. As a result, the best option was to uproot these costly mistakes. The most strident opponents of the American disclosure regime for securities regulation adopted a similar stance toward the SEC.

This envisaged radical return to the legal premises that structured nineteenth-century American marketplaces never had much of a chance. No highly regarded politicians stepped forward with proposals to repeal the Federal Trade Commission Act, the New Deal securities statutes, or the state legislation and local ordinances that had dotted America's institutional landscape with consumer protection agencies. If prominent elected officials had made such overtures, consumer organizations and labor unions would have howled in opposition. Even so strident an advocate of unregulated competition as the economist Milton Friedman carved out exceptions for duplicity. "There is one and only one social responsibility of business," Friedman argued in his best-selling 1962 book *Capitalism and Freedom*—"to increase its profits so long as it stays within the rules of the game, which is to say, engages in open and free competition without deception or fraud."[55] Nonetheless, many of the assumptions that undergirded conservative critiques of the antifraud state increasingly shaped policymaking within it.

This shift reflected the waxing influence of economics within antifraud agencies and government more generally. Beginning in the early 1970s, American business elites pushed for greater reliance on economic analysis in regulatory decision-making. The Chamber of Commerce, Business Roundtable, and National Association of Manufacturers all viewed such analysis as a way to constrain intrusive and expensive rules on workplace and product safety, environmental impacts, and consumer protection. As the Nixon, Ford, and Carter administrations grappled with the inflationary forces set off by the Vietnam War and the 1973 oil crisis, they all asked for careful appraisals of the costs imposed by government regulations. At those agencies with antifraud missions, leaders were also confronted with the criticisms leveled by Posner, Kripke, and others. As a result of these pressures, regulatory officials moved to hire more economists, to direct resources toward offices responsible for economic research, and to consult with advisory committees that included academic economists. The experts empowered by these developments advocated strategic planning processes and the use of formal assessments of benefits and costs to structure priority setting.[56]

More rigorous engagement with economic analysis percolated up to the highest levels of antifraud agencies, especially at the national level. One can see this intellectual process at work at the FTC, where Robert Pitofsky spearheaded a reorientation of antideception strategy that reflected Posnerian empiricism and logic. Like so many other post–World War II antifraud regulators, Pitofsky was a lawyer. After serving as executive director of the 1969 ABA inquiry into the FTC, where he collaborated with Posner, he became director of the FTC's Consumer Protection Division in 1970, a position he held until 1974, when he accepted a law professorship at Georgetown University. In 1978, President Carter nominated him to serve as an FTC commissioner, with the expectation that he would bring a moderating influence to bear on consumer protection issues. Pitofsky had received a basic grounding in economics as a New York University undergraduate, and undertook a self-taught crash course in more advanced principles when he started his legal career with a practice that defended corporate clients facing antitrust suits. At Georgetown, he delved into the economic dimensions of antitrust and trade regulation and helped to shape early research agendas within the law and economics movement (an emerging group of academics who wished to bring rigorous economic analysis into legal decision-making).[57]

This perspective suffused Pitofsky's approach to policing consumer fraud. The FTC, he argued, should remain committed to curbing marketing deceptions, but only those that harmed consumers, threatened trust in the marketplace, and generated misallocation of economic resources. There should be no more piddling cases prompted by puffery or promotional razzmatazz that allowed discounters to gain a foothold in "concentrated" retail markets, and perhaps no action against deceptive marketing for the lowest-priced goods. In such cases, the commission should trust the disciplinary and educative functions of the market. Thus, Pitofsky advocated that the FTC partially return to the standard of *caveat emptor*, because consumers could spot the most obvious "exaggerations and distortions." If false claims led to purchases of the cheapest goods, consumers would learn to avoid such impositions. The marketing of major corporations that reached national audiences deserved closer scrutiny; so too did advertising that targeted vulnerable populations, such as children and the elderly.[58]

This philosophy of more restrained and targeted antifraud regulation also shaped the federal government's responses to the demonstrated weaknesses in mandatory information disclosure. Drawing on findings from social psychology and economics, regulators and legislators sought to improve the design and implementation of disclosure standards. By the mid-1970s, social scientists, officials at antifraud agencies, and legislatures had all joined a debate about how to reduce excessive costs to businesses and better tailor the content and process of information provision so that it was more useful to relevant investors and consumers. A number of policy reforms ensued, including the SEC's Rule 175 on "Forward-Looking Statements," adopted in 1979; the SEC's development of a framework for integrated corporate disclosure, proposed in 1981; and the Truth in Lending Simplification and Reform Act, which passed Congress in 1980. Each of these reforms sought to ensure provision of relevant information and to moderate administrative burdens. The "Forward-Looking

Statements" rule facilitated corporate release of earnings projections by giving corporations that made good-faith forecasts a legal safe harbor against fraud suits based on incorrect predictions. Based on a decade's worth of studies and hearings, integrated disclosure reduced information overload and cut compliance costs by eliminating duplicative filing requirements. The Truth in Lending reform lessened legal risks faced by creditors by limiting the reach of private class actions. But it also authorized the Federal Reserve to create standard forms in the hopes of improving the comprehensibility and salience of consumer credit disclosures.[59]

More self-conscious applications of cost-benefit screens did not foreclose extensions of regulatory authority. The FTC adopted its holder in due course rule in the mid-1970s, and then placed a national spotlight on predatory marketing in the funeral business, leading to a funeral price disclosure rule that overcame ferocious industry opposition to curb the most abusive rip-offs.[60] Greater respect for market dynamics, however, signaled an important turning point in the history of American fraud policing, part of a broader skepticism about regulatory authority that would drive several decades of deregulatory fervor.

Better Business Bureaus and the Fraying of Self-Regulation

Even before Ronald Reagan's electoral victory in 1980 solidified the influence of market-based predispositions in American government, the more populist dimensions of a conservative revolt against activist government had important implications for self-regulatory institutions. To appreciate this aspect of renewed American faith in unleashed capitalism, we need to return to the post–World War II endeavors of the Better Business Bureaus. Those efforts always had significant limits. But insofar as the BBBs developed working partnerships with government antifraud agencies, they fostered smoldering resentments among their more conservative members that anticipated the wider revolt against regulation.

Ongoing efforts by BBB leaders to cultivate a brokering role among government antifraud agencies, militant consumer groups, and business groups exposed an organizational fault line along geographic and generational divides. BBB officials from the South and Southwest, along with some newly appointed executives elsewhere who had corporate backgrounds, blanched at the strategy of accommodating consumerism. According to local BBB heads such as Dan Berry of Nashville, Richard McClain of Houston, Ralph Smathers of Miami, and Jim White of Phoenix, the organization's troubles resulted from not embracing the views of the business establishment and becoming too focused on racket-busting. The Sun Belt faction, characterized by one of the older guard as "the younger conservative chaps in our group," hoped to attract greater backing from business by offering full-throated critiques of both overreaching government and paternalistic consumer groups, and insisting that robust self-regulation was the only workable constraint on commercial speech. Influenced by the tide of Goldwaterism sweeping over the Sun Belt, these voices saw no reason to give any ground to consumerism.[61]

The conservatives called on the BBBs to restrict their assistance to government prosecutors. By building cozy relationships with public regulatory agencies, these leaders maintained, BBB officials had cultivated too much of a reputation as de facto policemen, compromising their relationships with the business community. James Stephens was insistent on this point. "We in Atlanta," Stephens confided to Dan Berry in a 1965 letter,

> have long ago decided that our local problems can best be handled on a local basis and without the assistance of the FTC, SEC, . . . Food and Drug Administration, or whatever. . . . We do not receive one dime from the government and don't want any of their money. By the same token, we don't want any of their publicity. We are supposed to speak for business. . . . Our conversations should be business conversations, and our files should be business files, and our information should be business information, and our reports should be business reports, and our standards should be business standards. . . . If we are to play cops and robbers, then I think we should change the misnomer we call a slogan, 'Private Enterprise In the Public's Interest,' to 'Business Supported Agencies for the Purpose of Squealing on Business.'"

For Stephens, the only appropriate stance for the Bureaus was to remain "BUSINESS SPONSORED and BUSINESS ORIENTED." This perspective meant that BBBs needed to treat their files with greater respect for confidentiality and limit use of publicity as a sanction against firms, because exposés only heightened the pressure for more regulation. Wherever possible, Dan Berry implored, the Bureaus had to "solve our problems within the Bureau family and not, in a mood of haste or despair, run to outside agencies."[62]

BBB leaders who adopted this approach committed themselves to lobbying against new consumer legislation and to recruiting businesses targeted by such initiatives. One policy arena that attracted their attention concerned proposals in many local jurisdictions to ban door-to-door selling. Several local BBBs opposed the bans, arguing that one should not "cut off an arm to cure a boil," and that self-regulation of direct selling was a more appropriate means of addressing deception within the industry. After Kenneth Barnard's retirement in 1963, the Chicago BBB went so far as to inform businesses such as Encyclopedia Britannica and Avon of their efforts, and even to suggest that the National Association of Direct Sellers might assist in convincing its members to join BBBs in their marketing territories.[63]

Throughout the late 1960s and early 1970s, the Bureau's strategic response to consumerism vacillated. In 1970, Woodrow Wirsig, who had been an editor at *Printer's Ink* before taking the reins at the New York City BBB, publicly threw down the gauntlet to the consumer movement. Speaking at a national conference on consumer affairs, Wirsig characterized activists in both government and nonprofit organizations as whipping up "an atmosphere of hysteria" and creating "costly government bureaus" on the basis of "hunch and emotion." He further insisted, like Richard Posner, that consumers were not "helpless, ignorant, constantly in need of protection." At the end of his remarks, over one hundred executives in attendance gave him "loud applause," signaling the approval of the corporate establishment.[64]

Wirsig's speech, however, prompted a series of attacks by consumer groups and governmental officials on the BBB network. New York City's Commissioner of Consumer Affairs, Bess Myerson, dismissed the local BBB as incapable of separating itself from the firms it was supposed to police, and as "protect[ing] a lot of bad guys." Ralph Nader offered an even bleaker assessment, maintaining that "most local Better Business Bureaus—our own in Washington included—have been miserable failures." The sparks between BBB leaders and consumer activists prompted several in-depth stories by journalists at national newspapers such as the *New York Times*, the *Washington Post*, and the *Wall Street Journal*, all of which raised serious questions about BBB performance, anticipating the various criticisms leveled in the Rosenthal Report. The Bureaus, which since their inception had enjoyed fawning press because of close cooperation with establishment media, had never before faced this kind of sustained scrutiny. Dissemination of the Rosenthal Report only intensified negative press.[65]

The depth of public censure put many BBB officials on the defensive, as did the Nixon administration's moves to make the FTC a more effective regulator of deceptive practices, and the burgeoning number of state and local consumer protection agencies. For a time, these trends strengthened the hand of more moderate BBB reformers. As a result, the reorganization of BBB structures, implemented in 1971 and 1972, was overseen by former St. Louis BBB manager John O'Brien and Elisha Gray, chairman of the Whirlpool Corporation, both of whom called for the organization to improve its role in consumer protection. O'Brien went so far as to bring in one of Nader's Raiders, Dean Detterman, to assist in the organizational revamp. In some local BBBs, governance boards emulated this move, appointing new leadership directly out of the consumer movement. These actions would have been inconceivable as recently as the 1960s. Thus the New York City BBB shifted its resources toward consumer outreach and instituted a much tougher screening process for potential business members, while becoming more willing to sanction wayward members through expulsion, and even to publicize such internal policing.[66]

The conservative faction, however, continued to influence key policy decisions, reflecting the country's post-1968 political shift to the right and the growing assertiveness of corporate interests devoted to the tenets of market fundamentalism. In the late 1960s, for example, a two-year nationwide BBB investigation documented a trend among Sears's appliance departments to adopt bait and switch methods. But an eventual National BBB bulletin on the inquiry—a communication produced for BBB insiders—ignored the question of whether incentive structures and sales training contributed to problematic marketing practices. Some years later, similar complaints about Sears culminated in an FTC investigation and 1976 consent decree. In the intervening years, the Chicago BBB soft-pedaled the situation with Sears whenever customers or other bureaus inquired about it, insisting that BBB policy precluded discussion of ongoing governmental investigations that had not reached a final determination.[67]

Conservatives also forced out John O'Brien within two years of his taking the helm of the new Council of BBBs, replacing him with a CBS television executive. Allied with the largest national advertisers, they won a key debate over the constitution of the National Advertising Review Board, which in the end included only ten representatives of the public interest among its fifty members. Once the NARB had begun to function, they then relied on its operation to fend off calls for more stringent regulation of advertising by both the FTC and FCC, despite complaints by consumer activists about slow process, insufficient independence from corporate America, and a dearth of outreach to increase awareness and attract more consumer participation. Self-regulation of national advertising remained firmly in the hands of the business community.[68]

Conservatives also pushed through a national policy that allowed members to display BBB affiliation on store windows and in advertisements and to create a series of formal arbitration programs. These changes facilitated business recruitment, but also threatened to exacerbate adverse selection problems, because firms that used aggressive marketing had reason to join a BBB in order to flash its seal of approval. The second initiative also furthered the goal of moving dispute resolution outside the state, extending the BBB's capacity to deflect consumer dissatisfaction.[69] A 1973 marketing brochure that the Chicago BBB sent to prospective members made this point explicit, characterizing its consumer complaint mechanism as a "safety valve" and "a shock absorber."[70] As proposals for a federal Consumer Protection Agency lost steam in the mid-1970s, advertising self-regulation settled back into a channel of business influence.

The narrative of advertising self-regulation during the Cold War era reinforces the common pattern of interaction between regulatory pressures and the relative willingness of business elites to commit resources to nongovernmental mechanisms of commercial standard-setting and policing. The degree of support for the BBBs, financial and otherwise, tended to vary directly with the degree of threat that business leaders perceived from regulatory policy. In the face of the emerging consumer movement of the 1960s and early 1970s, and the associated rise of consumer protection measures by government, the business community made a concerted attempt to revamp the Bureaus, through reorganization, increased funding, and more aggressive provision of services to consumers.

The intensifying legalism of BBB operations also underscores the susceptibility of self-regulatory mechanisms to procedural values. In the early twentieth century, the first local groups of advertising professionals that formed to police marketing practices called themselves vigilance organizations. Deep into the twentieth century, some insiders still referred to their work in terms of "vigilante" policing. But rights consciousness was not only the province of civil rights activists, women's rights advocates, or postwar consumers. Business managers demanded their right to be heard and, if necessary, appeal to a forum of their peers, when BBBs questioned their business practices. As a result, the self-regulation of commercial speech lost some of its comparative advantage, relative to the state, in flexibility and institutional agility.

The experience of the BBBs in the mid-twentieth century further suggests the possibilities of, and the barriers to, genuine bureaucratic autonomy within self-regulatory institutions. Bestowed by the Great Depression with a corps of dedicated professionals, the BBBs fashioned an uneven independence during the 1940s and 1950s, allowing them to become significant regulatory protagonists. Drawing on their expertise and taking advantage of constrained enforcement budgets at antifraud agencies, BBB officials claimed the status of quasi-lawmakers and quasi-regulatory police. If one imagines a dodgy retailer visiting a savvy lawyer in 1958 to ask about the law of commercial misrepresentation, the BBBs would likely have come up in the discussion of both relevant rules and enforcement probabilities. For a time in the early 1970s, it even looked as if BBB leaders might forge deep bonds and shared strategy with figures in the consumer movement. There was not so much conceptual ground between the midlevel BBB manager who expressed contempt for merchants "whose technique is to trade upon and exploit human ignorance and credulity, and who as an automobile 'Medicine Man' pitches his 'snake oil' by mass advertising to today's Mortimer Snerds," and the young devotees of Ralph Nader.

The opportunity to build such linkages, however, ran afoul of two unfavorable contingencies. First, the BBB leaders most amenable to such partnerships were the ones who had seen what a collapse of public confidence looked like during the 1930s, who recognized that healthy markets and public trust depended on robust regulatory infrastructures, and who had learned to work with the modern regulatory state. But that group hit retirement age just as the dilemmas posed by consumerism demanded creative answers. Second, the newer generation of officials were shaped by the rejuvenated conservatism of the Sun Belt, which viewed markets as separate from and threatened by governmental regulation. Never a monolithic entity any more than other institutions of similar complexity, the BBB network of the 1970s had to navigate a profound political shift to the right. With that shift came renewed belief in free enterprise as a product of nature and an intensified impulse to deploy self-regulation as a shock absorber of consumer complaints and a safety valve against pressures for more stringent governmental action.

✳✳✳✳

In 1979, University of Wisconsin legal scholar Stuart Macaulay published a searching appraisal of the previous decade's formal expansion of legal protections for consumers. Macaulay wanted to assess how a major law had changed the nature of commercial transactions and the day-to-day practice of law. He initially chose the 1975 Magnuson-Moss Warranty Act and, with the help of a law student, conducted about a hundred interviews with Wisconsin lawyers to inquire about its impact. After some preliminary discussions, Macaulay realized that he would have to widen his scope to include all consumer protection–related matters. So few lawyers had heard of the new statute that specific inquiries about it would yield little salient evidence. Indeed, most attorneys knew very little about any of the consumer protection laws and regulations that had tumbled out of Congress, state legislatures, and regulatory bodies in Washington, DC, and Madison. The majority of interviewees did report some experience with consumer complaints; those in larger firms had defended businesses facing investigations by consumer protection agencies. In all such controversies, the lawyers focused on securing settlements, seeking to resolve disputes in a way that would "restor[e] social relations" without anyone losing dignity. Every so often, the formal shift toward *caveat venditor* intruded on interactions between a seller and an unhappy buyer or a state regulator, nudging negotiating leverage away from the seller. Business lawyers also did their best to help clients "comply with the disclosure requirements" that had multiplied since the 1960s. But throughout Wisconsin, legal and economic culture proved resistant to consumer protection reforms. These findings prompted Macaulay to wonder if one should view "most of the individual rights created by consumer protection laws . . . as primarily exercises in symbolism." Proponents of antifraud reforms, on this reading, "gained the pretty words in the statute books and some indirect impact, but the practice of those to be regulated was affected only marginally."[71]

Given the practical constraints on the most ambitious legal articulations of *caveat venditor*, this way of framing the historical significance of mid-twentieth-century American antifraud policies has obvious appeal. One must be leery, however, of equating consequences with aspirations. One must also consider the full mosaic of antifraud policies. For all of the antifraud state's limitations, the myriad educational efforts, wide-ranging extensions of legal obligations, sprouting of antifraud bureaucracies, deepening of regulatory networks and self-regulatory institutions, unprecedented attention to the frauds that victimized the poorest Americans, fashioning of novel enforcement tools, and periodic marshaling of targeted enforcement campaigns had a collective impact that exceeded the sum of the parts.

That impact added up to fraud containment. From the first days of the New Deal through the oil shocks and stagflation of the 1970s, the American economy continued to furnish ample opportunities for commercial imposture and misdirection. But whenever the scale of deception and fraud raised major hackles, there was sufficient political will and regulatory capacity to clamp down on offenders. The worst securities fraud and most abusive business opportunity scams led to prosecutions and convictions (even if penalties sometimes struck observers as modest, given the harms inflicted). By the 1970s, such enforcement actions included mechanisms for at least partial restitution to victims.[72] Regulators eventually shut down the Holland Furnace Company, Vigilant Protective Systems, and a host of similarly abusive firms.

Furthermore, the accumulated weight of antifraud efforts left a more diffuse imprint on social norms. All the declarations about the harms caused by business fraud deepened the discourse of consumer rights. Proliferating invocations of consumers as the bearers of rights that society was bound to respect encouraged the development of self-help strategies by CEPA and Consumer Action, as well as the crusading investigations of consumer reporters such as Marvin Zindler and the willingness of trial lawyers to take a chance on fraud-related class actions.[73] The broader climate of disapproval for commercial deceit also gave those more vigorous tactics legitimacy, increasing the pressure on the businesses that encountered leaflet-distributing pickets, embarrassing profiles on the six o'clock news, or fraud-related mass litigant civil suits.

Still, there were ironies. To the extent that the mid-twentieth century antifraud state contained fraud in the short to medium term, it lessened longer-term commitment to regulatory efforts. As institutional frameworks built greater trust in economic communication, there was always the danger that investors and consumers would become less wary and that political elites would see less need for investments in fraud policing. And as policy elites emphasized from different points on the political spectrum, no regulations come without costs. The most stringent rules and toughest enforcement against marketplace deceptions curbed competition, in part by pinching back the limbs and muffling the voices of would-be entrepreneurs. That trade-off would strike the arbiters of US regulatory policy as unacceptable in the closing decades of the twentieth century, with profound implications for American thinking about the always vexing problem of business fraud.

PART V

The Market Strikes Back (1970s to 2010s)

CHAPTER TWELVE

Neoliberalism and the Rediscovery of Business Fraud

Since the 1970s, the problem of business fraud has taken a firmer hold on the American imagination. According to Google Books, the frequency of the phrases "corporate fraud" and "business fraud" in published works has doubled every ten years since 1975.[1] Growth in the number of articles that use one of these phrases in the *New York Times*, *Wall Street Journal*, *Washington Post*, and *Los Angeles Times* reflects a similar exponential curve.[2] Every year, American newspapers, magazines, and blogs produce thousands of pages about specific fraud scandals and broader patterns of intentional economic duplicity, continuing the 150-year tradition of the journalistic fraud beat. Public officials have taken heed as well, whether through periodic prosecutions under existing law, inquiries into the extent and causes of fraudulent behavior, or consideration of reform proposals. During the past four decades, dozens of congressional hearings have examined fraudulent behavior that has harmed investors, consumers, other businesses, or the wider economy. This ever more intense focus on American business fraud has been prompted by a string of major fraud scandals involving allegations of intentional deception by corporations, including many large firms, against their counterparties.

Consider the following examples, all familiar to readers of either the old-fashioned financial pages or, for more recent events, economics blogs. Beginning in the mid-1970s, the United States encountered an epidemic of telemarketing fraud. The boiler room brigades extended their stock-in-trade beyond penny stocks into real-estate investments, "useless merchandise," "unnecessary insurance," and advance-fee scams involving sweepstakes and "credit repair" services. By 1994, one accounting organization estimated annual losses from telemarketing fraud at around $16 billion; a year later the FBI pegged a sum more than twice as high.[3] During the 1980s and 1990s, systematic strategies of overbilling generated billion-dollar contracting fraud scandals in defense procurement and the Medicare and Medicaid programs.[4] From the earliest days of the internet, latter-day Peter Funks have taken advantage of the explosive growth in online commerce, creating fake firms, rigging electronic auctions, selling counterfeit goods, and peddling web-based investment scams.[5]

The most far-reaching impositions occurred within the financial industry. During the late 1980s and early 1990s, financial improprieties at Savings and Loan associations led to dozens of failures. Although there were innumerable variations on the basic themes, most of these collapses followed the basic "Smash Bang" script developed at nineteenth-century financial institutions, with a few updates to take advantage of public deposit insurance and associated regulatory oversight: Attract deposits through comparatively high interest rates. Funnel the funds into investment projects controlled by bank insiders or their cronies. If necessary, arrange for generous appraisals to satisfy regulatory requirements for underwriting. Wherever possible, extract commissions, fees, and high salaries. And then, when an economic downturn exposes the house of cards, leave shareholders and government deposit insurance programs holding the bag. The final tally of direct costs from this period's S&L scandals exceeded $150 billion (in nominal dollars), with the most persuasive assessments attributing at least one-fifth and as much as one-half of this amount to systematic control frauds.[6]

In the late 1990s and early 2000s, American securities markets were beset by new twists on the old game of pump and dump. Several of the country's largest public corporations, including Cendant, WorldCom, Tyco, Health-South, and Enron, obscured unfavorable financial results through deceptive accounting. These firms treated loans as revenue, capitalized expenses, booked current profits on the basis of aggressive projections of future earnings, and manipulated stock prices through transactions with special-purpose entities controlled by company insiders. Their ability to hide financial problems was facilitated by professional gatekeepers. Investment bankers devised complex off-balance-sheet financing vehicles that hid poor results. Accountants (in many cases, the firm of Arthur Andersen) and lawyers blessed such sleights-of-hand as meeting disclosure obligations. Financial analysts, many with undisclosed conflicts of interest because of their firms' investment positions and role as underwriters, trumpeted buy recommendations predicated on the misleading financial reports. In the worst scandals, losses to investors topped $50 billion.[7]

During the early 2000s, two wonders of the financial world, Allen Stanford and Bernard Madoff, ensnared thousands of investors in massive Ponzi schemes that reached into the billions of dollars. Scores of promoters pulled off less grandiose pyramid scams, leading one regulator to describe an era of "rampant Ponzimonium."[8] The damage from fraud in the nation's housing markets achieved even more colossal dimensions, as intentional misrepresentations became business as usual within the chain of financing home mortgages. By 2006, every link in that chain, from home appraisals and mortgage brokerage, to loan securitization and bond rating, to the use of credit default swaps, was shot through with conflicts of interest, false claims about underlying assets and creditworthiness, and duplicitous marketing. At the end of the chain, investment banks and hedge funds engaged in complex manipulation of derivatives markets. Direct losses attributable to these misrepresentations and frauds ran into the hundreds of billions of dollars, implicating almost every large American bank and bringing down Lehman Brothers, Countrywide Financial, Washington Mutual, and a slew of other nonbank lenders. These failures placed severe stress on the banking system and triggered a global downturn that threw millions of people out of work and destroyed several trillion dollars of household wealth in the United States alone. Then, in the aftermath of the collapse, financial firms engaged in pervasive misrepresentations and outright lies about legal titles to properties in order to streamline foreclosures against nonpaying debtors.[9]

The enormity of these post-1980 scandals casts a different light on the business frauds of the preceding half-century, as well as the regulatory efforts to constrain them. From the mid-1930s into the 1980s, the most bald-faced consumer cheats were undertaken by small players operating on the margins of the economy, while the most substantial stock and commodities frauds involved obscure penny stocks or marginal companies. The worst frauds during the Cold War era, such as the Holland Furnace Company marketing scams or the market manipulations on the American Stock Exchange by the Re stockbrokerage firm, rarely inflicted losses reaching beyond the tens of millions (in inflation-adjusted current dollars). The very worst of the fraudulent business failures of the early 1970s, such as Equity Funding, cost investors around $150 million (or roughly $1.5 billion in 2015 dollars, calculated as an equivalent share of the overall economy). Over the past four decades, the most consequential fraud episodes have attained a much grander scale and scope, imposing direct costs an order of magnitude greater than those of the mid-twentieth century, and far more frequently embroiling large-scale corporations, including the country's biggest financial institutions.

With these business frauds being of such recent vintage, historians have yet to spill much ink about them. Within the historical guild, most scholars shy away from analysis of events until at least a generation or two has passed. As a result, few fine-grained historical case studies have appeared that would facilitate broader causal synthesis. But journalists, economic sociologists, political scientists, and legal scholars have been far less reticent, offering several assessments of more recent fraud episodes. Their accounts offer helpful building blocks for an overarching explanation of this dramatic inflection point, which must engage with how post-1975 deregulation widened the opportunities for large-scale business frauds. But any narrative must also take note of regulatory countercurrents, as the past four decades have also included significant antifraud initiatives, again both public and private. This chapter and book conclude with reflections on the contingent posture of post-2008 antifraud regulation and the implications of history for the elected officials, bureaucrats, and judges who confront the always-complex problem of marketplace masquerades.

The Many Faces of Deregulation

The occurrence of gigantic American business frauds after 1975 depended in part on structural shifts in modern capitalism. Rapid growth in telemarketing fraud was made possible by technological breakthroughs that drove down the costs of mass marketing over the phone lines. Similarly, the emergence of the internet as a platform for communication and commerce proved a godsend to con artists and scamsters. Anonymity within the online world complicated reputational checks; its many routes for bypassing legal borders muddled jurisdictional authority. The most extensive investment frauds involved complicated financial instruments that came into existence only because dramatic advances in computing power facilitated the underlying mathematical modeling. Processes of globalization constituted still another structural precondition for the largest financial frauds. The geographic expansion of integrated financial markets allowed intermediaries to sell more easily across oceans, increasing the potential for asymmetries of information. Steady growth in economic inequality since the early 1970s was an additional contributing factor. Stagnating incomes led to soaring household debt among less well-off Americans, opening up paths for debt-related frauds.

Demographic changes represent yet another explanatory variable. The rapid graying of America increased the size of a social group that has always served as a prime target for investment swindles and high-pressure selling. Con artists and fraudulent businesses sought out elderly Americans for the same reason that thieves seek out neighborhood financial institutions. The "nest eggs" of retired persons, like bank vaults, were where one could count on finding ready money, comprising roughly half of all US financial assets in 2000. This segment of the population also had time to answer phone calls or knocks at their doors, and those who were lonely tended to give sales personnel ample opportunity to make a pitch. Cognitive deficits associated with aging only heightened the appeal of steering deceptive marketing in this direction. Even when elderly Americans turned out not to be easy marks, those who took the bait had strong reasons to refrain from later voicing complaints. Defrauded senior citizens often worried about how their children might react to the news, which raised the specter of lost "independence through guardianship or nursing home placement." As a result, surveys found Americans over age sixty-five as much as three times as likely to be fraud victims as other adults, with vulnerability spiking further over age seventy-five.[10]

The most common theme running through accounts of large-scale American business frauds since 1975, however, has been the corrosive impact of deregulation, often linked to the insistent lobbying of firms and industry groups who pleaded for regulatory relief during the three decades that stretched from Jimmy Carter's election into the George W. Bush administration.[11] In popular discourse and political rhetoric, "deregulation" often refers to actions that curb governmental restraints on the maneuverability of firms. But the term requires careful parsing, because policymakers can take many different steps that relax regulatory fetters. This attention to detail is especially important in explaining post-1975 American business fraud. Different aspects of the more general deregulatory impulse have mattered more in encouraging some types of systematic corporate deception than others.

The most thoroughgoing form of deregulation uproots regulatory frameworks for specific industries, either by abolishing regulatory agencies or breaking down market partitions. This type of deregulatory policy, such as the repeal of the structures overseeing routes and rates for passenger airlines, railroads, and long-distance trucking that occurred during the Carter administration, played at least an indirect role in some fraud episodes. The removal of entry and pricing regulations over long-distance telephone rates and telephone equipment in the 1980s and 1990s, for example, facilitated the rapid expansion of firms such as WorldCom, whose aggressive pursuit of market share and short-term stock price appreciation led to deceptive accounting practices.[12] Similarly, the replacement of rigid energy pricing regulation with futures trading platforms gave Enron an opening to engage in the rigging of California energy spot markets, the sort of market manipulation that New Deal financial regulation had outlawed for stock and bond markets.[13]

Reconfigurations of rules structuring markets also sometimes encourage fraud outbreaks, as with the Savings and Loan crisis of the 1980s and early 1990s and the mortgage financing debacle of the mid-2000s. In the first of these episodes, persistent inflation during the 1970s weakened the financial position of S&Ls, which were locked in to long-term, low-rate mortgages. Congress responded in 1982 by easing previous limits on S&Ls' capacity to attract brokered deposits with aggressive interest rates, expanding their investment options to include commercial real-estate and business loans, and removing the requirement that Savings and Loans have at least four hundred shareholders. All of these changes contributed to the rapid expansion of speculative real-estate developments and fraudulent financing schemes.[14]

The subprime mortgage fiasco had important roots in several deregulatory statutes and administrative reforms. The former included the 1995 Private Securities Litigation Reform Act (PSLRA), the Graham-Leach-Bliley Act of 1999, and the 2000 Commodity Futures Modernization Act (CFMA). The PSLRA raised procedural and evidentiary hurdles associated with private securities fraud lawsuits against third parties such as accounting firms. Graham-Leach-Bliley repealed the New Deal prohibition on integrating the operations of commercial and investment banks. After 1999, the largest financial institutions could draw on commercial banking arms for capital, expanding their capacity to create and distribute mortgage-backed securities, as well as to finance non-bank lenders who supplied loans to securitize. This ready access to financing increased the supply of mortgage bonds and related derivatives, widening opportunities for deceptive practices in the debt markets. The CFMA exempted most over-the-counter derivatives from federal regulation, which left the sausage-making of securitization and credit default swaps in the shadows, and so enabled falsification and manipulation. A crucial deregulatory action that eased the path to "liars' loans" (mortgages predicated on false claims about borrower incomes) occurred in 1997, when the Office of Thrift Supervision replaced its underwriting standards for residential mortgages with unenforceable "guidelines."[15]

More subtle dimensions of American deregulation also promoted the proliferation of late twentieth-century business fraud. The impulse to loosen regulatory burdens often operated not so much through wholesale reconstruction of regulatory rules and institutions, but rather budget cuts or unwillingness to increase agency resources in the face of expanding market activity; appointment of officials committed to more cooperative relations with regulated businesses; and expanded delegation of fraud monitoring to private parties, including regulated entities themselves and third parties such as ratings agencies. These adjustments had dramatic impacts on antifraud enforcement.

Insufficient investment in policing played a central role in almost every major post-1975 fraud episode. The schemes undertaken by hundreds of S&L executives in the 1980s and early 1990s all depended on lax oversight by underfunded and overworked bank examiners.[16] Contractors who defrauded federal defense procurement and healthcare programs calculated that auditing mechanisms would not be able to keep up with sophisticated strategies to maximize billing.[17] At the SEC, budget cuts in the 1990s compromised its capacity to identify the accounting frauds that emerged amid the dot-com boom.[18]

During the George W. Bush administration, the FBI shifted scores of field investigators with a background in fraud cases to join the War on Terror.[19] Over those same years, Alan Greenspan's Federal Reserve declined to use its authority to crack down on deceptive tactics by mortgage brokers and lenders.[20]

The point here is not that every American antifraud professional looked the other way. Harry Markopolos, a midlevel securities executive in Boston, amassed evidence that Bernard Madoff was running a sophisticated Ponzi scheme as early as 1999, sharing his findings on several occasions with SEC officials and the New York State attorney general's office. At least two SEC staffers encouraged him to continue his research and statistical analysis. At Enron, internal auditor Sherron Watkins informed her superiors about indefensible inflation of earnings and obscuring of losses through the use of special-purpose entities and deceptive internal financial reports. Within the Federal Reserve, board member Edward Gramlich sounded alarms about lax oversight of the mortgage markets in 2000. His fears were echoed by a 2004 report by the FBI's mortgage fraud unit, which detailed widespread misrepresentations and outright duplicity. And the head of the Commodity Futures Trading Commission (CFTC), Brooksley Born, recognized the dangers lurking in unregulated derivatives such as credit default swaps and spearheaded an effort to regulate them in 2000.[21]

Such cautions, however, found unreceptive audiences among higher-level regulatory officials, prosecutors, and the most influential legislators. At large financial institutions, internal whistleblowers who raised concerns about mortgage fraud before 2008 were either stonewalled by management or fired.[22] In some instances, such as the Madoff case, this official skepticism reflected disinclination to take action against a well-connected member of the financial elite. In addition, the shift toward deregulatory premises in American policy-making reduced the salience of investor and consumer protection as officials sought to balance conflicting policy goals—at least until the economic ramifications of a specific kind of fraud became too obvious to ignore. Thus, the CFTC's attempt to regulate credit default swaps generated a firestorm of opposition from the financial industry, the Federal Reserve, Treasury Secretary Robert Rubin, and powerful members of Congress from both parties.[23] Attempts in 2000 and 2001 by Sheila Bair, then head of the Federal Deposit Insurance Corporation (FDIC), to create a voluntary set of mortgage underwriting standards were undermined by Federal Reserve officials.[24] Legislative efforts in both Georgia and New Jersey to tighten the regulation of mortgage lending in the early 2000s prompted furious objections from Wall Street powerbrokers and Washington regulators. After these two states made the securitizers of mortgage loans liable for damages if the underlying debts resulted from fraudulent transactions, ratings agencies refused to assess securitizations that included loans from New Jersey or Georgia, leading legislators to repeal key elements of their reforms. Federal banking regulators also moved to exempt federally chartered financial institutions from state oversight of mortgage practices.[25] At moments like these, the policy decisions that facilitated new avenues for fraud were refusals to impose new regulations, rather than repeal of long-existing rules or atrophy of hard-nosed enforcement.

One needs to place the evolving priorities of so many antifraud officials in the context of resurgent American antistatism. Throughout the twentieth century, conservative political thinkers had never lost their skepticism of onerous regulation, even as the consolidation of New Deal institutions marginalized this viewpoint. Antagonism toward heavy-handed, intrusive economic regulation regained some credence from the academic critiques of the regulatory state put forward by Marver Bernstein, Gabriel Kolko, George Stigler, and Richard Posner, as well as scores of additional studies that built on their premises. By the time of the Carter administration, expectations that regulatory agencies would bog down in bureaucratic morass had seeped into conventional wisdom. Social scientists across the political spectrum tended to portray those agencies as favoring big business at the expense of smaller competitors and consumers, whether by design, through continuous lobbying by corporate interests, or because officials came to identify with the firms they regulated.[26]

Macroeconomic developments intensified the appeal of these critiques, alongside companion proposals for formal deregulation. The persistent inflation caused by Vietnam War spending and Middle East oil shocks heightened concern about regulatory costs. With consumer prices rising 8 percent and then 15 percent a year in the 1970s, it became easier to argue that government officials could best look out for consumers by reducing regulatory burdens on corporations, because the latter responded to new rules by raising prices. Technological developments in some fields, such as telecommunications and banking, made existing regulatory frameworks seem like barriers to rapid adoption of efficiency-enhancing innovations in digital data services, cellular networks, financial data processing, and automatic teller machines. By the 1990s, the winds of globalization, fostered by global trading frameworks that reduced tariffs and nontariff trade barriers, also appeared in arguments for loosening up regulatory constraints. Unless America removed regulatory fetters, the argument ran, US firms would continue to lose out to less regulated competitors, whether in emerging markets or to longstanding rivals such as London's financial markets.[27]

Permeating these arguments was a deepening faith in the pervasiveness of economic rationality and the transformative power of markets.[28] Building on the arguments of George Stigler and Richard Posner, critics of restrictive regulation beseeched policymakers to reconsider how individuals made economic decisions and how markets adapted to problems such as deception. Most economic actors could look out for their own long-range interests. Absent regulatory mandates, companies would still disclose relevant financial data to lower their capital costs. Corporate executives would safeguard their good names by insisting upon trustworthy internal accounting, just as retailers would stand by promises in order to cultivate goodwill. For similar reasons, auditors, underwriters, and legal counsel would take care to sustain their reputations.

To the extent that fraudulent behavior intruded into marketplaces, critics of aggressive antifraud regulations adopted a Schumpeterian perspective, arguing that market discipline and entrepreneurial innovation offered the best means of addressing such problems. If firms misled investors or customers, any immediate gains would be counterbalanced by reputational consequences, especially in the case of settled businesses that had no intention of emulating the "fly-by-night" crowd. Over the long term, one could count on "informational intermediaries" to guide economic actors in assessing the trustworthiness of counterparties. This set of ideas, then, incorporated key dimensions of the earlier legal framework of *caveat emptor*. Adherents of this view also stressed the significance of long-term structural changes in American financial markets. By the 1980s, most purchasers of financial assets were not individuals, but rather mutual funds, pension funds, insurance companies, and hedge funds. Managers at these organizations presumably had the education, training, and moxie to look out for themselves, as well as the interests of the investors, workers, and policyholders whose capital they controlled.[29]

Policy elites did not always broadcast these understandings, beliefs, and more inchoate attitudes about business fraud. Indeed, public rhetoric sometimes masked private belief, which seems to have been the case for Alan Greenspan, the powerful member and then Chair of the Federal Reserve Board who served from 1987 to 2006. In his 2007 memoir, written as concerns about mortgage fraud were beginning to crest, Greenspan described the "rooting out of fraud" as "an area in which more rather than less government involvement is needed." Deceit, he proclaimed, was "the bane of the market system," a "destroyer of the market process itself because market participants need to rely on the veracity of other market participants." Accordingly, he advocated "greatly stepping up enforcement of anti-fraud and anti-racketeering laws." In private during the late 1990s and early 2000s, Greenspan seems to have sung a different tune. According to journalist Joe Nocera and former regulator Michael Greenberger, the Fed chair made clear in discussions about banking deregulation that "he didn't believe that fraud was something that needed to be enforced or was something that regulators should worry about," because "the market will figure it out and take care of the fraudsters."[30]

On occasion decision-makers did bring such thinking more fully into view. Federal Circuit Court Judge Edith Jones demonstrated how these assumptions could shape judicial reasoning in a 1997 securities fraud class action involving alleged misrepresentations by a Texas used-car-lot chain that focused on high-risk customers. As a partial justification for the court's decision to throw out this suit, which investors had brought against the corporation and its auditors, Coopers & Lybrand, Judge Jones found that the plaintiffs had not demonstrated the accounting firm's "motive" for certifying the adequacy of financial reports that they allegedly knew to be misleading. "Accounting firms," Jones conceded, "like all rational economic actors[,] seek to maximize their profits." But because "an accountant's greatest asset is its reputation for honesty," it was "extremely unlikely that Coopers & Lybrand was willing to put its professional reputation on the line by conducting fraudulent auditing work." For Jones, the legal default was that powerful economic players would not risk reputational capital.[31]

Entrepreneurial Innovation and Business Fraud in Greenspan's America

The tilting of regulatory discretion toward permissiveness after 1980, even in the face of credible evidence of far-reaching intentional deception, underscores the importance of more diffuse norms and cognitive defaults as shapers of business environments. At the height of America's recent age of deregulation, politicians and policymakers lionized risk-taking, innovation, short-term monetary incentives, and market discipline as the most desirable features of modern economic life. Such ideals, which also received a thorough airing in business schools and managerial discourse, seemed like a much-needed tonic for shaking off 1970s stagnation and meeting the stiff challenges of European and Japanese competition.[32]

Over the 1980s and 1990s, these shifts in public values encouraged aggressiveness among business executives. So did bold takeover campaigns by corporate raiders such as Michael Milken and Carl Icahn, who threatened sleepy corporations with leveraged buyouts. Investors channeled money and the business press directed plaudits toward brash, hard-headed managers. Both groups also advocated restructuring executive compensation to "align" the interests of managers with shareholders, whether through bonuses or stock options. Such compensation schemes spread rapidly in the 1990s, justified as ways to maximize shareholder value. Amid the resulting unforgiving, "hyper-competitive" environment, upper-level managers could more easily rationalize sharp business practices; those executives confronted insistent expectations from institutional investors for short-term stock performance. Executives, in turn, pressured middle managers to achieve ever more ambitious quarterly production goals and sales quotas. As one business ethics consultant summarized the general orientation of corporate America in the early 1990s, "The message out there is, Reaching objectives is what matters and how you get there isn't that important." By the late 1990s, "rank and yank" became a standard technique of assessing managerial performance at both brash new corporations such as Enron and many companies with a much older pedigree, such as General Electric. Managers with the best rankings received promotions and enviable remuneration; those in the middle received minimal raises and goads to improve; those at the bottom found themselves looking for new jobs. This approach to managerial evaluation generated strong incentives to shade internal financial statements, with some confidential surveys indicating that as many as one-third of corporate managers had intentionally falsified reports.[33]

In many of the biggest instances of corporate accounting manipulations of the late 1990s and early 2000s, midlevel managers and internal accountants alleged far more "coercive" pressure to assist in systematic deception. At companies such as WorldCom, Enron, Sunbeam, and HealthSouth, chief executive officers, chief financial officers, and other high-level executives badgered subordinates to deliver reports that would meet market expectations. At Health-South, according to an eventual federal criminal complaint, CEO Richard Scrushy and CFO Michael Martin set targets for earnings per share and then instructed internal accountants to find a way to meet the numbers. The resulting conclaves, referred to as gatherings of "the family," focused on how to fill the "holes" in the corporation's earnings with sufficient "dirt," by which prosecutors alleged they meant modes of inflating revenues.[34]

An analogous mindset filtered into the organizational culture of private gatekeepers such as accounting firms, investment analysts, ratings agencies, and law firms. These providers of business services came to stress profitability themselves, which eroded dedication to professional responsibility. Resulting conflicts of interest undermined commitments to transparency and investor protection.[35] The weakening of legal constraints and social norms against deceit unleashed a "Gresham's dynamic" in American financial markets: that is, duplicitous business practices drove out less ruthless approaches, in some contexts even fostering business cultures that normalized criminal behavior. The mantra of shareholder value, measured in terms of quarterly financial results, pushed the sensibilities of the used-car lot into corporate boardrooms and cubicles, the offices of white-shoe law firms, and the workplaces of auditors.[36]

Throughout the early twenty-first-century chain of American debt financing, sharp competition led thousands of businesses down this path. Real-estate agents and appraisers, mortgage brokers, loan underwriters, and analysts at credit rating agencies all grasped that if they balked at the prevailing strategies for feeding the maw of debt securitizers, they risked lost business, disapproving peers, and angry bosses. Real-estate agents and mortgage brokers who did not tout liars' loans and steer low-income Americans into abusive loan products gave juicy commissions away to their competitors. Appraisers who balked at signing off on inflated property-value estimates could look forward to lonely afternoons in their offices. Undertrained and understaffed employees at third-party loan-quality assessors learned how to say yes, and say it quickly, or found themselves holding pink slips. Within investment banks that oversaw the sausage-making of securitized debt instruments and the ratings agencies that assessed their riskiness, decision-makers contended with similar pressures. Investors had come to expect investment returns that only high volume could provide, and high volume required minimal regard for candor about the underlying quality of debt. Ratings agencies complied with demands that they certify collateralized mortgage instruments as investment-grade, even if they contained all manner of "trash" and "garbage." They knew that refusals meant a loss of extremely profitable business. As the CEO of Citigroup, Charles Prince, described the imperative of matching the business practices prevalent in the financial industry, "as long as the music is playing, you have to get up and dance."[37]

The central rationale for deregulation was to spur technological, organizational, and financial entrepreneurship, to unleash the creative energies of individuals and firms. But the longer trajectory of US business and legal history demonstrates enduring links between far-reaching commercial innovation—Joseph Schumpeter's process of creative destruction—and fraud. Fraudulent business practices and investment schemes have always clustered in sectors at the frontiers of economic change. This was so for Western real-estate development, railroad-building, and mail-order marketing in the nineteenth century; for early twentieth-century ventures in radio, aviation, and mutual stock funds; for mid-twentieth-century home improvement companies and franchising schemes. Consumers and investors confront significant asymmetries of information on the entrepreneurial margin, while the latter often prove less skeptical about dubious representations, because new technologies, marketing approaches, and organizational strategies encourage visions of killer capital gains. The disorder unleashed by transformative innovations, economist Paul Krugman noted in reflecting on the implications of Enron's collapse, "creates the kind of confusion in which scams flourish. How do you know whether a company has really found a highly profitable new-economy niche or is just faking it?" Whenever a cycle of creative destruction unleashes a speculative boom, the temptation to engage in profitable misrepresentation spreads, as does susceptibility to overconfident estimations of investment prospects by promoters and investors. When optimistic financial markets lead "the public [to] believe in magic," Krugman observed, "it's springtime for charlatans."[38]

Formal rules and informal norms, moreover, tend to be less clear in sectors undergoing entrepreneurial disruption, which makes it easier for economic actors to embrace strategies that strike counterparties and other observers as deceptive. Novel economic situations, such as nineteenth-century mail-order commerce, often lack established moral and legal anchors. Such circumstances amplify the incentives to take advantage of information asymmetries, while offering individuals ample ground to argue, to themselves and to others, that they did not transgress any established prohibitions. Indeed, research in cognitive psychology suggests that creative individuals—the sort likely to be at the forefront of entrepreneurial innovation—are more adept at rationalizing self-dealing and forms of commercial dishonesty, of "com[ing] up with good stories that help . . . justify . . . selfish interests," and "develop[ing] original paths around rules, all the while allowing" individuals to "reinterpret information in a self-serving way."[39] Insofar as innovation leads to newfangled financial instruments or unprecedented accounting questions, it also fosters ways to hide unanticipated problems behind a façade of hard-to-decipher accounting.

Some of the larger fraud episodes in the late twentieth and early twenty-first centuries fit this enduring historical pattern. The cluster of Medicare and Medicaid reimbursement scandals turned, in part, on the complex question of how to assign standardized payment codes to hospital treatments. On the margin, should back-office staff characterize services rendered to a patient with a bleeding ulcer as Diagnostic Related Group (DRG) 155, "Bleeding Ulcer," or DRG 154, "Bleeding Ulcer with Complications," the latter of which triggered higher payment from the government? During the 1990s, private hospital chains and many nonprofit healthcare providers answered that question by training billing staffs in "upcoding," the healthcare analogue of upselling. Instead of jawboning customers into purchasing pricier models, the idea was to find justifications for moving medical treatments into more expensive accounting categories, as by making sure that ulcer patients received nutritional workups.[40]

At Enron, executives embraced the goal of transforming a one-time energy pipeline company into a financial-services juggernaut dedicated to the inven-

tion of new derivatives contracts, energy market platforms, and modes of organizing business units. Enron's leaders touted the advantages of pursuing large-
scale projects and managing the resulting risks through complicated hedging
strategies. This invocation of entrepreneurial risk-taking, in combination with
"rank and yank" employee performance reviews, created strong incentives for
misleading depictions of business results, as well as manipulation of the new
energy markets. The labyrinthine nature of so many Enron activities and financial products facilitated these misrepresentations, as did the optimism fostered by internal breast-beating, years of outsized stock performance, and ac-
colades from the business press.[41]

The biggest business frauds of the post-1980 period depended on the opac-
ity that has so often accompanied the most abstruse financial innovations. Rot-
tenness in the chain of debt securitization depended on the complexity of collateralized debt obligations and credit default swaps. In the early 2000s,
financial engineers found even more intricate ways to construct securities out
of other financial assets, extending the risk-management principles of portfolio diversification. Investment bankers started with mortgage-backed securities (MBS), assets backed by scores of mortgages. From the 1960s through the
1980s, the MBS market was limited to securities marketed by the Federal National Mortgage Association (Fannie Mae) and the Federal Home Loan Mortgage Corporation (Freddie Mac), federal agencies that packaged loans meeting
strict government underwriting standards. During the 1980s and 1990s, Wall
Street bankers saw an opportunity to emulate this approach first with jumbo
mortgages, whose higher loan amounts made them ineligible for bundling by
Fannie Mae or Freddie Mac, and later with higher-risk subprime mortgages, as
well as car loans, credit-card balances, and commercial loans. Securitizers purchased pools of mortgages or other forms of debt and sliced them into different tranches, which possessed varying degrees of risk. The first tranche would
receive the initial slice of payments from the overall pool; the last would receive the very last payments, and so had the highest risk.

Once these debt-backed securities gained significant traction in the financial markets, some underwriters realized that they could extend this approach
by creating a new type of security, called a collateralized debt obligation
(CDO). This financial instrument would be made up of a given tranche from
many different collateralized obligations of a given type of debt. Some financial
alchemists went yet one step further, creating CDOs out of a pool of underlying CDOs. Others created credit default swaps, which gave CDO investors the
opportunity to hedge their positions through premium payments linked to estimations of default risk, and speculators a means of shorting a given debt
market. As soon as credit default swaps became commonplace, investment

banks came up with synthetic CDOs built out of pools of credit default swaps.[42] One insider described the process of assessing the quality of a plain vanilla CDO as akin to "taking 10 different vegetables and pureeing them in a food processor until you have something close to soup. Ask someone to identify the ingredients but don't let him taste it—make him rely strictly on his sense of sight. Your concoction is sure to make him wonder what's inside."[43] Each level of additional securitization further muddled the soup.

Even sophisticated American investors had great difficulty in scrutinizing the resulting financial stews. As a result, they tended to rely on the judgments of ratings agencies, which investment banks paid to assess the risk associated with these complex financial instruments. Despite the rickety foundations of underlying mortgages, car loans, or other debts, Moody's, Standard and Poor's, and Fitch Ratings all treated the upper tranches of synthetic CDOs as gilt-edged investments, reasoning that diversification and overcollateralization provided safety. They accordingly furnished them with AAA ratings, equivalent to the seals of approval given to the least risky corporations and sovereigns with unimpeachable credit. This rating made the complicated instruments eligible for the portfolios of insurance companies, pension funds, and other institutional investors that were prohibited from buying risky assets. Such analytical snake oil was facilitated by the novelty of collateralized debt and loan obligations, which posed new questions about how to assess their riskiness. Analysts at ratings agencies based their risk models on historical payment data that went back only to the late 1980s, when the market for them became sizable. That choice absolved them from reckoning with the possibility of a nationwide downturn in property values, something that had not occurred since the 1930s.[44]

Wall Street received a signal about the vulnerabilities of experienced corporate investors in evaluating complex structured-debt vehicles during the early 1990s, as a result of fraud allegations leveled against Bankers Trust by Gibson Greetings, Inc. and Procter & Gamble. Brokers at Bankers Trust convinced senior executives at both companies to enter into interest-rate swaps that they did not understand, leading Bankers Trust employees to joke about how they were taking advantage of their counterparties.[45] The far more convoluted structures of CDOs multiplied openings for sharp dealing, as demonstrated by the Abacus affair at Goldman Sachs. At the height of the real-estate bubble in 2007, a Goldman Sachs client, the Paulson hedge fund, wanted to short the subprime market, a strategy that Goldman was also employing. Goldman traders obliged by allowing Paulson to select several mortgage-backed securities with weak assets as the basis for a specific synthetic CDO in a class of financial instruments that the investment bank had dubbed Abacus. Goldman then sold the financial instrument to two European banks without disclosing Paulson's participation in the selection process—it instead emphasized the role of a third party that specialized in this work—and helped Paulson purchase credit-default swaps against the new security. This arrangement cost the banks nearly $1 billion, with Paulson profiting by a similar amount.[46]

Such predatory conduct recalls the tactics of Gilded Age promoters of fake companies and blind stock pools, or 1960s inner-city retailers who sold shoddy merchandise on credit before transferring debts to confederate finance companies. The fabulous bonuses available to wizards of the modern debt-trading desks encouraged this sort of behavior. But it is hard to see how such practices could have become standard operating procedure within Wall Street's loftiest firms without a quarter-century's worth of public veneration for imaginative financial invention. If the inventors of CDOs and synthetic CDOs, the analysts who rated them as AAA, or the salesmen who peddled them harbored any doubts about the propriety of their daily work, they could console themselves with reflections on the capacity of financial innovation to tame risk and sustain America's competitive position in the global economy.

POCKETS OF REGULATORY ACTION

Through several channels, then, neoliberal preferences to constrain government regulation encouraged businesses, including prominent corporations, to take greater liberties with marketing practices and financial reporting. But in spite of the dominant tendency toward deregulation and faith in unrestrained innovation, the period after 1975 also included moments of heightened regulatory stringency. These episodes often followed close on the heels of fraud scandals that garnered the attention of journalists, consumer groups, business elites, and governmental officials. Amid the moves toward regulatory disengagement, there were sporadic efforts to pin back opportunities for overbilling, phony accounting, and other forms of commercial or financial deceit.

One such regulatory counterstrike sought to root out government contracting fraud in defense procurement and healthcare reimbursement. Stung by revelations of massive overcharging by defense contractors and confronting hundred-billion-dollar annual deficits resulting from Reagan administration tax cuts, Congress enacted the Federal False Claims Act in 1986. Much like the Civil War–era statute on which it was based, the False Claims Act provided a mechanism for whistleblowers to bring fraudulent billing to light through private lawsuits. Ongoing post-Reagan budget deficits also heightened congressional concern about "waste, fraud, and abuse" in federal spending, which

prompted tighter regulatory oversight and expanded investigative and prosecutorial capacity in the Departments of Defense, Health and Human Services,
and Justice.[47]

A parallel burst of antifraud regulation occurred in response to the S&L
crisis. In this case, elected officials viewed tough regulatory action as vital because of potential costs to the United States Treasury resulting from public
deposit insurance. In 1989, President George H. W. Bush signed the Financial
Institutions Reform, Recovery, and Enforcement Act (FIRREA) into law. FIR-
REA created a new regulatory overseer of Savings and Loans, the Office of
Thrift Supervision, gave that agency authority to remove S&L officers and directors for malfeasance, and established new sanctions for false financial reports. It also increased civil and criminal penalties for the insider looting that
had driven so many thrifts into financial difficulties, created mechanisms for
disgorgement of assets illegally obtained by bank executives, and tightened
standards for loan-related appraisals of real estate. In addition, the S&L crisis
was one rationale for the statutory establishment of a Federal Sentencing Commission. Among other tasks, Congress charged the Commission with devising
formal sentencing parameters in cases involving white-collar crime, so that
individuals and organizations convicted of fraud and other forms of financial
malfeasance would not so readily avoid hefty fines and/or jail time. During the
late 1980s and early 1990s, federal agencies coordinated thousands of S&L-
related criminal investigations, which culminated in over one thousand felony
convictions. Mirroring the SEC's moves in the 1970s against gatekeepers who
abetted financial frauds, the FDIC also went after prominent accounting and
law firms that provided auditing and legal services to failed S&Ls, seeking
monetary recompense for their "breach of fiduciary duty and negligence." Settlements resulting from these cases reached as high as $400 million.[48]

The dot-com era's corruptions involving financial analysts and accounting
frauds generated still another intense round of antifraud policymaking. One
important locus of action occurred in New York State, where Attorney General
Eliot Spitzer directed investigations into Wall Street conflicts of interest. The
inquiry uncovered emails in which financial analysts described the high-flying
internet stocks that they publicly touted (and which brought their investment
banks lucrative underwriting fees) as "crap" and "dogs." These revelations led
to a global settlement with several large brokerages and investment banks,
which compelled them to pay more than $1 billion in fines, change compensa-
tion practices, and disclose financial interests linked to recommended stocks.[49]

That same year, Congress passed the Sarbanes-Oxley Act, which tightened
standards for corporate accounting, created a new oversight board for financial
reporting, prohibited auditing firms from undertaking consulting work that

created conflicts of interest, and mandated the medium-term rotation of external corporate auditors. In addition, the legislation delegated new regulatory responsibilities to corporate officials, requiring corporate attorneys to report instances of false accounts or other securities frauds, and mandating that corporate executives certify the truthfulness of financial reports. According to several leading legal scholars and economists, these new rules and monitoring structures improved the quality of internal and external auditing, as well as corporate financial reporting. Once large corporations implemented adjustments to internal audit systems, moreover, initial complaints about compliance costs dissipated.[50]

The most ambitious spurt of antifraud regulation occurred in the wake of the 2008 global financial crisis, centered on the Dodd-Frank Act of 2010. This mammoth statute sought to make the financial system more stable and reduce the risk of massive public bailouts for imperiled financial institutions. It also targeted the sort of deceptive marketing and fraudulent behavior that had helped to cause the 2008 crisis. Dodd-Frank authorized a well-funded, powerful new Consumer Financial Protection Bureau (CFPB), following the blueprint of then Harvard law professor Elizabeth Warren, who first proposed such an agency in 2007. Located in the Federal Reserve, the CFPB had a single director rather than the more cumbersome arrangement of multiple commissioners, obtained funding from the Fed independent of annual congressional appropriations, and received a broad mandate to combat deceptive practices in consumer and residential lending. Dodd-Frank also established new disclosure standards for mortgage lending and loan securitization, tightened oversight of debt ratings agencies, and required that corporations adopt mechanisms to claw back incentive-based executive compensation based on false financial results.[51]

Two additional overlapping antifraud initiatives have occupied elected officials and national regulators in the late twentieth and early twenty-first centuries, albeit with far less public fanfare. Congress, the FTC, state authorities, and consumer-oriented NGOs have waged intense campaigns against elder fraud (commercial or financial deceptions that target senior citizens) and internet fraud. Since 1980, these campaigns have spawned more than twenty congressional hearings, recurrent legislation and administrative rule-making, and large investments in public education. As a result of the Telemarketing and Consumer Fraud and Abuse Prevention Act of 1994 and subsequent FTC regulations, for example, telemarketers faced a much more restrictive legal environment. They were prohibited from using deceptive ice-breakers to disguise the sales focus of calls, misrepresenting "the cost, quantity, and other aspects of the offered goods or services," and offering "recovery services" that promised to aid aggrieved consumers in gaining refunds from previous scams. Businesses that ignored these rules were subject to injunctions, fines that could reach up to $11,000 per violation, and restitution orders. State attorneys general also received authority to bring enforcement cases in federal courts, which, as an observer of the industry noted, placed "51 new cops on the national telemarketing fraud beat."[52]

Even before the adoption of these regulations, the FBI, Justice Department, Postal Inspectorate, and state consumer protection agencies mounted major enforcement sweeps against fraudulent telemarketers, such as Operation Disconnect in 1993, Operation Sunstroke in 1994, and Operation Senior Sentinel in 1995. Adopting the same tactics as Anthony Comstock a century earlier, these campaigns used decoy customers and undercover employees to marshal evidence, and generated criminal prosecutions of hundreds of businesses and individuals. Once the FTC finalized its rules in 1995, it carried out further investigations in conjunction with state authorities through "Project Jackpot," which led to dozens of enforcement lawsuits in 1996 alone.[53] In the early 2000s, the FTC and SEC coordinated similar wide-ranging investigations of internet fraud, such as "Operation Top Ten Dot Cons" in 2000, "Operation Bidder Beware" in 2003, and "Operation Empty Promises" in 2011. Reflecting the international character of e-commerce, these endeavors drew on the assistance of not only federal and state agencies, but also consumer protection officials from many other countries.[54]

Outside the realm of governmental policy, the continuing salience of business fraud prompted extensive media coverage. Consumer groups continued their missions of education and cooperation with law enforcement, but now deployed online information clearinghouses and complaint mechanisms. Thus, the National Consumer League established Fraud.org in 1996, while the American Association of Retired Persons (AARP) beefed up its online antifraud initiative in the late 1990s. Like earlier organizations focused on consumer and investor protection, these websites offered compendiums of specific scams and more general warning signs, as well as guidance about how to make effective complaints. From as early as 1996, specific complaints to Fraud.org fed a national fraud database used jointly by the FTC and the National Association of Attorneys General. AARP also replicated earlier communal tactics of reliance on dispersed volunteers, encouraging its members to become official "fraud fighters" who educated neighbors about prevalent rip-offs and served as community sentinels.[55]

A growing number of firms also sought profitable angles in the public demand for fraud protection. One idea, pushed by several startups and some nonprofits, was to foster a market for "trustmarks." These third-party certifications would not only reassure consumers and businesses that online firms were real businesses, but also that they eschewed deceptive practices. Providers such as SquareTrade offered the use of a "digitally watermarked Seal," which sellers could obtain on the basis of reference checks, evidence about customer service, and a pledge to use the website's dispute resolution mechanism. A competing approach focused on giving consumers an outlet to "vent" anger toward firms that they viewed as having ripped them off or treated them shabbily. At sites such as RipoffReport.com, Scambook.com, My3Cents.com, and Pissed consumer.com, disgruntled Americans could tell their side of individual transactions gone sour, in their own unedited words. Their stories found audiences in the tens of thousands. Consumer sites less focused on fraud, such as Yelp and TripAdvisor, amplified the capacity of consumers to share marketplace experiences.[56] Through all of these online communities, scathing reviews mirrored the nineteenth-century signs that warned of Peter Funks, the cautions in early twentieth-century BBB newsletters, and leaflets distributed by CEPA members—they brought a communal hue and cry to bear on the online cheat.

Whether through certifying trustworthiness or magnifying consumer gripes, these innovations aimed to prevent sharp dealing through timely provision of information about the behavior of businesses. Yet there were also profound limitations to these modes of informal regulation. So many entities offered "trustmarks" that their value depreciated. Amid a scramble for market share, some certification schemes did minimal screening and so suffered from adverse selection, attracting businesses that needed a boost for compromised reputations. Sites with more stringent requirements often struggled to earn enough business to remain afloat.[57]

As soon as consumer complaint sites gained traction with web users, they drew criticism as constituting a new "Wild West." Spokespersons for some businesses pointed out that without editorial or regulatory filters, the truthfulness of reports remained open to question. Complaint sites could become platforms for false allegations by "disgruntled employees" or "rival companies." An emerging set of reputation management firms claimed that these websites engaged in a form of extortion reminiscent of the appliance repair scams of the 1950s and 1960s. After posting devastating reviews, these critics alleged, the sites offered to scrub them for a fee or in exchange for advertising placements. In 2011, by contrast, RipoffReport.com discovered that its site had been hacked by a reputation management firm, which then removed negative commentary about its clients.[58] After a comprehensive 2010 study, the Consumer Federation of America concluded that the great majority of complaints on the most reputable websites were genuine. But the report stressed a different shortcoming—

even when rants about abusive or fraudulent practices warned off future consumers, they did nothing to redress past injustices. The tellers of commercial tales of woe on Pissedconsumer.com could not count on site visitors to join them as they visited a place of business to seek redress, nor to participate in actual pickets if it was not forthcoming.[59]

Still other organizations and businesses focused on the burgeoning problem of deceit inside large-scale corporations. Concern over the accounting dimensions of the S&L crisis prompted Joseph Wells, a Texas CPA who had spent part of his career with the FBI, to establish the National Association of Certified Fraud Examiners (NACFE) in 1988. Headquartered first in Dallas, ground zero of the S&L debacle, NACFE gained thousands of members who saw the opportunity to offer specialized services to companies. The organization offered professional development courses, credentialed accountants who passed a two-day exam in forensic accounting, and kept its members abreast of financial innovations, ongoing fraud investigations, and shifts in regulatory policies. A few years after its launch, it dropped the word "National" to reflect its move onto the international stage, and began to commission annual studies of fraud costs, pegging them at $400 billion a year in the United States for 1994—roughly 6 percent of overall economic activity. Although this organization focused on aspects of occupational fraud, such as embezzlement, it also paid attention to the issues posed by corporate deceptions that harmed suppliers, customers, and investors. During the 1990s, the proliferation of deceit within the corporate world led major accounting firms to hire scores of ACFE-certified accountants.[60] It also prompted the emergence of boutique firms specializing in forensic accounting, and convinced some providers of general investigative services to corporations, such as Kroll Associates, to invest in fraud-related consulting services.[61]

After 1975, self-regulatory organizations continued to dot the American antifraud landscape. The Better Business Bureau network sustained its national coverage, though it experienced a slight drop in the number of local chapters, settling around 115. At the behest of business leaders who felt under siege from class-action lawsuits, local BBBs initiated formal dispute resolution programs in the late 1970s, and then encouraged members to handle unresolvable consumer complaints through BBB-trained arbitrators. The Bureaus also offered this service to consumers whose complaints it viewed as legitimate, and which were not resolved through initial mediation. Arbitration rapidly became a central BBB endeavor, with as many as one-third of member businesses in some metropolitan areas pledging to abide by its outcomes. Several national corporations also turned to the program to handle disputes over warranties. As a result, BBBs recruited thousands of attorneys and other volunteers across the country to serve as arbitrators.[62]

BBBs were also early movers into cyberspace, connecting local Bureaus to the Council of BBBs website, which offered "Scam Alerts," a library of "Tips" for avoiding rip-offs, searchable databases of business reviews, and the opportunity to file a complaint from one's keyboard. In the late 1990s, the organization created its own trustmark—an online BBB Torch available only to member firms, ostensibly testifying to integrity and fair dealing. A decade later, it introduced a more elaborate system of accreditation for all enterprises. BBB staff members based their system of letter grades (A to F) on information provided by businesses, the BBBs' own records of how they handled consumer complaints, and whether or not the firms were BBB members. These grades went into the BBB online database of business reviews. In 2014, the Council of Better Business Bureaus also launched "Scam Tracker." Drawing on the crowd-sourced input of consumers, this "free interactive online tool" gave consumers and law enforcement officials "a heat map showing where scams are being reported."[63]

Nonetheless, the criticisms leveled at the BBBs at the height of the 1970s consumer movement did not fall away. From the 1980s onward, the BBB's own marketing practices attracted media scrutiny. Journalists found that some local BBBs had pursued aggressive strategies to boost dues-paying membership, raising questions about conflicts of interest and flirtations with deception.[64] After the introduction of accreditation grades, more serious allegations surfaced that some BBBs would upgrade ratings if businesses agreed to become members. The sharpest allegations came from firms with poor BBB ratings, which portrayed the network as having become "a private interest" that pursued the sort of "pay for play scheme" that its leaders had long decried when practiced by others. After a 2010 exposé on the ABC news program *20/20*, which documented the ease with which fictional businesses could achieve BBB ratings of A or A+, the BBB network pledged to revamp its accreditation process, removing any advantages associated with membership.[65]

Toward the end of the twentieth century, new forms of antifraud business self-regulation emerged alongside the BBBs and the securities and commodities exchanges, lodged inside America's largest corporations. Within sectors dependent on government contracting, such as defense and healthcare, corporate leaders once again turned to self-regulatory experiments as a means of deflecting pressures for more statist regulatory oversight. As the press and Congress bore down on defense suppliers in the 1980s and healthcare providers the following decade, each developed elaborate internal "Ethics & Compliance" departments charged with reforming billing practices. These new bureaucracies took on all of the classic regulatory functions. They generated mission statements and more detailed codes of conduct, as well as training modules for corporate staff. Contractors created "ethics and compliance officers" at subsidiaries and within divisions, and established anonymous phone hotlines to encourage flows of information about problematic behavior in the ranks. Just as stock exchanges used the latest computer software to identify trading patterns that suggested illegal manipulation, defense and healthcare firms developed computer algorithms that identified evidence of suspect coding or billing patterns. Hospital companies centralized coding and billing operations, while nudging far-flung medical facilities to forge cultures of regulatory compliance and voluntarily disclose "problems affecting corporate contractual relations with government." In both defense and healthcare, leading firms forged industrywide organizations—the Defense Industry Initiative and the Health Care Compliance Association—to "share experiences" and hone best practices.[66]

Some corporations vulnerable to fraud or dependent on consumer confidence took even more elaborate steps to combat deceitful behavior. Credit-card companies confronted waves of fraudulent charges in the 1990s, both from unscrupulous businesses and as a result of stolen cards. To head off this threat, card issuers invested several hundred million dollars in security features, as well as computer systems that would identify suspicious purchasing patterns. Once alerted, company employees or automated calling systems contacted cardholders to verify that payments were legitimate.[67] As web commerce took off, the prevalence of online auction fraud threatened public confidence in new platforms for commercial transactions. The popular auction and direct sales site eBay responded by building a robust internal fraud unit directed by "a former prosecutor" and by fashioning an elaborate governance structure for online sellers and buyers. These systems relied on satisfaction ratings from buyers and sellers and sophisticated computer programs to identify individuals who engaged in bid-rigging, misrepresentation, or nondelivery of goods. Such measures improved eBay's ability to warn users about abusive sellers and shut down the worst offenders. When the company's CEO, Meg Whitman, become convinced that endemic deceit endangered profitability, she marshalled the financial resources and expertise to address the problem. As Whitman explained in a 1999 press release trumpeting "new upgrades" to the site's antifraud software, "eBay has zero tolerance for fraud." Noting that "fraud and other trust and safety issues are not new," she emphasized that "eBay's solutions are. We . . . will continue to commit resources to have the most comprehensive programs in order to keep eBay a safe harbor for online person-to-person trading."[68]

Ghosts of the Regulatory Past, Present, and Future

What to make of all this antifraud activity punctuating a neoliberal age? There are analytical dangers for historians who venture onto the terrain of the recent past, one reason so few have surveyed contemporary business culture, political economy, and regulatory institutions. Nonetheless, the longer arc of business fraud and antifraud regulation in the United States suggests some useful frames of reference. One important insight concerns an enduring feature in American political economy. Policymakers have never been comfortable with pure reliance on the checks and balances within markets to control duplicity. As the threat that business fraud poses to economic confidence becomes more obvious to journalists, academics, the business community, government officials, and the wider public, pressures for regulatory reform mount, and policy entrepreneurs come forward with specific plans of action.

Prevailing ideas about the trustworthiness of government nonetheless have channeled regulatory responses. During the Progressive Era, the New Deal, and the 1960s and 1970s, supporters of tougher measures against fraud thought in terms of administrative bureaucracy. By contrast, late twentieth-century policymakers manifested abiding skepticism about this institutional orientation. The move against contracting fraud was spearheaded by Charles Grassley, a conservative Iowa senator. He structured the 1986 False Claims Act around private legal actions by whistleblowers, who would share handsomely in any monies that the government recouped as a result of their revelations.[69] Federal policymakers also sought to delegate much of the responsibility for preventing fraudulent billing to contractors. The Reagan administration's Packard Commission, convened to devise ways to curb procurement fraud, prodded defense companies to embrace self-regulation. The movement to create Ethics and Compliance Departments gained a further boost from the 1991 Federal Sentencing Guidelines for criminal convictions, which promised easier treatment for corporations that could show good-faith efforts to rein in wrongdoing by their employees.[70] By the same token, private modes of regulation dominated responses to online business fraud, in part because government policymakers shied away from forceful actions during the web's formative years. As President Bill Clinton described this largely bipartisan consensus in a 1998 press briefing, "we will do nothing that undermines the capacity of emerging technologies to lift the lives of ordinary Americans."[71]

Experiences with American business fraud since the mid-1970s also replicated earlier patterns concerning the workings of self-regulatory organizations or self-regulatory mechanisms within corporations. When leaders of firms and industries saw that antifraud regulation mattered to policymakers, self-regulation could make a difference. So long as executives and trade association heads had to look over their shoulders at public regulators and prosecutors, they had strong reasons to make regulatory compliance a priority. This level of concern existed in the wake of defense and healthcare contracting scandals. The spotlight of congressional hearings and journalistic exposés, along with the pressure of whistleblower lawsuits and federal investigations, spurred meaningful commitments to clean up abuses. By contrast, reliance on self-regulation without a credible expectation of accountability furnished the thinnest of regulatory veneers, unless businesses deemed antifraud mechanisms as crucial to profitability. Defense contractors and eBay had reason to make self-regulation work; third-party mortgage-loan reviewers and credit ratings agencies did not.

Another recurring pattern involves the willingness of policymakers who dislike state regulation and who extol individual responsibility to make exceptions for consumers and investors whom they see as especially susceptible to fraud. During the height of adherence to a philosophy of *caveat emptor*, nineteenth-century prosecutors, judges, and juries demonstrated sympathy for allegations of fraud from elderly women or recent immigrants. Similar judgments led late twentieth-century conservatives such as Charles Grassley to support the deployment of public resources against elder fraud (along with pragmatic electoral considerations, given the high propensity of senior citizens to vote).[72]

As the economic, political, and intellectual fallout from the 2008 global financial crisis continues to unsettle the United States, the degree to which this episode represents a regulatory watershed remains an open question. The recent crisis most certainly shook confidence in the integrity of markets, among elites as well as the general public. Whether that jolt will prompt a fundamental reorientation of American regulatory policymaking away from the neoliberal premises of *caveat emptor* is less clear.

The establishment of the Consumer Financial Protection Bureau points toward a reassertion of the state's responsibilities to sustain public confidence in markets and protect the interests of vulnerable economic actors. Despite vehement political opposition from Republicans in Congress, which included a yearlong opposition to the appointment of former Ohio Attorney General Richard Cordray as its director, the CFPB has moved ahead on numerous regulatory fronts. Incorporating some former employees of the Office of Thrift Supervision, which Dodd-Frank eliminated, as well as a corps of experienced bank examiners, the Bureau also hired hundreds of highly educated, "idealistic" staff members, many with experience in the financial industry, who embraced its mission to bring consumer protection to credit markets. Over its first five years, it conducted detailed studies on financial literacy, arbitration, the student loan sector, and the impact of financial coaching, injected a new concern for consumer impacts in the regulatory monitoring of bank and non-bank lenders, and formulated several new regulatory rules. The most important of the latter clarified underwriting and disclosure standards for mortgages and several forms of consumer credit. The Bureau initiated scores of enforcement actions against lenders, loan originators, mortgage servicers, and collection agencies that engaged in abusive or deceptive behavior, resulting in restitution of $2.6 billion to millions of Americans through 2015, as well as more than $7 billion in additional relief to consumers. CFPB officials reached out to the segments of the credit markets that they regulated, soliciting feedback on every aspect of the Bureau's decision-making, and forged relationships with other federal agencies and state and local counterparts. The Bureau has also brought a new intellectual sophistication to consumer outreach, information disclosure, and enforcement strategy.[73]

The CFPB's policy innovations recall the flexibility and institutional creativity of many earlier antifraud institutions. The thorny nature of business fraud— the challenges associated with detection, the complexity of prosecutions, the protean character of scams and systemic misrepresentations—has often encouraged experimentation in regulatory design and strategy, driven by aspiring groups of experts and professionals. In the late nineteenth and early twentieth centuries, the key protagonists were accountants, scientists, a segment of the advertising community who wished to improve its status, and lawyers who built up regulatory bureaucracies. At the CFPB, this role has been taken up by a cluster of behavioral economists, cognitive psychologists, sociologists, and statisticians, working in conjunction with legal staff. These experts have focused on tailoring educational materials, online complaint databases, and lender disclosures to improve their salience for borrowers, as with a less-complex standard mortgage disclosure form that facilitates comparison shopping. They have also integrated analysis of complaint patterns into monitoring and enforcement, calibrating the degree of scrutiny that a lender, mortgage broker, or debt collector receives in light of its complaint profile.

At the same time, some CFPB staff members have expressed frustration with bureaucratic decision-making. The need to gain clearance from the chain of command to go forward with an enforcement action, such as multiple rounds of review for policy proposals, struck these young public servants as reflective of excessive timidity. "Important, productive initiatives," one former staff attorney recalled, "could get delayed all too easily by someone, seemingly at any level, suggesting it might make sense to wait for a more certain environment."[74] This comment evokes the now century-old trade-off between adopting the most effective means of curtailing commercial deception and retaining respect for fair regulatory process and the rule of law.

So too do critiques of Operation Choke Point, a joint effort begun by the Department of Justice and the Federal Deposit Insurance Corporation (FDIC) in 2013 to combat a host of fraudulent and other illegal or disreputable businesses by disrupting their ability to receive funds through online payment systems. Almost everything about this initiative harkens back to the Post Office's late nineteenth-century regulation of mail-order commerce. The categories of targeted businesses include "credit card schemes," "credit repair services," "debt consolidation scams," "get rich products," life-time guarantees," "lottery sales," "online gambling," "pharmaceutical sales," "Ponzi schemes," "pornography," "pyramid-type sales," and "telemarketing"—a list that echoes, eerily, the types of firms that Anthony Comstock and other postal inspectors attacked from the 1870s through the turn of the twentieth century. After identifying enterprises that fell into these categories, the officials responsible for Operation Choke Point pressured banks and third-party payment processors to stop online transfers of funds to them. As with the postal fraud order, the idea was to take away access to the basic infrastructure of commerce. Also like the postal fraud order in its first decades, this refusal of admission to economic life occurred without notice, hearings, or any other basic features of due process. Such actions could have devastating impacts on fraudulent businesses, but also on any other individuals or entities singled out as requiring regulatory discipline. They struck some observers, both conservative and liberal, as a turn to an "electronic Panopticon," a dystopian world of "limitation, control, and surveillance" that could ruin lawful as well as illicit firms, the next Richard Sears as well as the latest Sarah Howe or Charles Ponzi.[75]

If the early record of the CFPB and the dynamics of Operation Choke Point suggest comparisons to the late nineteenth-century postal inspectors' office, the New Deal SEC, or the most energetic state consumer protection agencies of the 1960s and 1970s, other aspects of antifraud regulation in the wake of the global financial crisis point in different directions. From late 2012 through 2014, the Justice Department negotiated a series of civil settlements with the largest financial institutions whose deceptive practices had helped to trigger the crisis. These settlements have clawed back tens of billions of dollars in fines, set aside billions more for restitution to still-struggling mortgage-holders, and included admissions of systematic nondisclosures and misrepresentations.[76] But as yet, almost no one within the financial world has faced criminal prosecution, whether for extensive efforts to generate a steady stream of subprime mortgages dressed up with false loan-application data and phony appraisals, the systemic misrepresentations of the resulting mortgage-backed securities, or the lies that greased foreclosures. From the mid-2000s into the first term of the Obama administration, federal investigations of mortgage frauds were hampered by insufficient manpower, the disinclination of some banking regulators to participate in criminal probes, and a skimpy conceptual definition of mortgage fraud that the FBI had agreed to as part of a partnership with the Mortgage Bankers of America. High-ranking members of the Obama administration, such as Treasury Secretary Tim Geithner, also worried about the impact that criminal prosecutions might have on systemic financial stability. For many critics, though, the lack of criminal prosecutions smacked of favoritism to the wealthy and powerful.[77]

When viewed against two centuries of American encounters with large-scale financial frauds, the Department of Justice's record-setting mortgage fraud–related settlements look a bit like payoffs from the "squawk fund" that companies facing fraud allegations have always been willing to make in order to quiet the angriest dupes. Even as the headline numbers for these settlements have inched closer to $100 billion, they still represent only a fraction of the profits earned from a system of deceptive practices in the six or seven years before the financial crisis. These deals also remain framed around "enterprise liability," doing little to touch the "immense wealth" accumulated by the bank executives "as a result of their control over the firm during the time of wrong-doing."[78] By foreclosing an airing of the evidence that underpins these complex cases, the settlements have also short-circuited public assessment of the problematic business practices and oversight failures that led to such pervasive and systemic frauds.

The same Congress that passed Dodd-Frank, moreover, enacted the 2012 Jumpstart Our Business Startups Act (JOBS). This bipartisan legislation expanded the number of companies exempted from the more onerous reporting requirements of the Sarbanes-Oxley Act, while slashing disclosure requirements for new companies looking to raise up to $50 million in capital.[79] Far from signaling a post-crisis intent to clamp down on dissembling promoters, the JOBS Act rather sought to address persistent economic slack by widening the scope to entice capital into new ventures. Consumer groups and voices for responsible investing have expressed worries about the law's potential exploitation by "the less than honorable fringe."[80] We can expect ongoing arguments about how to balance concerns about business fraud and facilitation of beneficial innovation. Some voices will point to the financial crisis's grave costs and demand smarter regulatory policies that improve the flow of usable information to consumers and investors, while prohibiting the worst deceptions. Where possible, those who see themselves as victims of deceit will seek redress from regulatory institutions. This has been the tack taken by thousands of former students who took out guaranteed federal loans to study at for-profit universities that made false claims about graduates' career paths. These individuals have pressed the Department of Education to void their debts, under a statutory provision that permits such action if former students show that schools lied in recruitment materials.[81] Others will argue that even if business fraud has increased as a result of deregulatory policies, the socioeconomic benefits of less-encumbered markets, greater maneuverability for entrepreneurs, and suitable wariness among investors and consumers outweigh any collateral increase in fraud. Where possible, those who rankle at overreaching regulatory institutions will do what they can to clip their wings. This perspective has underpinned the movement by major corporations to create contractual defaults that compel consumers to take any grievances to binding arbitration, outside the ambit of the state. In a pivotal 2011 case, *AT&T Mobility v. Concepcion*, a sharply divided US Supreme Court gave this corporate strategy a significant boost, ruling five to four that state legislatures lacked the authority to prohibit such clauses in consumer contracts. More recently, however, the CFPB has begun consideration of a new regulation that would ban compulsory arbitration as a feature of consumer financial products.[82]

In this and other policy debates about antifraud regulation, we can expect participants to engage in appeals to history. One struggles now to find anyone who would dispute the claim that during the past thirty years, the financial industry, along with the professional gatekeepers charged with keeping it honest, became far more hospitable to versions of Barnumesque humbuggery and Peter Funkism. But how should we account for this dramatic reputational decline? One recent explanation places much of the blame on the regulatory shift that the New Deal ushered in toward the principle of *caveat venditor*, which, on this view, reduced the incentives for corporations to take the standing of counterparties into account, because regulators could be trusted to discipline wayward firms. By the same token, professional gatekeepers such as law firms, external auditors, and ratings agencies no longer needed to safeguard their own reputations, because regulatory mandates compel corporate clients to retain their services. According to this interpretation, the way to restore reputational premiums would be to undertake more deregulation of the securities market and to direct the remaining regulatory energies toward structuring incentives that reward longer-term performance instead of short-term returns.[83]

This argument downplays the rise of limited liability partnerships within accounting, which removed the interests of accounting partners in monitoring activities elsewhere in the firm. It elides the semi-corporatization of law firms during the late twentieth century, as well as the shift of some investment banks from partnerships to limited liability corporations, moves that also shortened managerial time horizons. More significantly, it skirts the profound impact that deregulatory fervor had on social norms within the business community (helping to drive the relentless focus on short-term financial results that contributed to the 2008 financial crisis) and regulatory agencies (recalibrating the mission, organizational culture, and employment filters at institutions such as the SEC). Most importantly, the presumption that a fuller deregulation would prompt greater reliance on reputational checks ignores the lessons of the past two centuries of American encounters with business fraud. Such checks did not ward off rampant manipulations and deceptions in the New York City auction markets of the 1840s, on the San Francisco stock market of the 1870s, or on the Wall Street of the 1920s.

In the mid-1950s, the economist John Kenneth Galbraith surveyed the origins of the 1929 stock market collapse in his now-classic history, *The Great Crash*. Galbraith framed much of his analysis around capsule summaries of how "American enterprise in the twenties had opened its hospitable arms to an exceptional number of promoters, grafters, swindlers, impostors, and frauds. This, in the long history of such activities, was a kind of flood tide of corporate larceny." Such endemic violations of trust, we should remember, occurred in an era without any regulatory SEC mandates to interfere with the imperatives of investments in reputational capital. Toward the end of the volume, Galbraith mused about the inevitable progression of generational amnesia about the Great Crash and the Great Depression that it triggered. In the midst of the 1930s, he noted, the clarion call was "Never again." But with the passage of the years, one could anticipate that perceptions of the need for regulatory constraints would fade, as American aspirations were drawn to "some newly discovered virtuosity of the free enterprise system."[84]

Galbraith offers a formidable caution about reliance on historical memory as a guide to regulatory policymaking. And yet the complex narrative of American business fraud, filled with recurring motifs and tensions, but also profound evolutions in regulatory strategy, has much to offer the myriad regulatory protagonists who deal with the problem of economic deception on a regular basis. It has become a cast of thousands—the deputy attorney general in charge of consumer protection, SEC lawyer, and CFPB investigator; the BBB representative, AARP community volunteer, local consumer activist, and consumer affairs journalist; the certified public accountant, accredited forensic fraud specialist, and corporate general counsel; the trade association official for mortgage brokers, automobile dealers, and hundreds of additional sectors.

The history of American business fraud offers such regulatory actors a rich set of analytical perspectives.[85] These include: an appreciation for enduring psychological vulnerabilities and evolving social norms. Some sense of institutional possibilities and pitfalls. The importance of understanding prevailing regulatory ecologies before embarking on policy experiments or attempting to forge new policy coalitions. Cognizance of the fine legal lines that distinguish swindling from mistaken enthusiasm, and the frequent role of social status in shaping prosecutorial outcomes. A grasp of the trade-offs between facilitating innovation and curbing deceit. Mindfulness of the capacity of antifraud regulation to generate unforeseen consequences or become stuck in bureaucratic quagmires, as well as its potential to reshape conceptions of self-interest and restructure business routines in constructive directions. Awareness of how regulatory infrastructures can become outmoded or taken for granted in the face of socioeconomic, technological, and intellectual change. And always, assistance in asking the most useful question, or framing the most sensible menu of policy choices.

One can also identify enduring features of effective antifraud regulation. As important as reputational dynamics can be in constraining deceit, they will not, by themselves, forestall the sort of systematic frauds that can undermine public confidence in economic institutions. The regulation of business fraud has to have some punitive bite, both to stifle the most unscrupulous firms and to convince all market participants that the state is serious about fighting economic deceit. But regulators should direct resources toward well-designed public education that minimizes informational imbalances, the design of transactional defaults that empower investors and consumers, and the cultivation of market norms that stigmatize those willing to trade on reputation in the face of competitive pressure, or to construct enterprises on platforms of misrepresentation or conflict of interest. As they craft such strategies, policymakers should build networks that cut across levels of government (and now international boundaries) and leverage the creativity, local knowledge, and legitimacy of nongovernmental actors, including corporations, the press, professional gatekeepers, and private antifraud NGOs. No capitalist society will ever rid itself of clever, beguiling, charismatic flim-flammers, nor established firms that, in the face of new challenges, turn to deceptive marketing or dishonest accounting. But the history of American antifraud regulation shows that inventive governance can stay abreast of all the new twists on old games, shut down the worst frauds, fortify consumers and investors against imposition, and sustain, at reasonable cost, the social trust necessary for modern capitalism.

Abbreviations

❧❦❧

Newspapers & Periodicals

AC: Atlanta Constitution
AF: American Farmer
BET: Boston Evening Transcript
BL: Business Lawyer
BS: Baltimore Sun
CD: Chicago Defender
CIO: Chicago Inter Ocean
CT: Chicago Tribune
DMN: Dallas Morning News
DNT: Duluth News-Tribune
EMJ: Engineering and Mining Journal
HMM: Hunt's Merchants' Magazine
HW: Harper's Weekly
JM: Journal of Marketing
KCS: Kansas City Star
LAT: Los Angeles Times
MT: Macon Telegraph
NAR: North American Review
NOP: New Orleans Picayune
NPG: National Police Gazette
NYAN: New York Amsterdam News
NYH: New York Herald
NYT: New York Times
NYTR: New York Tribune
PI: Philadelphia Inquirer
PPL: Philadelphia Public Ledger
PT: Philadelphia Tribune
SEP: Saturday Evening Post
SFB: San Francisco Bulletin
WP: Washington Post
WSJ: Wall Street Journal

Academic Journals

AAPS: Annals of the American Academy of Political and Social Science
AHR: American Historical Review
ALJ: Albany Law Journal
BHR: Business History Review

CLR: Columbia Law Review
DLJ: Duke Law Journal
HLR: Harvard Law Review
JAH: Journal of American History
LHR: Law & History Review
MLR: Michigan Law Review
UPLR: University of Pennsylvania Law Review
YLJ: Yale Law Journal

Manuscripts & Collections

BBBMC: BBB of Metropolitan Chicago Records, ca. 1929–2003,
　　Chicago History Museum
Bell Papers: W. Dan Bell Papers, Denver Public Library
Consumers Research Papers: Special Collections Library, Rutgers University
Fraud Order Cases: Records of the Post Office Department, Record
　　Group 28, Entry 50, National Archives
Fraud Order Hearings: Records of the Post Office Department,
　　Record Group 28, Entry 55, National Archives
Gardner Papers: Paris Cleveland Gardner Papers, David M.
　　Rubinstein Rare Book and Manuscript Library, Duke University
HCF: Historical Clippings File, New York Better Business Bureau Archives
Kirstein Papers: Louis E. Kirstein Collection, Historical Collections,
　　Baker Library, Harvard Business School

Institutions

AACW: Associated Advertising Clubs of the World
AMA: American Medical Association
BBB: Better Business Bureau
DOJ: Department of Justice
FTC: Federal Trade Commission
FTCL: Federal Trade Commission Library
NA: National Archives
NAAG: National Association of Attorneys General
NBBB: National Better Business Bureau
NACM: National Association of Credit Men
NVC: National Vigilance Committee
NYSE: New York Stock Exchange
POD: Post Office Department
SEC: Securities & Exchange Commission
US HR: United States House of Representatives
US Sen.: United States Senate

Notes

❦

Chapter One: The Enduring Dilemmas of Antifraud Regulation

1. James Willard Hurst, *Law and Markets in United States History: Different Modes of Bargaining among Interests* (Madison, WI, 1982).

2. This point has become a commonplace among economic sociologists and historians of political economy. See, for example, Neil Fligstein, *The Architecture of Markets: An Economic Sociology of Twenty-First-Century Capitalist Societies* (Princeton, NJ, 2001); Hurst, *Law and Markets*, 1–90. But the view hardly represents a consensus among wider public opinion.

3. For sustained discussion of these themes and citations to the social science literature, see Edward J. Balleisen, "The Dialectics of Regulatory Governance," in Balleisen, ed., *Business Regulation*, 3 vols. (Cheltenham, UK, 2015), xxii–xxvii.

4. Michael Pettit furnishes a succinct overview of these three "short cons" in *The Science of Deception: Psychology and Commerce in America* (Chicago, 2013), 25–26.

5. On the conceptual issues suffusing the definition of fraud and white-collar crime, see John Braithwaite, "White Collar Crime," *Annual Review of Sociology* 11 (1985): 1–25; Susan Shapiro, "Collaring the Crime, Not the Criminal," *American Sociological Review* 55 (1990): 346–65; Robert Tillman and Henry Pontell, "Organizations and Fraud in the Savings and Loan Industry," *Social Forces* 73 (1995): 1439–44; William Black, *The Best Way to Rob a Bank Is to Own One: How Corporate Executives and Politicians Looted the S & L Industry* (Austin, 2005), 1–9. For important analyses of occupational fraud in nineteenth-century Britain, see George Robb, *White-Collar Crime in Modern England: Financial Fraud and Business Morality, 1845–1929* (New York, 2002); Ian Klaus, *Forging Capitalism: Rogues, Swindlers, Frauds, and the Rise of Modern Finance* (New Haven, 2014), 26–167.

6. Noah Webster, *A Dictionary of the English Language; Compiled for the Use of Common Schools in the United States* (Hartford, 1817), 135, 313.

7. For examples that span the decades of American history, see: Jane Kamensky, *The Exchange Artist: A Tale of High-Flying Speculation and America's First Banking Collapse* (New York, 2008); Roger Whitman, *The Rise and Fall of a Frontier Entrepreneur: Benjamin Rathbun, "Master Building and Architect,"* ed. Scott Eberle and David A. Gerber (Syracuse, 1996); Roger M. Olien and Diana Davids Olien, *Easy Money: Oil Promoters and Investors in the Jazz Age* (Chapel Hill, 1990); Forrest McDonald, *Insull* (Chicago, 1962); Kurt Eichenwald, *Serpent on the Rock* (New York, 1995).

8. Pettit, *The Science of Deception*, 8.

Chapter Two: The Shape-Shifting, Never-Changing World of Fraud

1. Ralph Lee Smith, *The Bargain Hucksters* (New York, 1962), 37.

2. "Detectives Watch Ward," *NYT*, May 10, 1884, 1; "More of Ward's Rascality," *NYT*, May 11, 1884, 1; "Ward Will Follow Fish," *NYT*, Oct. 29, 1885, 1; Russell Roberts, "The Wall Street Scandal of Grant & Ward," *Financial History* 81 (2004): 13–15, 36.

3. Charles Francis Adams, "A Chapter of Erie," *NAR* 109 (1869): 30–104; "The Dread of State Insurance by Rotten Life Insurance Companies," *Financier* 1 (May 18, 1872): 373; "Right and Wrong in Banking," *The Advance* 8 (Sept. 9, 1875): 913; "Life Insurance?," *The Sanitarian* 4 (Oct. 1, 1976), 443–44; Richard White, *Railroaded: The Transcontinentals and the Making of Modern America* (New York, 2012).

4. Edward Chancellor, *Devil Take the Hindmost: A History of Financial Speculation* (New York, 1999), 36–147.

5. The phrase "pump and dump" is of recent vintage, first appearing in the *Wall Street Journal* during 1988. Bruce Ingersoll, "School for Scam: Fraud Is Rife in Market for Pink Sheet Stocks," *WSJ*, Feb. 2, 1988, 1.

6. Herman Melville, *The Confidence-Man: His Masquerade* (London, 1857), 65; James K. Medbury, *Men and Mysteries of Wall Street* (Boston, 1870), 174–75.

7. C. Peter McGrath, *Yazoo: Law and Politics in the New Republic* (Providence, 1966); Henry William Herbert, *Tricks and Traps of Chicago* (New York, 1859), 29–43.

8. Louis Guenther, "Pirates of Promotion: Market Manipulation and Its Part in the Promotion Game," *World's Work* 37 (April 1919): 393–98; J. M. Friedlander, *Seventh Biennial Report of the State Corporation Department to the Governor of the State of California* (Sacramento, 1928), 12; "Old Turf 'Tip Fraud' Now Used in Stock Market Scheme," *AC*, Feb. 19, 1928, 8; "Tipster Sheet Warning Given," *LAT*, July 17, 1933, 7; "Boiler Room Boom," *WSJ*, Jan. 29, 1959, 1; Frank Gibney, *The Operators* (New York, 1969), 89–120.

9. Francis Flaherty, "Cyberspace Swindles: Old Scams, New Twists," *NYT*, July 16, 1994, 35; "Anatomy of a Swindle," *NYT*, Nov. 30, 1997, 50; Melynda Wilcox, "Online Stock Fraud Is on the Rise," *Kiplinger's Personal Finance Magazine* 53 (Feb. 1999): 20; Anthony Mason, "Using the Internet to Commit Stock Fraud," *CBS Evening News*, July 4, 2001.

10. Mitchell Zuckoff, *Ponzi's Scheme: The True Story of a Financial Legend* (New York, 2005).

11. Stewart L. Weisman, *Need and Greed: The Story of the Largest Ponzi Scheme in American History* (Syracuse, 1999); Diana B. Henriques, *The Wizard of Lies: Bernie Madoff and the Death of Trust* (New York, 2012).

12. On Sarah Howe and the Ladies Deposit Savings Bank, see "A Thoroughbred Fraud," *NPG* 37 (Oct. 30, 1880): 7; "Commencement at Boston of the Trial of Mrs. Howe," *CT*, April 22, 1881, 5; "The Lessons of the Boston 'Ladies' Deposit,'" *Popular Science Monthly* 19 (Sept. 1881): 698–703; George Robb, "Depicting a Female Fraud: Sarah Howe and the Boston Women's Bank," *Nineteenth-Century Contexts* 34 (2012): 445–59. On Fund W, see "The Fund W Swindle," *Michigan Farmer*, Oct. 31, 1883, 14; Alfred T. Andreas, *History of Chicago*, vol. 3 (Chicago, 1886), 271–72. On Miller and the Franklin Syndicate, see John Hill, Jr., *Gold Bricks of Speculation: A Study of Speculation and Its Counterfeits, and an Exposé of the Methods of Bucketshop and "Get-Rich-Quick" Swindles* (Chicago, 1904), 130–39; Arthur Train, "Colonel Ammon and the Franklin Syndicate," *American Illustrated Magazine* 41 (Dec. 1905): 204–13; and the extensive coverage in the *New York Times* through late 1899 and 1900.

13. Theodore Barrett and Louis Spaeth, *What about Dollars? Consumer Education* (New York, 1936), 171–82; I. Burton, "Memorandum for the Federal Trade Commission," May 14, 1943, Paris Gardner Papers, Box 3, Packet 2, In Re Clean-Rite Vacuum Stores, Box 3, Packet 2, Gardner Papers; R. L. Smith, *Bargain Hucksters*, 30–112; Harold Fay, Dan Mulholland, and Don Corpuz, *Bait and Switch Advertising: A Factual Report*

(Portland, OR, 1973); FTC, *Guides against Bait Advertising* (Washington, DC, 2000); "Alliance against Bait & Click," *Marketing Business Weekly*, Oct. 18, 2009, 228.

14. Joseph Newman, *What Everyone Needs to Know about Law* (Washington, DC, 1973), 87; Christine Winter, "Consumer Watch: Bait 'n' Switch Game," *CT*, May 18, 1975, W1–W2; Fleming Meeks, "Upselling," *Forbes* 145 (Jan. 8, 1990): 70–71.

15. Grant Gilmore, "The Commercial Doctrine of Good Faith Purchase," *Yale Law Journal* 63 (1954): 1057–122; David Caplovitz, "Breakdowns in the Consumer Credit Marketplace," *BL* 26 (1971): 795–800; David J. Benson and Al[phonse] M. Squillante, "The Role of the Holder in Due Course Doctrine in Consumer Credit Transactions," *Hastings Law Journal* 26 (1974): 427–59; Jodie Z. Bernstein and David A. Zetoony, "A Retrospective of Consumer Protection Initiatives," *Antitrust Law Journal* 7 (2005): 969–72.

16. Rolf Nugent and Leon Henderson, "Installment Selling and the Consumer: A Brief for Regulation," *AAPS* 173 (May 1934): 94–97; W. Bruce Cobb, "Consumer Credit as It Comes to the Legal Aid Society of New York, *AAPS* 196 (March 1938): 201–03.

17. R. L. Smith, *Bargain Hucksters*, 57–93; Warren G. Magnuson and Jean Carper, *The Dark Side of the Marketplace: The Plight of the American Consumer* (Englewood Cliffs, NJ, 1968), 3–9, 32–58; Philip G. Schrag, *Counsel for the Deceived: Case Studies in Consumer Fraud* (New York, 1972), 3–10, 116–62.

18. Other tactics included changing contractual terms by filling in blanks; quoting a rate for one rod, but then erecting several; and having customers sign a note and then cut off a portion, so as to change the meaning of its terms. "The Lightning Rod Swindle," *Albany Evening Journal*, July 20, 1867, 1; "Lightning Rods," *Farmer's Cabinet*, Sept. 3, 1878, 2; Bates Harrington, *How 'Tis Done: A Thorough Ventilation of the Numerous Schemes Conducted by Wandering Canvassers, Together with the Various Advertising Dodges for the Swindling of the Public* (Chicago, 1879), 195–216; "Swindling the Grangers," *Wheeling Register*, July 5, 1883, 4.

19. Untitled squib, *Indianapolis Sentinel*, June 23, 1873, 4; E. T. Roe, "Fence Stretcher Machine Fraud," *The New Standard American Business Guide: A Complete Compendium of How to Do Business by the Latest and Safest Methods* (New York, 1906), 345–46.

20. "Wage War on Sharpies," *Billboard* (Aug. 29, 1953): 94, 113. On opportunity scams, see *Humbug: A Look at Some Popular Impositions* (New York, 1859), 80–84; Harrington, *How 'Tis Done*, 217–43; "Book-Keeping in Three Weeks!" *AA* 46 (Oct. 1886): 445; Edwin Lawrence, "Swindling through the Post Office," *Outlook* 79 (Jan. 14, 1905): 123–25; John R. Gregory, "The Three Percent Home Loan Swindle," *WW* 46 (Sept. 1923): 486–90; E. Jerome Ellis and Frank W. Brock, *The Run for Your Money* (New York, 1935), 98–136; Beverly Beyette, "A Flowering of L.A. Consumer Scams," *LAT*, Feb. 10, 1982, G1.

21. Alfred D. Chandler Jr., *Henry Varnum Poor, Business Editor, Analyst, and Reformer* (Cambridge, MA, 1956), 113–15; "Extensive Frauds in Railroad Stocks," *Trenton State Gazette*, July 7, 1854, 2; "Parker Vein Coal Company," *Mining Magazine* 3 (July 1854): 91–93; "The Late Security Life," *The Independent* 29 (Jan. 25, 1877): 29; "The American Popular Failure," *NYT*, Apr. 24, 1877, 8; Paul M. Clikeman, *Called to Account: Fourteen Financial Frauds That Shaped the American Accounting Profession* (New York, 2009); Raymond B. Vickers, *Panic in Paradise: Florida's Banking Crash of 1926* (Tuscaloosa, 1994); W. T. Baxter, "McKesson and Robbins: A Milestone in Auditing," *Accounting, Business & Financial History* 9 (1999): 157–74; Hillel Black, *The Watchdogs of Wall*

Street (New York, 1962), 88–167; Kitty Calavita, Henry N. Pontell, and Robert H. Tillman, *Big Money Crime: Fraud and Politics in the Savings and Loan Crisis* (Berkeley, CA, 1997); Kurt Eichenwald, *Conspiracy of Fools: A True Story* (New York, 2005).

22. "Our Home Enterprises," *Clarksville Standard*, Jan. 15, 1859, 4.

23. Edward H. Smith, *Confessions of a Confidence Man: A Handbook for Suckers* (New York, 1923), 9.

24. Mark Twain, "Political Economy," in *Mark Twain's Sketches, New and Old* (Hartford, 1875), 21–27.

25. "'Bit' on Another Game," *Sioux City Journal*, Sept. 1, 1896, 2; "Lightning Rod Man is Abroad," Sept. 2, 1904, *DNT*, 6.

26. George Akerlof, "The Market for 'Lemons': Quality Uncertainty and the Market Mechanism," *Quarterly Journal of Economics* 84 (1970): 488–500; Caroline Gerschlager, ed., *Deception in Markets: An Economic Analysis* (New York, 2005).

27. "New York in Slices: The Mock Auction," *MT*, Sept. 9, 1848, 2; "Mock Auction," *The Water-Cure Journal* 13 (April 1852): 94.

28. "The Immigrant Society," *Albany Evening Journal*, June 6, 1843, 3; "The Shippers and the Runners," *NYH*, Nov. 13, 1856, 6; "Texas," *Appleton's Annual Cyclopaedia* 32 (1880): 831; "Trading on Ignorance," *NYH*, Aug. 21, 1887, 17.

29. John McLaren, "State Probe Here Will Target Fraud by Immigration Consultants," *San Diego Union-Tribune*, Feb. 25, 1987, A3; Shalin Hai-Jew and Patricia Quan, "Telemarketing Fraud Can Target Minorities," *Northwest Asian Weekly* 14 (Dec. 8, 1995), 1; Edwin McDowell, "F.T.C. Cracks Down on Travel Scams," *NYT*, April 6, 1997, E3; Keith B. Anderson, *Consumer Fraud in the United States: The Second FTC Survey* (Washington, DC, 2007), 26–32.

30. Charles Benjamin, "Want Ad Fakers Rob Millions," *CT*, July 30, 1905, E3; Jane Addams, "Wolves and Women," *DMN*, Oct. 7, 1907, 10; Frederic J. Haskin, "Work Frauds in Mails Exposed," *LAT*, Aug. 13, 1926, 7.

31. Whitney Young, Jr., "Consumer Frauds in the Ghetto," *CD*, June 24, 1967, 11; Len Lear, "Ghetto Residents Main Victims of Consumer Frauds," *PT*, Mar. 4, 1968, 1.

32. Marlys Harris, "Elder Fraud," *Money* 24 (Nov. 1995): 144–53; Gregory Church et al., "Elderscam," *Time*, Aug. 25, 1997, http://www.time.com/time/magazine/article /0,9171,986894,00.html, accessed Jan. 16, 2009; *Fraud: Targeting America's Seniors*, Hearings, Senate Committee on Commerce, Science, and Transportation, Aug. 4, 1999, 106th Cong., 1st. Sess.; "Broker Dealers, Dean Witter Officials Face NASDR Charges over Sales of Risky Bond Trust Investments," *BNA Securities Law Daily*, Nov. 21, 2000.

33. John Moody, "'Get Rich Quick' Schemes," *WP*, Nov. 11, 1906, RE2; Wirt D. Hord, *Lost Dollars: or, The Pirates of Promotion* (Cincinnati, 1924), 28; Frank Williams, "Sucker Traps," *McClure's Magazine* 62 (1928): 14–15; "Gyps & Swindles & Schemes," *Changing Times* 19 (June 1965): 29–34; Cynthia Kadonaga, "Doctors Called Easy Marks for Realty Schemes," *WP*, Jan. 13, 1979, E1.

34. Alfred D. Chandler, *The Visible Hand: The Managerial Revolution in American Business* (Cambridge, MA, 1977); Rowena Olegario, *A Culture of Credit: Embedding Trust and Transparency in American Business* (Cambridge, MA, 2006); Vincent P. Carosso, *Investment Banking in America: A History* (Cambridge, MA, 1970); Susan Strasser, *Satisfaction Guaranteed: The Making of the American Mass Market* (Washington, DC, 1989); Nancy F. Koehn, *Brand New: How Entrepreneurs Earned Customers*

Trust from Wedgwood to Dell (Cambridge, MA, 2001); Walter A. Friedman, *Birth of a Salesman: The Transformation of Selling in America* (Cambridge, MA, 2004).

35. Ian Klaus makes a similar argument in his *Forging Capitalism: Rogues, Swindlers, Frauds, and the Rise of Modern Finance* (New Haven, 2014), 4–6, 22–24, 229–33.

36. Melville, *The Confidence-Man*, 43.

37. Anthony Comstock, *Frauds Exposed; or, How the People Are Deceived and Robbed, and Youth Corrupted, Being a Full Exposure of Various Schemes Operated through the Mails* (New York, 1880), 69, 89, 92.

38. "The King of the Peter Funks," *NYT*, June 4, 1883, 5; Arthur H. Gleason, "Promoters and Their Spending Money," *Collier's* 48 (March 2, 1912): 13–14; Smith, *Confessions of a Confidence Man*.

39. P. T. Barnum, *Humbugs of the World: An Account of Humbugs, Delusions, Impositions, Quackeries, Deceits and Deceivers Generally, in All Ages* (1866, rpt. New York, 1965), 197–99; "Petrolea: A Stupendous Swindle Exploded," *NYT*, June 27, 1865, 8; "Swindling by Oil Stocks," *Ohio Farmer*, Mar. 25, 1865, 94; Henry B. Clifford, *Years of Dishonor: or, The Cause of the Depression in Mining Stocks* (New York, 1883), 6; Rev. T. De Witt Talmage, "The Age of Swindle," *Frank Leslie's Illustrated Magazine* 24 (Oct. 1888): 289. American promoters borrowed this tactic from their British counterparts. See George Robb, *White-Collar Crime in Modern England: Financial Fraud and Business Morality, 1845–1929* (1992, rpt. New York, 2002), 104–08.

40. Roger M. Olien and Diana Davids Olien, *Easy Money: Oil Promoters and Investors in the Jazz Age* (Chapel Hill, 1990), 76–91.

41. "Profitable Investments," *HMM* 43 (Oct. 1, 1860): 519; Joseph Daucus and James Buel, *A Tour of St. Louis* (St. Louis, 1878), 400–03; Walter L. Hawley, "The Temptation of Ten Percent," *Munsey's Magazine* 22 (Feb. 1900): 759–63; Frederic J. Haskin, "The Postal Service, XII: Driving out Frauds," *Salt Lake Telegram*, Dec. 4, 1913, 4; Louis Guenther, "On the Shoals of the Oil Boom," *Current Opinion* 46 (Apr. 1919): 269–70.

42. H. J. Barrett, *How to Sell More Goods: Secrets of Successful Salesmanship* (New York, 1918), 45–46; Edward Purinton, "The Efficient Salesman," *The Independent*, Sept. 18, 1916, 412.

43. "Stock Salesman Artist of the Get-Rich-Quick," *Kalamazoo Gazette*, Dec. 22, 1910, 14; Niklas Luhmann, *Trust and Power: Two Works by Niklas Luhmann* (1973/1975, rpt. Chichester, UK, 1979), 62.

44. See the circulars furnished by Laura Thomas's mail-order beauty business, *In Re Laura Thomas*, Fraud Order Cases, Box 3, Case 674.

45. *Memorandum for the Postmaster-General in Re H. H. Tucker, Jr.* (Washington, DC, 1908).

46. "The Fool and His Money," *Youth's Companion* 73 (Dec. 28, 1899): 686; Paul Tomlinson, "Safety and Seven Percent," *McClure's Magazine* 52 (Dec. 1920): 54–55; "Girl 'Ponzi' Held in Huge Stock Swindle," *AC*, Mar. 28, 1926, 3; "11 Arrested in Pyramid Clubs Probe," *LAT*, Jan. 18, 1949, 1; "The Man Who Swindled Akron," *Life* 72 (May 5, 1972): 40–44; Virgil Burke, "Of Pyramids and Pipe Dreams," *Black Enterprise* 19 (Aug. 1988): 68–73.

47. Mary Tabor, "In Scams, Some Immigrants Target Their Own," *Boston Globe*, Sept. 11, 1989, 17; Earl C. Gottschalk, "'Affinity' Groups Are Targeted by Con Artists," *WSJ*, Dec. 11, 1992, C1; "States Warn of Rise in Ethnic Affinity Fraud," *CD*, Nov. 17,

1997, 20; Amy Borrus, "The Fraternal Order of Fraud Victims," *Business Week*, Mar. 27, 2006, 50; Froma Harrop, "Madoff Case," *Providence Journal*, D7, Dec. 21, 2008.

48. North American Securities Administrators Association, *Preying on the Faithful: The False Prophets of the Investment World* (Washington, DC, 1989); Bill Broadway, "Fraud 'in the Name of God,'" *WP*, Aug. 11, 2001, B9; Susan Sachs, "Welcome to America, and to Stock Fraud," *NYT*, May 15, 2001, A1; Kevin DeMarrias, "Scams Targeting Latinos on Rise," *Bergen County Record*, July 31, 2005, B1.

49. "Extraordinary Swindle," *CIO*, Oct. 15, 1880, 2.

50. "Moral and Financial Ruin," *WP*, Feb. 29, 1896, 6; "Many Charge a Swindle," *CT*, Oct. 30, 1901, 5; "Religion Mixed with Frauds," *CT*, June 14, 1913, 3; "Preacher Must Do Six Years," *LAT*, Aug. 11, 1930, 6; "$200,000 Lost in Church Swindles," *CD*, Sept. 20, 1947, 1.

51. *Report of the Select Committee Appointed by the Legislature of New-York, to Examine into Frauds upon Emigrants* (Albany, 1847); "Hungarians Warned," *NYT*, July 10, 1885, 8; "Italians Roused by Swindle," *NYT*, Apr. 20, 1902, 40; "Immigrants Dupes in Weird Swindles," *NYT*, Nov. 28, 1923, 19.

52. William Thorp, "$100 Million a Year Stolen from Immigrants," *Colorado Springs Gazette-Telegraph*, Jan. 1, 1905, 17.

53. Harrington, *How 'Tis Done*, 202–03; "The Lightning Rod Man," *Lowell Daily Citizen*, Feb. 27, 1875, 1.

54. *San Antonio Express*, Feb. 12, 1899, 12; "Dr. Chambers' Remedy for Intemperance," *Baltimore Gazette and Daily Advertiser*, Nov. 6, 1827, 1; "Wright's Indian Vegetable Pills," *New Hampshire Gazette*, Apr. 16, 1844, 4; "Base Counterfeit of Hostetter's Stomach Bitters," *SFB*, May 31, 1860, 3.

55. Hill, *Gold Bricks of Speculation*, 113, 121; H. J. Kenner, *The Fight for Truth in Advertising: A Story of What Business Has Done and Is Doing to Establish and Maintain Accuracy and Fair Play in Advertising and Selling for the Public's Protection* (New York, 1936), 127–33.

56. Watson Washburn and Edmund S. De Long, *High and Low Financiers: Some Notorious Swindlers and Their Abuses of Our Modern Stock Selling System* (Indianapolis, 1932), 26–27.

57. Nelson Merritt, "The Tree Peddler," *Annual Report of the Colorado Horticultural and Forestry Association for the Years 1887–88*, vol. 4 (Denver, 1888), 542.

58. William Reddy, *The Navigation of Feeling: A Framework for the History of Emotions* (New York, 2001).

59. Circular, Lawrence & Co. / Circular No. 2, Bullion Gold and Silver Mining Company, both reprinted in Comstock, *Frauds Exposed*, 17, 129; "Buy before the Advance," *Overland Monthly* 57 (Dec. 1906): xxxviii; "A Sensational New Business," advertisement, *Popular Science* (Mar. 1934): 9.

60. "75% Profit," Wm. H. Morris & Co. advertisement, *AC*, Apr. 4, 1897, 10; "The Price of Secrecy," *Springfield Republican*, Nov. 27, 1909, 8; Martha Branagan, "Suckers Psyches," *WSJ*, Oct. 20, 1989, R12; Mara Der Hovanesian, "The Hedge-Fund Biz," *Business Week*, May 26, 2003, 86; Loch Adamson, "Anatomy of a Debacle," *Institutional Investor* 39 (Aug. 2005): 36–45.

61. James Harvey Young, *The Toadstool Millionaires: A Social History of Patent Medicines before Federal Regulation* (Princeton, 1972); Eric Boyle, *Quack Medicine: A History of Combating Health Fraud in Twentieth-Century America* (New York, 2013).

62. Dan Ariely, *Predictably Irrational: The Hidden Forces That Shape Our Decisions* (New York, 2008); Richard H. Thaler and Cass R. Sunstein, *Nudge: Improving Decisions about Health, Wealth, and Happiness* (New Haven, 2008); Daniel Kahneman, *Thinking, Fast and Slow* (New York, 2011).

63. Robert J. Shiller, *Irrational Exuberance* (Princeton, 2000), 153–55, 162–64; Jessica Cohen and William Dickens, "A Foundation for Behavioral Economics," *American Economic Review* 92 (2002): 335–38; Owen Jones and Timothy Goldsmith, "Law and Behavioral Biology," *CLR* 105 (2005): 405–502.

64. Shiller, *Irrational Exuberance,* 64–66; Robert Prentice, "Whither Securities Regulation? Some Behavioral Observations Regarding Proposals for Its Future," *DLJ* 51 (2002): 1476–78.

65. Daniel Kahneman, "Maps of Bounded Rationality: Psychology for Behavioral Economics," *American Economic Review* 93 (2003): 1449–75.

66. Amos Tversky and Daniel Kahneman, "Judgment under Uncertainty: Heuristics and Biases," *Science* 185 (Sept. 27, 1974): 1124.

67. Circular No. 2, Bullion Gold and Silver Mining Company, reprinted in Comstock, *Frauds Exposed*, 130; "THIS STOCK SHOULD MAKE A LIFE INCOME FOR YOU," *LAT*, Apr. 22, 1906, NE7; Pierre Bogardus, "Saving the Country $200,000,000 a Year," *Illustrated World* 26 (May 1917): 785–87; Richard Chen, "Microcap Deception: Stock Fraud Schemes in the Modern Age," *Journal of Investing* (Fall 2000): 19.

68. Charles P. Kindleberger, *Manias, Panics, and Crashes: A History of Financial Crises*, rev. ed. (New York, 1989), 86–107.

69. Ariely, *Predictably Irrational*, 23–48; Dan Ariely, George Lowenstein, and Drazen Prelec, "Tom Sawyer and the Construction of Value," *Journal of Economic Behavior and Organization* 60 (2006): 1–10.

70. Kenner, *Fight for Truth in Advertising*, 170–72; "Price Deception in Ads Attacked," *NYT*, Dec. 14, 1956, 52; FTC, *Guides against Deceptive Pricing* (Washington, DC, 1958); "Close-Out Sales Are Often Phony," *CD*, Feb. 4, 1958, 16; R. L. Smith, *Bargain Hucksters*, 1–18.

71. Amos Tversky and Daniel Kahneman, "The Framing of Decisions and the Psychology of Choice," *Science* 211 (1981): 453–58.

72. Comstock, *Frauds Exposed*, 128; US Congress, *Frauds and Deceptions Affecting the Elderly: Investigations, Findings, and Recommendations* (Washington, DC, 1965), 35–44.

73. Arthur H. Gleason, "The Modern Fairyland," *Collier's* 48 (March 12, 1912): 11.

74. Bogardus, "Saving the Country $200,000,000 a Year," 792–93.

75. Edward Jerome Dies, "The Fine Art of Catching the Sucker," Part III, *Outlook* 133 (1923): 674–78; Einar Barford, "Avoid This Fellow!" *Collier's* 27 (Jan. 2, 1926): 34–35; Kenner, *Fight for Truth in Advertising*, 86–89.

76. Harrington, *How 'Tis Done*, 12.

77. J. D. to Lawrence & Co., Nov. 21, 1878, reprinted in Comstock, *Frauds Exposed*, 58–59.

78. William R. Leach, *Land of Desire: Merchants, Power, and the Rise of a New American Culture* (New York, 1994); T. J. Jackson Lears, *Fables of Abundance: A Cultural History of Advertising in America* (New York, 1995).

79. On creative storytelling as mode of understanding, shaper of perceived interests, and prod to action, see Frederick W. Mayer, *Narrative Politics: Stories and Collective Ac-*

tion (New York, 2014). On the centrality of stories to economic deceit, see George Akerlof and Robert Shiller, *Phishing for Phools: The Economics of Manipulation and Deception* (Princeton, 2015), especially 45–46, 172–73.

CHAPTER THREE: THE POROUSNESS OF THE LAW

1. Phineas Taylor Barnum, *The Life of P. T. Barnum, Written by Himself* (New York, 1854), 28–35, 39, 75–76, 85–86, 99.

2. Paul Erickson probes this literature in "Honest Weights and Full Measures? Or, Learning How to Cheat Customers in Antebellum America," unpublished paper delivered at the Annual Meeting of the Business History Conference, March 26, 2010, Athens, Georgia.

3. The literature on Barnum's place in American society and culture mostly connects him to issues about race, urbanization, leisure/entertainment, the wider terrain of popular culture, and sectional identity. Barnum's role in accommodating consumers to the premises of *caveat emptor* receives extensive consideration in these writings. For the most part, however, these studies do not consider his significance for the long-term development of American legal or business culture. See: Neil Harris, *Humbug: The Art of P. T. Barnum* (Chicago, 1981); Bluford Adams, *E Pluribus Barnum: The Great Showman and the Making of U.S. Popular Culture* (Minneapolis, 1997); Benjamin Reiss, *The Showman and the Slave: Race, Death, and Memory in Barnum's America* (Cambridge, MA, 2001); James W. Cook, *The Arts of Deception: Playing with Fraud in the Age of Barnum* (Cambridge, MA, 2001); Michael Pettit, *The Science of Deception: Psychology and Commerce in America* (Baltimore, 2013), especially 9–12, 228–31.

4. This term seems to have first appeared in James Fenimore Cooper's 1838 novel *Home as Found*, becoming commonplace by the 1850s.

5. William Novak, "The Myth of the 'Weak' American State," *AHR* 113 (2008): 752–72; Harry Schieber, "Private Rights and Public Power: Law, Capitalism, and the Republican Polity in 19th Century America," *YLJ* 107 (1997): 823–61; William J. Novak, *The People's Welfare: Law and Regulation in Nineteenth-Century America* (Chapel Hill, 1996); Edward Balleisen, "Bankruptcy and the Entrepreneurial Ethos in Antebellum American Law," *Australian Journal of Legal History* 8 (2004): 61–82.

6. Melville M. Bigelow, *The Law of Fraud and the Procedure Pertaining the Redress Thereof*, 2 vols. (Boston, 1877). On anti-fraud policies within America's commonwealth tradition, see Novak, *The People's Welfare*, 88–95.

7. Bigelow's *Law of Fraud* furnishes a comprehensive overview of these various actions.

8. *Acts of the General Assembly of the State of Georgia* (Milledgeville, 1834), 192. On criminal fraud law in this era, see Francis Wharton, *A Treatise on Criminal Law*, 8th ed., vol. 2 (Philadelphia, 1880), 43–134.

9. "An Ordinance Regulating Auctions in the Town of Fredericksburg," *Virginia Herald*, Oct. 14, 1829, 3; "Auctioneers," *PPL*, May 9, 1838, 2.

10. "An Act to License and Tax Pedlars," *Acts, Resolutions, and Memorials Passed . . . the General Assembly of the State of Iowa* (Iowa City, 1848), 29–30; *Public Laws and Resolutions . . . of the State of North Carolina* (Raleigh, 1873), 234; C. C. Hine, *The Insurance Statutes of the United States and Canada* (New York, 1876).

11. Adam Chambers, *The Revised Ordinances of the City of Saint Louis* (St. Louis,

1843), 246–50; Peleg Chandler, *The Charter and Ordinances of the City of Boston* (Boston, 1850), 430–44; *A Digest of the Ordinances of the City Council of Memphis* (Memphis, 1857), 133–37.

12. Thomas M. Cooley, *The Compiled Laws of the State of Michigan*, vol. 1 (Lansing, 1857), 385–402.

13. *Casco Manufacturing Co. v. Dixon*, 57 Mass. Reports 407 (Massachusetts Supreme Court, 1849); James Kent, *Commentaries on American Law*, vol. 2 (9th ed., Boston, 1858), 645–49.

14. *Laidlaw v. Organ* 15 U.S. 178 (1817); "Commonwealth v. Samuel W. Hutchinson," *Pennsylvania Law Journal* 2 (Aug. 2, 1843): 241–46; "On False Pretences," *New York Legal Observer* 5 (Nov. 1847): 401–06; Kent, *Commentaries on American Law*, 642–69; Bigelow, *Law of Fraud*, 1: 8–9, 11–12, 14, 18, 32, 66–67, 70; "Effect of Fraud on Subscriptions to Stock," *American Law Review* 14 (Mar. 1880): 177–210; Morton J. Horwitz, *The Transformation of American Law, 1776–1860* (Cambridge, MA, 1977), 263; Paula Dalley, "The Law of Deceit, 1790–1860: Continuity amidst Change," *American Journal of Legal History* 39 (1995): 402–45; David M. Gold, "John Appleton of Maine and Commercial Law: Freedom, Responsibility, and Law in the Nineteenth-Century Marketplace," *LHR* 4 (1986): 55–69; Pettit, *Science of Deception*, 26–28.

15. *McFarland v. Newman*, 9 Watts 55 (Penn. Supreme Court, 1839); Robert E. Mensel, "'A Diddle at Brobdingnag': Confidence and Caveat Emptor during the Market Revolution," *University of Memphis Law Review* 38 (2007): 115–21.

16. *Farrell v. Lovett*, 68 Maine Reports 328 (1878). See also "Law Intelligence," *Albany Balance*, Oct. 29, 1811, 348; "Caveat Emptor—The Rule of the Common Law," *American Jurist* 12 (July 1834): 94–103.

17. Walter Hamilton, "The Ancient Maxim Caveat Emptor," *YLJ* 40 (1931): 1133–53; Mensel, "'A Diddle at Brobdingnag,'" 100–21.

18. Bigelow, *The Law of Fraud*, 1: 8–17; Wharton, *Treatise on Criminal Law*, 2: 45–56; "Miss Palmer Granted a New Trial," *Topeka Weekly Capital*, Jan. 12, 1893, 7; "The Law," *Daily National Intelligencer*, Nov. 25, 1834. A similar logic stymied proposals for more extensive regulation of marketing practices. See Joanna Cohen, "'The Right to Purchase Is as Free as the Right to Sell': Defining Consumers as Citizens in the Auction-House Conflicts of the Early Republic," *Journal of the Early Republic* 30 (2010): 41–59.

19. *People v. Crissie and Harvey*, 4 Denio 525 (New York Supreme Court, 1847). See, more generally, Wharton, *A Treatise on Criminal Law*, 101–06.

20. James Taylor, *Boardroom Scandal: The Criminalization of Company Fraud in Nineteenth-Century Britain* (New York, 2013), 28–34, 62–64, 132–34, 140–51.

21. Bigelow, *Law of Fraud*, 1: 9–10. In such contexts, jurists were more likely to embrace the sort of "jurisprudence of the heart" stressed by the legal historian Peter Karsten. See his *Heart versus Head: Judge-Made Law in Nineteenth-Century America* (Chapel Hill, 1997).

22. *Bowen v. State*, 68 Tenn. 50 (Supreme Court, 1876); "The Law of False Pretences," *HMM* 37 (July 1857): 61; "'Ordinary Prudence' in False Pretenses," *ALJ* 26 (Aug. 5, 1882): 105–07; Bigelow, *The Law of Fraud*, 1: 9, 280; Wharton, *Treatise on Criminal Law*, 560–61.

23. Taylor, *Boardroom Scandal*, 89–93, 98–100, 176–82.

24. Ibid., 16–22; H. G. Wood, "Misrepresentations as to Value," *ALJ* 13 (Mar. 4, 1876): 160–62; Dalley, "The Law of Deceit," 435–41.

25. James Kirke Paulding, *The Merry Tales of the Three Wise Men of Gotham* (New York, 1839), 114–65. No nineteenth-century commercial context was as shot through with misrepresentations as horse-dealing. See Steven M. Gelber, *Horse Trading in the Age of Cars: Men in the Marketplace* (Baltimore, 2008), 5–23.

26. On nineteenth-century republican citizenship, see Harry L. Watson, *Liberty and Power: The Politics of Jacksonian America* (New York, 1990); Daniel Rodgers, "Republicanism: The Career of a Concept," *JAH* 79 (1992): 11–38.

27. For instructive models of such empirical inquiry, see the following by Stewart Macaulay: "Non-Contractual Relations and Business: A Preliminary Study," *American Sociological Review* 28 (1963): 55–69; *Law and the Balance of Power: The Automobile Manufacturers and Their Dealers* (New York, 1966); "Lawyers and Consumer Protection Laws: An Empirical Study," *Law & Society Review* 14 (1979): 115–71.

28. *People v. McCord*, 46 N.Y. 470 (New York Court of Appeals, 1871), 473; Pettit, *Science of Deception*, 29–32.

29. "Employment Agencies," *NYH*, Jan. 13, 1882, 9.

30. "Case of Fraud," *New York Spectator*, Dec. 13, 1833, 3.

31. "Mock Auctions in New York," *NYTR*, Aug. 7, 1862, reprinted in *New Orleans Delta*, Aug. 22, 1862, 3.

32. "An Important Law Case," *Charleston Courier*, Aug. 6, 1803, 1; "Joseph Blount v. John Chester," *New Jersey Journal*, June 11, 1811; *Rose and Rogers v. Beatie*, 2 Nott & McCord 538 (South Carolina Constitutional Court, 1819); "Fraud in Cotton," *Baltimore Patriot*, Dec. 3, 1830, 2; "Miller v. Hemmingway," *NYH*, Jan. 1, 1845, 2; "Buying and Selling Produce," *BS*, Dec. 21, 1848, 1; "Legal Decision in Regard to Falsely Packed Cotton," *HMM* 31 (Oct. 1854): 456; "On 'Change,'" *New Orleans Times*, Aug. 21, 1868, 7; "Liability of Directors," *Banker's Magazine* 43 (Sept. 1888): 208–16; and the cases cited in Dalley, "Law of Deceit," and Bigelow, *Law of Fraud*.

33. *Ramsey & Parker v. J. B. Plauche & Co.*, *Lapeyre, Harrope Co. v. Buchannon*, *Carroll & Co.*, *Decisions of the New Orleans Chamber of Commerce* (New Orleans, 1857), 116–17, 319–20; *Nott & Co. v. Kirkman et al.*, 19 Louisiana Reports 14 (Louisiana Supreme Court, Eastern Dist., 1841); *Clarke et al. v. Lockhart et al.*, 10 Louisiana Reports 5 (Louisiana Supreme Court, 1845); "Of Falsely Packed and Unmerchantable Cotton," *HMM* 23 (July 1850): 111–12; *Mure v. Donnell*, 12 Louisiana Ann. 369 (Louisiana Supreme Court, 1857).

34. "A Horse Bought and Sold," *Barre Gazette*, Sept. 13, 1861, 1.

35. "Tricked for a Million," *CIO*, Nov. 26, 1889, 1; "A Mighty Swindle," *LAT*, Nov. 27, 1889, 4; "Wants Frederiksen's Securities," *CT*, Jan. 1, 1890, 6; "Frederiksen's Dupes at Law," *CT*, June 7, 1891, 3.

36. "Work of the Police," *BS*, Mar. 5, 1868, 1; "Work of the Police," *BS*, Apr. 3, 1868, 4; "Work of the Police," *BS*, May 4, 1868, 1; "Police Operations," *BS*, June 3, 1868, 1; "Arrests Made," *BS*, Aug. 4, 1868, 1; Police Operations," *BS*, Nov. 5, 1868, 1. From 1851 through 1853, New York City reported 434 arrests under the categories of "fraud" and "receiving goods under false pretenses," roughly one out of every three hundred arrests over that period. *Eleventh and Twelfth Report of the Prison Association of New York for 1855 and 1856* (New York, 1857), 126.

37. "The Fraudulent Insurance Cases," *BET*, Sept. 16, 1852, 2; "The Great Life Insurance Trial," *Flake's Galveston Bulletin*, Feb. 5, 1870, 6; "Another Udderzook Affair," *The Independent* 28 (Aug. 24, 1876): 28; "Louisville, Kentucky, Correspondence," *The Indica-*

tor 12 (Feb. 1893): 119. A survey of newspaper coverage of criminal false pretense cases in 1888, using the database *America's Historical Newspapers*, generated 343 instances of criminal proceedings, of which 273 offered at least some details about the nature of the alleged fraud. Of these 273 instances, only 119, or 43.7 percent, clearly involved allegations of fraud against businesses, while 38, or 13.9 percent, involved allegations of fraud by retailers against nonpaying consumers, and 33, or 12.1 percent, resulted from conflicts over nonpayment of personal loans.

38. Michael Hindus, "Black Justice under White Law: Criminal Prosecutions of Blacks in Antebellum South Carolina," *JAH* 63 (1976): 590.

39. *Annual Report of the Attorney General of the State of Michigan* (Lansing, 1866); *Annual Report of the Attorney General of the State of Michigan* (Lansing, 1873). In 1865–66, there were 20 convictions from 65 false pretenses indictments and 504 convictions from 765 larceny indictments. In 1872–73, there were 14 convictions from 79 false pretenses indictments and 488 convictions from 799 larceny indictments.

40. "Frauds upon the Manhattan Gas Company," *Brooklyn Eagle*, Sept. 29, 1853.

41. "Mock Auctions," *SEP*, Aug. 25, 1838, 2; George G. Foster, *New York in Slices* (New York, 1849), 33–36; "How We Furnished Our House," *HW* (Apr. 3, 1858): 209; "A Down Look," *SEP*, Sept. 22, 1860, 4; "Trade Morality," *PI*, Oct. 27, 1876, 4; Paul Prowler, "Glimpses of Gotham," *NPG*, May 24, 1879, 14; Corey Goettsch, " 'The World Is but One Vast Mock Auction': Fraud and Capitalism in Nineteenth-Century America," in Brian P. Luskey and Wendy A. Woloson, eds., *Capitalism by Gaslight: Illuminating the Economy of Nineteenth-Century America* (Philadelphia, 2015), 109–21.

42. The Alleged Mock Auction Frauds," *NYH*, Feb. 14, 1866, 5; "Alleged Mock Auction," *NYH*, Feb. 15, 1866, 2; "Zeno Burnham, the Mock Auctioneer," *NYT*, Feb. 17, 1866, 5.

43. "An Alleged Mock Auction Swindle," *NYT*, Oct. 7, 1865, 3; "The Alleged Mock Auction Frauds," *NYH*, Feb. 14, 1866, 5; "Alleged Mock Auction," *NYH*, Feb. 15, 1866, 2; "The Case of Burnham, the Mock Auctioneer," *NYT*, Feb. 16, 1866, 3.

44. "Burnham Case Again," *Brooklyn Eagle*, May 21, 1866, 2; "The Pardon of Zeno Burnham," *NYT*, May 25, 1866, 2; "Zeno Burnham again in Limbo," *NPG*, Feb. 16, 1867, 3; "Carnival of Crime," *Brooklyn Eagle*, Feb. 8, 1869, 1; "Furniture Funks," *NYT*, Mar. 13, 1871, 12; "Why Did Fenton Pardon Zeno Burnham?" *NYT*, Oct. 3, 1872, 12; "The Mock Auction Business," *NYT*, Oct. 18, 1879.

45. "An Extensive Swindle," *NYTR*, Dec. 8, 1866, 8; "Conspiracy to Cheat and Defraud," *NYT*, Mar. 3, 1867, 6; "The Alleged Great Dry Goods Swindle," *NYH*, Mar. 9, 1867, 8.

46. "Suit for $30,000 Damages for False Imprisonment," *NYH*, Oct. 28, 1868.

47. "Who Is Doctor Langley?" *Worcester Spy*, Mar. 26, 1879, 4; "An Important Arrest," *New Haven Register*, June 4, 1883, 3; "An Alleged Swindler," *Boston Journal*, June 4, 1883, 3; "The King of Peter Funks," *NYT*, June 4, 1883, 5; "The Boston Peter Funk," *CT*, June 7, 1883, 4; "Fraudulent Land-Selling Scheme," *CT*, July 21, 1888, 2; "He Was a Clever Swindler," *CT*, July 22, 1888, 13; "Another Failure to Convict," *NYT*, Oct. 10, 1888, 8; " 'Doc' Langley Arrested," *NYT*, Nov. 11, 1896, 3; "Langley Loses His Appeal," *NYT*, June 30, 1897, 3.

48. "Frauds upon Emigrants and Passengers," *New York Daily Tribune*, Nov. 14, 1859, 5; "The Ticket Swindlers and Judge Russell," *NYT*, Oct. 31, 1860, 8.

49. "Trial and Conviction of Dr. Dyott for Fraudulent Insolvency," *Daily National*

Intelligencer, June 7, 1839, 3; *The Highly Interesting and Important Trial of Dr. T.W. Dyott* (Philadelphia, 1839).

50. "Fraudulent Bankers Imprisoned in New Jersey," *NYH*, April 3, 1863, 5; "Justice," *HW* (Dec. 22, 1877): 999; "Benjamin Noyes Found Guilty," *NYT*, June 2, 1878, 2; "An Ex-Bank President in Prison," *NYH*, July 3, 1883; "The Wreckers Held," *PI*, Dec. 18, 1890, 3; "Banker Sawyer Is Guilty," *Kansas City Times*, Dec. 12, 1893, 1.

51. "Bank of Maryland Trials at Bel-Air," *Niles' Weekly Register* 50 (May 21, 1836): 202. A complete trial transcript ran in the *Baltimore Gazette* from June through September 1836. See also Robert E. Shalhope, *The Baltimore Bank Riot: Political Upheaval in Antebellum Maryland* (Urbana, 2009), 88–105. For later acquittals and decisions not to prosecute elites on fraud charges, see "Biddle, Cowperthwaite and Andrews Discharged," *PI*, Apr. 30, 1842, 2; "Bank Trial at Philadelphia," *NYT*, Dec. 22, 1858, 4; "Culver Trial," *NYTR*, Feb. 11, 1867, 8; "Insurance Officers Acquitted," *NYT*, Nov. 22, 1878, 5.

52. "Affair of the Schuylkill Bank," *PPL*, May 18, 1842, 2; "How Rogues Go Scot Free," *NYT*, Jan. 11, 1880, 12.

53. "No Cause for Action," *CIO*, Dec. 30, 1893, 5.

54. "Why Rogues Go Scot Free."

55. "Afraid of Wall Street," *NYT*, April 5, 1877, 4; *The Stock Market Rig: A Thorough Exposure of a Fascinating Fraud* (Brooklyn, 1875), 10–12; Joseph E. King, *A Mine to Make a Mine: Financing the Colorado Mining Industry, 1859–1902* (College Station, 1977); Cheryl Freeman, "Wanted: The Honorable William H. Cushman," *Colorado Magazine* 49 (1972): 35–54; Roger Whitman, *The Rise and Fall of a Frontier Entrepreneur: Benjamin Rathbun, "Master Building and Architect,"* ed. Scott Eberle and David A. Gerber (Syracuse, 1996).

56. "City Gleanings," *PPL*, May 11, 1841, 2; "Philadelphia," *BS*, May 17, 1841, 4; "Dr. Dyott," *Albany Argus*, reprinted in *Vermont Gazette*, May 18, 1841, 2; "Summary of News," *Farmer's Register*, May 13, 1841, 318.

57. Taylor, *Boardroom Scandal*.

58. Brian Luskey, "Central Intelligence Agencies: Negotiating Market Transactions and the Commodification of Labor in the Nineteenth-Century City," unpublished paper delivered to the Business History Conference, Athens, Georgia, March 26, 2010.

59. "Underwood v. Fetter (New York Supreme Court)," *New York Legal Observer* 6 (Feb. 1848): 66–69; "Arrest of a Swindler," *Mobile Herald*, Sept. 30, 1845, reprinted in *NPG* 1 (Oct. 11, 1845): 60; "Witnesses Spirited Away," *SFB*, Apr. 10, 1860, 4; "A Compromise," *Daily National Intelligencer*, Feb. 25, 1864, 3; "General Sessions," *NYT*, June 28, 1873, 2; "Amicably Settled," *NYH*, Apr. 8, 1886, 8. This dynamic parallels the creditor tactic of objecting to bankruptcy petitions as a way to extract payments from failed debtors. Edward J. Balleisen, *Navigating Failure: Bankruptcy and Commercial Society in Antebellum America* (Chapel Hill, 2001), 115–19.

60. "Falsely Packed Cotton," *Daily Alabama Journal*, Sept. 12, 1853, 2.

61. "Rewards to Policemen," *NPG* 2 (Aug. 21, 1847): 397; "A Baltimorean among the Peter Funks," *BS*, Aug. 26, 1853, 1; "Frauds of Intelligence Offices," *NYT*, Apr. 25, 1855, 8; "Mock Auctions in New York," *HMM* 37 (Sept. 1857): 393–94; "Affairs in New York," *BS*, Mar. 10, 1862, 4; "Contrite Swindlers," *CT*, Jan. 20, 1883, 7; "An 'Agent' in Trouble," *Kalamazoo Gazette*, Mar. 16, 1888, 4.

62. "On False Pretences," 401; "Pittsburgh," *NPG*, May 18, 1867, 3.

63. "Important Case," *Poulson's American Daily Advertiser*, Sept. 20, 1815, 3; "Cor-

respondence of the *Philadelphia North American*," *Charleston Southern Patriot*, Sept. 11, 1845, 2; coverage of the fraud conspiracy by the boot and shoe dealer M. Frank Paige in the *Boston Journal* (Jan. 11, Feb. 24, Mar. 8, 1879).

64. "Federal Baseness," *New Hampshire Patriot and State Gazette*, Feb. 6, 1838, 2; Peter J. Coleman, *Debtors and Creditors in America: Insolvency, Imprisonment for Debt, and Bankruptcy, 1607–1900* (Madison, 1974).

65. William Blackstone, *Commentaries on the Laws of England*, 12th ed. (London, 1795), 4: 4–5.

66. Allen Steinberg, *The Transformation of Criminal Justice: Philadelphia, 1800–1880* (Chapel Hill, 1989); Laura F. Edwards, *The People and Their Peace: Legal Culture and the Transformation of Inequality in the Post-Revolutionary South* (Chapel Hill, 2009).

67. "Another Falsehood of the *Clarmont Eagle*," *New Hampshire Gazette*, Feb. 6, 1838, 2; "Vermont Governor's Address to the Legislature," *Niles Weekly Register* 59 (Oct. 24, 1840): 115–16; "News Items," *Brattleboro Weekly Eagle*, Oct. 23, 1851, 2; "A New Way to Pay Old Debts," *Ohio State Journal*, Apr. 12, 1859, 2; "Abstract of New York Supreme Court," *ALJ* 14 (Nov. 21, 1874): 332–33; "Extradition—*Habeas Corpus*," *Central Law Journal*, Mar. 28, 1884, 252–56.

68. "Fay and Collins v. Oatley and Blodgett," 6 *Wisconsin Reports* 42 (1857).

69. *Message of James A. Beaver to the General Assembly* (Harrisburg, 1889), 53–54.

70. "Law of False Pretences," *PPL*, June 19, 1847, 2; June 30, 1847, 2; Jan. 21, 1848, 7; "Frivolous and Vexatious," *CT*, Sept. 3, 1857, 1; "Lecture upon Law," *PPL*, July 29, 1859, 1; "Judge Cowing's Charge," *NYT*, June 6, 1882, 3.

71. "Law of False Pretences," *HMM*, 63.

72. "Law Intelligence," *Albany Balance and State Journal*, Oct. 29, 1811, 348; "A Righteous Verdict," *Connecticut Courant*, Dec. 23, 1833, 2; "Obtaining Goods under False Pretences," *Daily National Intelligencer*, Nov. 9, 1843, 3; "Obtaining Goods under False Pretenses," *SFB*, Feb. 25, 1876, 2.

73. "Supreme Judicial Court," *Eastern Argus*, May 19, 1825, 2; "William Livermore," *Eastern Argus*, July 4, 1836, 3; "Commonwealth v. Hickey," *Pennsylvania Law Journal* 3 (Jan. 2, 1844): 86–94; "Enormous Swindling Transactions," *NYH*, Apr. 10, 1860, 4; "Wolf Case in the Criminal Court," *BS*, Mar. 10, 1868, 1; "Acquitted of Conspiracy," *NYH*, Dec. 6, 1884, 5.

74. *Monthly Law Reporter* 6 (Oct. 1848): 256–71.

75. On parallel tendencies of British creditors to pursue fraud allegations to obtain negotiating leverage, and of the British legal establishment to view such actions as perversions of process, see Taylor, *Boardroom Scandal*, 97, 147.

76. "Court of Oyer and Terminar," *NYT*, Feb. 6, 1866, 3; "Alleged Mock Auction," *NYH*, Feb. 15, 1866, 2; "Zeno Burnham Pardoned," *NYH*, May 16, 1866, 5; "Topics of Today," *Brooklyn Eagle*, Dec. 5, 1867, 2.

77. Tougher quality standards also constrained the ability of poorer planters to find a market, while the integration of inspectorships into local patronage networks produced grumbling about favoritism toward wealthy planters. Lynn Nelson and Peter Mancall, "Then the Poor Planter Hath Greatly the Disadvantage': Tobacco Inspection, Soil Exhaustion, and the Formation of a Planter Elite in York County, Virginia, 1700–1750," *Locus* 6 (1994): 119–41; Mary McKinney Schweitzer, "Economic Regulation and the Colonial Economy: The Maryland Tobacco Inspection Act of 1847," *Journal of Economic History* 40 (1980): 551–69; Newton Jones, "Weights, Measures, and Mercantilism:

The Inspection of Exports in Virginia, 1742 to 1820," in Darren B. Rutman, ed., *Old Dominion: Essays for Thomas Perkins Abernathy* (Charlottesville, 1964), 122–34.

78. "Tobacco Inspection," *Baltimore Patriot*, May 15, 1822, 2; "Tobacco Inspection," *Richmond Enquirer*, Mar. 31, 1831, 3; "Tobacco Inspection," *Missouri Republican*, Nov. 19, 1841, 2; "Tobacco Inspection," *Missouri Republican*, Nov. 23, 1841, 2; "Increased Tobacco Inspections," *BS*, Nov. 3, 1845, 4.

79. Jerome V. C. Smith, *Natural History of the Fishes of Massachusetts* (Boston, 1843), 16–17.

80. B. U. Coles, "Improvements in the Cultivation of Wheat and Flour," *AF* 2 (Feb. 2, 1821): 356–57; "Public Meeting," *BS*, Jan. 28, 1834, 2; Agricultural," *NYT*, Feb. 28, 1856, 3; "Flour Inspection," *NYTR*, Mar. 25, 1856, 4; "Flour Inspection at Philadelphia," *CT*, June 20, 1862, 4.

81. "O. Hunker," "The Inspection Laws," *The Pathfinder*, Mar. 25, 1843, 66; "The Inspection Laws," *NPG* 1 (July 4, 1846): 364; "Report on Inspections," *AF* 9 (Feb. 1854): 245–47; "Tobacco Inspection Laws of Maryland," *Monthly Journal of Agriculture* 3 (July 1857): 5–9; "Inspection of Beef and Pork," *San Joaquin Republican*, Mar. 24, 1860, 4; "Tobacco Inspection in Kentucky," *BS*, Feb. 5, 1872, 2; Nicholas Parillo, *Against the Profit Motive: The Salary Revolution in American Government, 1780–1940* (New Haven, 2013), 51–124.

82. "Inspection System," *BET*, Nov. 12, 1847, 2; "Massachusetts Mackerel," *Gloucester Telegraph*, July 22, 1848, 2; "Flour Inspection," *Daily Placer Times*, Nov. 8, 1853, 2; "Great Complaint," *Alta California*, Aug. 1, 1853, 7.

83. Moss et al. v. Mead et al., 1 Denio 378 (New York Supreme Court, 1845); "Flour and Provision Inspection," *Sandusky Journal*, Mar. 18, 1856, 2; Gunther & Rodewald v. Atwell, 19 *Maryland Reports* 157 (Maryland Court of Appeals, 1862); "Flour Inspection," *NOP*, July 12, 1870, 2. The best account of political reactions against activist government remains Louis Hartz, *Economic Policy and Democratic Thought: Pennsylvania, 1776–1860* (Cambridge, MA, 1948).

84. "The Flour Inspection Ordinance," *CT*, Dec. 1, 1863, 4.

85. "New Constitution of New York," *BS*, Oct. 22, 1846, 1; *Report of the Revisors of the Civil Code of Virginia* (Richmond, 1847), 489; "Voluntary Inspection," *NOP*, Jan. 8, 1852, 1; "Baltimore Board of Trade," *HMM* 27 (Nov. 1852): 626–28; "New Inspection Law of Maryland," *HMM* 31 (July 1854): 110–11; "Compulsory Inspection," *NOP*, Feb. 13, 1856, 3; *The General Statutes of the Commonwealth of Massachusetts* (Boston, 1860), 256–80; "A Word about the Inspection of Flour," *NOP*, Dec. 1, 1869, 2; Kelly Olds, "Public Export Inspections in the United States and Their Privatization," *Cato Journal* 19 (1999): 17–37.

86. *Debates and Proceedings in the New-York State Convention* (Albany, 1846), 398–400; *Proceedings and Debates of the Constitutional Convention* (Albany, 1868), 1368; "State Tobacco Inspection System," *BS*, Jan. 27, 1876, 2.

87. "Tobacco Inspection in Kentucky," *BS*, Feb. 5, 1872, 2; "Tobacco Inspection in the Legislature," *Southern Planter and Farmer* 36 (Feb. 1875): 113; "State Tobacco Inspection," *BS*, Feb. 20, 1879, 2; "Tobacco Inspection," *BS*, Jan. 14, 1884, 2.

88. *General Statutes of the Commonwealth of Massachusetts*, 256–80; "A Word about the Inspection of Flour," *NOP*, Dec. 1, 1869, 2; "The Inspection of Fish Laws," *Boston Journal*, Feb. 19, 1872, 4; J. Bryant Walker, *The Law of Municipal Corporations in the State of Ohio* (Cincinnati, 1871), 137–40.

89. "Zeno Burnham Again," *NYH*, Feb. 26, 1867, 8; "Mrs. Moore's Purchases," *NYH*, Sept. 25, 1879, 4. On threatened/imposed license revocations, see "New York," *BS*, Jan. 25, 1858, 4; "Peter Funked," *NYH*, Mar. 8, 1862, 3; "Municipal Affairs," *CIO*, Feb. 21, 1875, 2; "A Consistent Mayor," *Omaha Herald*, Feb. 16, 1888, 7.

90. "Mock Auctions," *Barre Gazette*, Sept. 12, 1845, 2; "Mock Auctions," *NPG*, Mar. 21, 1846, 248; "The Mayor and the Peter Funks," *NPG*, Oct. 3, 1846, 29; "The Mayor and the Mock Auctioneers," *NPG*, Jan. 23, 1847, 156. One New York auctioneer sought a court order to remove the warning sign outside his storefront, but lost his case. *Gilbert v. Mickle*, 4 Sandford 357 (New York Court of Chancery, 1846). On practice in London, see "Mock Auctions," *The Observer*, Apr. 20, 1828, 3.

91. "Mock Auctioneers," Jan. 24, 1862, 3; "Affairs in New York," *BS*, Apr. 24, 1862, 4; "Officer Wells and Peter Funk," *NYTR*, Nov. 11, 1862, 4.

92. "Affairs in New York," *BS*, Apr. 19, 1862, 4; "The Last of the Peter Funks," *New Orleans Delta*, Sept. 13, 1862, 1; "Peter Funk," *Lowell Citizen and News*, June 10, 1863, 2.

93. "False Pretences," *Cincinnati Gazette*, Dec. 6, 1867, 1; "Mock Auction Sales," *CT*, July 4, 1874, 11; "The Newest Swindle," *NYT*, Oct. 1, 1876, 16; "Mock Auction Sales," *NYT*, Nov. 12, 1876, 5; "Mock Auction Swindles," *NYT*, Nov. 26, 1876, 5; "Petty Swindling," *CT*, Dec. 14, 1882, 8; "Auction Sale of Cigars," *AA* 42 (Feb. 1883): 87; "A Mock Auction Store Closed," *NYT*, Aug. 9, 1884, 8; "Plying His Old Trade," *KCS*, July 28, 1992, 1.

94. "The Police Commissioners' Annual Report to the Board of Police," *NYH*, Jan. 5, 1864, 5. See also Goettsch, " 'World Is but One Vast Mock Auction,' " 122–26.

95. "Merchants Be on Your Guard," *Charleston City Gazette*, June 12, 1817, 2; "Fraud in Cotton Detected," *Charleston City Gazette*, Mar. 28, 1821, 2; "Fraud in Cotton," *Baltimore Patriot*, Nov. 14, 1828, 2; Ralph Haskins, "Planter and Cotton Factor in the Old South: Some Areas of Friction," *Agricultural History* 29 (1955): 1–4.

96. "Fraud in Packing Cotton," *Camden Southern Chronicle*, Apr. 9, 1825, 1; "From the *Mobile Register*," *Baltimore Patriot*, Mar. 25, 1829, 2; "False Packing of Cotton Wool," *Manchester Guardian*, Nov. 21, 1835, 2; *A Digest of the Laws of the State of Alabama* (Montgomery, 1836), 97.

97. "Frauds in Cotton Packing," *DeBow's Review* 1 (July 1851): 70; John Wrigley and Sons, "Letter to the Editor," *Manchester Guardian*, May 14, 1853, 8; "Sanded and Adulterated Cotton," *Manchester Guardian*, Oct. 5, 1859, 3; *Annual Report . . . of the Chamber of Commerce of the State of New York* (New York, 1860), 90–92; "Cotton," *Southern Cultivator*, 18 (May 1860): 147–48.

98. Judith Schafer, " 'Guaranteed against the Vices and Maladies Prescribed by Law': Consumer Protection, the Law of Slave Sales, and the Supreme Court in Antebellum Louisiana," *American Journal of Legal History* 31 (1987): 306–21; Dalley, "Law of Deceit," 430–32.

99. Harris, *Humbug*, 10–20; David Jaffee, "Peddlers of Progress and the Transformation of the Rural North, 1760–1860," *JAH* 78 (1991): 511–35; Joseph Rainer, "The 'Sharper' Image: Yankee Peddlers, Southern Consumers, and the Market Revolution," *Business and Economic History* 36 (1997): 27–44; Schafer, " 'Guaranteed against the Vices' "; Malcolm J. Rohrbough, *The Land Office Business: The Settlement and Administration of American Public Lands, 1789–1837* (New York, 1968); Peter R. Decker, *Fortunes and Failures: White-Collar Mobility in Nineteenth-Century San Francisco* (Cambridge, MA, 1978), 43–56; Daniel Pope, "Advertising as a Consumer Issue: An Historical

View," *Journal of Social Issues* 47 (1991): 41–56; Wendy A. Woloson. "Wishful Thinking: Retail Premiums in Mid-Nineteenth-Century America," *Enterprise & Society* 13 (2012): 790–831.

100. Balleisen, *Navigating Failure*, 95–96, 106–113; Susan Strasser, *Satisfaction Guaranteed: The Making of the American Mass Market* (Washington, DC, 1989); Stephen Mihm, *A Nation of Counterfeiters: Capitalists, Con Men, and the Making of the United States* (Cambridge, MA, 2007).

101. Robert Sobel, *The Big Board: A History of the New York Stock Market* (New York, 1965); King, *Mine to Make a Mine*; Glenn Vent and Cynthia Birk, "Insider Trading and Accounting Reform: The Comstock Case," *Accounting Historians Journal* 20 (1993): 67–82; Mark Wahlgren Summers, *The Era of Good Stealings* (New York, 1993).

102. Moritz Busch, *Wanderungen zwischen die Hudson und Mississippi 1851 und 1852* (Stuttgart, 1854), 107. See also Charles Dickens, *American Notes for General Circulation*, vol. 2 (London, 1842), 290–91; Foster, *New York in Slices*, 36.

Chapter Four: Channels of Exposure

1. On the economics of deception, see: Vincent-Antonin Lépinay and Ellen Hertz, "Preconditions of Economic Deception," in Caroline Gerschlager, ed., *Deception in Markets: An Economic Analysis* (New York, 2005), 269–96.

2. "False Packing," *NOP*, May 21, 1851, 2; "False Packed Cotton," *Daily True Delta*, Apr. 2, 1859, 2; "On 'Change,'" *New Orleans Times*, Aug. 21, 1868, 7.

3. "Sacking a Mock Auctioneer," *Newport Mercury*, Apr. 11, 1846, 2; "New York Mock Auctions," *MT*, Aug. 19, 1851, 4; "Peter Funk," *Ohio Statesman*, June 29, 1860, 1.

4. Robert Shalhope, *The Baltimore Bank Riot: Political Upheaval in Antebellum Maryland* (Urbana-Champaign, 2009), 61–87; E. P. Thompson, "The Moral Economy of the English Crowd in the Eighteenth Century," *Past and Present* 50 (1971): 76–136.

5. "Credit Obtained for Goods by Alleged Fraud," *HMM* 27 (1852): 205.

6. Rowena Olegario, *A Culture of Credit: Embedding Trust and Transparency in American Business* (Cambridge, MA, 2006); Vincent P. Carosso, *Investment Banking in America: A History* (Cambridge, MA, 1970); Alfred D. Chandler, *Henry Varnum Poor: Business Editor, Analyst, and Reformer* (Cambridge, MA, 1956); Susan Strasser, *Satisfaction Guaranteed: The Making of the American Mass Market* (Washington, DC, 1989); Richard S. Tedlow, *New and Improved: The Story of Mass Marketing in America* (New York, 1990); Nancy F. Koehn, *Brand New: How Entrepreneurs Gained Customers Trust from Wedgwood to Dell* (Cambridge, MA, 2001).

7. Steven C. Bullock, "A Mumper among the Gentle: Tom Bell, Colonial Confidence Man," *William & Mary Quarterly* 3rd Ser., 55 (1998): 231–58.

8. Rathbun's forgeries attracted coverage from New York papers and national journals; the Schuyler forgeries, like the Credit Mobilier scandal and the life-insurance frauds of the 1870s, consumed the work of journalists for months.

9. James Taylor, *Boardroom Scandal: The Criminalization of Company Fraud in Nineteenth-Century Britain* (New York, 2013).

10. "An Attempt to Swindle the Government," *NPG*, Nov. 21, 1846, 84; "Alleged Frauds in Certificates of Bank Shares," *NYT*, March 5, 1853, 6; "Robbing Merchants," *NYT*, May 14, 1874; "Forged Bonds on the Market," *NYT*, March 5, 1875, 8; "Swindling Devices," *NYT*, Dec. 18, 1876, 8; "Stranger Than Fiction," *NPG*, Nov. 6, 1880. See also

Wendy Woloson, "Wishful Thinking: Retail Premiums in Nineteenth-Century America," *Enterprise and Society* 13 (2012): 811.

11. Examples include: John Morgan, *A Warning against Quackery* (Boston, 1851); Henry William Herbert, *Tricks and Traps of New York City* (Boston, 1857); Henry William Herbert, *Tricks and Traps of Chicago* (New York, 1859); J. H. Holton, *The Rogues and Rogueries of New York* (New York, 1865); James K. Medbury, *Men and Mysteries of Wall Street* (New York, 1870); *The Swindlers of America: Who They Are and How They Work* (New York, 1875); Bates Harrington, *How 'Tis Done: A Thorough Ventilation of the Numerous Schemes Conducted by Wandering Canvassers* (Chicago, 1879); William W. Fowler, *Twenty Years of Inside Life in Wall Street* (New York, 1880); Anthony Comstock, *Frauds Exposed; or, How the People Are Deceived and Robbed, and Youth Corrupted* (New York, 1880); Joseph C. Grannan, *Grannan's Warning against Fraud* (Cincinnati, 1889); Peter R. Earling, *Whom to Trust: A Treatise on Mercantile Credit* (Chicago, 1890); E. G. Redmond, *The Frauds of America: How They Work and How to Foil Them* (Chicago, 1896); S. James Weldon, *Twenty Years a Fakir* (Omaha, 1899).

12. Joseph E. King, *A Mine to Make a Mine: Financing the Colorado Mining Industry, 1859–1902* (College Station, 1977), 44–46; Chandler, *Henry Varnum Poor*, 35–36; Woloson, "Wishful Thinking," 811–12; James Harvey Young, *The Toadstool Millionaires: A Social History of Patent Medicines in America before Federal Regulation* (Princeton, 1961), 76–88. For a mid-nineteenth-century critique of American newspapers as aiders and abettors of fraud, see Lambert A. Wilmer, *Our Press Gang: or, A Complete Exposition of the Corruptions and Crimes of the American Newspapers* (Philadelphia, 1859), 148–65, 340–52.

13. Mark Twain, *Roughing It* (New York, 1872), 306–11.

14. Mark Wahlgren Summers, *The Era of Good Stealings* (New York, 1993), 82–85; Richard White, "Information, Markets, Corruption: Transcontinental Railroads in the Golden Age," *JAH* 90 (2003): 19–43; Steven Fraser, *Every Man a Speculator: A History of Wall Street in American Life* (New York, 2005), 77–217.

15. Henry A. Boardman, *The Bible in the Counting-House* (Philadelphia, 1853), 25, 30–31.

16. For illustrations of such reporting in the *National Police Gazette*, see "Robert Sutton, *alias* Bob the Wheeler," Oct. 16, 1845, 1; "Dodger's 'Expositions,'" Aug. 10, 1867, 2; "A Female Fraud," Dec. 14, 1878, 10; "A Woman's Financial Scheme," Oct. 16, 1880, 2; "A Clever Adventuress," Nov. 17, 1894, 6.

17. Michael Pettit, "The Unwary Purchaser: Consumer Psychology and the Regulation of Commerce in America," *Journal of the History of the Behavioral Sciences* 43 (2007): 379–99.

18. "Beware of Fraud!" *Baltimore Patriot*, Jan. 1, 1815, 4; "Blake's Fire Proof Patent Paint," *NPG*, Nov. 2, 1850, 4; "The Ostermoor Patent Electric Felt Mattress," *Ladies Home Journal* 18 (May 1901): 17; Strasser, *Satisfaction Guaranteed*, 42–88.

19. "Flour Inspection," *NYT*, Feb. 13, 1856, 8; "Agricultural," *NYT*, Feb. 14, 1856, 6; "Flour Inspectors," *NYT*, Feb. 14, 1856, 3; "Market Reports," *NYT*, Feb. 25, 1856, 6; "Another Meeting about Flour Inspection," *NYT*, Feb. 28, 1856, 6; "Flour Inspection Meeting," *NYT*, Mar. 17, 1856, 3; "Eastern View of the Flour Inspection Reform," *NYT*, Mar. 21, 1856, 3; "Western View of the Flour Reform," *NYT*, Apr. 12, 1856, 3.

20. "Critical Notices," *Southern Quarterly Review* (Jan. 1855): 273; "Barnum's and Greeley's Biographies," *Christian Examiner* 23 (1855): 246, 257; "Lessons of Barnum's

Life," *NYT*, Dec. 16, 1854; "The English on Barnum," *British Advertiser*, reprinted in *Ohio Statesman*, Apr. 5, 1859, 1; Wilmer, *Our Press Gang*, 152–54; Neil Harris, *Humbug: The Art of P. T. Barnum* (Chicago, 1981), 152–54.

21. "Barnum Exploded," unnamed Albany paper, reprinted in *New Albany Ledger*, Feb. 12, 1856, 1; "Barnum Out-Barnumed," *Charleston Mercury*, Feb. 18, 1856, 2; "The Utter Failure of Mr. Barnum," *Wisconsin Free Democrat*, Mar. 26, 1856, 2; "The Barnum Correspondence," *NYH*, June 5, 1856, 4; "Financial and Political State of the Times," *NYH*, Sept. 10, 1857, 4.

22. P. T. Barnum, *Life of P. T. Barnum*; "A Distinction and a Difference," *NYTR*, Mar. 19, 1856, 4.

23. P. T. Barnum, *Humbugs of the World: An Account of Humbugs, Delusions, Impositions, Quackeries, Deceits, and Deceivers Generally, in All Ages* (New York, 1865), 21, 239.

24. Fowler, *Twenty Years of Inside Life in Wall Street*; Henry Clews, *Twenty-Eight Years in Wall Street: Fraud and Fair Dealing in Stocks! An Exposé* (New York, 1888), 88. See also Michael Pettit's discussion of Thomas Lawson's 1905 exposé, *Frenzied Finance*, in *The Science of Deception: Psychology and Commerce in America* (Baltimore, 2013), 46. These arguments dovetailed with the attacks that the era's defenders of speculation leveled against gambling. See Ann Fabian, *Card Sharps, Dream Books, and Bucket Shops: Gambling in Nineteenth-Century America* (Ithaca, NY, 1990).

25. Stephen Mihm, *A Nation of Counterfeiters: Capitalists, Con Men, and the Making of the United States* (Cambridge, MA, 2007), 209–55.

26. Typical articles in *Scientific American* include: "Scoundrelism in Patent Agents," Sept. 16, 1854, 5; "The Keely Motor Deception," July 17, 1875, 33; "Glucosed Leather," Sept. 6, 1884, 147.

27. Joris Mercelis, "Stages of Openness in the Development of Photographic Technology in Nineteenth-Century America," unpublished paper delivered to the Annual Meeting of the Business History Conference, March 14, 2014, Frankfurt, Germany.

28. Journals such as *The American Journal of Pharmacy*, *The Boston Medical and Surgical Journal*, and *Medical and Surgical Reporter* published hundreds of such articles in the nineteenth century; see also Young, *Toadstool Millionaires*, 144–67.

29. See, for example, *The American Bee Journal* 14 (1878): 29, 65, 130, 180, 211, 275, 352.

30. "Review," *American Journal of Dental Science* 12 (1879): 382.

31. "The Crystal Honey Fraud," *The American Bee Journal* 14 (Mar. 1878): 65.

32. John Tower, "Frauds in Guano and Other Manures," *The Genesee Farmer* 16 (1855): 242.

33. "The Golden Bee-Hive," *Gleanings in Bee Culture* 14 (Mar. 1, 1886): 179; "The Golden Bee-Hive," *Gleanings in Bee Culture* 14 (July 1, 1886): 330. One sees here the sort of sociable institutions identified by Yochai Benkler. See his "Law, Policy, and Cooperation," in Edward J. Balleisen and David A. Moss, eds., *Government and Markets: Toward a New Theory of Regulation* (New York, 2009), 299–334.

34. "A Fraud," *Railroad Gazette*, March 16, 1883, 167; "The Moral Effect of a Technical Education," *Iron Age*, Nov. 8, 1894, 804–05. The *Railroad Gazette* paid close attention to swindles by employees. See "A Pass Swindler," June 8, 1883, 370; "Underbilling," April 20, 1888, 249; "Another Fraud," Feb. 10, 1893, 103.

35. "Engineers' and Geologists' Reports," *EMJ*, April 15, 1876, 365–66; "Our Course Endorsed," *EMJ*, May 11, 1878, 323; "The Engineering and Mining Journal for 1879,"

EMJ, Dec. 21, 1878, 431; "Decline of the Mining Stock Market," *EMJ*, July 15, 1893, 50; "Growing Interest in Mining Investments," *EMJ*, Oct. 18, 1878; "Editorial Announcements," *EMJ*, Feb. 17, 1894, 146.

36. "Wild Cat," Jan. 26, 1878, 53; The Dauphin Island Scheme," Nov. 18, 1893, 516; "The Stephens Process," Oct. 22, 1898, 482.

37. Lewis Tappan to Lewis Tappan Stoddard, Feb. 6, 1843, quoted in Bertram Wyatt-Brown, *Lewis Tappan and the Evangelical War against Slavery* (Cleveland, 1969), 232.

38. "New York Swindles," *NYT*, Oct. 12, 1872, 6; "The Quack Gang," *NPG*, March 27, 1880, 2.

39. "Life Insurance," *NYT*, March 7, 1873, 2; "New York Swindles"; "A Warning," *SEP*, April 24, 1869, 3.

40. Mihm, *Nation of Counterfeiters*, 248–53.

41. "Fraud or No Fraud," Dec. 19, 1874, 6.

42. For an illustration of such pressure brought to bear on the *Engineering and Mining Journal*, see the coverage on the Poorman Mines of Silver City, Idaho, throughout 1894.

43. "Sundry Humbugs," *AA* 31 (Jan. 1872): 39.

44. "Editorial Announcements," *EMJ*, March 7, 1903; "The Poorman Consolidated," *EMJ*, July 7, 1894, 2.

45. On the problem of modern economic gatekeepers, see Susan P. Shapiro's articles "The Social Control of Impersonal Trust," *American Journal of Sociology* 93 (1987): 623–58; and "Collaring the Crime, Not the Criminal: Reconsidering the Concept of White-Collar Crime," *American Sociological Review* 55 (1990): 346–65. The concept of "reputation mining" has salience here. See George Akerlof and Robert Schiller, *Phishing for Phools: The Economics of Manipulation and Deception* (Princeton, 2015), 23–35.

46. "Adulterations in Food and Drugs," *HMM* 41 (1859): 654; "Guano," *The New England Farmer* 7 (1855): 333. For a similar observation, see Walter A. Friedman, *Birth of a Salesman: The Transformation of Selling in America* (Cambridge, MA, 2004), 53–55.

47. *NPG*, July 2, 1887, 14; Oct. 27, 1888, 14.

48. Mihm, *Nation of Counterfeiters*, 209–59; on bogus counterfeit detectors, see also "A New Swindle," *SEP*, Dec. 29, 1860.

49. Fowler, *Twenty Years of Inside Life in Wall Street*, 298–311.

50. King, *Mine to Make a Mine*, 38–39, 48–49; Dan Plasak, *A Hole in the Ground with a Liar at the Top: Fraud and Deceit in the Golden Age of American Mining* (Salt Lake City, 2006).

51. King, *Mine to Make a Mine*, 88–139; Donald Chaput, "Fraud at Fresno?," *Pacific Historian* 29 (1985): 47–58; William T. Jackson, "Dakota Tin: British Investors at Harney Peak," *North Dakota History* 33 (1966): 33–63; Clark C. Spence, *British Investments and the American Mining Frontier, 1860–1901* (Ithaca, NY, 1958), 22–72, 122–38.

52. "On the Valuation of Mines," Oct. 13, 1877, 272–73; "Growth of the Engineering and Mining Journal," April 14, 1877, 231; "What Is Needed to Float a Mine," April 4, 1878; 233–34, all in *EMJ*.

53. "The Secrets of Stock Jobbing," *NYT*, Mar. 9, 1857, 1; "History of a Stock Bubble," *NYT*, Mar. 26, 1857, 1; "What Is a Historian," *NYT*, Mar. 28, 1857, 4.

54. "The Equitable Ring and Its Hirelings of the Press," *New York Sunday Mercury*, Apr. 7, 1872, 4.

55. "An Unfortunate Speculator," *Wall Street Daily News*, Dec. 19, 1879, 1. For typi-

cal fraud coverage, see the same paper for "A New Swindle," Apr. 28, 1880, 1; "The Elevated Railroad Swindle," Oct. 17, 1881, 1.

56. On the parallel roles of British financial journals as both fraud monitors and boosters, see Ian Klaus, *Forging Capitalism: Rogues, Swindlers, Frauds, and the Rise of Modern Finance* (New Haven, 2014), 177–203.

57. "Newspaper Reports on Mines," *EMJ*, May 5, 1877, 292.

58. "New York Swindles," *NYT*, Oct. 12, 1872, 4.

59. Ibid.; "The Natural History of Swindles," July 10, 1875, 17.

60. "New York Swindles"; "New York Stock Broker," *Fraud and Fair Dealing in Stocks*, 14, 35–36.

61. Jürgen Habermas, *The Structural Transformation of the Public Sphere: An Inquiry into a Category of Bourgeois Society*, translated by Thomas Burger (Cambridge, MA, 1989).

62. "Life Insurance Frauds," *NYT*, Jan. 30, 1877, 4; "Latest Revelation," *NYT*, July 14, 1877, 4.

63. Barnum, *Life of P. T. Barnum*, 28, 39, 48–49, 74–76, 85–87, 93–105; "The Way the Company Managed the Affair," *NYT*, Dec. 8, 1872, 1; "False Packing," *MT*, Apr. 2, 1869, 2; Fowler, *Twenty Years of Inside Life in Wall Street*, 30–35, 260, 332–37, 460–61.

64. On this point, see Pettit, *Science of Deception*, 34–38.

65. "Scoundrelism in Patent Agents," *Scientific American*, Sept. 16, 1854, 5; "Sundry Humbugs" and "Going Right On," *American Agriculturist* 34 (April 1875): 126–27, quoted in Woloson, "Wishful Thinking," 827; Fowler, *Twenty Years of Inside Life in Wall Street*, 392–93; "Overcapitalization," *The Railroad Gazette*, March 16, 1888, 166; "Gold for Seawater," July 30, 1898; "False Pretenses of Quacks," *Medical and Surgical Reporter*, Sept. 3, 1870, 196; "Glimpses of Gotham," *NPG*, Jan. 24, 1880, 14.

66. "Robbing Merchants," *NYT*, May 14, 1874; "Commercial Chronicle and Review," *HMM* 35 (1856): 589; "Mining Speculation," *London Mining Journal*, reprinted in *Scientific American*, Feb. 24, 1872, 128; "A Bill for the Prevention of Fraud in the Organization of Mining and Other Companies," *EMJ*, July 22, 1876, 53; "New York Stock Broker," *Fraud and Fair Dealing in Stocks*, 62–69; "A Watch Night Sermon," *EMJ*, Dec. 31, 1898, 782.

67. *Manchester Times*, Nov. 11, 1837, quoted in Taylor, *Boardroom Scandal*, 59.

68. Edward Youmans, "A Foreign Lesson and a Domestic Application," *Popular Science Monthly* 5 (1974): 112.

69. "Humbugs," *Boston Advertiser*, Dec. 6, 1865, 2; "Library Table," *The Round Table* 11 (Nov. 18, 1865): 164. For a similar point, see Akerlof and Schiller, *Phishing for Phools*, 149–50.

70. "Barnum Tending Bar," *BET*, May 10, 1856, 1.

71. "Look out for Humbugs, *AA* 19 (Nov. 1860): 324; Edward Crapsey, "Nether World of New York," *Galaxy* 11 (1871): 659; "Frauds and Fools," *NPG*, Nov. 6, 1880, 7; "Protection for Fools," *NPG*, Nov. 6, 1880, 2; "Inside View of Western Mining Investments," *EMJ*, Jan. 20, 1877, 38; "Secrecy in Corporate Management," *Commercial and Financial Chronicle*, Sept. 20, 1879, 289; "Railroad Accounts," *Railroad Gazette*, March 23, 1888, 191–92; Steven Usselman and Richard R. John, "Protecting Small Savers: The Political Economy of Economic Security," in Richard R. John, ed., *Ruling Passions: Political Economy in Nineteenth-Century America* (University Park, 2006), 130–34.

72. Taylor, *Boardroom Scandal*, 159–248.

73. "Life Insurance Failures," *NYT*, Dec. 15, 1876, 4; "Bank Examiners and the Pacific Bank of Boston," *Commercial and Financial Chronicle*, March 29, 1884, 372–73.

74. See generally, Summers, *The Era of Good Stealings*. Anthony Comstock was a conspicuous exception to this tendency. As a governmental official charged with investigating swindlers, he evinced great confidence in the state and pleaded for both stricter laws and more expansive enforcement efforts.

75. "Mining Speculation."

76. This constraint suggests an extension to Akerlof and Schiller's notion of a "phishing equilibrium" in *Phishing for Phools*. Even if informational gaps and psychological vulnerabilities ensure some deception in capitalist markets, at some point rank duplicity imposes such great costs as to heighten popular suspicions.

77. Holly Cutting Baker, "Patent Medicine in Pennsylvania before 1906: A History through Advertising," *Pennsylvania Folklife* 26 (1977): 20–33; John G. Franzen, "Comfort for Man or Beast: Alcohol and Medicine Use in Northern Michigan Logging Camps, 1880–1940," *Wisconsin Archeologist* 7 (1995): 294–337; Joanna Cohen, " 'The Right to Purchase Is as Free as the Right to Sell': Defining Consumers as Citizens in the Auction-House Conflicts of the Early Republic," *Journal of the Early Republic* 30 (2010): 56–59; Philip Scranton, "The Horrors of Competition: Innovation and Paradox in Rhode Island's Jewelry Industry, 1860–1914," *Rhode Island History* 55 (1997): 47–55.

78. Steven M. Gelber, *Horse Trading in the Age of Cars: Men in the Marketplace* (Baltimore, 2008), 5–23.

79. Wendy Woloson stresses this point in "Wishful Thinking." See especially 824–28.

CHAPTER FIVE: THE BEGINNINGS OF A MODERN ADMINISTRATIVE STATE

1. On the economic theory of politics, see: Anthony Downs, *An Economic Theory of Democracy* (New York, 1957); James M. Buchanan and Gordon Tullock, *The Calculus of Consent: Logical Foundations of Constitutional Democracy* (Ann Arbor, 1962); Mancur Olson, *The Logic of Collective Action* (New York, 1971); George Stigler, "The Economic Theory of Regulation," *Bell Journal of Economics* 2 (1971): 3–21; Sam Peltzman, "Toward a More General Theory of Regulation," *Journal of Law and Economics* 19 (1976): 211–40. For critiques, see Jessica Leight, "Public Choice: A Critical Reassessment," in Edward J. Balleisen and David A. Moss, eds., *Government and Markets: Toward a New Theory of Regulation* (New York, 2010), 213–55.

2. On bureaucratic entrepreneurship, see Daniel P. Carpenter, *The Forging of Bureaucratic Autonomy: Reputations, Networks, and Policy Innovation in Executive Agencies, 1862–1928* (Princeton, 2001).

3. Edward Balleisen, "The Prospects for Effective Coregulation in the United States: A Historian's View from the Early Twenty-First Century," in Balleisen and Moss, eds., *Government and Markets*, 444–81.

4. For an incisive theoretical conceptualization of social movements, see Craig Calhoun, " 'Social Movements' of the Early Nineteenth Century," *Social Science History* 17 (1993): 385–42.

5. On regulatory change in this era, see: Morton Keller, *Affairs of State: Public Life in Late Nineteenth Century America* (Cambridge, MA, 1977); Morton Keller, *Regulating a New Economy: Public Policy and Economic Change in America, 1900–1933* (Cam-

bridge, MA, 1990); Marc Allen Eisner, *Regulatory Politics in Transition*, 2nd ed. (Baltimore, 2000).

6. "Army Frauds in Pennsylvania," *CT*, Oct. 23, 1861, 2; "American Contractors," *Manchester Guardian*, Jan. 29, 1862, 3; "Government Contracts," *NYT*, Feb. 6, 1862, 2; Stuart D. Brandes, *Warhogs: A History of War Profits in America* (Lexington, KY, 1997), 70–91; Mark Wilson, *The Business of Civil War: Military Mobilization and the State, 1861–1865* (Baltimore, 2006), 19–25, 149–56.

7. "Defrauding the Government," *BS*, June 4, 1861, 1; "Frauds upon the People," *New Hampshire Patriot*, Jan. 1, 1862, 2; "Republican Frauds," *Wisconsin Daily Patriot*, Feb. 19, 1862, 2.

8. Wilson, *Business of Civil War*, 154–55.

9. "Secretary of War," *NYTR*, Oct. 17, 1861, 7; "Shame! Shame!" *Sandusky Register*, Feb. 11, 1862, 2.

10. "Leeches," *HW* (Jan. 25, 1862): 53; Henry Morford, *The Days of Shoddy* (Philadelphia, 1863).

11. Brandes, *Warhogs*, 100; Wilson, *Business of Civil War*, 151; "Doom of Swindling Contractors," *NYT*, Jan. 18, 1862, 4.

12. *War Claims at St. Louis*, U.S. HR Exec. Doc. 94, 37th Cong., 2nd Sess. (1862); *Report of the Commission on Ordnance and Ordnance Stores*, U.S. Sen. Exec. Doc. 72, 37th Cong., 2nd Sess. (1862); Wilson, *Business of Civil War*, 108–10, 127–29, 164–65, 184–85.

13. John F. Callan, *The Military Laws of the United States* (Philadelphia, 1863), 547–50.

14. Wilson, *Business of the Civil War*, 183–87; "An Army Swindler Fitly Punished," *NYT*, Nov. 23, 1863, 4; Charles A. Dana, *Recollections of the Civil War* (New York, 1899), 162–64.

15. Dana, *Recollections of the Civil War*, 163–64; J. Matthew Gallman, *Mastering Wartime: A Social History of Philadelphia during the Civil War* (New York, 1990), 289–90.

16. "Grades of Grain and Rules of Inspection," *Chicago Daily Commercial Bulletin*, Aug. 17, 1871, 2; Guy Lee, "The Historical Significance of the Chicago Grain Elevator System," *Agricultural History* 11 (1937): 27–30; Harold Woodman, "Chicago Businessmen and the 'Granger' Laws," *Agricultural History* 36 (1962): 18–22.

17. *Reports Made to the General Assembly of Illinois* (Springfield, 1872), 465–69; *Reports Made to the General Assembly of Illinois* (Springfield, 1877), x–xi; *Seventh Annual Report of the Railroad and Warehouse Commission* (Springfield, 1877), 31–44; J. C. F. Merrill, "Classification of Grain into Grades," *AAPS* 38 (1911): 58–62; Benjamin F. Goldstein, *Marketing: A Farmer's Problem* (New York, 1928), 181; Woodman, "Chicago Businessmen," 23–24.

18. "Editorial," *CT*, Sept. 3, 1879, 4; "Grain Inspection," *CT*, May 30, 1879, 6.

19. "Grain Inspection," *CT*, June 26, 1880, 11; "Grain Receivers," *CT*, Jan. 30, 1881, 6; "On the Witness Stand," *CT*, Feb. 18, 1881, 6; "Grain Inspection," *CT*, July 6, 1883, 7; Frank Drake, "A Mean Attack," *CT*, June 12, 1885, 9; "To Improve Grain Inspection," *NYT*, Mar. 14, 1887, 1.

20. "Our Grain Inspection," *CT*, Mar. 15, 1885, 1; "State Inspection of Grain," Mar. 16, 1887, 4; "Our Grain Inspection," Mar. 21, 1887, 8; "St. Louis Men in Arms," *CT*, May

18, 1889, 5; "Civil Service Demanded," *CIO*, Sept. 23, 1896, 12; *Annual Report of the Railroad and Warehouse Commission of Minnesota* (St. Paul, 1895), 39–41.

21. "Grain Interests Stirred"; *CT*, Feb. 11, 1897, 12; *Report of the United States Industrial Commission on Transportation*, vol. 2 (Washington, DC, 1901), 257; W. Scott Cowen, "Grain Inspection in Illinois," *AAPS* 38 (1911): 78–82.

22. "Frauds in Artificial Manures," *Genesee Farmer* 18 (Mar. 1857): 75; *Ninth Annual Report of the Secretary of the Maine Board of Agriculture* (Augusta, ME, 1864), 96.

23. "Inspectors of Guano," *Southern Planter* 10 (May 1850): 150; *Report of the Commissioner of Patents, Part II: Agriculture*, U.S. HR Doc. 102, 32nd Cong., 1st Sess. (1852), 298; "History of Guano," *DeBow's Review* 13 (Dec. 1852): 627; "Cheating the Farmer," *Pennsylvania Farm Journal* 4 (Mar. 1854): 82; "Maryland Guano Inspection Law," *HMM* 31 (Aug. 1854): 232–33; Baltimore Board of Trade, *Ninth Annual Report* (Baltimore, 1858), 30–32; *First Report of Philip T. Tyson, State Agricultural Chemist* (Annapolis, 1860), 102–03; "Peruvian Guano," *Southern Planter and Farmer* 1 (May 1867): 107; "Special Manures," *New England Farmer* (May 1867): 216.

24. *First Report of Philip T. Tyson*, 132; James B. Chynoweth and William H. Bruckner, *American Manures; and Farmers' and Planters' Guide* (Philadelphia, 1871), 132.

25. *First Annual Report of Philip T. Tyson*, 132; Chynoweth and Bruckner, *American Manures*, 28.

26. Chynoweth and Bruckner, *American Manures*, 259–60; Samuel W. Johnson, "Agricultural Experiment Stations of Europe," *Annual Report of the Sheffield Scientific School of Yale College* (New Haven, 1875), 25–26. Fertilizer regulation thus reflected a transatlantic borrowing of the sort discussed by Daniel T. Rodgers in his *Atlantic Crossings: Social Politics in a Progressive Age* (Cambridge, MA, 2000).

27. Samuel W. Johnson, *Essays on Peat, Muck, and Commercial Manures* (Hartford, 1859); Samuel W. Johnson, "Report on Commercial Fertilizers," *Annual Report of the Ohio Board of Agriculture* (Columbus, 1869), 375–89.

28. "Inspection of Fertilizers," *Germantown Telegraph*, reprinted in *AF* 2 (Nov. 1860): 155; N. A. Pratt, *Ashley River Phosphates* (Philadelphia, 1868), 41; "Agricultural Society of Philadelphia," *Boston Journal of Chemistry* 2 (1867): 11–12.

29. P. B. Wilson, "Is It Needed?" *AF* (Feb. 1878): 47–48; *Fourteenth Annual Report of the Secretary of the Maine Board of Agriculture* (Augusta, ME, 1870), 207–20.

30. "Inspection of Fertilizers," *AF* (Mar. 1870): 43; Camm Patteson, "Commercial Fertilizers," *Southern Planter and Farmer* 7 (Sept. 1873): 3–5; John Carter, "Regulating the Sale of Fertilizers," *AF* (Mar. 1878): 85–86; "Commercial Fertilizers," *Maine Farmer* (Jan. 11, 1883): 1. On agrarian Populism, see: Lawrence Goodwyn, *Democratic Promise: The Populist Moment in America* (New York, 1976); Michael Kazin, *The Populist Persuasion: An American History* (New York, 1995), 27–48; Charles Postel, *The Populist Vision* (New York, 2009), 137–72.

31. On arrangements in Georgia and elsewhere, see *Revised Statutes of Connecticut* (Hartford, 1875), 527; "An Act to Prevent Fraud in the Manufacture and Sale of Commercial Fertilizers," *Act of the General Assembly of the Commonwealth of Kentucky* (Frankfort, 1880), 96–97; *A Supplement to the Code of Georgia* (Macon, 1878), 53–56; National Fertilizer Association, *The Fertilizer Movement during the Season 1882–83* (Baltimore, 1883), iii–lxxxiii.

32. "Importance of Analyses of Fertilizers," *Southern Cultivator* 39 (Sept. 1881): 334; John A. Myers, "Report of State Chemist," *Biennial Report of the . . . Agricultural and*

Mechanical College of Mississippi (Jackson, MS, 1885), 72–73; "Fertilizer Control and the Trade during 1887," *Tenth Annual Report of the North Carolina Agricultural Experiment Station* (Raleigh, 1888), 28–31; "Professor J. W. Sanborn on Fertilizers," *Popular Gardening and Fruit Growing* 3 (May 1888): 184; *Forty-First Annual Report of the Indiana State Board of Agriculture* (Indianapolis, 1892), 183; *Fifth Annual Report of the West Virginia Agricultural Experiment Station* (Fairmount, WV, 1897), 6.

33. "Analysis of Fertilizers," *Ohio Farmer* 12 (Nov. 1883): 312; Myers, "Report of State Chemist," 72–78; W. S. Dewolf, "How Frauds in Fertilizers Are Prevented," *MT*, Feb. 20, 1885, 7; *Tenth Annual Report of the West Virginia Agricultural Experiment Station* (Fairmount, WV, 1897), 62; Alan Marcus, "Setting the Standard: Fertilizers, State Chemists, and Early National Commercial Regulation," *Agricultural History* 61 (1987): 48–49.

34. "The Legislature and the Department of Agriculture," *AC*, Sept. 18, 1883, 4; *Maine Farmer* 52 (June 12, 1884): 1; "Report for 1887 on the Agriculture of North Carolina," *Diplomatic and Consular Reports on Trade and Finance, No. 340* (London, 1889), 2; "The Fertilizer Trade," *AA* 48 (Dec. 1889): 654.

35. *MT*, Mar. 19, 1881, 4; *Nineteenth Annual Meeting of the Vermont Dairymen's Association* (Montpelier, 1889), 30. See also "Matfield Fertilizer," *Maine Farmer* 44 (May 27, 1876): 4; "Bowker's Hill and Drill Phosphate," *Ohio Farmer* 90 (Mar. 11, 1882): 177; "Orchilla Guano," *Southern Planter* 46 (Jan. 1885): 61; "Cumberland Bone Co.," *Maine Farmer* 53 (Apr. 16, 1885): 4.

36. "Fertilizers," *Southern Cultivator* 32 (Apr. 1874): 157; P. B. Wilson, "Errors in Fertilizer Analysis," *AF* 5 (Apr. 1876): 109–11; National Fertilizer Association, *The Fertilizer Movement*, 6–8; Marcus, "Setting the Standard," 53–64.

37. *Proceedings of the Convention of Agricultural Chemists* (Raleigh, 1884), 6; *Methods of Analysis of Commercial Fertilizers* (Washington, DC, 1886); *Proceedings of the Ninth Annual Convention of the Association of Official Agricultural Chemists* (Washington, DC, 1892), 4–6; *Proceedings of the Eleventh Annual Convention of the Association of Official Agricultural Chemists* (Washington, DC, 1894), 7–10.

38. Marcus, "Setting the Standard," 52–53, 70–72.

39. John Panzar and Robert Willig, "Economies of Scope," *American Economic Review* 71 (1981): 268–72; Praveen Nayyar and Robert Kazanjian, "Organizing to Attain Potential Benefits from Information Asymmetries and Economics of Scope in Related Diversified Firms," *Academy of Management Review* 18 (1993): 735–59.

40. *Report of the Pennsylvania State Dairymen's Association, 1885* (Harrisburg, 1885), 13; *Proceedings of the Sixth Annual Convention of the Association of Official Agricultural Chemists* (Washington, DC, 1890), 11.

41. Mitchell Okun, *Fair Play in the Marketplace: The First Battle for Pure Food and Drugs* (DeKalb, 1986), 138–84.

42. James Harvey Young, *The Toadstool Millionaires: A Social History of Patent Medicines in America before Federal Regulation* (Princeton, 1961), 226–51; James Harvey Young, *Pure Food: Securing the Federal Food and Drug Act of 1906* (Princeton, 1989); Okun, *Fair Play in the Marketplace.*

43. Charles W. Dabney, *Proceedings of the Convention of Agricultural Chemists, Held at Atlanta, Ga., May 15th, 16th, 1884* (Raleigh, 1884), 29–30; "Commercial Fertilizers," *Twenty Third Annual Report of the Indiana State Board of Agriculture* (Indianapolis, 1884), 187.

44. "National Grain Grading," *CT*, July 29, 1892, 4; "Farmers Robbed by Inspection," *Grand Forks Herald*, Mar. 31, 1904, 1; "Federal Grain Inspection," *WSJ*, July 30, 1908, 2; "Grain Grades Not Satisfactory," *DNT*, Sept. 27, 1908, 11; "He'd Stop Grain Frauds," *KCS*, Jan. 2, 1909, 5; John O'Laughlin, "Charges Combine of Elevator Men Rules Grain Mart," *CT*, Mar. 4, 1914, 13; Alson Secor, "Standard Grades Needed," *Successful Farming* (July 1916): 12.

45. "Oppose National Grain Inspection," *DNT*, Jan. 7, 1904, 2; "Federal Grain Inspection," *DMN*, Dec. 27, 1908, 14; *Fifty Sixth Annual Report of the Commercial Exchange of Philadelphia* (Philadelphia, 1910), 69.

46. "Federal Grades," *Chicago Daily Tribune*, Aug. 22, 1913, 12; *Uniform Grading of Grain*, U.S. HR Agriculture Committee Hearings, 63rd Cong., 3rd Sess., Vol. 1 (Washington, DC, 1915), 4–10; *Agriculture Appropriation Bill*, U.S. HR Agriculture Committee Hearings, 64th Cong., 1st Sess. (Washington, DC, 1916), 1–68.

47. "U. S. Grain Standards Act," *San Jose Mercury*, Aug. 26, 1916, 6; "Prepare for Federal Grain Inspection," *KCS*, Oct. 17, 1916, 14; "Federal Grain Standards Act," *CLR* 17 (1917): 177–80.

48. "Give Grain Inspectors Tests," *Cleveland Plain Dealer*, Nov. 10, 1916, 6; "Grain Men Study Grading Problems," *The Oregonian*, Feb. 15, 1917, 20; "Need Experts for Grain Inspectors," *Grand Rapids Press*, Sept. 29, 1919, 10; "Forty Take Grain Course," *Perry Republican*, June 1, 1922, 1.

49. "5 Grain Inspectors Face Fraud Charges," *Fort Worth Star-Telegram*, June 3, 1918, 10; "Federal Supervisors to Demonstrate Grain Grading," *Lexington Herald*, Aug. 25, 1919, 13; "U. S. Grain Grades Get O. K. of Dealers," *Fort Worth Star-Telegram*, Mar. 22, 1922, 5.

50. Gerald Nash, "Government and Business: A Case Study of State Regulation of Corporate Securities, 1850–1933," *BHR* 38 (1964): 147–50.

51. The following account draws on "Mining on the Pacific Coast," *Overland Monthly* 7 (Aug. 1871): 151–58; "Rights of Stockholders," *San Francisco Evening Bulletin*, Dec. 29, 1871, 2; "Stock Speculation versus Legitimate Mining," *Salt Lake Tribune*, May, 5, 1877, 13; "Mining Mysteries and Iniquities," *Springfield Republican*, Aug. 26, 1879, 3; "Mining Interests and the Gorley Bill," *San Francisco Evening Bulletin*, Feb. 26, 1880, 2; "New York Mining Investments," *NYTR*, Mar. 15, 1880, 4; "Provisions of the Bill to Protect Mining Stockholders," *San Francisco Evening Bulletin*, April 13, 1880, 1; Nash, "Government and Business," 153–54; Glenn Vent and Cynthia Birk, "Insider Trading and Accounting Reform: The Comstock Case," *Accounting Historians Journal* 20 (1993): 67–82.

52. "The Nether Side of Life Insurance," *Scribner's Magazine* 14 (July 1877): 382–86; "The Last of the New Jersey Mutual Life," *The Independent* 29 (Oct. 18, 1877): 28; Julius Wilcox, "The Wrecking of Life Insurance Companies," *International Review* 9 (1880): 83–100.

53. "New Insurance Laws," *The Independent* 3 (Oct. 27, 1881): 24.

54. State of New York, *Annual Report of the Superintendent of the Insurance Department* (Albany, 1882), li–lii.

55. Morton Keller, "The Judicial System and the Law of Life Insurance," *BHR* 35 (1961): 317–35; William Lehrman, "Diversity in Decline: Institutional Environment and Organizational Failure in American Life Insurance," *Social Forces* 73 (1994): 613–17.

56. Herbert Wolfe, "Present Supervision of Life Insurance Companies," *NAR* 181

(1905): 11–19; "The Insurance Investigation," *The Independent* 59 (Nov. 23, 1905): 1233; *Report of the Joint Committee of the Senate and Assembly of the State of New York Appointed to Investigate the Affairs of Life Insurance Companies* (Albany, 1906); Burton Hendrick, "The Story of Life Insurance I," *McClure's Magazine* (May 1906): 36–49.

57. "Insurance Reforms," *NYT*, Dec. 6, 1906, 9; William H. Price, *Life Insurance Reform in New York* (Cambridge, MA, 1909).

58. Morton Keller, *The Life Insurance Enterprise, 1885–1910: A Study in the Limits of Corporate Power* (Cambridge, MA, 1963), 254–64.

59. Keyes Winter, "State Regulation of Corporations by Policing Sales of Securities," *AAPS* 129 (Jan. 1927): 149–55; Louis Loss and Edward M. Cowett, *Blue Sky Law* (Boston, 1958), 7–10; Daniel Holt, "Acceptable Risk: Law, Regulation, and the Politics of American Financial Markets, 1878–1930," Ph.D. diss., University of Virginia, 2008, 173–98.

60. John A. McCall, *The Regulation of Life Insurance in the United States and Foreign Countries* (New Haven, 1904), 16–18; Maurice Robinson, "Government Regulation of Insurance Companies," *American Economic Association Publications* 8 (1907): 137–44; William C. Johnson, "The Principles Which Should Govern the Regulation of Life Insurance," *American Economic Association Publications* 8 (1907): 155–88.

61. James Holbrook, *Ten Years among the Mail Bags* (New York, 1856), 258–66; "Operations of a Mayor's Police," *Weekly Wisconsin Patriot*, June 8, 1858, 2; "How the Credulous Are Swindled," *New York Evangelist*, June 2, 1864, 3; J. H. Holton, *The Rogues and Rogueries of New York* (New York, 1865), 9–12, 27–31, 96–101; Matthew Hale Smith, *Sunshine and Shadow in New York* (New York, 1870), 694–704.

62. "Gift Enterprise Swindles Broken Up," *New York Ledger*, Apr. 10, 1858, 4; "A Grand Swindle Exposed," *PI*, Nov. 20, 1860, 1; "The Cheap Watch Humbug," *AA* 21 (May 1862): 133; "Gift Enterprises," *NYT*, Mar. 30, 1866, 5.

63. "More Swindles Exposed," *Albany Journal*, June 8, 1858, 2; "A Swindle," *Sandusky Register*, Apr. 11, 1862, 2; "Facts for Fortune Hunters," *NYT*, Mar. 1, 1866, 8.

64. "Lottery Fraud," *Lowell Daily Citizen*, June 8, 1858, 2; Edward Crapsey, "The Circular Swindle," *The Galaxy* 11 (May 1871): 652–60.

65. "Bogus Lotteries," *Pittsfield Sun*, Apr. 22, 1858, 2; "A Caution against Gift Enterprises," *NYT*, Mar. 31, 1869, 10.

66. "Sundry Humbugs," *AA* 25 (1866): 244; "How the Verdant Are Swindled," *NYTR*, Jan. 7, 1868, 7; "Letter of the Solicitor of the Post Office," U.S. Sen. Doc. No. 57, 39th Cong., 1st Sess. (Feb. 14, 1866), 2.

67. D. D. T. Leech, *List of the Post Offices in the United States* (Washington, DC, 1857), 48; "More Swindles Stopped," *New Albany Ledger*, May 26, 1858, 2; "Mayor Tiemann's Police," *Milwaukee Sentinel*, June 18, 1858, 2.

68. "Powers of Postmasters," *Cleveland Plain Dealer*, June 12, 1858, 2; "An Important Opinion," *Easton Gazette*, Oct. 13, 1860, 1; "Case of Emory & Co.," *Official Opinions of Attorneys General of the United States*, vol. 9 (Washington, DC, 1869), 454–55.

69. "Post Office Department," *Daily National Intelligencer*, Dec. 8, 1864, 2; "An Important Post Office Bill," *Cincinnati Enquirer*, Feb. 5, 1866, 3; *Letter of the Solicitor of the Post Office Department*; "Frauds by Means of the Post Office," *PI*, Feb. 19, 1866, 4; "Facts for Fortune Hunters," *NYT*, 8.

70. "Illegal Use of the Mails," *Philadelphia Age*, Mar. 10, 1866, 2; "Lottery Tickets," *AA* 25 (Mar. 1866): 86; "A Wise Law," *New York Evangelist* 39 (Aug. 27, 1868): 1.

71. "Revision of the Postal Law," *NYT*, Dec. 8, 1870, 5; "An Act to Revise, Consolidate, and Amend the Statutes Relating to the Post Office Department," United States Congress, June 8, 1872, Sects. 300, 301; Dorothy Ganfield Fowler, *Unmailable: Congress and the Post Office* (Athens, GA, 1977), 55–65.

72. Anthony Comstock, "Suppression of Vice," *NAR* 135 (Nov. 1882): 484–89; Marshall Cushing, *The Story of Our Post Office* (Boston, 1893), 614–21; Nicole Kay Beisel, *Imperiled Innocents: Anthony Comstock and Family Reproduction in Victorian America* (Princeton, 1997): 25–53; Andrea Tone, *Devices and Desires: A History of Contraceptives in America* (New York, 2001), 5–28; Gaines M. Foster, *Moral Reconstruction: Christian Lobbyists and the Federal Legislation of Morality, 1865–1920* (Chapel Hill, 2002), 119–30.

73. "Our New York Letter," *PI*, Apr. 19, 1877, 3.

74. "Anthony Comstock," *Cincinnati Gazette*, Nov. 11, 1880, 4; Cushing, *Story of Our Post Office* 505–605.

75. "Killing of Lotteries," *PI*, Oct. 14, 1895, 8; *Annual Report of the Postmaster General* (Washington, DC, 1896), 59; "Frauds in Postal Affairs," *Omaha World Herald*, Nov. 7, 1897, 7; "Vigilance of Postal Inspectors," *Brooklyn Eagle*, Oct. 2, 1898, 15; Cushing, *Story of Our Post Office*, 619–21.

76. "Scientific Swindlers," *NYT*, Sept. 17, 1875, 8; *Letter from the Postmaster General in Reply to a Resolution of the House*, U.S. HR Doc. 22, 46th Cong., 2nd Sess. (Washington, DC, 1880), 1–17; "Day of Reckoning at Hand," *Omaha World Herald*, Dec. 9, 1893, 1; Cushing, *Story of Our Post Office*, 505–65; "After Patent Medicine Frauds," *NYT*, Nov. 10, 1894, 5; "Fake Concerns under the Ban," *WP*, Feb. 26, 1895, 6.

77. "An Unfortunate Speculator," *Wall Street Daily News*, Dec. 19, 1879, 1; "Millions Made by Fraud," *NYTR*, Dec. 30, 1879, 2; "Sundry Humbugs," *AA* 39 (Mar. 1880): 89.

78. "An Unfortunate Speculator"; "Millions Made by Fraud"; "Great Swindle Stopped," *NYT*, Dec. 31, 1879, 2; "Details of the Swindle," *WP*, Dec. 31, 1879, 2.

79. "Great Swindle Stopped"; "Bogus Brokers in New York," *BS*, Jan. 1, 1880, 4; *Letter from the Postmaster General*, 17–25.

80. "'Fund W' Finished," *CT*, Dec. 8, 1883, 7; "Swindlers Convicted," *Arkansas Gazette*, Dec. 8, 1883, 1; "The 'Fund W' Frauds," *Boston Journal*, 1883, 2; *United States v. Flemming et al.*, 19 Federal Reporter 908 (US Dist. Court for Northern Illinois).

81. "Using the Mails for Swindling Purposes," *NYT*, Feb. 9, 1879, 7; "More Fraud," *Brooklyn Eagle*, Apr. 7, 1885, 6; "A Great Swindle Stopped"; *Annual Report of the Postmaster General* (Washington, DC, 1890), 41; "Lottery and the Mails," *Cincinnati Commercial Tribune*, July 11, 1890, 1; Cushing, *Story of Our Post Office*, 521–25, 551–59; "Wanted Here for Swindling," *Brooklyn Eagle*, Aug. 28, 1897, 12; "Swindler Algernon Granville Convicted," *Pharmaceutical Era* 21 (May 25, 1899): 699.

82. "Easy Life in Jail," *CT*, July 27, 1884, 13; "How Swindlers Were Freed," *NYT*, Mar. 1, 1885, 1; Alfred Andreas, *History of Chicago*, vol. 3 (Chicago, 1886), 271–72.

83. "Lottery Traffic," *SFB*, May 16, 1885, 3; Cushing, *Story of Our Post Office*, 553.

84. "Swindling Devices," *NYT*, Dec. 18, 1876, 8; "Gambling for Farmers," *AA* 42 (July 1883): 347; "An Unequal Fight," *AA* 43 (Mar. 1884): 131; Patrick Woodward, *The Secret Service of the Post-Office Department* (Hartford, 1886), 437–40; "It's a Ten-Dollar Swindle," *Omaha World Herald*, Mar. 1, 1891, 1; Cushing, *Story of Our Post Office*, 523–34; "Defrauded by Fake Jewelers," *CT*, Dec. 16, 1894, 2; "Big Swindling Scheme Exposed," *NYH*, Mar. 27, 1895, 6.

85. Cushing, *Story of Our Post Office*, 527–28, 538–39, 562–65; "Lottery Business Abroad," *NYT*, Nov. 27, 1894, 16; *Report of the Postmaster General of the United States* (Washington, DC, 1896), 59–61.

86. "Used the Mail for Lottery Fraud," *CT*, Sept. 1, 1893, 3; "Crowding the Lottery Sharks," *CT*, Feb. 14, 1894, 5; John L. Thomas, *Lotteries, Frauds, and Obscenities in the Mails* (Columbia, MO, 1903), 343–44.

87. Fowler, *Unmailable*, 79–87; Foster, *Moral Reconstruction*, 124–27; Carpenter, *Forging of Bureaucratic Autonomy*, 109–10.

88. On action against bond investment firms: "A Glance at the Office of the Chief Post-Office Inspector," *Kalamazoo Gazette*, Jan. 9, 1890, 6; "Bond Investments Checked," *PI*, May 15, 1895, 3. On action against quackery: "Patent Medicines and the Post Office," *Outlook*, June 4, 1904, 240; "Uncle Sam Takes a Hand," *Ladies' Home Journal* 21 (Sept. 1904): 1; *The Nostrum Evil* (New York, 1905). On action against oil promotions: "Fraud Cases Set Record," *LAT*, May 16, 1920, V5; "Sees Oil Swindlers in Texas Dwindling," *WP*, July 15, 1923, 5; Roger M. Olien and Diana Davids Olien, *Easy Money: Oil Promoters and Investors in the Jazz Age* (Chapel Hill, 1990).

89. Holbrook, *Ten Years among the Mail Bags*, 270–74; "How Postmasters Are Tempted," *AA* 43 (Jan. 1884): 39.

90. "Facts for Fortune Hunters"; "Frauds. The Official List of Them," *NYTR*, Nov. 27, 1880, 2; "A New Fraud," *Printer's Ink* 6 (June 1892): 758.

91. Anthony Comstock, *Frauds Exposed: or, How the People Are Deceived and Robbed, and Youth Corrupted* (New York, 1880). See also Comstock's "The Suppression of Vice," *NAR* 85 (Nov. 1882): 484–89; "How I Came to Enter upon My Work," *Christian Advocate* 63 (May 17, 1888): 327; "Lotteries," *Christian Advocate* 65 (May 29, 1890): 343–44; "Lotteries and Gambling," *NAR* 154 (Feb. 1892): 217–24.

92. Comstock, *Frauds Exposed*, 571; "Fraud Orders," *The Youth's Companion* 78 (May 5, 1904): 222. The American Antiquarian Society's database, "America's Historical Newspapers," contains only seven stories with the phrase "fraud order" up to 1894; over the next six years, the number rises to 192; from 1901–1910, it goes to 667.

93. See the complaints in *In Re Artic Refrigerator Company of Cincinnati*, Fraud Order Cases, Entry 50, Box 12–3, Case 1310; *In Re Rockwell & Hammond*, and *In Re National Necktie Company of Philadelphia*, Fraud Order Cases, Box 8, Cases 1017, 1019–20; *In Re Mack Belting Company and United States Canvas and Rubber Co. of Cleveland*, Fraud Order Cases, Box 55, Case 3687; *Annual Report of the Postmaster General* (Washington, DC, 1916), 71.

94. "Swindlers Who Use the Mails," *NYT*, Sept. 27, 1883, 4; Cushing, *Story of Our Post Office*, 522.

95. Comstock, *Frauds Exposed*, 5; Woodward, *Secret Service of the Post-Office Department*, 421.

96. *Annual Report of the Post Office Department* (Washington, DC, 1913), 90; Winfield Fell, "It Keeps Uncle Sam Busy," *Trenton Times*, May 10, 1914, 13.

97. Charles McCurdy, "Justice Field and the Jurisprudence of Government-Business Relations: Some Parameters of Laissez-Faire Constitutionalism," *JAH* 61 (1975): 980–81; Michael Les Benedict, "Laissez-Faire and Liberty: A Re-Evaluation of the Meaning and Origins of Laissez-Faire Constitutionalism," *LHR* 3 (1985): 305–06, 327–31.

98. Charles McCurdy, "American Law and the Marketing Structure of the Large Corporation, 1875–1890," *Journal of Economic History* 38 (1978): 631–49; *State v. Agee*,

83 Alabama Reports 110 (Ala. Supreme Court, 1887); *In Re Schechter*, 63 Fed. Cases 595 (Circuit Court for the District of Minnesota, 1894). On deceptions by nursery agents, see: "Tricks of Tree Peddlers," *AA* 42 (May 1883): 259; Edson Goddard, "Marketing Trees and Plants," *Transactions of the Northern Iowa Horticultural Society* (Des Moines, 1890), 371–79.

99. *Ex Parte Jackson*, 96 U.S. 727 (1878); *Dauphin v. Key*, 1 McArthur & Mackay 203 (Supreme Court of the Dist. of Columbia, 1880); *U.S. v. Loring*, 91 Fed. Cases 881 (U.S. Dist. Court for the Northern Dist. of Illinois, 1884); *U.S. v. Finney*, 45 Fed. Cases. 41 (Dist. Court for the Dist. of Eastern Missouri, 1890); *Durland v. U.S.*, 161 U.S. 306 (1896); *Public Clearing House v. Coyne*, 194 U.S. 497 (1904); Thomas, *Lotteries, Frauds, and Obscenity in the Mails*, 227–351.

100. *Munn v. Illinois*, 94 U.S. 113 (1877); "Valid State Laws Incidentally Affecting Foreign and Inter-State Commerce," *Central Law Journal* 28 (Apr. 12, 1889): 337; Anthony Comstock, "Police Power," *Christian Advocate* 65 (Oct. 23, 1890): 697–98; *Patapsco Guano Co. v. Board of Agriculture*, 52 Fed. Cases 690 (U.S. Circuit Ct. for the Eastern District of North Carolina, 1892); Lewis Hochheimer, "The Police Power," *Central Law Journal* 44 (Feb. 19, 1897): 158–62.

101. Michael Pettit, *The Science of Deception: Psychology and Commerce in America* (Chicago, 2013), 121–32.

102. McCurdy, "American Law and the Marketing Structure of the Large Corporation."

103. Woodward, *Secret Service of the Post-Office Department*, 445–48.

CHAPTER SIX: INNOVATION, MORAL ECONOMY, AND
THE POSTMASTER GENERAL'S PEACE

1. Alfred D. Chandler, *The Visible Hand: The Managerial Revolution in American Business* (Cambridge, MA, 1977); Susan Strasser, *Satisfaction Guaranteed: The Making of the American Mass Market* (New York, 1989); Richard S. Tedlow, *New and Improved: The Story of Mass Marketing* (New York, 1990); William Leach, *Land of Desire: Merchants, Power, and the Rise of a New American Culture* (New York, 1993); Pamela Walker Laird, *Advertising Progress: American Business and the Rise of Consumer Marketing* (Baltimore, 1998); Nancy F. Koehn, *Brand New: How Entrepreneurs Earned Consumers' Trust from Wedgwood to Dell* (Cambridge, MA, 2001).

2. Boris Emmet and John E. Jeuck, *Catalogues and Counters: A History of Sears, Roebuck and Company* (Chicago, 1950), 63–64.

3. Telegram from Inspector Stuart to Chief Inspector M. D. Wheeler, Dec. 21, 1894, *In Re Sears, Roebuck et al.*, Fraud Order Cases, Box 3, Cases 659–60.

4. E. H. Gordon to Post Office Department, March 5, 1895, *In Re Sears, Roebuck & Co. et al.*

5. Louis E. Asher and Edith Heal, *Send No Money* (Chicago, 1942), 62–69; Emmet and Jeuck, *Catalogues and Counters*, 42–104.

6. Asher and Heal, *Send No Money*, 20–22, 31–46; Cecil C. Hoge, Jr., *The First Hundred Years Are the Toughest: What We Can Learn from the Century of Competition between Sears and Wards* (Berkeley, 1988), 30–39.

7. Richard W. Sears to Assistant Attorney General for the POD, Dec. 22, 1894, *In Re Sears, Roebuck et al.*

8. Emmet and Jeuck, 64, 110–14, 247–50.

9. Adam Smith, *An Inquiry into the Nature and Causes of the Wealth of Nations*, 4th ed., vol. 1 (London, 1806), 177.

10. Joseph A. Schumpeter, *Capitalism, Socialism, and Democracy* (London, 1943), 72–86, 121–30. See also Max Weber, *The Protestant Ethic and the Spirit of Capitalism* (New York, 1920, reprinted 1976), esp. 47–78.

11. Everett Dick, *The Lure of the Land: A Social History of the Public Lands from the Articles of Confederation to the New Deal* (Lincoln, NE, 1970); Stephen Mihm, *A Nation of Counterfeiters: Capitalists, Con Men, and the Making of the United States* (Cambridge, MA, 2007); Dan Plazak, *A Hole in the Ground with a Liar at the Top: Fraud and Deceit in the Golden Age of American Mining* (Salt Lake City, 2006); Roger M. Olien and Diana Davids Olien, *Easy Money: Oil Promoters and Investors in the Jazz Age* (Chapel Hill, 1990).

12. J. H. Holton, *The Rogues and Rogueries of New York* (New York, 1865), 96–106; "Local Agencies," *American Agriculturist* 48 (Aug. 1889): 417.

13. "Extracts from the Memorial of the Auctioneers of New-York," *Patron of Industry*, Jan. 20, 1821, 2; Asa Greene, *The Perils of Pearl Street: Including a Taste of the Dangers of Wall Street* (New York, 1834), 52–55; "Tricks of Trade," *Charleston Southern Patriot*, Nov. 10, 1837, 2.

14. "Another Fraudulent Life and Health Insurance Company," *Sandusky Register*, Feb. 16, 1853, 2; "Extensive Insurance Swindle," *BS*, Sept. 6, 1854, 1; "Bogus Insurance Companies," *BET*, July 13, 1855, 2; "A Bogus Insurance Company," *Wisconsin Free Democrat*, Sept. 26, 1855, 2; "Bogus Insurance Companies," *NYH*, June 3, 1860, 4.

15. *In Re The Bank Depositors Insurance Company, of Washington, D.C. et al.*, Fraud Order Cases, Box 36, Case 3002; Fraud Order Cases, Box 38, Case 3207; "Post Office Fraud Order Issued against Wedderburn & Company," *Scientific American* 77 (Nov. 20, 1897), 323; George B. Cortelyou, "Financial Frauds: The Story of 'Fund W,'" 47 *Colliers* (April 22, 1911): 34.

16. "Salesmen," *Minneapolis Journal*, Feb. 5, 1898, 7; "Salesmen," *The Oregonian*, April 24, 1898, 7; "Salesmen," *Birmingham Age Herald*, Sept. 4, 1898, 8; "Agents," *Springfield Republican*, Mar. 19, 1899, 3; "Salesmen," *Trenton Evening Times*, June 17, 1899, 5; "100 Weekly and Expenses," *Literary Digest* 19 (July 15, 1899), 87.

17. Homer Canfield to D. W. Canfield, April 1, 1899; Memorandum from Assistant Attorney General James N. Tyner, July 12, 1899; Report from Harvey Wiley, Bureau of Chemistry, Department of Agriculture, Sept. 12, 1899; all in *In Re Artic Refrigerating Co.*, Fraud Order Cases, Box 12–13, Case 1310.

18. "Artificial Ice," *Scientific American* 40 (June 28, 1879): 405; "Domestic Refrigeration," *The Century Magazine* 28 (Aug. 1884): 637; "The Cold Storage System," *MT*, Oct. 24, 1888, 5; Edward Nichols, "The Production of Artificial Cold," *The Chautauquan* 11 (Apr. 1890): 42–47; "The Ice Man's Foe," *Kalamazoo Gazette*, Aug. 22, 1893, 3; "Coolness to Order," *CIO*, July 7, 1895, 12.

19. "A Career of Fraud Stopped," *NYT*, Apr. 3, 1884, 1; "Still Looking Them Up," *CT*, July 23, 1887, 15; "Mr. Unverzagt's Aladdin's Lamp," *NYH*, Dec. 11, 1893, 3; "Still Undismayed," *The Independent* 46 (Jan. 18, 1894): 23; "A Monte Sharp's Bluff," *Traveler's Record* 30 (Jan. 1895): 3; "Twenty Miles of Gold," *Munsey's Magazine* 45 (June 1911): 408–09; "Gold Put on Sale at $4.50 an Ounce," *Morning Oregonian*, Sept. 5, 1921, 15; *In Re Charles H. Unversagt et al.*, Fraud Order Cases, Entry 50, Box 77, Case 4612.

20. David Hochfelder, " 'Where the Common People Could Speculate': The Ticker, the Bucketshop, and the Origins of Popular Participation in Financial Markets, 1880–1920," *JAH* 93 (2006): 335–58.

21. Hugh R. Conyngton, *Financing an Enterprise, Vol III: The Financing* (New York, 1923), 540–41.

22. Edward H. Smith, *Confessions of a Confidence Man: A Handbook for Suckers* (New York, 1923), 275.

23. Colin Camerer and Dan Lavallo, "Overconfidence and Excess Entry: An Experimental Approach," *American Economic Review* 89 (1999): 306–18.

24. Orange Smalley, "Market Entry and Economic Adaptation: Spiegel's First Decade in Mail Order," *BHR* 35 (1961): 380–86.

25. "Something for Nothing," *Knoxville Journal*, Jan. 12, 1894, 8; "Fraudulent Shoe Scheme," *Albuquerque Citizen*, Jan. 24, 1900, 4; John Olson, "Combating Mail Order Competition," *Salesmanship* 9 (Oct. 1907): 116; "Mail Order Fakes," *Idaho Falls Times*, Nov. 12, 1907, 13; George H. Powell, *Powell's Practical Advertiser: A Practical Work for Advertising Writers and Business Men* (New York, 1908), 125–26; POD, *Annual Report for the Fiscal Year Ended June 30, 1910* (Washington, DC, 1911), 49–55; "Mail Order Houses Offer Enticing Bait," *San Jose Mercury News*, May 26, 1915, 6; Arthur Jerome Eddy, *The New Competition*, 4th ed. (New York, 1920), 65–67; Saul Engelbourg, *Power and Morality: American Business Ethics, 1840–1914* (Westport, CT, 1980), 75.

26. Smalley, "Market Entry and Economic Adaptation," 397–98.

27. Clowry Chapman, *The Law of Advertising and Sales and Related Business Law*, vol. 1 (Denver, 1908), 71; Earnest Elmo Calkins and Ralph Holden, *Modern Advertising* (New York, 1905), 257–59.

28. Gene Gressley, "The French, Belgians, and Dutch Come to Salt Creek," *BHR* 44 (1970): 498–519; Earl Zarbin, "Dr. A. J. Candler: Practitioner in Land Fraud," *Journal of Arizona History* 36 (1995): 173–88; William Warren Rogers, "The Power of the Written Word and the Spoken Word in the Rise and Fall of William Lee Popham," *Florida Historical Quarterly* 76 (1998): 265–96; Plazak, *A Hole in the Ground with a Liar at the Top*, 132–45.

29. "Misleading Brands Discussed by Bar," *NYT*, Apr. 6, 1923, 28; "Drive against Fake Names for Fur," *WP*, July 18, 1926, S11; H. J. Kenner, *The Fight for Truth in Advertising* (New York, 1936), 240–47.

30. George Akerlof, "The Market for Lemons: Quality Uncertainty and the Market Mechanism," *Quarterly Journal of Economics* 84 (1970): 488–500.

31. "Grangers Beware!" *CT*, Nov. 8, 1873, 3; "Montgomery, Ward, & Co.," *CT*, Nov. 10, 1873, 3; "Montgomery Ward," *Sioux City Journal*, Nov. 13, 1873, 2; "Montgomery, Ward & Co.," *Chicago Tribune*, Dec. 24, 1873, 5. See also the uproar over oleomargarine: Henry Bannard, "The Oleomargarine Law: A Study in Congressional Politics," *Political Science Quarterly* (1887): 545–55; Geoffrey Miller, "Public Choice at the Dawn of the Special Interest State: The Story of Butter and Margarine," *California Law Review* 77 (1989): 83–131.

32. Richard Brief, "Nineteenth-Century Accounting Error," *Journal of Accounting Error* 3 (1965): 12–21; Brief, "The Origin and Evolution of Nineteenth-Century Asset Accounting," *BHR* 40 (1966): 1–6; Engelbourg, *Power and Morality*, 42–46; Richard White, "Information, Markets, and Corruption: Transcontinental Railroads in the Gilded Age," *JAH* 90 (2003): 19–43.

33. "Railway Reform for the West and the East," *Milwaukee Journal of Commerce*, Oct. 21, 1874, 2; "The English Association of American Bond and Share Holders," *London Times*, Mar. 17, 1885, 11; "The Mysteries of American Railway Accounting," *NAR* 128 (Feb. 1879): 135–47; Alfred D. Chandler, *Henry Varnum Poor: Business Editor, Analyst, and Reformer* (Cambridge, MA, 1956), 168–71.

34. "Capitalizing Fictitious Railroad Profits," *Railway Times* 21 (June 12, 1869): 191; "Report of the Massachusetts Railroad Commissioners," *Van Nostrand's Eclectic Engineering Magazine* 14 (Apr. 1876): 343–48; Thomas Greene, "Railway Accounting," *Political Science Quarterly* 7 (1892): 598–612.

35. "The Management of Railways," *Merchant's Magazine and Commercial Review*, June 1, 1870, 415; "Railroad Securities," *New York Herald Tribune*, Mar. 19, 1877, 4; "The Week," *The Nation* 53 (Oct. 8, 1891): 269; White, "Information, Markets, and Corruption," 34–35.

36. *In Re Modelle Miller*, Fraud Order Cases, Box 3, Case 696; *In Re Madame C. J. Walker*, Fraud Order Hearings, June 17, 1919, Entry 55, Box 39, Case 131; *In Re Crown Motor Car and Hercules Motorcar Companies*, Fraud Order Hearings, Nov. 24, 1914, Box 23, Case 60.

37. *In Re Charles H. Young*, Fraud Order Hearings, May 7–8, 1927, Box 39, Case 137, 145–75.

38. "Instructions for Branch Managers," *In Re Modelle Miller*. On creative marketing by early beauty entrepreneurs, see Kathy Peiss, *Hope in a Jar: The Making of America's Beauty Culture* (New York, 1998), 60–96.

39. On moral opposition to such methods, see "An Endless Chain, Indeed," *Zion's Herald* 76 (July 20, 1898): 29; "Fraudulent Shoe Scheme," *Albuquerque Citizen*, Jan. 24, 1900, 4; "Something for Nothing," *Colman's Rural World* 54 (July 10, 1901): 8; "Swindlers by Mail Often Exposed," *Montgomery Advertiser*, Aug. 24, 1902, 2.

40. J. Owen Stalson, *Marketing Life Insurance: Its History in America* (Cambridge, MA, 1942), 482–537; "Hosiery Sales Plan Pronounced Legal by Court," *NYT*, July 26, 1925, 29.

41. *In Re Charles H. Young*, 135–37; Richard W. Sears to John L. Thomas, July 18, 1895, *In Re Sears, Roebuck*.

42. Report of Postal Inspector William McMechen, *In Re Orphan Boy Extension Mine et al.*, Fraud Order Cases, Box 5, Case 752. See also *In Re White Swan Mines Co, and Letson Balliet*, Fraud Order Cases, Box 18, Case 1790.

43. J. Overton Paine to Post-Office Solicitor Lamar, Sept. 16, 1916, *In Re J. Overton Paine and the Paine Statistical Corporation*, Fraud Order Hearings, Box 36, Case 120, 4–12.

44. "The Outlook," 73 *Zion's Herald* (Sept. 11, 1895): 1. "Something for Nothing," 54 *Colman's Rural World* (July 10, 1901): 8; Daniel Carpenter, *The Forging of Bureaucratic Autonomy: Reputations, Networks, and Policy Innovation in Executive Agencies, 1862–1928* (Princeton, 2001), 84–87.

45. "Getting Something for Nothing," *CT*, June 3, 1891, 4; "Fraud Run to Earth," *CT*, Dec. 10, 1893, 6; "Federal Offenses," *Central Law Journal* 38 (May 4, 1894): 393; *In Re State Mutual Insurance Company*, Fraud Order Cases, Box 1, Case 555.

46. *In Re The Interstate Tracer et al.*, Fraud Order Cases, Box 8, Case 1042; *In Re The Merchants' National Union*, Fraud Order Cases, Box 8, Case 1044.

47. James and Walter Brown to John L. Thomas, March 26, 1895, *In Re Mrs. E. E.*

Mercer et al., Fraud Order Cases, Box 3, Case 682; J. Overton Paine to Solicitor Lamar, *In Re Paine Statistical Corporation et al.*, 5–6.

48. W. S. Daily to Postmaster General, Dec. 31, 1894; John S. Dillon to John L. Thomas, May 31, 1895; G. E. McAllister to John L. Thomas, Dec. 21, 1895; R. L. Beatty to John L. Thomas, May 1, 1896; all in *In Re Sears, Roebuck et al.* On legal definitions shaping social perceptions and identities, see Robert Gordon, "Critical Legal Histories," *Stanford Law Journal* 36 (1984): 57–125.

49. POD, "Report of the Assistant Attorney General," *Annual Reports for the Fiscal Year Ended June 30, 1907* (Washington, DC), 69–71.

50. Sidney Morse, *The Siege of University City: The Dreyfus Case of America* (University City, MO, 1912); George Graham Rice, *My Adventures with Your Money* (New York, 1911); "Promoter E. G. Lewis, 81, Who Made Millions, Dies," *LAT*, Aug. 11, 1950, 26; Plazak, *Hole in the Ground*, 253–86.

51. Morse, *The Siege of University City*, 298–336; "Bank Was a Fraud," *WP*, July 10, 1905, 1. See also the extensive *Los Angeles Times* coverage of Lewis's bankruptcy and mail fraud trial from 1925 through 1928.

52. "Millions in Margins Gone at Scheftels," *NYT*, Oct. 1, 1910, 9; "Brokers Had Squawk Sheet," *WP*, Nov. 15, 1911, 1; Louis Guenther, "The Pirates of Promotion: George Graham Rice," 36 *WW* (Oct. 1918): 584–91; "Rice's Conviction as Tipster Upheld," *NYT*, Nov. 5, 1929, 20.

53. Morse, *The Siege of University City*, 284–85, 391–95, 405–11, 478–79, 635–40; Edwin C. Madden, *The U.S. Government's Shame: The Story of the Great Lewis Case* (Detroit, 1908), 151–64, 177–78.

54. Rice, *My Adventures with Your Money*, 271, 290–307; "'Tex' Rickard Testifies," *LAT*, Jan. 20, 1912, 19; "Graham Rice Assails Prosecutor," *NYT*, Jan. 16, 1920, 3; "Rice Resumes Stock Promotions," 50 *WW* (June 1925): 137–38.

55. For an example of such contrition, see Frank Arbuckle to Postmaster General Wilson, May 21, 1895, and Report of Inspector William McMechen, May 21, 1895, *In Re Orphan Boy Extension Mine et al.*

56. Richard W. Sears to John L. Thomas, Jan. 23, 1895, *In Re Sears, Roebuck et al.*

57. Morse, *The Siege of University City*, 165–66, 385–89, 441, 495, 673–74; "Millions in Margins Gone at Scheftels"; "Rice Resumes Stock Promotions"; "Rice to Face Trial on Fraud Charges," *NYT*, July 16, 1927, 22.

58. *In Re Charles H. Young*, May 7–8, 1927 Hearing, 113–39; "Will Shield Him No More," *NYH*, Nov. 11, 1894, 7; News coverage of Rice's legal woes frequently noted his youthful criminality. See for example, "Nat Goodwin's Wicked Partner," *NYT*, Feb. 5, 1911, B4.

59. *In Re Charles H. Young*, May 7–8, 1927 Hearing, 14–44, 173–201.

60. Richard W. Sears to R. W. Haynes, July 18, 1895, *In Re Sears, Roebuck et al.*; Modelle Miller to Postmaster General, April 16, 1895; B. F. Shively to Postmaster General, May 15, 1895, *In Re Modelle Miller*; Senator Palmer to Postmaster General, Jan. 6, 1896; Representative Cannon to Postmaster General, Jan. 9, 1896, *In Re Interstate Tracer et al.*

61. On social networks in American business, see Pamela Walker Laird, *Pull: Networking and Success since Benjamin Franklin* (Cambridge, MA, 2006). On pardon culture, see Karin A. Shapiro, *A New South Rebellion: The Battle against Convict Labor in the Tennessee Coal Fields, 1871–1896* (Chapel Hill, 1998), 47–78; on the significance of con-

nections to post-bankruptcy commercial careers, see Edward J. Balleisen, *Navigating Failure: Bankruptcy and Commercial Society in Antebellum America* (Chapel Hill, 2001), 165–201.

62. J. T. Hanna to Acting Postmaster General F. H. Jones, July 14, 1894, *In Re State Mutual Life Insurance Company of Illinois et al.*; *In Re Laura Thomas*, Fraud Order Cases, Box 3, Case 674.

63. Guenther, "Pirates of Promotion: George Graham Rice," 590; "Graham Rice Assails Prosecutor," *NYT*, Jan. 16, 1920, 3; "Trial of Rice Opens on Fraud Charges," *NYT*, Nov. 15, 1928, 18.

64. Morse, *The Siege of University City*, 354–56, 571–80, 664–65; Madden, *The U.S. Government's Shame*, 13, 19–21.

65. Lewis, *Order Number 10*, 9–13; Madden, *The U.S. Government's Shame*, 19–21; Rice, *My Adventures with Your Money*, 308–09, 322–23, 354; "Scheftels's Counsel Speaks of Enemies," *NYT*, Nov. 14, 1911, 7; "What Delaney Said," *LAT*, Nov. 14, 1911, I13.

66. Morse, *The Siege of University City*, 326–29, 364–84; "Cortelyou on Stand," *WP*, Feb. 10, 1912, 4.

67. "Curb Lambs Caught by Ely Central," *NYT*, Nov. 10, 1909, 3; Rice, *My Adventures with Your Money*, 301–40; "Business Bureau Reports on Frauds," *NYT*, March 9, 1926, 32; BBB of New York City, "Special Bulletin No. 16: George Graham Rice Sentenced," Jan. 14, 1929."

68. A. S. Burrell to John L. Thomas, Dec. 26, 1896, *In Re Interstate Tracer et al.*; A. S. Burrell to Thomas, Jan. 23, 1897, *In Re National Mercantile Union*, Fraud Order Cases, Box 8, Case 1044. On the role of D. H. Conley in shutting down his competitors in the mail-order cosmetics business, see James & Walter Brown to John L. Thomas, March 4, 1895, *In Re E. E. Mercer*, Fraud Order Cases, Box 3, Case 692.

69. "Charge Fraud against N. Y. Cotton Exchange," *NYT*, Jan. 3, 1907, 1.

70. D. E. Christiansen to John L. Thomas, July 3, July 12, 1895, July 27, 1895, *In Re Sears, Roebuck et al.*

71. Richard W. Sears to John L. Thomas, April 3, July 18, Oct. 12, 1895, May 8, 1896, *In Re Sears, Roebuck*.

72. Rice is more easily characterized as unabashedly criminal. See Plazak, *Hole in the Ground*, 253–86.

73. "How the Mails Are Used to Catch the Unwary," *NYT Magazine*, Sept. 12, 1909, 8; Lewis, *Order Number 10*, 17–21.

74. Allen Steinberg, *The Transformation of Criminal Justice: Philadelphia, 1800–1880* (Chapel Hill, 1989); Laura F. Edwards, *The People and Their Peace: The Reconstitution of Governance in the Post-Revolutionary South* (Chapel Hill, 2009).

75. Cortelyou, "Frauds in the Mails," 810.

76. Craig Muldrew, "The Culture of Reconciliation: Community and the Settlement of Economic Disputes in Early Modern England," *The Historical Journal* 39 (1996): 915–42; Cynthia B. Herrup, *The Common Peace: Participation and the Criminal Law in Seventeenth-Century England* (Cambridge, UK, 1987); Max Gluckman, *The Judicial Process among the Barotse of Northern Rhodesia* (Glencoe, IL, 1955); June Starr, *Dispute and Settlement in Rural Turkey: An Ethnography of Law* (Leiden, 1978); Laura Nader, *Harmony Ideology: Justice and Control in a Zapotec Mountain Village* (Stanford, 1990).

77. Chandler, *The Visible Hand*, 230–32.

78. "Sears, Roebuck, & Co. Charged with Fraud," *Wilkes-Barre Times*, Dec. 13, 1907,

12; "Great Firm Accused of Slick Ways," *Olympia Record*, March 6, 1918, 1; Strasser, *Satisfaction Guaranteed*, 216–17.

79. *In Re Charles H. Young*, 137.

CHAPTER SEVEN: THE BUSINESSMEN'S WAR TO END ALL FRAUD

1. For typical notices of the previous week's radio fraud topics in the summer of 1933, see *Dallas BBB Bulletin*, July 28, 1933, NYSE Archives, New York City.

2. Stephen Fox, *The Mirror Makers: A History of Advertising and Its Creators* (New York, 1984); Roland Marchand, *Advertising the American Dream: Making Way for Modernity, 1920–1940* (Berkeley, 1985); Pamela Walker Laird, *Advertising Progress: American Business and the Rise of Consumer Marketing* (Baltimore, 1998); Inger L. Stole, *Advertising on Trial: Consumer Activism and Corporate Public Relations in the 1930s* (Urbana, 2006).

3. My point is not to challenge these venerable interpretations of business-government relations, laid out in key works such as: Robert H. Wiebe, *Businessmen and Reform: A Study of the Progressive Movement* (Cambridge, MA, 1962); Gabriel Kolko, *The Triumph of Conservatism: A Re-Interpretation of American History, 1900–1916* (New York, 1963); Ellis W. Hawley, *The Great War and the Search for a Modern Order: A History of the American People and Their Institutions, 1917–1933* (New York, 1979); Morton Keller, *Regulating a New Economy: Public Policy and Economic Change in America, 1900–1933* (Cambridge, MA, 1990). Powerful business interests *did* frequently and vociferously oppose regulatory action, especially with regard to labor conditions; they *did*, especially after the cooperative experience of World War I, frequently seek government assistance in facilitating industrywide standard-setting; they *did* sometimes fervently desire governmental regulation, as with the creation of the Federal Reserve. In addition, "business" almost always contained fault lines, with industries and firms taking different sides of regulatory issues. I seek not a new framework for "lumping," but rather some additional "splitting" about regulatory aspirations and the extent to which they bore institutional fruit.

4. "Financial Crime Loss Is Three Billions Yearly," *NYT*, July 6, 1924, H5; "Debit 3 Billions a Year to Crooks," *Current Opinion*, Oct. 1, 1924, 510; "War on the White Collar Bandits," *Literary Digest*, Mar. 6, 1926, 11–12; E. Jerome Ellison and Frank W. Brock, *The Run for Your Money* (New York, 1935), 3–4.

5. Edward H. Smith, "Profit in Loss," *SEP*, Feb. 5, 1921, 14–15, 59–70; Edward H. Smith, "The Credit Trimmers," *SEP*, May 13, 1922, 88–100; NACM, *Commerce and the Credit Crook* (New York, 1925).

6. Louis Guenther, "Pirates of Promotion: Market Manipulation and Its Part in the Promotion Game," *WW* 37 (1919): 393–98; Edward Jerome Dies, "The Fine Art of Catching the 'Sucker,'" *Outlook*, Mar. 28, Apr. 4 and 11, 1923, 590–93, 631–33, 674–78; Edward H. Smith, *Confessions of a Confidence Man: A Handbook for Suckers* (New York, 1923); "Tipster Publications Direct Investors' Money into Specially Prepared Channels," Special Bulletin No. 10, New York City BBB, Aug. 15, 1924; "Boston Curb Exchange," Special Bulletin of the NBBB, Mar. 17, 1927.

7. William Wright, *The Oil Regions of Pennsylvania* (New York, 1865), 207–26; "Spouters Are Rare," *Deming Herald*, Oct. 15, 1901, 5; Paul Lucier, *Scientists and Swindlers: Consulting on Coal and Oil in America, 1820–1890* (Baltimore, 2008), 249–59;

Roger M. Olien and Diana Davids Olien, *Easy Money: Oil and Promoters in the Jazz Age* (Chapel Hill, 1990).

8. Lewis Guenther, "The Pirates of Promotion: Methods of the Industrial Promoters," *WW* 37 (Jan. 1919): 317–18; "Caution! Trial of Southern Motors Case," NBBB Special Bulletin, Dec. 22, 1926.

9. Marshall D. Beuick, "Who Pays for Credit Frauds?" *CM* 28 (May 1926): 9; George Alger, "Unpunished Commercial Crime," *American Lawyer* 12 (Sept. 1904): 380.

10. H. J. Kenner, *The Fight for Truth in Advertising* (New York, 1936), x; Merle Sidener, "Patrolling the Avenues of Publicity," *WW* 35 (1918): 638; "Advertising as Power for Good," *Utica Daily Press*, Mar. 12, 1924, in HCF; R. S. Sharp, "A Suggestion for Curbing the Pirates of Promotion," *WW* 45 (1919): 354–56; *The Boston Better Business Commission* (Boston, 1922), 1–2; "The Financial Situation," *Commercial and Financial Chronicle* (Feb. 11, 1922), in Cromwell Scrapbooks, vol. 2, NYSE Archives; "Caution! Trial of Southern Motors Case."

11. H. J. Kenner, "Letter to the Editor," *Printer's Ink*, May 8, 1924; "Fighting Frauds and Fakes," *Wilmington Journal*, July 3, 1926, both in HCF; "Stock Frauds Seen as Spur to Bolshevism," *NYT*, Feb. 22, 1919, in Stock Fraud Scrapbook, NYSE Archives.

12. J. H. Tregoe, *Pioneers and Traditions of the National Association of Credit Men* (New York, 1946); Kenner, *Fight for Truth in Advertising*; Julia Ott, "The 'Free and Open' 'People's Market': Public Relations and the New York Stock Exchange, 1913–1929," *Business and Economic History Online* 2 (2004): 1–42; Rowena Olegario, *A Culture of Credit: Embedding Trust and Transparency in American Business* (Cambridge, MA, 2006).

13. Robert N. Mayer, *The Consumer Movement: Guardians of the Marketplace* (Boston, 1989); Lisabeth Cohen, *A Consumer's Republic: The Politics of Mass Consumption in Postwar America* (New York, 2003); Stole, *Advertising on Trial*.

14. James K. Medbury, *Men and Mysteries of Wall Street* (Boston, 1870), 18; "The New York Stock Exchange," *International Review* 2 (Nov. 1875): 822; Jonathan Lurie, *The Chicago Board of Trade, 1859–1905: The Dynamics of Self-Regulation* (Urbana, 1979), 209.

15. Medbury, *Men and Mysteries of Wall Street*, 83–138, 197–99; *The Stock Privilege Rig: A Thorough Exposure of a Fascinating Fraud* (Brooklyn, 1875); *Fraud and Fair Dealing in Stocks!* (New York, 1880); Henry Clews, *Twenty-Eight Years in Wall Street* (New York, 1887), 19–24, 201–08, 213–22, 700–10.

16. "No Quarter," *CIO*, Feb. 7, 1878, 6; "Broker Billups Brings Suit against the Cotton Exchange," *NYH*, Feb. 2, 1884, 8; "Expelled by the Board of Trade," *CT*, June 17, 1891, 3; "Edward Morton Expelled," *Boston Advertiser*, Apr. 4, 1895, 1.

17. "Packing Cotton," *MT*, Aug. 13, 1869, 4; "False Packed Cotton," *Galveston Tri-Weekly News*, Dec. 17, 1869, 4; "Cotton Exchange Convention," *Cincinnati Gazette*, June 12, 1874, 5.

18. "To Prosecute Fraudulent Failures," *BS*, Dec. 10, 1897, 10; "To Fight Fraud," *BS*, July 6, 1899, 10; "Tregoe the Busy Man," *WP*, June 4, 1905, F6; "J. H. Tregoe Dead," *NYT*, Oct. 6, 1935, 47.

19. "Boosters Rule at Devils Lake," *Aberdeen Weekly American*, Mar. 12, 1913, 4; "Would Discard 'Caveat Emptor,'" *DNT*, Feb. 3, 1915, 12; "Truth Is the Rule in Ads," *Kansas City Times*, Nov. 10, 1915, 5; "Kenner Acts as a Watchman," *DNT*, Feb. 8, 1920, 9; James C. Auchincloss, *The Better Business Bureau: Its Growth and Work* (New York,

1927), 7–8; Kenner, *Fight for Truth in Advertising*, 44–59; "H. J. Kenner," *NYT*, Jan. 9, 1973, 42.

20. Daniel Nelson, *Frederick W. Taylor and the Rise of Scientific Management* (Madison, WI, 1980); Paul J. Miranti, *Accountancy Comes of Age: The Development of an American Profession, 1886–1940* (Chapel Hill, 1990); John Duffy, *The Sanitarians: A History of American Public Health* (Urbana, 1992); Regina G. Kunzel, *Fallen Women, Problem Girls: Unmarried Mothers and the Professionalization of Social Work, 1890–1945* (New Haven, 1993); Andrea Tone, *The Business of Benevolence: Industrial Paternalism in Progressive America* (Ithaca, 1997).

21. "Advertising Imperils Consumer Confidence," *NVC Bulletin*, July 17, 1925; "Salesman's Statements and Advertising Claims," *NBBB Bulletin*, Sept. 15, 1927; Alger, "Unpunished Commercial Crime," 379; Edward Roberts, "How to End Stock Swindling," *Bangor Maine News*, Dec. 15, 1923, in Cromwell Scrapbooks, vol. 2, NYSE Archives; "Ignorance Supports Financial Fraud," *NBBB Bulletin*, July 1929.

22. "Share Fakers Set a Record," *New York Sun*, May 23, 1920, in Stock Fraud Scrapbook, NYSE Archives; AACW, *The Most Dangerous Enemy of the Oil Industry* (New York, 1919?); Charles S. Dewey, *Federal Cooperation to Prevent Fraud* (St. Louis, 1926), 2–4; "Are You an Easy Mark," Kansas City BBB, *Better Business Bulletin* (May 31, 1926); J. H. Tregoe, "Credit Protection and Financial Statements," *CM* 28 (Feb. 1926): 23; Circular to Exchange Employees, May 3, 1927, Records of the New York City BBB, NYSE Archives.

23. E. H. H. Simmons, *Security Frauds: A National Business Liability* (New York, 1927), 7; Edwin Lawrence, "Swindling through the Post Office," *Outlook* 79 (Jan. 14, 1905): 121–26; E. D. Hulbert, "Advertising Ethics and the General Welfare," *Survey* 22 (1909): 325–26; Harry New, "The Use of the Mail for Fraudulent Purposes," *AAPS* 125 (May 1926): 58–59.

24. Alger, "Unpunished Commercial Crime," 381; Maurice W. Sloan, "Prosecution of Fraudulent Debtors," *BNACM* 9 (1909): 348; Andre Tridon, "The Post Office: Guardian Angel to the 'Easy,'" *HW* 56 (Nov. 6, 1910): 12; John K. Barnes, "Harvest Time for the Get-Rich-Quick Promoter," *WW* 35 (Dec. 1917): 158–59; E. H. H. Simmons, "Security Frauds," *Independent* 114 (Dec. 1925): 731.

25. Kenner, *Fight for Truth in Advertising*, 3–15; Editorial, *BNACM* 14 (Mar. 1914): 143; "Some Observations Suggested by a Study of Fraud Cases," *BNACM* 21 (June 1919): 346–47; Jules Hart, "Compromise with Fraud Always Poor Business," *CM* 25 (Aug. 1923): 34–35; Keyes Winter, "Fools and Their Money," *Harper's Magazine* 151 (Aug. 1927): 371.

26. Tregoe, *Pioneers and Traditions*; C. H. Arnold, "False Statements," *BNACM* 6 (Oct. 1906): 36–37; Otis A. Pease, *The Responsibilities of American Advertising: Private Control and Public Influence, 1920–1940* (New Haven, 1958), 44–48; Michael E. Parrish, *Securities Regulation and the New Deal* (New Haven, 1970), 4–40.

27. Gerard C. Henderson, *The Federal Trade Commission: A Study in Administrative Law and Procedure* (New York, 1924), 16–26; Tony Allan Freyer, *Regulating Big Business: Antitrust in Great Britain and America, 1880–1990* (New York, 1992), 154–58.

28. "May Stop 'Ad' Frauds," *WP*, Nov. 24, 1915, 2; FTC, *Annual Report* (Washington, DC, 1924), 24; Henderson, *Federal Trade Commission*, 167–200; Milton Handler, "False and Misleading Advertising," *YLJ* 39 (Nov. 1929): 42–43; Carl F. Taeusch, *Policy and Ethics in Business* (New York, 1931), 402–31; C.D.P., "Federal Trade Commission—False

and Misleading Advertising," *MLR* 31 (1933): 804–17; Richard Tedlow, "From Competitor to Consumer: The Changing Focus of Federal Regulation of Advertising, 1914–1938," *BHR* 40 (1981): 38–48.

29. Louis Guenther, "The Pirates of Promotion: The Wreckage," *WW* 37 (Mar. 1919): 512; "Preventing Stock Frauds," *Cheyenne Tribune*, Jan. 28, 1923, in Cromwell Scrapbooks, vol. 2, NYSE Archives.

30. Bernard G. Priestly, "Checkmating the Get-Rich-Quick Promoter," *Bankers' Magazine* 111 (Mar. 1925): 317–23; "War Declared!" *Buffalo BBB Bulletin*, Aug. 12, 1925; Edward L. Greene, *Activities of the National Better Business Bureau, 1927–28* (New York, 1928), 15–16; Kansas City BBB, *Protecting Legitimate Business and the Public: Annual Report* (Kansas City, 1928): 15–19; Columbus BBB, *Annual Report* (Columbus, 1929), 1; BBB of Los Angeles, *Second Annual Report* (Los Angeles, 1931).

31. BBB of St. Louis, *Telling the Public* (St. Louis, 1926).

32. "Making Loss Prevention a Systematic Business," Rhode Island Hospital Trust Company, *The Netopian*, Mar. 1 1927; "The Road to Safe Investment," *Newark Call*, Jan. 13, 1924; Edson B. Smith, "Investors Must Learn to Patronize Reliable Firms," *Boston Traveler*, Mar. 30, 1924, all in HCF.

33. William Gregg, "Help the Doctor! Increasing the Curative Work of Credit Protection Fund," *CM* 28 (1926): 9; J. H. Tregoe, "A Dozen Rules for Sound Credit," *Bankers' Magazine* 112 (Mar. 1926): 384; Affiliated BBBs, *A Guide for Retail Store Advertising* (Boston, 1932).

34. Dorchester Mapes, *Why I Am a Member!* (New York, 1900); John Field, *Personality: An Address to the 5th Annual Convention of the NACM* (New York, 1900): 8–9; Herbert Houston, "The New Morals of Advertising," *WW* 28 (1914): 384–88; "Cromwell Says Blue Sky Laws Easily Evaded," *Rochester Post Express*, Oct. 13, 1922, in Cromwell Scrapbooks, vol. 2, NYSE Archives.

35. Richard Maxwell Brown, *Strains of Violence: Historical Studies of American Violence and Vigilantism* (New York, 1975); Cindy Higgins, "Frontier Protective and Social Network," *Journal of the West* 42 (2003): 63–73; Stephen Mihm, *A Nation of Counterfeiters: Capitalists, Con Men, and the Making of the United States* (Cambridge, MA, 2007), 300–02; Nicole Kay Beisel, *Imperiled Innocents: Anthony Comstock and Family Reproduction in Victorian America* (Princeton, 1997): Andrea Tone, *Devices and Desires: A History of Contraceptives in America* (New York, 2001), 4–25.

36. Garrett W. Cotter, "New Styles in Credit Crime," *CM* 27 (Feb. 1925): 44; Elaine Abelson, *When Ladies Go A-Thieving: Middle-Class Shoplifters in the Victorian Department Store* (New York, 1992), 145–46; Michael Willrich, *City of Courts: Socializing Justice in Progressive Era Chicago* (New York, 2003), 133–71.

37. "Report of the Investigation and Prosecution Committee," *BNACM* 21 (1919): 630–40; *Commerce and the Credit Crook*, 8–9; "The Campaign Starts!," *CM* 31 (Feb. 1929): 15–16; Tregoe, *Pioneers and Traditions*, 71–90; Auchincloss, *Better Business Bureau*, 8; Carl H. Getz, "Fighting the Wildcat Advertiser," *Bankers' Magazine* 106 (1923): 70–74; John Richardson, "Business Policing Itself through Better Business Bureaus," *Harvard Business Review* 10 (1931): 69–73.

38. "Sees Public Faith Growing through More Honest Ads," *New York Daily News*, Mar. 9, 1923; G. F. Olwin, "Advertising Censor Guards the Public," *Indianapolis Star*, Jan. 2, 1922, both in HCF; "Guide for Boston Better Business Shoppers," Box 11, Folder A-9-10-2, Kirstein Papers.

39. "Making Loss Prevention a Systematic Business"; Boston Better Business Commission, *Our Accomplishments in 1924: Third Annual Report* (Boston, 1924), 5.

40. J. H. Tregoe, "General Letters to Members," Aug. 1, 1924, Baker Library, Harvard Business School; W. A. Williams, "Keep Crooks out of Business," *CM* 30 (Mar. 1928): 7–8, 24; *BNACM* 14 (Dec. 1914): 980.

41. "Credit Protection Counsels," *CM* 28 (Sept. 1928): 36; "A New Rogue's Gallery," *CM* 30 (1928): 32; Simmons, *Security Frauds*, 14. For a typical nationwide investigation, see the 1928 correspondence between Henry Jay Case, of the NYSE Committee on Records and Investigations, and W. P. Collis, of the New York BBB, in Records of the New York City BBB, NYSE Archives.

42. New York City BBB, *Safeguarding the Integrity of Business* (New York, 1928), 9; NACM, *About the National Fund for Credit Protection* (New York, 1925), 7; "Suppressing Credit Crime," *CM* 27 (Jan. 1925): 8.

43. "Would Broaden Work of Better Business Bureaus," *Printer's Ink*, Sept. 11, 1924, in HCF; Kansas City BBB, *Protecting Legitimate Business and the Public: 1928 Annual Report* (Kansas City, 1928), 3–5, 10–11; New York City BBB, *Facts, Then Action: A Merchandise Report, 1925–1930* (New York, 1930). This graduated approach to disciplinary action represents an early example of "responsive regulation." See Ian Ayres and John Braithwaite, *Responsive Regulation: Transcending the Deregulation Debate* (New York, 1995); John Braithwaite, *Restorative Justice and Responsive Regulation* (New York, 2001).

44. Ralph M. Hower, *The History of an Advertising Agency: N. W. Ayer & Sons at Work, 1869–1949* (Cambridge, MA, 1949), 503; Boris Emmet and John E. Jeuck, *Catalogues and Counters: A History of Sears, Roebuck and Company* (Chicago, 1950), 595.

45. Abelson, *When Ladies Go A-Thieving*, 142; "Shoplifters Are Bane of Stores," *LAT*, Dec. 11, 1910, IIIE; "Halycon Days of Shoplifters Gone," *WP*, July 9, 1916, E9; "Thwarting the Shoplifter," *WP*, Mar. 29, 1925, 75; Theodore D. Irwin, "Guarding the Nation's Railroads," *WP*, Dec. 14, 1930, SM2.

46. FTC, *Annual Report* (Washington, DC, 1930), 24–25.

47. Tregoe, "General Letters to Members"; "When Guerilla Efforts Failed," *CM* 27 (1925): 9; "The Fight against Commercial Crime," *CM* 27 (Apr. 1925): 10; Simmons, *Securities Frauds*, 15–16. On the era's public health campaigns, see Duffy, *The Sanitarians*; Margaret Humphreys, *Yellow Fever and the South* (New Brunswick, NJ, 1992); Margaret Humphreys, *Malaria: Poverty, Race, and Public Health in the United States* (Baltimore, 2001).

48. "Vigilantia and Fidelitas: The Credit Man's 1926 Resolution," CM 28 (Jan. 1926): 20–21; H. J. Kenner, "The Bureau's Purpose," *Kansas City BBB Bulletin*, Feb. 2, 1927; Boston BBB, "How Frauds Hurt Business," *Bulletin* 1 (Oct. 3, 1929); Buffalo BBB, "Detective Agency Decision Reversed," *Bulletin*, May 13, 1931; Oklahoma City BBB, *Report of Better Business Bureau Activities* (Oct. 1930), 6; Auchincloss, *Better Business Bureau*, 14.

49. "The National Policeman," *CM* 28 (May 1926): 9.

50. "President Coolidge on Truth-in-Advertising," *Accuracy* 2 (Nov. 1926): 7; "Anti-Fraud Campaign Has Coolidge Support," *NYT*, Sept. 22, 1924, HCF; "Herbert Hoover Approves," *CM* 27 (Apr. 1925): 10; " 'Deserving of the Support of the Business Public,' " *CM* 27 (Apr. 1925): 11; "A. W. Mellon to W. H. Pouch," *CM* 31 (Mar. 1929): 13; "Honorable Charles H. Tuttle," *Accuracy* 3 (Apr. 1927): 1.

51. "Mattuck to Direct War on Swindlers," *NYT*, Oct. 5, 1925, 5; "Heads Stock Fraud

Bureau," *NYT*, Feb. 12, 1929, 18; "Schwab's Bureau of Investigation," *NYT*, Oct. 24, 1926, E7; "Credit Protection Counsels," 36; "Credit Men Meet," *NYT*, June 21, 1937, 30; "Buckner to Fight Business Frauds," *NYT*, Mar. 19, 1925, 23; "Florida Facts for New Yorkers," Member News Bulletin No. 43, New York City BBB, June 9, 1926; "Better Business in Securities," *Wall St. News*, Apr. 5, 1927; "Fighting Frauds," *Xenia* [OH] *Republican*, Apr. 23, 1927, both in HCF.

52. "Credit Men's Dinner," *NYT*, Apr. 23, 1897, 2; "Dinner to Fraud Fighters," *NYT*, Feb. 6, 1906, 7; "Investors Put on Right Track," *Brooklyn Eagle*, Mar. 3, 1924; "Would Broaden Work of Better Business Bureaus," *Printers' Ink*, Sept. 11, 1924; "National Business Group Convention," *Indianapolis Star*, Sept. 21, 1925, all in HCF; "Noted Visitor Coming," *Charlotte Observer*, Dec. 12, 1913, 6; "Suppressing Credit Crime," *CM* 27 (Jan. 1925): 8; Edward F. Lamb, "An Honest Commerce Crusade," *CM* 28 (Aug. 1926): 18; John E. Norvell, "Forward for the Fund!" *CM* 28 (Sept. 1926): 19.

53. *St. Louis BBB Bulletin*, June 18, 1941.

54. Craig Calhoun, " 'New Social Movements' of the Early Nineteenth Century," *Social Science History* 17 (1993): 385–427; Frederick Mayer, *Narrative Politics: Stories and Collective Action* (New York, 2014), 101–41.

55. On communitarian versus individualistic/market framing, see Dan Ariely, *Predictably Irrational: The Hidden Forces That Shape Our Decisions* (New York, 2009), 67–88.

56. Butler D. Shaffer, *In Restraint of Trade: The Business Campaign against Competition, 1918–1938* (Lewisburg, PA, 1997).

57. G. Cullom Davis, "The Transformation of the Federal Trade Commission, 1914–1929," *Mississippi Valley Historical Review* 49 (1962): 437–55; Morton Keller, "The Pluralist State: American Economic Regulation in Comparative Perspective, 1900–1930," in *Regulation in Perspective: Historical Essays,* ed. Thomas K. McCraw (Cambridge, MA, 1981), 56–94.

58. Seymour Cromwell's scrapbooks at the NYSE Archives furnish abundant evidence of the Exchange's antagonism to "blue-sky" proposals. The creation of the New York City BBB followed a 1921 wave of failures among marginal brokerage firms, which heightened pressure for tougher oversight of Wall Street. AACW, *Most Dangerous Enemy,* 4.

59. Ellis Hawley, "Three Facets of Hooverian Associationalism: Lumber, Aviation, and Movies, 1921–1930," in *Regulation in Perspective*, ed. McCraw, 95–123; H. J. Kenner, *Business Self-Discipline* (New York, 1927), 1.

60. On the politics of Southern segregation, see J. Morgan Kousser, *The Shaping of Southern Politics: Suffrage Restriction and the Establishment of the One-Party South, 1880–1910* (New Haven, 1974); Glenda Elizabeth Gilmore, *Gender and Jim Crow: Women and the Politics of White Supremacy in North Carolina, 1896–1920* (Chapel Hill, 1996); J. Douglas Smith, *Managing White Supremacy: Race, Politics, and Citizenship in Jim Crow Virginia* (Chapel Hill, 2002).

61. Keller, "The Pluralist State"; Tony Allan Freyer, *Regulating Big Business: Antitrust in Great Britain and America* (New York, 1992); Gerald Berk, "Communities of Competitors: Open Price Associations and the American State, 1911–1929," *Social Science History* 20 (1996): 375–400.

62. *Jones, Collector of Revenue, v. Better Business Bureau of Oklahoma City*, 123 Fed. 2nd 767 (U.S. Court of Appeals for the 10th Circuit, 1941).

63. H. J. Kenner, *You and the Integrity of Business: An Address to the Rotary Club of New York* (New York, 1929).

64. Boston BBB, "No Libel Action Lost," *Bulletin*, Nov. 7, 1929; Richardson, "Business Policing Itself," 74; Kenner, *Fight for Truth in Advertising*, 264–65; Auchincloss, *Better Business Bureau*, 6; *Artloom Corporation v. National Better Business Bureau et al.*, 48 Fed. 2nd 897 (U.S. District Court for the Southern District of New York, 1931); *McCann v. New York Stock Exchange et al.*, 107 Fed. 2nd 908 (U.S. Court of Appeals for the 2nd Circuit, 1939).

65. William F. Egelhofer, "Credit and Commercial Crime," *Central Law Journal* 21 (1928): 28; Elmer Leslie McDowell, "No Quarter for Creditors," *NAR* 236 (1933): 148; "Credit Men at Seattle Discuss War on Fraud," *NYT*, June 13, 1928, 31; "Fraud Fight Convicts 734," *NYT*, June 17, 1929.

66. "Trade Honesty Gain Reported," *Christian Science Monitor*, Feb. 3, 1927, in HCF; "Periodical Men Act to Curb Ad Frauds," *NYT*, Oct. 10, 1928, 31; "Magazines Rejected $2,000,000 in Ads," *NYT*, Jan. 5, 1930, 2; New York City BBB, *Facts, Then Action*; Buffalo BBB, "New Codes of Advertising Practices," *Bulletin* 2 (May 31, 1933); "New Frauds Court Called a Success," *NYT*, July 21, 1923, 5; Phillip Ives, "Prompt Prosecution of Commercial Fraud," *CM* 25 (Apr. 1923): 15; "Sees Speedy Trials Best Curb on Fraud," *NYT*, Jan. 22, 1929, 51.

67. E. B. Moran, "Facts, Not Opinions," *CM* 25 (July 1925): 30; "Avoided Loss of $920," *CM* 27 (Feb. 1925), 13; "Department Store Has Accuracy Meeting," *Accuracy* 1 (Sept. 1925): 1; Kansas City BBB, "Cooperates with Bureaus," *Bulletin*, Nov. 29, 1926; Kenner, *Fight for Truth in Advertising*, 167–68.

68. "The Campaign Starts!," *CM* 31 (Feb. 1929): 16; Tregoe, "General Letters to Members," June 1, 1926; Philadelphia BBB, "Protecting the Commercial Reputation of Philadelphia," *Bulletin* 443, Dec. 1931; Kenner, *Fight for Truth in Advertising*, 169–70; Oklahoma City BBB, *Report of Better Business Bureau Activities*, 6. The businessmen's war on fraud thus generated what John Braithwaite and Peter Drahos refer to as regulatory "webs of dialogue" and regulatory "webs of reward and coercion." *Global Business Regulation* (New York, 2000), 553–59.

69. Cuthbert Greig, "All in the Same Boat," *CM* 30 (Nov. 1928): 5–6; Louis Kirstein, "Better Business Bureaus and How They Serve," Manuscript text of speech before the Incorporated Association of Retail Distributors, London, Apr. 21, 1925, Kirstein Papers; Victoria de Grazia, *Irresistible Empire: America's Advance through Twentieth-Century Europe* (Cambridge, MA, 2005), 15–74, 130–83.

70. Edward F. Lamb, "Ten Months of the Fund," *CM* 28 (June 1926): 51; "One Out of 117 Wanted to Prosecute," *CM* 30 (July 1928): 3; Elizabeth Frazer, "The Dynamiters," *SEP* 201 (Nov. 17, 1928): 16–17, 52, 54, 56; "Getting Rich by Going Broke," *Literary Digest* 101 (Apr. 27, 1929): 65–67; Richardson, "Business Policing Itself," 71–72; New York City BBB, *Blocking the Return of the Stock Swindler* (New York, 1933); McDowell, "No Quarter for Creditors"; Ellison and Brock, *Run for Your Money*, 3–4; Kenner, *Fight for Truth in Advertising*, 202–04.

71. "Wallbrook Presbyterians," *BS*, Jan. 14, 1898, 10; "Tregoe the Busy Man"; "Booze Worst Foe to Business," *Kansas City Times*, Jan. 18, 1917, 2; "Warns of Alien Bandits in Trade," *PI*, Oct. 11, 1920, 18; "Tregoe Rebukes Gompers," *NYT*, June 13, 1922, 4.

72. Sidener, "Patrolling the Avenues of Publicity," 638.

73. Williams, "Keep Crooks out of Business," 8; Smith, "The Credit Trimmers," 92;

C. D. West, "Commercial Crook Meets His Waterloo," *CM* 25 (1923): 32; Edward F. Lamb, "An Honest Commercial Crusade," *CM* 28 (Aug. 1926): 18. On public health experts' antagonism toward immigrants, see Alan M. Kraut, *Silent Travelers: Germs, Genes, and the "Immigrant Menace"* (Baltimore, 1995).

74. Ferdinand Pecora, *Wall Street under Oath: The Story of Our Modern Money Changers* (New York, 1939); John Kenneth Galbraith, *The Great Crash* (New York, 1955); Forrest McDonald, *Insull* (Chicago, 1962); and John Brooks, *Once in Golconda: A True Drama of Wall Street, 1920–1938* (New York, 1969).

75. "The Better Business Bureau and Investment Trusts," *Journal of Commerce*, July 20, 1927, in HCF. Although the *Journal of Commerce* printed Kenner's retraction, it also asserted that the previous story reflected "the explicit and reiterated assurances" from the quoted employee that "he was an officer of that organization and authorized to speak for it." On investment trust frauds, see "Trust Heads Indicted," *WSJ*, Jan. 18, 1930, 6; "Investment Trust Faces Fraud Writ," *NYT*, July 18, 1930, 18; "U. S. Indicts Bob for $7,000,000," *CT*, Apr. 29, 1931, 2; Watson Washburn and Edmund S. De Long, *High and Low Financiers: Some Notorious Swindlers and Their Abuses of the Stock-Selling System* (New York, 1932), 229–49.

76. "Business Bureau Elects," *NYT*, June 20, 1930, 44. On Whitney's fall from grace, see Galbraith, *The Great Crash*, 161–65.

77. Quoted in "Department Store Has Accuracy Meeting."

CHAPTER EIGHT: QUANDARIES OF PROCEDURAL JUSTICE

1. Official Despotism," *Pomeroy's Democrat*, Apr. 4, 1874, 2; "Anthony Comstock," *Pomeroy's Democrat*, Apr. 11, 1874, 1; "Bravely Done," *Pomeroy's Democrat*, Apr. 20, 1878, 2.

2. D. M. Bennett, *The World's Sages, Thinkers, and Reformers* (New York, 1876), 1072–73; D. M. Bennett, *The Champions of the Church: Their Crimes and Persecutions* (New York, 1878), 1010–11; "Letter from Alfred E. Giles," in Benjamin Tucker, *Proceedings of the Indignation Meeting Held in Faneuil Hall* (Boston, 1878), 57; Letter from "A New York Pastor," *NYTR*, Feb. 12, 1880, in Anthony Comstock, *Frauds Exposed: Or How the People Are Deceived and Robbed, and Youth Corrupted* (New York, 1880), 541; Alfred E. Giles, *Societies for the Suppression of Vice: Are They Beneficial or Injurious?* (Boston, 1883).

3. "Spy System," *New York Commercial Advertiser*, April 10, 1837, 2; "Beauties of the Credit System," *Circular* 5 (Aug. 14, 1856): 120; "Commercial Black Lists," *PPL*, Feb. 20, 1860, 2; "Commercial Agencies," *NYH*, Apr. 5, 1869, 5; "Commercial Agencies," *Pomeroy's Democrat*, June 29, 1870, 4; Thomas Francis Meagher, *The Commercial Agency "System" of the United States and Canada Exposed: Is the Secret Inquisition a Curse or a Benefit?* (New York, 1876); Scott A. Sandage, *Born Losers: A Cultural History of Failure in America* (Cambridge, MA, 2005), 106–08, 171–84; Rowena Olegario, *A Culture of Credit: Embedding Trust and Transparency in American Business* (Cambridge, MA, 2006), 70; Marc Flandreau and Gabriel Geisler Mesevage, "The Untold History of Transparency: Mercantile Agencies, Law, and the Lawyers (1851–1916)," *Enterprise and Society* 15 (2014): 222–25.

4. Edward T. Freedley, *Money: How to Get, How to Keep, and How to Use It* (London, 1853), 79.

5. Bernard Bailyn, *The Ideological Origins of the American Revolution* (Cambridge, MA, 1992); Harry L. Watson, *Liberty and Power: The Politics of Jacksonian America* (New York, 1990); Michael F. Holt, *The Political Crisis of the 1850s* (New York, 1983).

6. Olegario, *Culture of Credit*, 71, 74–76.

7. Comstock, *Frauds Exposed*, 526–39, 547–48; "The Suppression of Vice," *NYT*, Jan. 21, 1885, 5.

8. "The Mercantile Agency," *HMM* 24 (1851): 46–53; "Money Market and Commercial News," *The Independent* (Apr. 26, 1855): 334–35; "The Mercantile Agency System," *Bankers' Magazine* 12 (1858): 545–49; *Commercial and Statistical Review of the City of Burlington, Iowa* (Burlington, 1882), 106.

9. "Mercantile Agencies," *ALJ* (Aug. 2, 1873): 65–66; "Credit Organizations and Meddlesome Legislation," *Commercial and Financial Chronicle* 18 (Apr. 4, 1874): 338–39; "Malice Necessary to a Libel," *NYT*, Mar. 6, 1884, 8; Louis Greeley, "What Publications of Commercial Agencies Are Privileged," *American Law Register* 35 (Nov. 1887): 681–93; Flandreau and Mesevage, "Untold History of Transparency," 240–46.

10. "Exposure of Fraud and Crime," *New York Evangelist* 52 (Jan. 13, 1881): 4; Charles Norton, "Professional Swindling," *Christian Union* 23 (Feb. 23, 1881): 177–78; "Fools and Knaves," *Boston Advertiser*, Jan. 25, 1881, 2; "Anthony Comstock's Law," *NYT*, May 18, 1888, 3.

11. " 'In Purity There Is Power,' " *Boston Journal*, Mar. 28, 1879, 1; "Suppression of Vice," *Cincinnati Gazette*, May 6, 1879, 8; "Suppression of Vice," *Christian Advocate* 45 (Jan. 29, 1880): 69; "A Year's Work in Suppressing Vice," *NYTR*, Jan. 23, 1884, 2; "Anthony Comstock Vindicated," *Christian Union* 37 (Jan. 26, 1888): 116; *Northern Christian Advocate*, Jan. 29, 1891, 36; "Year's Fight with Vice," *NYT*, Jan. 23, 1896, 9.

12. "An Attempt to Kill A. J. Comstock," *NYTR*, Nov. 2, 1874, 12; Comstock, *Frauds Exposed*, 294–306; "Anthony Comstock Arrested," *NYT*, Sept. 17, 1881, 3; "Anthony Comstock Victorious," *New Haven Register*, Oct. 22, 1881, 1; "A Suit against Anthony Comstock," *New York Herald-Tribune*, May 4, 1896, 13.

13. "Fraud Orders Held Back," *NYH*, Feb. 2, 1895, 4; "No Early Decision in Lottery Cases," *St. Louis Republic*, Jan. 6, 1896, 8; *Annual Reports of the Post-Office Department* (Washington, DC, 1897), 38.

14. J. T. Hanna to F. H. Jones, Acting Postmaster General, *In Re State Mutual Life Insurance Company of Illinois*, Fraud Order Cases, Entry 50, Box 1, Case 555; "Post-Office Despotism," *Printer's Ink* 6 (Apr. 27, 1892): 541–42; John Irving Romer, "A Hypocritical Fraud," *NYT*, Oct. 9, 1892, 12; "Our Post Office," *Advertisers' Guide*, reprinted in *Printer's Ink* 17 (Dec. 23, 1896): 29.

15. "Linsey & Co. Want to Enjoin the Postal Department," *CIO*, Sept. 23, 1896, 11; "Judge Grosscup Takes up the Fraud Order Cases," *CIO*, Oct. 21, 1896, 11.

16. Amy Dru Stanley, *From Bondage to Contract: Wage Labor, Marriage, and the Market in the Age of Slave Emancipation* (New York, 1998), 98–137; Mary Ellen Curtin, *Black Prisoners and Their World: Alabama, 1865–1900* (Charlottesville, 2000), 42–61; Lucy E. Salyer, *Laws Harsh as Tigers: Chinese Immigrants and the Shaping of Modern Immigration Law* (Chapel Hill, 1995).

17. "New Fraud Order Policy," *Wilkes-Barre Times*, June 25, 1897, 3; "Report of the Postmaster General," *Post Office Annual Reports* (Washington, DC, 1905), 29.

18. "Less Mail Swindling," *Tacoma News*, Oct. 11, 1898, 6.

19. *Report of the Fourth Assistant Postmaster-General J. L. Bristow on the Investiga-*

tion of Certain Divisions of the Post-Office Department (Washington, DC, 1903), 36–69; "New Indictments in Postal Frauds," *LAT*, Oct. 6, 1903; "Miller and Johns Appear in Court," *LAT*, Oct. 9, 1903, 3. For extensive coverage of the Tyner-Barrett trial, see the *Springfield Republican*, the *Kansas City Star*, and the *Washington Post* in May 1904.

20. "Senator Burton Is Indicted for Accepting Bribe," *San Antonio Express*, Jan. 24, 1904, 1; "Jury Convicts Him," *DMN*, Mar. 29, 1904, 1; "Senator Burton Sentenced to Jail," *Current Literature* 36 (May 1904): 488–89.

21. "Kansas Oil Men's Burden," *KCS*, Mar. 12, 1906, 1; "Uncle Sam Mail Released," *KCS*, May 31, 1907, 1; *Memorial of the Uncle Sam Oil Company Relating to Its Business Transactions with the Standard Oil Company*, U.S. Sen. Doc. 503, May 18, 1908, 60th Cong., 1st Session, 4–12; "Espouses Cause of Oil Concern," *DMN*, May 23, 1908, 3; "Says Standard Controls Post-Office Department," *Tulsa Daily World*, Jan. 15, 1911, 1.

22. For correspondence between Lewis and Goodwin and a purported affidavit by a private detective sent by Lewis to assess Goodwin's willingness to take on mail fraud cases, see Edwin C. Madden, *The U.S. Government's Shame: The Story of the Great Lewis Case* (Detroit, 1908), 279–98.

23. Edward G. Lewis, *Order Number Ten: Being Cursory Comments on Some of the Effects of the Great American Fraud Order* (St. Louis, 1911), 40–41, 58, 108; Sidney Morse, *The Siege of University City: The Dreyfus Case of America* (University City, MO, 1912), 411–18, 430–35, 466–68, 633–34; Madden, *U.S. Government's Shame*, 166–74.

24. "Postal Law Reform," *Health* 59 (May 1909): 213–14.

25. *The Public* 6 (July 18, 1903): 227–28; Franklin Pierce, *Federal Usurpation* (New York, 1908), 359–62; Edward F. Browne, *Socialism or Empire: A Danger* (Omaha, 1906), 2, 197. See also "Autocracy at the Post Office," *Review of Reviews* 36 (Oct. 1907): 407; Harry E. Byrd, "The Decay of Personal Rights and Guarantees," *Report of the Thirteenth Annual Meeting of the Maryland State Bar Association* (Baltimore, 1908), 24–37.

26. "Mob Law Discussed," *Colorado Springs Gazette*, Mar. 31, 1904, 1; "Crumpacker's Speech," *Montgomery Advertiser*, Feb. 25, 1905, 10; Speech of Rep. Crumpacker, Apr. 11, *Congressional Record* 40 (1906): 4103; "Fraud Order Legislation," *Morning Olympian*, Jan. 2, 1907, 2; "Czar-Like Power," *AC*, Mar. 11, 1908, 2.

27. *Lewis Publishing Company*, House Committee on Expenditures in the Post Office Department (Washington, DC, 1913); *Uncle Sam Oil Co.*, House Committee on Expenditures in the Post Office Department (Washington, DC, 1912); "Finds Post Office Abuses," *NYT*, June 16, 1912, 9.

28. Henry Castle, "Defects and Abuses in Our Postal System, II" *NAR* 175 (July 1902): 122–23; Edwin Lawrence, "Swindling through the Post Office," *Outlook* 83 (Jan. 14, 1905): 121; *Annual Reports of the Post-Office Department* (Washington, DC, 1905), 28–30; *Annual Reports of the Post-Office Department* (Washington, DC, 1906), 28–30; *Memorandum by the Assistant Attorney General for the Post-Office Department on Postal 'Fraud Order' Law* (Washington, DC, 1906). George Cortelyou, "Fraud in the Mail: Fraud Orders and Their Purposes," *NAR* 184 (Apr. 19, 1907): 809–15; *Post-Office Department Annual Reports* (Washington, DC, 1907), 68–70.

29. "Fraud Orders," *Youth's Companion* 78 (May 5, 1904), 222–23; "Patent Medicine and Postal Department," *Medical News* 84 (June 11, 1904): 1133–34; "Postal Fraud Laws," *Outlook* 83 (Jan. 14, 1905): 111; John Callan O'Laughlin, "Crumpacker Bill Shown as Menace," *CT*, Jan. 14, 1907, 1; "Big Power," *NYT*, Jan. 26, 1907, 8; "The People

vs. the Swindlers," *Outlook* (Jan. 12, 1907): 48–49; "Losing Sixteen Millions a Year," *LAT*, Nov. 30, 1908, 11.

30. *American School of Magnetic Healing v. McAnnulty*, 187 U.S. 94 (1902); *Public Clearing House v. Coyne*, 194 U.S. 497 (1904).

31. *Missouri Drug Co. v. Wyman*, 129 Fed. Cases 623 (Circuit Ct. for the E.D. of Missouri, 1904); *People's United States Bank v. Gilson et al.*, 140 Fed. Cases 1 (E.D. of Missouri, July 19, 1905); *Hall v. Wilcox*, 225 Fed. Cases 333 (Circuit Ct. for S.D. of New York, 1906); *Appelby et al. v. Cluss*, 160 Fed. Cases 984 (Circuit Ct. for Dist. of New Jersey, 1908); *People's United States Bank v. Gilson*, 161 Fed. Cases 286 (Circuit Ct. for E.D. of Missouri, 1908); *Putnam v. Morgan*, 172 Fed. Cases 450 (Circuit Ct. for S.D. of New York, 1909), *Degg v. Hitchcock*, 35 App. D.C. 219 (DC Court of Appeals, 1910); Jed S. Rakoff, "The Federal Mail Fraud Statute (Part I)," *Duquesne Law Review* 18 (1980): 771–822.

32. "Will Review Postal Frauds," *Charlotte Observer*, Jan. 8, 1907, 1; "To Stop Fraud Orders," *NYT*, Jan. 8, 1907, 14; John Callan O'Laughlin, "Thaw Case Evils Shock Roosevelt," *CT*, Feb. 12, 1907, 4; "Bills Sent to Next Congress," *DMN*, Feb. 26, 1907, 8; Dorothy Ganfield Fowler, *Unmailable: Congress and the Post Office* (Athens, GA, 1977), 94–95.

33. *Annual Report of the Postmaster-General* (Washington, DC, 1910), 12–13; "We'll Put Mail Swindlers behind Bars," *NYT Magazine*, Nov. 27, 1910, 8; "Reaching after Stock Swindlers," *PI*, Nov. 27, 1910, 8.

34. "Postal Raids Show Vast Stock Frauds," *NYT*, Nov. 22, 1910, 1; "New York Men Charged with Huge Swindle," *DNT*, Nov. 22, 1910, 2; "Mr. Hitchcock's War upon Swindlers," *The Independent* 69 (Dec. 1, 1910): 1221; "Watching Uncle Sam's Mails," *Anaconda Standard*, Feb. 12, 1911, 1. The category of Nolle Prosequi refers to cases that postal prosecutors chose to discontinue.

35. Franklin Escher, "The Government and the Get Rich Quick Industry," *HW* (Oct. 12, 1910): 30; "'We'll Put Mail Swindlers behind Bars': American Medical Association Publishes 'Nostrums and Quackery,'" *NYT Sunday Magazine*, Jan. 14, 1912, 7.

36. *Annual Report of the Postmaster General* (Washington, DC, 1912), 27.

37. *Annual Report of the Postmaster-General* (Washington, DC, 1910), 77; *Annual Report of the Postmaster-General* (Washington, DC, 1912), 63.

38. *Annual Report of the Postmaster-General* (1912), 63.

39. "Indictments Expected," *LAT*, Jan. 9, 1914, I12; "$239,000,000 Lost in Mail Frauds," *Biloxi Daily Herald*, Oct. 20, 1915, 3; "Spending Thousands to Avenge Hundreds' Loss," *LAT*, Jan. 9, 1916, I11.

40. *Annual Report of the Postmaster General* (Washington, DC, 1913), 36–37; "Plan to Stop Mail Swindles," *LAT*, Jan. 5, 1914, I3; "Indictments Expected," *WP*, Jan. 9, 1914, I12.

41. *Annual Report of the Postmaster General* (Washington, DC, 1913), 64–65; "Mail Swindlers Get $351,000,000," *NYT Magazine*, Feb. 14, 1915, 19.

42. Frank Koester, *The Price of Inefficiency* (New York, 1913), 27–29; George S. Coleman, "Public Service Commissions," in *Some Legal Phases of Corporate Financing, Reorganization, and Regulation* (New York, 1916), 363.

43. *Annual Report of the Postmaster General* (Washington, DC, 1915), 44, 85–88; AMA, *Medical Mail Order Frauds* (Chicago, 1915); "Merchant Gets Two-Year Sentence in Fraud Case," *Bulletin of the NACM* 16 (Jan. 1916): 18; Merle Sidener, "Patrolling the Avenues of Publicity," *World's Work* 35 (Apr. 1918): 640.

44. *Annual Report of the Postmaster General* (Washington, DC, 1916), 71; *Annual Report of the Postmaster General* (Washington, DC, 1919), 112.

45. Warren Waite and Ralph Cassady, Jr., *The Consumer and the Economic Order* (New York, 1939), 111–14.

46. "Report on the Better Business Bureaus," Foreman's National Detective Agency, in J. L. Foreman to F. J. Schlink, June 10, 1932; "National Businessmen's Protective Council to Secretary," Consumers Research, Jan. 6, 1931; both in Box 170, Consumers Research Papers.

47. Frank Dalton O'Sullivan, *Rackets: An Exposé of the Methods and Practices of the Better Business Bureaus* (Chicago, 1933), 21–29, 41–42, 59–61; Edwin C. Riegel, *The Indictment of the Better Business Bureau Conspiracy* (New York, 1931), 10–16; Manhattan Board of Commerce, *Do Better Business Bureaus Better Business?* (New York, 1930).

48. O'Sullivan, *Rackets*, 40; "'Shoppers' as Snoopers," *The Lance* 1 (June 1933): 8.

49. *Acid Truths about the Better Business Bureau of Saint Louis* (St. Louis, 1930); O'Sullivan, *Rackets*, 90–91, 122–25; "Self-Appointed Censors of Business," *The Lance* 1 (June 1933): 11; Riegel, *Indictment of the Better Business Bureau Conspiracy*, 2–3, 7, 34–42.

50. George Graham Rice, *My Adventures with Your Money* (New York, 1911), 358–59; "G. G. Rice Runs Foul of the Law," *NYT*, Jan. 6, 1926, 25; "Rice Put on Trial," *NYT*, Nov. 14, 1928, 16; NBBB, "Tipster Sheets," *Bulletin*, Sept. 30, 1928; "Prosecutor's Raid Uncovers Conspiracy," *The Detroit Better Business Bureau Factfinder*, June 1932.

51. H. J. Kenner, *You and the Integrity of Business* (New York, 1929), 12–13; James C. Auchincloss, *The Better Business Bureau: Its Growth and Work* (New York, 1927), 6; "Mr. Riegel Comes to St. Louis," *St. Louis BBB Bulletin* 4 (July 9, 1931); "Prosecutor's Raid Uncovers Conspiracy."

52. Columbus BBB, *The Pig Squeals!* (Columbus, 1934?); "'War' Declared on Better Business Bureaus!" *Report of the Chicago Better Business Bureau* 2 (Nov. 30, 1930): 1–2; H. J. Kenner, *The Fight for Truth in Advertising* (New York, 1936), 131–34; 264–65; Ellison and Brock, *Run for Your Money*, 252–54.

53. "R. H. Macy & Co. Calls Attention to Their Own Make of Gentlemen's Shirts," *Puck* 7 (May 5, 1880): 159; *The Record: Recounting the Advertising Price Claims of R. H. Macy & Company, Inc., and the Position of the Better Business Bureau of New York City, Inc., in Respect Thereto* (New York, 1926), 1–9; Tom Mahoney, *The Great Merchants* (New York, 1955), 165.

54. Percy Straus to Bayard Dominick, Apr. 21, 1926, in *The Record*, 10–14.

55. Straus to Dominick, in *The Record*, 14–17.

56. "Store War," *Time*, Oct. 12, 1931, 58–59; Kenneth Barnard, "Personal and Confidential Memorandum to the Affiliated Better Business Bureaus," Nov. 26, 1930, Box 8, Bell Papers; Milton Handler to F. J. Schlink, Oct. 6, 1931, Box 170, File 12, Consumers Research Papers; *A Guide for Retail Store Advertising* (Boston, 1932), 6; Ruth P. Mack, *Controlling Retailers: A Study of Cooperation and Control in the Retail Trade with Special Reference to the NRA* (New York, 1936), 41–42; H. J. Kenner, *The Fight for Truth in Advertising* (New York, 1936), 205–09.

57. *The Record*, 3–4.

58. "New Code of Advertising Practices Adopted by National Advertisers," *Buffalo BBB Bulletin* 2 (May 31, 1933): 1.

59. "Outline of National Better Business Bureau Activities, 1931," *NBBB Bulletin*, Dec. 31, 1931.

60. "Advertising Field to Have 'High Court,'" *NYT*, Dec. 11, 1932, 29; "Ad Review Board to Enforce Ethics," *NYT*, Feb. 2, 1933, 33; "Acts to Enforce Advertising Code," *NYT*, Apr. 13, 1933, 31; "Consider Two Plans for Ad Censorship," *NYT*, Dec. 9, 1934, N15; Alfred McClung Lee, *The Daily Newspaper in America* (New York, 1937), 332–33.

61. New York City BBB, *Helping Business and the NRA* (New York, 1933), 4–7; "Expert Is Sent Here to Avert Code Cheating," *WP*, Aug. 13, 1933, 3; "Accord on Code Is Now Indicated," *NYT*, Aug. 25, 1933, 10; "H. J. Kenner Aids Board," *NYT*, Nov. 18, 1933, 6; "Better Business Bureau Will Act as NRA Mediator," *CT*, Dec. 4, 1933, 15; Mack, *Controlling Retailers*, 217, 258–61; H. J. Kenner, "The Search for NRA's Successor," *Nation's Business* 25 (Nov. 1937): 33.

62. FTC, *Annual Report* (Washington, DC, 1916), 6–12; John L. Meachum, "Procedure and Practice before the Federal Trade Commission," *MLR* 21 (1922): 127–40; Gerald C. Henderson, *The Federal Trade Commission: A Study in Administrative Law and Procedure* (New York, 1924), 49–55, 61, 70–77.

63. Henderson, *Federal Trade Commission*, 58–60, 62–65.

64. Ibid., 83–84.

65. FTC, *Annual Report* (Washington, DC, 1917), 8; Henderson, *Federal Trade Commission*, 86–90.

66. Huston Thompson, "Protecting the Public by Informing the Investor," Address to the Thirteenth Annual Meeting of Life Insurance Presidents, Dec. 5, 1919, *Speeches of Commissioner Huston Thompson*, FTCL; Henderson, *Federal Trade Commission*, 175–76, 232–34.

67. "Trade Commission Adopts Policy of Greater Secrecy," *AC*, May 1, 1925, 4; Silas Bent, "Trade Commission Has Adopted New Methods," *NYT*, May 3, 1925, XX12; FTC, *Annual Report* (Washington, DC, 1925), 110–11; William Humphrey, "A New Spirit in Federal Trade Cases," *Nation's Business* 15 (July 1927): 30–31.

68. William Humphrey, "Address before the National Petroleum Association," Atlantic City, Sept. 17, 1926, in *Speeches of Commissioner William Humphrey*, FTCL; William Humphrey, "We Quit Playing Tag with Fraud," *Nation's Business* 18 (Jan. 1930): 39–42.

69. James Young, "Sales Policies and the Federal Trade Commission," *AAPS* 115 (1924): 22; Henderson, *Federal Trade Commission*, 78–82, 244; "Seeks to Check Fraud in Selling," *NYT*, Aug. 15, 1926, E14; "Dishonest Advertising," *WP*, June 15, 1928, 6; "American Business Widens Self-Rule," *NYT*, Dec. 10, 1928, 8; "Trade Rules Parley," *WSJ*, June 24, 1931, 3; *Annual Report of the Federal Trade Commission* (Washington, DC, 1939), 93–97.

70. FTC, *Annual Report* (Washington, DC, 1929), 55–56; FTC, *Annual Report* (Washington, DC, 1931), 111–13; C. D. P., "Federal Trade Commission," 816–17.

71. Humphrey, "Address to the National Petroleum Association."

72. Henry Ward Beer, "The FTC and Its Due Process of Law," *Notre Dame Lawyer* 7 (1932): 170–84.

73. Albert Venn Dicey, *Lectures Introductory to the Study of the Law of the Constitution* (London, 1886), 174.

74. Daniel Ernst, "Ernst Freund, Felix Frankfurter, and the American *Rechtsstaat*: A

Transatlantic Shipwreck," *Studies in American Political Development* 23 (Oct. 2009): 171–75, 185–86.

75. Ernst, "Ernst Freund, Felix Frankfurter," 184–85, 187–88; James Willard Hurst, *The Growth of American Law: The Law Makers* (Boston, 1950), 419–36; Ernst, "The Politics of Administrative Law: New York's Anti-Bureaucracy Clause and the O'Brien-Wagner Campaign of 1938," *LHR* 27 (2009): 338–39.

76. On the lawyerly impulse to sustain the Constitutional principle of checks and balances, see James Willard Hurst, *Law and Markets in United States History: Different Modes of Bargaining among Interests* (Madison, 1982), 96–98; Edward A. Purcell, *Litigation and Inequality: Federal Diversity Jurisdiction in Industrial America, 1870–1958* (New York, 1992).

77. E. P. Thompson, *Whigs and Hunters: The Origin of the Black Act* (New York, 1975), 219–69; Clive Emsley, "Repression, 'Terror' and the Rule of Law in England during the Decade of the French Revolution," *English Historical Review* 100 (1985): 801–25; Rande Kostal, "A Jurisprudence of Power: Martial Law and the Ceylon Controversy," *Journal of Imperial and Commonwealth History* 28 (2000): 1–34; Richard Horowitz, "International Law and State Transformation in China, Siam, and the Ottoman Empire during the Nineteenth Century," *Journal of World History* 15 (2004): 445–86; Sally Falk Moore, "Treating Law and Knowledge: Telling Colonial Officers What to Say to Africans about Running 'Their Own' Native Courts," *Law & Society Review* 26 (1992): 11–46; Edward Berenson, *The Trial of Madame Caillaux* (Berkeley, 1993); Eugenia Lean, *Public Passions: The Trial of Shi Jianqiao and the Rise of Popular Sympathy in Republican China* (Oakland, 2007), 106–40; Thomas Dubois, "Rule of Law in a Brave New Empire," *LHR* 28 (2008): 287–317.

78. H. L. A. Hart, *The Concept of Law* (New York, 1961), 20–32; Lon L. Fuller, *The Morality of Law*, revised edition (New Haven, 1969), 33–94; John Rawls, *A Theory of Justice* (New York, 1971), 235–43.

79. My thinking along these lines has been shaped by discussions with Jonathan Ocko and David Gilmartin.

CHAPTER NINE: MOVING TOWARD *CAVEAT VENDITOR*

1. Franklin D. Roosevelt, "Message to Congress," March 29, 1933, available at Gerhard Peters and John T. Woolley, *The American Presidency Project*: http://www.presidency.ucsb.edu/ws/?pid=14602.

2. These two phrases only appeared regularly in the *New York Times* from 1933. A Google Books "Ngram" also indicates initial usage then, with exponential growth in the 1960s, reflecting the wave of consumerism.

3. Julia C. Ott, *When Wall Street Met Main Street: The Quest for an Investors' Democracy* (Cambridge, MA, 2011).

4. Robert Reed, " 'Blue Sky' Laws," *AAPS* 88 (1920): 177–87; Robert Reed and Lester Washburn, *Blue Sky Laws: Text and Analysis* (New York, 1921), ix–xvi; "Blue Sky Laws," *CLR* 24 (1924): 79–86; Harper Leech, "Take-a-Chance Men Built U.S.," *CT*, Sept. 26, 1924, 29; Michael E. Parrish, *Securities Regulation and the New Deal* (New Haven, 1970), 1–20; Daniel Holt, "Acceptable Risk: Law, Regulation, and the Politics of American Financial Markets, 1878–1930," Ph.D. diss. (University of Virginia, 2008), 188–246.

5. *Annual Report of the Attorney General of the State of New York* (Albany, 1926), 9–11; "State Starts War on Stock Frauds," *NYT*, Jan. 18, 1923, 1.

6. *Annual Report of the Attorney General of the State of New York* (Albany, 1931), 30–35; Watson Washburn, "Control of Securities Selling," *MLR* 31 (1933): 768–84.

7. Keyes Winter, "Fools and Their Money," *Harper's Monthly Magazine* (Aug. 1, 1927): 363–71; "George Graham Rice Enjoined," *WSJ*, Feb. 21, 1927, 12; Keyes Winter, "Parasites of Finance," *NAR* 224 (Nov. 1929): 516–21; "Market Corner Held as Fraud," *WSJ*, Jan. 4, 1930, 14; "Stricter Curb Asked on Investing Trusts," *NYT*, Dec. 26, 1930, 15.

8. Samuel Untermeyer, "The Farcical Martin Act," *NYT*, July 20, 1923, 12; *Annual Report of the Attorney General of the State of New York* (Albany, 1930), 29; *Annual Report of the Attorney General of the State of New York* (Albany, 1931), 34; Lawrence P. Simpson, "The New York Blue Sky Law and the Uniform Act," *New York University Law Quarterly Review* 8 (1930): 465–80.

9. Forrest McDonald, *Insull* (Chicago, 1962), 280–95, 320–28.

10. John Kenneth Galbraith, *The Great Crash: 1929* (New York, 1961), 78–86; John Brooks, *Once in Golconda: A True Story of Wall Street, 1920–1938* (New York, 1968), 65–74; Joel Seligman, *The Transformation of Wall Street: A History of the Securities and Exchange Commission and Modern Corporate Finance*, 3rd ed. (New York, 2003), 16–22.

11. John T. Flynn, *Investment Trusts Gone Wrong!* (New York, 1930); John T. Flynn, "The Investment Trusts and the Suckers," *New Republic* 95 (June 15, 1938): 158–59; Galbraith, *Great Crash*, 52–69.

12. Brooks, *Once in Golconda*, 186–90; Seligman, *Transformation of Wall Street*, 34; Steven Fraser, *Every Man a Speculator: A History of Wall Street in American Life* (New York, 2005), 428–31.

13. Vincent Carosso, *Investment Banking in America: A History* (Cambridge, MA, 1970), 264–65; Seligman, *Transformation of Wall Street*, 28.

14. SEC, *Twenty-Fifth Annual Report* (Washington, DC, 1959), xv–xviii; Carosso, *Investment Banking in America*, 278–79, 330–31; Seligman, *Transformation of Wall Street*, 24–27.

15. Hamilton Ward, "Address," *New York State Bar Association Bulletin* 1 (1929): 389.

16. Thomas W. Lawson, *Frenzied Finance: The Crime of Amalgamated* (New York, 1905); George Graham Rice, *My Adventures with Your Money* (New York, 1911); Edwin Lefevre, *Reminiscences of a Stock Operator* (New York, 1923); William Z. Ripley, *Main Street and Wall Street* (Boston, 1927); John T. Flynn, "Dishonest Business," *Forum* 82 (Dec. 1929): 351–55; Flynn, *Investment Trusts Gone Wrong!*.

17. Galbraith, *The Great Crash*, 161–63; Carosso, *Investment Banking in America*, 325–35; Seligman, *Transformation of Wall Street*, 12–38; Michael Perino, *The Hellhound of Wall Street: How Ferdinand Pecora's Investigation of the Great Crash Forever Changed American Finance* (New York, 2010).

18. Louis Loss, *Securities Regulation* (Boston, 1951); Michael E. Parrish, *Securities Regulation and the New Deal* (New Haven, 1970), 108–44; Seligman, *Transformation of Wall Street*, 39–100.

19. Emmanuel Stein, *Government and the Investor* (New York, 1941), 144–46; Paul S. Grant, "The National Association of Securities Dealers: Its Origins and Operation,"

Wisconsin Law Review (1942): 597–609; Seligman, *Transformation of Wall Street*, 183–89.

20. "The Investment Company Act," *CLR* 41 (1941): 269–85; Chelcie Bosland, "The Investment Company Act of 1940," *Journal of Political Economy* 49 (1941): 477–529; E. L. Kohler, "Protection for Investors," *The Accounting Review* 15 (1940): 446–52; H. Lawrence Wilsey, "The Investment Advisers Act of 1940," *Journal of Finance* 4 (1949): 286–94.

21. *In Re Cady, Roberts, & Co.* 40 SEC 907 (1961); *SEC v. Texas Gulf Sulphur*, 401 F. 2d 833 (2nd Circuit, 1968); Alan Bromberg, *Securities Law: Fraud-Rule 10b-5* (New York, 1967); Manuel F. Cohen, "The Development of Rule 10b-5," *BL* 23 (April 1968): 593–98.

22. Thomas McCraw, "With Consent of the Governed: The SEC's Formative Years," *Journal of Policy Analysis and Management* 1 (1982): 346–70; Thomas K. McCraw, *Prophets of Regulation: Charles Francis Adams, Louis D. Brandeis, James M. Landis, Alfred E. Kahn* (Cambridge, 1986), 169–203; Seligman, *Transformation of Wall Street*, 112–23, 167–79.

23. Richard Jennings, "Self-Regulation in the Securities Industry: The Role of the Securities and Exchange Commission," *Law and Contemporary Problems* 29 (1964): 663–90.

24. FTC, *Digest of Decisions* (Washington, DC, 1940); FTC, *Trade Practice Submittals* (Washington, DC, 1925); Carl F. Taeusch, *Policy and Ethics in Business* (New York, 1931); Frank Chapman Sharp and Philip G. Fox, *Business Ethics: Studies in Fair Competition* (New York, 1937); *Annotation and Cases on What Constitutes False, Misleading, or Deceptive Advertising or Promotional Practices* (Rochester, 1959).

25. "The Extent of the Jurisdiction of the Federal Trade Commission," *CLR* 23 (1923): 758–61; C. D. P., "Federal Trade Commission: False and Misleading Advertising," *MLR* 31 (1933): 812–16.

26. *FTC v. Standard Education Society et al.*, 302 U.S. Reports 112 (1937). In 1941, the Supreme Court curbed the FTC's authority by ruling that it lacked jurisdiction over deception in intrastate trade: *FTC v. Bunte Bros.*, 312 U.S. Reports 349.

27. Richard Tedlow, "From Competitor to Consumer: The Changing Focus of Federal Regulation of Advertising, 1914–1938," *BHR* 55 (1981): 35–58.

28. Barney Lefferts, "Good Cop," *Barron's National Business* 32 (Dec. 29, 1952): 5, 10; "Trade Rules and Trade Conferences: The FTC and Business Attack Deceptive Practices, Unfair Competition, and Antitrust Violations," *YLJ* 62 (1953): 912–53; FTC, *Guides against Deceptive Pricing* (Washington, DC, 1958); FTC, *Guide against Bait Advertising* (Washington, DC, 1959); FTC, *Guides against Deceptive Advertising of Guarantees* (Washington, DC, 1960).

29. *Gelb v. FTC*, 144 F. 2d 580 (2nd Circuit Court of Appeals, 1944); *FTC v. Mary Carter Paint Co.*, 382 U. S. Reports 46 (1965); *FTC v. Colgate-Palmolive*, 380 U.S. 374 (1965); Lawrence Laurent, "Fadeout Is Ordered for Ad Trickery on TV," *WP*, Jan. 6, 1962, A1.

30. *General Motors v. FTC*, 114 F. 2d 36; FTC, *Manual for Attorneys*, 3rd ed. (Washington, DC, 1966), 106–11. On judicial deference to FTC findings of deception, see: Glen E. Weston, "Deceptive Advertising and the Federal Trade Commission: Decline of Caveat Emptor," *Federal Bar Journal* 24 (1964): 549–59; "Developments in the Law: Deceptive Advertising," *HLR* (Mar. 1967): 1030–58.

31. "War Frauds Unit Set up by Biddle," *NYT*, Feb. 5, 1942, 6; "Drive to Stamp out War Frauds," *CT*, July 15, 1942, 6; "Vast Sums Saved by Frauds Unit," *Edwardsville Intelligencer*, Jan. 9, 1943, 2; Paul Ward, "63 Prosecuted in War Frauds," *BS*, July 18, 1943, 9; David Fain and Richard Watt, "War Procurement—A New Pattern in Contracts," *CLR* 44 (1944): 127–215; Mark Wilson, " 'Taking a Nickel out of the Cash Register': Statutory Renegotiation of Military Contracts and the Politics of Profit Control during World War II," *LHR* 28 (2010): 343–83.

32. "Text of General Maximum Price Regulation," *WSJ*, April 29, 1942, 8; Chester Bowles, "OPA Volunteers: Big Democracy in Action," *Public Administration Review* 5 (1945): 350–59; Martin Hart-Landsberg, "Popular Mobilization and Progressive Policy-Making: Lessons from World War II Price Control Struggles in the United States," *Science & Society* 67 (2004): 414–21; Meg Jacobs, " 'How about Some Meat?': The Office of Price Administration, Consumption Politics, and State-Building from the Bottom Up," *JAH* 84 (1997): 921–28.

33. James Marlow and George Zielke, "Racket in Radios," *Burlington Daily Times-News*, June 20, 1944, 9; "OPA Moves to Curb Used Auto Frauds," *NYT*, June 23, 1944, 21; "Huge Fraud Bared in Meat Coupons," *NYT*, Jan. 25, 1945, 21; NBBB, "Report of the War Activities Committee," June 14, 1945, Box 4, Bell Papers.

34. H. H. Hannah, "The Fur Products Labeling Act," *Stores* (May 1952): 20; "New Fabric Labeling Law Will Go into Effect Today," *BS*, March 3, 1960, 17; "Federal Laws Affecting Automobile Dealers," *National Association of Automobile Dealers Magazine* 34 (Nov. 1962): 11–14.

35. "Reveals Frauds in 11 Billion GI School Setup," *CT*, June 5, 1951, 17; Sylvia Porter, "Manpower Training Act Puts New Life into School Rackets," *LAT*, Aug. 16, 1962, A6; Paul Weissberg, "Shifting Alliances in the Accreditation of Higher Education: On the Long Term Consequences of the Delegation of Government Authority to Self-Regulatory Organizations," Ph.D. diss. (George Mason University, 2009), 102–17.

36. Council of State Governments, *Occupational Licensing in the States* (Chicago, 1952); "The Regulation of Advertising," *CLR* 56 (1956): 1057–72; Spencer Kimball and Bartlett Jackson, "The Regulation of Insurance Marketing," *CLR* 61 (1961): 152–57, 165–200; "Regulation of Consumer Credit: The Credit Card and the State Legislature," *YLJ* 73 (1964): 886–904; "Developments in the Law: Deceptive Advertising," 1119–22.

37. *Donaldson v. Read Magazine*, 333 U.S. 178 (1948); *Reilly v. Pinkus*, 338 U.S. 269 (1949); Robert Ague, "Intent to Defraud in Postal Fraud Order Cases," *Temple Law Quarterly* (Fall 1964): 61–71.

38. "Regulation of Advertising," 1038–43; "Postal Inspectors Lauded in Battle on Fraud," *WP*, Oct. 29, 1963, C3.

39. "Bar Payola," *Salt Lake City Tribune*, Jan. 1, 1960, 1; Charles Siepmann, "Moral Aspects of Television," *Public Opinion Quarterly* 24 (1960): 12–18; L. S. T., "Federal Communications Commission: Control of 'Deceptive Programming,' " *UPLR* 108 (1960): 868–73; Richard Tedlow, "Intellect on Television: The Quiz Show Scandals of the 1950s," *American Quarterly* 28 (1976): 483–95; Kent Anderson, *Television Fraud: The History and Implications of the Quiz Show Scandals* (Westport, CT, 1978), 137–69; Donald Mabry, "The Rise and Fall of Ace Records: A Case Study in the Independent Record Business," *BHR* 64 (1990): 445–47.

40. See: Donn Layne, "Boom Time for Gyp Schemes," *Nation's Business* 34 (April

1946): 58; Bob Crossley, "Get Set for the Two-Legged Termites!" *Better Homes & Gardens* 25 (April 1947): 59; Don Wharton, "Five Frauds to Watch out For," *Reader's Digest* 67 (1955): 101–04; "Don't Be Fooled When You Invest," *Changing Times* 10 (Aug. 1956): 37–40; Arthur Wesley Baum, "Beware Those Phony Stock Salesmen!" *SEP* 229 (June 22, 1957): 19.

41. Ralph Lee Smith, *The Health Hucksters* (New York, 1960); Ralph Lee Smith, *The Bargain Hucksters* (New York, 1962); Frank Gibney, *The Operators* (New York, 1960); Sidney Margolius, *Buyer, Be Wary!* (New York, 1965). These works dovetailed with Vance Packard's critique of mass-media manipulation, *The Hidden Persuaders* (New York, 1957), which showed how advertisers used psychological techniques to impel purchases.

42. "Two-County Anti-Fraud Unit Urged," *LAT*, May 31, 1959, 20; Sal Nuccio, "Sellers' Conscience Looks Back," Oct. 16, 1962, 71; Don Smith, "Bureau Forms to Curb Shady Business Deals," *LAT*, Sept. 26, 1965, OC1. In the early 1960s, the BBBs distributed two million booklets and 350,000 posters annually, while their leaders gave two thousand speeches. *Facts You Should Know about Your Better Business Bureau: Public Service in the Public Interest* (New York, n.d.); NBBB, *Advertising Topics*, Box 2, Folders 4–6, BBBMC.

43. For scripts from 1952 and 1956, see BBBMC, Box 32, Folder 5; Box 33, Folder 1.

44. Colston Warne, "The Influence of Ethical and Social Responsibilities on Advertising and Selling Practices," *American Economic Review* 51 (1961): 527–39; "The 'Plastic Paint' Racket," *Consumers' Research Bulletin* (Mar. 1956): 28–29; "Mail-order Gyps," *Consumer Bulletin* (Apr. 1964): 34–36.

45. Janice Williams Rutherford, *Selling Mrs. Consumer: Christine Frederick and the Rise of Household Efficiency* (Athens, GA, 2003); Kathy Peiss, "American Women and the Making of Modern Consumer Culture," *Journal of Multimedia History* 1 (1998), available at: http://www.albany.edu/jmmh/vol1no1/v1n1.html, accessed Aug. 19, 2014.

46. Elinor Lee, "Who Is Boss?—It's Mrs. Consumer," *WP*, Oct. 5, 1955, 33; "Mrs. Consumer!—IGA Ad," *WP*, Apr. 24, 1958, A15. On organizing by middle-class suburban women, see especially Sylvie Murray, *The Progressive Housewife: Community Activism in Suburban Queens, 1945–1965* (Philadelphia, 2003).

47. "New Bill in Senate Would Label Furs," July 6, 1947, 33; US Sen., *Fur Labeling: Hearings before a Subcommittee of the Committee on Interstate and Foreign Trade* (Washington, DC, 1949); US HR., *Hearings before a Subcommittee of the Committee on Interstate and Foreign Commerce* (Washington, DC, 1949); "Fur Industry Favors New Labeling Rule," *NYT*, Feb. 9, 1952, 24; "Ask Single Labeling Law," *NYT*, Mar. 5, 1956, 33; Alan Stone, "The Politics of Trade Regulation: Toward a Theory of Regulatory Behavior," Ph. D. diss. (University of Chicago, 1972), 299–321.

48. Mabry, "Rise and Fall of Ace Records," 446–47; Kerry Segrave, *Payola in the Music Industry: A History* (Jefferson, NC, 1994); Joeri Mol and Nachoem Wijnberg, "Competition, Selection, and Rock and Roll: The Economics of Payola and Authenticity," *Journal of Economic Issues* 41 (2007): 709–11.

49. On capture, see William Novak, "A Revisionist History of Regulatory Capture," in Daniel Carpenter and David A. Moss, *Preventing Regulatory Capture: Special Interest Influence and How to Limit It* (New York, 2013), 25–49.

50. Association of BBBs, *A Guide for Retail Advertising and Selling* (New York, 1956); Willard Linn Thompson, "Self-Regulation in Advertising," Ph. D. diss. (University of Illinois, 1958), 179–80, 189–220.

51. C. W. Dessart to C. B. Smith, Texas, May 16, 1957, in Box 10, Folder 14, BBBMC.

52. "President Truman's Message," *BS*, Jan. 6, 1949, 6; Alonzo Hamby, "The Vital Center, the Fair Deal, and the Quest for a Liberal Political Economy," *AHR* 77 (1972): 653–78.

53. "Text of Eisenhower's Congress Message," *LAT*, Feb. 3, 1953, 6.

54. "Ike Calls TV Rigging 'Terrible,'" *WP*, Oct. 23, 1959, A3; "The President's News Conference at Augusta, Georgia, Oct. 22, 1959," *The American Presidency Project*, available at http://www.presidency.ucsb.edu/ws/?pid=11564, accessed Feb. 5, 2016.

55. "Hi Sucker!" *Newsweek* 27 (Jan. 21, 1946): 73–74; Frank Brock and Henry Lee, "Don't Fall for It!" *BS*, Oct. 15, 1950, WM10; Fletcher Platt, "The Grift Goes Legit," *Harper's Magazine* 210 (June 1955): 65; William Slocum, "Sucker Traps," *Collier's* 125 (Jan. 28, 1950): 36–37; Harry Wilson, "The Suckers Came Running!" *SEP* (Feb. 10, 1951): 104, 107; Al Thrasher, "Saga of 10 Percenters Winds to Sorry Finale," *LAT*, Apr. 24, 1961, 2, 24.

56. Carlton Brown, "Confidence Games," *Life*, Aug. 12, 1946, 45; Joseph Marshall, "Look before You Leap," *Norfolk Journal and Guide*, July 28, 1956, 11.

57. Gibney, *The Operators*, 8–9; Walter Wagner, *The Golden Fleecers* (Garden City, NY, 1966), 7; F. J. Schlink to Percival Wilde, Aug. 30, 1948, Box 124, File 19; "Memorandum Re: Land Sale Scheme," Sept. 13, 1965, Box 164, File 27, both in Consumers Research Papers.

58. "Don't Fall for These Frauds and Gyps," *Changing Times* 14 (July 1960): 7–14; William Lydgate, "Don't Be Too Sure," *Redbook* (Oct. 1947): 34–35, 83–86; Laurence Van Ness, "What to Do if You're Cheated," *BS*, May 10, 1959, WM17.

59. Argus Advisory Service, *Monthly Newsletter of Current Frauds and Swindles* 1 (Jan. 1946): 1.

60. Burton Crane, "Stock Sale 'Boiler Rooms' Thrive," *NYT*, Oct. 31, 1954, F1.

61. Donald Rothschild and Bruce Throne, "Criminal Consumer Fraud: A Victim-Oriented Analysis," *MLR* 74 (1976): 769.

62. Stuart Macaulay, "Lawyers and Consumer Protection Laws," *Law & Society Review* 14 (1979): 121–25; "Consumer Protection under the Iowa Consumer Fraud Statute," *Iowa Law Review* 54 (1968): 342–43; Bronson Lafollette, "Consumer Fraud and Consumer Protection in Wisconsin," in FTC, *National Consumer Protection Hearings* (Washington, D.C., 1969), 246; Ralph Mooney, "Attorney General as Counsel for the Consumer: The Oregon Experience," *Oregon Law Review* 54 (1975): 126.

63. "Bogus Stocks from Canada," *Changing Times* (July 2, 1949): 13–14; D. C. L., "The Promotion and Sale of Foreign Securities by Foreign Broker-Dealers: The 'Canadian Situation,'" *Virginia Law Review* (1952): 208–10; Christopher Armstrong, "Canadian Promoters and American Markets: Regulating the Irregular, 1945–55," *Business History* 34 (1992): 96–101.

64. Lloyd Wendt, "Not All Fur Trappers Are up North," *CT*, Oct. 27, 1940, I9; John Kobler, "Terrible Williamsons," *SEP* 229 (Oct. 27, 1956): 26–27, 55–62; H. J. Maidenberg, "Roof-Repair Fraud," *NYT*, Apr. 6, 1967, 53; Max Skidmore, "The Folk Culture of 'The Travelers': Clans of Con Artists," *Journal of American Culture* 20 (Fall 1997): 73–80.

65. "The Regulation of Advertising," *CLR* 56 (1956): 1040–41; "Translating Sympathy for Deceived Consumers into Effective Programs for Protection," *UPLR* 114 (1966): 424–26; Robert Rabin, "Agency Criminal Referrals in the Federal System: An Empirical Study of Prosecutorial Discretion," *Stanford Law Review* 24 (1972): 1047–50; Rothschild

and Throne, "Criminal Consumer Fraud," 679–81; David Silver, Oral History Interview with Irving Pollack, Jan. 16, 2002, SEC Historical Society, 9–10, available at http://www.sechistorical.org/museum/oral-histories/o-r/, accessed June 24, 2014.

66. Gibney, *The Operators*, 19–21, 52–53; Theodore Hendricks, "Fraud Jury Dismissed in Mistrial," *BS*, Mar. 25, 1961, 32; "Defense of the White Collar Accused: A Judge's View," *American Criminal Law Quarterly* 3 (Spring 1965): 124–28.

67. "State Control of Bait Advertising," *YLJ* 69 (1960): 839–40.

68. Lester Velie, "Fantastic Story of the Tucker Car," *Collier's* 123 (June 25, 1949): 13–15, 68–72; "Tucker, 7 Associates Indicted," *WSJ*, June 11, 1949, 8; William Clark, "Lawyer Calls Tucker Honest Man of Vision," *CT*, Jan. 20, 1950, A13; George Eckel, "Jury Is Locked up in Tucker Car Case," *NYT*, Jan. 22, 1950, 33; George Eckel, "Tucker and Aides Cleared of Fraud," *NYT*, Jan. 23, 1950, 1.

69. "Fraud Charge against Steel Man Dismissed," *CT*, Oct. 24, 1956, C4; "McGurren Freed," *BS*, Dec. 5, 1963, 54; Edmund Rooney, "Krebiozen Developer Is Acquitted," *WP*, Feb. 1, 1966, A3.

70. "Term Suspended in $169,000 Fraud," *BS*, Apr. 28, 1950, 36; "TV Repair Men Go Free," *NYT*, June 18, 1954, 18; "Garfield Gets Suspended Sentence, $50,000 Fine," *WSJ*, Dec. 7, 1964, 6; Wagner, *Golden Fleecers*, 8–10; Robert Ogren, "The Ineffectiveness of Criminal Sanctions in Fraud and Corruption Cases: Losing the Battle against White-Collar Crime," *American Criminal Law Review* 11 (1973): 961–69.

71. Philip Schrag, *Counsel for the Deceived: Case Studies in Consumer Fraud* (New York, 1972), 50–51; Michael Jensen, "Light Penalty for White-Collar Crime," *NYT*, Sept. 22, 1973, 37, 41; Les Gapay, "When the SEC Slaps Your Wrist," *WSJ*, Nov. 27, 1973, 24.

72. "Fraud Case Convictions Overturned," *WP*, Jan. 3, 1964, A10; Alan Dessoff, "S&L Case Convictions Overturned," *WP*, Sept. 15, 1964, A1.

73. Ferral Heady, "State Administrative Procedure Laws," *Public Administration Review* 12 (1952): 10–20; Bernard Schwartz, "The Model State Administrative Procedure Act: Analysis and Critique," *Rutgers Law Review* 7 (1953): 431–58; James Brazier, "An Anti-New Dealer Legacy: The Administrative Procedure Act," *Journal of Policy History* 8 (1996): 206–26; Joanna Grisinger, *The Unwieldy American State: Administrative Politics since the New Deal* (New York, 2012).

74. See postwar annual reports for these two agencies.

75. The case files of FTC lawyer Paris Cleveland Gardner, which range from 1941 through 1962, document this sluggish pace. Gardner Papers. See, for example, *In Re Clean-Rite Vacuum Stores*, Box 3, Packet 2.

76. F. J. Schlink to Harry Riehl, July 21, 1953, Box 34, File 9, Consumers Research Papers; "Howery Reports FTC Streamlined Procedure," *WSJ*, Aug. 19, 1954, 1; Julius Duscha, "New Chief Scores FTC Duplication," *WP*, Mar. 15, 1961, A4; "FTC Increases Base of Power," *KCS*, June 26, 1961, 12; Weston, "Deceptive Advertising," 561–63; Edward Cox, Robert Fellmouth, and John Schulz, *The "Nader Report" on the Federal Trade Commission* (New York, 1969), 71–86; *Report of the American Bar Foundation to Study the Federal Trade Commission* (Washington, DC, 1969), 15–31.

77. *In Re Holland Furnace Company*, 55 FTC Reports 55 (July 7, 1958); "Selling by Scare," *Consumer Reports* 30 (Oct. 1958): 509–10; Warren Magnuson and Jean Carper, *The Dark Side of the Marketplace: The Plight of the American Consumer* (New York, 1968), 21–22.

78. "Holland Does Hot Job," *Newsweek* 8 (Nov. 7, 1936): 36–37; "Attention Workers,"

Ogden Standard-Examiner, June 20, 1951, 17; "Holland Company Denies Unfair Sales Practices," *Benton Harbor News-Palladium*, July 19, 1954, 11; "Salesmen Wanted," *Kelispell* [MT] *Daily Inter Lake*, Apr. 20, 1956, 10; "FTC Orders End of 'Scare' Sales," *BS*, Aug. 7, 1958, 34; "Furnace Man Gets the Heat," *CT*, Jan. 16, 1962, 5; John O'Brien, "Holland Furnace Firm and 3 Ex-Aides Guilty," *CT*, Jan. 28, 1965, A11; "Plan to Appeal Sentence, Fines," *Holland Evening Sentinel*, Jan. 28, 1965, 1; Joseph Tydings, "Fair Play for Consumers," *Trial* 6 (Feb./March 1970): 37.

79. SEC, *First Annual Report* (Washington, DC, 1935), 35; SEC, *Sixteenth Annual Report* (Washington, DC, 1950), 153; DOJ, *Summary of National Conference on Antitrust Problems and Consumer and Investor Protection* (Washington, DC, 1961), 65. The FTC only started a newsletter with summaries of deception cases in 1961; four years later, it also began regularly informing attorneys general about enforcement trends. "U.S. Plans Campaign on Consumer Frauds," *LAT*, June 15, 1965, 17.

80. McCraw, "With Consent of the Governed," 346–70; Joel Seligman, "Cautious Evolution or Perennial Irresolution: Stock Market Self-Regulation during the First Seventy Years of the Securities and Exchange Commission," *BL* 59 (2004): 1347–69.

81. Philip Loomis, "Enforcement Problems under the Federal Securities Laws," *BL* 14 (April 1959): 667.

82. Silver, Oral History Interview of Irving Pollack, 41–42.

83. Thompson, "Self-Regulation in Advertising"; Earl Kintner, "Some Encouraging Signs of Self-Regulation in Advertising," Speech to Advertising Club of St. Louis, July 26, 1960; "Raising the Level of Advertising in Minneapolis," Speech to Minneapolis Advertising Club; "1961: Armageddon for Advertising?" Speech to the Advertising Federation of America, May 30, 1961, all in Earl W. Kintner Collection, American Heritage Center, University of Wyoming.

84. "Critical Consumers," *WSJ*, Nov. 8, 1960, 1; *Facts You Should Know*; Edward Gallagher, "Old Paths and New Roads for the Better Business Bureaus," Confidential Address, ABBB Annual Conference, June 1959, 3, Box 4, Bell Papers; David Boldt, "It's No Bargain, Lady," *WSJ*, April 7, 1965, 1; Testimony of Richard Maxwell, Nov. 25, 1968, FTC, *National Consumer Protection Hearings* (Washington, DC, 1969), 192–93.

85. Neil J. Ross to St. Louis, Kansas City, and Springfield BBBs, June 23, 1933, Bell Papers; Victor Nyborg, "Practices in the Home Improvement Field," Statement to U.S. Sen. Committee on Banking and Currency, July 15, 1954, Box 107, Folder 1, BBBMC. See also Edward Gallagher, "Fifty Years of Consumer Protection by BBBs: For Those Who Don't Know So That Others May Not Forget" (unpublished manuscript, 1971), 63–69; Box 9, Bell Papers."

86. W. Dan Bell to Victor Nyborg, Feb. 1, 1960, Box 5, Folder 24, BBBMC.

87. The Federal Trade Commission and the Reform of the Administrative Process," *CLR* 62 (1962): 680–85; FTC, *Manual for Attorneys*, 3rd ed. (Washington, DC, 1966), 18; *Report of the American Bar Association*, 26–40; Cox et al., *The "Nader Report,"* 134–58; Jack Anderson, "U.S. Protective Agencies Are Remiss," *WP*, Nov. 28, 1969, C27.

88. Wayne Green, "The Securities Cops," *WSJ*, Feb. 25, 1969, 1; Kenneth Bacon and Les Gapay, "SEC's Top Cops," *WSJ*, July 9, 1973, 1; Irving Pollack, Oral History Interview with Stanley Sporkin, Sept. 23, 2003, SEC Historical Society, available at: http://www.sechistorical.org/museum/oral-histories/s-t/, accessed June 24, 2014; Hillel Black, *The Watchdogs of Wall Street* (New York, 1962); Susan P. Shapiro, *Wayward Capitalists: Targets of the Securities and Exchange Commission* (New Haven, 1987), 160–91.

89. Luther Huston, "Brownell Sets up Office," *NYT*, Oct. 7, 1954, 1; "He's Uncle Sam's Top Fraud Fighter," *Carroll Daily Times Herald*, Jan. 13, 1956, 3; *National Conference on Antitrust Problems*, 68–71; Wallace Turner, "135 Land Frauds Studied by U.S.," *NYT*, Mar. 30, 1963, 9; "Nathaniel Kossack, " 'Scam': The Planned Bankruptcy Racket," *New York Certified Public Accountant* 35 (1965): 417; Nathaniel Kossack and Sheldon Davidson, "Bankruptcy Frauds, Alliance for Enforcement," *Journal of the National Conference of Referees in Bankruptcy* 40 (Jan. 1966): 12–18; "Nathaniel E 'Tully' Kossack," *WP*, Dec. 2, 1992, C5.

90. "Upsurge in Chain Letters," *Oshkosh Daily Northwestern*, Mar. 14, 1946, 21; "McDonald to Speak," *Brooklyn Daily Eagle*, Aug. 27, 1951, 2; "Variety of Mail Fraud Schemes," *Reading Eagle*, Sept. 23, 1962, 54; William MacDougall, "Mail Swindlers Face Scientific Crackdown," *LAT*, Oct. 31, 1963, 15; William Borders, "Drive against Consumer Frauds," *NYT*, Aug. 20, 1964, 46; "U. S. Using a Computer to Fight Filth and Fraud," *CT*, Sept. 19, 1965, A6.

91. Harry Ferguson, "How Postal Inspectors Protect You from Gyps," *Norfolk New Journal and Guide*, Sept. 21, 1963, 7; Thomas Foley, "Postal: Little Known, Most Effective," *LAT*, Sept. 17, 1972, E1.

92. On Bell: see his scrapbooks and retirement and death notices, Box 3, Bell Papers. On Willson: "Willson Retires As NBBB President," *NBBB Bulletin* (June 1968). On Nyborg: "Foes of Rackets Pick Officers," *LAT*, June 27, 1941, 13; "Top Officers Are Reelected to Better Business Bureaus," *NYT*, May 22, 1965, 41. For bios of hundreds of Bureau officials, see Dan Bell's unpublished Biographical Notes, Box 5, Bell Papers.

93. Kenneth Barnard to Clyde Kemery, March 23, 1960, Box 6, Folder 1, BBBMC.

94. Howard Westwood and Edward Howard, "Self-Government in the Securities Business," *Law and Contemporary Problems* 17 (1952): 533–38; Frank Cormier, *Wall Street's Shady Side* (Washington, DC, 1962), 72–75; Ezra Levin and William Evan, "Professionalism and the Stock Broker," *BL* 21 (Jan. 1966): 349–53; William Conway, "Quack Is a Rare Bird," *WP*, May 4, 1947, B2; J. W. Davis, "Medical Quackery," *San Antonio Express and News*, Oct. 1, 1961, 81.

95. Paul Windels, "Our Securities Markets: Some S.E.C. Problems and Techniques," *New York Law Forum* 8 (1962): 169.

96. "Recommendations for the Advertising and Sale of Plastic Slip Covers," Sept. 3, 1965, Box 4, Folder 10, BBBMC. For other examples, see: "Wax Trade to Confer," *NYT*, Aug. 17, 1948, 28; FTC, *Annual Report* (Washington, DC, 1955), 62–67; "FTC Defines Functions of Industry Advisory Groups," *WSJ*, Sept. 30, 1955, 18; "Industry Conference," *Bridgeport Post*, Sept. 23, 1963, 16; "Hearing Aid Industry Gets Ethics Code," *Syracuse Post-Standard*, Aug. 2, 1965, 13.

97. "Report to Dealers," *Facts*, March 18, 1957, Box 8, Folder 1, BBBMC.

98. Earl Kintner: "Self-Discipline or Stricter Government Control," Speech to the Advertising Federation of America, Feb. 5, 1960, 39; "The Unsoiled Sell," Speech to Los Angeles BBB, Apr. 29, 1960, 5; "Responsibilities of Broadcasters and Their Counsel," Speech to Federal Communications Bar Association," June 9, 1960, 18; "Some Encouraging Signs," 11; all in Kintner Collection.

99. Blake Clark, "Be Sure You Know What's In Your Health and Accident Policy," *Reader's Digest* 65 (July 1954): 1115–19; Rodney Crowther, "FTC Charges 17 Companies," *BS*, Oct. 24, 1954, 17; Charles McCarter, "Recent Misleading and Deceptive Mail-Order Accident and Health Insurance Policies and Advertising," *Insurance Law Journal*

(April 1956): 247–52, 260–61; Christy Chapin, "Ensuring America's Health: Publicly Constructing the Private Health Industry," Ph. D. diss. (University of Virginia, 2011), 64–151.

100. "FTC Plans Insurance Rules Parley," *WP*, Dec. 16, 1955, 2; Charles Moore, "Insurance: Federal Regulation," *MLR* 57 (1958): 289–91; McCarter, "Recent Misleading and Deceptive Mail-Order," 262, 267–69; Jon Hanson and Thomas Obenberger, "Mail Order Insurers: A Case Study in the Ability of the States to Regulate the Insurance Business," *Marquette Law Review* 50 (1966): 193–215; Chapin, "Ensuring America's Health," 207–15. For similar dynamics within the tire industry and among hearing-aid dealers, see Earl Kintner, "Self-Discipline or Stricter Government Control," 30–33; "Buyers Guide to Tires," *Changing Times* 15 (July 1961): 25–28; "Developments in the Law: Deceptive Advertising," 1131.

101. "TV Sales Pitch Lands Los Angeles Used Car Dealer and Aide in Jail," *WSJ*, May 25, 1955, 3; Howard Berquist to C. W. Dessart, May 9, 1957, and Kenneth Barnard to Robert Bauer, Oct. 18, 1957, Box 10, Folder 14; Memo from Ken Barnard to BBB Managers, April 25, 1962, Box 7, Folder 3; BBBMC; Jim Foree, "Buyers Beware," *CD*, June 20, 1957, 1; James Lewis, "Dropping Car 'Pack' May Aid Sales Ethics," *WP*, March 14, 1958.

102. "Six Insurance Companies Accused of Overcharging," *WSJ*, March 19, 1957, 2; Warren Unna, "Auto Gouging Charged at Senate Quiz," *WP*, March 20, 1957, A2; "Insurance Overcharges Aired on Hill," *WP*, Aug. 10, 1958, C11; "Car Owners Get Refunds on Insurance," *CD*, Oct. 14, 1959, 4.

103. See enforcement statistics compiled in SEC and POD annual reports; Shapiro, *Wayward Capitalists*, 147–62.

104. John N. Makris, *Silent Investigators: The Great Untold Story of the United States Postal Inspection Service* (New York, 1959), 43, 278; Raymond Daniel, "Inspector Notes Mail Fraud Rise," *NYT*, Aug. 27, 1964, 14; E. J. Kahn, Jr., *Fraud: The United States Postal Inspection Service and Some of the Fools and Knaves It Has Known* (New York, 1973), 1–10.

105. "Boiler Room Tactics on Wane," *WP*, Jan. 5, 1961, D6; SEC, *Twenty-Seventh Annual Report* (Washington, DC, 1961), 164–72, 259; Windels, "Our Securities Markets," 179–86; Louis Lefkowitz, "New York: Criminal Infiltration of the Securities Industry," *AAPS* 347 (May 1963): 54–56; SEC, *Thirty-First Annual Report* (Washington, DC, 1965), 131–35; "U. S. Rackets Convictions Rise to 546," *BS*, Jan. 10, 1965, 3.

106. On these promoters and the period's crackdown on securities fraud, see Black, *Watchdogs of Wall Street*.

107. "Advance-Fee Game," *Time* 72 (July 28, 1958): 64; "Officials Eye Advance Fee Racketeering," *Charleston Gazette-Mail*, July 19, 1959, 44; "Mail Fraud," *Changing Times* 13 (July 1959): 41–42; "Government Cracks down on Real Estate Frauds," *WP*, Nov. 10, 1962, D15; Loreene Beasley, "Mail Order Swindles Work 2 Ways," *San Mateo Times*, Jan. 26, 1965, 4.

108. James Clayton, "Three Agencies Unite to Thwart Across-Border Mail Order Frauds," *WP*, Oct. 23, 1961, A2; "U.S. Aims at Radio Ad-Mail Gyps," *Tucson Daily Citizen*, Nov. 20, 1961, 9.

109. Murray Bloom, "Don't Be a Sucker with Your Savings!" *Reader's Digest* 80 (May 1962): 75–78; Gene Blake, "Land Swindlers," *LAT*, Oct. 2, 1962, A2; "Savings, Loan Scandals," *BS*, Dec. 23, 1962, BF16; Trevor Armbrister, "Land Frauds," *SEP* 236 (Apr. 27, 1963): 17–23; "Cheating Creditors," *WSJ*, May 20, 1963, 1; "Bankruptcy Caper," *News-*

week 61 (June 10, 1963): 31; "When There's Gold in Bankruptcy," *Business Week* (May 23, 1964): 52–56.

110. Stipulation with Logan Appliance & Furniture Mart, April 11, 1952, Box 5, Folder 11, BBBMC.

111. Carl Dalke, "How to Improve the Value of Automobile Advertising," n.d., Box 9, Folder 2, BBBMC; Thompson, "Self-Regulation in Advertising," 306–09.

112. NBBB, *Advertising Topics*, April 1963.

113. See, for example, the BBB's moves against David Ratke, whose serial mail-order ventures sold fake radios, low-grade cosmetics, worthless battery additives, and an invasive weed tree that Ratke falsely described as a scarce and valuable plant: "Seven Firms Charged with False Claims for Battery Additive," *York Gazette and Daily*, Dec. 8, 1958, 32; Jack Roth, "Ad Fraud Charged to Promoter Who Sold Items to Last 'Forever,'" *NYT*, Aug. 19, 1959, 1; "Don't Fall for These Frauds and Gyps," 14 *Changing Times* (July 1960): 8; "3 Convicted of $1.3 Million Fraud," *Des Moines Register*, Apr. 22, 1970, 16; "Investigate before You Invest," *Atchison Daily Globe*, Oct. 25, 1970, 16.

114. Peter Bart, "Sturdy Watchdog Fifty Years Old," *NYT*, Jan. 28, 1962, 118; "History of Legal Actions against BBBs," May 1, 1963, Memo, Box 8, Bell Papers; "Responses to Survey on Lawsuits," Box 8, Bell Papers.

115. Los Angeles BBB, "Truth in Advertising," 1947, Box 10, Folder 14; Victor Nyborg to Kenneth Barnard, Jan. 9, 1961; Draft Report, "Advertising Improvement Committee," July 25, 1961, Box 6, Folder 6, BBBMC.

116. Fritzel Case, Box 89, Folders 13–14, BBBMC.

117. Chicago BBB, *The Report* (February 1964): 5; News Clippings on Fritzel Case, Jan. 1964; Box 89, Folder 14.

118. For illustrative cases, see files on: Hub Vacuum Stores (Box 112, Folders 1–2) and Keystone Chevrolet (Box 122, Folder 21), BBBMC.

119. Dalke, "How to Improve the Value"; "Report to Dealers"; "Critical Consumers." On the advance advice emanating from the SEC, see McCraw, *Prophets of Regulation*, 214–15.

120. Seymour Ginsburg to Ben Ugelow, Box 41, Folder 12, BBBMC. See also negotiations between several BBBs and Ritholz optical businesses, Box 178, Folder 3; and *In Re Penn Poultry Service*, Box 6, Packet 5, Gardner Papers.

121. Very few FTC cases handled by Paris Gardner led to formal hearings. He also closed dozens of files because of insufficient evidence, lack of complaints from competitors, good reputations by firms, or lack of "public interest."

122. "Trade Rules and Trade Conferences," 915–16; "Federal Trade Commission and the Reform of the Administrative Process," 686–700; FTC, *Advisory Opinion Digests, June 1, 1962 to December 31, 1968* (Washington, DC, 1969).

123. Kenneth Culp Davis, "Administrative Powers of Supervising, Prosecuting, Advising, and Declaring, and Informally Adjudicating," *HLR* 63 (1949): 206–12, 225–27; "Regulation of Advertising," 1043; "Administrative Declaratory Orders," *Stanford Law Review* 13 (1961): 310–11; "Translating Sympathy for Deceived Consumers," 440–43; "Developments in the Law: Deceptive Advertising," 1072.

124. Earl Kintner, Speech at the FTC Conference on Public Deception, Dec. 21, 1959, 2, in Box 1, Kintner Collection; Paul Rand Dixon, Speech to the International Radio and Television Society, Mar. 3, 1965, quoted in Jerrold Van Cise, "Regulation—By Business or Government?" *Antitrust Bulletin* 12 (1967): 8

CHAPTER TEN: CONSUMERISM AND THE REORIENTATION OF ANTIFRAUD POLICY

1. David M. Potter, *People of Plenty: Economic Abundance and the National Character* (Chicago, 1958), 172–88; Lawrence R. Samuel, *Brought to You By: Postwar Television Advertising and the American Dream* (Austin, 2002); Lizabeth Cohen, *A Consumer's Republic: The Politics of Mass Consumption in Postwar America* (New York, 2003); Meg Jacobs, *Pocketbook Politics: Economic Citizenship in Twentieth-Century America* (Princeton, 2006); Janice M. Traflet, *A Nation of Small Shareholders: Marketing Wall Street after World War II* (Baltimore, 2013).

2. Stewart Ewen, *PR! A Social History of Spin* (New York, 1996), 346–98; William Bird, *"Better Living": Advertising, Media, and the New Vocabulary of Business Leadership, 1935–1955* (Evanston, 1999); Kim Phillips-Fein, *Invisible Hands: The Businessmen's Crusade against the New Deal* (New York, 2009).

3. Ralph Blumenthal, "Consumer Frauds Thrive in Ghettos," *NYT*, Aug. 20, 1966, 1; Warren Magnuson, "The Ghetto Gets Gypped," *Ebony* 23 (Sept. 1968): 112–20; Thomas Lippman, "Fraud War Pledged by Flannery," *WP*, June 6, 1969, A1; "How to Squelch Fraud Schemes," *Better Homes & Gardens* 48 (1970): 30; "Warning on 11 Common Frauds & Gyps," *Changing Times* 26 (Nov. 1972): 17–18; Sidney Margolius, *The Innocent Consumer vs. the Exploiters* (New York, 1967); James Bishop Jr. and Henry W. Hubbard, *Let the Seller Beware* (Washington, DC, 1968); Amram M. Ducovny, *The Billion $ Swindle: Frauds against the Elderly* (New York, 1969); Robert S. Rosefsky, *Frauds, Swindles, and Rackets: A Red Alert for Today's Consumers* (Chicago, 1973).

4. "Home Improvement Frauds," Feb. 20, 1968, 1; "Signing of Blank Contracts Can Get Car Buyers in a Peck of Trouble," June 8, 1968, 1; "Medical Swindlers Often Demand Your Money," July 9, 1968, 7; "Insurance Frauds," Oct. 21, 1968, 3; "Insurance Industry Accused of Overcharging," Jan. 16, 1969, 1; "On Mr. Help," Feb. 2, 1971, 2.

5. "TV5 to Air Special Series on 'Rip-Offs,'" *Atlanta Daily World*, Jan. 16, 1977, 10; "The Guide," *WP*, Nov. 21, 1971, 19.

6. "State Control of Bait Advertising," *YLJ* 69 (1960): 830–46; "Translating Sympathy for Deceived Consumers into Effective Programs for Protection," *UPLR* 114 (1966): 395–450; "Developments in the Law: Deceptive Advertising," *HLR* 80 (1967): 1005–63. "Consumer Legislation and the Poor," *YLJ* 76 (1967): 745–92; "Extrajudicial Consumer Pressure: An Effective Impediment to Unethical Business Practices," *DLJ* (1969): 1101–57; "A Case Study of the Impact of Consumer Legislation: The Elimination of Negotiability and the Cooling Off Period," *YLJ* 78 (1969): 618–61; "'Corrective Advertising' Orders of the Federal Trade Commission," *HLR* 85 (1971): 477–506; "Direct Loan Financing of Consumer Purchases," *HLR* 85 (1972): 1409–38.

7. David Caplovitz, *The Poor Pay More: Consumer Practices of Low-Income Families* (New York, 1963), 137–54; *Report of the National Advisory Commission on Civil Disorders* (Washington, DC, 1968), 274–77; Louis Hyman, *Debtor Nation: The History of America in Red Ink* (Princeton, 2012), 173–84.

8. "The New Look in 'Consumer Protection,'" *Changing Times* 20 (Nov. 1966): 13; "West Phila. to Hash out Consumer Fraud," *PT*, Jan. 11, 1969, 32; Morton Mintz, "Gulled Consumer Has Disparate Champions," *WP*, June 8, 1969, B5; Angela Parker, "Black Community Has Its Own Ralph Nader," *CT*, May 9, 1971, A5; Robert McClory, "Grass Roots Consumerism," *CD*, May 20, 1972, 6; "Consumer Action Groups Make Your

Voice Heard," *Oakland Post*, Dec. 27, 1972, 8; "CEPA Has Long Been Fighting Battles for Local Consumers," *PT*, Dec. 23, 1975, 4.

9. "Lefkowitz to Recommend Bill to Curb Fraud," *NYT*, Dec. 17, 1959, 75; "Attorney Gnl Probes Food Freezer Fraud," *NYAN*, Nov. 19, 1966, 28; "Lefkowitz Seeking New Credit Laws," *NYT*, July 25, 1969, 26; Louis Lefkowitz, "Protecting the Consumer," *NYT*, Sept. 15, 1971, 46.

10. "Lefkowitz Asks Fight on Frauds," *NYT*, July 6, 1960, 21; George Brown, "Fraud and Bogus Businesses," *New Pittsburgh Courier*, Oct. 6, 1962, 1; "Connecticut Sets Sweeping Shifts," *NYT*, May 10, 1959, 60; Leonard Ingalls, "Governor Points to Consumer Aid," *NYT*, Sept. 30, 1962, 61; Gene Oishi, "Governor Urges Probe for Fraud," *BS*, Oct. 8, 1967, 26; "Stronger Laws Sought," *Atlanta Daily World*, Jan. 7, 1973, 4; Jerry Gillam, "Reagan Calls for Seven Point Consumer Protection Program," *LAT*, Mar. 6, 1970, E11.

11. "Clark Spearheads Actions against Frauds," *CD*, Dec. 13, 1966, 23; Oswald Johnson, "Consumer Office Opens," *BS*, June 12, 1967, C8; Robert Morgan, "People's Advocate in the Marketplace—The Role of the North Carolina Attorney General in the Field of Consumer Protection," *Wake Forest Intramural Law Review* 6 (1969): 1–20; Sheila Wolf, "State Is Leader in Consumer Fraud Fight," *CT*, July 29, 1970, 8; Christopher Bayley, "Consumer Protection," *Washington State Bar News* 24 (May 1970): 7–8, 21–22; Jeffrey Tannenbaum, "New Muscle," *WSJ*, Jan. 7, 1972, 1; James Bassett, "State's Attorney General Post Packs a Wallop," *LAT*, Jan. 30, 1972, 1; Press Release, Office of Slade Gorton, Feb. 17, 1972, in File 8, Box 162, Consumers Research Papers.

12. President John F. Kennedy, "Special Message to Congress on Protecting the Consumer Interest," March 15, 1962, The American Presidency Project, http://www.presidency.ucsb.edu/ws/?pid=9108, accessed April 25, 2014.

13. President Lyndon B. Johnson, "Special Message to the Congress on Consumer Interests," March 21, 1966, The American Presidency Project, http://www.presidency.ucsb.edu/ws/?pid=27505, accessed April 25, 2014.

14. President Richard M. Nixon, "Special Message to the Congress on Consumer Protection," Oct. 30, 1969, The American Presidency Project, http://www.presidency.ucsb.edu/ws/?pid=2299, accessed July 8, 2014.

15. Esther Peterson, "Representing the Consumer Interest in the Federal Government," *MLR* 64 (1966): 1323–28.

16. "Betty Furness Urges Action," *NYT*, May. 28, 1969, 41; Joseph Slevin, "Important Consumer Aids," *WP*, Oct. 29, 1968, D8.

17. John Morris, "Justice Department Establishes a Section on Consumer Affairs," *NYT*, Dec. 16, 1970, 30; "Mrs. Knauer Likens Fraud to a Cancer," *NYT*, Dec. 17, 1969, 42; Robert Gray, "Virginia Knauer: What She Tells the President about Consumers," *Nation's Business* 58 (July 1970): 34–38; Alexander Auerbach, "Mrs. Knauer," *LAT*, July 30, 1970, B14.

18. Political science research on agenda-setting offers some important caveats here. There has been a half-life to public interest in issues identified by US presidents, measured in months rather than years. But sustained efforts by presidents that reach across more than one administration and across the partisan divide have broad impacts. John W. Kingdon, *Agendas, Alternatives, and Public Policies* (Boston, 1984); Jeffrey Cohen, "Presidential Rhetoric and the Public Agenda," *American Journal of Political Science* 39 (1995): 87–107; George Edwards III and B. Dan Wood, "Who Influences Whom: The

President, Congress, and the Media," *American Political Science Review* 93 (1999): 327–44; Matthew Eshbaugh-Soha, *The President's Speeches: Beyond Going Public* (Boulder, 2005).

19. Warren G. Magnuson and Jean Carper, *The Dark Side of the Marketplace: The Plight of the American Consumer* (Englewood, NJ, 1968), xv.

20. Edward Brown Williams, "The Proposed Regulatory Restrictions on Packaging and Labeling," *BL* 21 (Nov. 1965): 99–106; Robert Albright, "Fair Label Bill Passed by Senate," *WP*, June 10, 1966, A1; Marilyn Hart, "Short Weight," *CT*, May 18, 1969, SCL11; "Lending Bill Stalemate Criticized," *BS*, March 7, 1965, 3; Kenneth McLean, "The Federal Consumer Credit Protection Act," *BL* 24 (Nov. 1968): 199–207; David Fouquet, "Mail Order Land Fraud Probed," *WP*, May 19, 1964, A22; Dorothy Cohen, "New Consumer Product Warranty Law," *Marketing News* 8 (Mar. 28, 1975): 12; Michael R. Lemov, *People's Warrior: John Moss and the Fight for Freedom of Information and Consumer Rights* (Lanham, MD, 2011).

21. U.S. Sen., *Consumer Protection, Parts I and II*, Hearings before the Consumer Subcommittee of the Commerce Committee, 91st Cong., Dec. 16 and 17, 1969, Feb. 3 and 5, March 17–19, April 9, 1970 (Washington, DC, 1970); Erma Angevine, "The Consumer Federation of America," *Journal of Consumer Affairs* 3 (1969): 152–55; Robert Herrmann, "Consumerism: Its Goals, Organizations, and Future," *JM* 34 (1970): 58–60; Clinton Warne, "The Consumer Movement and the Labor Movement," *Journal of Economic Issues* 7 (1973): 307–16. On parallel policy ferment in the states, see Young Lawyers Section, Seattle–King County Bar Association, "Memorandum to the Washington State Legislature," January 12, 1970, File 6, Box 190, Consumers Research; Susan Silbey, "Consumer Justice: The Massachusetts Attorney General's Office of Consumer Protection, 1970–1974," Ph.D. diss. (University of Chicago, 1978), 110–201; Mark Budnitz, "The National Consumer Law Center from Its Birth to 2013," unpublished paper available at: http://papers.ssrn.com/sol3/papers.cfm?abstract_id=2700720, accessed Feb. 10, 2016.

22. Edward Cox, Robert Fellmouth, and John Schulz, *The "Nader Report" on the Federal Trade Commission* (New York, 1969); Justin Martin, *Nader: Crusader, Spoiler, Icon* (Cambridge, MA, 2002); Eduardo Canedo, "The Rise of the Deregulation Movement in Modern America, 1957–1980," Ph. D. diss. (Columbia University, 2008); Benjamin Waterhouse, *Lobbying America: The Politics of Business from Nixon to NAFTA* (Princeton, 2014), 141–73.

23. James Harvey Young, *The Medical Messiahs: A Social History of Health Quackery in the Twentieth Century* (Princeton, 1967), 390–422; "Developments in the Law: Deceptive Advertising," 1101–16; David Cantor, "Cancer, Quackery and the Vernacular Meanings of Hope in 1950s America," *Journal of the History of Medicine and Allied Sciences* 61 (2006): 324–36.

24. "Quackery in California," *Stanford Law Review* 11 (1959): 265–96; Ruth Roemer, "Legal Systems Regulating Health Personnel: A Comparative Analysis," *Milbank Memorial Fund Quarterly* 46 (1968): 431–71; Eric Boyle, *Quack Medicine: A History of Combating Health Fraud in Twentieth-Century America* (Santa Barbara, 2013), 92–150.

25. "Truth in Lending," *U.S. News and World Report* (May 27, 1968): 92–93; "Truth in Lending Act," *Federal Reserve Bulletin* 54 (June 1968): 497–504; "The New Key to Credit Shopping," *Consumer Reports* (July 1969): 67; "Truth-in-Packing under the Fair Packaging and Labeling Act: An Untapped Source of Consumer Protection," *Columbia*

Journal of Law and Social Problems 6 (May 1970): 280; Steven Dorsey, "Regulation of Interstate Land Sales," *Stanford Law Review* 25 (1973): 605–21.

26. Margaret Dana, "Waiting Period Can Deflate High-Pressure Salesmen," *LAT*, Sept. 24, 1967, D12; "Case Study of the Impact of Consumer Legislation"; Michael Knight, "Aid to Consumers Growing in Nation," *NYT*, Aug. 9, 1970, 1; NAAG, *State Programs for Consumer Protection* (Washington, DC, 1973), 51–53; Thomas Hogarty, "Survey of Non-Federal Consumer Protection Groups," *Journal of Consumer Affairs* 9 (1975): 107–13.

27. Michael Mintrom and Phillipa Norman, "Policy Entrepreneurship and Policy Change," *Policy Studies Journal* 37 (2009): 649–67.

28. Frank Cormier, *Wall Street's Shady Side* (Washington, DC, 1962), 14–38.

29. Milton Cohen, "Reflections on the Special Study of the Securities Markets," Speech to the New York Practicing Law Institute, May 10, 1963, available at: http://www.sec.gov/news/speech/1963/051063cohen.pdf, accessed July 13, 2014.

30. SEC, *Special Study of Securities Markets*, Parts 1–6, House Document 95, 88th Cong., 1st Session (Washington, DC, 1963); "SEC Warns Securities Industry to Toughen Its Self-Regulation," *WSJ*, Nov. 29, 1962, 2; "Policing the Stock Markets," *WP*, April 6, 1963, A10; Robert Nichols, "SEC Calls for Legislation to Tighten Rein on O-T-C," *LAT*, June 5, 1963, B9.

31. Arden Cooper, "New Securities Bill Is Only Start for SEC," *LAT*, Aug. 23, 1964, L1; "House Group O.K.s Stock Fraud Curb," *BS*, May 8, 1964, 30; Richard Phillips and Morgan Shipman, "An Analysis of the Securities Acts Amendments of 1964," *DLJ* 13 (1964): 1139–70; SEC, *Annual Report* (Washington, DC, 1965), 1–19; Seligman, *Transformation of Wall Street*, 280–361.

32. "Ancillary Relief in SEC Injunction Suits for Violation of Rule 10b-5," *HLR* 79 (1966): 656–71; "SEC Disciplinary Rules and the Federal Securities Laws: The Regulation, Role, and Responsibilities of the Attorney," *DLJ* (1972): 969–1022; David S. Ruder, "Multiple Defendants in Securities Law Fraud Cases: Aiding and Abetting, Conspiracy, *Pari Delicto*, Indemnification, and Contribution," *UPLR* 120 (1972): 597–600; J. Vernon Patrick, Jr., "The Securities Class Action for Damages Comes of Age," *BL* 29 (March 1974): 159–66; David Silver, Oral History Interview with Irving Pollack, Jan. 16, 2002, SEC Historical Society, 22–25, 31–33, available at: http://www.sechistorical.org/museum/oral-histories/o-r/, accessed June 24, 2014.

33. Kenneth Durr, Oral History Interview with David Silver, March 22, 2006, 12, available at: http://www.sechistorical.org/museum/oral-histories/o-r/, accessed June 24, 2014. The broader collection of oral histories undertaken by the SEC Historical Society teems with references to this *esprit de corps*.

34. James E. Rice, ed., *The Franchising Phenomenon* (Ann Arbor, 1969); Thomas Dicke, *Franchising in America: The Development of a Business Method, 1840–1940* (Chapel Hill, 1994).

35. Kenneth Slocum, "Franchise Flourish," *WSJ*, Dec. 21, 1960, 1; Jordan Ray, "Current Franchising Problems: A Rollback of Caveat Emptor," *American Business Law Journal* 8 (1971): 231–46; FTC, *Franchise Business Risks* (Washington, DC, 1972); E. J. Kahn, *Fraud: The United States Postal Inspection Service and Some of the Fools and Knaves It Has Known* (New York, 1973), 260–70.

36. David Krischer, "Franchise Regulation: An Appraisal of Recent State Legislation," *Boston College Industrial and Commercial Law Review* 13 (1972): 539–52; Bernard

Goodwin, "Franchising Law Matures," *BL* 28 (April 1973): 703–20; David Black, "New Federal Trade Commission Franchise Disclosure Rule," *BL* 35 (Jan. 1980): 409–33.

37. Sylvia Porter, "Consumer Milestone," *Benton Harbor News Palladium*, Jan. 16, 1974, 41; Carol Shifrin Washington, "FTC Institutes New Enforcement Plans," *WP*, Jan. 7, 1976, C7; "Oliver Jones," "Holder in Due Course Doctrine Gone," *CT*, May 29, 1976, 17; Gerald Udell and Philip Fischer, "The FTC Improvement Act," *JM* 41 (April 1977): 81–86.

38. Dorothy Cohen, "Remedies for Consumer Protection: Prevention, Restitution, or Punishment," *JM* 39 (Oct. 1, 1975): 27; FTC, *Staff Report to the Federal Trade Commission on the Ad Substantiation Program* (Washington, DC, 1972); "Corrective Advertising—The New Response to Consumer Deception," *CLR* 72 (1972): 415–31; Robert Dyer and Philip Kuehl, "The 'Corrective Advertising' Remedy of the FTC: An Experimental Evaluation," *JM* 38 (Jan. 1974): 48–54.

39. Gene Bylinsky, "Consumer Cops," *WSJ*, Nov. 11, 1960, 1; William Lovett, "State Deceptive Trade Practice Legislation," *Tulane Law Review* 46 (1972): 724–60; NAAG, *State Programs*, 1–15; William Bruns, "The Role of State and Local Consumer Protection Agencies in Advertising Regulation," in Fredric Stuart, *Consumer Protection from Deceptive Advertising* (Hempstead, NY, 1974), 26–40.

40. Richard F. Dole, Jr., "Merchant and Consumer Protection: The Uniform Deceptive Trade Practices Act," *YLJ* 76 (1967): 485–506; William Lovett, "Private Actions for Deceptive Trade Practices," *Administrative Law Review* 23 (1971): 271–90; Richard F. Dole, Jr., Ray D. Henson, and George R. Richter, Jr., "The Uniform Consumer Sales Practices Act," *BL* 27 (Nov. 1971): 139–51.

41. Ann Blackman, "Agencies to Fight Market Fraud Multiply," *LAT*, Dec. 14, 1969, 8–9; Philip McCombs, "Suburban Offices Going to Bat for the Consumer," *WP*, March 2, 1972, G1–G3; Bruns, "Role of State and Local Consumer Protection Agencies," 41–50.

42. Denver Area BBB, "'After Hours' with Dan Bell," April 18, 1961; Dan Bell, "Memo to Better Business Managers," April 27, 1961, Box 9; Dan Bell, "Are You Listening? Do You Hear?," Address to AMR Conference, June 17, 1970, Box 3, Bell Papers.

43. Edward Gallagher, "Old Paths and New Roads for the Better Business Bureaus," Confidential Address, ABBB Annual Conference, June 1959, 3, Box 4, Bell Papers; Kenneth Barnard to George Dennison, Pittsburgh BBB, Jan. 6, 1960, Box 13, Folder 12; BBB of Oklahoma City Resolution, Feb. 25, 1960, ABBI Annual Meeting, Box 5, Folder 24; BBBMC; James Stephens to Dan Berry, Jr., Aug. 26, 1965, Box 9; Dan Berry, Jr., "There Are Termites in the Basement!" Memo to BBB Executives, Aug. 30, 1965, Box 4, Bell Papers; Knight, Gladieux, & Smith Confidential Report to Association of BBBs, Sept. 2, 1969, Box 1, Bell Papers. Council of BBBs, *Challenge to American Business* (New York, 1971).

44. "Campaign Is Urged Exposing 'Gyp' Ads," *NYT*, June 25, 1958, 47; "F.T.C. Will Carry 'Big Stick' on Ads," *NYT*, Dec. 22, 1959, 22.

45. Vernon Libby, "The Better Business Bureaus and the Consumer Movement," ABBB Annual Conference, May 17, 1865, Box 4, Bell Papers; Elisha Gray, Chairman of the Board, Whirlpool Corporation, "Building Better Bridges," Keynote Address, ABBBI Annual Conference, June 3, 1969, Box 2, Bell Papers; "Roper Poll," NBBB *Advertising Topics*, June 1967; H. Bruce Palmer, "A Fresh Approach to Consumerism," *Association Management* (Nov. 1971), reprinted by CBBB, Box 3, Bell Papers; Papers; Knight, Gladieux, & Smith Confidential Report, 24–27.

46. Kenneth Barnard to Joseph Meek, May 1, 1961; Kenneth Barnard to A. B. Johnston, Aug. 10, 1961, Box 15, Folder 2, BBBMC; Richard McClain to Lane Breidenstein, Nov. 16, 1969, Box 3, Bell Papers.

47. Eric Zanot, *The National Advertising Review Board, 1971–1976* (Minneapolis, 1979).

48. FTC Press Release, June 17, 1966; Victor Nyborg to W. Dan Bell, Sept. 2, 1966, Box 4, Bell Papers. On longstanding judicial suspicion of self-regulation that included compulsory sanctions, see Jerrold Van Cise, "Regulation—By Business or Government," *Harvard Business Review* (April 1966): 53–63.

49. "Consumerism," *Time*, Sept. 18, 1972, 87; Douglas Cray, "Consumer Protection," *NYT*, June 18, 1972, F17; Bettina Gregory, "Help for Long Island Consumer, *NYT*, July 7, 1974, 70; Narda Trout, "Fern Jellison," *LAT*, Sept. 23, 1974, B1; "Jane Byrne," *CT*, July 13, 1975, H12, H24, H26, H28.

50. "Consumer's Guardian," *NYT*, June 26, 1969, 32; W. Stewart Pinkerton, "Curbing Fraud," *WSJ*, Jan. 9, 1970, 1; Bess Myerson, "Caveat Vendor," *NYT*, Jan. 7, 1973, 49, 72; Matthew Seiden, "A Model for Others," *BS*, Feb. 13, 1973, C24.

51. Daniel Bessner, "The Night Watchman: Hans Speier and the Making of the National Security State," Ph.D. dissertation (Duke University, 2013); Elizabeth Brake, "Uncle Sam on the Family Farm: Farm Policy and the Business of Southern Agriculture, 1933–1965," Ph.D. diss. (Duke University, 2013); Matthew Murray, "Broadcast Content Regulation and Cultural Limits, 1920–1962," Ph.D. diss. (University of Wisconsin, 1997); Ronald Bottini, "The Self-Regulation of Motion Picture Content," Master's thesis (University of Missouri, 1966); William Goldsmith, "Public Goods, Private Watchmen: The Origins and Evolution of Federal Reliance on Private Accreditors in U.S. Education and Healthcare," unpublished paper in the possession of the author, 2014. See also Marc Allen Eisner, "Discovering Patterns in Regulatory History: Continuity, Change, and Regulatory Regimes," *Journal of Policy History* 6 (1994): 171–75; William Novak, "The Myth of the 'Weak' American State," *AHR* (2008): 113 (2008): 752–72; Edward J. Balleisen, "Rights of Way, Red Flags, and Safety Valves: Regulated Business Self-Regulation in America, 1850–1940," in Peter Collin, Gerd Bender, Stefan Ruppert, Margrit Seckelmann, and Michael Stolleis, eds., *Regulierte Selbstregulierung in der westlichen Welt des späten 19. und frühen 20. Jahrhunderts / Regulated Self-Regulation in the Western World in the Late 19th and the Early 20th Century* (Frankfurt, 2014), 75–127; Brian Balogh, *The Associational State: American Governance in the Twentieth Century* (Philadelphia, 2015).

52. Sylvia Porter, "Caveat Venditor," *Emporia Gazette*, Feb. 6, 1961, 5; Colston Warne, "Advertising: A Critic's View," *JM* 26 (Oct. 1, 1962): 14; News Release, Attorney General Louis Lefkowitz, March 30, 1963, File 16, Box 189, Consumers Research Papers.

53. Morton J. Simon, *The Advertising Truth Book* (New York, 1960), 6; Advertisement of J. T. O'Connell, *Newport Daily News*, Aug. 7, 1964, 3; Armstrong Cork Company, *Annual Report* (Lancaster, 1972), 1; U.S. Chamber of Commerce, *A Handbook on White Collar Crime: Everyone's Problem, Everyone's Loss* (Washington, DC, 1974), 7–8.

54. "The Nixon Brand of Consumerism," *CT*, Nov. 2, 1969, 28.

55. Nixon, "Special Message to the Congress on Consumer Protection"; U.S. Chamber of Commerce, *Handbook on White Collar Crime*, 9.

56. "Annual Conference Panelists Commend Bureaus' Role in Auto Advertising," Chicago Business Bureau, *The Report*, Aug. 13, 1962, 1.

57. See, for example, Reed, "Consumer Protection in Washington"; Alabama Office of Consumer Protection Newsletters from 1975 through 1978 (especially March 1977), File 12, Box 188, Consumers Research Papers.

58. Morton Mintz, "There Are Caveats to 'Caveat Emptor,'" *WP*, Dec. 18, 1968, A20; Elizabeth Fowler, "Vendors Cautioned," *NYT*, April 3, 1971, 39; John King, "Rising Consumerism Restoring Competitive Nature to Markets," *Marketing News* 8 (Dec. 1, 1974): 5.

59. The papers of Consumers' Research testify to the avalanche of materials sent out by state antifraud agencies and nongovernmental organizations. On consumer curricula, see Judy Roberts, "Class Tells Consumers How to Put Law to Use," *CT*, Jan. 3, 1971, S9; Marian Heath Mundy, "Teaching Buyer to Be Wary," *NYT*, May 28, 1972, 72; California State Department of Education, *California Basic Adult Education: Examples of Lesson Plans in Elementary Subjects for Adults* (Sacramento, 1972), 10; New Jersey Center for Consumer Education, *Selected Audio-Visual Materials for Consumer Education* (Edison, NJ, 1974). On public outreach by medical authorities about quackery, see Eric Boyle, *Quack Medicine: A History of Combating Health Fraud in Twentieth-Century America* (Santa Barbara, 2013), 128–40.

60. Argus Advisory Service, *Monthly Newsletter of Current Frauds and Swindles* 1 (Feb. 1946), 1; M. C. Phillips to Charles W. Stickle, Nov. 24, 1965, File 16, Box 189, Consumers Research Papers; California DOJ, *What to Do When You Have Been Cheated* (Sacramento, 1965); Bay Area Neighborhood Development, *Protect Others Too* (San Francisco, 1966); Martha Cole, "You, the Consumer," *Miami Daily News-Record*, Apr. 4, 1968, 10; Pennsylvania Bureau of Consumer Protection, *Conrad Consumer's Sock-It-to-'Em Survival Guide* (Harrisburg, 1969); California Trial Lawyers Association, *How Not to Be Cheated and Who to Contact If You Are* (Sacramento, 1972); Pennsylvania DOJ, *How to Be an Effective Complainer* (n.d., circa 1972), in File 3, Box 190, Consumers Research Papers.

61. New York Department of Law, *The Fine Art of Fraud* (Albany, 1966), available at: https://www.youtube.com/watch?v=evVjxKKwcSg, accessed July 24, 2014.

62. FTC, *Report on District of Columbia Consumer Protection Program* (Washington, DC, 1968); Lee Benton, "Aiding the Poor," *WSJ*, Jan. 4, 1968, 1; "Better Business Bureau in Harlem," *NYAN*, Mar. 30, 1968; Aurelia Toyer, "Consumer Education and Low-Income Families," *Journal of Consumer Affairs*, June 1968, 107–14; "FTC Sees Some Direct Action," *Albuquerque Journal*, Nov. 22, 1968, 48; Isadore Barmash, "Buyers in Harlem Warned by Movie," *NYT*, Apr. 16, 1969, 62; "Consumer Aid Specialist," *Ebony* 26 (Oct. 1971): 7; Lesly Jones, "We're Being Robbed," *NYAN*, Nov. 20, 1971, A1; Grace Lichtenstein, "Co-op City Stages a Consumer Fair," *NYT*, Jan. 31, 1972, 17; Eve Sharbutt, "Consumer Specialist Challenges Big Business," *Fitchburg Sentinel*, June 18, 1973, 16.

63. Len Lear, "CEPA Appears to Be Best Equipped to Fight Consumer Fraud," *PT*, Apr. 16, 1968, 1; "NAACP Officials Meet," *PT*, May 11, 1968, 36; "Consumer Party Woman Candidate," *Somerset* [PA] *Daily American*, Nov. 2, 1970, 11. Like the Better Business Bureau network, inner-city consumer activists regularly used the term "gyp" without any qualms about the ethnic slur that it conveyed.

64. "Finan to Ask State Police Racket Unit," *WP*, Feb. 4, 1962, A3; Walter Wagner, *The Golden Fleecers* (Garden City, NY, 1966), 4; "State Agency Fights Fraud," *Los Angeles Sentinel*, Jan. 26, 1967, A1; Bronson Lafollette, "Consumer Fraud and Consumer Protection in Wisconsin," in FTC, *National Consumer Protection Hearings* (Washington, D.C.,

1969), 250–52; John Kazanjian, "Consumer Protection by State Attorneys General: A Time for Renewal," *Notre Dame Lawyer* 49 (Dec. 1973): 416; NAAG, *State Programs*, 31–34; Patrick Leahy, "White-Collar Crime and the Consumer," *Bennington Banner*, Mar. 27, 1974, 5; Louis Lefkowitz, "Some Reflections on Consumer Protection: The Role of the Attorney General," *New York State Bar Journal* (Aug. 1974): 336; "Crime Fighters Persist," *Oakland Tribune*, Nov. 24, 1974, 100.

65. "Brooklyn D.A. Hits FTC," *Advertising Age*, Mar. 21, 1956, 29; "Caruso, 6 Aides in Guilty Pleas," *LAT*, Oct. 2, 1957, B1; William Witt, "Regulation of Retail Automobile Sales in the District of Columbia," *George Washington Law Review* 29 (1961): 761–81; "Crackdown Set on 'Salesmen,'" *BS*, Dec. 2, 1962, C6; "State Atty. General in New Crackdown," *CD*, Mar. 28, 1964, 7; Wagner, *Golden Fleecers*, 103–06; Len Lear, "D. A. Cracks Down," *PT*, Aug. 16, 1969, 32; Steve Emmons, "Fraud in TV Repair," *LAT*, Dec. 5, 1971, OC3; Charles Elwell, "Covina Drive on Fraud," *LAT*, July 9, 1972, SG1; Christopher Bayley, "One Prosecutor's Battle Plan," *LAT*, July 8, 1973, G6.

66. See, for example: the New York attorney general's newsletter, *Consumer Action*; John Occhiogrosso, "Consumer Protection, Information, and Education: A County's View," *San Diego Law Review* 8 (1971): 41–44; James M. Lorenz, "Consumer Fraud and the San Diego District Attorney's Office," *San Diego Law Review* 8 (1971): 55–59; James Jeffries, "Protection for Consumers against Unfair and Deceptive Practices," *Marquette Law Review* 57 (1974): 592–607; California Department of Consumer Affairs, *Annual Report* (Sacramento, 1976), 7; and the annual reports of the Kansas Consumer Fraud Division, available at: http://ag.ks.gov/about-the-office/document-center/annual-reports /consumer-protection/page/4, accessed Aug. 5, 2014.

67. Wayne King, "Glenn Turner," *NYT*, Jan. 13, 1972, 59; "Michigan Arrests 14 Distributors of Turner," *WSJ*, June 13, 1972, 14; Wayne King, "A Distinct Smell of Snake Oil," *NYT*, Sept. 3, 1972, E4; "G. W. Turner Activities Face Additional Curbs," *WSJ*, Sept. 7, 1972, 6; "Collapse of the Pyramids," *Newsweek* 82 (Sept. 3, 1973): 76–77; Ralph Mooney, "Attorney General as Counsel for the Consumer: The Oregon Experience," *Oregon Law Review* 54 (1975): 126–31; Rudy Maxa, *Dare to Be Great* (New York, 1977).

68. Gilbert Geis, ed., *White Collar Criminal: The Offender in Business and the Professions* (New York, 1969); John E. Conklin, *"Illegal But Not Criminal": Business Crime in America* (Englewood, NJ, 1977).

69. "Letters to the *Times*: Sentencing of C. Arnold Smith," *LAT*, June 20, 1975, D4.

70. Philip Schrag, *Counsel for the Deceived: Case Studies in Consumer Fraud* (New York, 1972), 79–96, 179–80, 187.

71. "Consumer Protection Comes to Westside," *CD*, Sept. 11, 1969, 6; Sheila Wolfe, "State Is Leader in Consumer Fraud Fight," *CT*, July 29, 1970, 8; Bruns, "Role of State and Local Consumer Protection Agencies," 27–48.

72. Ward Welsh, "Fraud Bureau Is Short-Changed," *PI*, clipping (n.d.), File 4, Box 190, Consumers Research Papers; James MacNees, "Consumer Aid Bill Offered," *BS*, Mar. 12, 1968, A11; "New York Leads the Consumer Crusade," *Business Week* (Jan. 31, 1970): 52; Jeanne Voltz, "New Consumer Voice," *LAT*, Feb. 11, 1971, G3; Alexander Auerbach, "Can Agency Be Protective on a Shoestring?," *LAT*, Feb. 22, 1971, G10; "Consumers Battle at the Grassroots," *Business Week* (Feb. 26, 1972): 88; Michael Burns, "Agencies Get 100 Complaints Weekly," *BS*, Nov. 12, 1972, A16.

73. John Darnton, "City's Consumer Agency Beset by Internal Strife," *NYT*, Sept. 18, 1974, 1.

74. Philip Dougherty, "Sellers vs. Consumers," *NYT*, May 7, 1972, F15.

75. "Report on the Better Business Bureaus," *Congressional Record* 111 (Dec. 17, 1971), 47781–95; Knight, Gladieux, and Smith, "Confidential Report."

76. Young Lawyers Section, "Memorandum to the Washington State Legislature."

77. On these aspects of mid-twentieth-century middle-class women's civic action, see Meg Jacobs, *Pocketbook Politics: Economic Citizenship in Twentieth-Century America* (Princeton, 2006), 179–220; Sylvie Murray, *The Progressive Housewife: Community Activism in Suburban Queens, 1945–1965* (Philadelphia, 2003).

78. "Many Here Seek Fraud Unit's Aid," *NYT*, Aug. 3, 1958, 82; "Housewives and State to Fight Sales Frauds," *NYT*, Sept. 22, 1958, 18; "Urge Housewives to Watch Business," *NYAN*, Apr. 18, 1959, 14; "Attorney General's First Course for Law Students," *New York State Bar Journal* 39 (1967): 550; Occhiogrosso, "Consumer Protection, Information, and Education," 46; Lilly Bruck, *NCJW Journal* 34 (Feb. 28, 1972): 3; Celeste Durant, "Specialists to Check Store Ads," *LAT*, Oct. 2, 1973, OC2; "New Help for Consumers," Jan. 14, 1973, 85; Lefkowitz, "Some Reflections on Consumer Protection," 336.

79. Oswald Johnston, "Consumers' Office Open," *BS*, June 12, 1967, C8; Michael Burns, "2 Counties' Consumer Units Need Manpower," *BS*, Nov. 12, 1972, A16; John Gregory, "Consumer Protection," *LAT*, Oct. 4, 1971, C1; Gerald Gold, "Consumerism," *NYT*, Jan. 22, 1974, 41; Leslie Berkmann, "You're a Consumer and You've Got a Complaint," *LAT*, Dec. 28, 1975, OC1.

80. Eric Steele, "Fraud, Dispute, and the Consumer: Responding to Consumer Complaints," *UPLR* 123 (1975): 1180.

81. Steele, "Fraud, Dispute, and the Consumer," 1137–68; D. W. Maurer, "The Argot of Confidence Men," *American Speech* 15 (1940): 116; Occhiogrosso, "Consumer Protection, Information, and Education," 45; Sacramento County Consumer Protection Bureau, "Truth in Bureaucracy: The Day in the Life of a Consumer Protection Bureau" (1973), Box 190, File 14, Consumers Research Papers; Steve Kline, "Consumers' Don Quixote," *LAT*, Aug. 22, 1973, OCB1; Mooney, "Attorney General as Counsel for the Consumer," 131–60; Silbey, "Consumer Justice," 309–405.

82. Testimony of Barnett Levy, New York Assistant Attorney General; Michael Padnos, Director, Atlanta Legal Aid Society; John Occhiogrosso, Commissioner, Nassau County Office of Consumer Affairs; and Bruce Craig, Wisconsin Assistant Attorney General, *National Consumer Protection Hearings*, 55, 126–27, 165; Steele, "Fraud, Dispute, and the Consumer," 1168–79.

83. See Annual Reports from the Kansas State Consumer Protection Division, State of Kansas, for 1975 through 1977. See also: "'White Collar Bandits' Keep Robbing Community of Millions," *New Pittsburgh Courier*, Mar. 7, 1964, 3; New York Bureau of Consumer Frauds and Protection, *1972 Annual Report* (Albany, 1972), 5–10; Alabama Office of Consumer Protection, *1974 Annual Report* (Montgomery, 1974); "Got a Complaint? Call Your State Consumer Office," *Changing Times* 29 (1975): 43–46; "L.A. Consumers Get Restitution," *BS*, Oct. 27, 1975, B5; Silbey, "Consumer Justice," 349–53, 490–93.

84. "Translating Sympathy for Deceived Consumers," 42; U.S. Chamber of Commerce, *Handbook on White Collar Crime*, 5–6; Don Oakley, "Crackdown on White Collar Crime," *Leavenworth Times*, May 25, 1976, 4; "'White Collar' Crimes," *Bridgeport Telegram*, Oct. 6, 1977, 1; Jack Anderson, "Rich Man, Poor Man Justice," *WP*, Apr. 30, 1978, B7.

85. "Developments in the Law: Deceptive Advertising," *HLR* (Mar. 1967): 1126–27;

Schrag, *Counsel for the Deceived*, 118–19; Martha Willman, "Consumer Crackdown Near," *LAT*, Dec. 9, 1973, SFA7; Mooney, "Attorney General As Counsel for the Consumer," 149; "Consumer Protection: New Hope Following Failure of Civil and Criminal Remedies," *Journal of Criminal Law & Criminology* 66 (1975): 11; Silbey, "Consumer Justice," 396.

86. Schrag, *Counsel for the Deceived*, 185.

CHAPTER ELEVEN: THE PROMISE AND LIMITS OF THE ANTIFRAUD STATE

1. Philip Schrag, *Counsel for the Deceived: Case Studies in Consumer Fraud* (New York, 1972), 117–61; "Telephone Solicitors," *Brooklyn Eagle*, Dec. 5, 1952, 21; "Five Indicted on Food Fraud," *Oneonta Star*, Apr. 5, 1955, 1; "Acts in Food Club Case," *NYT*, Feb. 15, 1956, 14; "Admits Freezer Fraud," *NYT*, June 21, 1956, 26; "Curbs Home Burglar Alarm Sales Scheme," *NYAN*, June 28, 1969, 51; Grace Lichtenstein, "Alarm Concern Accused of Fraud Fails," *NYT*, Aug. 1, 1971, 52; Barbara Campbell, "Burglar Alarm Company Here Charged," *NYT*, Oct. 9, 1971, 35; Richard Phalon, "Alarm Concern Making Refunds," *NYT*, Apr. 28, 1971, 49; "Sol Rosen and Pro-Tech Programs," *SEC News Digest*, Apr. 29, 1977, 2.

2. Jean Carper, "Philadelphia Consumers Picket against Cheating," *Spokane Daily Chronicle*, Mar. 16, 1970, 4; John Maginnis, "Some Are Finding Headaches with Consumer, Education and Protective Association," *Gettysburg Times*, Mar. 31, 1971, 7; Len Lear, "CEPA Pickets GMAC in New York," *PT*, July 8, 1972, 5; Andrea McCardle, "Jersey Justice and Discourses of Power: Consumer Rights, Good-Mother Citizenship, and the Cold War," Ph.D. diss. (New York University, 2010), 111–14.

3. Fred Swartz, "Consumer Calls off Picket of Lit's," Aug. 27, 1966, 1; Len Lear, "CEPA Cracks Down Hard," Oct. 10, 1967, 3; Len Lear, "CEPA Pickets Force Used Car Dealer to Take Back Automobile," May 18, 1968, 26; Len Lear, "D.A. Cracks Down," Aug. 16, 1969, 32; "CEPA Puts Heat on Food Freezer Operator," Jan. 20, 1970, 4; Len Lear, "Area Woman Wins $820 after 'Fraud' by Korvette's," Nov. 7, 1972, 4. For coverage elsewhere, see: Bob Queen, "Robbing Innocent People," *Baltimore Afro-American*, Sept. 24, 1966, 17; Warren Magnuson, "How the Ghetto Gets Gypped," *Ebony* (Sept. 1968): 117–18; Morton Mintz, "Gulled Consumer Has Disparate Champions," *WP*, June 8, 1969, B5; Martha Jablow, "Lemon Car Owners Learning," *BS*, Mar. 25, 1973, T1.

4. Tom Ehrbar, "Consumers Band Together for Protection," *Cleveland Call and Post*, Dec. 11, 1971, 11; "Black Community Has Its Own Ralph Nader," *CT*, May 9, A5; Robert McClory, "Community Club: Grass Roots Consumerism," *CD*, May 20, 1972, 6; "Consumer Action Groups Make Your Voice Heard," *Oakland Post*, Dec. 27, 1972, 8; Henry Weinstein, "Inside a Consumer Group," *NYT*, Feb. 9, 1975, 149; "Citizens with a Wallop," *Changing Times* (May 1977): 32; Gregory Wilson and Elizabeth Brydolf, "Grass Roots Solutions: San Francisco Consumer Action," in Laura Nader, ed., *No Access to Law: Alternatives to the American Judicial System* (New York, 1980), 417–59.

5. Craig Fallon, "Cheating a Customer Is a Risky Business," *WSJ*, Jan. 6, 1972, 1; "New Consumer Plan Working," *Bryan* [TX] *Eagle*, Jan. 13, 1972, 12; Nicholas Chriss, "Texas Tornado," *LAT*, Jan. 22, 1972, A1; "Consumer Battle at the Grassroots," *Business Week*, Feb. 26, 1972, 86; "'Let the Seller Beware,'" *Deer Park* [TX] *Progress*, Aug. 3, 1972, 1; John Durham, "Marvin Zindler: Consumer Lawman," *Texas Monthly* (Feb. 1973): 52–57.

6. "Extrajudicial Consumer Pressure: An Effective Impediment to Unethical Business Practices," *DLJ* (1969): 1011–57; Len Lear, "Fighting Consumer Frauds: Part II," *PT*, Mar. 19, 1968, 1; "CEPA Gets Injunction Overruled," *PT*, July 14, 1970, 14; Weinstein, "Inside a Consumer Group."

7. "Marvin Zindler to Address to Friendswood Optimist's Club," *Friendswood* [TX] *News*, May 16, 1974, 2; William Martin, "In Houston, They Dial M for Marvin," *People* 1 (June 17, 1974): 58. Zindler later gained national attention through reporting that exposed a brothel outside Houston frequented by politicians and law enforcement officials, an episode that furnished the basis for the Hollywood film *The Best Little Whorehouse in Texas*.

8. Michael Mattice, "Media in the Middle: A Study of the Mass Media Complaint Managers," in Nader, ed., *No Access to Law*, 485–522.

9. "Life Cigarettes Are Deceptively Advertised," *WSJ*, Dec. 14, 1959, 5; R. W. Apple and Everett Martin, "The Unsoiled Sell," *WSJ*, March 4, 1960, 1; "FTC Lathers Shaving Ad," *BS*, Jan. 4, 1962, 4.

10. Lewis Lowenfels, "Expanding Public Responsibilities of Securities Lawyers: An Analysis of the New Trend in Standard of Care and Priorities of Duties," *CLR* 74 (1974): 412–38; Apple and Martin, "The Unsoiled Sell."

11. Hubert Hooper, "A Study of the Evolution of the Legal Liability of Accountants with Implications for the Future of the Profession," Ph.D. diss. (Tulane University, 1976), 127–36; Oral History Interview with Theodore Sonde, Apr. 4, 2005, SEC Historical Society, 9–15, available at: http://www.sechistorical.org/museum/oral-histories/s-t/, accessed Aug. 9, 2014.

12. John Gillis, "Accountants under Siege," *Financial Analysts Journal* 29 (Sept.–Oct. 1973): 18–19, 22, 90–91; Lowenfels, "Expanding Public Responsibilities," 418–24; Ray Garrett, "New Directions in Professional Responsibility," *BL* 29 (1974): 9–10. A number of these cases related to Robert Vesco's use of an unregistered investment company to defraud offshore mutual funds, which ensnared several prominent lawyers and Nixon's attorney general, John Mitchell.

13. Garrett, "New Directions," 12; Interview with Sonde, 15–34; SEC Release No. 5404 (June 18, 1973), 5.

14. David Ruder, "Multiple Defendants in Securities Law Fraud Cases: Aiding and Abetting, *In Pari Delicto*, Indemnification, and Contribution," *UPLR* 120 (1972): 598–665; J. Vernon Patrick, Jr., "The Securities Class Action for Damages Comes of Age," *BL* 29 (1974): 159–66; Daniel Fischel, "Secondary Liability under Section 10(b) of the Securities Act of 1934," *University of California Law Review* 69 (1981): 81–111.

15. Robert Rosenblatt, "How Accountable Are Accountants?" *LAT*, Sept. 19, 1976, H1; Samuel Gruenbaum and Marc Steinberg, "Accountants' Liability and Responsibility: Securities, Criminal and Common Law," *Loyola of Los Angeles Law Review* 13 (1980): 277–87; John Burton, "The Profession's Institutional Structure in the 1980s," *Journal of Accountancy* 145 (Apr. 1978): 63.

16. J. Gordon Clooney, "The Implications of the Revolution in Securities Regulation for Lawyers," *BL* 29 (Mar. 1974): 129–35; "Angry Lawyers Blast the SEC," *Business Week* Aug. 10, 1974: 102–03; Arthur Mathews, "Liabilities of Lawyers under the Federal Securities Laws," *BL* 30 (Mar. 1975): 105–55; Paul Steiger, "SEC Enforcers" *LAT*, Oct. 30, 1975, A1; Lowenfels, "Expanding Public Responsibilities," 436–37; "Judge and Jury," *Barron's* (Feb. 21, 1977): 3–6.

17. "Impact of SEC's New Disclosure Rules," *Business Week* (Jan. 6, 1973): 58–60; William Foster, "The Current Financial Reporting Environment," *CPA Journal* 44 (Mar. 1974): 34.

18. Wayne Green, "Supreme Court Softens Liability of Audit Firms," *WSJ*, Mar. 31, 1976, 4; John Berry, "President Can Help Shape SEC," *WP*, June 22, 1980, H1; Stan Crock, "SEC's Shad Shows Pro-Business Tilt," *WSJ*, Sept. 16, 1981, 29; Daniel Fischel, "Secondary Liability under Section 10(b) of the Securities Act of 1934," *California Law Review* 69 (1981): 80–111.

19. Francis Wheat, "The Impact of SEC Professional Responsibility Standards," *BL* 34 (1979): 973.

20. Frederick Andrew, "Peat Marwick Is the First Big CPA Firm to Submit to 'Quality Review,'" *WSJ*, June 17, 1974, 8; "Speech of AICPA President Wallace E. Olson," *Journal of Accountancy* 140 (Sept. 1975): 6–8; "Speech of Wallace E. Olson," *Journal of Accountancy* 141 (May 1976): 82–85; Paul M. Clikeman, *Called to Account: Fourteen Financial Frauds That Shaped the American Accounting Profession* (New York, 2009), 69–80.

21. Richard Cunningham, "Class Action Treatment of Securities Fraud Suits under the Revised Rule 23," *George Washington Law Review* 36 (1968): 1150–68.

22. "Los Angeles Board Told Rigged Meters Cost Riders $1.9 Million," *Santa Cruz Sentinel*, July 22, 1964, 5; "Probers Refuse Action as Taxi Hearing Ends," *Pasadena Independent*, Nov. 10, 1964, 22.

23. *Daar v. Yellow Cab Co.*, 67 California Reports 2nd Ser. 695 (California Supreme Court, Nov. 15, 1967); Gene Blake, "Supreme Court Permits Suit," *LAT*, Nov. 29, 1967, A6; Rudy Villasenor, "Yellow Cab Settles Suit," *LAT*, Nov. 24, 1970, B2; "Class Action Lawyer," *LAT*, Jan. 24, 1971, G1; "Yellow Cab Must Reduce Customers Rates," *Fremont Argus*, Jan. 27, 1971, 9.

24. "Two Legal Reforms to Protect Shoppers' Rights," *Changing Times* 24 (Apr. 1970): 23–24; Mark Green, "Appropriateness and Responsiveness: Can the Government Protect the Consumer?" *Journal of Economic Issues* 8 (1974): 322.

25. Myrna Oliver, "Class Action—Setback Not a Lethal Blow," *LAT*, Sept. 22, 1974, 1.

26. Robert Lindsey, "Investors' Lawyer-Sleuth," *NYT*, Mar. 21, 1976, 107; Craig Stock, "Law Firm Rides to the Aid of Investors," *PI*, Oct. 3, 1983, D3.

27. "High Court Bolsters Agencies," *NYT*, Jan.10, 1979, D1; "Twenty Cited in Suit over Westec Trading Agree to Partial $1.6 Million Settlement," *WSJ*, Aug. 1, 1972, 2; "Aldon Industries Sets Class Suit Settlement Totaling $1.1 Million," *WSJ*, Apr. 13, 1976, 33; "Union Bancorp to Settle Civil Lawsuits," *LAT*, July 14, 1978, F23; Ted Vollmer, "Court Approves 2 U. S. Financial Suit Settlements," *LAT*, Nov. 29, 1978, E15.

28. Richard Dole, "Consumer Class Actions under the Uniform Deceptive Practices Act," *DLJ* (1968): 1103; Arthur Travers, Jr., and Jonathan Landers, "The Consumer Class Action," *Kansas Law Review* 18 (1970): 811–38; Lou Ashe, "Class Action: Solution for the Seventies," *New England Law Review* 7 (1971): 1–24; James Hinds, "To Right Mass Wrongs: A Federal Consumer Class Action Act," *Harvard Journal on Legislation* 13 (1976): 776–844.

29. Morris Macey, "Award of Attorney Fees as a Stimulant to Private Litigation under the Truth in Lending Act," *BL* 27 (Jan. 1972): 593–601; "Class Actions under the Truth in Lending Act," *YLJ* 83 (1974): 1410–38; William Whitford, "Structuring Consumer Protection Legislation to Maximize Effectiveness," *Wisconsin Law Review* (1981):

1037–39. For illustrative lawsuits, see: "Untruth in Lending," *Cleveland Call and Post*, July 4, 1970, A1; Richard Phalon, "Credit Suits May Result in Refunds," *NYT*, Sept. 19, 1970, 18; "Bank in Violation of '68 Truth Act," *NYAN*, July 10, 1971, A12; "Class Action Suit Settled," *KCS*, Mar. 2, 1973, A4.

30. Lewis Popper, "The New Federal Warranty Law: A Guide to Compliance," *BL* 32 (Jan. 1977): 399–416; Wilson Herndon, "Consumer Class Actions and the Effect of Magnuson-Moss," *Forum* 15 (1980): 926–29; "Magnuson-Moss Class Action Provisions: Consumers' Remedy or Empty Promise," *Georgetown Law Journal* 70 (1982): 1399–1403.

31. John Morris, "U. S. Consumer Unit Asks Easier Access to Courts," *NYT*, Sept. 29, 1973, 21; Linda Greenhouse, "Consumer Class-Action Bill Argued," *NYT*, Feb. 14, 1974, 33; "Are Consumer Class Actions Dead?" *Consumer Reports* 39 (Aug. 1974): 583–85; "Consumer Bill Killed by House," *WSJ*, Feb. 9, 1978, 2.

32. Richard Lesher, "The Voice of Business," *Lubbock Avalanche-Journal*, Sept. 18, 1977, G2; Benjamin C. Waterhouse, *Lobbying America: The Politics of Business from Nixon to NAFTA* (Princeton, 2014), 151–73.

33. Nancy Bernstine, "Prosecutorial Discretion in Consumer Protection Divisions in Selected State Attorney General Offices," *Howard Law Journal* 20 (1977): 263–72; Robert Skimick and Patricia Avery, "State Court Class Action: A Potpourri of Differences," *Forum* 20 (1985): 750–72.

34. "Cost Allocation in California Class Actions," *California Western Law Review* 13 (1977): 65–68; Douglas Roberts and Gary Martz, "Consumerism Comes of Age: Treble Damages and Attorney Fees in Consumer Transactions," *Ohio State Law Journal* 42 (1981): 956–60; Joseph Moldovan, "New York Creates a Private Right of Action to Combat Consumer Fraud: Caveat Venditor," *Brooklyn Law Review* 48 (1982): 509–92.

35. Craig Zabala, "Sabotage and General Motors' Van Nuys Assembly Plant, 1975–1983," *Industrial Relations* 20 (1989): 16–32; "Management Practices, Relational Contracts, and the Decline of General Motors," *Journal of Economic Perspectives* 28 (2014): 49–72.

36. GM's move represented a classic example of what the economists George Akerlof and Robert Schiller refer to as "reputation mining." *Phishing for Phools: The Economics of Manipulation and Deception* (Princeton, 2015), 223–35.

37. "GM Ordered to Tell Buyer of Switches," *BS*, Mar. 13, 1977, A9; Andrea Pawlyna, "Great Engine Switch," *BS*, June 19, 1977, T1; "Great Engine Switch and Other Magic Tricks," *Consumer Reports* 43 (Apr. 1978): 190–91.

38. "Attorneys General Ask G.M. Payment," *NYT*, July 16, 1977, 27; Mitchell Locin, "States Join in Suing GM over Engine," *CT*, Oct. 15, 1977, A5; "Engine Switch Pact to Cost GM $40 Million," *CT*, Dec. 20, 1977, B1; "Great Engine Switch and Other Magic Tricks," 190–91.

39. "Settlement with GM on Engine Switch Is Upset," *WSJ*, Feb. 27, 1979, 12; Anne Keegan, "Joe Siewek and His 'Chevymobile,'" *CT*, Mar. 13, 1981, 1; "Jury Orders G.M. to Pay 10,000," *NYT*, June 28, 1981, 25; "1,200 in State to Get $400 Each," *CT*, Mar. 2, 1984, A8.

40. Jonathan Sheldon and George Zweibel, *Survey of Consumer Law* (Washington, DC, 1978), 74–115.

41. Jane G. Schubert and Robert E. Krug, *Consumer Fraud: An Empirical Analysis* (Washington, DC, 1979), 8–67.

42. Marver H. Bernstein, *Regulating Business by Independent Commission* (Princeton, 1955); Gabriel Kolko, *The Triumph of Conservatism: A Reinterpretation of American History, 1900–1916* (New York, 1963).

43. Edward Cox, *The Nader Report on the Federal Trade Commission* (New York, 1969); American Bar Association, *Commission to Study the Federal Trade Commission* (New York, 1969).

44. Frank Angell, "Some Effects of the Truth-in-Lending Legislation," *Journal of Business* 44 (1971): 78–85; Griffith Garwood, "Truth-in-Lending: A Regulator's View," *BL* 29 (Nov. 1973): 198–99; George Day and William Brandt, "Consumer Research and the Evaluation of Information Disclosure," *Journal of Consumer Research* 1 (1974): 21–32.

45. George Day, "Assessing the Effects of Information Disclosure Requirements," *JM* 40 (Apr. 1976): 42–52; Noel Capon and Richard Lutz, "A Model and Methodology for the Development of Consumer Information Programs," *JM* 43 (Jan. 1979): 58–67.

46. Kenneth McNeil, John Nevin, David Trubek, and Richard Miller, "Market Discrimination against the Poor and the Impact of Consumer Disclosure Laws: The Used Car Industry," *Law & Society Review* 13 (1979): 695–720.

47. George Stigler, "Public Regulation of the Securities Markets," *BL* 19 (1964): 721–53; David Clurman, "A Report . . . on New Issues of Securities" (1969), available at http://www.sechistorical.org/collection/papers/1960/1969_0901_NYNewIssues.pdf, accessed April 26, 2016; George Benston, "The Value of the SEC's Accounting Disclosure Requirements," *Accounting Review* 44 (1969): 515–32; Lyn Pankoff and Robert Virgil, "Some Preliminary Findings from a Laboratory Experiment on the Usefulness of Financial Accounting Information to Security Analysts," *Journal of Accounting Research Supplement* (1970): 1–61; Elliot Weiss, "Disclosure and Corporate Accountability," *BL* 34 (Jan. 1979): 579–81; Homer Kripke, *The SEC and Corporate Disclosure: Regulation in Search of a Purpose* (New York, 1979).

48. Renee Friedman, "Regulation of Interstate Land Sales: Is Full Disclosure Sufficient?" *Journal of Urban and Contemporary Law* 20 (1980): 153–58.

49. Angell, "Some Effects of Truth-in-Lending Legislation," 82–83; "Consumer Credit Regulation: Illusion or Reality?" *BL* 33 (Feb. 1978): 1148.

50. George Benston, "Required Disclosure and the Stock Market: An Evaluation of the Securities and Exchange Act of 1934," *American Economic Review* (1973): 132–55.

51. Gregory Alexander, *Honesty and Competition: False-Advertising Law and Policy under FTC Administration* (Syracuse, 1967).

52. Richard Posner, "The Federal Trade Commission," *University of Chicago Law Review* 37 (1969): 61–82.

53. George Benston, "An Appraisal of the Costs and Benefits of Government-Required Disclosure: SEC and FTC Requirements," *Law and Contemporary Problems* 41 (1977): 39–41; Homer Kripke, *The SEC and Corporate Disclosure: Regulation in Search of a Purpose* (New York, 1979), 62–68, 232–42.

54. Posner, "Federal Trade Commission," 61–64; Kripke, *SEC and Corporate Disclosure*, 117–33.

55. Milton Friedman, *Capitalism and Freedom* (Chicago, 1962), 133.

56. Kripke, *SEC and Corporate Disclosure*, 68–70, 96–116; Marc Eisner, "Institutional History and Policy Change: Exploring the Origins of the New Antitrust," *Journal of Policy History* 2 (1990): 261–89.

57. Brooksley Born, "Oral History Interview with Robert Pitofsky," Oct. 28, Dec. 2, 19, 2003, Feb. 20, Mar. 10, May 20, 2004, Historical Society of the District of Columbia Circuit, 27–31, 42–48, 67, 73–75, available at: http://dcchs.org/RobertPitofsky/robert pitofsky_complete.pdf, accessed Feb. 16, 2010.

58. Robert Pitofsky, "Beyond Nader: The Regulation of Advertising," *HLR* 90 (1977): 664–92.

59. Kimberly Till, "The SEC Safe Harbor for Forecasts—A Step in the Right Direction?" *DLJ* (1980): 607–40; "SEC to Simplify Reports by Firms, *Toronto Globe and Mail*, Aug. 5, 1981, B6; Michael Ferry, "The Truth-in-Lending Simplification and Reform Act: An Overview," *Journal of the Missouri Bar* 38 (1982): 417–25.

60. Born, "Oral History Interview of Robert Pitofsky," 57, 78–82; Michael Pertschuk, *The Revolt against Regulation: The Rise and Pause of the Consumer Movement* (Berkeley, 1982), 80–85, 98–106, 113–17.

61. John O'Brien to W. Dan Bell and Woodrow Wirsig, Nov. 20, 1969, Box 9, Bell Papers; "Protective Government 'Paralyzes' Consumers," clipping from *Advertising Age*, Oct. 10, 1966, Box 31, Folder 5, BBBMC; Richard McClain to Victor Nyborg, Dec. 20, 1968, Box 3, Bell Papers; Jim Hyatt, "Friend or Foe?" *WSJ*, Sept. 18, 1970, 1.

62. Stephens to Barry; Dan Berry, Jr., "The Roof Is Leaking," Memo to BBB Executives, Aug. 23, 1965, Box 4, Bell Papers.

63. John Madsen to Encyclopedia Britannica, Feb. 23, 1966; John Madsen to Avon, Feb. 23, 1966; Earl Lind to Lloyd Delke, President, National Association of Direct Sellers, April 24, 1967, Box 150, Folder 15, BBMC.

64. Peter Millones, "Harassment Laid to Consumerism," *NYT*, Feb. 18, 1970.

65. Peter Weaver, "The Better Business Bureau Isn't Always Better," *WP*, Mar. 7, 1971, F15; "Promoting Self-Policing," *Time*, June 14, 1971; Jack Anderson, "Better Business Units Faulted," *WP*, Sept. 7, 1971, C21; David Levy, "The Better Business Bureau: Whom Does It Really Protect?" *WP*, Nov. 7, 1971, B49; Hyatt, "Friend or Foe?" Grace Lichtenstein, "Better Business Bureaus Seek to Counter Criticism," *NYT*, May 22, 1972, 1; Isadore Barmash, "City Business Bureau Is 50," *NYT*, May 2, 1972, 57.

66. Levy, "The Better Business Bureau"; Frances Cerra, "New Better Business Chief Is Consumer Oriented," *NYT*, Jan. 8, 1978, 40; Ralph Blumenthal, "Better Business Unit Drops 15 Companies," *NYT*, Apr. 12, 1978, B2; Ralph Blumenthal, "Consumer Activists Who Mean Business," *NYT*, Aug. 15, 1979, CI.

67. Chicago BBB Report on Sears Roebuck, Oct. 1974, Box 209, Folder 5; Earl Lind to J. B. Myers, Memphis BBB, Box 209, Folder 4, BBBMC. "Sears Roebuck Consents to Order by FTC Barring 'Bait-and-Switch' Sales Tactics," *Wall Street Journal*, Oct. 2, 1976, 13.

68. Jack Anderson, "Better Bureaus Are No Better," *WP*, Feb. 12, 1972, D15; Eric Zanot, *The National Advertising Review Board, 1971–1976* (Minneapolis, 1979), 7–21; John Morris, "F.C.C. Rejects Three Requests to Expand Role," *NYT*, Oct. 10, 1971, F4; Philip Dougherty, "Problems of a Review Board," *NYT*, Aug. 4, 1972, 38; Philip Dougherty, "N.A.R.B. Is Scored," *NYT*, Feb. 11, 1974, E7; Stanley Cohen, "Consumerist Group Raps NAD Delays," *Advertising Age*, April 22, 1974, 2; Alexander Auerbach, "Ad Self-Regulation Is Set Back," *LAT*, Mar. 9, 1975, E9.

69. Grace Lichtenstein, "Business Bureaus Back Arbitration," *NYT*, May 28, 1972, 79; William Jones, "Arbitration Setup Offered by BBBs," *WP*, June 25, 1974, D10; James Simison, "Arbitration for Consumers Is Spreading," *WSJ*, Apr. 21, 1975, 30; Jane Bryant Quinn, "Arbitration Panel Aids Complainant," *WP*, Mar. 8, 1976, D7.

70. Chicago Better Business Bureau, *WHO Will Be the GO-BETWEEN?* (Chicago, 1974), Box 28, Folder 5, BBBMC.

71. Stewart Macaulay, "Lawyers and Consumer Protection Laws," *Law & Society Review* 14 (1979): 116–71.

72. After the Equity Funding accounting fraud broke in 1973, more than twenty corporate officers and external accountants faced criminal indictments, with sixteen receiving jail time of up to eight years. Investors victimized by the fraud eventually received between fifteen and forty cents on the dollar in restitution, paid by the accounting firms that certified the company's financial statements, underwriters of Equity securities offerings, and former Equity executives in their personal capacities. "A $20-Million Suit Is Filed by Trustee of Equity," *NYT*, Apr. 2, 1975, 58; Al Delugach, "Last 3 Equity Defendants Given 3-Month Jail Terms," *LAT*, July 17, 1975, D11; "$57 Million Tentative Settlement Drafted," *NYT*, Jan. 6, 1977, 47.

73. On the significance of "rights discourse" for consumer activism, see McCardle, "Jersey Justice," 116.

CHAPTER TWELVE: NEOLIBERALISM AND THE REDISCOVERY OF BUSINESS FRAUD

1. For this, Google Ngram, see: https://books.google.com/ngrams/graph?content =corporate+fraud%2Cbusiness+fraud&year_start=1976&year_end=2008&corpus=17 &smoothing=3&share=&direct_url=t1%3B%2Ccorporate%20fraud%3B%2Cc0%3B .t1%3B%2Cbusiness%20fraud%3B%2Cc0.

2. Searches of the "Proquest Historical Newspapers" and "Proquest Newspapers" databases yielded the following number of hits: 1976–1985: 139; 1986–1995: 237; 1996–2005: 378; 2006—Feb. 2014: 1,019.

3. Federal Bureau of Investigation, *Senior Sentinel Telemarketing Fraud* (Washington, DC, 1995); Mark Allan Baginskis, "Telemarketing Fraud upon the Elderly Shows No Signs of Slowing," *Loyola Consumer Law Review* 11 (1998): 5; Fred Huebner, "Fifty Ways to Scam Your Brother," *Washington State Bar News* 52 (Mar. 1998): 16–17; David Anderson, "The Aggregate Burden of Crime," *Journal of Law and Economics* 42 (1999): 637–38.

4. "Scams, Frauds, and Overruns: How Can the Pentagon Cope," *Providence Journal*, May 15, 1985, A15; Paul Jesilow, Gilbert Geis, and John C. Harris, "Doomed to Repeat Our Errors: Fraud in Emerging Health-Care Systems," *Social Justice* 22 (Summer 1995): 125–38.

5. Miriam Albert, "E-buyer Beware: Why Online Auction Fraud Should Be Regulated," *American Business Law Journal* 39 (2002): 575–601. See also the annual reports of the FBI's Internet Crime Complaint Center, available at: https://www.ic3.gov/media /annualreports.aspx.

6. George Akerlof and Paul Romer, "Looting: The Economic Underworld of Bankruptcy for Profit," *Brookings Papers on Economic Activity* (1993): 1–73; Robert Tillman and Henry Pontell, "Organizations and Fraud in the Savings and Loan Industry," *Social Forces* 73 (1995): 1439–63; William Black, *The Best Way to Rob a Bank Is to Own One: How Corporate Executives and Politicians Looted the S&L Industry* (Austin, 2005). Some economists demurred from this analysis, arguing that most S&L losses reflected ill-judged speculation rather than managerial looting. Robert Rosenblatt, "Just How Massive Was the Fraud in the S&L Disaster?" *LAT*, July 21, 1990, 1; Bert Ely and Vicki Van-

derhoff, *Lessons Learned from the S & L Debacle: The Price of Failed Public Policy* (Lewisville, TX, 1991), 12. For a compelling rejoinder, see Henry Pontell, "White-Collar Crime or Just Risky Business? The Role of Fraud in Major Financial Debacles," *Crime, Law, and Social Change* 42 (2005): 311–15.

7. "When the Numbers Don't Add up," *The Economist* 362 (Feb. 9, 2002): 57–60; Larry Ribstein, "Market vs. Regulatory Responses to Corporate Fraud: A Critique of the Sarbanes-Oxley Act of 2002," *Journal of Corporation Law* 28 (2002): 4–7; John Kroger, "Enron, Fraud, and Securities Reform: An Enron Prosecutor's Perspective," *University of Colorado Law Review* 76 (2005): 57–138. Gary Giroux, "What Went Wrong? Accounting Fraud and Lessons from the Recent Scandals," *Social Research* 75 (2008): 1205–38.

8. Amir Afrati, Tom Lauricella, and Dionne Searcy, "Top Broker Accused of $50 Billion Fraud," *WSJ*, Dec. 12, 2008, A1; Steve Sacklow, "Ponzi Schemes Proliferate," *WSJ Europe*, Jan. 29, 2009, 19; Tom Fowler and Mary Flood, "Stanford Group Now Accused of Ponzi Scheme," *Houston Chronicle*, Feb. 29, 2009, A1; Kevin McCoy, "Economic Troubles Reveal Ponzi Plague," *USA Today*, Apr. 17, 2009, B1; Alan Abelson, "Ponzi's Legacy," *Barron's* 92 (July 16, 2012): 7.

9. Paul Muolo and Matthew Padilla, *Chain of Blame: How Wall Street Caused the Mortgage and Credit Crisis* (New York, 2010); David Dayen, *Chain of Title: How Three Ordinary Americans Uncovered Wall Street's Great Foreclosure Fraud* (New York, 2016).

10. American Association of Retired Persons, *A Report on the Survey of Older Consumer Behavior* (Washington, DC, 1990); Regina Haasis and Lori Shelby, "Seniors: The Con's Deepest Pockets," *Experience* 5 (Winter 1995): 5–11; Keith Slotter, "Hidden Faces: Combating Telemarketing Fraud," *FBI Law Enforcement Bulletin* 67 (Mar. 1998): 13; Lauren Dake, "How Seniors Can Spot a Fraud More Easily," *Christian Science Monitor*, July 24, 2006, 13.

11. On "corrosive" regulatory capture, see Daniel Carpenter and David A. Moss, eds., *Preventing Regulatory Capture: Special Interest Influence and How to Limit It* (New York, 2013), 16–18.

12. J. Gregory Sidak, "The Failure of Good Intentions: The WorldCom Fraud and Collapse of American Telecommunications after Deregulation," *Yale Journal on Regulation* 20 (2003): 227–46.

13. Harry Trebing, "Assessing Deregulation: The Clash between Promise and Reality," *Journal of Economic Issues* 38 (2004): 14–16; Woodrow Clark, Jr. and Istemi Demirag, "US Financial Regulatory Change: The Case of the California Energy Crisis," *Journal of Banking Regulation* 7 (2006): 75–93.

14. Stephen Pizzo, Mary Fricker, and Paul Muolo, *Inside Job: The Looting of America's Savings and Loans* (New York, 1991), 21–54; Sinan Cebenoyan, Elizabeth Cooperman, and Charles Register, "Deregulation, Reregulation, Equity Ownership, and S&L Risk-Taking," *Financial Management* 24 (Autumn 1995): 63–76; Kitty Calavita, Henry N. Pontrell, and Robert Tillman, *Big Money Crime: Fraud and Politics in the Savings and Loan Crisis* (Berkeley, 1997), 1–15.

15. G. Mitu Gulati, Jeffrey Rachlinski, and Donald Langevoort, "Fraud by Hindsight," *Northwestern University Law Review* 98 (2004): 773–825; L. Randall Wray, "Lessons from the Subprime Meltdown," *Challenge* 51 (Mar.–Apr. 2008): 40–57; John Coffee, Jr. and Hillary Sale, "Redesigning the SEC: Does the Treasury Have a Better Idea?," *Virginia Law Review* 95 (2009): 710–20; Patricia McCoy, Andrey Pavlov, and Susan Wachter,

"Systemic Risk through Securitization: The Result of Deregulation and Regulatory Failure," *Connecticut Law Review* 41 (2009): 1327–76; James Lieber, "Up in Smoke," *Village Voice*, Jan. 28, 2009, 13–18, 20; Financial Crisis Inquiry Commission, *The Financial Crisis Inquiry Report* (New York, 2011), 52–66; William Black, "The Department of Justice 'Chases Mice While Lions Roam the Campsite': Why the Department Has Failed to Prosecute the Elite Frauds That Drove the Financial Crisis," *UKMC Law Review* 80 (2012): 53.

16. Kitty Calavita and Henry Pontrell, "'Heads I Win, Tails You Lose': Deregulation, Crime, and Crisis in the Savings and Loan Industry," *Crime and Delinquency* 36 (1990): 328–29; Black, *The Best Way to Rob a Bank Is to Own One*, 17–40, 256–65.

17. Carrington, "Seven Defense Contractors Submitted Millions of Dollars of Dubious Bills," *WSJ*, May 16, 1985, 12; "Panel to Probe Abuses by Defense Contractors," *Seattle Times*, June 18, 1985, A2; "Few Defense Fraud Cases Prosecuted," *Houston Chronicle*, July 29, 1985, A2; Richard Halloran, "Trouble with Defense Contractors," *NYT*, Dec. 8, 1985, A1; Spencer Rich, "Medicare Fraud Said to Cost Hundreds of Millions," *WP*, Oct. 3, 1991, A21; Pamela Bucy, "Health Care Reform and Fraud by Health Care Providers," *Villanova Law Review* 38 (1993): 1003–38; Peter Mitchell, "Faulty Claims Mar Medicare," *WSJ*, June 7, 1995, F1.

18. Adrian Michaels and Peter Spiegel, "Agency Underfunded," *Financial Times*, July 1, 2002, 26.

19. "Georgia Struggles with Rising Tide of Mortgage Fraud," *Knight Ridder Tribune Business News*, Feb. 6, 2005, 1; Daniel Lathrop, "FBI Lacks Resources to Fight Boom in Mortgage Fraud," July 5, 2007, A1.

20. *Financial Crisis Inquiry Report*, 94–95.

21. Michele Derus, "Mortgage Fraud Takes Heavy Toll," *Milwaukee Journal Sentinel*, Apr. 11, 2005, 1; Edward Gramlich, *Subprime Mortgages: America's Latest Boom and Bust* (Washington, DC, 2007); Richard Schmitt, "FBI Saw Threat of Loan Crisis," *LAT*, Aug. 25, 2008, A1; Harry Markopolos, *No One Would Listen: A True Financial Thriller* (Hoboken, 2010); Mimi Swartz and Sherron Watkins, *Power Failure: The Inside Story of the Collapse of Enron* (New York, 2004).

22. William D. Cohan, "Wall Street Whistleblowers," *FT.com* (May 30, 2014), available at: http://www.ft.com/cms/s/2/ce216134-e6c7–11e3–9a20–00144feabdc0.html #axzz3C2o23blr, accessed Aug. 31, 2014.

23. *Frontline*, "The Warning," originally aired on PBS October 20, 2009, available at http://www.pbs.org/wgbh/pages/frontline/warning/, accessed April 26, 2016.

24. *Financial Crisis Inquiry Report*, 79–80.

25. David Reiss, "Subprime Standardization: How Ratings Agencies Allow Predatory Lending to Flourish in the Secondary Mortgage Market," *Florida State Law Review* 33 (2006): 1023–53.

26. Jessica Leight, "Public Choice: A Critical Reassessment," in Edward Balleisen and David Moss, eds., *Toward a New Theory of Regulation* (New York, 2009), 213–55; Edward J. Balleisen, "Introduction: The Dialectics of Modern Regulatory Governance," in Balleisen, ed., *Business Regulation*, vol. 1 (Cheltenham, UK, 2015), xlii–xlvi, lii–lvi.

27. Richard Vietor, *Contrived Competition: Regulation and Deregulation in America* (Cambridge, MA, 1994); Daniel T. Rodgers, *Age of Fracture* (Cambridge, MA, 2011), 60–63; Luigi Zingales, Robert Glauber, Robert Litan, Allan Ferrell, and Andrew Kuritz-

kes, *Interim Report of the Committee on Capital Market Regulation* (New York, 2007), available at: http://capmktsreg.org/press/interim-report/, accessed Aug. 26, 2014.

28. On the wider intellectual currents involving the "rediscovery of the market," see Rodgers, *Age of Fracture*, 41–69.

29. Michael Darby and Edi Karni, "Free Competition and the Optimal Amount of Fraud," *Journal of Law & Economics* 16 (1973): 67–88; Frank Easterbrook and Daniel Fischel, "Mandatory Disclosure and the Protection of Investors," *Virginia Law Review* 70 (1984): 674–77, 688–90; Richard A. Posner, *Economic Analysis of Law*, 3rd ed. (New York, 1986), 422–24; Stephen Choi, "Regulating Investors, Not Issuers: A Market-Based Proposal," *California Law Review* 88 (2000): 279–83.

30. Alan Greenspan, *The Age of Turbulence: Adventures in a New World* (New York, 2007), 375; *Frontline*, "The Warning," script available at: http://www.pbs.org/wgbh/pages/frontline/warning/etc/script.html, accessed Aug. 26, 2014.

31. *Melder et al. v. Morris et al.*, 27 Fed. 3rd Series 1097 (5th Circuit Court of Appeals, 1997).

32. Thomas J. Peters and Robert H. Waterman, *In Search of Excellence: Lessons from America's Best-Run Companies* (New York, 1982); Thomas J. McCoy, *Compensation and Motivation: Maximizing Employee Performance with Behavior-Based Incentive Plans* (New York, 1992); James M. McTaggart, *The Value Imperative: Managing for Superior Shareholder Returns* (New York, 1994); Rakesh Khurana, *From Higher Aims to Hired Hands: The Social Transformation of American Business Schools and the Unfulfilled Promise of Management as a Profession* (Princeton, 2007); Kimberly Phillips-Fein, *Invisible Hands: The Making of the Conservative Movement from the New Deal to Reagan* (New York, 2009), 185–262.

33. K. Labich and T. Ehrenfeld, "The New Crisis in Business Ethics," *Fortune* 125 (Apr. 20, 1992): 167; Reed Abelson, "Companies Turn to Grades," *NYT*, Mar. 19, 2001, A1; Michelle Conlin, "Compensation Is Getting Personal," *Business Week* (Dec. 6, 2002): 1; Alex Berenson, *The Number: How the Drive for Quarterly Earnings Corrupted Wall Street and Corporate America* (New York, 2003), 71–149.

34. Chad Terhune, Carrick Mollenkamp, and Ann Carns, "Inside Alleged Fraud at HealthSouth," *WSJ*, Apr. 3, 2003, A1; Brooke Masters, "Worldcom Exec Tells of 'Pressure,'" *WP*, Feb. 15, 2002, 15; Carrie Johnson, "Prosecutors, Regulators Step up Pace of Auditor Probes," *WP*, Jan. 28, 2003, E1; Berenson, *The Number*, 180–218.

35. "How Corrupt Is Wall Street?" *Business Week*, May 13, 2002, 36–42; Gretchen Morgenson, "The Enforcers of Wall St?" *NYT*, June 20, 2002, C1; William Grider, "The Enron Nine," *The Nation* 274 (May 13, 2002): 18–22; Paul Healey and Krishna Palepu, "How the Quest for Efficiency Corroded the Market," *Harvard Business Review* 81 (July 2003): 76–85; John C. Coffee, *Gatekeepers: The Professions and Corporate Governance* (New York, 2006), 15–77, 146–64, 226–29, 283–92; Jonathan R. Macey, *The Death of Corporate Reputation: How Integrity Has Been Destroyed on Wall Street* (Upper Saddle River, NJ, 2013), 123–89.

36. James Donegan and Michele Ganon, "Strain, Differential Association, and Coercion: Insights from the Criminological Literature on Causes of Accountants' Misconduct," *Accounting and the Public Interest* 8 (2008): 1–20; William Black, "Neo-Classical Economic Theories, Methodology, and Praxis Optimize Criminogenic Environments and Produce Intensifying Crises," *Creighton Law Review* 44 (2011): 597–645; Tomson H. Nguyen, *Fraud and the Subprime Mortgage Crisis* (El Paso, 2011). On the social contexts

that legitimize deceptive practices, and the diffusion of new forms of deception, see: Cynthia Koller, "Diffusion of Innovation and Fraud in the Subprime Mortgage Market," Ph.D. diss. (University of Cincinnati, 2010). Dan Ariely describes such diffusion of dishonesty as "moral infection": *The (Honest) Truth about Dishonesty: How We Lie to Everyone—Especially Ourselves* (New York, 2012), 191–216.

37. "Bullish Citigroup Is 'Still Dancing' to the Beat," *Financial Times*, July 10, 2007, 1; Richard Bitner, *Confessions of a Subprime Lender: An Insider's Tale of Greed, Fraud, and Ignorance* (Hoboken, 2008), 41–125; Muolo and Padilla, *Chain of Blame*; Mark Gillispie, "The Subprime House of Cards," *Cleveland Plain Dealer*, May 11, 2008, A1; Kevin Hall, "How Moody's Sold Its Ratings," *McClatchy Newspapers*, Oct. 18, 2009, available at http://www.mcclatchydc.com/2009/10/18/77244/how-moodys-sold-its-ratings-and.html, accessed Oct. 19, 2009; Drew DeSilver, "Reckless Strategies Doomed WaMu," *Seattle Times*, Oct. 25, 2009, available at http://seattletimes.com/html/businesstechnology/2010131911_wamu25.html, accessed Oct. 16, 2009; Bethany McLean and Joe Nocera, *All the Devils Are Here: The Hidden History of the Financial Crisis* (New York, 2010); Financial Crisis Inquiry Commission, *The Financial Crisis Inquiry Report*, 102–212; Koller, "Diffusion of Innovation and Fraud," 91–106; Nguyen, *Fraud and the Subprime Mortgage Crisis*, 75–114; Neil Fligstein and Alexander Roehrkasse, "All the Incentives Were Wrong: Opportunism and the Financial Crisis," unpublished paper delivered to Law and Ethics Conference, Yale University, Feb. 15, 2013, available at http://sociology.berkeley.edu/sites/default/files/faculty/fligstein/All%20The%20Incentives%20Were%20Wrong%20for%20Financialization%20Workshop.pdf, accessed Sept. 17, 2014.

38. Paul Krugman, "Two, Three, Many?" *NYT*, Feb. 1, 2002, A25. Jonathan Coopersmith has made a similar argument. See his unpublished paper, "Creative Construction: The Importance of Fraud and Froth in Emerging Technologies," available at: http://the-bhc.org/sites/default/files/webform/pre-meeting-papers/BHC%20June%202015%20Coopersmith.pdf, accessed July 5, 2015.

39. Ariely, *The (Honest) Truth about Dishonesty*, 163–89. See also Malcolm Salter, *Innovation Corrupted: The Origins and Legacy of Enron's Collapse* (Cambridge, MA, 2008), especially 305–17.

40. Lucette Lugnado, "Hospitals Profit by 'Upcoding' Illnesses," *WSJ*, Apr. 17, 1997, B1; Eva Rodriguez, "In Columbia Inquiry, a Fine Line Defines Fraud," *WSJ*, Aug. 11, 1997, A3; Edward J. Balleisen, *Scenes from a Corporate Makeover: Health Care Fraud and the Refashioning of Columbia-HCA, 1992–2001* (Durham, 2003), Part 1, 15–18.

41. D. N. Ghosh, "Wall Street Capitalism and the World of Professional Managers," *Economic and Political Weekly* 37 (2002): 3803–09; Robert Prentice, "Enron: A Brief Behavioral Autopsy," *American Business Law Journal* 40 (2003): 427–33; Kurt Eichenwald, *Conspiracy of Fools: A True Story* (New York, 2005); Malcolm S. Salter, *Innovation Corrupted: The Origins and Legacy of Enron's Collapse* (Cambridge, MA, 2008).

42. Adam Ashcraft and Til Schuermann, "Understanding the Securitization of Subprime Credit," Staff Report 318, Federal Reserve Bank of New York (2008); John Martin, "A Primer on the Role of Securitization in the Credit Market Crisis of 2007," unpublished paper, 2009, available at: http://www.sba.pdx.edu/faculty/danr/danraccess/courses/fin562/martin_2009_securitization_primer.pdf, accessed Aug. 29, 2014.

43. Bitner, *Confessions of a Subprime Lender*, 109.

44. David Reiss, "Ratings Failure: The Need for a Consumer Protection Agency in

Rating Agency Regulation," *Banking & Financial Services Policy Report* 28 (Nov. 2009): 12–22; SEC, *Summary Report of Issues Identified in the Commission Staff's Examination of Select Credit Rating Agencies* (Washington, DC, 2008); Bruce Jacobs, "Tumbling Tower of Babel: Subprime Securitization and the Credit Crisis," *Financial Analysts Journal* 65 (May/June 2009): 17–30.

45. Gary Rhodes, "Gibson Sues over Swap Loss," *Cincinnati Post*, Sept. 13, 1994, D5; Thomas Paulette, "Procter & Gamble Sues Bankers Trust," *WSJ*, Oct. 28, 1994, A6; Donald Langevoort, "Selling Hope, Selling Risk: Some Lessons from Behavioral Economics about Stockbrokers and Sophisticated Investors," *California Law Review* 84 (1996): 627–701; Macey, *Death of Corporate Reputation*, 55–81.

46. Michael Lewis, *The Big Short: Inside the Doomsday Machine* (New York, 2010), 70–82; Macey, *Death of Corporate Reputation*, 41–51.

47. David Nadler, "Suspension and Debarment of Government Contractors: The Current Climate," *National Contract Management Journal* 22 (Winter 1989): 9–16; Sandra Sugawar, "Training Bigger Guns on Corporations," *WP*, Mar. 2, 1990, A1; William Gregory, "The Defense Procurement Mess," *Internal Auditor* (Apr. 1990): 49–55; John Ruhnka and Edward Gac, "The 'New' False Claims Act," *The CPA Journal* 68 (1998): 40–45; Balleisen, *Scenes from a Corporate Makeover*, Part 1, 18–32.

48. Donald Wood, Loye Young, Frederick Frost, and Pamela Nichols, "Overview of FIRREA," *Practical Real Estate Lawyer* 6 (July 1990): 43–54; Raymund Kawasaki, "Liability of Attorneys, Accountants, Appraisers, and Other Independent Contractors under the Financial Institutions Reform, Recovery, and Enforcement Act," *Hastings Law Journal* 42 (1990): 249–84; Stephen Albert, "Federal Sentencing Guidelines," *The Internal Auditor* 49 (1992): 49–50; Patrick Crawford, "Inefficiency and Abuse of Process in Banking Regulation: Asset Seizures, Law Firms, and the RICOization of Banking Law," *Virginia Law Review* 79 (1993): 205–42; Arthur Leibold, "Lawyers at Risk: Lawyer Asset Freezes and Other Chilling Experiences," *Review of Litigation* 12 (1993): 573–618; Kitty Calavita and Henry Pontell, "The State and White-Collar Crime: Saving the Savings and Loans," *Law & Society Review* 28 (1994): 297–324; Stephanie Strom, "Accounting Firm Settles Federal Auditing Charges," *NYT*, Aug. 10, 1994, D1; Michelle Singletary, "Justice Dept. Hails Prosecutions at Banks," *WP*, Nov. 14, 1995, A10.

49. Charles Gasprino, "Wall Street Has an Unlikely New Cop," *WSJ*, Apr. 25, 2002, C1; Randall Smith and Aaron Luchetti, "How Spitzer Pact Will Affect Wall Street," *WSJ*, May 22, 2002, C1; "Spitzer on Analysts, Predators, and Politics," *American Banker* (May 29, 2002): 11.

50. Mark High, "Looking under the Rocks: Due Diligence after Sarbanes-Oxley," *Business Law Today* 15 (Sept.–Oct. 2005): 12–17; Don Langevoort, "Internal Controls after Sarbanes-Oxley: Revisiting Corporate Law's 'Duty of Care as Responsibility for Systems,'" *Journal of Corporation Law* 31 (2006): 949–73; John Coates, "The Goals and Promise of the Sarbanes-Oxley Act," *Journal of Economic Perspectives* 21 (2007): 91–116; Melissa Maleske, "8 Ways SOX Changed Corporate Governance," *Inside Counsel* (Jan. 2012); "Survey Finds Improvement in Internal Control over Financial Reporting Since Passage of Sarbanes-Oxley," *Investment Weekly News*, June 23, 2012, 702; Paul Sweeney, "Sarbanes-Oxley—A Decade Later," *Financial Executive* (July/Aug. 2012), available at: http://www.financialexecutives.org/KenticoCMS/Financial-Executive-Magazine/2012_07/Sarbanes-Oxley—A-Decade-Later.aspx#axzz3C54bfNoF, accessed Aug. 28, 2014.

51. John Heasley, "Executive Summary of the Dodd-Frank Act," *Texas Banker* 99 (Sept. 2010): 28, 33; Linda Singer, Zachary Best, and Nina Simon, "Breaking Down Financial Reform: A Summary of the Major Consumer Protection Portions of the Dodd-Frank Wall Street Reform and Consumer Protection Act," *Journal of Consumer and Commercial Law* 14 (2010): 2–15; Hema Rao, John McDonald, and Dean Crawford, "The Dodd-Frank Wall Street Reform and Consumer Protection Act," *The CPA Journal* 81 (Mar. 2011): 15–25; Lydia DePillis, "A Watchdog Grows Up: The Inside Story of the Consumer Financial Protection Bureau," *WP Blogs*, Jan. 12, 2014.

52. Anthony Ramirez, "A Crackdown on Phone Marketing," *NYT*, Feb. 10, 1995, D1; "New Rules to Reduce Telemarketing Fraud," *Consumers' Research Magazine* 78 (Oct. 1995): 33; Chad Rubel, "Stiffer Rules for Telemarketers," *Marketing News* 30 (Feb. 26, 1996): 1; Tara Flynn, "Current Trends in Telemarketing Fraud," *Bank Security & Fraud Prevention* 4 (Oct. 1997): 3–5.

53. Slotter, "Hidden Faces," 14–16; D'Jamila Salem, "U. S. Cracks Down on Telephone Con Artists," *LAT*, Mar. 20, 1996, A1; Flynn, "Current Trends in Telemarketing Fraud," 5; Gene Tharpe, "FTC Pits 'Peach Sweep' on Scam Calls," *AC*, July 15, 1997, G3; Jeff Leeds and Amanda Elk, "66 Firms Accused of Telemarketing Fraud," *LAT*, Aug. 12, 1998, 3.

54. Cheryl Winokur, "SEC Files Flurry of Suits," *American Banker* (Oct. 29, 1998): 3; James Frank, "Scam Artists on Internet Warned," *CT*, Mar. 24, 2000, A4; Bob Keefe, "Online Auctions Feel Gavel Crackdown," *Atlanta Journal-Constitution*, May 1, 2003, C1.

55. Rory O'Connor, "Consumer Fraud Group Moves onto the Net," *PI*, Feb. 29, 1996, C3; "AARP Plots New Measures to Foil Telemarketing Fraud," *Orange County Register*, Feb. 19, 1998, A17; Cassandra Lane, "Seniors Deputized in Fraud Fight," *New Orleans Times Picayune*, Feb. 25, 1999, A8; Thomas Kimble, "Become an AARP Fraud Fighter," *Michigan Chronicle*, Sept. 30, 2009, C6; Thomas Peck, "Consumer Complaint Sites Warn about Disreputable Companies," *Information Today* 27 (July/Aug. 2010): 34–35.

56. John Hall, "One Place You Don't Want to See Your Name," *Air Conditioning, Heating & Refrigeration News* 219 (June 23, 2003): 31; Kristina Fiore, "LI Native Is Keeping 'em Honest," *Newsday*, Sept. 4, 2006, A34; Jeff Gelles, "Websites Let Consumers Vent," *Pittsburgh Post-Gazette*, June 13, 2010, C2.

57. Emilio Boulianne and Charles Cho, "The Rise and Fall of Webtrust," *International Journal of Information Systems* 10 (2009): 229–44.

58. "The March Group Protects Clients from Scams," *Telecommunications Business* (Apr. 14, 2010): 109; "Ripoff Report Shuts Out 'Reputation Management' Hacker," *PR Newswire*, Aug. 19, 2011; "Court Declines to Enjoin Negative Consumer Review Site," *Computer and Internet Lawyer* 29 (Mar. 2012): 15–19; "Reputation Changer," *PR Newswire*, Sept. 18, 2012.

59. CFA, "Consumer Complaint Websites: An Assessment" (June 2010), available at: http://www.consumerfed.org/elements/www.consumerfed.org/file/Complaint_Website_Report2010.pdf, accessed May 24, 2014. Search engine companies have invested significant resources to develop algorithms that can identify fraudulent consumer reviews; this arena has also attracted growing attention from academics. See the resources provided at the website "Opinion Spam Detection: Detecting Fake Reviews and Review-

ers," maintained by University of Illinois–Chicago computer scientist Bing Lui, https://www.cs.uic.edu/~liub/FBS/fake-reviews.html, accessed May 26, 2016.

60. Elizabeth Fowler, "Forensic Accountants in Demand," *NYT*, July 16, 1991, D17; Zabihollah Rezaee, E. James Burton, and Thomas Strickland, "Careers in Fraud Investigation," *Management Accounting* 74 (1993): 46–47; Christy Chapman, "ACFE Publishes Landmark Fraud Study," *Internal Auditor* 53 (Apr. 1996): 9; Rocco Vanasco, "Fraud Auditing," *Managerial Auditing Journal* 13 (1998): 4–71; Robert Thompson, "Fraud Costs Employers Dearly," *HRMagazine* 43 (Nov. 1998): 10.

61. "The Kroll-O'Gara Company Announces Acquisition of Lindquist Avey McDonald," *PR Newswire*, June 16, 1998, 1; "Kroll Returns Focus to Risk Consulting," *Mergers and Acquisitions* 36 (July 2001): 14–16.

62. "BBB Arbitrates Repair Disputes," *Los Angeles Sentinel*, Oct. 11, 1979, A11; Jay Hamburg, "Court of Common Sense, Fairness," *Orlando Sentinel*, Nov. 17, 1986, B1; Lisa Belkin, "An Arbitration Plan Gains," *NYT*, May 31, 1984, C3; Margo Harakas, "Help the System: Be an Arbitrator," *Fort Lauderdale Sun Sentinel*, Mar. 2, 1992, D1; Alan Walsh, "BBB Auto Line," *Lancaster Intelligencer Journal*, Jan. 9, 1995, 6.

63. Don Oldenburg, "BBB New Online Seal," *Fort Lauderdale Sun Sentinel*, June 7, 1997, D12; Patricia Sabatini, "BBB Seal Helps Resolve Online Trouble," *Pittsburgh Post-Gazette*, May 2, 2002, E1; Eileen Ambrose, "BBB Starts Using Letter Grades," *BS*, Mar. 10, 2009, A10; Benjamin Edelman, "Adverse Selection in Online 'Trust' Certifications and Search Results," *Electronic Commerce Research and Applications* 10 (Dec. 2010): 17–25; "BBB Scam Tracker Is Important New Tool in the Fight against Scams and Fraud," BBB Press Release, Nov. 10, 2015, available at: https://www.bbb.org/news-release-bbb-scam-tracker/, accessed May 26, 2016.

64. John Emshwiller, "If You Can't Trust the BBB," *WSJ*, Jan. 15, 1988, 1; Glenn Collins, "Watchdog's Deal Raises Revenue and Eyebrows," *NYT*, Aug. 19, 1994, D1; Chris Knapp and Jan Norman, "BBB Has a Spotty Record," *Orange County Register*, June 12, 2002, A1.

65. Ben Mook, "Better Business Bureau's Rating System Attacked," *Baltimore Daily Record*, Nov. 12, 2010; Paul Muschick, "Grading the Better Business Bureau," *Allentown Morning Call*, Dec. 5, 2010, A6; "Mesa Law Group Joins Growing Community Accusing the Better Business Bureau Rating System as a Business Scam," *Real Estate & Investment Business* (Dec. 25, 2010): 233; David Segal, "But Who Will Grade the Grader?" *NYT*, Feb. 27, 2011, B6.

66. Thomas Monahan and Cary Claiborne, "Self-Policing Strategies for Defense Contractors," *Internal Auditor* (Dec. 1988): 17–20; Nancy Kurland, "The Defense Industry Initiative: Ethics, Responsibility, and Accountability," *Journal of Business Ethics* 12 (1993): 137–45; Balleisen, *Scenes from a Corporate Makeover*, Part III, 3–18.

67. James Cummings, "High-Tech Systems Help Thwart Crime," *Dayton Daily News*, May 29, 1996, B5; Keith Slotter, "Plastic Payments: Trends in Credit Card Fraud," *FBI Law Enforcement Bulletin* (June 1997): 1–7; "Visa to Spend $200 Million on Anti-Fraud Measures," *Cards International* (Nov. 4, 2005): 2.

68. "EBay Launches the Most Comprehensive Trust and Safety Upgrades," *PR Newswire*, Jan. 15, 1999, 1; Jim Carlton and Ken Bensinger, "Phony Bids Put eBay on Defensive," *WSJ*, May 24, 2000, B1; Nick Wingfield, "EBay's Battle against Fraud," *WSJ*, Sept. 16, 2002, 7; "Software Ferrets out Likely Fraud," *LAT*, Dec. 11, 2006, C2; Dawn Gregg and Judy Scott, "The Role of Reputation Systems in Reducing On-Line Auction Fraud,"

International Journal of Electronic Commerce 10 (Spring 2006): 95–120. Google has un-dertaken analogous efforts to combat those "unscrupulous people [who] sometimes try to use the Google brand to scam and defraud others." See "Avoid and Report Google Scams," available at: https://support.google.com/faqs/answer/2952493?hl=en, accessed May 26, 2016.

69. John Phillips, "Changing the Rules to Fight Plunder in Procurement," *WSJ*, Apr. 22, 1986, 22; Richard Reeves, "Resurrected False Claims Act," *Fort Lauderdale Sun Sen-tinel*, Oct. 3, 1986, A14; Howard Berman and Charles Grassley, "Defense Procurement: Exposing Crime Pays," *WSJ*, Sept. 6, 1988, 1.

70. Lynette Khalfani, "Federal Sentencing Guidelines Turn Ethics Training into Cottage Industry," *Daily Record*, Oct. 9, 1996, 9; John Ruhnka and Heidi Borstler, "Gov-ernmental Incentives for Corporate Self-Regulation," *Journal of Business Ethics* 17 (1998): 315–26; Diana Murphy, "The Federal Sentencing Guidelines for Organizations: A Decade of Promoting Compliance and Ethics," *Iowa Law Review* 87 (2002): 697–718; Robert Roberts, "The Rise of Compliance-Based Ethics Management," *Public Integrity* 11 (2009): 269.

71. John Broder, "Ira Magaziner Argues for Minimal Internet Regulation," *NYT*, June 30, 1997, 1; Leslie Walker and Robert O'Harrow, "Web Firms Urged to Self-Regulate," *WP*, Dec. 1, 1998, D3.

72. "Congress Puts the Spotlight on Telemarketing Fraud," *Credit Card News* 6 (Oct. 15, 1993): 3; Joan Mitric, "'Predatory' Lending Practices Target Elderly," *WP*, Apr. 14, 1998, Z22; Lawrence Knutson, "Clinton Proposes Legislation to Protect Older Ameri-cans," *Milwaukee Journal Sentinel*, Apr. 1999, 8; Martin Anderson, "Iowa's Main Street Republican," *Insight on the News*, Nov. 12, 2002, 24–26.

73. Rob Blackwell, "How the Specter of Regulatory Capture Shaped the CFPB's First Year," *American Banker*, July 10, 2012; Apryl Motley, "A Work in Progress," *Independent Banker* 62 (July 2012): 41–45; Rob Blackwell, "Cordray Defends Complaint Database," *National Mortgage News* 36 (July 16, 2012); Stephen Agostini, "CFPB Says Agency Using Resources Wisely," *National Mortgage News* 37 (July 15, 2013): 4; Mike Rose, "CFPB Developments Continue," *Collector* 79 (Sept. 2013): 29–30; CFPB, "Enforcing Consumer Protection Laws," July 15, 2015, available at: http://files.consumerfinance.gov/f/201507_cfpb_enforcing-consumer-protection-laws.pdf, accessed Dec. 12, 2015.

74. Depillis, "A Watchdog Grows Up."

75. US Department of Justice, "Holding Financial Institutions Accountable for Fraud," press release, March 27, 2015, available at: https://www.justice.gov/opa/blog/holding-financial-institutions-accountable-fraud, accessed May 22, 2016; Norbert Mi-chel, "The House Should Be Commended for Effort to Stop Operation Choke Point," *Forbes Magazine*, Feb. 8, 2016, available at: http://www.forbes.com/sites/norbert michel/2016/02/08/the-house-should-be-commended-for-effort-to-stop-operation-choke-point/2/#a66b63724d46, accessed May 2, 2016; Sarah Jeong, "How a Cashless Society Could Embolden Big Brother," *The Atlantic*, April 8, 2016, available at: http://www.theatlantic.com/technology/archive/2016/04/cashless-society/477411/#article-comments, accessed April 9, 2016; Charles J. Cooper, "Operation Choke Point and the Bureaucratic Abuses of Unaccountable Power," in Dean Reuter and John Yoo, eds., *Lib-erty's Nemesis: The Unchecked Expansion of the State* (New York, 2016), 81–90. The cri-tiques of Operation Choke Point from the Right emphasize classic libertarian themes; those from the Left are filled with the sorts of arguments that Michel Foucault leveled at

the modern state. See generally his *Discipline and Punish: The Birth of the Modern Prison*, translated by Alan Sheridan (New York, 1977).

76. Kate Davidson, "Settlements against Banks over Crisis Abuses," *American Banker*, Feb. 10, 2012, 1; "JP Morgan Signs $13 Billion Global Settlement," *Mortgage Banking* 74 (Dec. 2013): 12–14; Sheelah Kolhatkar, "Citigroup Settlement Gives the Government a Financial-Crisis Win," *Business Week*, July 14, 2014, available at: http://www.businessweek.com.proxy.lib.duke.edu/articles/2014–07–14/citigroup-settlement-gives-the-government-a-financial-crisis-case, accessed Aug. 31, 2014; U.S. DOJ Press Release, "Bank of America to Pay $16.65 Billion in Historical Justice Department Settlement for Financial Fraud Leading up to and during the Financial Crisis," Aug. 21, 2014.

77. Matt Taibbi, "Why Isn't Wall Street in Jail?," *Rolling Stone* (Mar. 3, 2011): 44–51; Gretchen Morgenson and Louise Story, "In Financial Crisis, No Prosecutions of Top Figures," *NYT*, Apr. 14, 2011, available at: http://www.nytimes.com/2011/04/14/business/14prosecute.html?pagewanted=all&_r=0, accessed Aug. 31, 2014; Black, "The Department of Justice 'Chases Mice While Lions Roam,'" 1012–16; Henry Pontell, William Black, and Gilbert Geis, "Too Big to Fail, Too Powerful to Jail?: On the Absence of Criminal Prosecutions after the 2008 Financial Meltdown," *Crime, Law, and Social Change* 61 (2014): 1–13. Prosecutors have gained criminal verdicts against the perpetrators of major pyramid schemes, such as Bernard Madoff and Allen Stanford; they have also continued to prioritize action against insider trading. In both of these contexts, moreover, judges have proved more amenable to multi-year jail sentences. Madoff and Stanford each received terms of over one hundred years; the average sentence for insider trading went up over 30 percent between 2009 and 2013, with some approaching ten years. Clifford Krauss, "Financier Is Sentenced to 110 Years for Fraud," *NYT*, June 15, 2012, B1; Nate Raymond, "Insider Traders in U.S. Face Longer Prison Terms," Reuters, Sept. 2, 2014, available at: http://www.reuters.com/article/us-insidertrading-prison-insight-idUSKBN0GX0A820140902, accessed May 29, 2016.

78. Donald Langevoort, "On Leaving Corporate Executives 'Naked, Homeless, and without Wheels': Equitable Remedies, and the Debate over Enterprise versus Individual Liability," *Wake Forest Law Review* 42 (2007): 630.

79. Stephen Barlas, Mike Osheroff, Dennis Whitney, and Kathy Williams, "JOBS Act Exemptions for Emerging Growth Companies," *Strategic Finance* 93 (May 2012): 27–28; Frank Zarb, "The JOBS Act Provides New Flexibility in Public and Private Offerings," *Insights* 26 (Nov. 2012): 9–15.

80. Tim Stuhldreher, "JOBS Act Reforms Trigger Concerns," *Central Penn Business Journal* 28 (April 13, 2012): 1, 4; Eileen Ambrose, "JOBS Act Lets Startups Crowdfund for Money," *BS* Apr. 15, 2012, C1; Cathy McKitrick, "Loosening Reins on Startups Triggers Raves, Warnings," *Salt Lake Tribune*, May 7, 2012.

81. Josh Mitchell, "Thousands Want Student Loans Canceled," *WSJ*, Jan. 21, 2016, A3.

82. *AT&T Mobility v. Concepcion*, 563 U.S. 333 (2011); "CFPB Considers Proposal to Ban Arbitration Clauses That Allow Companies to Avoid Accountability to Their Customers," CFPB press release, Oct. 7, 2015, available at: http://www.consumerfinance.gov/about-us/newsroom/cfpb-considers-proposal-to-ban-arbitration-clauses-that-allow-companies-to-avoid-accountability-to-their-customers/, accessed May 22, 2016; Jessica Silver-Greenberg and Robert Gebeloff, "Arbitration Everywhere, Stacking the Deck of Justice," *NYT*, Nov. 1, 2015, A1.

83. Macey, *Death of Corporate Reputation.*

84. John Kenneth Galbraith, *The Great Crash: 1929* (New York, 1954), 193–95.

85. For a more general discussion of the advantages that historical awareness can bring to regulatory decision-making, see Edward Balleisen and Elizabeth Brake, "Historical Perspective and Better Regulatory Governance: An Agenda for Institutional Reform," *Regulation & Governance* 8 (2014): 222–45.

Index

Note: Italics indicate the location of an illustration.